Leonard Broom Australian National University
Philip Selznick University of California, Berkeley
Sociology:

Sociology: A Text with Adapted Readings

Sixth Edition
A Text with Adapted Readings

Harper & Row, Publishers

New York   Hagerstown   San Francisco   London

Sponsoring Editor: Alvin A. Abbott
Project Editor: Robert Ginsberg
Production Supervisor: Stefania J. Taflinska
Photo Researcher: Helena Frost
Compositor: Ruttle, Shaw & Wetherill, Inc.
Printer and Binder: Kingsport Press
Art Studio: e h Technical Services

Sociology: A Text with Adapted Readings, Sixth Edition

Library of Congress Cataloging in Publication Data

Broom, Leonard.
    Sociology.

    Includes bibliographies and indexes.
    1. Sociology. I. Selznick, Philip, Date-
joint author. II. Title.
HM51.B86 1977   301   76-50126
ISBN 0-06-040965-7

Acknowledgments

The chapter on *SOCIALIZATION* was written, with our collaboration, by Gertrude Jaeger, who also contributed extensively to *RELIGION* and to other sections of the book.

For generous collaboration on this or earlier editions we extend thanks to Robert Blauner, Burton R. Clark, Donald R. Cressey, Dorothy Broom Darroch, Saul Geiser, Norval D. Glenn, Helen Beem Gouldner, Paul Jacobs, F. Lancaster Jones, Yuriko Kitaoji, William Kornhauser, Richard T. Morris, Philippe Nonet, Byron Sansom, Jerome H. Skolnick, and Ralph H. Turner.

We are greatly indebted to Gretchan N. Broom for her creative and unstinting collaboration in editing and writing, and for carrying the burden of administrative tasks.

In addition to others whose help we acknowledged in previous editions, we express our appreciation for the assistance and guidance of Alvin A. Abbott, Mary Archondes, Samuel Baum, Robert Cushing, Russell K. Darroch, Doris Fine, Helena Frost, Robert Ginsberg, Peter Glasner, Charles Y. Glock, Hironobu Kitaoji, Howard Leiderman, Larry H. Long, Patrick McDonnell, Pamela Utz, and Paul Van Seters.

The first four editions of this book owed much to the high editorial standards and the indefatigable efforts of Phyllis M. Barnett. We are conscious of her continuing imprint on this edition, and we shall always be grateful for her patient guidance and personal commitment.

Other debts are recorded in footnotes and credit lines, but we wish especially to express our indebtedness to the authors of the original works upon which our Adaptations are based.

L. B.
P. S.

Chapters

Contents

Sociology: A Text with Adapted Readings

Part One
Elements of Sociological Analysis

1 | The Sociological Perspective

Section one elements and themes

Beyond common sense Some aspects of society are well known to most people, and almost everyone has intimate and personal knowledge of social situations: a family, a work setting, a congenial group, or a life-style. The sociologist respects this common-sense knowledge and often depends upon it in research, for instance, by interviewing people to learn about their social experiences, beliefs, and interpretations. However, common sense understandings based on fragmentary impressions have serious limitations. For example, almost everyone is aware of racial prejudice and discrimination. But in the ordinary course of events, individuals may not learn much about what lies behind these feelings and actions. Nor are they likely to have a very accurate idea of how widespread racial antagonism is, what forms it takes, how it differs from place to place and among different groups, and whether such sentiments are increasing or declining in extent and intensity.

Sociological research tries to be more exact and more systematic than common sense. To do so, sociologists must often go beyond the categories of everyday speech to interpret events and experiences in a fresh light. For example, *friendship* is a common-sense term, but *primary group* is a sociological concept that includes the idea of friendship, but also much more. Similarly, such sociological concepts as *deviance, stratification*, or *role* make possible more searching inquiry than common sense allows.

The person and the group in context The individual-in-context is a human being interacting with his or her social environment. To understand how people behave and how they change, the social context must be closely observed. For example, a contextual approach to mental illness shifts attention from the remote influences of early childhood, which preoccupy conventional psychiatry, to the effect upon the patient of stresses in the present environment (Laing and Esterson, 1964).

Columbia University lecture hall: An intricate network of social decisions lies behind this academic gathering

The sociology of education considers the human environment of learning, which includes not only the school itself as a social setting but the influence of the child's home on his school performance. A large-scale study of inequality in American education stressed that "schools bring little influence to bear on a child's achievement that is independent of his background and general social context" (Coleman et al., 1966:325). (See EDUCATION,[1] p. 362.)

The social environment of industry includes the attitudes people have toward work; the responsibilities they feel toward their families; traditions regarding the employment of women; educational opportunities; the absence, presence, and militancy of trade unions; and many other factors. To the sociologist, the business firm is an enterprise-in-context, an organization that may try to pursue specialized goals but in doing so must respond to forces and conditions in the social environment.

The person and the group in action The sociological perspective is sensitive to the acting person and the acting group. The acting person is a specific human being who pursues goals, interprets experience, responds to opportunities, and confronts difficulties. The individual-in-action does not necessarily stay within neat boundaries. A sociologist studying what it means to be a prison warden would go beyond a formal description of the rules and routines of the job. The warden's day-to-day life would be closely observed to see what he or she does in action, how the various forces at work in the prison are balanced and how one goes about gaining the cooperation of inmates, supporting the morale of guards, and maintaining satisfactory relations with the public. An analysis of the inmate-in-action would

[1] To simplify cross-reference, chapter titles are given thus: EDUCATION.

produce a picture of prison life as experienced by the prisoner.

The perspective of action is a gateway to sociological realism. Sociology claims to be realistic because it removes the decorative wrappings of social experience. The work of a judge is usually described in the language of ideals and aspirations—what a judge is supposed to be and do. The idealized definition is an important beginning, but a full understanding requires a specific description of how cases are handled, including the influence of the judge's personal experience and social background. In this way the sociological perspective encourages the study of law-in-action.

The plurality of social experience The sociological emphasis on context and action points to the concreteness of human experience. In the world as it is experienced there are no abstract human beings; there are only unique persons who live out their lives at a particular time in history. It follows from this perspective that action is creative. To act over a period of time is to build up a unique social reality. Every individual has a history of failures and victories, private perceptions, and distinctive ways of expressing personality and relating to others.

From the starting point of individual history, it is but a step to see that people who share similar life experiences create distinctive group realities and their own social worlds. The sociologist recognizes that much apparent uniformity obscures a complex and diverse group life. Some of the most stimulating sociological research describes the variety of social worlds and shows how they emerge from action in context. For example, a sociological study of unemployment (Bakke, 1935) delineated how the unemployed man during the depression of the 1930s, in pursuing his own goals within a restricted social setting, developed a pattern of conduct that made sense to him even though it was rejected and misunderstood by official society.

Awareness of plurality is an essential part of the sociological imagination. It sharpens sensitivity to the innovations that take place as people work out new ways of relating and new styles of life. The diversity of social experience is the seed bed of change, an ever-present reminder of the openness and richness of human alternatives.

Patterns and configurations There is a tension in sociology between the general and the particular, the abstract and the concrete. Much of sociology presses for detailed analysis of specific settings and events, for example, life in street corner society (Adaptation 10, p. 137, and Adaptation 11, p. 141), the account of a race riot (Adaptation 19, p. 234), or the social history of a religious movement (Adaptation 31, p. 391). On the other hand, even highly specific studies strive to find a larger generalization in concrete details. The case study is not an end in itself. Details are needed to show how things happen and to take account of the context. But the objective of inquiry is always a sociological lesson, a general idea that can become part of the sociologist's store of insights, concepts, and findings.

"Architecture and Social Order" (p. 6) depicts the patterning of privilege and subordination in the organization of a Victorian upper-class country house.

Sociology goes beyond case studies, however revealing they may be, to the larger pattern of human society. Human action is indeed specific, focused, and diverse, but there are also broad general patterns. For example, modern society is sometimes called the organizational society or the managed society. These summary tag names are meant to suggest that large, bureaucratic organizations tend to dominate the social scene: Most people, as employees or consumers, students or soldiers, have their choices limited by the decisions of distant, impersonal officials, both private and public. Hence the protest against treating people as if they were punch cards: "Do not fold, spindle, or mutilate."

Bureaucracy is a societal pattern and a human context; it limits alternatives, sets goals to which people aspire, and otherwise creates a conditioning framework for everyday life.

Social patterns are of many varieties: the composition of populations, the relative political power of social groups, the emergence of suburbia, the rise of the "multiversity," the distribution of prestige and privilege, the enduring structure of values and attitudes. To discover these patterns and to monitor their changes calls upon the entire range of sociological methods and the full exercise of sociological sensibility.

Unintended effects Sociology is a probing discipline. It looks beneath the surface to find the springs of action, the obscure sources of motivation and control, the latent patterns that foreshadow things to come. Thus the idea of latency is an important part of the sociological perspective.

One way of probing is to look for unin-

tended meanings and effects. Instead of accepting at face value what people say they do and what they say they accomplish, the sociologist studies what they actually do and what unspoken or unintended consequences ensue (Merton, 1968:Chap. 3). For example, a large college class is often divided into sections led by teaching assistants in order to give students an opportunity to meet in small groups and have some degree of personal contact with at least a junior instructor. But that is not all that happens. An unintended effect of the section format may be to dilute the authority of the professor and decrease his or her interaction with the students.

Sometimes the study of latent effects is a kind of debunking, especially when a professed goal or justification is interpreted as a smokescreen for hidden motives. In recent years the professed aim of rehabilitating prisoners has been attacked as masking the "true" objective of increasing the power of prison officials and parole boards, who have

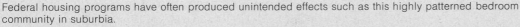

Federal housing programs have often produced unintended effects such as this highly patterned bedroom community in suburbia.

Architecture and social order

*Victorian country houses were
enormous, complicated, and highly
articulated machines for a way of life
which seems as remote as the stone
age, served by a technology as
elaborate as it is now obsolete. The
houses were complicated partly
because they had to contain so many
people but mainly because the activities
and interrelationships of their
occupants were so minutely organized
and subdivided. In an age when
government was organized into*

Source: Abridged from *The Victorian Country
House* by Mark Girouard (Oxford: Oxford
University Press [Clarendon Press], 1971),
pp. 19–20. Home plan at p. 23. Used by
permission of Oxford University Press.

*departments, the middle classes into
professions, science into different
disciplines, and convicts into separate
cells, country-house life was neatly
divided into separate parcels.*

*The largest houses had fifty or more
indoor staff; anything eligible for the
title of a country house was unlikely
to have fewer than eight. In the period
between the reduction of infant
mortality and the introduction of birth
control, families of twelve or more
children were by no means uncommon,
and children had their own retinue of
governesses, tutors, nannies, and
nursery maids. The new railways made
it easy for friends and relatives to
come to stay in large quantities, the
men each bringing his own valet and
the women her lady's maid. A great*

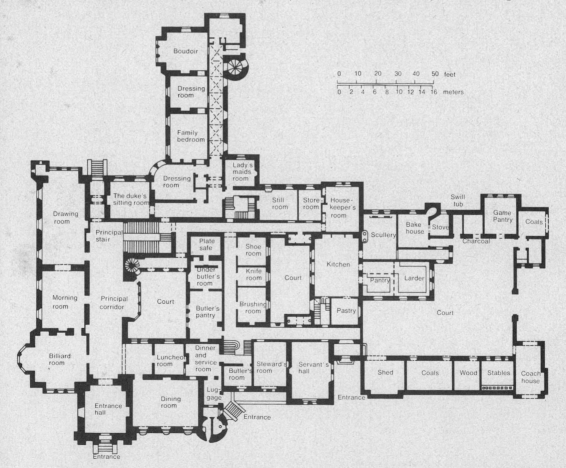

country house at its busiest might contain 150 people, and a population of forty or fifty would not be out of the ordinary.

These large numbers of people were carefully stratified and subdivided. There were territories reserved for each stratum and territories common to one or more. Each territory was subdivided according to the activities that went on in it. This analysis of activities became more and more exact, and more and more activities were given a separate room. The household was divided into family, guests, and servants; the servants were divided into upper and lower servants; the family, into children and grown-ups; the children, into schoolroom and nursery. It was considered undesirable for children, servants, and parents to see, smell, or hear each other except at certain recognized times and places. Guests and family met on common ground, but each had private areas to retire to.

Owing to these subdivisions the activity of eating became complicated. The main meals might have to be served in five different places: the dining room, the schoolroom, the nursery, the steward's room (for the upper servants), and the servants' hall (for the lower servants). Outside eating hours the sex division was important. The mistress of the house had her boudoir to work in, the master, his study or business room. The drawing room (or rooms) was considered the ladies' territory, but the gentlemen were allowed in; the opposite was the case with the library. The billiard room tended to become exclusively male territory. Among guests, the bachelors were kept in a separate corridor from the unmarried ladies. Even more important, the men-servants slept separately from the maids and often did not even have the pleasure of passing them on the stairs, separate men's and women's staircases being provided.

authority to decide when a man is rehabilitated. However, debunking is likely to offer an overly simple and partial explanation. While the gap between ideals and reality is often real enough, it is usually unintended.

Unintended effects produce social configurations. As people pursue their private and immediate objectives, a "fallout" occurs of which they are unaware. The composition of the population is such a configuration, the consequence of numerous private decisions and actions: An unbalanced ratio of males to females may be the result of selective migration in response to job opportunities; the number of dependent young and very old people is an unintended outcome of private decisions to marry early or late, to have children or not to have them.

Karl Marx called attention to the unintended effects of industrial organization. He argued that many separate decisions by capitalist entrepreneurs resulted in the concentration of workers in large factories, which in turn created the conditions for labor organization and for class consciousness. (See SOCIAL STRATIFICATION, p. 185.)

Social dynamics Finally, the sociological perspective involves close analysis of the sources of change—the pressures for new ways and the characteristics that make societies receptive toward or resistant to new influences. Specifically, sociologists recognize that, at least in complex societies, social unity is a precarious papering-over of potential conflicts.

The study of change may range from a small-scale analysis of how farm people accept new ideas (Loomis and Loomis, 1967) to a broad overview of master trends, such as the rise of postindustrial society (Bell, 1973). In each case, the ultimate focus is on human relations: Who communicates with whom and to what effect? What new styles of life or new associations emerge? What new demands or expectations arise?

The sources of change are characteristically remote from their social effects. New religious doctrines, such as those of Luther and Calvin in the sixteenth century, contributed to an economic individualism from which those early Protestant reformers would have recoiled; technological developments, such as the automobile, beginning as limited conveniences, transformed the entire round of life; the growth of population and of cities doomed the long-standing political and economic dominance of small-town America.

In the sociological perspective change is considered normal, not abnormal. Every society is at least potentially in flux, for each must respond to challenges from the outside and to the play of forces within it. Moreover, every segment of society has its inner dynamic, its inherent tensions, such as the conflicts that are built into social roles. (See p. 36.) Not all of these tensions result in major social change, but they create openings or "soft spots" for the reception of new influences. Indeed, society can be perceived as the sometimes successful but often unsuccessful "management of tensions" (Moore, 1963:10).

Section two knowledge for what?

Sociology is a human enterprise carried on by limited and error-prone people. It too can be studied in context and in action, with full recognition of the strains and problems that characterize the discipline. There is a constant risk that sociological thought may become too abstract, too specialized, too remote from urgent social concerns. Warnings on this score have been sounded in *Knowledge for What?* (Lynd, 1939) and *The Sociological Imagination* (Mills, 1959). These and other writings argue for a vigorous, committed sociology capable of looking beyond the details of social life to the conditions that affect the fate of the individual in twentieth-century society.

RELEVANCE AND RESPONSIVENESS

A responsive discipline As part of the social world, the discipline of sociology is caught up in major events and crises. Since the end of World War II much research has been done on the emerging nations of the Third World, reflecting the postwar breakup of colonial empires. Racial conflict, crime and delinquency, population pressure—these and many other urgent social topics give focus and direction to sociological research. The choice of problems for study has always been largely determined by what is going on in the world. In this sense, sociology is responsive to changing historical conditions and has a clear relevance to social issues.

But relevance and responsiveness are ambiguous ideas. Responsive to whom? Relevant to what? Some kinds of relevance are challenged today, such as the use of social science knowledge to aid military or counterinsurgency operations. The impulse to be relevant and practical may in some cases compromise the independence of the sociologist and limit his or her capacity to serve as a critic of contemporary society.

When the researcher can accept the premises of practical people, such as government officials, business executives, or political leaders, it is easy to do relevant research. The sociologist can then help make institutions more efficient, for example, by studying absenteeism in industrial employment or morale in military units. Research on absenteeism or morale can have a larger significance. It may lead to new insights and generalizations that build sociological knowledge; it may even result in critical analysis of the way institutions are run. Nevertheless, there is a risk that when sociological research focuses on such limited problems as efficiency, it may neglect to inquire into the basic assumptions of social policy.

On many issues, American sociology has been in the forefront of public opinion. Sociologists have responded to perceived needs and to the contradictions of belief and action in American society. In the 1920s and

1930s, long before the larger society was ready, most sociologists opposed segregation and discrimination and in their classrooms helped prepare opinion for the tidal change against racism and prejudice. One of the most influential documents of social science, the culmination of the work of many social scientists over many years, was Gunnar Myrdal's collaborative work *An American Dilemma* (1944), which exposed to a large audience the workings of racism and the heritage of oppression. In addition, sociologists helped lay the foundations for many social programs, such as Head Start, which reflects sociological understanding of the importance for the child of the early learning environment. Sociological ideas and research have strongly influenced most of the major presidential commissions on social issues, such as the Kerner Commission report on civil disorder. It is probable that most sociologists have thought of themselves as critics with a mission of enlightenment, especially against intolerance.

On other issues, sociologists have been less clear and less effective. Sociology has always been concerned about poverty, for example, but the tendency has been to see poverty as a result of temporary dislocations, to be dealt with through individual welfare rather than by basic changes in the structure of opportunity.

Sociologists cannot help being influenced by their social surroundings, especially by the ideas current in their generation. Some of this influence is beneficial. The black revolution that began in the 1960s has stirred a reassessment of older assumptions about the cohesion of American society and the prospects for racial integration. On the other hand, some influences, such as the widespread confidence in the American economy that prevailed in the 1950s and the largely unquestioning acceptance of foreign policy assumptions (perhaps a heritage of the great national consensus of the war against Japan and Nazi Germany) have tended to limit perspectives.

To correct these limitations, sociology needs a continuous renewal of its critical spirit. For sociology is inherently critical: In going beyond common sense it resists being bound by the categories of conventional wisdom; in its awareness of the plurality of social experience sociology teaches that no social arrangement is inevitable or beyond question.

Critical responsiveness An open, responsive, self-critical discipline requires both intellectual independence and social sensitivity. These ideals involve each other. To be independent a sociologist must be sensitive to the restrictions imposed by personal involvements; to be fully aware of new issues and possibilities he or she must be able to expand horizons and shift perspectives. The sociologist must be as free-wheeling as possible yet try to take in as much of the social world as insight and imagination will allow.

Not every sociologist is (or should be) a broad-ranging theorist and social critic. There are also painstaking scholars who want to know not only whether an idea is interesting or relevant but also whether it can be tested and whether it will stand up under close analysis. If there is to be reliable knowledge about inequality, population growth, or discrimination, researchers must devise methods of measurement and analyze the research results. Furthermore, many sociologists are profitably occupied in attempting to reinterpret the common-sense world in an effort to discover, for example, the religious component of political life or the unspoken rituals of social interaction. These efforts may take them far afield from direct social criticism. It is the discipline as a whole, not the individual sociologist, that should be held accountable for contributing to human betterment.

Nothing is more central to the scientific spirit than the idea of self-correction. Social scientists cannot claim to be purely objective. Scholars inevitably bring to their work some element of choice, some limitation on their capacity to look at the world objectively. But the scientific enterprise does not need to be assured of absolute objectivity. It is only necessary that the discipline be open and pluralistic; that there be opportunity for criticism of assumptions, findings, and interpretations; and that there be receptiveness to new ideas. Self-correction, not purity, is the scholarly ideal.

CONTRASTING MODELS OF SOCIETY

Although most sociologists share a general perspective, there are important differences of emphasis and outlook. Many scholars place bets, so to speak, on one or another approach in the hope that it will offer a key to sounder knowledge or greater insight. As a result, the newcomer to sociology soon hears competing voices. An attentive listener can detect recurrent themes that present different views of man and society.

Consensus v. conflict One may begin the study of society by asking: What holds it all together? What keeps it steady? Or one may ask: What pulls society apart? What makes for change? These alternative starting points seem neutral enough, but they contain the seeds of controversy (Dahrendorf, 1958).

No sociologist seriously doubts the importance of conflict in society. But some take conflict for granted and give their main attention to what they consider the fundamental sources of social cohesion: shared ideas, shared traditions, shared ways of perceiving and understanding the world. These ingredients of social order are summed up in the assumption that every group is held together by a consensus, by agreement on basic rules and values. These agreements extend to the details of everyday life, the assumptions people must share even when they sit down together at the dinner table.

The consensus model gives considerable weight to the persistence of shared ideas. Major social change is thought to come rather slowly and to depend on large-scale shifts in attitude and belief. Hence consensus has a somewhat conservative overtone. It

seems to suggest that many proposals for change are unrealistic because they do not sufficiently take into account the underlying structure of community beliefs. For example, it might be argued that any effort to radicalize American workers must run up against a deep resistance to anticapitalist ideologies.

The conflict approach, on the other hand, holds that the most important aspect of social order is the domination of some groups by others, that society is best understood as an arena of actual and potential conflict, and that when things look peaceful, it is only because someone is sitting on the lid. Conflict theorists do not ignore consensus and belief, but they emphasize that popular attitudes are often sustained and manipulated by groups in power. They focus attention on who controls the communication media or the educational system and how these controls are used to induce acceptance of official doctrines.

A conflict model appeals to proponents of change for two reasons. First, it identifies the potential for change, especially the rise of new groups capable of challenging existing institutions. Second, the conflict model suggests that a strategic shift in power can decisively affect social history. These themes are prominent in the writings of Marx, whose work is the clearest example of the application of a conflict model to the study of society. (See pp. 185–188.) Broadly speaking, conflict theorists in modern sociology tend to be influenced by Marxism, although they do not necessarily accept all of it. Consensus theorists are more likely to follow in the tradition of the French sociologist Emile Durkheim. (See Adaptation 3, pp. 45–58.)

Most sociologists would say that they are sensitive to both consensus and conflict. Only a minority identify themselves exclusively with one approach or the other. However, there is a tendency for sociologists to lean toward the consensus model, because an awareness of "the social"—the influence of shared contexts and shared experiences on the human mind and self—has been so

Boston, 1975: Prayer and anger, solidarity and conflict, mark this mass protest against busing schoolchildren for racial integration.

large a part of the sociological tradition. The conflict model serves as a corrective to over-emphasis on consensus.

Structure v. process Another source of tension in sociological thought stems from an inherent problem in social analysis. To analyze society is to break it up into components for study: social roles, social strata and classes, institutions, culture, organizations, communities. These are concepts that identify *structural* units of society. Yet in the last analysis, society is made up of individual human beings. To discuss abstract social units, necessary though it may be, carries the risk that the human individual will be forgotten or neglected.

One school of thought that concentrates on *process* and tries to keep the individual at the center of attention is known as *symbolic interactionism* (Blumer, 1969). Symbolic interactionists argue that the core of social reality is the active human being trying to make sense of social situations. To make sense of a situation is to interpret it, to lend it meaning. The individual does not respond to the social world directly. His experience takes form from the meaning he places on his own acts and on the acts of others. The act of interpretation gives interaction its symbolic character: A gift is interpreted as an act of love, a stone is interpreted as a religious object.

Symbolic interactionism as a point of view calls attention to the detailed, person-centered processes that take place within the larger units of social life. Many aspects of the social order can be illuminated without fully specifying, or even considering, what happens to particular human beings. For example, one can understand the distribution of opportunities by studying population movements and technological change. But to understand why some people respond to opportunities and others do not, it is necessary to know the individual's particular situation and the interpretation he or she gives to that experience.

Strictly speaking, structure v. process is a false distinction. There can be no structure without process, nor does it make sense to study process without considering the nature of the situation and the framework within which choice and action take place. The issue is one of emphasis and sensitivity. The interactionist argues that a preoccupation with structural units may dull sensitivity to the way the individual-in-action modifies and even creates his social environment.

A structural perspective suggests an image of society in which individuals are seen as determined by the forces that play upon them, by their social backgrounds, and by group memberships. An interactionist per-

spective studies social life from the point of view of the actor, how he makes sense of his experience and copes with his environment. This is a perspective that encourages sympathy for the outcast and the underdog. Most sociologists share that concern, although they come to it in different ways.

Conclusion The conflict model and symbolic interaction speak to the same basic issues. They are voices of resistance to an image of society as stable and self-renewing, capable of imposing a common mold on its members. Insofar as people derive from sociology such a restricted and faulty image of the social world, the criticism is justified. On the other hand, social knowledge cannot proceed without analysis of structure; and an understanding of what holds society together is necessary even for those who dislike the bonds and would gladly break them. Consensus *and* conflict, structure *and* process remain major themes of sociological inquiry.

Adaptation 1: Reading a table

A statistical table is a laborsaving device. Quantitative information in a properly laid-out table is more clearly, more concisely, and more simply presented than in several paragraphs of words. A good table has unambiguous signposts, and if you follow the directions carefully, you can avoid needless work and confusion. Table 1:1 shows what the main features of a table are, and this adaptation tells how to read it.

TITLE
This title says that the table summarizes information on poverty for the population of the United States in 1974 by age groupings, by sex, and by race and that the data are presented as rates, that

Source: Suggested by Wallis and Roberts, 1956:270–274.

is, percentages. Further information is given in the headnote, in footnotes, and in the source.

HEADNOTE
The bracketed headnote explains that the rates pertain to money income both of people who live alone and in families. (For a nonfarm family of four persons, the poverty line in 1974 was $5,038.) By implication, payment in kind, such as free rent or farm produce, is not counted as money income. Races other than black and white are excluded from the table.

FOOTNOTES
Footnote [a] (to the headnote) tells where to find more information about how income and poverty

Table 1:1 Poverty rates by age, race, and sex, United States, 1974, in percentages

[Unrelated individuals and persons in families with money income in 1974 below the poverty line. Races other than blacks and whites are omitted.][a]

PERCENT IN POVERTY

Age	White			Black			Both races[b]		
	Male (Col. 1)	Female (Col. 2)	Both sexes (Col. 3)	Male (Col. 4)	Female (Col. 5)	Both sexes (Col. 6)	Male (Col. 7)	Female (Col. 8)	Both sexes (Col. 9)
16–21	8	10	9	34	35	35	11	13	12
22–44	5	8	7	12	28	21	6	10	8
45–54	4	6	5	16	28	23	5	8	7
55–59	6	9	8	18	28	24	7	11	9
60–64	7	10	8	21	31	26	8	12	10
65 and over	10	16	14	29	42	36	12	18	16
16 and over	6	9	8[b]	20	31	26[b]	8	12	10

Source: U.S. Bureau of the Census, Current Population Reports, Series P-60, No. 99, "Money Income and Poverty Status of Families and Persons in the United States: 1974" (Advance Report: Table 19). Based on a Current Population Survey sample of about 45,000 households conducted in March 1975 by the U.S. Bureau of the Census.

[a] For definitions and explanations of money income, see original source, pp. 2–3, and Current Population Reports, Series P-60, No. 97. For discussion of the poverty classification, see original source, p. 3, and Current Population Reports, Series P-60, No. 98. For discussion of reliability of estimates, see original source, p. 3, and Current Population Reports, Series P-60, No. 97 and No. 98.
[b] Computed from data in original source.

are defined and how reliable the estimates are. Whereas footnote [a] refers to the whole table, footnote [b] refers only to the panel with the heading "Both races" and in the bottom row to the summary entries for "Both sexes." Footnote [b] states that the information in the panel for both races and the summary figures for both sexes for ages 16 and over in the bottom row were not copied directly from the original source, but were calculated by the authors.

SOURCE

The source note points out that the data are drawn from a large sample survey conducted by a division of the U.S. Bureau of the Census, which is careful about specifying the reliability of its statistics. For a brief discussion about sampling in the census, see *POPULATION*, p. 264.

The data in Table 1:1 are taken directly from an original source, but the authors of this book computed some of the entries. The original source, the Bureau of the Census, is one of the most competent statistical agencies in the world. The report is

identified as an "advance report," and it is possible, but not likely, that the final report might present corrected data. There is no rule about where such explanations should be given, but they should be given somewhere.

HEADINGS AND STUBS

There are two levels of headings in the table: first, by race (white, black, and both races); second, by sex, grouped under each of the three racial categories. Headings instruct us to look down the columns. The stubs, in this case referring to ages, tell us to read across the rows.

UNITS

This table reports its data in percentages, that is, in rates per 100 persons. The primary source also reports population numbers, but they are not presented here to keep the table small and easy to understand. Tables may report data in whole numbers or percentages, and numbers may also be reported in thousands or in millions.

MARGINALS

When you examine the numbers in the table, it is a good idea to work from the outside in. In other words, begin by looking at the "marginals," that is, the figures at the margins of the table. These figures provide summary information.

Thus the extreme right margin (column 9) shows the variation in poverty by age groups for the whole population being studied. The overall average percent in poverty for all ages 16 and over, both sexes, and both races is given in the lower right corner as 10. By studying column 9 you can see that the oldest age group has the highest poverty rate and the youngest the next highest. Reading across the bottom margin, the last row, you can see that blacks have higher poverty rates than whites and that females have higher poverty rates than males of the same race.

CELLS

To make more detailed comparisons, examine specific cells in the body of the table. For example, you might want to know whether white females (column 2) in any given age bracket have a higher or lower poverty rate than white males (column 1) of the same age group. In every case females have a higher rate. Now compare rates for blacks of both sexes (column 6) with those for whites of the same ages (column 3). Without exception, white rates are lower, age for age. As a matter of fact in comparing all the cells in the black and white panels, only one age group of black males (column 4) age 22–44 (row 2) has a lower poverty rate than any of the white age/sex categories. The single white category with a worse poverty rate is for white females (column 2) age 65 and over (row 6). This comparison indicates the degree to which blacks are economically disadvantaged, and this kind of analysis is expanded in *SOCIAL STRATIFICATION,* pp. 164–165.

FACTS FROM THE TABLE

Much more information can be teased out of this table, but a few facts can be briefly stated.

1. The poverty rates in 1974 for persons 16 years and older averaged 10 percent.

2. There was a wide variation by age, race, and sex, ranging from a high of 42 percent for black females age 65 and over to a low of 4 percent for white males age 45–54.

3. Poverty rates were highest for the oldest groups and next highest for the youngest groups.

4. Poverty rates were higher for females than for males of the same race.

5. They were higher for blacks than for whites.

Section three plan of this book

This text has been designed to provide a systematic introduction to sociology. Reference to the detailed table of contents will be helpful in following this comment and in using the book most efficiently.

PART ONE: ELEMENTS OF SOCIOLOGICAL ANALYSIS

The first nine chapters cover the basic topics in the subject matter of sociology. Taken together, these Part One chapters present the main ideas with which the sociologist approaches any special area, the chief skills and interests that make up the sociologist's tools of analysis.

The topics in this book are organized to achieve an orderly and systematic presentation of the basic ideas and findings of sociology. The chapters are not neat and watertight compartments. For example, the fundamental aspects of social organization are introduced in Chapter 2, but broadly conceived the topic includes the study of primary groups, associations, and social stratification. These aspects of society are also treated in separate chapters.

Each chapter includes case studies as well as concepts, application to real-life situations as well as theory. For example, to illustrate basic principles *ASSOCIATIONS* discusses political parties and factories, and *PRIMARY GROUPS* discusses friendship networks in a black ghetto.

PART TWO: ANALYSIS OF MAJOR INSTITUTIONS

Part Two brings sociological analysis to bear on four institutions: the family, education, religion, and law. In these chapters many of the ideas and methods discussed in Part One are elaborated and applied. For example, *EDUCATION* includes further material on the micro-order, bureaucracy, and social stratification—all topics introduced in Part One. At the same time, the chapter provides an introduction to the sociology of education.

In modern society, family life, education, religion, and law are subject to great strains. These institutions take the brunt of social change. As a consequence, each is the focus of major policy debates. In recognition of this fact, a section on social policy and social change concludes each of the Part Two chapters.

PART THREE: MASTER TRENDS

Four major themes characterize modern society: (1) the growing significance of race and ethnic origin in advanced and developing nations; (2) the development of the city as a general site of human residence, association, and work; (3) the ascendance of an industrial order with new problems of organization and control; and (4) the transformation of the political order. These trends are the subjects of related chapters that form the final larger unit of the book. The chapters are presented within a framework emphasizing social change; at the same time they introduce the student to the main ideas and findings about minorities, the city, and industrial and political sociology. Illustrations are drawn from emergent as well as advanced societies, from nations still at the threshold of modernity as well as the more fully developed industrial societies. These chapters are titled *RACE AND ETHNICITY, URBANIZATION, TECHNOLOGY AND CIVILIZATION,* and *POLITICS AND SOCIETY.*

FORMS OF PRESENTATION

The subject matter is handled in two ways: in text and in adapted readings, referred to as Adaptations. The text consists of self-contained sections, which can be studied as independent modules and which together form a systematic treatment of major topics.

At the end of many sections are separately identified Adaptations. These report key aspects of important studies previously published in books, monographs, and professional journals. Whenever the material was originally written in technical and abstract language for academic readers, we have simplified, condensed, and codified it to make it readily understandable for students beginning sociology. In some Adaptations we present the most important theme of a major work or our own summary and interpretation of a classic book. In every case, Adaptations develop and illustrate points covered in the text.

Most of the Adaptations are case studies included for their factual detail:

Cannibalism and Religion:
    The Case of the Andes Survivors
Pets, People, and the Food Supply
Police Tactics and Crowd Destruction
Riot in Watts: Los Angeles 1965

Other Adaptations are more theoretical:

Mead on Mind, Self, and Society
Tocqueville on the Democratic Age
Piaget on the Child's Conception of Justice
Durkheim on Suicide and Social Integration

Brief illustrative materials, or, in the language of the printer, text inserts, highlight particular topics and are set off from the rest of the text:

Sojourner Truth: Free Woman
A Case of Jitters
The Case of the G.E. Babies

Charts and tables are used to summarize material in a clear form. They should be studied with the same care as pages of words. See "Reading a Table" (Adaptation 1) and "Interpreting a Figure" (pp. 16–17).

Interpreting a figure

Graphic figures are visual aids for quickly understanding quantitative data that might otherwise be presented as equations or statistical tables. Such charts are particularly useful for describing changes over a period of time or approximate differences of such a characteristic as income or education between two or more populations. Although specialized graph papers and plotting machines make it possible for data to be read from some statistical diagrams with precision, diagrams are not customarily used that way in sociology. If exact data are needed it is best to refer to the original tabulations.

Figure 1:1 is a good example of a visual summary. It presents in brief form information that would take a relatively large number of words or several tabular columns of numbers.

Title In this figure, the title declares that this is a report of the percentage illiterate of the total U.S. population and of two major racial categories for a century.

Sources The base figures are estimates from the decennial census figures for the years 1870–1930 and sample surveys from Current Population Surveys for 1947, 1952, 1959, and 1969. Statistics for 1940 were estimated from both census data and sample surveys. Data that reach back for a century and are compiled in different ways should be treated with caution even when the sources are respected.

Assumption Because illiteracy is related to educational attainment, the surveys assumed that everyone who completed six or more years of school (in 1947, five or more years) was literate. This assumption is supported by the findings that 57.4 percent of persons who had not completed a year

of school, but only 2.3 percent of those who had completed five years of school, were illiterate.

Comparability Differences in methods of compiling or changes made for administrative or technical reasons may affect the strict comparability of data compiled over a period of time.

1. Some of the data are from the census; other data are from the Current Population Survey, which used various procedures over the years.

2. Members of the armed forces are excluded from the surveys but not from census estimates.

3. Inmates of institutions are excluded from surveys but included in the census.

4. The census excluded persons below age 10; the surveys excluded those below age 14.

5. The change in 1969 from "nonwhite" to "black only" reflects the concern of policy makers to have a body of well-substantiated facts about blacks. For the years before 1969, Asians, American Indians, and blacks (Negroes), were often grouped in statistical reports as "nonwhites" or "Negro, and other races." The census continues to use "Negro," but this text uses "black" wherever appropriate.

In summary, there is a certain amount of "noise" that impairs strict comparability, but the relative rates over the period between the large racial categories can be accepted as a reasonable indication of the facts.

Trend In 1870 one person in five aged ten years and older was illiterate. By 1900 the figure had been cut in half, and around 1925 it had been halved again. By November 1969 the illiteracy rate was about one person in 100, or one-twentieth the rate in 1870.

Racial differences The figure shows the drastically higher illiteracy for

tion of the campus be discovered. Further-more, any social organization is a dynamic, living thing, changing from year to year even though the formal rules may change slowly.

SOCIAL SYSTEMS

In pursuing the study of social organization, the sociologist often uses the term *social system*. This idea emphasizes the interdependence of social phenomena. Separate social facts or units are studied as parts of larger, interconnected wholes.

The idea of social system invites attention to relationships that are not ordinarily visible and for which there are no common-sense names. For example, the interdependence of police and informers constitutes a social system. Social systems may cut across or extend beyond what are conventionally defined as social units. Thus the intersection of military, political, and industrial life may form a significant unity or complex and may properly be thought of as a social system.

Social systems may be small or large, stable or unstable. Indeed, the most important thing about a system may be its internal stresses and tensions, that is, the sources of instability that are breaking it down or changing it into something else.

For example, in studying the social system of a family—how its members respond to one another, how their activities are organized, how they depend on one another—the sociologist is interested in the tensions within the family as well as the smooth accommodations that have taken place. Similarly, when Marx analyzed what he called the capitalist system he was interested in both the forces that held it together and its latent internal conflicts. He saw the system as producing a class struggle and thereby generating problems it could not solve.

LEVELS OF SOCIAL ORGANIZATION

It is helpful to think of the patterns of social organization (or social systems) at three levels: the interpersonal, the group, and the

social order. Figure 2:1 shows the elements of social organization occurring at each of the three levels. The figure also shows how the elements may be grouped into the micro-order and the macro-order.

1. Interpersonal relations and the micro-order An interpersonal relation is the most elementary social bond occurring between two persons, such as friend/friend, leader/follower, or neighbor/neighbor. Interpersonal means between persons and does not necessarily imply that the relation is intimate. It may be quite the opposite.

Interpersonal relations are the building blocks of social structure. From a common-sense point of view, a group is composed of people. From the sociological perspective, a group is indeed composed of people, but it is also an organization of roles and forms of interaction. In any group, some are in authority and others are followers, some are friends and some antagonists. The sociologist is interested not only in what goes on in specific groups but in more general types of interaction, such as leadership and friendship. It is hoped that through discovering the conditions that sustain interpersonal relations and the strains to which they are subject, knowledge may be gained that will be applicable to all groups of a given kind.

Figure 2:1
Levels and elements of
social organization

Levels	Elements	
Interpersonal level	Patterned interactions	Micro-order
	Role behavior	
Group level	Primary groups	
	Interpersonal relations in organized groups and institutions	
	Intergroup relations	Macro-order
Social order level	Comprehensive patterns of social organization	
	Communities and societies	

2. Group relations The middle level of social organization, as depicted in Figure 2:1, refers to the group structure of society, that is, the variety of groups and the relations among them. At any given time, there are dominant groups and subordinate ones, allies, enemies, and neutrals. Some are strategically located and can communicate with or influence many parts of the community; others are on the fringes with limited access to other groups. Knowing the pattern of group relations is essential to understanding a community or society.

3. The social order When for a large part of its history a society is characterized by distinct patterns of social organization, it is identified as a social order, which is a comprehensive social system. In these circumstances particular kinds of interpersonal relations, such as those involved in kinship, slavery, or feudalism, pervade the entire society. A historical example is European feudalism, which had a number of key features: a personal tie of loyalty between lord and vassal, the binding of serfs and villeins to the soil, a manorial system of agriculture, and decentralized military control by barons who dominated the countryside from fortified castles. These and other features define the ingredients of the feudal order in Europe from about the ninth to the fourteenth centuries. (See Section Five.)

Sociologists are also interested in the distinctive features of other social orders: nomadic societies, the modern industrial society, and totalitarian social organization. Such large social systems are not readily reducible to a few simple elements, but it is possible to outline how the social order functions, the chief sources of its strength, and the main points of weakness and inner conflict.

The study of social systems can also be applied to more limited areas of life. The medical world, for example, is strongly controlled by professional organizations, by a specialized technology requiring centralization of many activities in large hospitals, by the doctor-patient relationship, and by the

way the private physician cooperates with hospital personnel. Anyone interested in medical care needs to understand this network of social relations that extends from the doctor at his patient's bed to the social ranking of hospital personnel.

No sharp separation can be made between studying large institutional settings and small-scale situations. The social organization of the medical world reaches into the hospital ward and affects the human relations within it, just as the social organization of feudalism left its mark on personal interaction in the baronial halls and in the fields.

Section Two presents an interpretation of the formation and dynamics of the micro-order and analyzes patterns of interaction at the interpersonal level. Section Three treats social status and social roles, and Section Four covers social participation; taken together these two sections provide a bridge between the micro-order and macro-order. Section Five discusses comprehensive patterns of social organization.

Section two interaction and the micro-order

To bring the social world into perspective the sociologist often uses a wide-angle lens. The camera takes in a broad landscape: the system of social stratification, the institutional order, and the organization of industry, politics, education, or religion. Society is observed at a distance. With such a perspective, important as it is, the individual's immediate life situations may be obscured.

This section sharply narrows the field of view. Social order is seen up close as an aspect of everyday life. The small-scale behavior setting within which human contact occurs is the center of attention. The pattern of these settings, the *micro-order*, is based upon social interaction, that is, the process of acting in awareness of others and adjust-

There are immediate gratifications in being "one up," to say nothing of the long-term benefits of special privilege. Even the low man on the totem pole may gain satisfaction from belonging to a group of higher status than another group.

From the standpoint of the person, one who gives deference may benefit from showing respect for someone genuinely esteemed. On the other hand, deference may be degrading and dehumanizing if it means that a human being is treated as a thing or if it involves "stripping the self." (See *SOCIALIZATION*, pp. 97–99.) From the standpoint of the group, ranking may aid communication, as when people accept the orders of a ship's captain, or it may interfere with communication, as when no one wants to tell bad news to the boss. (See Adaptation 15, p. 203.) Close attention to the micro-order reveals the gains and the losses to the individual and to the group.

In giving deference and demanding it, *social distance* is manipulated (Goffman, 1967:62–76). People of higher rank often feel entitled to take liberties, trespassing on a lower-ranking person's privacy or personal space. For example, women employees are often treated with a familiarity—in humor, in physical contact, and in the use of first names—that their male co-workers would not accept. Such a pattern underscores the low status of the subordinate while protecting the dignity and inviolability of the superior. One party in the interaction is exposed and vulnerable, the other is more secure.

Cooperation and reciprocity

Social order is created when people need each other, but cooperation is always potentially unstable (Blau, 1964:26). Cooperation raises such questions as: Who needs whom? Who is dependent on whom? What resources do the parties have for social exchange? Thus *dependency* and *reciprocity* are key conditions that affect how much cooperation there will be and the form it will take.

There is a difference between casual or market reciprocity and the kind that sustains a pattern of interaction. Buying a newspaper is a form of exchange reciprocity, but as a purely economic transaction no micro-order need be involved. The exchange might take place mechanically by putting money in a slot. On the other hand, buying a newspaper is a meaningful interaction if the purchase is part of an established relationship between a regular customer and a storekeeper.

Cooperation has a positive connotation and seems to be a good thing in itself, but it may be based on unequal power and dependency. A social exchange is not necessarily evenly balanced: It may be oppressive and exploitative. If A has many alternatives and B has none, then B is the more dependent and may have to submit to harsh or humiliating terms. In other words, the idea of exchange does not imply that partners enter into interaction with equal resources, wit, or power. There is often a poignant asymmetry in human exchanges. A woman may love a man and consider his very presence a great benefit; he may be interested in maintaining the connection but only because he receives sexual or housekeeping service. Needless to say, it can work the other way around. Psychiatrists and family therapists have a professional interest in identifying the stress points in such micro-orders. Thus patterns of dependency and exchange may have clinical applications as well as general sociological interest.

PERSPECTIVES ON THE MICRO-ORDER

In the foregoing discussion, which is informed by an interactional perspective, the micro-order is seen as emerging from the give-and-take of human adaptation. But it is sometimes difficult to maintain an interactional perspective (Blumer, 1969:Chap. 1). Individuals are perceived as having learned a set of rules through the process of socialization, and once learned, the rules are assumed to be part of the standard equipment people carry around with them. When con-

they are used most of the time by loners and occasional couples looking for a private spot. Largeness and formality of furniture arrangements are the most commonly cited lounge characteristics discouraging casual small group use. High viewing distance, light levels, high ceilings and visual access from the hall entrance, make the lounge awkward as a dating parlor, and impossible as a group study space (Van der Ryn and Silverstein, 1967:44).

Another illustration of ecological awareness is Winston Churchill's defense of the architectural form of the British House of Commons (see *COLLECTIVE BEHAVIOR*, p. 232). Churchill realized that the size and shape of the chamber contributed to a desired form of interaction among members of Parliament. Quantitative studies of interaction among office workers confirm that spatial arrangements have a significant influence on the frequency of social interaction and friendship (Gullahorn, 1952; Wells, 1965).

The deliberate design of interactional settings suggests a connection between group ecology and the definition of the situation. Much architectural design is oriented to the management of impressions, helping people to create desirable images of themselves. For example, office spaces are often arranged to help sustain the "masks" and "performances" people engage in at work (Goffman, 1959:17 ff.). A top executive is provided with private spaces, such as an executive washroom, and buffer zones of secretarial offices, so that he can control how he appears before others:

He must have private space to which he can retreat, either to prepare for the next performance or to rest from the last. . . . Outside contacts with the executive are preceded by contact with the secretary. She screens potential telephone calls, letters, and entrants. She will forewarn the executive of a visitor in terms of his status and function. The executive may then assume the appropriate stance for the encounter. With his status-equals he may be casual, with underlings "the boss," with visitors a "company representative," with his wife a husband, or with his boss an employee. Each may require a moment of preparation—psychological and physical (Roizen, 1969:13–14).

Ranking and deference All societies and most enduring human groups rely for social order, at least to some extent, on distinctions of rank and on inequalities of power and privilege. Patterns of domination are common among many animal species, and it has been argued that ranking is a "principle of organization without which a more advanced social life cannot develop in higher vertebrates" (Lorenz, 1966:40). In the study of subhuman primates domination is an important theme:

Although expressions of dominance vary widely from one species to another, between groups within the same species, and even in the same individual at different times, it is clear that dominance interactions are fundamental to primate behavior and that they are especially prominent in the Old World monkeys, apes, and man. It is in the primarily ground-dwelling species such as baboons and macaques that dominance behavior is most apparent, and it is in the social groups of these species that dominance hierarchies exert the most influence in social organization (DeVore, 1968:355).

Ethology (the study of animal behavior) gives much attention to social organization. Recent investigations, some involving painstaking observation of animals in their natural habitats, have reawakened appreciation for the continuity of human and other animal species. Indeed, a new field of scientific study, sociobiology, has recently emerged. Sociobiology brings together the work of zoologists, geneticists, and students of human behavior (Wilson, 1975).

The continuities of human and other animal species are especially striking with respect to such basic behavior patterns as nurturing the young and expressing social domination. Among humans, one of the most important social and psychological foundations of ranking is that people want to have self-respect and to be respected.

pends on many detailed transactions among patients, physicians, and staff (Strauss et al., 1963). In labor relations, bargaining between union and employer does not stop when a formal settlement is reached and a contract is signed. Negotiation continues as part of the everyday life of the plant in the form of "fractional bargaining" over specific grievances (Kuhn, 1961:Chap. 5).

Ethnomethodology resembles certain developments in anthropology, such as ethnosemantics or ethnobotany. Ethnosemantics refers to "the system of meanings—the tacit theory of the world—lying behind a language and its usages" (Kay, 1970:20). As in ethnomethodology, the perspective of persons (or groups) is adopted to learn how they interpret the world. Ethnobotany studies the way plants are described and used by the people,

especially members of non-Western or preliterate societies.

Caution The main principles of ethnomethodology are consistent with the discussion of interaction and the micro-order in this chapter. However, if treated as the only way to understand the totality of social organization, ethnomethodology may be misleading. All social organization involves interaction, but the conditions of interaction and the framework in which it takes place may depend on such impersonal forces of the macro-order as technology, industrial organization, migration, conquest, and economic power. The approach of ethnomethodology can throw light on the micro-order, but it cannot provide an adequate account of the macro-order.

Adaptation 2 Goffman: Rituals of interaction

The writings of Erving Goffman bring a fresh perspective to the study of everyday life. Two themes are central in Goffman's work: (1) the fate of the self in the course of interaction, that is, the way the individual is put at risk in encounters with others and how he or she manages those risks, and (2) the fate of the micro-order, that is, the many devices that are used, often unconsciously, to sustain the continuity of social life at the level of human interaction.

In pursuing these themes, a number of ideas are prominent in Goffman's thought, among them life as episode and as theater, the management of

impressions, and the significance of ritual in human encounters.

THE EPISODIC NATURE OF THE MICRO-ORDER
⌈The micro-order may be conceived of as made up of millions of minute and transient episodes of social life.⌉Even where people have long-standing relationships over many years, the actual time they are in communication consists of relatively brief encounters and occasions. In this sense "society" is not an abstraction—it is made up of very specific activities and communications, many of which are fleeting and precarious. To some degree, society as it is really lived is continuously coming into being and passing out of existence.

"A sociology of occasions is here advocated. Social organization is the central theme, but what is organized is the co-mingling of persons and the temporary interactional enterprises that can arise therefrom. A normatively stabilized structure is at issue, a 'social gathering,' but this is a shifting en-

Source: A summary and interpretation of works on the micro-order by Erving Goffman. His analyses appear in the following volumes: *The Presentation of Self in Everyday Life* (Garden City, N.Y.: Doubleday Anchor Books, 1959); *Encounters: Two Studies in the Sociology of Interaction* (Indianapolis: Bobbs-Merrill, 1961); *Behavior in Public Places: Notes on the Social Organization of Gatherings* (New York: The Free Press of Glencoe, 1963); *Interaction Ritual: Essays on Face-to-Face Behavior* (Garden City, N.Y.: Doubleday Anchor Books, 1967); *Relations in Public: Microstudies of the Public Order* (New York: Harper Colophon Books, 1971). Quoted material, some of which is abridged, is used by permission of the author and copyright holder. This adaptation was prepared by Saul Geiser.

tity, necessarily evanescent, created by arrivals and killed by departures" (1967:2).

Being episodic, the micro-order must be created anew at each successive encounter. Re-creation is accomplished through an exchange of cues and gestures by which the participants indicate to each other their own intended roles in the situation as well as what they expect the others' roles to be. This working consensus will differ from one interaction setting to another. "Thus, between two friends at lunch, a reciprocal show of affection, respect, and concern for the other is maintained. In service occupations, on the other hand, the specialist often maintains an image of disinterested involvement in the problem of the client, while the client responds with a show of respect for the competence and integrity of the specialist" (1959:10).

INTERACTION AS THEATER

In an important sense, therefore, social interaction is much like theater. There is an expressive, dramatized element designed to project a definition of reality as much as to carry out practical tasks. Shakespeare's metaphor "all the world's a stage" can be developed into a dramaturgical model of the micro-order, showing how everyday life is pervaded by features of a theatrical performance. Thus, many social establishments are divided into "front-stage" and "backstage" regions. In front-stage areas, such as living rooms and food counters, an idealized display of decorum and cleanliness is affected whenever outsiders are present; backstage, in bedrooms and kitchens, performers can relax in guarded secrecy. Social performances are often staged by teams, such as the husband and wife hosting a dinner party or the doctor and nurse showing spotless clinical efficiency in the presence of patients.

THE MANAGEMENT OF IMPRESSIONS

If interaction is like theater, then individuals must be like actors. The individual as effective "actor" in social encounters must be skilled in the art of "impression management"—controlling his or her image in the eyes of others so as to create a favorable definition of the situation. "For example, in American society we find that eight-year-old children claim lack of interest in the television programs that are directed to five and six year olds,

but sometimes surreptitiously watch them. We also find that middle-class housewives may leave *The Saturday Evening Post* on their living room end table but keep a copy of *True Romance* ('It's something the cleaning woman must have left around') concealed in their bedroom. . . .

"In their capacity as performers, individuals will be concerned with maintaining the impression that they are living up to the many standards by which they and their products are judged. But qua performers, individuals are concerned not with the moral issue of realizing these standards, but with the amoral issue of engineering a convincing impression that these standards are being realized" (1959:42, 251).

THE HAZARDS OF IMPRESSION MANAGEMENT

Once the individual has projected an impression of himself or herself to others, the others will expect this impression to be maintained throughout the remainder of the encounter as well as in any subsequent encounters.

"The expressive coherence that is required in performances points out a crucial discrepancy between our all-too-human selves and our socialized selves. As human beings we are presumably creatures of variable impulse with moods and energies that change from one moment to the next. As characters put on for an audience, however, we must not be subject to ups and downs. A certain bureaucratization of the spirit is expected so that we can be relied upon to give a perfectly homogeneous performance at every appointed time" (1959:56).

However, such expressive coherence is often difficult to sustain. The individual may make *faux pas* and boners that give away his or her act; the audience may come into possession of past information about the individual which is inconsistent with the character presently portrayed; outsiders may accidentally enter backstage regions, catching a team in the midst of activity at odds with their front-stage image. A fundamental theme that runs through Goffman's work is the ever-present danger that someone will see through, contradict, or otherwise disrupt a performance.

"When these disruptive events occur, the interaction itself may come to a confused and embarrassed halt. At such moments the individual whose presentation has been discredited may feel

ing responses to the way others respond. Thus, study of the micro-order focuses on the human individual in the behavior setting (Barker and Barker, 1961:Chap. 15).

An illustration of the micro-order is the phenomenon of civil inattention (See Adaptation 2, p. 29.) In Western society there are informal rules limiting eye contact between persons who are unacquainted. These rules are associated with public places such as elevators, streets, and rest rooms. When people encounter one another in such places, they are expected to glance at each other, but not long enough to suggest that the other is an object of special interest. Too much eye contact, or staring, may be embarrassing.

In traditional India, where eye avoidance is a manifestation of the caste system, it is the obligation of persons of high and outcaste statuses to avoid visual contact. Failure to do so results in contamination of the higher-caste individual who may then be obliged to undergo purification.

In these cases the micro-order is patterned by rules that govern how people behave and what they expect. Such rules are often unspoken; most are never written down or discussed, even in the most exhaustive book of etiquette. Moreover, the rules of the micro-order are often vague and subject to negotiation. When two people meet they have to work out for themselves the terms of their interaction, acting within commonly accepted guidelines. The character of the interaction and the significance of the encounter for each of the parties depends on cues and nuances, on detailed ways of showing deference, maintaining distance, or overcoming barriers to communication.

THE CREATION OF MICRO-ORDERS

Although much can be learned from close study of the rules or norms that govern interaction, the social order, including the micro-order, is more than a set of rules. When people interact they do so not as puppets but as living persons with wants and needs and problems, who are strong in

some ways and weak in others, who must act in a specific world of practical opportunities and limits. These circumstances suggest that the structure of the micro-order is a complex product of social expectations and personal adaptations, of spontaneous responses and calculated strategies.

The following paragraphs review some of the main ways interaction is patterned and a micro-order produced.

Definition of the situation "If men define situations as real they are real in their consequences." With this much-quoted sentence W. I. Thomas (1928:572) meant that to a large extent people create their own social realities. When human beings act and interact, they bring to bear their own assessments and interpretations. They act on their understanding of what is going on and what a situation requires, for example, whether to be serious or relaxed. To define the situation is to give it meaning and thus to make it part of social order.

Social order exists when people share the same definition of the situation. They then have similar expectations and know how to orient their conduct. Most of these shared definitions are acquired unconsciously. They constitute "a world taken for granted" (Schutz, 1962:74). The reality of that world can be dramatically revealed if without warning people behave in unexpected ways, challenging the unconsciously accepted definition of the situation.

A sociologist asked his students to spend an evening at home behaving as if they had just been introduced to their parents, using formal terms of address like Mr. and Mrs. and being as polite as one would ordinarily be with new acquaintances. The students were instructed to maintain the pose for an entire evening without explaining what they were doing. So strong was the pressure against this disruptive conduct that most students found it impossible to complete the assignment, and quite a few parental tempers had to be cooled with explanations (Garfinkel, 1967:Chap. 2). Such exercises show how the micro-order often operates without our awareness and becomes revealed only when expectations are violated and when people react to violated expectations.

But the definition of the situation is not always taken for granted. Many situations are more open and fluid than others; the meaning they have for the participants must be worked out in the course of interaction. People may compete with one another to establish a definition of the situation that will serve their interests. A person entering an interaction may try to convey an impression of authority or sincerity, of being "with it" or "available." In doing so he or she tries to control how others respond, that is, how they define the situation. The phrase "management of impressions" has been applied to the personal strategies people use in creating self-serving definitions of the situation (Goffman, 1959:208–237).

If an individual's definition of the situation is too personal and idiosyncratic, it will create difficulties. For example a person who persists in treating a gathering as a party when everyone else is trying to hold a meeting imposes strains on everyone, including himself. On the other hand, if enough people define the situation as a party, the chances are it will become one. This is an example of what Thomas meant by saying that a situation defined as real is real in its consequences. The definition of the situation becomes a "self-fulfilling prophecy": If people believe that a bank is not solvent and withdraw their funds, the bank will soon be in trouble. Teachers who believe that ghetto children cannot learn and treat them as though they cannot learn help make their predictions come true.

The concept of defining the situation points to a *subjective* source of social order: Interaction is patterned by states of mind, by the beliefs and interpretations people bring to the situation, by the meanings they give to their own actions and the actions of others. This is fundamental, for ultimately all groups and societies are held together by shared beliefs and perceptions.

On the other hand, subjective states of mind are influenced by *objective* conditions. The work people do, the communities they live in, the opportunities they have—these conditions are objective in the sense that they set limits to the way people can interpret the world and encourage some interpretations rather than others. The environment of interaction, the setting within which behavior takes place, is important in delineating the micro-order. The effect of physical arrangements on neighborliness is an example of the influence of ecological environment (man-made as well as natural) on the form and quality of interaction.

Ecological patterning Because architects are in the business of designing environments within which social interaction goes on, they are concerned with ecological patterning. The architect Richard J. Neutra once claimed that he could so design a house that conflict would be created between the most compatible spouses. It is not known whether he ever published this ecological prescription for domestic disaster, but the claim makes sociological sense. However, if architects are mainly preoccupied with efficient spaces or with designs for the overall structure, they may give insufficient attention to the micro-order and its significance for human satisfaction (Van der Ryn, 1969). For example, a study of recently built student dormitories found that the designers were insensitive to the realities of student life in a number of ways. The use of built-in furniture tended to limit the variety of room arrangements and therefore the possibilities of facilitating or limiting interaction among roommates to suit individual needs, such as avoiding eye contact when studying. It was also found that rooms intended for large groups were ill designed:

The main lounge and library do little to develop overlapping social groups among the residents;

out the conversational rituals of speaking and listening in turn, social interaction would degenerate into chaotic babble.

A second basic function of interpersonal ritual is to ensure that one's self will escape relatively unscathed when one enters interactional traffic. Each new interactional episode poses a potential threat to the self-image the individual attempts to project; and the self is therefore a "ritually delicate object," ever alert to offenses and slights that would reflect unfavorably upon it. Even having one's remarks ignored in conversation can be taken as a sign that one's self is somehow deficient; conversational etiquette requires that one's remarks, however trivial, be acknowledged.

"The complete withholding of ritual supports is often inclined to but rarely achieved. Without such mercies, conversation would want of its fundamental basis of organization—the ritual interchange—and everywhere unsatisfactory persons would be left to bleed to death from the conversational savageries performed on them" (1971:68–69).

Third, the principle of reciprocity is built into the very structure of interpersonal ritual. It has a "dialogistic" character; that is, it typically involves a standardized exchange of moves and countermoves, or dialogue, between two or more actors: "Hi, how are you?" "Fine, thanks. And you?" Together these moves make up a little ceremony in which both selves receive ritual support; it is like holding hands in a circle, in which one gets back in the left hand what he or she gives with the right. Because such ritual exchanges occur so often in everyday interaction, they provide repeated opportunities for actors mutually to ratify their projected identities and thereby to sustain a workable, if idealized, definition of the situation. Interpersonal ritual thus involves a tacit teamwork, allowing each individual room to construct and uphold his own chosen identity. It is a curious twist. Though individuals are selfishly concerned to sustain a favorable impression of themselves, their efforts must be ritually expressed as altruistic regard for the identities of others: "His aim is to save face; his effect is to save the situation" (1955/1967:39).

THE CONSERVATIVE NATURE
OF THE MICRO-ORDER

Because of its episodic and fleeting character, the

micro-order may seem to be rather flimsy and unstable, lacking a consistent influence upon the behavior of the individual. In some senses this is true. Since the ritual order depends primarily on informal sanctions to effect conformity, anyone with enough self-assurance can override attempted sanctions simply by not allowing himself or herself to be emotionally affected. Ethnomethodologists profess to see the seeds of a "revolutionary" viewpoint in this analysis: The micro-order exists only because people *believe* it exists; social order is really quite precarious.

Yet Goffman's work has a conservative ring. He is at pains to show how interaction constrains people and why such constraints are necessary if people are to create a shared and consistent definition of reality:

"By entering a situation in which he is given a face to maintain, a person takes on the responsibility of standing guard over the flow of events as they pass before him. He must ensure that a particular *expressive order* is sustained—an order that regulates the flow of events, large or small, so that anything that appears to be expressed by them will be consistent with his face. . . . While his social face can be his most personal possession and the center of his security and pleasure, it is only on loan to him from society; it will be withdrawn unless he conducts himself in a way that is worthy of it. Approved attributes and their relation to face make of every man his own jailer; this is a fundamental social constraint even though each man may like his cell" (1955/1967:9–10).

Perhaps the most conservative element in Goffman's account of the micro-order is his emphasis on shared values as the social glue by which society is held together. Unlike theorists of a more radical persuasion who see society as marked by continual conflict and held together by force, he locates the basis of social order in the values people hold in common. Ritual is important insofar as it is a means of ceremonially reaffirming these values. Yet unlike earlier conservative theorists such as Durkheim, who emphasized abstractly shared values and ritual, Goffman shows how ritual performances are a pervasive feature of everyday life:

"To the degree that a performance highlights the common official values of the society in which it occurs, we may look upon it . . . as a ceremony—as an expressive . . . reaffirmation of the moral values of the community. Furthermore, insofar as the expressive bias of performances comes to be accepted as reality, then that which is accepted at the moment as reality will have some of the characteristics of a celebration. To stay in one's room away from the place where the party is given, or away from where the practitioner attends his client, is to stay away from where reality is being performed. The world, in truth, is a wedding" (1959:35–36).

Section three social status and social role

The concepts of status and role provide indispensable starting points for the analysis of social structure. Briefly, a social status is a position within a social system; a social role is the pattern of behavior associated with that position. The words *professor* and *student* indicate statuses; the associated roles are what professors and students do, how they act out the expectations and meet the problems that go with the statuses. Thus status and role involve each other; role "represents the dynamic aspect of status" (Linton, 1936:114).

THE IDEA OF STATUS

The definitions above are necessarily broad since they must embrace a wide variety of statuses and roles, some of which may be temporary or unstable. For example, in a group of three persons, one may have a special status in that he or she is liked and respected by the other two, who are less keen about each other. Sociologists are more often concerned with statuses that are stable enough and significant enough to generate beliefs and expectations. For this reason, a status is often identified by the rights and obligations that are assigned to it.

Salient status A major significance of status in society is that it can and does determine social identity. A status is salient and tends to fix the identity of the person who occupies it if a large part of the individual's life is organized around it or if the status has a special symbolic significance. Thus, for many people an occupation or profession is a salient status. For many others, however, the job is less salient and consequently tells little about the individual who fills it except how a living is earned. A transitory or occasional social position—for example, a student's summer job—has little impact upon social identity. Researchers of occupational careers recognize this fact and put such jobs in a separate category from the person's basic career history.

Traditional society depended for its stability on salient statuses. There was widespread belief in the rightness and permanence of one's "station" in life. Occupational status was stable and transmitted from generation to generation; the cobbler kept to his last and taught his trade to his son. Social discipline was maintained by inculcating the view that every person had a proper place in the social scheme of things. Salient status was also *fixed* status.

Fixed status is not so dominant a principle of social organization in contemporary Western society. Life is more fluid, and people occupy many different statuses at the same time and through the life cycle. But a status may still be relatively salient, at least for a certain period of life. Sometimes the salient status is voluntary or self-determined, as when a person is devoted to a demanding profession, a public occupation, or becoming an artist. On the other hand, many salient statuses are nonvoluntary, or *ascribed*.

An ascribed status is one assigned to the individual by legal or other social criteria, without regard to the individual's choice, activities, or special characteristics. The social criteria may be age, sex, race, inheritance, or anything else that permits some people to be classified as significantly different from others. Thus being an adult, a man, and black are all ascribed statuses. Of these, being black may be salient from the

Lazarsfeld, Paul F., William H. Sewell, and Harold L. Wilensky
1967 The Uses of Sociology. New York: Basic Books.

Merton, Robert K., Leonard Broom, and Leonard S. Cottrell, Jr. (eds.)
1959 Sociology Today: Problems and Prospects. New York: Basic Books.

Nisbet, Robert A.
1966 The Sociological Tradition. New York: Basic Books.

Park, Robert E. and Ernest W. Burgess
1924 Introduction to the Science of Sociology. Chicago: University of Chicago Press.

Schneider, Louis
1975 The Sociological Way of Looking at the World. New York: McGraw-Hill.

Theodorson, George A. and Achilles G. Theodorson
1969 Dictionary of Sociology. New York: Crowell.

Annual Review of Sociology
Palo Alto, Calif.: Annual Reviews, Inc. Began publication in 1975.

Encyclopedia of the Social Sciences
1938 New York: Macmillan.

International Encyclopedia of the Social Sciences.
1968 New York: Macmillan.

Statistical Abstract of the United States. Published annually since 1878 by the U.S. Bureau of the Census.

Periodicals

This is an abbreviated list of journals of general sociological interest. They contain articles on topics pertinent to each of the chapters in this book and are not separately listed in succeeding chapters.

American Journal of Sociology
American Sociological Review
Annals of the American Academy of Political and Social Science
British Journal of Sociology
Canadian Journal of Sociology
Canadian Review of Sociology and Anthropology
Contemporary Sociology
Current Sociology
New Society
Rural Sociology
Social Forces
Social Problems
Social Science Quarterly
Society (formerly transaction)
Sociological Abstracts
Sociology (British)
Sociometry

For an extended list of journals in sociology and related fields see:

Rhoades, Lawrence J.
n.d. The Author's Guide to Selected Journals. Washington, D.C.: American Sociological Association.

2 | Social Organization

Section one introduction

By itself the word *organization* connotes a technical arrangement of parts and does not suggest the complexity and dynamics of human association. The adjective *social* before *organization* emphasizes that individual and group relations are adaptive outcomes of social processes. Social organization, the pattern of individual and group relations, emerges out of day-to-day interactions, out of problem solving, conflict, cooperation, and accommodation.

Social organization is often called "the social fabric," which suggests that human relations are closely interwoven and that strains on one part may weaken the whole fabric in unexpected ways. This figure of speech further suggests an emphasis on social harmony and social cohesion, but social organization also consists of relations that involve disharmony and conflict. The social organization of a business may be an efficient linking of production and distribution departments, but it may create disharmony by segregating blue-collar from white-collar employees and creating conflicts of interest among various groups within the enterprise. What is good for the business may not be equally good for all of the employees, for management, for the stockholders, or for the customers.

To grasp the general idea of social organization, consider the familiar case of an American university. On the campus there is a wide variety of groups, some permanent and formally recognized, others formed for special tasks and purposes. Less visible are the lines of communication and influence among groups and their members, and these communication networks are well known only to the most active participants in campus life. The student government may be a "sand box" with little power and with weak communication with the student body. Or it may provide effective leadership to the students and significantly influence the way the university is run. The patterns of communication and influence are not likely to be revealed in an official description of student organization, power, and responsibility. Only through actual experience or through systematic research can the social organiza-

standpoint of the society, while being an adult may be salient from the point of view of the individual. These interpretations come into conflict when a black man is called "boy" because he is black.

Status and ranking In common speech and in much sociological discussion, *status* is used to designate a position within a system of social ranking. Sergeants rank higher than privates, and the whole set of military ranks may be referred to as a "status system."

Many other statuses, for example, those of mother or friend, do not necessarily carry the connotation of higher or lower. Still, it is true that social positions tend to be differently rewarded and esteemed, and a system of fixed statuses is especially likely to emphasize rank and to maintain distinctions of place and privilege. In other words, ranking is often associated with a system of statuses, and it is easy to understand why the distinction between rank and status is often blurred. In strict terms, ranking should be considered as one important attribute or aspect of some statuses.

ROLES AND ROLE SETS

In its most familiar connotation, a role is a part in a play. The actors and actresses have assigned roles and their performances consist in conveying an impression of reality while reading the playwright's lines and following the instructions. The sociological meaning of role—a pattern of behavior associated with a status or social position—also suggests acting out. The individual does what is called for by the position occupied. However, he or she does so not as an actor or actress speaking someone else's lines but as a person responding to genuine expectations and problems.

Role as a pattern of behavior associated with a social status includes the following elements:

1. The socially prescribed or ideal role The ideal role prescribes the rights and duties belonging to a social position: It tells what is expected of a father or mother, to whom he or she has obligations, and upon whom she or he has rightful claims.

2. The perceived role What the individual believes should be done in a particular position—how he or she defines the situation—may not fully coincide with the conventional image or ideal. Similarly the specific people with whom one interacts may have different ideas. The interactional perspective on roles does not take it for granted that social norms are always accepted or perceived by everyone in the same way.

3. The performed role What the individual actually does in the role—the practical course of conduct—depends on more than beliefs, expectations, and perceptions. Actual role behavior is always subject to the pressures and opportunities of a specific social setting at a specific time. It is also conditioned by the individual's personality and past experience.

An adequate analysis of any social role, even one as well established and clearly defined as the role of a judge, must take account of all three elements: prescription, perception, and performance.

Emergent roles Conventional or prescribed roles are so numerous and so important that they dominate the social landscape. It is easy to forget that a great many roles are informal and new ones are always emerging. For example, in small-group interaction one person may be a spark plug or idea person, another a joker who helps relieve tension, still another an informal leader or negotiator. Emergent roles are not necessarily based on clearly defined expectations. They may cut across or be independent of formally defined positions; they tend to be expressive of personality and of rather immediate group or interactional needs; and there is often no conventional name for the role. Goffman refers to a "sidekick" role:

[On] back-wards in mental hospitals one can find attendant and patient who have grown old together and find that the patient is required to be the butt of the attendant's jokes at one moment, while receiving an aligning collusive wink from him at another, this therapeutic support being given the attendant whenever he is pleased to demand it. . . . Some members of street-corner gangs and some executive assistants in the cour s that form around Hollywood producers provide other illustrations (1959:206).

Emergent roles may be found at every level of social structure. A large organization may have a problem deciding how to conceive its own role—what business it is really in. General Electric's slogan, "Progress Is Our Most Important Product," may be dismissed as public relations, but it reflects an awareness that technological innovation may be as important a competence or role to advertise as a specific product. Similarly the different political and pressure-group organizations that make up a social movement, such as the civil rights movement, may develop roles appropriate to the distinctive mission of the organization.

The same logic applies to the emergent roles of organization members especially members of an organization that has not yet clearly defined its task or role. It is not always apparent at the outset how member's role will develop or be conceived. The role of the Peace Corps volunteer has been a continuing problem for the Peace Corps, especially whether the volunteer should be an agent of change or merely one who gives assistance but does not rock any boats, whether the volunteer should be involved in social concerns or restricted to technical matters. Whether one role or another emerges has significant implications for the training of volunteers and for the Peace Corp's relations with local communities and national leaders.

The roles of high officials may also be problematic and emergent. A business executive may gradually define his role as an "outside man," mainly concerned with getting business or negotiating with govern ment or labor; or he may be an "inside man," giving most attention to production or internal administration.

Role sets Most roles and statuses are more complex than they appear to be at first glance. A mother is a mother in relation to a child; yet being a mother is more than just one social relation. It is a bundle of relations to other members of the family and to the community, as well as to the child. Part of the role of mother may involve membership in the Parent-Teachers Association, just as part of the role of employer may involve membership in a Chamber of Commerce.

The concept of role set suggests the complex nature of roles and recognizes that a given status generates more than one role. A single status, such as husband, involves "an array of associated roles" (Merton, 1968:423). Someone entering a new status usually acquires not a unitary role but a role set in order to meet the expectations of a number of different people. A person does not marry his or her in-laws, but they become role partners and the relations with the role partners form a role set that is associated with the status of husband or wife.

STRAIN AND CONFLICT

Because of the diverse demands contained in a role set, the individual who occupies a status is subject to competing pressures. The demands of one role partner may conflict with the demands of others. Much more is entailed than individual or personality differences. Rather, the role set in one status binds the person to other people who occupy different statuses and, as a result, are subject to their own demands and limitations. A professor's role set embraces relations to undergraduates, graduate students, teaching colleagues, research colleagues, administrators, publishers, and others who occupy differing statuses. Luckily, not all of these role partners make the same or conflicting demands at the same time. And the professor can learn with experience to develop strategies for coping with the pressures of the system (Goode, 1960:486–490; Merton, 1968:425–433).

The strains and conflicts in role behavior are only partly accounted for by competing pressures in the role set. Some strains arise because the role itself requires different and inconsistent kinds of conduct. For example, a role may call for friendship or intimacy but also require impersonal judgment or command. To the extent that a professor's role leads him or her to influence some students deeply, he or she needs to be on friendly terms with them, to treat them as unique persons, and to develop a sense of mutual loyalty. But the professor must also be a judge who evaluates the work of the student and makes decisions that may affect the latter's career. These conflicting demands can require painful adjustments on the part of both participants.

Role conflicts in industry and military life are revealed when the attempt is made to create a communications bridge from the commanding group to those who must obey. Many noncommissioned officers in the army and foremen in industry play this bridging role. They must communicate orders from above, but they must be close enough to the working group to understand how these orders will be received; they must have the confidence of the working group lest fear and hostility undermine effective communication and the will to cooperate. At the same time, these lower-level leaders must be able to take the point of view of their superiors whose orders are to be communicated and enforced. The result is a continuing necessity to take account of two approaches to daily experience and of two sets of interests that are often in conflict. (The adaptive strategies of foremen are discussed in Adaptation 15.)

Thus strains and inconsistencies are built into the role. When these built-in conflicts are known, the problems posed for the individual by the role are also known. The role makes demands, limits the choice of alternatives, and creates problems to be solved. This point illustrates the dynamic, motivating, and problem-setting nature of social organization.

ROLES AND PATTERN VARIABLES

Close study of social roles has shown that a relatively few basic themes or patterns occur with high frequency. Among these is a set of contrasts called pattern variables. The term *pattern variable* was introduced by Parsons and Shils (1951:76–91) and Parsons (1951:45–67). However, similar contrast conceptions and some of the specific pattern variables, for example, ascription–achievement, instrumental–expressive, have long been familiar in sociology. Primary–secondary (see p. 126), caste–class (see p. 182), and *Gemeinschaft–Gesellschaft* (see p. 152) are examples of paired alternatives similar to the pattern variables identified and analyzed by Parsons and Shils. A pattern variable is a *pair of alternative modes of orientation*, that is, contrasting ways of relating to oneself and to others. Like yin

Figure 2:2 yin/yang

In classical Chinese philosophy, yin and yang are complementary principles or forces. Yin represents darkness, femaleness, cold, water, earth, passivity; yang is brightness, maleness, warmth, fire, activity. "This was not a dualism of the Occidental sort, like that between good and evil or spirit and matter. On the contrary yin and yang complemented each other to maintain the cosmic harmony, and might transform into each other; thus winter, which is yin, changes into summer, which is yang (Creel, 1953:173)."

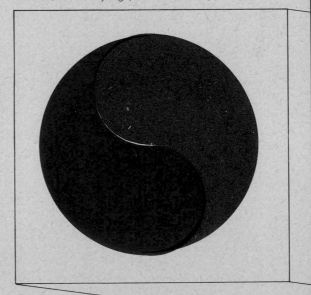

and yang, they are opposites that involve and complement each other. Therefore the pattern variables point to recurrent tensions or dilemmas in social action and social organization.

Four of the best understood and most widely cited pattern variables are the following: (1) universalism–particularism, (2) instrumentalism–expressiveness, (3) specificity–diffuseness, and (4) ascription–achievement.

Universalism–particularism

The college entrance requirements of a state university are supposed to be applied uniformly to all who seek higher education, excluding no one except on grounds relevant to educational qualifications. Such criteria are called *universalistic* because they transcend the special interests of persons or groups. They are based on general rules or principles and are to be applied uniformly to all members of an appropriate category, in this case, applicants for admission.

A *particularistic* criterion, on the other hand, recognizes the claim of an individual to be treated in a special way. If one chooses a physician or lawyer because he is a friend who needs the business, then one has made a particularistic choice. The classic example of particularism is nepotism, the hiring of relatives. Notice that there may be a norm of particularism: People may feel that it is right and proper to be loyal to friends or relatives, even at the loss of efficiency or fairness.

Universalism and particularism are competing principles, and the tension between them accounts for many difficulties in role behavior. It is usually assumed, probably correctly, that universalism is the more fragile of the two orientations and needs the greater protection. Because most people have their deepest commitments to other persons who are committed to them in turn rather than to abstract ideas, roles based on universalistic principles are often elaborately protected against the intrusion of particularism. For example, judges and simi-

lar officials are expected to disqualify themselves if relatives or close associates appear before them or if they have financial interest in a case.

Instrumentalism–expressiveness

Many roles demand a rational, utilitarian, cost-accounting approach to oneself, to other people, and to objects in the world. Action is *instrumental* when it is governed by principles of efficiency and effectiveness, when things are weighed for their worth as means to preconceived ends.

A student who comes to college with a definite vocational objective in mind has an instrumental orientation. On the other hand, those who perceive themselves in a process of growth and change and respond spontaneously to new experiences and opportunities have an *expressive* orientation. The gratifications of expressiveness flow from action and response itself rather than from the attainment of a fixed goal. Individuals acting expressively invest their personalities in the acts; consequently conduct is less controlled and less efficient from the standpoint of achieving a specific objective at minimum cost.

A satisfactory balance of the expressive and the instrumental is essential for efficiency accompanied by personal satisfaction. The idea of meaningful work presumes such a balance: To be meaningful, work should offer opportunity for self-realization, that is, for a sense of continuity between the requirements of the task and the organization of personality. In alienated work, instrumentalism predominates, and the individual becomes an adjunct of the machine, including the bureaucratic machine. (See *TECHNOLOGY AND CIVILIZATION*, p. 522–523.)

Specificity–diffuseness

The parties to a contract try to set down exactly what they do and what they will be responsible for. Their obligations are defined and limited. Thus contractual commitments are *specific* rather than diffuse; they are limited and determined, not open-ended. Because it is

ample, that unmarried people are "freer" to choose suicide as a response to despair than are married people because the unmarried are relatively isolated from controlling social bonds.

The effects of social isolation were explored in a comparative study of the "propensity to strike." The following questions were raised: In what industries do strikes occur? Are certain industries more consistently free of strikes? Are others more consistently strike-prone? Data on man-days lost from strikes and lockouts were collected from 11 countries. It was found that, irrespective of the country, certain industries were characterized by frequent strikes and others by relatively few.

In industries with a high propensity to strike the workers are relatively isolated from the larger society. The miners, the sailors, the longshoremen, the loggers, and, to a much lesser extent, the textile workers form isolated masses, almost a "race apart." They live in their own separate communities: the coal patch, the ship, the waterfront district, the logging camp, the textile town. These communities have their own codes, myths, heroes, and social standards. There are few neutrals in them to mediate the conflicts and dilute the mass. All people have grievances, but what is important is that all the members of each of these groups have the same grievances: industrial hazards or severe depression, unemployment or bad living conditions (which seem additionally evil because they are supplied by the employer), or low wages or intermittent work (Kerr and Siegel, 1954:191–192).

Social isolation is not by itself a cause of strikes, but when it is combined with strongly felt grievances and the opportunity for collective action, it accounts for the greater number of strikes in some industries than in others. Isolation tends to release the individual or the group from outside social ties that would otherwise be restraining.

DEVIANCE AND THE SOCIAL BOND

Deviance is a product of both organization and disorganization; it reveals the weakness of social structure and at the same time shows how alternative patterns are created and sustained.

Deviance refers to any conduct that violates social expectations. It therefore includes much more than crime or officially defined delinquency. A married couple is deviant if, contrary to expectations, they reverse occupational and domestic roles. It follows that deviance is a relative idea. An action is deviant from the standpoint of standards set by a particular group or community. From the standpoint of another group, the behavior in question may be conformist, not deviant.

The following discussion considers three aspects of deviance: (1) the loosening of social bonds, (2) the formation of new bonds that run counter to the control system of the official society, and (3) the deviance-creating uses of official power.

Social disorganization The disruption or breakdown of a social system is called social disorganization (Cohen, 1959:474 ff.). What was once organized, such as a ball game or a college dance or a church congregation, becomes disorganized if people stop coordinating their activities, ignore the rules, or lose interest. The main effect of social disorganization is the weakening of membership: Ties to the group become loosened and people do not readily submit to group control. In this sense, social disorganization is not an evaluative idea. Social disorganization may be considered good or bad depending on how one feels about the merits of the group or of participation in it.

The concept of disorganization has an important place in research on delinquency. Rates of delinquency tend to be highest in urban areas that show many signs of social instability: physical deterioration, overcrowding, poor housing, recent immigration of aliens or minorities, unemployment, partial employment, broken families, and chronic dependency (Shaw and McKay, 1942; Lander, 1954).

English transvestites at drag ball

A study of Chicago areas with the highest increases in rates of delinquency over the period 1927–1961 showed that in one area a largely middle-class white population was replaced by a black population.

[In] the areas of greatest increase there was serious role disruption. Opportunities to participate in local political and economic institutions were not available, at least for some period of time, and the not too strong family structure was further weakened by the complex problems of urban life (McKay, 1967:115).

The central fact was not racial composition but the disruption of community organization. Delinquency rates *decreased* in areas where the black population had lived for several decades. These areas were apparently moving toward institutional stability.

Similarly, a study of delinquency areas in New York City found that rapid changes in the population involving replacement of one ethnic community with another produced great strains in social organization. There was "marked social and psychological isolation of the youth from the world of adults" and widespread community support for delinquency and other forms of deviation (Martin, Fitzpatrick, and Gould, 1970:162).

Although some urban areas show high delinquency rates when compared to others, most children in a "delinquency area" do not become delinquent. This fact has encouraged research on the specific differences between delinquents and nondelinquents who reside in the same areas but nevertheless have dissimilar backgrounds and experiences. A study that compared 500 delinquent and 500 nondelinquent boys from the same underprivileged neighborhoods found that the home life of the delinquents tended to be more disorganized in household routines, in maternal supervision, and in emotional ties (Glueck and Glueck, 1950).[2]

The weakening of parental control is a form of disorganization that probably has a significant impact on delinquency rates among affluent children as well as among poor children (Toby, 1967:140). If children are not strongly bound into the family circle, supervision will be inadequate and they will be free to give their main loyalty to their peer group, which is not subject to the kind of control that can be exercised over the individual family member.

Differential association The theory of social disorganization helps account for some aspects of deviance, especially the weakening of ties that bind the individual into an established order. However, much deviant behavior is organized activity rather than detached individual behavior. Furthermore, people learn how to be deviant in groups, and they are sustained in their deviance by association with others.

The theory of *differential association* holds that deviance results from intensive participation in group life, but in groups whose norms run counter to those of the official community (Sutherland and Cressey, 1974:Chap. 4). It emphasizes that delinquent behavior results not so much from the social isolation of juveniles as from their involvement in the social world of the street gang. The gang promotes delinquency by encouraging attitudes of hostility toward agencies of social control, teaching techniques of crime, assigning high prestige to criminal daring and skill, and serving as a medium of contact between beginners, more experienced delinquents, and older professional criminals.

The theory of differential association is a valuable corrective to an overemphasis on social disorganization. First, it views social organization as pluralistic, involving many groups and social worlds, often with competing moralities and standards of conduct. Certain forms of conduct, legal and illegal, take on value and meaning for the individual within the context of the group experience.

Second, the theory of differential association considers the way people are converted to a deviant perspective. The differential as-

[2] For a critical assessment of the method and findings of the Glueck study, see Hirschi and Selvin, 1967.

Baby and friend in New Orleans

sociation theory leads to the study of deviant alternatives, for example, gangs, rackets, and drug "scenes" (Becker, 1963).

<u>Labeling</u> A third view of the relation between social organization and deviance has developed partly as a reaction against the use of official statistics like arrest records and court convictions to measure rates of delinquency. Although official records indicate much higher rates of delinquency among lower-class than among middle-class youth, there is impressive evidence that the lower-class child is more likely to be picked up by the police, more likely to be sent to juvenile court, more likely to be convicted, and more likely to be institutionalized if convicted, than a middle-class child who has committed the same offense.

As a result of such findings, sociologists have turned their attention to another aspect of deviance—the discretionary power exercised by official agencies of social control. The police, the courts, and the schools have the power to classify individuals as deviant, incorrigible, delinquent, criminal, or mentally ill. The exercise of this power often leads to the transformation of a casual or occasional deviant into a confirmed outsider. This view is known as *labeling theory* because it draws specific attention to the way officials classify or label the suspected men and women with whom they come into contact.

Labeling reflects social organization in two ways. First, it manifests the power of organized society to impose its stamp upon the world through official agencies. Second, the weaker elements of society are the ones who must submit to the labeling process. Lower-class youth typically lack the influence others can bring to bear in resisting deviant labels.

The three theories of deviance discussed above are sometimes presented as opposing perspectives; in fact, each accounts for a different aspect of deviance as a social phenomenon.

Adaptation 3 Durkheim: Suicide and social integration

The French sociologist Emile Durkheim was interested in the varieties of social integration and in social disorganization, the weakening of social bonds. He used rates of suicide as an index of social integration. The suicide rate was higher for Protestants than for Catholics, higher for the unmarried than for the married, higher for soldiers than for civilians, higher for noncommissioned officers than for enlisted men, higher in times of peace than in times of war or revolution, and higher in times of both prosperity and recession than in times of economic stability.

Durkheim reasoned that since different groups have different suicide rates, there must be something in their social organization that prevents or fails to deter people from suicide or which may even prompt them to it. He acknowledged that individual reasons were many and varied: financial distress, disappointment in love, failing to pass an examination, ill health, and so on. But these reasons did not explain why some groups have higher suicide rates than others.

Durkheim suggested that the degree to which the individual was integrated into group life determined whether he could be motivated to suicide. However, he recognized that no single set of circumstances explains suicide. The individual can be motivated to suicide at either of two extremes: if he is highly integrated or if he is only superficially integrated into society.

ALTRUISTIC SUICIDE

When the individual is tightly bound into a highly integrated group with a strong sense of solidarity,

he accepts the values and norms of the group as his own. He does not distinguish between his interests and those of the group, nor is he likely to think of himself as a unique individual with a life separate from the group. Under these circumstances what would prompt him to commit siucide?

He will be willing to sacrifice his life for group goals. The Japanese *kamikaze* of World War II is an example of military self-sacrifice. Japanese airmen crashed their planes onto enemy ships in order to disable them, despite the fact that it meant certain death. In highly integrated societies where there is a strong sense of social solidarity, self-destruction may be looked upon as self-affirmation and fulfillment; death, as well as life, has meaning

In addition to his study of suicide, Emile Durkheim (1858–1917) is best known for his *Division of Labor in Society* and *The Elementary Forms of the Religious Life* (see p. 380).

Source: A summary and interpretation of Emile Durkheim, *Le Suicide* (Paris: Alcan, 1897). English translation and introduction by George Simpson (New York: Free Press, 1951).

and value. Closely related to this kind of suicide is ritualistic self-sacrifice. In India a practice called *suttee,* now outlawed, was sometimes performed, in which the Hindu widow threw herself on her husband's funeral pyre.

If the individual fails to meet group standards, death may appear preferable to life. Identification with the group can be so intense that group condemnation is tantamount to self-condemnation. Failure in such a case is total and absolute. The individual puts all his eggs in one basket. He stakes his entire self-respect on approval of one particular group; when that is withdrawn, he has no other basis for self-esteem.

Suicide that results from an excessive degree of group integration Durkheim called *altruistic:* It is committed for the sake of the group or according to group norms of conduct. Altruistic suicide may be a manifestation of overinvolvement in one group and social isolation from other groups.

Durkheim used his theory of altruistic suicide to explain why the suicide rate was higher for soldiers than for civilians, higher for noncommissioned officers than for enlisted men, and higher for volunteers and those who reenlisted than for conscripts. He suggested that suicide increases as the soldier identifies himself more completely with the values and norms of military life. The officer is better integrated into the military organization than the ordinary soldier, the volunteer more involved with military life than the conscript. The more fully the soldier is integrated into military life, the greater is his isolation from other groups in society; the more dedicated he is to military values, the more he stakes his self-respect on success in the army. No other paths are open to him.

EGOISTIC SUICIDE

What happens to the individual when he is only weakly attached to the social order?

1. He lacks the restraints that intense participation in group life imposes on him. If he has an inclination to commit suicide, he is not deterred because of deeply felt obligations to others. Nor does he consider the consequences of his suicide for the group. An individual not bound to others is free of any claims that they may have on his survival.

2. The individual lacks the emotional attachments to others that make life worthwhile and less self-centered.

3. The individual lacks the emotional supports

that deep immersion in group life can provide. He is thrown back upon his own resources. He gains no satisfaction from the achievements of the group; success or failure are his alone. Wrongdoing is not defined solely by group standards but is a matter of personal judgment and responsibility. Under the burden of individual responsibility, the individual is susceptible to the emotional disturbances which may lead to suicide, and he cannot fall back upon relations with others to help him over a personal crisis.

This kind of suicide Durkheim called *egoistic.* It is self-centered rather than group-centered. Altruistic suicide occurs because the individual is overly involved in group life; egoistic suicide occurs when the individual is uninvolved and detached.

According to Durkheim, the relatively higher rate of Protestant suicide could be explained as egoistic. Both Catholicism and Protestantism condemn suicide, but Catholicism makes its injunction effective by attaching the individual to the church as a social institution. Protestantism, on the other hand, makes salvation a matter of individual faith and religious belief, of personal responsibility. It tends to detach the individual from all religious constraint except his own conscience. In doing so, however, it removes the very social restraints that would be most effective in deterring him from suicide.

The relatively higher suicide rate among the unmarried is also an instance of egoistic suicide. The unmarried have fewer responsibilities as well as fewer attachments. The married are restrained by both formal obligations and emotional ties. They are also apt to be less self-centered. Their lives are perforce taken up with the care of others, and they develop shared interests and values and find emotional support in interpersonal relations.

During wars and revolutions people are led to forget themselves and their troubles in uniting for a common effort. At least temporarily, social crises result in a stronger integration of society. For this reason, Durkheim claimed, the suicide rate tends to fall during social disturbances and wars.

ANOMIC SUICIDE

A highly integrated and unified group develops norms to regulate behavior and interpersonal relations. The group provides the individual with a sense of security by establishing clear rules of right and wrong and by limiting his aspirations to what he can hope to achieve.

Durkheim believed that an ever-present source of acute anxiety is unrestrained aspiration. When people live without established, attainable goals and definite alternatives, when there is "only empty space above them," they are subject to emotional distress. When group norms are weakened, the individual feels less restraint on his aspirations and conduct. At the same time, he loses the security that group control and regulation provide. His ambitions soar beyond possible fulfillment, and he is uncertain of what is right and wrong.

According to Durkheim, a society that lacks clear-cut norms to govern men's aspirations and moral conduct is characterized by *anomie*, which means "lack of rules" or "normlessness." Suicide resulting from anomie Durkheim called *anomic*.

Anomic and egoistic suicide both spring from low social integration, but they are nevertheless independent. Although the egoistic suicide does not have the personal bonds that would deter him from the act, he has not necessarily rejected social norms. On the contrary, the egoistic suicide may be a highly moralistic person who feels a deep sense of personal responsibility for his behavior. His morality, however, stems from principle rather than from felt loyalties to other persons or institutions. Indeed, one of the sources of his emotional disturbance may be that he is overdisciplined, that he conforms in an overly rigid way. According to Durkheim, egoistic suicide is apt to occur among intellectuals and professionals, people who are primarily concerned with ideas and are only loosely attached to specific persons or groups.

In anomic suicide, on the other hand, the individual may be deeply involved in society, but group life fails to provide him with controlling standards of behavior. Life may be unbearable to the egoistic suicide because of *excessive* self-discipline; life may be unbearable to the anomic suicide because of *inadequate* self-discipline.

Durkheim offered two kinds of evidence to support his theory that a lack of limiting norms would result in a high suicide rate.

1. He noted that the rate was higher in countries that permitted divorce than in countries that did not permit it, and the rate was still higher where divorce was frequent. Durkheim reasoned that by allowing divorce a society weakened an important regulatory principle.

When the relation of suicide to divorce is considered, a distinction must be made between the fact of divorce and the possibility of it. The fact of divorce tends to isolate the individual and thereby contributes to the rate of egoistic suicide. The possibility of divorce reflects permissive norms that open up alternatives and generate anxiety; therefore it is relevant to anomic suicide.

2. Durkheim also noted that suicide is associated with economic conditions. In periods of depression the suicide rate is high. However, the cause is not the hardship of poverty but rather the dislocation attendant upon economic crises. In the nineteenth century, Spain was much poorer than France but had only a tenth as many suicides, and rates were generally low in areas of persistent poverty.

Durkheim felt that any abrupt economic changes, whether of boom or of depression, would unsettle established expectations. Sudden prosperity is unsettling, for it brings increased desire and excitability. "Poverty protects against suicide because it is a restraint in itself. . . . Wealth, on the other hand, by the power it bestows, deceives us into believing that we depend on ourselves only. Reducing the resistance we encounter from objects, it suggests the possibility of unlimited success against them. The less limited one feels the more intolerable all limitation appears" (1951:254).

Durkheim's generalization about poverty was correct. The high suicide rates during depressions are due to the suffering that accompanies a *relative* loss of wealth or social standing. But his hypothesis about prosperity is rather weakly supported in *Suicide* and has not been confirmed.

CONCLUSION

His study of suicide furthered Durkheim's broader interest in the nature of social order and social disorganization. The significance of Suicide *is the light it casts on human relatedness, both to groups and to group norms. The types of suicide—altruistic, egoistic, anomic—point to the phenomena of integration and isolation.*

The concept of anomie has a prominent place in contemporary sociological thought. It has helped focus attention on the personal disorientation of people who lack a sense of belonging to a secure moral order (Clinard, 1964).

Suicide was published in 1897 and was based on data that seem crude by modern standards. On the other hand, many of Durkheim's conclusions have been supported by later studies, and the ingenuity of his analysis and interpretation is a continuing challenge to contemporary social scientists.[3]

Section five the group structure of society

This section considers some elementary aspects of the macro-order, that is, the larger patterns and units of social organization.

GROUPS AND SOCIAL CATEGORIES

The word group has a very general meaning. It refers to any collection of persons who are bound together by a distinctive set of social relations. This includes everything from members of a family, adherents to Catholicism, or participants in a mob to citizens of a national state. Two persons form a group if they are friends or partners or otherwise held together and set apart from others by their relationship. Groups can be highly organized and stable or fluid and temporary.

People who have similar incomes or who are alike in other ways, such as age, occupation, or reading habits, do not necessarily form social groups. Such classifications may be called statistical aggregates or social categories. A persistent interest of sociology is the study of the conditions under which various social categories may become or produce social groups.

The aged are a significant social category, and there is considerable interest today in the kinds of groups older people are likely to form or accept (Rosow, 1967). Is there an old-age style of life that can provide the natural basis for separate housing? Or do older people feel little sense of identity with each other despite their similar age and dependency? There have been some old-age political pressure groups, such as the Townsend movement of the 1930s. Should more and increasingly powerful groups of this sort be expected as the number of older people in the population rises? What effect would

this have on the political order? These questions indicate the kinds of problems raised by exploring the group-forming potential of a social category.

Although *consciousness of kind*, the awareness of belonging to a certain category, is an important element in the formation of groups, it is not indispensable. Many workers belong to lodges, bowling clubs, and other groups that are distinctively working-class in character; yet if asked, they would not necessarily identify themselves as belonging to any particular social category. Nevertheless they unconsciously enter and create ways of group life based on similarities of occupation, income, and life-styles. Similar experiences lead to social interaction and the formation of groups, even though people are not aware of why and how this takes place. In the chapters that follow, especially *PRIMARY GROUPS, SOCIAL STRATIFICATION, ASSOCIATIONS,* and *COLLECTIVE BEHAVIOR,* the major types of groups are examined in detail.

BASIC PATTERNS OF SOCIAL ORGANIZATION

Students of social organization attempt to describe the general features of whole societies or social orders. They try to identify the most important institutions, the most pervasive social relations, the basic social trends.

Because human societies are so complex, it is difficult and risky to generalize about broad patterns or trends in social organization. Nevertheless, much scholarship has been devoted to this task, and it is possible to state some conclusions with confidence.

Five key forms of social organization are:

[3] A number of findings are reviewed in Henry and Short, 1954: Appendix 1. See also Gibbs and Martin, 1964.

Above, purposive activity among Peruvians at a community development meeting. *Contrast below,* an American family watches TV; the sculpture garden at the Museum of Modern Art, New York City.

(1) kinship, (2) fealty, (3) status, (4) contract, and (5) rational coordination. In various societies or historical periods one or another of these modes of organization has tended to give the society or age its distinctive character. But no matter how dominant a particular principle of order may be, all of the key forms occur to some degree.

Kinship In many societies kinship is the most important social bond, and the family is the basis of social organization. The family firm and the family farm are reminders of economic activities based upon the family. Only a few centuries ago in England, families vied for preeminence in politics, for the right to rule as the royal house, or to be counted among the more favored nobility.

Societies may be called familistic when the family is the dominant type of social group and carries the chief burden of maintaining order, producing goods, and propitiating the gods. In such a society individuals are dependent on relatives. They are the chief sources of practical aid, and they hold the keys to social esteem. The interests of the family—wealth, honor, continuity—are placed above the interests of the individual.

Fealty Another fundamental social bond is the personal relation of follower and leader. Fealty is the recognized obligation of one person to be faithful to another. More than a contract of service is involved. Fealty presumes a personal commitment to do whatever may be needed to serve the interests of the leader, to take the bad with the good. In a limited sense, it is like a marriage. And indeed, oaths of fealty have sometimes matched the sacredness and binding character of marriage vows.

In Europe and England, for about 400 years fealty was a principal social bond. This was the epoch of feudalism, which may be roughly dated from about the tenth century, when its outlines were already clear, to the thirteenth century, when it began a gradual decline.

A chief characteristic of feudal life was lordship—a system of political obligation in which a group of followers, allies, and servile dependents owed personal loyalty and service to a powerful individual. An especially powerful lord might be called a duke or a king. In the heyday of feudalism, a great hierarchy of lords and their dependents, all knit together by bonds of loyalty and protection, gave the social order a remarkable symmetry and a precarious cohesion.

The development of lordship presumed that no effective central authority existed, and this was so in western Europe and England after the decline of Roman power. Moreover, lordship was an alternative to the bond of kinship. Some men sought the protection of lords who were not their relatives, because there was no kin group capable of establishing order at the local level (Gibbs, 1953:21).

Functions of fealty The bond of fealty had a dual importance. First, fealty helped create a small but devoted band of personal followers for the king or local lord. In the formative period of feudalism, power was in the hands of small bodies of armed men. The lord was the leader of such a band, and his influence depended on his capacity to maintain continuing loyalty. The development of a code of honor, with loyalty to the lord a supreme virtue, was helpful in sustaining this relationship. As feudalism evolved, increasing emphasis was placed on the loyalty of a man to his lord, and the most important crime was treason against a lord.

Second, fealty was a way to maintain the cohesion of a society made up of local domains, each ruled by a supreme personal leader. As feudalism matured, the local barons became entrenched in their power. They were vassals of the king and took an oath of fealty to him, but they had independent power, with troops and resources of their own. Fealty and vassalage were in effect ways of recognizing an alliance or creating a federation. It was as if the governors of the 50 states were considered personal rulers and recognized the central government by taking an oath of personal loyalty and submission to the president.

As a social bond, fealty belongs not only to a remote and exotic age but also to contemporary society. Many executives of large enterprises rely on the personal loyalty of a few staff members. An executive who is promoted or moves to another organization often takes along the key assistants who can be relied upon to help establish control over the organization.

Ties of fealty are of continuing significance in modern political life. Because elections are often popularity contests and center on the person rather than on the party, politics tends to be based on personal leadership. In many areas, candidates create their own political organizations to supplement the work of the regular political party. To build campaign organizations often requires ties of personal loyalty.

trary, they tend to form configurations that point to *types of society*. Thus, in modern society, roles tend to be universalistic, instrumental, specific, and achievement-oriented. This patterning reflects a world of specialization, bureaucracy, and rationality. In a traditional or folk society, social relations tend to be particularistic, expressive, diffuse, and ascriptive.

Section four participation and social control

Social organization may be viewed as an opportunity structure and as a system of social control. Individuals gain from involvement in social life, but there is always a price: acceptance of restraints on the freedom to do as one pleases.

OPPORTUNITY AND CONSTRAINT

The amount and kind of an individual's participation depend largely on the range of available opportunities. For some there may be many alternatives—many chances to try again after failure. For others, alternatives are few, and failure is catastrophic.

The distribution of opportunities is a major topic in *SOCIAL STRATIFICATION*. However, the idea of an opportunity structure is relevant to the broadest study of society. If legitimate opportunities are closed, people may turn to illegitimate ways of meeting their needs. It has been observed that racketeers and mobsters were largely drawn from immigrant groups.

There is little question that men of Italian origin appeared in most of the leading roles in the high drama of gambling and mobs, just as twenty years ago the children of East European Jews were the most prominent figures in organized crime, and before that individuals of Irish descent were similarly prominent (Bell, 1953:150–151).

These experiences point to the existence of illegitimate as well as legitimate oppor-

tunity structures. Access to gangs and rackets is a kind of opportunity, just as is the availability of conventional education or conventional jobs. Both kinds of opportunity contribute to the social organization of a community and affect the likelihood of crime and the forms it takes (Cloward and Ohlin, 1960:150 ff.).

Freedom and dependency To take advantage of opportunities is to fit oneself into society. The result is both freedom and constraint. When young people marry they exchange the constraints of independent responsibility for the constraints of parental control. But the new responsibilities may be liberating, if they provide fresh opportunities for the enlargement of self.

Social organization produces social control mainly because people are dependent on each other. One way of mapping the social structure of a group or community is to explore the pattern of mutual dependencies (Emerson, 1962:31–41). The more people an individual is dependent upon for satisfactions, the more claims there will be to exercise self-restraint lest those who are needed be offended.

Dependency is not necessarily an expression of narrow self-interest. It may invoke ideals that might otherwise be inoperative. The social ideals of parenthood do not have much influence on a bachelor. His behavior cannot be restrained by responsibility to children he does not have. It is only through relations to others and by participating in social institutions that responsibilities arise; only in this way do ideals become effective governors of motivation and conduct.

Isolation and control Social isolation weakens social control. Persons uninvolved with others have few occasions to assess the consequences of their actions either for themselves or for others. Durkheim's explanation of the different rates of suicide (Adaptation 3) is grounded in a theory of social organization. He pointed out, for ex-

specific, the contract as a legal device is well adapted to the market economy. Executives know what they are getting into and can calculate costs.

In enduring social relations, however, it is difficult to maintain a principle of limited commitment (Selznick, 1969:52–57). And executives may be reluctant to insist upon the strict terms of a contract or to work out all obligations in advance:

Disputes are frequently settled without reference to the contract or potential or actual legal sanctions. There is a hesitance to speak of legal rights or to threaten to sue in these negotiations. Even where the parties have a detailed and carefully planned agreement which indicates what is to happen if, say, the seller fails to deliver on time, often they will never refer to the agreement but will negotiate a solution when the problem arises apparently as if there had never been any original contract. . . . Businessmen may welcome a measure of vagueness in the obligations they assume so that they may negotiate matters in light of actual circumstances (Macaulay, 1963:61, 64).

The underlying truth is that obligations tend to become *diffuse* and open-ended when an enduring association is contemplated. It is easy enough to specify obligations when a single act is involved, such as the purchase of a house. But when buyer and seller expect to do business over a long period and depend on each other for cooperation, it is more difficult to work out all details in advance or to be sure just what obligations will arise. Executives who are willing to take the risks of uncertainty often disagree with their lawyers who try to minimize risks by making all obligations as specific as possible.

In Western society the obligations of marriage are not precisely defined, although there is a trend toward more specific expectations. (See *THE FAMILY*, p. 333.) In the traditional marriage the parties do not guarantee that they will remain sexually attractive, in good health, or good providers. Quite the contrary, they promise they will stick together no matter what the luck and even if the marriage sours. But there are limits to the open-endedness of marital obligation, and many marriages fail because specific expectations are not fulfilled. Thus even roles that are predicated on diffuseness and unlimited commitment display tension between specificity and diffuseness.

Ascription–achievement Ascription is a way of relating to others by *placing them into categories* and thus assigning to them certain virtues, deficiencies, rights, or other qualities. People in categories are responded to as they are presumed to be rather than on the basis of what they actually perform or achieve. Ascription is the labeling side of ascribed status. (See p. 44 and *SOCIAL STRATIFICATION*, p. 182.)

Ascriptive labeling is an ever-present feature of role behavior because people tend to confound the role and the person. A label such as teacher or hard hat may elicit conclusions regarding personal characteristics. To classify someone is to establish a basis for routine response. Cues such as dress or manners facilitate classification, and people then adjust their conduct to the presumed qualities associated with the classification.

Ascription runs up against the competing principle of *achievement,* or performance. If a person does not do what he is supposed to do, the label is not validated and expectations are disappointed. Parents and children are supposed to love each other, and those who do not may try to cover up the absence of such love. But in the end some performance is necessary if expectations are to be upheld.

Western society, committed to unceasing industrial growth, has made achievement a dominating cultural theme. But every society requires some orientation to achievement, if only the demand that the breadwinner meet his or her responsibilities. The relation between ascription and achievement poses problems in all societies.

Relations among the pattern variables The alternative orientations discussed above are not independent of each other. On the con-

Status In a society based on fixed status, personal qualities and expectations depend on social rank. Traditional Japan offers a good example:

At all levels the lamentable principle prevailed that a man's status was irrevocably fixed at birth; and to the present day Japanese life is governed by the subtle ubiquity of the concept of *mibun* (personal position); a person's *mibun*, which depends on his sex, age, birth, education, rank, and occupation, governs his behavior at all stages. This means that the same conduct can be praiseworthy, indifferent, or actually reprehensible, depending on a person's *mibun*. The merchant's duty is to enrich himself, but a samurai who concerns himself with money is unworthy of the name; a second son is permitted amorous adventures; indeed they earn him applause and respect; his elder brother, however, is expected to behave irreproachably (Maraini, 1959:240).

As European and English feudalism matured, status became more important as the foundation of social order. In the earlier period, kingship was highly personal, and the hereditary principle was not well established. A king was a king because he won and maintained the personal loyalty of a group of followers. Later a subtle and decisive transformation took place. The king received loyalty as a right *because he was king*. At the same time, hereditary monarchy, based on status fixed by birth, was strengthened. Thus status joined fealty as a cardinal principle of feudal order.

In the contemporary world fixed statuses are less important to the social order, but the desire to achieve status and the effects of status are continuing features of everyday life. The assignment of status remains a powerful device for allocating respect and defining an individual's social worth. The allocation of status in modern society is treated in *SOCIAL STRATIFICATION.*

Contract In the postfeudal era there was a basic trend toward contract as a principle of social organization. By the sixteenth century, society was beginning to be seen in a new light. The Renaissance, the Protestant Reformation, and the growth of business enterprise all helped give the individual a new hold on the political, economic, and philosophical imagination. More and more, the basis of obligation was sought in the agreements made by freely acting, personally responsible individuals. This perspective advanced steadily and reached its greatest influence in the nineteenth century.

When the principle of contract is a dominant feature of social organization, private initiative and autonomy are encouraged. Especially during the nineteenth century, contract became almost a sacred principle to those who believed most strongly in individualism and in private rather than government initiative.

In today's commercial civilization, contract remains a significant part of social organization. It is the institutional mainstay of the market economy. Nevertheless, there are signs that unregulated, voluntary agreement is losing ground within the social order. Government is assuming an increasingly active role in limiting freedom of contract by setting standards, especially where the parties to the bargain are unequal in power. The most striking examples are in labor relations, but the trend is growing in the fields of environmental protection, consumer economics, and food and drug administration and in the regulation of rates charged by telephone and power companies. (Friedmann, 1959:Chap. 4).

Bureaucracy The principle of social organization most characteristic of twentieth-century industrial society may be called *rational coordination*. In this pattern people are brought together in complex organizations run by professional managers. The managers are often called bureaucrats and the organizations they run are known as bureaucracies.

During the past two generations, many writers have called attention to the increasing bureaucratization of human activity. They mean that more and more spheres of

The work of Max Weber (1864–1920) has left a major impress on many fields of contemporary sociology, including the study of bureaucracy, law, politics, social stratification, religion, economic development, and the theoretical foundations of social science.

ments the coordination of specialists in accordance with an impersonal logic of efficiency is highly developed. The same trend may be observed in educational institutions and in church organization.

Where bureaucracy develops, there is increased specialization, impersonality, reliance on general rules, and distance between top management and the ordinary worker, citizen, or soldier. Up to a point, this is usually associated with increased efficiency, but there is growing evidence that new techniques are needed to offset some of the characteristics of bureaucracy that tend to limit initiative and personal satisfaction. (See ASSOCIATIONS, pp. 208–209.)

THE MASTER TREND

Over many centuries, Western society has shifted from an emphasis on kinship and fixed status to a reliance upon more impersonal, more instrumental, more fluid ways of life. There is less reverence for established institutions. People are more mobile and more isolated. At the same time, modern society has created powerful and centralized governments, corporations, trade unions, and other large-scale systems of coordination and control.

Taken together, these two overarching themes—the breakdown of traditional, person-centered unities of kinship, locality, and occupation and the emergence of bureaucracy and mass society—have posed the great issues of modern society. Much of sociology and therefore many of the themes of this book deal with those issues.

life are dominated by large organizations, and increasing numbers of people are employees of the big corporation or government. The organization society produces the "organization man" (Whyte, 1956).

Few aspects of modern society can be studied without reference to the bureaucratic trend. Most obviously, in the business world and in modern military establish-

References

Barker, Roger G. and Louise Shedd Barker
1961 "Behavior units for the comparative study of cultures." Pp. 457–476 in Bert Kaplan (ed.), Studying Personality Cross-Culturally. New York: Harper & Row.

Becker, Howard S.
1963 Outsiders: Studies in the Sociology of Deviance. New York: Free Press.

Bell, Daniel
1953 "Crime as an American way of life." Antioch Review 13 (June):131–154.

Blau, Peter M.
1964 Exchange and Power in Social Life. New York: Wiley.

Blumer, Herbert
1969 Symbolic Interactionism: Perspective and Method. Englewood Cliffs, N. J.: Prentice-Hall.

Cicourel, Aaron V.
1968 The Social Organization of Juvenile Justice. New York: Wiley.

Clinard, Marshall B. (ed.)
1964 Anomie and Deviant Behavior. New York: Free Press.

Cloward, Richard A. and Lloyd E. Ohlin
1960 Delinquency and Opportunity: A Theory of Delinquent Gangs. New York: Free Press.

Cohen, Albert K.
1959 "The study of social disorganization and deviant behavior." Chap. 21 in Robert K. Merton, Leonard Broom, and Leonard S. Cottrell, Jr. (eds.), Sociology Today. New York: Basic Books.

Daniels, Arlene Kaplan
1970 "The social construction of military psychiatric diagnoses." Pp. 182–205 in Hans Peter Dreitzel (ed.), Recent Sociology No. 2: Patterns of Communicative Behavior. London: Macmillan.

DeVore, Irven
1968 "Primate behavior." Pp. 351–359 in International Encyclopedia of the Social Sciences 14.

Dewey, John
1938 Logic: The Theory of Inquiry. New York: Holt, Rinehart and Winston.

Dreitzel, Hans Peter (ed.)
1970 Recent Sociology No. 2: Patterns of Communicative Behavior. London: Macmillan. See articles on ethnomethodology.

Durkheim, Emile
1897/1951 Suicide. Translated by George Simpson. New York: Free Press. First published in French.

Emerson, Richard M.
1962 "Power-dependence relations." American Sociological Review 27 (February):31–41.

Friedmann, W.
1959 Law in a Changing Society. Berkeley and Los Angeles: University of California Press.

Garfinkel, Harold
1967 Studies in Ethnomethodology. Englewood Cliffs, N. J.: Prentice-Hall.

Gibbs, Jack P. and Walter T. Martin
1964 Status Integration and Suicide. Eugene: University of Oregon Books.

Gibbs, Marion
1953 Feudal Order. New York: Abelard-Schuman.

Glueck, Sheldon and Eleanor T. Glueck
1950 Unraveling Juvenile Delinquency. New York: Commonwealth Fund.

Goffman, Erving
1955 "On face-work: an analysis of ritual elements in social interaction." Psychiatry: Journal for the Study of Interpersonal Processes 18 (August):213–231. Also as pp. 5–45 in Goffman, 1967.
1956 "The nature of deference and demeanor." American Anthropologist 58 (June):473–502. Also as pp. 47–95 in Goffman, 1967.
1959 The Presentation of Self in Everyday Life. Garden City, N. Y.: Doubleday (Anchor Books).
1963 Behavior in Public Places. New York: Free Press.
1967 Interaction Ritual: Essays on Face-to-Face Behavior. New York: Doubleday (Anchor Books).
1971 Relations in Public: Microstudies of the Public Order. New York: Harper Colophon Books.

Goode, William J.
1960 "A theory of role strain." American Sociological Review 25 (August):483–496.

Gullahorn, J. T.
1952 "Distance and friendship as factors in the gross interaction matrix." Sociometry 15:123–134.

Henry, Andrew F. and James F. Short, Jr.
1954 Suicide and Homicide. New York: Free Press.

Hirschi, Travis and Hanan C. Selvin
1967 Delinquency Research: An Appraisal of Analytic Methods. New York: Free Press.

Kay, Paul
1970 "Some theoretical implications of ethnographic semantics." Bulletin of the American Anthropological Association 3 No. 3, part 2:19–31.

Kerr, Clark and Abraham Siegel
1954 "The interindustry propensity to strike—an international comparison." Pp. 189–212 in Arthur Kornhauser, Robert Dubin, and Arthur M. Ross (eds.), Industrial Conflict. New York: McGraw-Hill.

Kuhn, James W.
1961 Bargaining in Grievance Settlement. New York: Columbia University Press.

Lander, Bernard
1954 Towards an Understanding of Juvenile Delinquency. New York: Columbia University Press.

Linton, Ralph
1936 The Study of Man: An Introduction. Englewood Cliffs, N. J.: Prentice-Hall.

Lorenz, Konrad
1966 On Aggression. New York: Bantam Books.

Macaulay, Stewart
1963 "Non-Contractual Relations in Business: A Preliminary Study." American Sociological Review 28 (February):55–67.

McKay, Henry D.
1967 "A note on trends in rates of delinquency in certain areas in Chicago." Pp. 114–118 in The President's Commission on Law Enforcement and Administration of Justice, Task Force Report: Juvenile Delinquency and Youth Crime. Washington, D.C.: GPO.

Maraini, Fosco
1959 Meeting with Japan. New York: Viking Press.

Martin, John M., Joseph P. Fitzpatrick, and Robert E. Gould
1970 The Analysis of Delinquent Behavior: A Structural Approach. New York: Random House.

Merton, Robert K.
1968 Social Theory and Social Structure. New York: Free Press.

Parsons, Talcott
1951 The Social System. New York: Free Press.

Parsons, Talcott and Edward A. Shils
1951 Toward a General Theory of Action. Cambridge: Harvard University Press. Cited to Harper Torchbook, 1962.

Pfeiffer, John E.
1969 The Emergence of Man. New York: Harper & Row.

Roizen, Ronald P.
1969 "Office layout and the behavior of office workers." Unpublished paper.

Rosow, Irving
1967 Social Integration of the Aged. New York: Free Press.

Schutz, Alfred
1962 Collected Papers, I: The Problem of Social Reality. The Hague: Martinus Nijhoff.

Selznick, Philip
1969 Law, Society, and Industrial Justice. New York: Russell Sage.

Shaw, Clifford R. and Henry D. McKay
1942 Juvenile Delinquency and Urban Areas. Chicago: University of Chicago Press.

Strauss, Anselm, Leonard Schatzman, Rue Bucher, Danuta Ehrlich, and Melvin Sabshin
1963 "The hospital and its negotiated order." Pp. 147–169 in E. Friedson (ed.), The Hospital in Modern Society. New York: Free Press.

Sutherland, Edwin H. and Donald R. Cressey
1974 Criminology. Philadelphia: Lippincott. Eighth Edition.

Thomas, W. I. and Dorothy S. Thomas
1928 The Child in America. New York: Knopf.

Toby, Jackson
1967 "Affluence and adolescent crime." Pp. 132–144 in President's Commission on Law Enforcement and Administration of Justice, Task Force Report: Juvenile Delinquency and Youth Crime. Washington, D.C.: GPO.

Van der Ryn, Sim
1969 "College live-in." Trans-action 6 (September):63–69.

Van der Ryn, Sim and Murray Silverstein
1967 Dorms at Berkeley: An Environmental Analysis. Berkeley: University of California Center for Planning and Development Research.

Wells, B. W. P.
1965 "The psycho-social influence of building environment: sociometric findings in large and small office spaces." Building Science 1:153–165.

Whyte, William H., Jr.
1956 The Organization Man. New York: Simon & Schuster.

Wilson, Edward
1975 Sociobiology. Cambridge: Harvard University Press.

Sources and readings

Banton, Michael
1965 Roles: An Introduction to the Study of Social Relations. New York: Basic Books.

Biddle, Bruce J. and Edwin J. Thomas, eds.
1966 Role Theory: Concepts and Research. New York: Wiley.

Blau, Peter M.
1964 Exchange and Power in Social Life. New York: Wiley.

Coser, Lewis
1964 The Functions of Social Conflict. New York: Free Press.

Douglas, Jack D.
1967 The Social Meanings of Suicide. Princeton: Princeton University Press.

Etzioni, Amitai
1968 The Active Society. New York: Free Press.

Gerth, H. H. and C. W. Mills
1953 Character and Social Structure, Part Three. New York: Harcourt Brace Jovanovich.

Gutman, Robert (ed.)
1972 People and Buildings. New York: Basic Books.

Homans, George C.
1950 The Human Group. New York: Harcourt Brace Jovanovich.
1974 Social Behavior: Its Elementary Forms. New York: Harcourt Brace Jovanovich. Revised edition.

Merton, Robert K.
1968 Social Theory and Social Structure. New York: Free Press.

Morris, Desmond (ed.)
1969 Primate Ethology. New York: Doubleday (Anchor Books).

Parsons, Talcott
1966 Societies: Evolutionary and Comparative Perspectives. Englewood Cliffs, N. J.: Prentice-Hall.

Weber, Max
1922/1947 The Theory of Social and Economic Organization. New York: Oxford University Press.

Williams, Robin M., Jr.
1970 American Society: A Sociological Interpretation. Third Edition. New York: Knopf.

Section one the concept of culture

The idea of culture has a rich intellectual background. In the philosophical, literary, and historical tradition, culture refers mainly to ideals of enlightenment and refinement in the realms of learning, morality, and art. This humanist view of culture emphasizes creativity and excellence: The cultured person is one who can appreciate and perhaps contribute to the richness of the cultural tradition (Kroeber and Kluckhohn, 1963; Williams, 1960).

In the nineteenth century, especially in Germany, a connection was made between culture as an intellectual ideal and culture as the *ethos,* or fundamental character, of a people or an epoch (Kroeber and Kluckhohn, 1963: Part 1; Mosse, 1961; Mazlish, 1966). Styles of art, conceptions of law, philosophical systems, religious orientations, and literary themes were studied for the way they revealed this ethos. While the emphasis on intellectual, aesthetic, and moral attainment remained, the idea of culture began to be applied to a whole society at a stage of its history.

Nineteenth-century anthropologists often used the words *culture* and *civilization* interchangeably, and they were fascinated by the possibility that society had evolved from lower to higher stages. Culture was something humanity attained as it developed skills and rational capacities. Gradually, however, the meanings of culture and civilization were disentangled (Stocking, 1963; 1966). Civilization retained its evaluative connotation, and culture came to refer to the distinctive way of life of a people, whatever that might be.

At the same time that evolutionary theories of society were being debated, anthropologists were trying to identify the human races and assess the influence of race differences on human accomplishment. Some attempted to account for different ways of life by the influence of biological heredity, and the achievements of Western civilization were attributed to a presumed inherent superiority of the white race. For example, in the middle of the last century, Gobineau, in his *Essay on the Inequality of Human Races,* argued that white Aryans or Nordics were responsible for the development of civilization.] These and similar writings were used to justify the racist ideology of Nazi Germany under Adolf Hitler.

Anthropologists like Boas, however, read the lesson of cultural variation differently (Boas, 1912/1955). They showed that biological heredity was of minor importance compared to social heredity. The difference between one people and another was a matter of historical opportunity, not of biological endowment.

[Anthropologists wanted a concept of culture that would (1) be descriptive, free of value judgments, useful for analyzing any people's way of life, no matter how crude or primitive it might seem; and (2) direct attention to social rather than biological influences on human nature and achievement.]

By the early decades of the twentieth century the anthropological concept of culture had come to refer to the social heritage taken as a whole (Tylor, 1913). The humanist concept, with its selective emphasis on ideas and the arts, was set aside as unsuitable for anthropological inquiry:

Culture is not restricted to certain special fields of knowledge; it includes ways of behaving derived from the whole range of human activity. The designs for living evident in the behavior of the Eskimos, the natives of Australia, or the Navahos are as much a part of culture as those of cultivated Europeans and Americans. Culture includes not only the techniques and methods of art, music, and literature, but also those used to make pottery, sew clothing, or build houses. Among the products of culture we find comic books and popular street songs along with the art of a Leonardo da Vinci and the music of a Johann Bach. The anthropologist does not employ the contrast "cultured versus uncultured," for this distinction of popular usage represents only a difference in culture, not its absence or presence (Beals and Hoijer, 1965:266).

This viewpoint rejects provincialism and underscores the receptiveness of the social scientist in studying cultures other than his own. A comprehensive, inclusive idea of culture avoids invidious distinctions. It assumes that humanity may be achieved through any sustained social experience. A forest pygmy, an Eskimo, an ancient Roman, an advertising account executive, a member of a delinquent gang, or a hippie are all equally human and all possess culture.

Thus the history of anthropology and its moral concerns have encouraged a comprehensive view of culture as equivalent to the entire social heritage, that is, all the knowledge, beliefs, customs, arrangements, and skills that are available to the members of a society. In recent years, scholars have come to agree that culture should be defined somewhat more narrowly, to distinguish it from social organization (Kroeber and Parsons, 1958; Jaeger and Selznick, 1964; Williams, 1970:25–26). In this book culture refers to shared ways of thinking, believing, perceiving, and evaluating. Culture is the realm of ideals and ideas, values and symbols. In a nutshell, [culture is the symbolic order; social organization is the relational order. Culture is the design for living, which produces a distinctive way of life (Kluckhohn, 1951:86); social organization is the actual pattern of individual and group relations.]

THE SYMBOLIC ORDER

Social life can exist without symbols as it does among other animals, but only humans have culture because only they are capable of creating symbols.

A symbol may be broadly defined as anything that stands for or represents something else. The word *pencil* is a symbol: It stands for the idea of a pencil or for a specific object. The meaning of a symbol is social in origin: Meaning is given to a symbol by those who use it. Thus symbols are always man-made. While words are the most common symbols, acts or objects can be symbols too, for example, a threatening gesture or a river that marks a boundary.

For the purpose of understanding culture, two kinds of symbols should be distinguished, the referential and the expressive. Referential symbols are *denotative*; they are words or objects that have a specific reference; they are instrumental. "Portable type-

INTERPERSONAL RITUALS

The main foundation of social order lies in the minute interpersonal rituals—hellos, goodbys, courtesies, compliments, apologies, and handshakes—that punctuate everyday interaction. "The gestures which we sometimes call empty are perhaps in fact the fullest things of all" (1967:91).

In the context of religion, "ritual" denotes standardized conduct through which an individual shows respect and regard to an object of ultimate value (usually a supernatural being) or to its stand-in (for example, an idol or a priest). In other words, rituals have mostly ceremonial, but little practical value. Nevertheless, as Durkheim—to whom Goffman owes a theoretical debt—pointed out, ritual and ceremony play an essential role in holding society together; through ritual worship of a common totem, members of primitive tribes reaffirmed their mutual commitment and collective solidarity.

Religious rituals have declined in importance in modern, secular societies, but despite their passing, many kinds of interpersonal rituals remain in force and perform the same function.

There are several types of interpersonal rituals. *Presentation* rituals include such acts as salutations, invitations, and compliments, by which the actor depicts his appreciation of the recipient.

"When members of the [hospital] ward passed by each other, salutations would ordinarily be exchanged, the length of the salutation depending upon the period that had elapsed since the last salutation and the period that seemed likely before the next. At table, when eyes met, a brief smile of recognition would be exchanged; when someone left for the weekend, a farewell involving a pause in on-going activity and a brief exchange of words would be involved. In any case, there was the understanding that when members of the ward were in a physical position to enter into eye-to-eye contact of some kind, this contact would be effected. It seemed that anything less would not have shown proper respect for the state of relatedness that existed among members of the ward" (1956/1967:71).

Avoidance rituals, on the other hand, are practices in which the actors respect the privacy of others by such distancing behaviors as limiting eye contact between persons who do not know each other.

"In performing this courtesy the eyes of the looker may pass over the eyes of the other, but no 'recognition' is typically allowed. Where the courtesy is performed between two persons passing on the street, civil inattention may take the special form of eyeing the other up to eight feet, during which the sides of the street are apportioned by gesture, and then casting the eyes down as the other passes—a kind of dimming of the lights. In any case, we have here what is perhaps the slightest of interpersonal rituals, yet one that constantly regulates the social intercourse of persons in our society" (1963:84).

Maintenance rituals reaffirm the well-being of a relationship, for example, where persons with a long-standing relationship who have not seen one another for a time arrange an encounter: "It is as if the strength of a bond slowly deteriorates if nothing is done to celebrate it, and so at least occasionally a little invigoration is called for" (1971:73).

Ratification rituals, such as congratulations at marriage and commiserations at divorce, mark the passage of an individual from one status to another: "Ratificatory rituals express that the performer is alive to the situation of the one who has sustained change, that he will continue his relationship to him, that support will be maintained, that in fact things are what they were in spite of the acknowledged change" (1971:67)

Access rituals, such as greetings and farewells, are commonly employed to mark the transition of persons to and from a state of increased access to one another: "The enthusiasm of greetings compensates for the weakening of the relationship caused by the absence just terminated, while the enthusiasm of farewells compensates the relationship for the harm that is about to be done to it by separation" (1955/1967:41).

Different rituals serve different specific functions, but they all have one essential feature in common: They are a conventionalized means by which the actor portrays ceremonial respect and regard for the self of another. Interpersonal rituals are important for three main reasons: First, they may be likened to traffic signs that serve to keep the flow of interaction moving smoothly and direct it away from areas that could prove dangerous. Like "do not enter" signs, avoidance rituals prevent us from being conversationally accosted in public places and so leave us free to go about our business. Like a green light, invitations and greetings tell us when our interaction is welcome and appropriate. With-

ashamed while the others present may feel hostile, and all the participants may come to feel ill at ease, nonplussed, out of countenance, embarrassed, experiencing the kind of anomy that is generated when the minute social system of face-to-face interaction breaks down.

"While the likelihood of disruption will vary widely from interaction to interaction, . . . there is no interaction in which the participants do not take an appreciable chance of being slightly embarrassed or a slight chance of being deeply humiliated. Life may not be much of a gamble, but interaction is" (1959:12, 243).

THE SPECIAL INTENSITY OF FACE-TO-FACE INTERACTION

Face-to-face interaction has a kind of multiplier effect, serving to raise both the emotional intensity as well as the hazards of social interaction. By being in the physical presence of others, the individual gives off information not only by verbal expressions but by clothing, gestures, and physical demeanor; as a result, face-to-face interaction is potentially more threatening to projected definitions of self than interaction mediated by telephone or writing, since more information about the individual is available to the observer.

"Each individual can *see* that he is being experienced in some way, and he will guide at least some of his conduct according to the perceived identity and initial response of his audience. Further, he can be seen to be seeing this, and can see that he has been seen seeing this. Ordinarily, then, to use our naked senses is to use them nakedly and to be made naked by their use. Copresence renders persons uniquely accessible, available, and subject to one another" (1963:16, 22).

Interaction ritual, Japanese style

Left, Irven DeVore meets a troop of baboons. In the course of 1,200 hours of field observations, DeVore came to know about 80 baboons by sight. *Right,* an adult male asserts his dominance with a threatening gesture. "Baboons are reasonably tolerant of scientists, but one thing you must never do is frighten an infant. DeVore did just that by accident one day, the infant yelped, and immediately several large angry males dashed to the spot slapping the ground and lunging at him. Fortunately he knew the appropriate signal. He smacked his lips loudly, which is a pacifying gesture among baboons and can be translated roughly as follows: 'Sorry about that. It was a mistake. No harm intended.' " (Pfeiffer, 1969:254)

and respond, they sort out and classify their experiences. They do so not in the interests of science, but as a way of dealing with needs and problems. Thus people classify their associates as friends or acquaintances or place them in other categories, and the categories they use offer clues to the way social life is organized.

Sensitivity to practical classification has stimulated some interesting studies, especially of official conduct: Police or probation workers classify offenders as good kids, punks, or incorrigibles, and psychiatrists decide who is to be labeled mentally ill (Cicourel, 1968; Daniels, 1970; on labeling, see p. 44). The main point of these analyses is that the sorting reflects the way officials respond to pressures—for instance, when military psychiatrists succumb to the pressures of commanding officers in determining who is psychologically unfit for duty.

3. Negotiated meanings The world of everyday life is concrete, not abstract. Thus general ideas are insufficient as guides to action. The meaning of the word *student,* for example, has to be filled in to reflect the condition of being a student at a particular institution at a particular time. This process of filling in meanings is negotiated in the sense that the meaning emerges out of the give-and-take of interaction. The concept of negotiated meaning encourages appreciation of the way general ideas are both specified and redefined in practical life.

The process of negotiating meanings is of special importance in authority situations. The acceptance of a general idea—you are my boss; I follow your orders—helps maintain the system of authority. The negotiated meaning—being a boss does not mean you can breathe down my neck—modifies the employee's situation and helps make it bearable.

4. Negotiated order Social order is not easily imposed. A process of bargaining usually takes place, even when one partner is apparently dominant. Thus parents and children, husbands and wives, and friends and lovers negotiate the conditions of affection and support. In more formal settings like hospitals, effective coordination de-

fronted with immediate situations, the individual more or less automatically is supposed to select the appropriate rule and follow its prescriptions. And because others are also assumed to have learned the same rules, a predetermined framework for orderly social behavior is taken for granted.

A great deal of interaction is in fact effectively guided by preexisting rules, many of which are learned unconsciously, as in the example of civil inattention. However, many sociologists are doubtful about the blueprint approach to interaction. They see it as only a partial explanation for interaction and one that does not necessarily account for the most important aspects of the micro-order. Rules often provide only a general framework within which the actual terms of interaction are worked out.

Limits of consensus Another limitation of the blueprint approach is that it overestimates social consensus. A focus on rules exaggerates the degree to which people agree on how to behave. Modern societies are extremely diverse, and the rules of the established order do not reflect the aspirations, interests, or life experiences of everyone. Racial minorities and youth groups are often troublesome partners in a legal or public engagement just because they do not share the blueprints of the dominant social groups. But even people who usually accept the dominant values and would like to live by the rules do not always do so. In the day-to-day pursuit of their own goals and satisfactions, following the rules does not always seem sensible or practical. For them, following the rules is only one element in the situation, to be weighed against others.

The fundamental limitation of the blueprint approach is that it cannot adequately account for the flux and uncertainty of social interaction. It cannot explain how a micro-order develops when participants have different interpretations of the rules to be followed. On very formal occasions, such as public ceremonies and church rituals, people know beforehand (or are shown then and there, sometimes by a printed program) exactly what is expected of them; but on most other occasions there is room for several interpretations. When a particular encounter brings together persons of different backgrounds and outlooks, they may have different ideas about how to conduct themselves, or no clear idea at all.

ETHNOMETHODOLOGY

The point of view of this section underlines the tentative and problem-solving nature of human interaction. With some differences in emphasis, this general perspective has been restated and specified in a school of thought recently named ethnomethodology (Garfinkel, 1967; Dreitzel, 1970).

The Greek word *ethnos* means nation, people, tribe, or race. Hence, ethnomethodology refers to the methods or practical understandings people acquire and use in the course of action and interaction.[1] In everyday life people learn how to cope with the social world and how to relate to others. Ethnomethodologists argue that the understandings people gain — even though they may be unsystematized — should be the point of departure for studying social organization. This is another way of stressing the importance of the definition of the situation.

The following are basic principles of ethnomethodology:

1. Background expectancies or assumptions Actors make sense of the world by calling upon a store of tacit assumptions. In the situations of everyday life, background expectancies are taken for granted and are often not brought to the surface unless disruption occurs. (See p. 30.)

2. People as knowers When people act

[1] Writings of the German philosopher Alfred Schutz (1899–1959) are cited as the major inspiration of ethnomethodology (1962). Schutz recognized his affinity with the symbolic interactionist position (see p. 11) and especially with the American philosophers William James, George H. Mead, and John Dewey. Dewey's chapter "Common Sense and Scientific Inquiry" (1938) is especially pertinent.

Doing sociology A study guide[2] has been prepared as a companion to this text. It gives instructions for group and individual projects on a variety of topics, such as sex-role socialization, primary relations among the elderly, violation of personal space, and the control of collective behavior. Elementary research techniques appropriate to the projects are presented. In addition *Doing Sociology* includes review materials keyed to this text and study aids found in conventional workbooks.

References In this book citations to articles and books are identified in parentheses by author, publication date, and often page of the source. The style is commonly used in sociological publications and eliminates most footnotes without losing necessary bibliographic information. References fulfill the scholarly obligation to record where ideas and information come from, to document statements, and also to provide leads to further reading on a topic.

In a few cases two publication dates are given: (1904/1976). This means that the original printing, the first date, is not readily available and reference is therefore being made to the later printing. The date of first publication communicates a historical sense of the place of the work in sociological thought.

Sources and readings In addition to the References, a selected bibliography for further study may be found at the end of each chapter. These "Sources and readings" identify general works and monographs, classic studies as well as more recent research. Usually the list includes one or more anthologies and specialized texts with more extended reading lists in specific areas.

References

Bakke, E. Wight
1935 The Unemployed Worker. New York: Dutton.

Bell, Daniel
1973 The Coming of Post-Industrial Society. New York: Basic Books.

Blumer, Herbert
1969 Symbolic Interactionism: Perspective and Method. Englewood Cliffs, N.J.: Prentice-Hall.

Coleman, James S., Ernest Q. Campbell, Carol J. Hobson, James McPartland, Alexander M. Mood, Frederic D. Weinfeld, and Robert L. York
1966 Equality of Educational Opportunity. Washington, D.C.: GPO.

Dahrendorf, Ralf
1958 "Toward a theory of social conflict." Journal of Conflict Resolution 2 (June):170–183.

Laing, R. D. and A. Esterson
1964 Sanity, Madness and the Family. Middlesex, England: Pelican Books.

Loomis, Charles P. and Zona K. Loomis
1967 "Rural sociology." Pp. 655–691 in P. F. Lazarsfeld, W. H. Sewell, and Harold L. Wilensky, The Uses of Sociology. New York: Basic Books.

Lynd, Robert S.
1939 Knowledge for What? Princeton: Princeton University Press.

Merton, Robert K.
1968 Social Theory and Social Structure. New York: Free Press.

Mills, C. Wright
1959 The Sociological Imagination. New York: Oxford University Press.

Moore, Wilbert E.
1963 Social Change. Englewood Cliffs, N.J.: Prentice-Hall.

Myrdal, Gunnar, with the assistance of Richard Sterner and Arnold Rose
1944 An American Dilemma. New York: Harper & Row.

Wallis, W. Allen and Harry V. Roberts
1956 Statistics: A New Approach. New York: Free Press.

[2] Darroch, Dorothy Broom, *Doing Sociology: Chapter Guides, Projects, Tool Kit,* 2nd ed. (New York: Harper & Row, 1977).

Sources and readings

Aron, Raymond
1965 Main Currents in Sociological Thought. New York: Basic Books. 2 vols.

Bottomore, T. B.
1971 Sociology: A Guide to Problems and Literature. New York: Pantheon.

Coser, Lewis A.
1971 Masters of Sociological Thought. New York: Harcourt Brace Jovanovich.

Faris, R. E. L. (ed.)
1964 Handbook of Modern Sociology. Chicago: Rand McNally.

Gould, Julius and William L. Kolb (eds.)
1964 Dictionary of the Social Sciences. New York: Free Press.

Figure 1:1 Percentage illiterate by race: United States, 1870–1969

Data for 1870–1940 are for the population 10 years old and over; data for 1947–1969 are for the population 14 years old and over. Data for 1940 are estimated.

Source: Current Population Reports, Series P-20. No. 217, March 10, 1971.
a Black only in 1969.

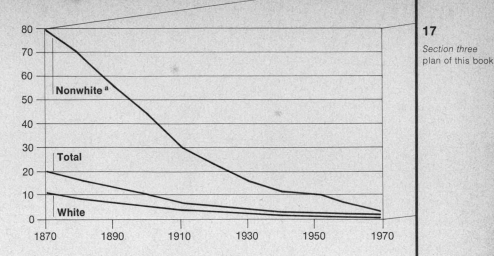

nonwhites compared with whites after the Civil War—a difference of about 68 percentage points in 1870. If a horizontal line is drawn across the graph from the highest illiteracy rate for whites (over 11 percent) in 1870, it intersects the curve for nonwhites about 1940. In other words, in 1940 blacks (and other nonwhite races combined) had reached the level where whites had stood 70 years earlier. Or considered another way, they had made up a very large part of the deficit. But in the meantime, white illiteracy had declined to 2 percent, so there was additional ground to be made up.

A horizontal line drawn from the black illiteracy rate in 1969 intersects the curve for whites between 1920 and 1930, indicating that in 1969 blacks reached the literacy level whites had occupied 45 years earlier—significant progress but still a significant lag. The difference between whites and blacks in percentage illiterate declined from 68 points in 1870, to 38 in 1900, to 13 in 1930, to 6 in 1959, and to 3 in 1969. In 1969 white illiteracy was approaching zero, and black illiteracy was on the threshold of final eradication. Because most illiterates are over 45 years of age, and because almost all persons now complete elementary school, black illiteracy should fall below 1 percent before the end of this century.

writer" is a referential symbol; it is a convenient way of referring to a specific class of
objects.

Expressive symbols are *connotative.* They
evoke associations that are diffuse and open-
ended rather than specific and limited. The
word *professor* denotes one who holds a
position on a faculty, but the same word
connotes a wide range of associations, not
fully specified, suggesting authority, knowledge, and wisdom, or perhaps subversion
and impracticality. The word *cross* denotes
a physical arrangement, but it connotes religious martyrdom and the perspectives of
Christianity.

Expressive symbols have a special importance for culture. When symbols are narrowly denotative and technical—for example, a code for filing books in a library—
they do not readily sustain personal and
group identity. A symbol invested with connotation evokes responses that are personally meaningful: The connotations are
experienced by the person as comforting or
threatening, uplifting or degrading. Thus
home is a more expressive symbol than
house; boss probably conveys more person-
centered meanings than *employer; convoca-
tion* evokes associations of a ritual occasion,
while *meeting* is more narrowly referential.
Expressive symbolism is capable of contributing to social solidarity by defining and
reinforcing shared ideals and perspectives.

George Orwell's novel *1984* depicts the
decay of social relations and culture in a
totalitarian society dominated by "Big
Brother." A phase of that decay is described
in "Newspeak and Expressive Symbolism"
(p. 58).

Symbolism and the arts In all societies,
though in varying degrees, expressive symbolism is sustained and enriched by aesthetic activity—dance, music, sculpture. The
arts help celebrate occasions that are significant to the group. The artist is a specialist in creating symbolic representations that
convey the spirit of a culture or an age,
though he may be unaware that he is doing

The technocratic age finds symbolic expression in this
light-space modulator, a mobile metal construction, by
Laszlo Moholy-Nagy.

so. Artistic creations are therefore important
to the student of culture. In the study of expressive symbolism the humanist and the
social scientist find common ground.

However, expressive symbolism is not restricted to the arts. Any repetitive human
act, any object, however simple or routine,
can have expressive meaning. A meal, a style
of dress, a greeting, a dwelling, a public
gathering place—any of these may be rich
with connotation.

CULTURAL VALUES AND NORMS

[A cultural value may be defined as a widely
held belief or sentiment that some activities,
relationships, feelings, or goals are important to the community's identity or well-
being.] Because they are often held unconsciously, or are expressed as themes cutting
across specific attitudes, the values of a
people are not immediately apparent.

Newspeak and expressive symbolism

The name of every organization, or body of people, or doctrine, or country, or institution, or public building, was invariably cut down into the familiar shape: that is, a single easily pronounced word with the smallest number of syllables that would preserve the original derivation. In the Ministry of Truth, for example, the Records Department was called Recdep, the Fiction Department was called Ficdep, the Teleprograms Department was called Teledep, and so on. Even in the early decades of the twentieth century, telescoped words and phrases had been one of the characteristic features of political language; and it had been noticed that the tendency to use abbreviations of this kind was most marked in totalitarian countries and totalitarian organizations.[1] It was perceived that in thus abbreviating a name one narrowed and subtly altered its meaning, by cutting out most of the associations that would otherwise cling to it. The words Communist International, for instance, call up a composite picture of universal human brotherhood, red flags, barricades, Karl Marx, and the Paris Commune. The word Comintern, on the other hand, suggests merely a tightly knit organization and a well-defined body of doctrine. Comintern is a word that can be uttered almost without taking thought, whereas Communist International is a phrase over which one is obliged to linger at least momentarily. In the same way, the associations called up by a word like Minitrue are fewer and more controllable than those called up by Ministry of Truth.

What was required, above all for political purposes, were short clipped words of unmistakable meaning which could be uttered rapidly and which roused the minimum of echoes in the speaker's mind. For the purposes of everyday life it was no doubt necessary, or sometimes necessary, to reflect before speaking, but a Party member called upon to make a political or ethical judgment should be able to spray forth the correct opinions as automatically as a machine gun spraying forth bullets. His training fitted him to do this, the language gave him an almost foolproof instrument, and the texture of the words, with their harsh sound and a certain willful ugliness, assisted the process still further.

The Newspeak vocabulary was tiny, and differed from almost all other languages in that its vocabulary grew smaller instead of larger each year. Each reduction was a gain, since the smaller the area of choice, the smaller the temptation to take thought. Ultimately it was hoped to make articulate speech issue from the larynx without involving the higher brain centers at all. This aim was frankly admitted in the Newspeak word duckspeak, meaning "to quack like a duck." Provided that the opinions which were quacked out were orthodox ones, it implied nothing but praise, and when the Times referred to one of the orators of the Party as a doubleplusgood duckspeaker it was paying a warm and valued compliment.

[1] For example, Gestapo from Geheime Staatspolizei; Comintern from Communist International; Agitprop from Agitation and Propaganda department.

Source: From "The Principles of Newspeak," Appendix to 1984 by George Orwell (New York: Harcourt Brace Jovanovich, 1949), pp. 309–311. Used with permission.

The world of things joins the world of symbols.

Here is one attempt to summarize the major values of North Americans:

1. American culture is organized around the attempt at *active mastery* rather than *passive acceptance.* Into this dimension falls the low tolerance of frustration; the refusal to accept ascetic renunciation; the positive encouragement of desire; the stress on power; the approval of ego-assertion, and so on.

2. It tends to be interested in the *external world* of things and events, of the palpable and immediate, rather than in the inner experience of meaning and affect. Its genius is manipulative rather than contemplative.

3. Its world-view tends to be *open* rather than closed: it emphasizes change, flux, movement; its central personality types are adaptive, accessible, outgoing and assimilative.

4. In wide historical and comparative perspective, the culture places its primary faith in *rationalism* as opposed to *traditionalism*; it de-emphasizes the past, orients strongly to the future, does not accept things just because they have been done before.

5. Closely related to the above is the dimension of *orderliness* rather than unsystematic *ad hoc* acceptance of transitory experience. (This emphasis is most marked in the urban middle classes.)

6. With conspicuous deviations, a main theme is a *universalistic* rather than a *particularistic* ethic.

7. In interpersonal relations, the weight of the value system is on the side of *"horizontal"* rather than *"vertical"* emphases: peer-relations, not superordinate-subordinate relations; equality rather than hierarchy.

8. Subject to increased strains and modifications, the received culture emphasizes *individual personality* rather than group identity and responsibility (Williams, 1970:501–502).

Thus a whole culture is sometimes characterized by values that reinforce each other and create a distinctive ethos.

Norms Cultural values are supplemented by norms, which are specific guides to conduct. The society may value privacy, but the particular norms governing privacy in the handling of mail or the administration of public toilets necessarily depend on the situation and circumstances. While some norms apply to narrowly specified situations that may

William Graham Sumner (1840–1910), author of *Folkways* and *The Science of Society* (with A. G. Keller). Sumner's work emphasized the conservative influence of custom. He was also a staunch conservative on both political and economic issues. Perhaps the best-known chapter title in social science is from *Folkways:* "The Mores Can Make Anything Right and Prevent Condemnation of Anything."

occur only rarely, others apply to the most common activities of everyday life. When the occurrence is rare, as in the case of funerals and other ceremonies, specialists are needed to instruct the participants on proper conduct.

Culturally salient norms, such as prohibitions of murder and incest, have been called *mores.* Sumner observed that "the Romans used *mores* for customs in the broadest and richest sense of the word, including the notion that customs served welfare and had traditional and mystic sanction so that they were properly authoritative and sacred" (1906/1960:48). [The Latin singular of mores is *mos,* but the singular has not been adopted by sociologists. It is more usual to say "one of the mores."]

Sumner distinguished mores from *folkways,* which are less salient norms. The intensity of feeling associated with folkways is relatively low, and conformity is more nearly optional. Norms specifying appropriate dress, for instance, evoke little emotion, except where the deviance is perceived as extreme.

CULTURE AND SOCIAL ORGANIZATION

Social organization is made up of interpersonal and group relations. The family is a unit of social organization, but the form of the family and much familial behavior are prescribed by the culture. One culture may value a kind of family in which the father is dominant; another may relegate him to a lesser role. Culture is the design and the prescription, the composite of guiding values and ideals. Hence, culture and social organization are interdependent. The separate treatment of the subjects is a matter of selective interest and emphasis.

On the other hand, much of social organization is not culturally prescribed but arises out of the give-and-take of personal and group interaction. For example, a hierarchy of social classes may be sharply defined as it was in medieval Europe. In American society, stratification exists, but it has much less cultural support.

The interrelations between culture and social organization are well illustrated by the Tanala, a hill tribe of Madagascar (Linton, 1936:348–355; 1933). Originally they subsisted by dry rice cultivation. They cut down and burned jungle growth, thus clearing the land for planting. After one or two crops, the land had to be abandoned until the jungle overran it again. The jungle about a village was thus exploited until it was exhausted, and then the village was moved. There was no individual ownership of land; the village as a whole held the territory. Within the village joint families—groups of households connected through a common head—were the chief units of organization. Joint-family members worked as a group and owned the crops from the land they cleared. The head of the joint family divided the crops among the households, and there was little variation in wealth between families. Forest products, such as game, belonged to anyone who took them.

The adoption of wet rice cultivation from a neighboring people disrupted Tanala culture and social organization. Because at the outset wet rice planting was done on relatively small plots, it was cultivated by single households and, unlike the dry rice system, the land was in continuous cultivation. The idea of exclusive ownership of real estate developed, and because there was only a limited amount of suitable land, two classes —landowners and landless—became distinguished. Those who held wet rice land no longer needed to be involved in the large joint-family effort in jungle clearing, and they did not want the villages to be moved. The landless, who continued dry rice cultivation, had to move into the jungle too far to return to the village at night. As a result they too began to develop separate household organization. There were numerous other effects: changes in the kinship and marriage system, in the practice of warfare, in the design of villages and village defense, in slavery, and in the growth of a centralized authority with autocratic control.

The Tanala case shows how changes in social relations are affected by changes in the key activities of a group and how the particular forms of adaptation and interaction are embedded in custom. When the food-gathering technology was changed, the social system changed along with it. The sequence of changes was initiated by a modification in the technology—the shift from dry to wet rice cultivation. This was accompanied by changes in social organization: greater emphasis on the individual household, declining emphasis on the large joint family, and the stabilization of the site of the village. Accompanying these changes were shifts in cultural values: The joint family was displaced by the household as the chief object of loyalty, and land became valued

as something not to be used temporarily but to be possessed permanently. Thus culture and social organization interact as people work out their relations to the physical environment and each other.

Section two the impact of culture

The experience of the Tanala with rice cultivation portrays culture as a dependent variable, something altered by other determining forces. Technological change affected social organization, which in turn influenced the culture—the Tanala conceptions of property and the symbolic meaning of the land. But culture can also be an independent variable, a determinant of social patterns.

PERVASIVENESS OF CULTURE

Culture creates a world taken for granted. It forms the unconscious assumptions of thought and action. It is pervasive, touching every aspect of life. The pervasiveness of culture is manifested in two ways. First, culture provides an unquestioned context within which individual action and response take place. Even rational action is subject to the cultural definition of what a meaningful goal is and what suitable means are. Emotional responses are governed by cultural norms that prescribe appropriate expressions of grief, pride, or love. Culturally determined responses are built into the very physiology of the organism, for example, conditioning the individual to feel nauseated by certain sights, smells, or tastes or to be sexually aroused by certain objects (Hall, 1959; 1966; see Adaptation 4).

Second, culture pervades social activities and institutions. There is a strain toward consistency in culture (Sumner, 1906/1960:21, 49–50)—consistency of perception and style, as well as of values. This is the thesis of Ruth Benedict's discussion of integrating themes in three preliterate, relatively simple societies. Benedict based her analysis on the following argument:

A culture, like an individual, is a more or less consistent pattern of thought and action. Within each culture there come into being characteristic purposes not necessarily shared by other types of society. In obedience to these purposes, each people further and further consolidates its experience, and in proportion to the urgency of these drives the heterogeneous items of behavior take more and more congruous shape (Benedict, 1946:42).

Although a strain toward consistency is probably universal in all cultures, the degree of consistency is highly variable. As Benedict recognized, the more complex the society and the more exposed it is to differing influences, the harder it is to identify and make generalizations about culture themes.

When radically different customs are compared, the impact of culture is obvious. But it is often necessary to examine the details of interaction, and the interdependence of language and thought, to grasp the depth of cultural influence. (See Adaptation 4.)

LANGUAGE AND CULTURE

Ordinarily language is taken for granted as a way of expressing ideas and feelings and of communicating messages. Because language appears to place no restraint on the flow of ideas, we assume that it is a medium equally fitted to convey any idea. According to this common-sense view, the various spoken languages of the world are merely different inventories for the same underlying reality; although different names and sounds are used in each language, the things named are actually the same. Though the "codes" may vary, the "messages" or thoughts expressed are fundamentally equivalent.

Such a conception of languages has been challenged by a number of linguists and anthropologists. Inspired especially by the work of Whorf, social scientists have come to believe that language is more than a ve-

hicle of thought: It pervades the content and style of thought itself. Language is not simply a set of labels for preexisting objects. Rather, language constructs reality by determining the kinds of objects we carve out of experience. Languages are not merely different codes for the same messages; they shape the kinds of messages that can be conveyed and even the kinds of messages that can be conceived.

Language is a guide to "social reality." Though language is not ordinarily thought of as of essential interest to the students of social science, it powerfully conditions all our thinking about social problems and processes. Human beings do not live in the objective world alone, nor alone in the world of social activity as ordinarily understood, but are very much at the mercy of the particular language which has become the medium of expression for their society. . . . No two languages are ever sufficiently similar to be considered as representing the same social reality. The worlds in which different societies live are distinct worlds, not merely the same world with different labels attached (Sapir, 1929/1958:162).

While this statement may be somewhat exaggerated, it does point to one of the most important ways culture as a symbolic realm influences the human mind.

Selective attention By sensitizing the individual to certain aspects of the external world, language accentuates some features at the expense of others. An illustration is the use of verbs. In English, tense is an important aspect of conjugation. Since in English a verb must have tense, the speaker is cognizant of a time dimension whenever he uses the language. However, the Hopi Indian language conjugates its verbs for validity rather than time (Whorf, 1940/1956:217). In naming an action, the Hopi must indicate the nature of his evidence, that is, whether he is reporting (1) a direct experience, (2) a belief or expectation, or (3) a generalization about experience. For example, having watched a boy running down a footpath, the Hopi uses the verb form *wari* ("running," statement of direct

Figure 3:1
Languages dissect
nature differently

The different isolates of meaning
(thoughts) used in English and in the
American Indian language Shawnee, in
reporting the same experience, that of
cleaning a gun by running the ramrod
through it. The pronouns "I" and
"it" are not shown by symbols, as they
have the same meaning in each language.
In Shawnee *ni-* equals "I"; *-a* equals "it."

Source: Redrawn after Whorf, 1940/1956.

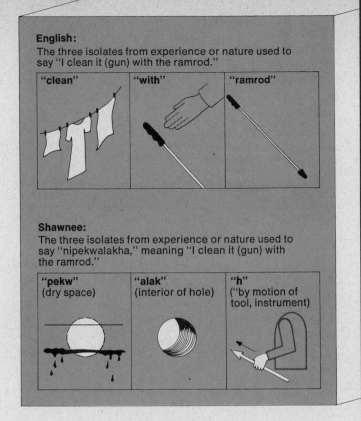

English:
The three isolates from experience or nature used to
say "I clean it (gun) with the ramrod."

| "clean" | "with" | "ramrod" |

Shawnee:
The three isolates from experience or nature used to
say "nipekwalakha," meaning "I clean it (gun) with
the ramrod."

| "pekw" (dry space) | "alak" (interior of hole) | "h" ("by motion of tool, instrument) |

observation); *wari* may be translated either
as "He is running" or "He ran," since the
time of the action is unspecified. If the Hopi
believes the boy is running down the footpath but has no direct evidence for this, he
uses the form *warikni* ("running," statement
of expectation); this form may refer to a past,
present, or future action. Finally, if the
speaker knows the boy runs as a matter of
custom or habit, perhaps as a participant in
racing games, he uses the form *warikngwe*
("running," statement of a generalization or
law). The Hopi language thus encourages
the speaker to check his sources of information.

Language and status Many cultural premises are deeply embedded in language.
Among these are patterns of dominance and
subordination. In revising this book, the
authors have done their best to respond to a
new awareness that the English language
takes male preeminence for granted. For a
very long time, those who treated *man* as a
synonym for *humanity* and freely used *he*
to represent any person, male or female,
ignored the subtle effects of language on female self-esteem. Similarly, the words used
by racial or ethnic groups both to identify
themselves and to identify others reflect the
sensitive interplay of language and belief.
(See the discussion of the vocabulary of race,
pp. 443–446.)

In Japanese, there are a number of sets of
verbal triplets that denote the same action,
one form indicating a humble attitude on the
part of the speaker toward the listener, another an attitude of politeness, and the
third a plain or abrupt attitude (Shodara,
1962:31–32). For example, *iku*, which is the
plain form of "to go," becomes *irrasharu* in
the polite form and *mairu* in the humble

The Culture Shock of Quiet Death

I had become friendly with a farm family who also ran a little cafe out on the road where the buses stopped. One morning I was sitting around waiting for a bus to take me down to the next village when one of the farmer's sons and his wife sat down by me. She was holding a baby in her arms who was dying of pneumonia, and I sat there listening to that unbearable gasping struggle for breath while the family calmly gathered around the child and watched. Only the mother seemed to be upset.

I was sure that they were waiting for the bus to rush the baby to a doctor, but as the bus came closer and finally into sight they made no move. And suddenly using the most beautiful Spanish of my life, completely out of control I was screaming at them, "Your baby's going to die; you've got to get him to a doctor. Now. Now."

The young mother began to pant; her husband looked to his father who simply nodded his head in a sort of permission without saying anything, and the young couple ran down to the road and stopped the bus.

When I got back that night they told me that the baby was dead.

The next afternoon I was about a mile from town buying some pineapples from a small farmer—just past the graveyard. As I was coming back I met the funeral procession, the toylike coffin painted in white and sprinkled with a silver dust being negligently packed on a farmer's shoulder.

Behind him and strung out for a hundred yards the family and their friends followed. The men carried bottles of traigo, stumbling and reeling in the mud of the trail. But while they advanced with a sort of dignity, there was also something slapstick about it. Some of them stopped to offer me a drink.

The statistics, of course, I knew— that in the country areas [Ecuador] three out of five babies die before their third year. And I was also aware of the Catholic philosophy which makes these deaths bearable to the country people. They hold the profound belief that when a baby dies, it dies in a state of grace and flies directly to heaven.

Within this framework then, the death of a child is something to celebrate; he has been released without sin from a life of suffering and poverty to become one of God's angels.

But knowing all this, I still could not accept it. Two mornings later, drinking coffee in the same little open air cafe and once more waiting for a bus, I had to leave and stand in a drizzle of rain to keep from watching another baby dying. The calmness with which they accepted his death was obscene to me.

I began to develop a grudge against the town and would make wild generalizations in my mind about the town and the people in it. By the end of the second week I had pretty much decided that I really didn't much like the people and that it would be impossible to work with them.

What I was going to do in that unrewarding spot for 18 more months was something that when I seriously thought about it sent me reeling into a real depression. I locked myself in my room for about three days. . . .

Well, I got straightened around, but it took a little time; it took at least a month. And I write about this experience now not because it is particularly interesting, but because it is so typical of a volunteer's first reactions to another, a different culture. It is a hard and unpleasant time, but I think almost all volunteers at one time or another go through it.

Source: Moritz Thomsen, "The Culture Shock of Quiet Death," *This World,* San Francisco *Chronicle,* April 25, 1965, p. 26. Used by permission.

form; *taberu* ("to eat," plain form) becomes *agaru* (polite form) and *itadaku* (humble form). Since the speaker is obligated to take into account the status of the listener, the abrupt or plain form is used in the presence of inferiors, the polite form in the presence of peers, and the humble form in the presence of superiors. In effect, the Japanese is placed in the social hierarchy simply by using a verb form. European languages, too, have formal and informal modes of address, as in the French *vous—tu* and the German *Sie—du*.

Modes of discrimination Selective attention enforced by language reflects the distinctive problems and experiences of the society. In English, for example, the same word is used for falling snow, snow on the ground, snow packed hard like ice, slushy snow, wind-driven flying snow, and so on (Whorf, 1940; 1956:216). An Eskimo is acutely aware that these various types of snow are distinct phenomena, each presenting its own problems and opportunities. The more inclusive word is not useful in the Eskimo's environment, and the Eskimo language includes a large vocabulary of specific terms.

Language and thought Because languages accentuate some features of experience and lend the world a special cast, they tend to produce different conceptions of reality and different thoughtways. The fact that some words are not translatable from one language to another "is merely the outward expression of inward differences between two peoples in premises, in basic categories, in the training of fundamental sensitivities, and in the general view of the world" (Kluckhohn, 1964:145). Consider the idea of time. There is evidence that many peoples conceive of time differently. For example, the language of the Kachin people of North Burma seems to contain no single word that corresponds to the English *time* (Leach, 1966:124). Instead, there are numerous partial equivalents. In the following expressions the Kachin equivalent of *time* differs in every case:

The time *by the clock*	*ahkying*
A long time	*na*
A short time	*tawng*
The present time	*ten*
Spring time	*ta*
The time *has come*	*hkra*
In the time *of Queen Victoria*	*lakhtak, aprat*
At any time *of life*	*asak*

A Kachin is encouraged by his language to be aware of these distinctions.

Conceptions of time, space, and other aspects of the world are rooted in language. Concealed in the structure of each language is a set of implicit assumptions. By emphasizing features of experience, vocabulary and grammar carry an implicit message: This is important. That is not important. Always distinguish *A* from *B* (Kluckhohn, 1964:145).

The extent to which language influences thought is not fully understood. It is clear, however, that the structure of language leaves its imprint on the consciousness and the thoughtways of a people.

CULTURE SHOCK

To the extent that persons are imbued with cultural values, act according to cultural assumptions, and lack awareness of alternative ways, they are said to be culture bound. Everyone is culture bound, at least to some degree.

When unquestioned expectations are shaken, culture shock may ensue. Culture shock is the experience of disorientation and frustration that occurs when individuals find themselves among people who do not share their fundamental premises. Usually, disagreement over abstract ideas or variation in modes of dress, eating habits, and other daily routines can be learned and adjusted to fairly readily. Acute culture shock is most likely to be experienced when expectations about personal feelings and interaction are violated. A case in point is the description by a Peace Corps volunteer in "The Culture Shock of Quiet Death."

Jeremy Bentham (1748–1832), no conformist, was a persistent critic of tradition and urged that all social practices be assessed according to their utility in maximizing pleasure and minimizing pain. In his gift to the University of London, he required that his remains be preserved in University College, where his clothed skeleton is kept on display in a glass case.

CONFORMITY AND DEVIATION

Although culture is an important determinant of thought and feeling, it does not absolutely govern behavior.

Human beings participate in culture to different degrees and are more or less responsive to values and norms because most human action takes place in specific situations and involves solving specific problems. People spend most of their time dealing with the problems, stresses, and opportunities of everyday life. Therefore, culture is always mediated by or filtered through routine activities and interactions.

People are not culturally determined automatons who merely act out values and follow rules. They take rules into account and are often guided by them, but they also deviate from rules, both deliberately and unwittingly.

Some norms are more specifically stated than others; some have wider ranges of application than others; some permit individual interpretation to a greater extent than others. Limits are indeed set by norms, but variation in conformity is often permitted, and exceptions are also provided for. A person may have to choose between one norm and another. For example, a driver who hits another automobile to avoid hitting a child violates one norm in order to conform to another. That he does so "automatically" shows how deeply ingrained the underlying values are. In this case the relative importance of the norms is clear and there is no conflict. On the other hand, a student who sees a friend cheating on an examination must choose between conflicting norms, especially if the school has an honor system. One norm instructs the student to see that honesty is upheld, the other to be loyal to a friend.

Norms in conflict Few acts are more repugnant to Western peoples than murder and cannibalism, few assertions more readily accepted than "Self-preservation is the first law of nature." What happens when these two norms directly conflict?

During the seventeenth century a small fishing party was driven far out to sea by a storm in the Caribbean (Cox, 1886:629). Their few provisions were soon exhausted, and it became evident that it would take many days to reach land. One of the men proposed that lots be cast and that the loser sacrifice himself to be eaten so that the others might live. Lots were cast, and it so happened that the original proposer lost. However, no one would act as executioner and butcher, and it was necessary to cast lots again. A butcher was thus chosen, and the man was killed and eaten. After 17 days the small boat reached port at a French island where the magistrate did not hold the survivors. Because they were English, their case was again examined by an English judge on the island of St. Kitts. He released the prisoners outright saying ". . . the inevitable necessity had washed away the crime."

Can it be taken as a general principle that under the compulsion of necessity the strongest of laws and mores may be over-ridden? Examine this case from an incident in 1884.

At the trial of an indictment for murder it ap-peared, upon a special verdict, that the prisoners D. and S., seamen, and the deceased, a boy be-tween seventeen and eighteen, were cast away in a storm on the high seas, and compelled to put into an open boat; that the boat was drifting on the ocean, and was probably more than 1000 miles from land; that on the eighteenth day, when they had been seven days without food and five without water, D. proposed to S. that lots should be cast who should be put to death to save the rest, and that they afterwards thought it would be better to kill the boy that their lives should be saved; that on the twentieth day D., with the assent of S., killed the boy, and both D. and S. fed on his flesh for four days; that at the time of the act there was no sail in sight nor any reason-able prospect of relief; that under these circum-stances there appeared to the prisoners every probability that unless they then or very soon fed upon the boy, or one of themselves, they would die of starvation (*Regina* v. *Dudley and Stephens*, in Cox, 1886:624–638; cf. Cahn, 1955:61–71).

The court held the prisoners guilty of murder and sentenced them to death. On the argument that the killing was an act of necessity, the court said:

Who is to be the judge of this sort of necessity? By what measure is the comparative value of lives to be measured? Is it to be strength, or intellect, or what? It is plain that the principle leaves to him who is to profit by it to determine the necessity which will justify him in deliberately taking an-other's life to save his own. In this case the weak-est, the youngest, the most unresisting, was chosen. Was it more necessary to kill him than one of the grown men? The answer must be "No" (Cox, 1886:637).

Although sentence of death was passed, it was afterward commuted by the Crown to six months' imprisonment. The original sen-tence defended a principle regarded as essential to the moral order; the commuta-tion of the sentence acknowledged the ex-ceptional circumstances of the crime.

Adaptation 4 Hall: The silent language

Much cultural behavior is so deeply ingrained that the individual is unaware of it. Even such funda-mental matters as dealing with space and time are approached with subtle and profound variations in different cultures. In The Silent Language, *an-thropologist Edward T. Hall treats the nonverbal aspects of communication.*

THE VOICES OF TIME

Time talks. It speaks more plainly than words. The message it conveys comes through loud and clear.

Source: Abridged and adapted from *The Silent Language* by Edward T. Hall (New York: Doubleday, 1959), Chaps. 1, 9, 10. Used in this form by permis-sion of the author and Doubleday.

Not long ago I learned from the superintendent of the Sioux that he had been born on the reservation and was a product of both Indian and white cul-tures, having earned his B.A. at one of the Ivy League colleges.

During a long and fascinating account of the many problems his tribe was having in adjusting to our way of life, he asked: "What would you think of a people who had no word for time? My people have no word for 'late' or for 'waiting,' for that mat-ter. They don't know what it is to wait or to be late." He then continued: "I decided that until they could tell time and knew what time was they could never adjust themselves to white culture. So I set about to teach them time. There wasn't a clock that was running in any of the reservation classrooms. So I first bought some decent clocks. Then I made the school buses start on time, and if an Indian was two minutes late that was just too bad. The bus started at 8:42 and he had to be there."

He was right, of course. The Sioux could not adjust to European ways until they had learned the meaning of time. The superintendent's methods may have sounded a bit extreme, but they were about the only ones that would work. The idea of starting the buses off and making the drivers hold to a rigid schedule was a stroke of genius; much kinder to the Indian, who could better afford to miss a bus on the reservation than lose a job in town because he was a day late. There is, in fact, no other way to teach time to people who handle it as differently from us as the Sioux. The quickest way is to get very technical about it and make it mean something.

In the United States, a girl feels insulted when she is asked for a date at the last minute by someone whom she doesn't know very well, and the person who extends an invitation to a dinner party with only three or four days' notice has to apologize. How different from the people of the Middle East, with whom it is pointless to make an appointment too far in advance, because their informal

time system places everything beyond a week into a single category of "future," in which plans tend to "slip off their minds."

Even physiological urgency is handled quite differently by people around the world. In many countries, people need less of what Americans would call urgency in order to discharge a tension. In the United States, the need must be highly critical before people act. The distribution of public toilets in America reflects our tendency to deny the existence of urgency even with respect to normal physiological needs. I know of no other place in the world where anyone leaving home or office is put to periodic torture because great pains have been taken to hide the location of rest rooms. Yet Americans are the people who judge the advancement of others by their plumbing.

PUNCTUALITY

Informally, for important daytime business appointments between equals in the eastern United States, punctuality has a variety of meanings: on time and 5, 10, 15, 20, 30, 45 minutes, and one hour early or late. In regard to being late there are "mumble something" periods, slight apology periods, mildly insulting periods requiring full apology, rude pe-

Figure 3:2
The language of gesture

A study of immigrant communities in New York described cultural variations in nonverbal communications. Left, a traditional southern Italian gesture that can signify "Please, I pray you to shut up, I want to talk." Right, a Jewish immigrant way of making a conversational point with a companion's hand. The study found that such gestural patterns were rapidly lost in succeeding generations.

Source: Efron (1941, Figs. 19, 65). Illustrations after Stuyvesant Van Veen.

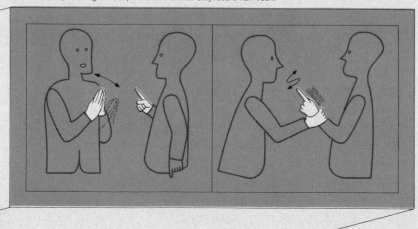

riods, and downright insulting periods. No right-minded American would think of keeping a business associate waiting for an hour; it would be too insulting. No matter what is said in apology, there is little that can remove the impact of an hour's heel-cooling in an outer office.

Even the five-minute period has its significant subdivisions. When equals meet, one will generally be aware of being two minutes early or late but will say nothing, since the time in this case is not significant. At three minutes a person will still not apologize or feel that it is necessary to say anything (three is the first significant number in the one-to-five series); at five minutes there is usually a short apology; and at four minutes before or after the hour the person will mutter something, although he will seldom complete the muttered sentence. The importance of knowing this aspect of informal culture is driven home if one pictures an actual situation.

An American ambassador in an unnamed country interpreted incorrectly the significance of time as it was used in visits by local diplomats. An hour's tardiness in their system is equivalent to 5 minutes by ours, 50 or 55 minutes to 4 minutes, 45 minutes to 3 minutes, and so on for daytime official visits. By their standards the local diplomats felt they couldn't arrive exactly on time; this punctuality might be interpreted locally as an act relinquishing their freedom of action to the United States. But they didn't want to be insulting—an hour late would be too late—so they arrived 50 minutes late. As a consequence the ambassador said, "How can you depend on these people when they arrive an hour late for an appointment and then just mutter something? They don't even give you a full sentence of apology!" He couldn't help feeling this way, because in American time, 50 or 55 minutes late is the insult period, at the extreme end of the duration scale; yet in the country we are speaking of it's just right. If he had been taught the details of the local time system just as he should have been taught the spoken language, it would have been possible for him to adjust himself accordingly.

SPACE SPEAKS

As one travels abroad and examines how space is handled, startling variations are discovered—differences we react to vigorously. Literally thousands of experiences teach us unconsciously that space communicates. Yet this fact would probably never have been brought to the level of consciousness if it had not been realized that space is organized differently in each culture. The associations and feelings that are released in a member of one culture almost invariably mean something else in the next. When we say that some foreigners are "pushy," all this means is that their handling of space releases this association in our minds.

"It's as much as your life is worth to ride the streetcars. They're worse than our subways. What's more, these people don't seem to mind it at all." As Americans, we have a pattern which discourages touching, except in moments of intimacy. When we ride on a streetcar or crowded elevator we "hold ourselves in," having been taught from early childhood to avoid bodily contact with strangers. Abroad, it's confusing when conflicting feelings are being released at the same time. Our senses are bombarded by a strange language, different smells, and gestures, as well as a host of signs and symbols.

The Latin house is often built around a patio that is next to the sidewalk but hidden from outsiders behind a wall. It is not easy to describe the degree to which small architectural differences such as this affect outsiders. American foreign aid technicians living in Latin America used to complain that they felt left out of things, that they were "shut off." Others kept wondering what was going on "behind those walls." In the United States, on the other hand, propinquity is the basis of a good many relationships. To us the neighbor is actually quite close. You can borrow things, including food and drink, but you also have to take your neighbor to the hospital in an emergency. In this regard he has almost as much claim on you as a cousin.

Another example has to do with the arrangement of offices. In this case one notices great contrast between ourselves and the French. In the United States, the pattern is to take a given amount of space and divide it up equally. When a new person is added in an office, almost everyone will move his desk so that the newcomer will have his share of the space. This may mean moving from positions that have been occupied for a long time and away from favorite views. The point is that the office force will make its own adjustments voluntarily. In fact, it is a signal that they have acknowledged the presence of the new person when they start rearranging the furniture. Until this happens, the boss can be sure that the new person has not been integrated into the group.

The French, by contrast, do not make way for each other in the unspoken, taken-for-granted way that we do. They do not divide up the space with a new colleague. Instead they may grudgingly give him a small desk in a dark corner looking toward the wall. This action speaks eloquently to Americans who have found themselves working for the French. We feel that not to "make a place" accents status differences. If the rearrangement which says, "Now we admit you to the group, and you are going to stay," fails to take place, Americans are likely to feel perilously insecure.

CONVERSATIONAL DISTANCE

Spatial changes give a tone to a communication, accent it, and at times even override the spoken word. The normal conversational distance between strangers illustrates how important are the dynamics of space interaction. If a person gets too close, the reaction is instantaneous and automatic—the other person backs up. And if he gets too close again, back we go again. I have observed an American backing up the entire length of a long corridor while a foreigner whom he considers pushy tries to catch up with him. This scene has been enacted thousands of times—one person trying to increase the distance in order to be at ease, while the other tries to decrease it for the same reason, neither one being aware of what was going on. We have here an example of the tremendous depth to which culture can condition behavior.

This was suddenly brought into focus one time when I had the good fortune to be visited by a very distinguished and learned man who had been for many years a top-ranking diplomat representing a foreign country. After meeting him a number of times, I had become impressed with his extraordinary sensitivity to the small details of behavior that are so significant in interaction. Dr. X was interested in some of the work several of us were doing at the time and asked permission to attend one of my lectures. He came to the front of the class at the end of the lecture to talk over a number of points made in the preceding hour. While talking he became quite involved in the implications of the lecture as well as what he was saying. We started out facing each other and as he talked I became

dimly aware that he was standing a little too close and that I was beginning to back up. Fortunately I was able to suppress my first impulse and remain stationary because there was nothing to communicate aggression in his behavior except the conversational distance. His voice was eager, his manner intent, the set of his body communicated only interest and eagerness to talk. It also came to me in a flash that someone who had been so successful in the old school of diplomacy could not possibly let himself communicate something offensive to the other person except outside of his highly trained awareness.

By experimenting I was able to observe that as I moved away slightly, there was an associated shift in the pattern of interaction. He had more trouble expressing himself. If I shifted to where I felt comfortable (about 21 inches), he looked somewhat puzzled and hurt, almost as though he were saying, "Why is he acting that way? Here I am doing everything I can to talk to him in a friendly manner and he suddenly withdraws. Have I done anything wrong? Said something that I shouldn't?" Having ascertained that distance had a direct effect on his conversation, I stood my ground, letting him determine the distance between us.

In Latin America the interaction distance is much less than it is in the United States. Indeed, people cannot talk comfortably with one another unless they are very close to the distance that evokes either sexual or hostile feelings in the North American. The result is that when they move close, we withdraw and back away. As a consequence, they think we are distant or cold, withdrawn and unfriendly. We, on the other hand, are constantly accusing them of breathing down our necks, crowding us, and spraying our faces.

Getting over a spatial accent is just as important, sometimes more so, than eliminating a spoken one. Advice to the foreign traveler might be: Watch where people stand, and don't back up. You will feel funny doing it, but it's amazing how much difference it makes in people's attitudes toward you.

CONCLUSION

1. Units of time gain their meaning in social situations that are culturally defined. Being an hour late in one culture is equivalent of being five minutes late in another.

2. Comfortable interpersonal distance for a

Latin American connotes undue intimacy or aggression to a North American.

3. Nonverbal communication may be as decisive as words in determining the effectiveness of

interaction. Time and distance elements of a culture should therefore be studied as closely as the overt symbolic behavior of gesture, speech, and writing.

Section three cultural diversity

Studies of history and anthropology compel the conclusion that humanity is both *one* and *many*. Everywhere the human being is the same in biological and psychic nature. But upon that foundation is built a remarkable diversity of motivation, custom, and belief. The interplay of human oneness and plurality, uniformity and diversity, is considered in this section.

THE CONSTANT AND THE VARIABLE

No feature of life in society is exempt from cultural variability—from language to physical posture, from concepts of property to ways of making love, from great ideas to the details of etiquette. To the reader of this book, many unfamiliar customs would be reasonable or even attractive alternatives, for example, wearing an Indian sari or having more than one spouse. Other variations would be hard to accept or even to think about without pain, such as circumcision rites for adolescent boys and girls or eating live witchetty grubs.

Not all variations are equally important. Variations in dress, for example, may or may not be salient to a culture. In some places costume has symbolic significance; elsewhere it is almost neutral, and changes in style are easily accepted. What is salient can be known only if the culture as a whole is understood.

Cultural universals Despite manifest and even rampant diversity, there is striking uniformity. Murdock has listed the following common elements in all known cultures, arranged in alphabetical order:

Age-grading, athletic sports, bodily adornment, calendar, cleanliness training, community organization, cooking, cooperative labor, cosmology, courtship, dancing, decorative art, divination, division of labor, dream interpretation, education, eschatology, ethics, ethnobotany, etiquette, faith healing, family, feasting, fire making, folklore, food taboos, funeral rites, games, gestures, gift giving, government, greetings, hair styles, hospitality, housing, hygiene, incest taboos, inheritance rules, joking, kin-groups, kinship nomenclature, language, law, luck superstitions, magic, marriage, mealtimes, medicine, modesty concerning natural functions, mourning, music, mythology, numerals, obstetrics, penal sanctions, personal names, population policy, postnatal care, pregnancy usages, property rights, propitiation of supernatural beings, puberty customs, religious ritual, residence rules, sexual restrictions, soul concepts, status

Anthropologist at work: Margaret Mead as a young fieldworker among the Manus of the Admiralty Islands off the north coast of New Guinea.

differentiation, surgery, tool making, trade, visiting, weaning, and weather control (Murdock, 1945:124).

This list could be extended if the items were analyzed further. For example, the word *authority* does not appear, as it would if the items "community organization" and "cooperative labor" were broken down into their elements.

When the constant and the variable are considered together, a more balanced response to strange customs is possible than when either aspect is considered alone. Among the polar Eskimo of northwest Greenland, a man may lend his wife to a friend for the night, and the temporary exchange of wives is common (Murdock, 1934:213). The idea of sexual property is maintained (the wife is not supposed to lie with another man without permission), but there is evidently no great value placed on exclusive physical intimacy. To someone reared in another tradition, wife lending is a startling variation in what human beings can tolerate.

On the other hand, the ideal of hospitality appears to be common to all cultures. Such cultural universals are general, however, not specific social forms. The content remains to be specified. Thus hospitality, the general phenomenon, may be offered in many different ways, of which wife lending is one. What gives the Eskimo culture its distinctiveness is the particular way of extending hospitality and the special sensibilities associated with it. A culture is always made up of unique adaptations and elaborations. The universals, however, show that all peoples belong to the human species and the societies they create are *human* societies.

Cultural universals can be accounted for in three ways:

1. The psychic unity of humanity Despite individual differences and cultural variation, all human beings are alike in being subject to conditioning, in having a similar range of emotions, in the need for security and response, in the capacity to symbolize, and in many other ways. This psychic unity does not determine specific adaptations; it does not make cultures identical, but it is a source of cultural similarities. When the same kind of organism responds to roughly similar circumstances, it is understandable that there are similar outcomes.

2. Requirements of group life Social life has functional necessities, that is, requirements that must be met if groups are to survive and flourish. Reciprocity, leadership, communication, specialization, and symbolic affirmations of group identity are not mere accidental developments. They are solutions to problems, rediscovered innumerable times as ways of dealing with the ever-present necessities of organization and solidarity. Here again, the common elements or universals are general, not specific. The particular form of leadership or feasting or exchange of goods reflects the experiences of the society.

3. Limited possibilities Action and choice always take place within a framework of limited alternatives. Some limitations are set by the physical environment, especially when the society is isolated and has a low level of technology. In the polar North, shelters may be made of ice or skins, but few other alternatives are available. The principle of limited possibilities applies most clearly to the technical arts. There are many ways of making a boat or an oar, but certain conditions must be met if the boat is to float or the oar to pull; if, in addition, the quest is for a speedy boat or the most efficient oar, the technological limitations are even more severe. "The fewer the possibilities . . . the more likely are similar solutions" (Goldenweiser, 1937:125). The principle of limited possibilities also applies to language, which must have some sort of grammar; to social organization, which must adapt to physical and demographic resources; and even to ritual, which relies for solemnity or exuberance on available modes of congregation, dance, and incantation.

Selective adjustment and elaboration Cultural diversity means cultural selection.

From a broad range of possibilities, each people selects ends and means that make up its way of life. "All cultures constitute so many somewhat distinct answers to essentially the same questions posed by human biology and by the generalities of the human situation" (Kluckhohn, 1962b:317). Every culture faces similar problems, but each culture solves those problems in its own way. Some challenges must be met if the community is to survive; others may be neglected or not even perceived. Whether something is conceived as a problem—for example, whether a standard of living or birthrate is felt to be satisfactory—largely depends on cultural assessments.

ETHNOCENTRISM AND CULTURAL RELATIVISM

Each group tends to consider its way the natural and the best way. Strange people, beliefs, or practices are treated with suspicion and hostility simply because they are strange. Identification with the familiar and devaluation of the foreign is called *ethnocentrism*. It is the feeling that one's own culture is the best in all respects and that others are in varying degrees inferior—barbaric, heathen, or outlandish. Extreme ethnocentrism supports attitudes that lead to rejection of some people as less than human, against whom any violence may be justified.

In less virulent form, ethnocentrism appears as a cultural nearsightedness that takes one's own culture for granted and passively, rather than actively, rejects others. Even a book like this, which tries to be sensitive to such problems, falls into ethnocentric terminology in using *American* to mean a national of the United States. The word is the common property of all the peoples of North and South America, and Latin Americans sometimes resent the proprietary use of a word that applies equally to them. In polite parlance, they call U.S. nationals *Norteamericanos*, which also betrays a mild ethnocentrism on their part because they lump together citizens of Canada and the United States. But there is no convenient name for a citizen of the United States of America as there is for Canadians or Mexicans.

The critique of ethnocentrism is often approached from the moral and intellectual position called *cultural relativism*. Sumner expressed this point of view when he said, "Everything in the mores of a time and place must be regarded as justified with regard to that time and place. 'Good' mores are those which are well adapted to the situation. 'Bad' mores are those which are not so adapted" (1906/1960:65). According to Sumner, there is no universal standard an outside observer can use to evaluate cultures or cultural norms as good or bad. Each culture must be seen in its own terms, and the worth of a custom can be judged only by the contribution it makes to the culture of which it is a part. In that sense, judgments and interpretations are relative; they must begin with an understanding of the social setting.

Social science looks to the cultural context to make moral sense of a particular practice, whether it is cannibalism or television commercials. Cultural relativism encourages both a tolerant perspective on foreign ways and a closer inspection of what those ways are and how to understand them.

Although cultural relativism is an important point of view for social science, certain limitations should be noted:

1. It is sometimes said that cultural relativism precludes the belief that some values are good for all humanity. On the contrary, cultural relativism itself posits a fundamental value: respect for cultural differences. Implicit in the doctrine is the view that all people need and deserve respect as a warrant of their common humanity.

2. Although it is proper to insist that cultural facts be interpreted according to their settings, it is nevertheless possible to discover aspects of morality that are cross-cultural:

Considering the exuberant variation of cultures in most respects, the circumstance that in some particulars almost identical values prevail throughout mankind is most arresting. No culture tolerates indiscriminate lying, stealing, or violence within the in-group. The essential universality of the incest taboo is well known. No culture places a value upon suffering as an end in itself. . . . In spite of loose talk (based upon an uncritical acceptance of cultural relativity) to the effect that the symptoms of mental disorder are completely relative to culture, the fact of the matter is that all cultures define as abnormal individuals who are permanently inaccessible to communication or who consistently fail to maintain some degree of control over their impulse life (Kluckhohn, 1962a:294–295).

These considerations should give pause to an extreme interpretation of relativism (Bidney, 1962:436–453).

SUBCULTURES

Complex societies like the United States contain not one homogeneous culture but a multitude of ethnic, regional, and occupational subcultures with which people identify and from which they derive many distinctive values and norms, as well as social relationships and life chances. Some sociologists have even suggested that there is no such thing as American culture, but instead only a conglomeration of subcultures. American culture can be thought of in several ways: as including all the subcultures, as consisting of only those elements that all subcultures share, or as restricted to the values and orientations that are subscribed to by a dominant element or the majority of the population.

A subculture is a pattern that is in significant respects distinctive but that has important continuities with a host or dominant culture. In other words, a subculture contains some of the dominant cultural values but also contains values, perspectives, or life-styles peculiar to itself. Every group has some patterns of its own, but if the patterns do not affect the total life of the members, they do not comprise a subculture. A subculture has a general influence on attitudes and life-styles and tends to give the person a discernible identity.

A subculture may be based on an occupation, especially one that provides a total context for everyday life. Thus military subcultures are supported by the isolation of military garrisons, intensive training affecting deportment and outlook as well as skills, long-term career orientations, and the absorption of families into the military social system. Occupations that require special life-styles, setting the members off from the rest of the community, are especially likely to develop subcultures.

More typical, however, is a subculture based on residential, ethnic, or social-class conditions. These subcultures tend to coincide with local communities and thus provide a setting for the entire round of life.

Continuities and discontinuities The concept of subculture has made a useful contribution to the study of juvenile delinquency. Some theories of delinquency stress the continuity of the delinquency-breeding subculture with its host society (Cohen, 1955; Matza, 1964); other theories place greater emphasis on the uniqueness of the subculture (Miller, 1958).

A special sort of subcultural continuity is identified in one interpretation of delinquent boys. The argument begins with a description of differences. The boy from the slums grows up in a world that takes no great stock in self-discipline, high aspirations, deferred gratification, or community responsibility. "There is little interest in long-run goals, in planning activities and budgeting time, or in activities involving knowledge and skills to be acquired only through practice, deliberation, and study" (Cohen, 1955:30). An immediate, close-knit world of family or gang dominates life, and the rest of the world is seen as made up of victimizers and victims. These subcultural orientations are real, but the members of the subculture are not isolated from the larger society. When they come into contact with the middle-class school and such other middle-class institutions as government agencies and large employers, they meet disapproval and rejection. The delinquent behavior pattern is an aggressive reaction against this disapproval, both a hitting out against middle-class culture and an attempt to establish criteria of worth which the individual can meet, thus repairing his damaged self-respect.

The delinquent subculture functions simultaneously to combat the enemy without and the enemy within, both the hated agents of the middle class and the gnawing internal sense of inadequacy and low self-esteem. It does so by erecting a counterculture, an alternative set of status criteria (Bordua, 1961:125).

As a counterculture, a reaction formation, the delinquent subculture shows its continuity with the host community. According to this theory, delinquent subcultures can be understood only by seeing their relation to the larger culture within which they develop.

A contrasting view emphasizes the autonomy and distinctiveness of lower-class culture. On this theory, the delinquent boy and his gang do not react against middle-class standards but act out values, such as masculinity, which are a positive aspect of lower-class traditions.

Implications Just as sociology attempts to eliminate ethnocentrism in the treatment of different cultures, so must it avoid the same bias in analyzing subcultures. Because subcultures interact with and incorporate parts of the host culture, observers may fail to recognize the existence and the viability of distinctive subcultural patterns. This failure may result in misleading assessments. For example, the phrase *culturally deprived* is often applied to lower socioeconomic strata in the United States and elsewhere. The term signifies that the cultural milieu does not prepare the members to compete in the larger social and economic world. Other writers charge that use of terms like *cultural*

deprivation is but another instance of ethnocentrism, in this case class ethnocentrism. They point out that while lower- and working-class environments may indeed leave their members ill-prepared to compete in the middle-class world, these environments constitute a distinctive subculture, having their own worth as adaptations to lower-class conditions of deprivation and discrimination.

In the assessment of lower-class subcultures, there is a tension between two values. The sensitive observer wishes to appreciate diversity and accept alternative life-styles. On the other hand, the sensitive observer wants to recognize that the practical conditions of life may lead to impoverished social experience. The first perspective emphasizes culture while the second views social organization as the major determinant. An example of the latter approach is found in *Tally's Corner* (see Adaptation 10), a study of the black ghetto in Washington, D.C., in which the author concludes:

Whether the world of the lower-class Negro should be seen as a distinctive subculture or as an integral part of the larger society . . . is much more than an academic question and has important consequences for "intervention." . . . Many similarities between the lower-class Negro father and son (or mother and daughter) do not result from "cultural transmission" but from the fact that the son goes out and independently experiences the same failures, in the same areas, and for much the same reasons as his father. . . . The problem is how to change the conditions which, by guaranteeing failure, cause the son to be made in the image of the father (Liebow, 1967:219, 223).

There can be no rule for deciding in advance when to treat a subculture as autonomous and when to see it as dependent upon or reacting against the larger cultural setting. Both perspectives can be valuable; each must be assessed for the light it sheds on a particular situation.

Adaptation 5: Negro–pygmy relations

The Ituri forest is inhabited by two kinds of people, Negroes and pygmies, who maintain an almost symbiotic relationship, based on trade. A Negro village may own approximately 100 square miles of forest territory. In this territory are the Negro village and the pygmy village. The former is permanent, in a clearing; the latter is temporary, under the forest trees. In maintaining their relationship, it is the pygmies' job to take in honey and meat, while the Negroes' obligation is to give them plantains. In addition, the pygmies may bring in a certain amount of wild baselli fruit in season, or roofing leaves, or rattan and fibers for net making; in return they may acquire ax blades, knives, and arrowheads from the Negroes.

There is no strict process of barter involved, and no accounting kept, other than through general observation. If the pygmies are stingy, the Negroes will hold back their bananas. If the Negroes are stingy, the pygmies will leave the territory and go to live with other pygmies serving other Negro hosts.

This relationship is interfamilial, between a pygmy family and a Negro family. It is a matter of close personal relations, inherited, on both sides, from father to son. These alliances may change from time to time, but when they do there are usually hard feelings; if a man's pygmy leaves him to serve another host, it is a kind of divorce. In the old days, a frequent cause of intervillage warfare among the Negroes was the luring away of each other's pygmies.

Before the Belgians stopped intervillage and intertribal warfare, the most important single duty of the pygmy was to act as scout and intelligence agent in the forest. As soon as he became aware of a raiding party crossing the boundary of his host's territory, he would hotfoot it to the village to give warning. This eternal vigilance on the part of the pygmy was probably of more value to his hosts than the meat that he brought in. Now that the need of this has ceased he is fulfilling only half of his contract; the Negro, who still provides plantains

and manufactured objects, is still fulfilling all of his. Yet both are satisfied.

Ordinarily, the pygmy keeps inside the territory of his Negro hosts. Individuals and small family groups may go outside to visit relatives in other bands, but this causes no disturbance because the visitors turn in their game to the hosts of the kinsmen whom they are visiting. This constant milling about evens up on the whole, and the number of pygmies in any band at any one time is about the same. There are occasions, however, when the hunters of a band may have a strong reason to pass beyond the landmarks which designate their hosts' territorial boundaries. If there is a lot of game just over the border and no pygmies there to catch it, the pygmies will tell their Negroes, who in turn tell the Negroes owning that part of the forest. An agreement will be made between the two groups of Negroes, and the pygmies will be allowed to take the game, provided that they pay a part of it to the owners of the forest, and another part to their own hosts. This kind of economic treaty, therefore brings the pygmies of a given band into contact with two groups of Negroes, and may initiate new relationships.

When the pygmy camp is close to the Negro village, some of the pygmies may come in every evening. They will leave a couple of old men to stay behind in the camp as guards, smoking hashish, and the rest will go into the village, usually around four o'clock in the afternoon, after the day's hunting is over. From then until dark a few pygmies are usually to be seen hanging about the women's quarters. If a white man arrives, however, they quickly disappear, through fear that he will confiscate their antelope or any other game that they may have brought with them.

These mass visits are made particularly if it is going to be a moonlit night, and if wine drinking is going on. If there is a moon they will stay and dance; if not, they will come home at dark. The Negroes give them wine in a condescending way, and the pygmies put on what the Negroes consider to be wild, barbaric dances.

Sometimes the pygmy camp is as much as two days' journey from the village. In this case the pygmies go in seldom, and browbeat their wives to make them go in to get plantains.

Source: Abridged and adapted from "The Pygmies of the Ituri Forest," pp. 323–325 in Carleton S. Coon (ed.), *A Reader in General Anthropology* (New York: Holt, Rinehart and Winston, 1948). Patrick Putnam, who lived with the peoples for nearly two decades, narrated this account to Coon, who condensed it for his *Reader*.

Ituri pygmies carrying bunches of plantain from a village in Zaïre, formerly Belgian Congo

A visitor to a Negro village can nearly always see bunches of plantains lying around on the ground: they have been placed there for the pygmies, who pick them up and carry them home. There is no need for any special bargaining or designation; the pygmies know which bunches are for them.

PYGMY ATTITUDE TOWARD THEIR NEGROES

The pygmies consider themselves inseparably attached to their hosts and think it their duty to provide them with meat. Although they feel that they are supposed to turn over all honey and elephant meat, in each case they eat all they can before taking it into the village. They never preserve or store any food. Their duty of feeding the Negroes meat is therefore regarded as somewhat of a nuisance. On the other hand, when the pygmy wants something from a Negro, he wheedles and "begs" for it. He may thus "borrow" a mortar, a skin-headed drum for dancing, etc., and will not return it until the Negro comes after it or sends for it. He will not put any of these things under cover, or care for them; he leaves them out in the rain to mildew and rot. The owner has to see that his property is cared for, and this forms a subject on which the Negro can make fun of the pygmy.

The form of this relationship is therefore a grudging duty in the case of giving, and a wheedling begging in the case of receiving. These outer forms fail to reveal the inner feeling of loyalty and affection between the parties concerned, but rather symbolize the existing situation in which the Negro is at the top of the scale and the pygmy at the bottom.

NEGRO ATTITUDE TOWARD THEIR PYGMIES
The Negroes distinguish four ranks or orders of living beings: people, pygmies, chimpanzees, and other animals. The pygmies are thus considered a species apart, neither human nor animal, but in between. The main point of distinction lies not in their size or physique, but in the fact that the pygmies do no cultivation.

The Negroes think of their pygmies as barbaric and uncultured, but at the same time they are often fond of them. A Negro may occasionally marry a pygmy woman, and the children are considered real children, complete human beings; they are brought up with the Negro's other children. The Negroes say that pygmy women are good in bed, cheap, and prolific, but that they are useless for women's work—cultivation and cooking. For a pygmy woman it is a great rise in the scale of living to marry a Negro as his second or third wife, despite the fact that pygmy wives are usually the butt of humor from the Negro wives. This is, however, a one-way process; no Negro woman could endure the pygmy way of living, and none of them ever marries a pygmy.

The interplay between Negroes and pygmies may be illustrated by a number of examples in which they disagree on historical facts. The Negroes say that the pygmies once went naked, like animals. The pygmies hotly deny this and assert that they always wore loincloths. The Negroes admit that they themselves were once cannibals, but say that the pygmies ate more human flesh than they did. This, too, the pygmies deny; they claim that they never ate human flesh except when the Negroes gave it to them.

In addition to the exchange of food and, formerly, protection, which form the basis for Negro–pygmy interaction, there is another activity which helps to cement their relationship. The Negroes have a circumcision school, of the usual Negro variety. This school is held about once in four or five years. There is no specific interval; it is probable that they wait until there are enough boys ready to form a class of the right size. These boys are anywhere from nine to fourteen years of age. Now the pygmies associated with these Negroes may send their boys through this same school with the sons of their hosts. Thus, the pygmy boys are away from home for several months, are in close association with the Negro boys, and are taught the same secrets that the Negro boys learn. At the end they are all circumcised together, and their parents come to the Negro village to dance and get drunk with the parents of the Negro boys.

The pygmies are thus age-graded like the Negroes. Each class has its own cheer, or song, as in American colleges. Each class also has its own name, such as "Hurricane" or "great army worm," depending on some event which occurred during its period of isolation. This not only forms a strong bond between the pygmies and their hosts but it gives them a formal sequence of age-grades in their own society. It is a common experience to hear one person asking another, when strangers meet, "What class were you in? I am a Hurricane."

Section four the transformation of culture

Themes of development and deterioration, growth and decay, have had a special place in the study of culture. For example, the idea of cultural evolution has had a prominent place in the history of thought. (For an overview and critique, see Nisbet, 1969.) This section considers the attenuation, destruction, and renewal of culture.

CULTURE UNDER FIRE

Under certain conditions, cultures may be weakened or destroyed. A culture may lose its strength and vitality as a result of internal social change, or it may be overwhelmed by outside influences. In either case, there is likely to be a substantial human cost.

Vulnerability of the symbolic order The cultural symbols of language, ritual, and belief are viable only so long as people accept them. Therefore the symbolic order is sensitive to change that erodes tradition and opens up alternatives. Sometimes the established order is challenged directly, as, for example, in the nineteenth-century conflict between religion and science. Other influences may be more remote and subtle, such as the effect of computer technology on the significance of work.

Culture is vulnerable when (1) a breakdown of authority is threatened; (2) there is a serious gap between cultural ideals and social realities; (3) individuals' lives are fragmented, so that they lack the sense of participating in a coherent and sustaining symbolic order; and (4) beliefs or practices hitherto valued for themselves—that is, expressive of personal or group identity—become more narrowly instrumental.

Acculturation: threat and opportunity Acculturation is the adoption of new traits or patterns in the course of culture contact. Ideally, acculturation is the way one people learns from another and thereby enriches its own life. Although many primitive peoples have lived in isolation, others have traveled and traded extensively, communicating a wide variety of beliefs and practices—from knowledge of navigation to ideas for tracing descent and inheriting property. Culture contact among peoples who share a roughly similar style of life is more likely to be experienced as opportunity than as threat:

Minor variations in cultures, when they appear and function in the historical contact of peoples, seem to be among the most powerful incentives of development and progress. But there is a limit to the cultural disparity between two groups in contact which can be resolved with relative safety. When the disparity is extreme . . . there is danger (Goldenweiser, 1937:428).

The contact of primitive or folk communities with more cosmopolitan and more technologically advanced societies poses the question of cultural integrity in a sharp and poignant form. A striking illustration within modern American society is the plight of the Old Order Amish (Wittmer, 1971).

The Amish are a Mennonite religious community committed to the idea that a simple, rural, traditional way of life is an essential condition of salvation. Their rearguard struggle to maintain a distinctive, preindustrial life-style has been frustrated at many points.

The Amish want to limit the education of their children so as not to spoil them for farm life; in this they run up against compulsory education laws and the modern consolidated school. They prefer the horse and buggy, but horses do not last long on hard-surfaced roads now replacing dirt and gravel. The Amish want to do without electricity, but the standards set by outside milk inspectors limit their opportunity to sell milk for extra income.

An Amishman feels close to God when tilling the soil, and farming is the sanctioned occupation. Until recently, Amish farmers have been able to buy farms from retiring non-Amish neighbors, often lending one another money at 2 or 3% in order to help the young Amish farmer obtain land. Non-Amish farmers in the community resent this. Perhaps for this reason, many public auctions of farm lands are now being held on Sunday, eliminating the Sabbath-abiding Amishman from the bidding. Because of the scarcity of land, many Amishmen have recently taken jobs in factories sanctioned by the church. Since the Amish religion does not permit a member to join the union, these jobs are usually short-lived (Wittmer, 1971:106).

When the Amish strive to isolate their children, they are protecting the authority of traditional norms and traditional leaders; when they try to maintain a homogeneous life-style, with everyone engaged in farming, they are upholding more than a religious ideal. The dispersion of the community into factory work or into commerce tends to undermine the individual's commitment to the community, eroding the experience of participating in a coherent way of life.

The Amish are a special case in that they are, to some extent, an "intentional" community. (See PRIMARY GROUPS, p. 155.) For religious reasons, they are self-conscious about maintaining a distinctive cultural identity. Most preindustrial communities, lacking this determination, have been more receptive to external influences.

The costs and benefits of acculturation can be assessed only by considering specific historical circumstances. It cannot be assumed, for example, that the European impact on indigenous communities has always been destructive. For example, a summary of culture change since the Spanish conquest in the Mexican village of Tepoztlán concluded that "on the whole, but particularly in the field of material culture [technology], the new culture elements in all periods did not supplant but were added to the old, making for a richer and more heterogeneous culture" (Lewis, 1951:440).

On the other hand:

We have seen that in the increased contact with the outside world in recent years, Tepoztecans have taken many new traits of modern life. They now have Coca-Cola, aspirin, radios, sewing machines, phonographs, poolrooms, flashlights, clocks, steel plows, and some labor saving devices. They also have a greater desire to attend school, to eat better, to dress better, and to spend more. But in many ways their world view is still much closer to sixteenth-century Spain and to pre-Hispanic Mexico than to the modern scientific world. They are still guided by superstition and primitive beliefs; sorcery, magic, evil winds, and spirits still dominate their thinking. It is clear that, for the most part, they have taken on only the more superficial aspects and values of modern life. Can western civilization offer them no more? (Lewis, 1951:448).

Cultural borrowing is always selective, but what is selected is crucial for the survival of a way of life.

Attenuation of culture Various expressions have been used by anthropologists to refer to the weakening of culture: *cultural disorganization* (Redfield, 1941), *deculturation* (Steward, 1955), *cultural deterioration* (Goldenweiser, 1937), *spurious culture* (Sapir, 1924). There is an understandable uneasiness in using such terms, because they appear to pass judgment upon the quality or worth of a culture. But no serious problem

of objectivity arises if (1) it is understood that any culture is placed in jeopardy when social change takes place, and (2) the alleged points of weakness and the forces that produce them are spelled out with care so that they can be tested in the light of evidence and argument.

A study of cultural change in Yucatán (Redfield, 1941) compared four communities: an isolated Indian tribal village (Tusik), a peasant village (Chan Kom), a town (Dzitas), and a city (Mérida). The communities varied along a gradient—the "folk-urban continuum." From Tusik at the folk extreme to Mérida at the urban end, the investigators found an increasing attenuation of traditional culture: People were more open to outside influences; their way of life was less steady and less homogeneous. The result was, progressively, (1) a weakening of cultural coherence, (2) an increase of secularization, and (3) a more individualized society.

Cultural disorganization, a term used in the Yucatán study to indicate a loss of cultural coherence, is illustrated by the conversion of some families in Chan Kom to Protestantism, which introduced a distinction between religious affiliation and community membership. Two strands of culture, religion and community consciousness, were separated. "The community no longer acted as a unit in its religious life, and the principal leaders, who remained Catholic, felt the weakness and often expressed their sorrow and chagrin" (Redfield, 1941:145).

Yet a certain amount of reorganization also occurred. After a while, the Protestant families relaxed their separatism and participated in some of the traditional Catholic rituals:

While maintaining their separate prayer-meeting, the Protestants began to attend novenas of their neighbors. . . . When All Souls' Day came around, the Protestants held a prayer-meeting with a table decorated much as they had decorated tables on such occasions before conversion; and, while they did not set out food for the dead or call upon them by name, their prayer-meeting was

Cultural impoverishment in affluence and in extreme
deprivation

felt to have the same ghost-averting function as its more traditional predecessor. . . . So the community remained a single community, although with alternate cults for certain classes of occasions, and with an unresolved conflict as to the sanctity and value of the santos (Redfield, 1941:145).

Whenever institutional differentiation occurs—for example, the separation of religion from government or of family life from occupation—cultural coherence tends to be weakened. The weakening may be welcomed, however, in the interest of other values such as individual freedom.

Secularization is revealed in a loss of symbolic meaning—in the conduct of church festivals, in growing and handling maize, in carrying on traditional occupations. The affairs of life become less expressive and more instrumental. Holy days become holidays—occasions for secular entertainment, for attracting visitors and making money.

Individualization appears in a breakdown of traditional forms of collective labor dedicated to civic enterprises and religious worship, in the emergence of more individual rights in land, and in a narrowing of the sense of kinship to more immediate relatives. "In the villages it is relatively easy to say 'the family did this' or 'the community did that'; in Mérida it is not so easy" (Redfield, 1941:356).

These conclusions help specify the meaning of cultural attenuation. They should not be read as necessarily implying that all isolated villages are similar to Tusik in having a deeply rooted folk culture, nor that exposure to outside influences always produces the same effects. (A comparison with Guatemala may be found in Tax, 1939.) Lewis's later study of Tepoztlán in Mexico, although otherwise critical, confirmed Redfield's findings, "particularly in regard to the trend toward secularization and individualization, perhaps less so in regard to disorganization" (Lewis, 1951:440).

The attenuation of culture is a matter of degree, and assessment of it depends very much on a balancing of values. Industrial society has indeed eroded culture, but it has

also opened new opportunities and new horizons to millions of people. Participation in a "genuine" culture, as in a tight community, can be a source of personal enrichment, but it may also make the individual more limited and more parochial. Furthermore, a people may survive and even flourish under conditions of cultural disorganization, secularization, and individualization.

Destruction of culture A more clearly tragic outcome of culture under fire is the destruction of culture. The rapid and radical collapse of a way of life has frequently occurred when technologically advanced societies have impinged on primitive communities. Economic exploitation is only part of the colonialist and imperialist story. In addition, the indigenous cultures were often shattered. Traditional crafts, around which a large part of the symbolic order was built, could not survive competition with Western technology. And the authority of the old institutions was undermined as they lost credibility.

The island of Tahiti was the scene of such a destruction:

The chief trouble was that there was now nothing for the Tahitians to do. Before the Europeans arrived they had their own occupations and had enlivened their days with their own rituals and entertainments, but now all these had been taken away from them, and the singing of Christian hymns was really not enough to compensate. In that soft soporific climate it was impossible to make the people work for long. . . . The missionaries imported a weaving machine, and for a month or two the girls worked it with great enthusiasm. Then the novelty wore off and the machine was left to rust away in its palm-leaf hut. It was the same with the attempts to start cotton and sugar-cane growing; after the first season or two the workers drifted away. Their own arts and crafts had long since been forgotten; no one could make cloth from the bark of a tree and there no longer seemed any point in building the great double-canoes with their high carved prows: a crude boat hacked out of a tree-trunk was good enough (Moorehead, 1966:87–88).

When Captain Cook arrived at the island in

1769, the people numbered about 40,000. Less than a century later, the population was only 6,000. The destruction of the culture had a direct effect on health and longevity. "It almost seemed that the heart had gone out of the people, and that they had lost the will to survive. Pulled one way by the missionaries, another by the whalers, and now another by the French officials they subsided with a sigh" (Moorehead, 1966:93).

This conclusion probably refers to the loss of motivation that occurs when activities are robbed of symbolic meaning. Loss of motivation brings with it personal disorganization: the psychic inability to take care of oneself, relate to others, keep up a garden, hold a job, and resist self-destructive gratifications, such as excessive use of alcohol. As a result, especially when new diseases are introduced, the indigenous population may decline dramatically, at least for a time.

Early in this century, a substantial depopulation of the islands of Melanesia was noted, and some observers attributed the decline to the erosion of culture and a consequent "loss of interest in life" (Rivers, 1922: Chap. 8). It is difficult, however, to disentangle such influences from the catastrophic effects of newly introduced diseases. In any event, populations that appeared to be near extinction when Rivers wrote have now rebounded, and overpopulation has become a serious problem throughout the Pacific.

Resilience and renewal While the human cost of cultural destruction cannot be dismissed or treated lightly, it is important to avoid a morbid fascination with cultural decline. As noted above, any change in social organization—arising, for example, from a new method of agriculture—carries some risk that the traditional culture will be weakened. In many cases, that is a necessary prelude to the emergence of new values and life-styles.

In modern Israel, the youth are ethnically the same as the Jews of pre-Zionist times, but their experiences and aspirations have generated a new outlook and self-image. They tend to reject the withdrawn, ironic, defensive style of the Jew as victim. The native *sabra* is very different from his grandfather—in speech, in humor, in cast of mind. He is apparently less intellectual, less doctrinaire, more pragmatic—in a way less "Jewish." At the same time, other strands of cultural continuity are being developed, mainly through the shared experiences of nation-building (Elon, 1971). Thus whatever cultural attenuation may be taking place must be considered in the context of renewal.

In contemporary America, there is a groping for new ways of reestablishing the values of a more integrated culture, as suggested in the following contrast (Bennis, 1970):

From	Toward
Achievement	Self-actualization
Self-control	Self-expression
Independence	Interdependence
Endurance of stress	Capacity for joy
Full employment	Full lives
Mechanistic forms	Organic forms
Competitive relations	Collaborative relations

The newer ideals, if they become securely grounded in the realities of social organization, may lead in time to a substantial transformation of culture. But even the achievement of such ideals cannot be equated with the experience of living in an "old-time" culture, small in scale and slow in pace, based upon stability, homogeneity, and sacredness. Modern man may be able to learn from the fate of culture, but he "can't go home again."

References

Beals, Ralph L. and Harry Hoijer
1965 An Introduction to Anthropology. New York: Macmillan. Third Edition.

Benedict, Ruth
1946 Patterns of Culture. Baltimore, Md.: Penguin Books.

Bennis, Warren
1970 "Warren Bennis, a conversation." Psychology Today 3 (February):48–54, 68–71.

Bidney, David
1962 "The concept of value in modern anthropology." Pp. 436–453 in Sol Tax (ed.), Anthropology Today: Selections. Chicago: University of Chicago Press.

Boas, Franz
1912/1955 Race, Language and Culture. New York: Macmillan.

Bordua, David J.
1961 "Delinquent subcultures: sociological interpretations of gang delinquency." Annals of the American Academy of Political and Social Science 338 (November):119–136.

Cahn, Edmond
1955 The Moral Decision. Bloomington, Ind.: Indiana University Press.

Cohen, Albert K.
1955 Delinquent Boys. New York: Free Press.

Cox
1886 Criminal Law Cases. Vol. XV. London.

Efron, David
1941 Gesture and Environment. New York: Kings Crown Press.

Elon, Amos
1971 The Israelis. New York: Holt, Rinehart and Winston.

Goldenweiser, Alexander
1937 Anthropology. New York: Appleton.

Hall, Edward T.
1959 The Silent Language. New York: Doubleday.
1966 Hidden Dimension. New York: Doubleday.

Jaeger, Gertrude and Philip Selznick
1964 "A normative theory of culture." American Sociological Review 29 (October):653–669.

Kluckhohn, Clyde
1951 "The study of culture." Pp. 86–101 in Daniel Lerner and Harold Lasswell (eds.), The Policy Sciences. Stanford, Calif.: Stanford University Press.
1962a Culture and Behavior. New York: Free Press.
1962b "Universal categories of culture." Pp. 304–320 in Sol Tax (ed.), Anthropology Today: Selections. Chicago: University of Chicago Press.
1964 Mirror for Man. Greenwich Conn.: Fawcett. First published in 1944.

Kroeber, A. L. and Clyde Kluckhohn
1963 Culture: A Critical Review of Concepts and Definitions. New York: Vintage Books.

Kroeber, A. L. and Talcott Parsons
1958 "The concepts of culture and of social system." American Sociological Review 23 (October):582–583.

Leach, E. R.
1966 Rethinking Anthropology. London: Athlone Press.

Lewis, Oscar
1951 Life in a Mexican Village: Tepoztlán Restudied. Urbana, Ill.: University of Illinois Press.

Liebow, Elliot
1967 Tally's Corner. Boston: Little, Brown.

Linton, Ralph
1933 The Tanala: A Hill Tribe of Madagascar. Anthropological Series Vol. XXII. Chicago: Field Museum of Natural History.
1936 The Study of Man. New York: Appleton.

Matza, David
1964 Delinquency and Drift. New York: Wiley.

Mazlish, Bruce
1966 The Riddle of History: The Great Speculators from Vico to Freud. New York: Harper & Row.

Miller, Walter B.
1958 "Lower-class culture as a generating milieu of gang delinquency." Journal of Social Issues 14 (July):5–19.

Moorehead, Alan
1966 The Fatal Impact. New York: Harper & Row.

Mosse, George L.
1961 The Culture of Western Europe. Chicago: Rand McNally.

Murdock, George Peter
1934 Our Primitive Contemporaries. New York: Macmillan.
1945 "The common denominator of cultures." Pp. 123–142 in Ralph Linton (ed.), The Science of Man in the World Crisis. New York: Columbia University Press.

Nisbet, Robert A.
1969 Social Change and History. New York: Oxford.

Redfield, Robert
1941 The Folk Culture of Yucatan. Chicago: University of Chicago Press.

Rivers, W. H. R.
1922 Essays on the Depopulation of Melanesia. Cambridge: Cambridge University Press.

Sapir, Edward
1924 "Culture, genuine and spurious," American Journal of Sociology 29 (January):401–429.
1934 "Symbolism." Encyclopedia of the Social Sciences 14: 492–495.
1929/1958 "The status of linguistics as a science." Pp. 160–165 in David G. Mandelbaum (ed.), Selected Writings of Edward Sapir. Berkeley, Calif. and Los Angeles: University of California Press.

Shodara, Hide
1962 "Honorific expressions of personal attitudes in spoken Japanese." Center for Japanese Studies, Occasional Papers, No. 2. Ann Arbor, Mich.: University of Michigan Press.

Steward, Julian H.
1955 Theory of Culture Change. Urbana, Ill.: University of Illinois Press.

Stocking, George W., Jr.
1963 "Matthew Arnold, E. B. Tylor, and the uses of invention." American Anthropologist 65 (August):783–799.
1966 "Franz Boas and the culture concept in historical perspective." American Anthropologist 68 (August):867–882.

Sumner, William Graham
1906/1960 Folkways. New York: New American Library.

Tax, Sol
1939 "Culture and civilization in Guatemalan societies." Scientific Monthly 48 (May):463–467.

Tylor, Edward B.
1913 Primitive Cultures: Researches into the Development of Mythology, Philosophy, Religion, Language, Art and Custom. London: Murray. Fifth edition.

Whorf, Benjamin Lee
1940/1956 Language, Thought, and Reality. New York: Wiley.

Williams, Raymond
1960 Culture and Society, 1780–1950. Garden City, N.Y.: Doubleday.

Williams, Robin M., Jr.
1970 American Society: A Sociological Interpretation. New York: Knopf. Third edition.

Wittmer, Joe
1971 "The Plight of the Old Order Amish." Current Anthropology 12 (February):106–107.

Sources and readings

Benedict, Ruth
1946 Patterns of Culture. Baltimore, Md.: Penguin Books.

Hymes, Dell
1964 Language in Culture and Society. New York: Harper & Row.

Kluckhohn, Clyde
1964 Mirror for Man. Greenwich, Conn.: Fawcett. First published in 1944.

Kroeber, A. L. and Clyde Kluckhohn
1963 Culture: A Critical Review of Concepts and Definitions. New York: Vintage Books.

Leach, E. R.
1970 Political Systems of Highland Burma. London: Athlone Press. First published in 1954.

Linton, Ralph
1936 The Study of Man. New York: Appleton.

Malinowski, Bronislaw
1931 "Culture." Pp. 621–645, vol. 4, Encyclopedia of the Social Sciences. New York: Macmillan.

Mead, Margaret
1935 Sex and Temperament in Three Primitive Societies. New York: Morrow.

Murdock, George P.
1935 Our Primitive Contemporaries. New York: Macmillan.

Sahlins, Marshall D. and Elman R. Service (eds.)
1960 Evolution and Culture. Ann Arbor, Mich.: University of Michigan Press.

Singer, Milton
1968 "The Concept of Culture." Pp. 527–541, vol. 3, International Encyclopedia of the Social Sciences. New York: Macmillan.

Tax, Sol (ed.)
1962 Anthropology Today: Selections. Chicago: University of Chicago Press.

White, Leslie A.
1959 The Evolution of Culture: The Development of Civilization to the Fall of Rome. New York: McGraw-Hill.

Periodicals

American Anthropologist

Comparative Studies in Society and History

Current Anthropology

Human Organization

Man (Journal of the Royal Anthropological Institute)

RAIN (Royal Anthropological Institute News)

4 Socialization

By *Gertrude Jaeger*
in collaboration with L. B. and P. S.

Section one introduction

From the perspective of society, socialization is the process of fitting new individuals into an organized way of life and an established cultural tradition. Socialization begins very early and is a lifelong process. As individuals participate in social forms and institutions, they learn disciplines and develop values. Parents as socializing agents are themselves socialized as they learn the disciplines and experience the rewards of the parental role.

From the perspective of the individual, socialization is the process by which the human animal becomes a human being and acquires a self. Through interaction with others, the individual gains an identity; takes on ideals, values, and aspirations; and under favorable circumstances becomes capable of self-realizing activity. Socialization is the indispensable condition for self-awareness and for the formation of individual identity, and if it fails, personal development will be impaired. Thus socialization represents two complementary processes: the transmission of a social and cultural heritage and the development of personality.

BIOLOGICAL BASIS OF SOCIALIZATION

The species Homo sapiens is by nature social. The capacity and need for group life are integral parts of the human biological makeup and are the products of a long evo-

Wire and cloth mother surrogates

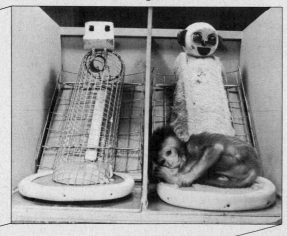

lutionary development (Pfeiffer, 1972). Thus, for Homo sapiens socialization is both possible and necessary. For example, the human neurological equipment for language makes socialization possible. Without socialization, however, biological readiness to use and create signs and symbols would remain unrealized.

Following are some of the key biological characteristics of the human animal on which socialization is based:

Absence of instincts In the nineteenth century, after the appearance of Darwin's evolutionary theory and the development of the biological sciences, the concept of instinct gained favor as a way of accounting for human behavior. Society was explained by a herding instinct, the role of women by a maternal instinct, property by an acquisitive instinct, war by an aggressive instinct, and so on. After a time a reaction set in, and for a while the word *instinct* was virtually banned from scientific discourse. At present in its strict sense, instinct refers only to those relatively complex behavior patterns for which some species are biologically programmed. Nest building among birds is a familiar example: It is called an instinct because it contains both the impulse to build a nest (under suitable stimulation) and the readiness to respond to the environment in patterned ways that result in the construction of a particular kind of nest. While some learning may intervene even in nest building, it cannot significantly alter the species-specific pattern for nests. Nest-building techniques vary greatly among species, but not within species.

Like all living things, humans have innumerable built-in physiological reflexes, only a few of which, such as eye blinking or sweating, are readily observable. If human beings possessed biologically fixed behavior patterns comparable to nest building, they would limit learning and make humans inaccessible to socialization. Humans have biological drives rather than instincts. A drive, such as hunger or sex, is an organic

tension that is felt as discomfort or impulse but does not direct behavior to specific goals or touch off a predetermined sequence of coordinated activities leading to need-satisfaction. A drive impels activity but does not determine it in detail. Though drives are biological imperatives, they tend to produce only restlessness and searching behavior unless they are focused and directed by the learning process.

Social contact needs That humans are basically social beings is supported by recent experimental work with rhesus monkeys. These experiments have demonstrated an infant need for physical contact clearly independent of the gratifications associated with feeding. Satisfaction of this need appears to be a strong biological drive: Rhesus monkeys deprived of bodily contact and interaction in early life developed behavioral aberrations and, as adults, both males and females were unable to respond to each other with appropriate mating postures. A few females were eventually impregnated by a normally reared male but were incapable of appropriate maternal behavior and often beat, bit, and otherwise maltreated their young.

In the basic experiment, each infant monkey was taken from its biological mother and placed in a cage with two mock "mothers" constructed of wire, one with the wire exposed, the other covered with soft cloth (Harlow, 1959). Some monkeys were fed by bottles attached to the wire mother, others by bottles attached to the cloth mother. But even those infants fed by the wire mother spent most of their time clinging to the cloth mother.

The biological and psychological functions of clinging became apparent when the infant monkeys, confronted with unfamiliar objects, fled to the cloth mother. As their fears diminished, they explored new objects, occasionally returning to the mother. If no mother or only a wire mother was present, the infants cowered in terror, screaming, sucking their fingers or toes, and otherwise showing fear and withdrawal. The cloth mother allayed fear; the wire mother did not.

Monkeys raised with cloth mothers did not show normal development, however, unless they played with other infant monkeys. Only then did they develop into socially and sexually competent adults. "The failure of infants to form infant–infant affectional relations delays or destroys adequate adult heterosexual behavior" (Harlow and Harlow, 1965:328). Like humans, some of the primates are social animals by nature, requiring the give-and-take of social interaction for realization of their biological potentialities.

The results of the rhesus monkey experiments are consistent with findings from studies of children deprived of sustained human contact. A study of the effects of relative social isolation compared the progress of a group of 61 infants in a foundling home, where there was a minimum of social contact and stimulation, with three other groups in more normal environments. A measure called the Development Quotient (DQ) was used which assessed six sectors of personality: perception, body mastery, social relations, memory, relations to inanimate objects, and intelligence (Spitz, 1945 and 1947/1964). The foundling-home infants had an average DQ of 124 for the first four months of their lives, the second highest of the four groups. Within the first year, their average DQ fell to 72, whereas the DQs of the other groups did not change. By the end of the second year, the average DQs of the foundlings deteriorated to 45, which "would qualify these children as imbeciles" (Spitz, 1964:418).

Two years after the end of the study, the foundling home was revisited. Of the 21 children between the ages of two and four years who were observed, only five could walk unassisted, only one dressed alone, and only one spoke in sentences; most could not talk at all or knew only a few words. Lack of body stimulation and contact in infancy appeared to inhibit and prevent the development of their higher learning functions.

Childhood dependence Humans have a much longer period of physical dependence and sexual immaturity than their fellow primates, and this is another condition that makes extensive socialization possible. Human dependency is further prolonged by the need to acquire the skills of social living. This long period of relative helplessness during which the child is cared for, controlled, and vulnerable to others leads to an emotional dependence that lasts throughout life.

Capacity to learn Dependence would count for nothing if the human animal were not highly educable. Humans can learn more than other animals and can continue to learn more over a longer period of time. Although abilities vary from one individual to another, a high level of intelligence is an innate human biological potentiality. For a few years young chimpanzees learn as well as, and in some respects better than, human infants of the same age, but their relative rate of learning soon declines.

Language The ability to learn is directly related to the human capacity for language. Other animals have intelligence, but humans alone can reason because they have language. It has recently been shown that chimpanzees can learn at least a rudimentary sign language and communicate by combining gestures into simple "sentences" (Kellog, 1968). Furthermore, when chimpanzees fit poles together to secure otherwise unobtainable food, they have insight into solving a problem. But without genuine language they cannot reflect upon their discovery, elaborate it, or convey it *as a principle* to other chimpanzees.

Language also expresses and arouses emotion, conveying feelings, values, and attitudes as well as knowledge. Whether as a vehicle for knowledge or for attitudes, language is the key factor in the creation of human society. By making possible the communication of ideas, it frees response and interaction from purely biological limits. It makes possible the symbolic interaction upon which human society depends.

AIMS OF SOCIALIZATION

The content of socialization is as diverse as human society itself. The Eskimo child must be taught how to cope with the Arctic cold, the Berber child with the desert sun, but whatever the environment and cultural context, socialization has certain common aims.

1. Socialization inculcates basic *disciplines*, ranging from toilet habits to the methods of science. Undisciplined behavior is prompted by impulse. It ignores future consequences and satisfactions in favor of immediate and perhaps transitory gratifications. Disciplined behavior restricts immediate gratifications either by postponing, foregoing, or modifying them, sometimes to gain social approval, sometimes for the sake of a future goal.

Disciplines can even modify physiological responses. Many people waken early whether they want to or not, and individuals often become physically incapable of performing socially prohibited acts. A person may become ill after eating tabooed food, or sexually impotent as a result of deeply internalized social prohibitions.

2. Socialization instills *aspirations* as well as disciplines. Because disciplines are often arduous and unrewarding in themselves, they are best sustained when the individual sees them as means to realizing goals. Every society instills in each of its members a variety of aspirations corresponding to the statuses the individual will occupy because of sex, age, group affiliation, or family origin. In preindustrial society, a cobbler would try to instill in his son the desire to be a good cobbler on weekdays, a faithful attendant at Sunday services, a good trencherman on feast days, and a leader of the cobblers' guild in his mature years. His daughter would have been brought up to be a pious churchgoer, a diligent and capable housekeeper, and a devoted wife and mother. This illustration is a reminder that, especially in traditional societies, socialization may both restrain and encourage aspirations.

3. Socialization provides individuals with *identities*, largely through the aspirations it encourages or discourages. Many upper-class young Englishmen were once taught upper-class etiquette by their valets. But knowledge of upper-class manners could not make the "gentleman's gentleman" upper class, either in his own eyes or in the eyes of others. Although he knew how to act like a gentleman perhaps better than the gentleman, he did not have the identity of a gentleman.

In contemporary industrial society, aspirations are less securely fixed than in preliterate and traditional society. One consequence appears to be a weaker sense of identity. In modern society, a sense of personal identity seems to be achieved later in life than in past eras; individuals now have more options, and socialization is less closely dependent on such factors as sex, ethnic origin, and family status.

Section two dynamics of socialization

Socialization is carried out in many different ways, by numerous people, and in a variety of social contexts. Parents, playmates, teachers, fellow students, co-workers, lovers, spouses, children all contribute, and they do so in all possible settings. Socialization may be deliberate or unintended, formal or informal. It may require face-to-face encounters, but it is also carried on at a distance, through letters, books, and the mass media. The persons being socialized may be relatively passive or active, depending on the extent to which they are able to influence the socializer or guide their own socialization. Socialization may be carried on for the benefit of the one being socialized or for the benefit of the socializer; and the two interests may be compatible or opposed. Socialization often goes along smoothly with little awareness of shaping or being shaped, controlling or being controlled. But it can also be abrasive, even brutal, with mutual awareness of coercion and conflict.

Different ways of learning and different socializing agencies follow one another in a more or less orderly way as the individual

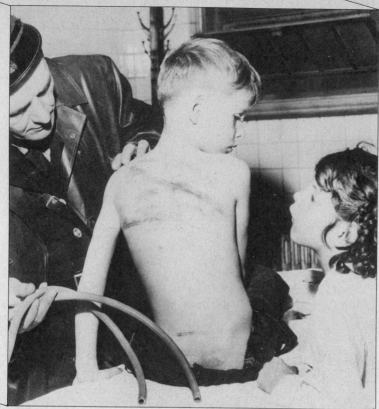

The battered child may be one result
of faulty parental socialization.

passes from one stage in the life cycle to the next. In homogeneous societies, where the various groups that socialize the individual tend to share the same values, socialization can give the individual a sense of living out an unbroken life career, in which each stage gives rise to the next, and all experience fits together into a meaningful pattern. But in heterogeneous societies, where groups with different values compete for the same individuals, socialization often entails a complementary process of desocialization whereby individuals are encouraged to reject their past socialization and the groups from which they came. In such societies, socialization is marked by discontinuities, and life can become a series of difficult choices and painful self-assessments rather than a smooth passage from birth to death.

PARENT–CHILD INTERACTION

In every society socialization of the infant and young child necessarily takes place in face-to-face contexts of nurturing, caring for, and watching over. In Western industrial society, the modal child-rearing environment consists of the nuclear family composed only of parents and children, residing in a dwelling separate from others, from which the husband-father is absent most of the day. Several consequences important for socialization flow from this arrangement. Parents tend to be the only adults with direct and constant access to infants and young children; conversely, they tend to be the only persons to whom their offspring can turn for help, affection, and instruction. In sharp contrast to many preliterate and folk societies, day-to-day care of the young child is primarily in the hands of only one person, the mother; thus mother and child form a socially isolated dyad for long periods, each having only limited opportunities for social interaction with their age-mates. Moreover, what goes on in the home is largely unobserved and unmonitored by the rest of society. This places great responsibilities and burdens of self-control upon parents and leaves children vulnerable to the psychological and social limitations of their immediate families.

Responses to the child How the infant's physical needs are met is largely socially determined. Feeding patterns, for example, vary from culture to culture, from one social group to another, and, in a complex urban society, from mother to mother. The infant may be fed whenever it cries, only at rigidly prescribed intervals, or erratically at the mother's convenience. It may be breast-fed until well into childhood or weaned early.

Evidence connecting the experiences of early infancy with adult personality is not yet clear. Nevertheless, many students of human behavior believe that individuals gain an image of the world as stingy or indulgent, capricious or reliable, depending on the way their primary biological needs are met in infancy and early childhood.

From birth, the infant has social and psychological significance for others and is responded to in an emotional way. Attitudes of rejection or acceptance, approval or disapproval, and tension or relaxation color the physical care he or she receives. The act of feeding or cleaning is accompanied by facial expressions, emotions, and physical gestures prompted by cultural values and attitudes. In the 1920s, the middle-class culture of the United States dictated a degree of aloofness and rigidity toward the child; in the 1940s, permissiveness was actively encouraged. Depending on the society, the social group, and the individual family, child care may be regarded as a nuisance and a disruption of adult interests or as a natural and fulfilling aspect of marriage and adult life.

As the infant grows to childhood, adult responses shift from efforts to satisfy the child's bodily needs to expressions of approval and disapproval designed to encourage self-control. There are also emotion-laden responses to the child's appearance, intelligence, and temperament. The parents have cultural and personal images of what they themselves are and what they expect the child to be. They respond to the child in terms of their own psychological needs; their position in the class, status, and role structure of society; and their ambitions for the child. Few societies compare with contemporary Western societies in the extent to which they place responsibility for the fate of the child on the biological parents. It is small wonder, therefore, that the parent–child relation tends to carry a high emotional charge and is widely regarded by psychologists as the dominating factor in personality formation.

Responses of the child Infants and young children are in many respects extremely dependent on and vulnerable to their social environments. However, as suggested above, human infants are equipped at birth with a repertory of reflexes and responses that make them capable of social interaction very early in life and therefore of being participants, however unequal, in their own socialization.

The earliest reactions of human infants are biological responses to their own inner states of comfort and discomfort. When they cry, they neither know that they cry nor do they cry to gain attention. Gradually, however, they associate crying with the attention and satisfaction they receive. They learn to cry purposively to bring a ministering response. By employing the cry to stimulate response in another, the infant enters into interpersonal communication. Later the child is able to forego crying and say instead, "I am hungry."

The capacity of the human animal to express feelings and emotions is of central importance to socialization. Besides giving even young infants the ability to communicate and participate in elementary forms of social interaction, the biological capacity of Homo sapiens to respond to events emotionally is the essential core around which human personality develops. It is difficult to conceive of personality apart from the expression of feeling. However, the free expression of raw emotion can be self-destructive and socially disruptive, and therefore learning how to cope with and reshape feelings is one of the primary goals of socialization. Another goal of socialization is to enlarge the range and subtlety of human emotions.

Three emotions or affects, the raw material out of which human personality and social bonds are created, appear to be basic to the human animal:

1. Rage The human organism does not suffer deprivation and frustration passively. It reacts by manifesting rage and aggression. For the infant and child, these are resources for exercising some measure of control over others. As children mature and are expected to control their impulses, they express hostility and resentment against other children and adults who are the source of their frustration. One of the important problems the child faces in the course of socialization is the management of frustration and aggressive impulses.

2. Anxiety Rage and hostility are immediate, sharply defined emotional responses, capable of being "discharged" by some act of aggression against the offending object. Anxiety, in contrast, is a diffuse emotional state. It is a vague, uneasy apprehensiveness experienced when one feels threatened by an unknown danger or when the outcome of a situation is in doubt. It should not be confused with fear, which is a response to a definite danger.

Homo sapiens has been called the rational animal, the social animal, and also the anxious animal. Modern Western society, which places a premium on independence and self-sufficiency, continually introduces new sources of anxiety as children mature. Before they enter school, children are expected to be independent of their mothers to the extent of feeding themselves, managing bodily

functions, and controlling aggressions and expressions of rage and hostility. They are then introduced to a formal and competitive system of education, where further demands are made on self-control. They are supposed to set goals for themselves and to achieve them. Later, they are expected to choose a career, trade, or profession, to leave the parental home, and to make their own way. At every hand, they face the possibility of rejection and failure, and a corresponding burden of anxiety.

3. Love The study of rhesus monkeys (Section One) suggests the extent to which the human infant takes an active part in loving and being loved (Harlow, 1959). In addition, the human infant's early capacity to smile and make responsive sounds are additional resources for establishing relations of mutual affection and pleasure. The rhesus monkey experiments are doubly important, however, because they confirm what has long been suspected from the study of delinquent and maladjusted children: Children have an imperative need to evoke positive feelings from their parents or substitute parents. Clinical studies have found that failure to evoke love in the parents may result in the atrophy of the ability to love and in what has been called a "fear of loving" (Redl and Wineman, 1951). In extreme cases, even when removed to environments of love and attention, some delinquent children were unable to return positive feelings with anything but hostility. In less extreme cases, the failure to evoke love results in anxiety, in a sense of uncertainty, threat, and personal inadequacy. The evident need for love, respect, and self-esteem has led to the suggestion that these requirements for full human development are so basic that they should be called "instinctoid"—that is, like instincts (Maslow, 1965:33).

Static and dynamic adaptation Part of socialization is more or less routine learning and adjustment, in which habits are formed and perceptions of the self and the world are acquired. Some adjustments have deeper impact upon the personality and generate inner tensions, needs, and strivings. This difference between surface learning and depth responses is sometimes expressed as the difference between static and dynamic adaptation:

By static adaptation we mean such an adaptation to patterns as leaves the whole character structure unchanged and implies only the adoption of a new habit. An example of this kind of adaptation is the change from the Chinese habit of eating to the Western habit of using fork and knife. A Chinese coming to America will adapt himself to this new pattern, but this adaptation in itself has little effect on his personality; it does not arouse new drives or character traits.

By dynamic adaptation we refer to the kind of adaptation that occurs, for example, when a boy submits to the commands of his strict and threatening father—being too afraid of him to do otherwise—and becomes a "good" boy. While he adapts himself to the necessities of the situation, something happens in him. He may develop an intense hostility against his father, which he represses, since it would be too dangerous to express it or even to be aware of it. This repressed hostility, however, though not manifest, is a dynamic factor in his character structure. It may create new anxiety and thus lead to still deeper submission; it may set up a vague defiance, directed against no one in particular but rather toward life in general. . . . This kind of adaptation creates something new in him, arouses new drives and new anxieties (Fromm, 1941:15–16).

In part because of dynamic adaptation, there is often a considerable discrepancy between what parents want their children to be and the way they actually turn out.

MODES OF SOCIAL LEARNING

The specific mechanisms of socialization are only beginning to be understood (Goslin, 1969). At least four different modes of social learning may be identified: conditioning, identity taking, modeling-after, and problem solving.

Conditioning Much of learning is based on the principle of association. An organism is said to be conditioned when a response pattern is built into the organism as a result of environmental stimuli. Normally, conditioning requires repetitive associations of stimulus and response, but a response pattern may result from a single significant experience.

Classical conditioning, associated with the name of Ivan Pavlov (1849–1936), builds upon an existing stimulus-response pattern. In dogs (and people) the connection between salivation and food tasting is an unlearned or unconditioned response. The salivation response can be conditioned, however, by introducing another stimulus that is maintained, for a time, in constant association with the original stimulus. Thus if a bell is sounded repeatedly when food is presented to a dog, the dog learns to salivate in response to the bell. This response is then a conditioned response (Pavlov, 1927/1960).

Thus classical conditioning varies the stimulus while the response remains constant. The dog continues to salivate but the stimulus is different. Similarly, it has been shown that ten-day-old babies can "learn" to blink at the sound of a tone if the sound is systematically paired with a puff of air directed at the baby's eyes (Lipsitt, 1971:88).

In contrast, *operant* or *instrumental* conditioning tries to control the response. Certain animal responses, such as turning left in a rat maze, can be effectively extinguished if they are systematically followed by the infliction of pain, for example, from an electric shock; others, such as taking a right turn in a maze, can be made routine or habitual by rewarding the animal with food or even by withholding the electric shock that would otherwise be forthcoming. By using operant conditioning, animals have been induced to perform in uncharacteristic ways—seals to blow horns, dogs to dance, chimpanzees to do simple arithmetic (Kelleher, 1965:232).

The word *operant* suggests work done, an effect produced. Hence behavior is operant when it is guided by an anticipated result, for example, moving to avoid a blow or opening the door to walk outside. These examples point to an important distinction. Operant conditioning is the creation of a built-in response pattern as a result of systematic reinforcement, including negative reinforcement. Moving out of the way to avoid a blow is often a pattern established by operant conditioning. On the other hand, a simple means-end action, such as opening a door, is an example of operant or instrumental *learning*, but not necessarily of conditioning.

Conditioning offers a valid if limited perspective on social learning. We rely on conditioning to establish the routine patterns that sustain a host of everyday activities, such as driving a car or getting along with other people. But the establishment of stimulus-response patterns, whether by classical or operant conditioning, does not do justice to the complexity of social learning.

Identity-taking Studies of European and American children show that children only gradually acquire the idea of the stability of objects, the immutability of species, and the unchangeability of biological sex (Kohlberg, 1966:96). However, by the time they are five, most children correctly identify themselves and others by sex and behave in the conventional ways assigned to men and women by the societies of which they are members. Some students of socialization believe that sex-typed behavior emerges largely through operant conditioning. They reason that children first engage in a wide range of behaviors, only gradually learning to inhibit those assigned to the other sex.

While approval and disapproval, reward and punishment, undoubtedly play a large part in socialization for maleness and femaleness, it is doubtful that conditioning alone accounts for sex differences in behavior. With the acquisition of language and cognitive skills, children can hear themselves being called a boy or girl, accept the label, learn by observation and report what boys and girls do, and behave accordingly. Without a foundation of conditioning—

associating conformity with approval and deviance with disapproval—labeling would be ineffective as a socialization device. Nevertheless, once the basic ground rules have been learned, labeling on the part of others and identity taking on the part of the individual constitute a process by which traditional social roles are readily transmitted. Throughout life, the individual takes on a number of identities and assumes responsibility for learning the "official" role requirements of student, spouse, or employee.

Modeling-after A nonroutine, often emotion-laden form of identity-taking is the selection of an admired, loved, or feared figure to model oneself after. Modeling-after appears to be a typical stage in the formation of personality and in the development of both personal autonomy and social involvement (Bandura, 1969). By means of a model of one's own choice, the individual gains some independence from his or her immediate environment and, at the same time, establishes a unique relation with a selected portion of the social world. The person acquires a self-chosen identity which is valued and which contributes to self-esteem. Through a model, behavior acquires meaning and becomes something more than conformity to conventional expectations.

This form of deep social influence has a liberating effect insofar as the individual gains from the model personal standards of excellence and choice. On the other hand, when identification with the model is accompanied by strong dependency feelings, options may be foreclosed and personal development inhibited.

Problem solving The mechanisms discussed above are, for the most part, modes of *internalization* (Aronfreed, 1969; Scott, 1971). They are the ways that norms and values—including deviant norms and deviant values—become part of personality and establish the individual's characteristic way of responding. But social learning is something more than the internalization of norms and values. It is also learning to participate in cooperative activities and in activities where there is conflict, to cope with new situations, and to achieve goals in a context of opportunity and constraint.

A problem-solving orientation is necessary for effective social participation, especially in a complex and fluid society. Yet such an orientation is often difficult to achieve. Psychological difficulties get in the way, as when a person is more interested in "ego trips" than in the task at hand. Social norms may also be counterproductive if they become ways of programming conduct in detail rather than providing general frameworks within which effective action can take place.

In this context, problem solving is not an intellectual operation, like solving a problem in mathematics; it is action taken to change the environment or oneself. It is applied to a problematic social situation, one that makes the individual uncomfortable and calls for a response.

The American philosopher and social psychologist John Dewey (see *EDUCATION*, p. 342) was a strong advocate of a problem-solving approach to social learning. This approach requires an understanding of cognitive and moral development, that is, the conditions under which people gain the capacity for effective and self-preserving social participation. The writings of George Herbert Mead and Sigmund Freud (see Section Three) and Jean Piaget (see Adaptation 32) speak to this topic.

Limitations No single mode of social learning accounts for all socialization. For example, with the acquisition of language, children are soon able to understand the idea of reward and punishment and do not have to be conditioned. They become capable of controlling their own behavior.

Perhaps more important is the fact that each mode of social learning has distinctive limitations, and no single mode can be completely relied upon. Even where conditioning is effective, it may produce maladaptive response patterns. The overly conditioned individual may be at a serious disadvantage in complex societies, in periods of social change, or in novel situations that require flexibility. The main limitation of identity taking is the possibility of great discrepancy between the individual's personality and the identity which he or she takes on. It does not matter much whether children are born with certain temperaments or acquire them during the first few years of life; in either case they are equipped very early with an inner nature that may be seriously frustrated by the conventional roles and labels assigned to them by society. Modeling-after has its characteristic problems: for the person, the risk of excessive dependency, and for the society, the possible glorifying of destructive heroes. Finally, problem solving, since it encourages a critical spirit, may erode existing norms and values. Training in problem solving is to some extent a process of desocialization for it involves unlearning the easy truths of childhood and criticizing established ways.

REPRESSIVE AND PARTICIPATORY SOCIALIZATION

Two broad patterns of socialization can be identified in American society (Bronfenbrenner, 1958; Kohn, 1959). These are presented in Table 4:1 as a set of contrasts. One pattern, oriented toward obedience, may be called repressive socialization; the other, oriented toward gaining the participation of the child, participatory socialization.

Reward and punishment play a part in all learning, but one rather than the other may be stressed. Repressive socialization emphasizes punishing wrong behavior; participatory socialization rewards and thus reinforces good behavior. In toilet training, for example, parents may look for mishaps to admonish or concentrate on praising self-control.

If the modes of socialization are compared with operant conditioning of animals, repressive socialization is similar to admin-

Table 4:1   Two modes of socialization

Repressive socialization	Participatory socialization
Punishing wrong behavior	Rewarding good behavior
Material rewards and punishments	Symbolic rewards and punishments
Obedience of child	Autonomy of child
Nonverbal communication	Verbal communication
Communication as command	Communication as interaction
Parent-centered socialization	Child-centered socialization
Child's discernment of parent's wishes	Parent's discernment of child's needs
Family as significant other	Family as generalized other

istering an electric shock to an experimental rat when it takes a wrong turn in a maze. Participatory socialization resembles giving the rat a pellet of food when it selects the right path. Both forms of conditioning extinguish "wrong" behavior, one by the negative act of punishment, the other by the positive act of reward.

In principle, participatory socialization gives children freedom to try things out for themselves and explore the world on their own terms. This does not mean that the child is left alone. On the contrary, a great deal of adult supervision is required, but the supervision is general rather than detailed and intrusive. Repressive socialization also requires supervision, indeed so much detailed supervision that it tends to be greatly modified in practice. As a result, punishment from the child's viewpoint is arbitrarily applied, depending on whether he or she is caught misbehaving and whether the parent is in a mood to administer punishment.

Repressive socialization emphasizes obedience, respect for authority, and external controls. Parents may indulge the child but also use corporal punishment, shame, and ridicule. Two-way conversation between parent and child is not encouraged. Communication tends to be downward from parent to child and to take the form of command. Gesture and nonverbal communication are conspicuous (Bernstein, 1958). The child must learn to discern the seriousness of the parent's command to "shut up" or "get down" by taking account of tone of voice, facial expression, and physical posture.

In participatory socialization, communication takes the form of dialogue in which children are expected to make known their needs and desires as well as responses to the adult world. Participatory socialization is child-centered rather than parent-centered: The adult assumes responsibility for discerning the child's needs rather than expecting the child to discern the parent's wishes.

The two modes of socialization are illuminated by G. H. Mead's distinction between "significant others" and "the generalized other" (see Adaptation 7, p. 104.) When obedience is the keynote, socialization tends to remain at the level of the significant other. The child takes its cues from particular persons, mainly parents, who dominate the social and psychological environment. When cooperation for shared goals is emphasized, socialization is less directly dependent on imitation or on compliance with specific rules. The understanding of means–end relations is stressed rather than the performance of prescribed roles. For a similar contrast, see Piaget's analysis of the morality of constraint and the morality of cooperation in Adaptation 32.

RESOCIALIZATION

Over the total life span, people change their attitudes, values, and self-conceptions as they assume new roles and undergo new experiences.

Adult change that is gradual and partial is called continuing socialization. Resocialization denotes change that is more basic and more rapid, especially the abandonment of one way of life for another that is not only different from the former but incompatible with it. Important examples of attempts at resocialization are brainwashing, the rehabilitation of criminals, and the conversion of "sinners" to a religious way of life. In these cases, the aim is to make the person over in fundamental ways and to effect a break with the past. Certain occupational and life roles demand extensive and intensive socialization, and training for them approaches resocialization. The role of priest or nun traditionally required that the new religious life be all-encompassing and that religious novices make a thorough break with their past lives and with the ways of the secular society.

Total institutions Resocialization of the mature individual usually takes place in what is called a total institution. A total institution is all-encompassing and usually isolated from the community. Examples are mental hospitals, prisons, military units, religious orders, and some political groups. Adaptation 6 discusses the fate of the self in organizations that try to establish full control over the individual. While the Adaptation points to some common characteristics of such institutions, the differences among them are significant. The assault on identity that takes place in a prison or mental hospital has something in common with the mortification of a military recruit or a religious novitiate, but the impact on the person may be quite different. When self-abasement is voluntary and sustained by theology or patriotism, there may be little or no psychological damage.

Adaptation 6 Goffman: Stripping the self

The recruit comes into the establishment with a conception of himself made possible by certain stable social arrangements in his home world. Upon entrance, he is immediately stripped of the support provided by these arrangements. In the accurate language of some of our oldest total institutions, he begins a series of abasements, degradations, humiliations, and profanations of self. His self is systematically, if often unintentionally mortified. He begins some radical shifts in his *moral career,* a career composed of the progressive changes that occur in his beliefs concerning himself and significant others.

The processes by which a person's self is mortified are fairly standard in total institutions; analysis

of these processes can help us to see the arrangements that ordinary establishments must guarantee if members are to preserve their civilian selves.

BREAKING WITH THE PAST

The barrier that total institutions place between the inmate and the wider world marks the first curtailment of self. In many total institutions, the privilege of having visitors or of visiting away from the establishment is completely withheld at first, ensuring a deep initial break with past roles. A report on cadet life in a military academy provides an illustration:

For two months the swab (new recruit) is not allowed to leave the base or to engage in social intercourse with noncadets. This complete isolation helps to produce a unified group of swabs, rather than a heterogeneous collection of persons of high and low status. Uniforms are issued on the first day, and discussions of wealth and

Source: Abridged from *Asylums: Essays on the Social Situation of Mental Patients and Other Inmates* by Erving Goffman (Garden City, N.Y.: Doubleday, 1961), pp. 14–23. Published in this form by permission of the author and publisher.

family background are taboo. The role of the cadet must supersede other roles the individual has been accustomed to play. There are few clues left which will reveal social status in the outside world.

PEOPLE PROCESSING

The inmate, then, finds certain roles are lost to him by virtue of the barrier that separates him from the outside world. The process of entrance typically brings other kinds of loss and mortification as well. We very generally find staff employing what are called admission procedures: taking a life history; photographing, weighing, fingerprinting, assigning numbers, searching, and listing personal possessions for storage; ordering the recruit to undress, bathe, and be disinfected; haircutting;

issuing institutional clothing; instructing as to rules; and assigning to quarters. Admission procedures might better be called trimming or programming, because in thus being squared away the new arrival allows himself to be shaped and coded into an object that can be fed into the administrative machinery of the establishment, to be worked on smoothly by routine operations. Many of these procedures depend upon attributes such as weight or fingerprints that the individual possesses merely because he is a member of the largest and most abstract of social categories, that of human being. Action taken on the basis of such attributes necessarily ignores most of his previous bases of self-identification.

THE OBEDIENCE TEST

Because a total institution deals with so many aspects of its inmates' lives, with the consequent complex admission procedure, there is a special need to obtain initial cooperativeness from the recruit. Staff often feel that a recruit's readiness to be appropriately deferential in his initial face-to-face encounters with them is a sign that he will take the role of the routinely pliant inmate. The occasion on which staff members first tell the inmate of his deference obligations may be structured to challenge the inmate to balk or to hold his peace forever. Thus these initial moments of socialization may involve an obedience test and even a will-breaking contest: An inmate who shows defiance receives immediate visible punishment, which increases until he humbles himself.

Admission procedures and obedience tests may be elaborated into "the welcome," a form of initiation where staff or inmates, or both, go out of their way to give the recruit a clear notion of his plight. As part of this rite of passage he may be called by a term such as *fish* or *swab,* which tells him that he is merely an inmate and, what is more, that he has a special low status even in this low group.

The admission procedure can be characterized as a leaving off and a taking on, with the midpoint marked by physical nakedness. Leaving off, of course, entails a dispossession of property, important because persons invest self-feelings in their possessions. What is perhaps the most significant of these possessions is not physical at all: one's full name. Whatever one is called thereafter, loss of one's name can be a great curtailment of self.

STANDARD ISSUE

Once the inmate is stripped of his possessions, at least some replacements must be made by the establishment, but these take the form of standard issue, uniform in character and uniformly distributed. These substitute possessions are clearly marked as really belonging to the institution and in some cases are recalled at regular intervals to be, as it were, disinfected of identifications. With objects that can be used up—for example, pencils—the inmate may be required to return the remnants before obtaining a reissue. Failure to provide inmates with individual lockers and the periodic search and confiscation of accumulated personal property reinforce property dispossession. Religious orders have appreciated the implications for self of such separation from belongings. Inmates are sometimes required to change their cells once a year so as not to become attached to them.

IDENTITY KIT

One set of the individual's possessions has a special relation to self. The individual ordinarily expects to exert some control over the guise in which he appears before others. For this he needs cosmetic and clothing supplies, tools for applying, arranging, and repairing them, and an accessible, secure place to store these supplies and tools—in short, the individual needs an identity kit for the management of his personal front. He also needs access to decoration specialists such as barbers and clothiers.

On admission to a total institution, however, the individual is likely to be stripped of his usual appearance and of the equipment and services by which he maintains it, thus suffering a personal defacement. Clothing, combs, needle and thread, cosmetics, towels, soap, shaving sets, bathing facilities—all may be taken away or denied him, although some may be kept in inaccessible storage, to be returned if and when he leaves. In the words of the Rule of St. Benedict, which governs the Benedictine monks:

Then forthwith he shall, there in the oratory, be divested of his own garments with which he is clothed and be clad in those of the monastery. Those garments of which he is divested shall be placed in the wardrobe, there to be kept, so that if, perchance, he should ever be persuaded by the devil to leave the monastery (which God forbid), he may be stripped of the monastic habit and cast forth.

As suggested, the institutional issue provided as a substitute for what has been taken away is typically of a coarse variety, ill-fitting, often old, and the same for large categories of inmates. The impact of this substitution is described in a report on imprisoned prostitutes:

First, there is the shower officer who forces them to undress, takes their own clothes away, sees to it that they take showers and get their prison clothes. . . .

There is not a sadder sight than some of the obese prisoners who, if nothing else, have been managing to keep themselves looking decent on the outside, confronted by the first sight of themselves in prison issue.

In addition to being stripped of one's identity kit, loss of a sense of personal safety is common. Beatings, shock therapy, or, in mental hospitals, surgery—whatever the intent of staff in providing these services for some inmates—may lead many inmates to feel that they are in an environment that does not guarantee their physical integrity.

MORTIFICATION

Corresponding to the indignities of speech and action required of the inmate are the indignities of treatment others accord him. The standard examples here are verbal or gestural profanations: Staff or fellow inmates call the individual obscene names, curse him, point out his negative attributes, tease him, or talk about him or his fellow inmates as if he were not present.

Whatever the form or the source of these various indignities, the individual has to engage in activity whose symbolic implications are incompatible with his conception of self. In prisons, denial of heterosexual opportunities can induce fear of losing one's masculinity or femininity. In military establishments, the patently useless make-work forced on fatigue details can make men feel their time and effort are worthless. In religious institutions, there are special arrangements to ensure that all inmates take a turn performing the more menial aspects of the servant role. An extreme is the concentration camp practice of requiring prisoners to administer whippings to other prisoners.

Section three the social self

Self is an Anglo-Saxon word that originally meant "same" or "identical." Applied to the human being, the term acquired the connotation of uniqueness, a distinctive identity persisting through time. In Western culture, to be human is to have a self, an inner, unchanging personal identity that remains essentially the same despite the vicissitudes of social experience. Thus conceived, the self is the thinker of one's thoughts, the planner of one's actions, the sufferer of one's feelings.

This concept of selfhood is by no means universal. Even in Western society some categories of people — women, slaves — have frequently been defined as incapable of possessing a self or soul. In preliterate or folk societies, individuals are sometimes considered not the authors of their own acts and thoughts but the agents of other beings and forces. In extreme situations, people are believed to be possessed by demons or spirits; in more routine circumstances they are seen less as self-motivated actors than as re-enactors of traditional roles, representatives in the present of both past and future.

Nevertheless, every culture endows its members with a self of some sort. The *content* of the self is variable but the *process* by which the self is created is universal. The quest for an understanding of that process is a major theme of social psychology.

MEAD ON SELF AND SOCIETY

During the nineteenth century, there was a revolt against an excessively individualistic, antisocial conception of mind. New understandings developed, shared by Marx, that the human being is a historical creature whose very nature is derived from his or her unique social experiences. According to this view, the content of human consciousness cannot be separated from the society in which it is formed. Mead (1863–1931), the American pragmatist philosopher, is the outstanding twentieth-century representative

of this approach. However, in contrast to his forerunners, who emphasized the impact of culture or large social structures on the content of mind, Mead turned his attention to the microprocesses of day-to-day socialization. In tracing out how language, social interaction, and role-taking create the human mind, he laid the conceptual foundations for social psychology. An outline of Mead's point of view is presented in Adaptation 7.

In revising past philosophic concepts, Mead emphasized the following:

1. Mind and self are indivisible   In Mead's words, "the unity of the mind is . . . an abstraction from the more inclusive unity of the self" (1934:144). In concrete terms, Mead recognized that in the course of being socialized, the child cannot help but learn facts and their social meanings simultaneously. One might suppose it possible to teach a fact simply as a fact, devoid of social meaning. However, to teach a fact as a fact is to convey an attitude toward it, namely, that it is simply a fact and ought to be learned on that account alone. Inevitably, as socializers present children with an array of real or alleged facts, they present an array of attitudes toward the facts. In taking on and responding to those attitudes, the child acquires a social self. Thus the acquisition of mind is part of a process that creates and forms a self.

2. Minds and selves are developmental outcomes of social processes   For Mead, as for many earlier philosophers, the defining characteristic of the self is that "it is an object to itself" (1934:136). In other words, people are conscious, and conscious that they are conscious. But Mead was unique in stressing the role that *social others* play in creating the self. "The individual experiences himself as such, not directly, but only indirectly, from the particular standpoints of other individual members of the same social group or from the generalized standpoint of the social group as a whole" (1934:138).

Mead saw two stages in the development of the self. In the first stage, the child is too immature to cooperate with others in joint activities or comprehend shared, socially negotiated purposes. Young children relate only to specific individuals in specific social acts; their social interactions are limited to interpersonal relations. At this stage, Mead says, the self is only incompletely social.

If the given human individual is to develop a self in the fullest sense, it is not sufficient for him merely to take the attitudes of other human individuals toward himself and toward one another . . . he must also . . . take their attitudes toward the various phases or aspects of the common social activity or set of social undertakings in which, as members of an organized society or social group, they are all engaged (1934:154–155).

The second stage can begin only when the child is mature enough to be a functioning member of a social group. Gradually, the individual is able to perceive the attitudes that other members of society take toward the social roles and shared activities that constitute social life and to comprehend the bearing these attitudes have on the common social life in which the child and all other members of the child's society are implicated. Society is more than an association of individuals; it is a complex organization of social attitudes and as such enters into and shapes the developing self.

FREUD ON SELF AND SOCIETY

The writings of Freud (1856–1939), the founder of psychoanalysis, have left a deeper imprint on present-day conceptions of the nature of the self than have those of Mead. Mead and Freud were contemporaries, but while one was teaching philosophy at the University of Chicago, the other was practicing a new kind of psychotherapy in Vienna. Their views are not incompatible, but they looked at the self and the social group from different perspectives and for different purposes. As a philosopher, Mead explored the positive role that society plays in the emergence of human rationality and selfhood. As a psychoanalyst, Freud stressed the role of society in the genesis of mental

and emotional disorders. Mead emphasized the cooperative aspects of social life as well as the potential unity of the individual self; Freud emphasized the conflicts inherent in group life and the struggles that go on within the self.

Both Mead and Freud divided the self into parts. Mead described the self as in part conventional, as an "organization of social attitudes" (1934:173). But Mead saw another part as spontaneous and creative. He called this part of the self the active 'I'; the more conventional or socially controlled part of the self he called the 'me'. If group life is rigid and restrictive, the 'me' dominates the 'I' and individuality is minimal. But, under appropriate social conditions, the 'I' influences and restructures the social process. Indeed, there are occasions when the 'me' encourages the free expression of the 'I', and these, Mead said, provide "the most exciting and gratifying experiences" (1934:213).

Freud divided the self into three parts: the id, the ego, and the superego. Each of these parts may be thought of as standing for a different kind of demand experienced in society: instinctual gratification, rational self-preserving action, and social conformity. As individuals experience conflicts among these demands, they become self-conscious; in the course of coping with these conflicts, a variety of selves, character structures, and personalities are formed.

In Freud's scheme, the id is the biological core of the self; it stands for urgencies inherent in the animal nature of human beings. These are the sexual and aggressive instincts which continually press upon the individual for satisfaction regardless of social proprieties. The id is therefore the part of the self that society tries to control but never succeeds in thoroughly domesticating.

Although Freud postulated an instinctual id as the core and mainspring of the self, he insisted that instincts could not be trusted to guide behavior. Being blind and knowing nothing, they are bound to lead to self-destruction regardless of whether they are directed toward sex or aggression. As a result, the individual develops an ego. The ego is a name for the capacity to take account of the facts; to reason, calculate consequences, postpone gratification, avoid danger—in short, to engage in rational actions in accordance with a "reality principle."

The ego is a kind of mediator trying to effect a compromise between the individual's biological demands and the demands of society. It has to do with the integrative, controlling functions of the self. Table 4:2 lists some of these functions together with the ways they would be handled by an adequate and by an inadequate ego.

[The superego is roughly equivalent to Mead's 'me'. It stands for society and its demands, for all those social norms and prohibitions experienced as the voice of conscience.] Aware that his sexual theories offended many people, Freud pointed to the superego as the locus of moral and aesthetic ideals, as humanity's higher nature (1923:26).

However, he also saw the superego as less than benign. According to Freud, the repression routinely called for in socialization frequently gets out of hand; excessive guilt may create painful neuroses or distort behavior in other ways. For example:

In many criminals, especially youthful ones, it is possible to detect a very powerful sense of guilt which existed before the crime, and is therefore not its result but its motive. It is as if it was a relief to be able to fasten this unconscious sense of guilt on to something real and immediate (Freud, 1923:42).

[Freud's theory of the superego helps to explain how socialization can be harmful, leading the individual to punish himself by self-denigrating or self-destructive behavior. The morality of the superego can be harsh and repressive.]

From the point of view of instinctual control, or morality, it may be said of the id that it is totally

Table 4:2 Functions of the ego

Ego function	Adequate ego	Inadequate ego
Tolerating frustration	Can substitute another goal for one that is blocked	Has a temper tantrum
Coping with insecurity, anxiety, and fear	Can develop psychological defense mechanisms	Can only flee or attack
Resisting temptation	Can defer gratifications	Seeks immediate gratification
Assessing reality	Adjusts behavior to particular circumstances and people	Regards authority figures as replicas of parents
Facing guilt	Has guilt feelings and can right a wrong	Has few guilt feelings and tries to evade them
Establishing inner controls	Can substitute inner control when external supervision is withdrawn	Becomes disorganized when outside controls are removed
Resisting group intoxication	Is slow to respond to group excitement	Loses control under impact of group excitement
Responding to rules and routines	Interprets rules and routines realistically as social necessities.	Interprets rules and routines as directed against self
Dealing with failure, mistakes, and success	Can correct a mistake and is proud of success	Interprets a mistake as worthlessness and success as absolute worth
Maintaining ego identity	Expresses, but does not lose, own values in group activity	Gives in easily to the authority of the group

Source: Adapted from Redl and Wineman, 1951:74–140. This is a study of delinquent children with severe psychological and social difficulties.

non-moral, of the ego that it strives to be moral, and of the superego that it can be super-moral and then becomes cruel as only the id can be. . . . But even ordinary normal morality has a harshly restraining, cruelly prohibiting quality (Freud, 1923:44).

According to one psychoanalytic interpretation, when adult socializers have themselves undergone severe repression, they may find themselves resenting and fearing children. This occurs because children remind them of the instinctual pleasures they have had to renounce, and such memories are both painful and tempting. Such a dynamic, usually unconscious, tends to produce cruel socialization practices; a beating, it has been said, punishes both parent and child.

The autonomous ego Freud's writings emphasized the vulnerability of the ego, caught between a punitive superego and an insistent id. Since Freud's time, psychoanalytic thought has devoted much attention to the problems of the embattled ego, and many psychotherapists now see therapy less as an exploration of the unconscious than as a building-up of ego strength. Adjusting to society has more and more faded into the background as a valid goal either of psychotherapy or of socialization. Instead, psychotherapists now tend to see the creation of a self capable of controlling and directing its own behavior as a strategic goal of socialization.

THE SITUATIONAL SELF

As conventionally understood, the self is a coherent and continuing entity. It persists through time as an unbroken chain of memories and a constancy of motivation and identity. Yet the self is always to some degree situational: It is neither wholly unified nor wholly continuous in time.

Even if there is a deeper core of uniqueness and identity, everyone has a repertory of selves to match a variety of roles and audiences. Similarly, all individuals acquire a

succession of selves as they pass from one stage of life to another. The point was made by James (1842–1910):

[The individual] has as many different social selves as there are distinct groups of persons about whose opinion he cares. Many a youth who is demure enough before his parents and teachers, swears and swaggers like a pirate among his "tough" friends. We do not show ourselves to our children as to our club-companions, to our customers as to the laborers we employ, to our own masters and employers as to our intimate friends. From this there results what practically is a division of the man into several selves (James, 1891:294).

The idea that a situation can bring out the best, or the worst, in a person is a recognition of the fluidity of the self. But in such cases the self is situational in only a limited sense, for there is no forming or re-forming of the person.

The self is situational in a more profound sense when it takes on a pattern in response to situational demands. To use James's example, where swaggering is part of the male youth culture, males are apt for a time to be, and not merely pretend to be, swaggering youths; only some will be engaging in a social performance merely for the sake of conformity. But the swaggering self is situational: It is readily replaced when another year brings a new style in youthful behavior.

Recognition of the situational self has led to new perspectives on deviance, mental health, and the unity of the self. Deviance, once viewed as the result of a basic character defect, is increasingly interpreted as situational in origin. Many of the "crazy" responses of the mentally ill, for example, are now seen as normal responses to crazy environments. In other words, more attention is being given to possible pathologies in the individual's situation. Lack of a unified coherent self—of a clear sense of identity—has long been regarded as a personal and social tragedy. This view is now being called into question on a number of grounds (Lifton, 1968; Berger, 1971):

1. Society has undergone and will con-

tinue to undergo rapid social change. To seek a fixed identity during such change is to risk unhappiness and maladjustment. In certain historical epochs, such as the period of industrialization, stability of character and purpose may have been essential for accumulating capital resources. Some argue that socialization should now strive to inculcate flexibility and resilience of self.

2. Society is becoming ever more heterogeneous in values and life-styles. A single consistent identity tends to limit opportunities for social participation and personal development.

3. A truly democratic society should encourage each individual to perform a variety of social roles, ranging from simple household tasks to community leadership. In contemporary society, having a unified self and a consistent identity may reflect a poverty of social experience.

Adaptation 7 Mead: Mind, self, and society

George Herbert Mead never presented his ideas in book form, and the four volumes published under his name are for the most part stenographic reports of lectures. Mind, Self, and Society *represents notes taken during 1927 and 1930 in Mead's social psychology lectures, a course he had given since 1900.*

Both as philosopher and social psychologist, Mead was concerned with socialization. As a philosopher he was interested in the question: Which came first, the individual or society? Many philosophers in trying to account for the existence of society, assumed that individuals endowed with mind and self-consciousness could exist prior to or outside society.

On the other hand, Mead considered the human self as the product, not the creator, *of society. "The self . . . is essentially a social structure, and it arises in social experience. After a self has arisen, it in a certain sense provides for itself its social experiences, and so we can conceive of an absolutely solitary self. But it is impossible to conceive of a self arising outside of social experience" (1934:140).*

Mead thought the distinctive task of social psychology is to explain how society gets into the individual, determines behavior, and thus becomes part of psychological makeup or selfhood. He also advanced specific hypotheses concerning

stages in the development of the self from the narrow capacity to take on the attitudes of other individuals to the more generalized capacity to relate to the community.

PREVERBAL INTERACTION

Social interaction precedes language, mind, and self-consciousness. Among many animal species, sexual union and care of the young make necessary at least some continuing interaction among individuals; thus, rudimentary family life exists among species lower than man. In most cases common cooperation is made necessary by biological differences in capacity or function, of which sexual and age differentiation are the most striking examples.

Among ants and bees, some individuals are biologically specialized to perform a single function, such as reproduction or food getting. The survival of both individual and species depends upon the interaction of highly specific biological roles in a complex pattern of cooperative acts. In this way ant and bee societies arise. But their organization is, strictly speaking, a biological one, and interaction is based on physical and chemical cues.

Nonverbal communication must precede language. Interaction, even on the biological level, is a kind of communication; otherwise, common acts could not occur. A dancing male bird does not deliberately intend to communicate a readiness to mate; yet communication occurs because it is

Source: A summary and interpretation of George H. Mead, *Mind, Self, and Society* (Chicago: University of Chicago Press, 1934). Quotations by permission of the University of Chicago Press.

more or less guaranteed by the nervous system of the species. As a rule, the dance arouses an appropriate response in a female, much as if she understood the meaning of the male's behavior.

The dance communicates because it stands for something else. It is not an isolated, meaningless bit of behavior. It is a natural sign, a product and manifestation of a state of organic tension, of a physiological readiness to mate. The tensions behind the mating dance require for their relief appropriate behavior on the part of the female. Thus, because the dance is a natural sign directed toward another, it can be viewed as a gesture, that is, as nonverbal communicative behavior.

If human beings could not first participate in a nonverbal "conversation" of gestures, they could never communicate by means of language. Before language can convey meaning *to* the child, the mother's behavior must have meaning *for* the child. Children could never understand the meaning of *angry* or *hungry* unless they first understood angry or nurturing gestures. Nor would the mother's gesture have meaning for the child unless both were participants in a joint activity. The emergence of language depends upon the existence of already established social interaction.

THE IMPORTANCE OF LANGUAGE

Language creates minds and selves. Despite interaction and communication, neither mind nor self-consciousness need be present in these primitive social acts; indeed, without language they cannot be. Language alone makes possible ideas and communication by ideas.

The male bird's mating dance has meaning for the female when it prompts an answering response from her, but it cannot be said to have meaning for the dancing male. He is simply behaving. He is not telling the female he is ready to mate; if anything tells the other, it is the dance and not the dancing bird. The bird's behavior communicates, but not the bird.

Language makes it possible to replace behavior with ideas. The mother can teach her child the meaning of "I am angry" only by behaving in appropriate ways, but once the child learns the words, the mother need not behave in an angry fashion in order to communicate displeasure. Because mother and child now share an idea, the child can respond to what the mother says as well

George Herbert Mead (1863–1931) disagreed sharply with the atomistic conception of man characteristic of seventeenth- and eighteenth-century "scientific" philosophy. This perspective conceived of individuals "forming" society the way atoms form matter. Mead refuted the atomistic analogy and showed that the individual is dependent upon society for the distinctive attributes of a human being, that is, for mind and self.

as to what she does. It is the mother (not merely her behavior) who now communicates.

Furthermore, having the idea of anger, the child can think about his mother's anger; it can have meaning even when she is absent or not angry. Thus as the child acquires language he acquires mind. He also becomes self-conscious as he reflects not only about his mother's anger but about himself and his own behavior. Thus he acquires a self. As he matures, the child no longer adjusts merely to immediate expressions of approval and disapproval. He *takes the attitudes of others* into himself as enduring guides and standards, as part of his own personality.

THE SOCIAL SELF

Mind and self are social. Much of language is factual, simply identifying objects about which people communicate. But through language children also learn the attitudes and emotions with which objects are viewed by their parents and others. Some of these attitudes help the child deal with the physical environment; for example, attitudes of caution may go along with *dog* and *fire*. Others are more distinctively social. Factually, *cow* means the same to a Hindu as to an American, but to the Hindu child the meaning of *cow* also includes attitudes of religious reverence and respect. Thus, in learning language, children are initiated into a world of social meanings; they share the meanings objects have for their social group.

Just as the child learns to take the same attitudes toward objects in the environment that others take toward them, so he learns to take the same attitudes toward himself that others take toward him. When the mother tells the child that he has done something good or bad, right or wrong, she is not trying to teach him merely what the words mean. She treats the child as an object toward which she takes a certain attitude and tries to induce the child to do the same. He is encouraged *to take himself as an object.* He evaluates and controls himself in the same way that he evaluates and controls other objects, and he does so from the standpoint of someone else. He is taught, in short, to make appropriate or prescribed responses to his own behavior just as he has been taught to make appropriate or prescribed responses to other objects in his environment.

Because this control occurs through taking the attitudes of others toward oneself, because it is control from the standpoint of someone else, it is distinctively social in nature. This is how society gets into the individual. Of all the animals, only the human animal is able to exercise self-criticism; but all self-criticism is social criticism insofar as the principles that guide it are the result of internalizing the attitudes of others toward oneself.

Before he can use the attitudes of others to think about himself, the young child is not *self-conscious.* As an animal, the human child is conscious. He has sensations, feelings, and perceptions of which he is aware. It is by thinking about himself in the light of the attitudes of others toward him that the individual becomes *self*-conscious and begins to acquire a social self.

MATURATION AND RESPONSE TO THE OTHER

As the individual matures he develops the capacity to respond to significant others and to a generalized other. All higher forms of communication depend upon the capacity of each to put himself in the place of the other, that is, to control his own responses in terms of an understanding of what the other's responses are likely to be. As he learns to control his behavior in the light of another individual's attitudes either toward that behavior or toward the environment, the individual learns *to take the role of the other.* He responds to himself and to the world as he anticipates the other would respond. The capacity to put oneself in the place of the other emerges only with maturity and in the process of social interaction and communication.

The child first internalizes the attitudes of particular individuals, primarily his parents, toward himself. At this stage he does not have the capacity to participate in organized group life or to engage in complex, cooperative games governed by impersonal rules. Social interaction is limited to interaction with specific individuals, and behavior is largely determined by the child's experience with those who are not merely others but *significant others* for him. At this stage of development, play consists largely of simple role taking. The child plays at being a mother, father, doctor, or postman, reenacting the behavior and attitudes of others as individuals.

Gradually the child learns a less personalized, more complex form of role taking as expressed in his developing ability to participate in organized games. In baseball, for example, the acting out of a highly specific individual role is not required. The player adjusts from moment to moment and does so in the light of what a number of others are doing and of the rules and purposes of the game. In performing this role, the child as player responds to a *generalized other.*

Mead used this term to designate "the organized community or social group which gives to the individual his unity of self" (1934:154). One who takes the standpoint of the generalized other knows what is required to keep the group to its distinctive aims and rules. The individual sees not only his own role, not only the roles of particular others, but the ways roles are related in determining the outcome of group activity. Gradually the individual becomes capable of taking on the point of view of the community as a whole.

THE 'I' AND THE 'ME'
The social self has a creative, spontaneous aspect. To stress the essentially social nature of the

self may seem to imply that the self is completely determined by the internalized attitudes of others. This is not so. To be sure, the internalized attitudes of others represent what the individual takes into account when he acts; they are the demands that group life actually or supposedly makes upon him. Nevertheless, human behavior has a large element of freedom and spontaneity. The demands of the social situation pose a problem to the acting individual, but there is considerable leeway in how he deals with the problem. Furthermore, the individual can never predict precisely what his response in a given situation will be. The baseball player wants to play good ball; in this sense behavior is determined by accepting the demands and standards of the group. But whether he will make a brilliant play or an error neither he nor anyone else knows beforehand.

Mead called the acting self the 'I'. The 'me', on the other hand, is that part of the self that is an organization of the internalized attitudes of others. The 'I' represents the self insofar as it is free and has initiative, novelty, and uniqueness. The 'me' represents the conventional part of the self. The 'I' responds to the 'me' and takes it into account, but it is not identical with it.

There may be varying amounts of 'I' and 'me' in behavior. In impulsive behavior, the 'me' is absent; in Freudian language, the 'I' is not being censored by the 'me'. Social control is present to the extent that the 'I' is controlled by the 'me'. The oversocialized individual is overdetermined by his 'me'. In more normal circumstances, the individual responds to a situation in its social aspects but does so with some regard for his own unique capacities and needs. The most gratifying experiences are those in which the demands of the 'me' — or of the social situation — permit the expression and realize the potentialities of the 'I'.

The enlargement of the self is dependent upon and in turn supports the breadth of community values. What the self is and how it develops depends upon the nature of the community whose attitudes the individual has internalized. Membership in a community is more than physical presence in it; the small child belongs to a play group, not to the city in which he lives: ". . . until one can

respond to himself as a community responds to him, he does not genuinely belong to the community" (1934:265).

The self will be isolated and alienated from other selves if it is a member of a socially isolated group or one with narrow or provincial values. The self becomes enlarged to the extent that it belongs to a group engaged in activities that bring it into contact with other groups. Nationalism, which seems to be and often is a constraining and limiting influence, has nevertheless played its part in creating broader human communities. Similarly the self becomes enlarged to the extent that it belongs to a community that subscribes to universal values, such as the objective standards of science or a religious belief in human brotherhood.

SUMMARY

1. *Language is a biologically given human potentiality. But humanity could not develop this potentiality without first being able to interact socially and communicate with others in a nonverbal, gestural way within shared, ongoing activities. Without social interaction, language would not be possible. Out of social interaction, accompanied by language, human reason and self-consciousness emerge.*

2. *Social interaction, when accompanied and facilitated by language, leads "naturally" to social control and the development of human society.*

3. *Through language the individual takes on or internalizes the attitudes of others toward both the environment and self. In this way, the human being acquires a social self. The young child internalizes the attitudes of those who are significant others. With maturity the individual learns to relate to a generalized other, that is, to organized group activity and the community as a whole.*

4. *The individual need not and indeed cannot be totally controlled by the internalized attitudes of others, that is, by the 'me' part of the self. The individual is also an 'I', that is, someone who takes account of the 'me' but is not necessarily dominated by it. The 'I' may act upon, influence, and modify the social process.*

Section four discontinuities and failures

It is easy to come away from a general discussion of socialization with the erroneous impression that it is uniformly effective. To be sure, humans are inescapably social animals, and everyone is socialized to some degree. But the implicit aims of socialization outlined in Section One are seldom fully achieved. Moreover, some of these aims are mutually antagonistic. The smooth transmission of culture is to some extent counteracted by the effort to create unique and fully developed human personalities.

As some writers have observed, there is a temptation for sociology to communicate an "oversocialized conception of man" (Wrong, 1961; Berger, 1963). The temptation is understandable, because sociology has a special obligation to explore the many ways a biological organism, through social influences, becomes a functioning human being.

It should never be forgotten, however, that scientific study is governed by the principle of variation. The lesson of sociology is not that men conform. Rather, conformity is an important phenomenon that varies both in degree and in kind. Sociology tries to discover the many different kinds of conformity and control, how effective they are under varying conditions, and what differences they make for personality and society.

When social processes are studied in detail, it is impossible to ignore the contingencies, hazards, and breakdowns that beset socialization. Research on deviance, mental health, inequality, and many other topics takes for granted that socialization often fails from the standpoint of the individual or from the standpoint of society.

INEFFECTIVE TRANSMISSION

In a small, homogeneous, tradition-bound society, the transmission of culture may be smooth and uniform. Even then, the smoothness of transmission is easy to exaggerate; but in more complex societies, socialization is always problematic. A few indications are suggested in the following paragraphs.

Competition of socializing agencies In primitive and folk societies, a great part of the culture has access to children. The life of the society is lived out before their eyes; very little is not open to direct observation. Most of the agencies support each other in socializing children, and there is little competition for access to them. On the other hand, in a large and heterogeneous society, the agencies of socialization are faced with the problem of gaining access to the individual and of establishing the conditions that make for deep rather than superficial influence.

If the groups that reach the individual (family, school, peer groups) have similar values and goals, they are mutually supportive, and socialization is reinforced. If, however, they compete for the opportunity to impress their values, the individual must choose between them and may be less than effectively socialized by any group. For example, children of immigrants are often exposed to two sets of sharply divergent values, one held by the parents, the other by the host society. Because the values of the larger society are unsupported at home or in the ethnic community, the child may understand and accept them only in an incomplete and superficial way. The person caught between two cultures, not fully socialized by either, has been called the "marginal man" (Stonequist, 1937; Golovensky, 1952).

Inadequate reinforcement A point of view akin to the fallacy of oversocialization is the fallacy of "normative determinism."

At its most naive level, normative determinism takes the fact that norms *are meant* to control behavior as the basis for assuming that they *do* control it. The only task of social science is then to discover the particular norms in any given society (Blake and Davis, 1964:461).

In fact, the effectiveness of social norms varies a great deal. Norms that are widely accepted and strongly felt tend to be self-enforcing: A violation evokes immediate rebuke and social sanction. But not all norms are strongly felt; many are enforced only by official agencies, leaving much everyday violation uncontrolled. Even when norms are widely accepted, society is not always able to motivate individuals to do what is expected of them. For example, high school students must exercise a considerable degree of self-control and defer many gratifications if they are to be good students. But if what they are asked to study has little connection with what they are likely to do when they graduate, the chances of effective socialization are greatly diminished. A study of a California high school drew the following conclusions:

Whenever present activity fails to make sense by being clearly connected to future increments of status, the student tends to become expressively alienated and rebellious. The student who grasps a clear connection between current activity and future status tends to regard school authority as legitimate, and to obey. . . . The system of symbols on which school authority depends are those of age-grading, that is, symbols that distinguish adults from children and justify school authority by pointing to age differences. When these symbols fail to elicit loyalty because the student rejects the picture of himself as an adolescent, expressive alienation results (Stinchcombe, 1964:9).

More generally, socialization cannot be fully effective if it is not reinforced by social conditions that make conformity both possible and rewarding.

The antisocial personality Perhaps the most striking indicator of ineffective cultural transmission is the individual without a conscience. In the official terminology of the American Psychiatric Association, this is an *antisocial personality:*

This term is reserved for individuals who are basically unsocialized and whose behavior pattern brings them repeatedly into conflict with society. They are incapable of significant loyalty to individuals, groups, or social values. They are grossly selfish, callous, irresponsible, impulsive, and unable to feel guilt or to learn from experi-

In some societies males are socialized to treat female strangers as sexual objects.

ence and punishment. Frustration tolerance is low. They tend to blame others or offer plausible rationalizations for their behavior. A mere history of repeated legal or social offenses is not sufficient to justify this diagnosis (American Psychiatric Association, 1968:43).

An earlier edition of this diagnostic manual referred to much the same constellation as a *sociopathic personality*, and still earlier editions used the term *psychopathic personality*. The names have been changed in a somewhat futile effort to avoid derogatory labeling. *Sociopath* is still in use among psychiatrists as a synonym for *antisocial personality* (Chodorkoff and Baxter, 1969:1142).

The essential element of the antisocial personality is the psychic capacity to injure others without guilt or remorse. While such individuals are socialized in many other ways—language, skills, personal aspirations—they have failed to develop effective superego and ego controls. The precise causes of such failure are obscure. In some cases, people with antisocial personalities have had parents who unconsciously encouraged resentment of authority. More important, perhaps, is the absence or erosion of ties of affection and trust within the family. A compelling account has been written of the experience and background of two such men who murdered a whole family in cold blood (Capote, 1965).

Caution While it is highly probable that neglectful and emotionally unsupportive parents increase the risk that antisocial personalities will develop, such conditions are not sufficient to account for extreme superego and ego failure. Most people from such backgrounds do *not* become sociopaths.

SOCIALIZATION FOR DISADVANTAGE

From a democratic perspective, socialization is deficient when it perpetuates the disadvantaged position of one group relative to another. In the United States, being nonwhite or female constitutes an ascribed status to which are attached certain socialization practices that serve to channel nonwhites and women into subordinate roles relative to whites and men. Moreover, disadvantaged groups tend to perpetuate themselves and to do so through the socialization practices they engage in. In effect, they cooperate in their own and their children's subordination.

Sometimes parents frankly accept an inferior status. In traditional societies, children are taught not to aspire above their station in life, not only because it is unrealistic to do so but because the parents believe in the traditional system of social order. At other times, parental cooperation consists in "cooling out" children, getting them to accept their lot in life. Until recently, at least, this was a very common experience among black children.

In the 1940s, prior to the upsurge of the civil rights movement, 150 black children were interviewed in New York and St. Louis regarding their difficulties with whites. They reported a total of 487 instances of "ridicule, physical ill-treatment, aggression, rude treatment, discrimination, and indirect disparagement" in encounters with whites (Goff, 1949:22). The children said they had reported 298 of these instances to their parents. "The instructions most frequently received, appearing in 61 percent of the instances, was to withdraw" (Goff, 1949:57). In another 26 percent of the instances, the advice of the parent was to avoid further encounters with whites, thus implicitly placing responsibility on the children rather than on those who had degraded them. Cooling out the child is an understandable socialization strategy for oppressed groups that face physical danger.

Parental cooperation is often unwitting and unintended. Parents may simply not recognize disadvantage for what it is. This is evident in the socialization of girls, who are rarely encouraged to develop top-level occupational skills. Parents believe they are doing their best for a daughter when they prepare her for a good marriage rather than a good occupation; they do not see that they may be foreclosing her options and preparing her for a lifetime of dependency.

Socialization for personal independence and autonomy requires (1) an orientation of mastery toward the environment, (2) self-esteem and self-confidence, (3) aspirations that serve to expand rather than constrict the self, and (4) adequate levels of skill and knowledge.

Mastery Socialization that seriously inhibits the human impulse to explore the environment and engage in problem-solving activities is training for passivity, helplessness, and dependence. Recent research indicates that women are socialized to seek affiliation rather than mastery as a source of satisfaction (Hoffman, 1972). Socialization for affiliation is consistent with the adult role traditionally assigned to women: Women are supposed to confine themselves to the home, to take care of others, and to find satisfaction in interpersonal relations and domesticity rather than in an occupation or the larger society.

However, there is evidence that girls do not adopt the traditional and restrictive female role as readily as boys adopt the traditional male role. Various studies of children's play preferences support the view that, at least between the ages of three and ten, "boys more strongly prefer the stereotyped male role than girls prefer the stereotyped female role" (Hartup and Zook, 1960:424). In other words, girls more often like so-called boys' games than boys like so-called girls' games (Brown, 1957; Rosenberg and Sutton-Smith, 1960). This is understandable in light of the greater freedom and adventuresomeness in boy-appropriate as compared with girl-appropriate play. One study showed a consensus among preadolescents, both boys and girls, that domestic activities such as washing dishes were what girls do and hitching a ride on the back of a truck and other risky acts were what boys do (Hartley and Hardesty, 1964:48). It has been said that "the typical woman regards herself

as less adequate and more fearful than most men" because of the greater freedom, power, and value assigned to the male role (Kagan, 1964:142). It might also be added that the play activities assigned to girls do not encourage exploration and problem solving; by limiting the life space of the female they serve to limit her sense of mastery and independence.

Self-esteem Prejudice tends to perpetuate itself by creating a negative self-image among the disadvantaged. This fact played a role in the 1954 decision of the Supreme Court outlawing school segregation. The decision has been described as having been

based primarily on considerations of ego development. It recognized that school and other public facilities cannot be "separate and equal" because enforced and involuntary separateness that is predicated on purely arbitrary criteria necessarily implies an inferior caste status, and thereby results in psychological degradation and injury to self-esteem (Ausubel and Ausubel, 1963:109).

In a footnote, the Supreme Court decision referred to several studies showing that the negative evaluation of dark skin color prevalent in the society was accepted by black children. A study in the early 1940s presented 253 black children with four dolls, identical except for color: Two were brown with black hair, two were white with yellow hair. The children were then asked to give the experimenter the doll "that you like to play with best," "that is a nice doll," "that looks bad," "that is a nice color." In responding to each of the requests, a majority of the black children displayed a preference for the white doll. However, the study also reported that compared to the northern children, "the southern children, in spite of their equal favorableness toward the white doll, are significantly less likely to reject the brown doll (evaluate it negatively)" (Clark and Clark, 1947:178).

Two decades later, a white psychiatrist observed blacks and whites, both children and adults, involved in instances of school desegregation in the South. He asked the

Left, a white girl by Ruby. *Right,* self-portrait by Ruby.

children to draw pictures. Following are some of his comments on Ruby, a black child, who began to draw for the psychiatrist when she was six years old:

For a long time—four months, in fact—Ruby never used brown or black except to indicate soil or the ground; even then she always made sure they were covered by a solid covering of green grass. It was not simply on my account that she abstained from these colors; her school drawings showed a similar pattern. She did, however, distinguish between white and Negro people. She drew white people larger and more lifelike. Negroes were smaller, their bodies less intact. A white girl we both knew to be her own size appeared several times taller. While Ruby's own face lacked an eye in one drawing, an ear in another, the white girl never lacked any features. Moreover, Ruby drew the white girl's hands and legs carefully, always making sure that they had the proper number of fingers and toes. Not so with her own limbs, or those of any other Negro children she chose (or was asked) to picture. A thumb or forefinger might be missing, or a whole set of toes. The arms were shorter, even absent or truncated (Coles, 1967:47).

Aspirations Black people, Mexican-Americans, and women tend to have low aspirations, thereby perpetuating their disadvantage. For example, even though many young women have the ability to be physicians, they do not aspire beyond becoming nurses. Ironically, when disadvantaged children do express high aspirations, they are apt to be unrealistic.

The relatively low aspirations of stigmatized groups reflect the low expectations others have of them and they are socialized to have of themselves. These low expectations are frequently expressed directly, as when girls and nonwhites are encouraged by parents, high school counselors, and others to enter clerical and manual occupations on the ground that they are mentally or emotionally unsuited for higher-level jobs. However, low expectations are conveyed very early to the child in more subtle ways. While they appear to express kindness and concern, they have the effect of inhibiting the child's achievement and thus justifying low expectations. A number of studies suggest that one of the most important means of conveying low expectations, damaging self-esteem, and reducing achievement is through overpraising the child, accepting mediocre performances, and permitting the child to avoid difficult problems (Coopersmith, 1967).

Skills In recent years, psychologists and sociologists have cast a jaundiced eye on standard intelligence tests, school grades, and the concept of IQ, arguing that these reflect only one kind of intelligence and creativity. Nevertheless, this kind of intelligence is highly valued in modern industrial societies and is rewarded with power, prestige, and privilege.

The tendency of some minority groups, such as blacks or Mexican-Americans, to score relatively low on IQ tests is well documented (Coleman et al., 1966:217–233). The causes of this tendency are still being debated, with some taking the position that they are genetic (Jensen et al., 1969). However, most social scientists hold that group differences in intelligence are not genetic but the product of differences in socialization. It has been repeatedly demonstrated that improvements in the environment of young children are usually accompanied by improvements in IQ. These findings have recently been duplicated with laboratory rats. Rats raised in more interesting environments containing various kinds of "toys" have been shown to be more alert and intelligent than rats raised in environments providing little stimulation (Hunt, 1969:193).

Preschool programs such as Head Start, which are primarily for minority children, are based on the recognized need to reach such children at an earlier age than is now possible through regular school channels. Such programs are oriented not to inculcating specific skills, such as reading, but to improving what might be called the infrastructure of achievement. This infrastructure is, in effect, learning to learn. It includes learning to use language to give and receive information and to express needs, adopting attitudes of experimentation and curiosity, and coping with frustration in problem-solving situations.

Section five culture, personality, and human nature

Through socialization each culture places its distinctive mark on human personality. The more homogeneous the culture, the more likely it is to produce a characteristic type of person who reflects the dominant ethos or culture theme. In one society the representative personality may be relaxed and easygoing, careless of time, and tolerant of uncleanliness. In another society, quite opposite characteristics occur.

This observation has been the commonplace experience of travelers for many centuries, and untrained observers may leap easily to generalized images or stereotypes. Americans are apt to think of the English as stuffy and unemotional, the English to think of Americans as brash and crude, and both to think of Latins as undependable and volatile. Everyone thinks of everyone else as lacking humor.

BASIC PERSONALITY

Anthropologists and sociologists approach the subject of representative personalities with caution because of the wide variation in personality observed within cultures and the difficulty of defining what is representative. The concept of representative personality (sometimes called basic personality, modal personality, or social character) points toward a common core of traits by members of a society, but there is some disagreement about the meaning of this idea.

1. Representative may mean simply the statistically frequent. Any item of behavior exhibited by a large number of people in a

Table 4:3 Socialization and social character

Social character	Who socializes?	What guides behavior?	Psychological mechanism of conformity	Life-style
Tradition-directed	The clan the tribe, the village	Detailed norms of village life learned by direct observation	Shame; wrongdoing is a transgression against the group	Politically indifferent; subsistence-oriented
Inner-directed	The parents	General principles laid down early in life; freedom for nonconformity within these limits; built-in gyroscope steers individual	Guilt; wrongdoing is a violation of personal ideals	Politically moralistic; production-oriented
Other-directed	The peer group	Cue taking in particular situations; built-in radar steers individual	Anxiety; the ultimate evil is being unloved and unapproved	Politically manipulative; consumption-oriented

Source: Adapted from Riesman, 1950.

society would then be part of its representative personality.

2. Representative personality may consist of those common characteristics of personality which exist despite differences in overt behavior (Kardiner, 1945). Attention is then directed not toward the minutiae of observable behavior and response but toward basic underlying orientations and outlooks, for example, Riesman's tradition-directed, inner-directed, and other-directed types. (See Table 4:3.)

3. Representative personality sometimes means the personality which most fully expresses the spirit or ethos of a culture. In this sense the representative personality may be shared by only a minority. It is a kind of personality most easily integrated into dominant social institutions. The cultivated English man or woman, products of a distinctive system of education, are representative in this sense.

SEX AND TEMPERAMENT

All societies distinguish between the roles of men and women, assigning to each sex special tasks, duties, and prerogatives. In Western society, differences in the roles of men and women are associated with sharp and contrasting differences in temperament.

The female is regarded as naturally non-aggressive and passive, the male as naturally aggressive and active. The contrasting temperaments of men and women have been associated with the dominance of one and the submission of the other. Thus, the more dominating a man, the more masculine he is considered; the more passive and pliant a woman, the more feminine she is.

Margaret Mead analyzed three societies (Arapesh, Mundugumor, and Tchamubuli) on the island of New Guinea to determine whether temperamental differences between males and females are universal (Mead, 1935).

The ideal Arapesh, man or woman, is gentle, responsive, unaggressive, and maternal. A child is not regarded as the result of a single act of impregnation but must be fed and shaped in the mother's womb by repeated unions of mother and father. The verb *to bear a child* may refer either to a man or a woman. After an infant is born, the husband lies down at his wife's side and is said to be "in bed having a baby." Husband and wife together observe the taboos and perform the ceremonies that accompany the birth of a child. Later, the husband shares in child care.

The minute day-by-day care of little children, with its routine, its exasperations, its wails of misery that cannot be correctly interpreted, these are as congenial to the Arapesh men as they are to the Arapesh women. And in recognition of this care, as well as in recognition of the father's initial contribution, if one comments upon a middle-aged man as good-looking, the people answer: "Good-looking? Ye-e-s? But you should have seen him before he bore all those children" (Mead, 1935:39).

Sexual aggressiveness is attributed to neither sex. Rape is unknown among the Arapesh; their image of male sexuality makes it psychologically alien to them. The Arapesh permit polygyny (one husband, several wives), but it is not regarded as an ideal.

Among the Mundugumor, both men and women are aggressive, harsh, and violent. In the structure of Mundugumor society the father and his daughters form one group, the mother and her sons another. Pregnancy is welcomed by neither parent, for the father fears a son and the mother a daughter. The crying infant is suckled only as a last resort, with the mother in a strained, standing position. Infants are removed as soon as they stop suckling. Weaning consists of slapping and thrusting the child away.

Both sexes are regarded as sexually aggressive, and sex play, especially in premarital encounters in the bush, takes the form of mutual scratching and biting. Polygyny is an ideal. Wives bring wealth and power by growing and curing tobacco, but new marriages are a further stimulus to hostility. Throughout life there is antagonism between the sexes. In this battle women

are believed to be just as violent, just as aggressive, just as jealous [as men]. They simply are not quite as strong physically, although often a woman can put up a very good fight, and a husband who wishes to beat his wife takes care to arm himself with a crocodile-jaw and to be sure that she is not armed (Mead, 1935:210).

Among the Tchambuli, sharply divergent roles are prescribed for the sexes and are accompanied by marked temperamental differences. The roles reverse Western notions about what is naturally male and female temperament. Tchambuli economic life is supervised by the women, and the men de-

vote themselves in separate establishments to art and ceremony. The women work together in easy and bantering camaraderie, and the men are anxious, distrustful of each other, and given to catty remarks. The women are efficient and unadorned, the men self-conscious and arrayed in feathers. The women work and support the community; the men arrange ceremonies and dances to entertain and amuse the women.

Women are regarded as more actively and urgently sexed than men. The men's emotional life centers around the women. One source of this emotional dependence is the experience of the young male child. In infancy and early childhood he lives as an integral part of the women's community, where his experiences are pleasant and intimate. For a number of years, when he is considered too old to spend all his time with the women but still too young to be accepted into the adult male community, he lives in a kind of emotional limbo. His earliest and deepest ties, which are to women, are never counterbalanced by his experiences in the male community.

Caution Although men and women do take on distinctive personality traits in different cultures, in no society is there a dead level of temperament. Among the Arapesh, for example, there were noticeable differences in the degree to which individuals were unaggressive and nonviolent. Nevertheless, even the most active Arapesh child is less aggressive than a normally active American child.

HUMAN NATURE

Because one's own responses seem spontaneous and natural, we often regard them as part of our essential humanity rather than as the result of a particular training and experience. On the other hand, once the efficacy of socialization is understood, it is easy to fall into the opposite fallacy and to deny that there are limits to human malleability.

The "nature" of wood and water means that they respond in ascertainable ways to known conditions. If too large a nail is driven into hardwood, it may crack; if water is heated to 100 degrees Celsius at sea level, it will boil. To know the nature of anything is to know also its potentialities and limits. The problem of human nature should be understood in the same matter-of-fact way.

The idea of human nature is clear enough when it refers to the study of humans as physical organisms. The more we learn about body chemistry and physiology, the more we can say about the organism's responses to the invasion of bacteria and to changes in temperature, stress, and nutrition. Similarly, various psychological phenomena, such as learning and perceiving, seem to follow laws that are characteristic of the whole species. But human beings also have personality, characterized by dispositions to respond in emotional ways, by the development of a self, and by psychological defenses.

Turning to the socially relevant aspects of psychic structure, such challenging questions as the following are raised: Are there universal psychological characteristics which affect the way humans relate to each other? Do these characteristics, if they exist, set limits on the kinds of social arrangements that are psychologically acceptable? Or are psychic tolerances so broad that *any* kind of social organization is possible? Are some aspirations, such as the quest for power, part of essential human nature, or are they products of socialization in a given culture? Some of these questions have been explored in such comparative studies of personality and society as Mead's investigations of sex and temperament.

Another approach to the study of human nature attempts to identify emotional needs which demand satisfaction in social arrangements. Fromm asserts that human beings have a fundamental need for belonging, for being securely part of a community which can provide them emotional support (Fromm, 1941; 1947). The growth of economic and political freedom in Western society has tended to isolate the individual and to bring about the withdrawal of older social supports. Fromm's analysis, which is based on neo-Freudian psychology, recognizes the importance of social influences but maintains that the human psychic structure is naturally fragile, because it grows out of and depends upon social interaction. The continued support of others through love, affection, and social approval is needed. The neo-Freudians hold that humans are anxiety-prone and that social groups must provide conditions that alleviate anxiety. If these supports are lacking, the individual will seek a way out of anxiety, sometimes with serious consequences for political order. Anxiety may manifest itself in several ways: in overaggressiveness, submission to authority, or in apathetic withdrawal.

A common human nature does not necessarily lead directly to uniformities in behavior. What is observed depends on the conditions within which response takes place, and what is learned is the disposition of the person to respond. If the need for personal security is a fundamental part of human nature, the need will be revealed in a wide variety of ways. An understanding of the underlying psychic condition can reveal much about potential responses of children and adults to anxiety-provoking situations.

In Adaptation 8 the psychic unity of mankind is poignantly revealed.

Adaptation 8 Kroeber: Ishi in two worlds

On August 29, 1911, in the California gold country, an emaciated, middle-aged Indian was found crouched against a corral fence. The sheriff was called, saw that the "wild" man was near starvation and suffering from exhaustion and fear. When he was unable to communicate with Ishi, he took him to jail to protect him from curiosity seekers. Undoubtedly Ishi expected to be killed as a result of his capture by his enemy, the white man.

Anthropologist T. T. Waterman went to the jail and established a rudimentary communication with him with the aid of a phonetically transcribed list of Yana words, which were from a dialect of the language Ishi spoke. The University of California received permission from the Indian Bureau in Washington, D.C., to take Ishi to the University Museum of Anthropology in San Francisco, which became his home until he died, four-and-a-half years later.

Ishi was the last wild Indian in North America and the last surviving member of the lost tribe of the Yahi, a subgroup of the Yana nation, whose ancestral lands were in northern California. The coming of the white man brought death to the California Indians. In the single year of 1864, most of the two or three thousand Yana, other than the Yahi, had been murdered and massacred by white settlers. In 1865, when Ishi was a small child, the extermination of the Yahi began. By the 1870s, only a handful were still alive. In order to survive and to maintain their identity as a people, these few Yahi entered upon the Long Concealment. With rare exceptions, they were never again seen by strangers. They hid in the brush of the canyons, avoiding all encounters, but their struggle for survival was doomed. By the turn of the century, apparently only five Yahi remained, among them Ishi, his mother, and his sister (or cousin). Finally, the only survivors were Ishi and his mother. After she died, he was without human companionship from November 1908 until August 1911.

Source: Abridged from *Ishi in Two Worlds: A Biography of the Last Wild Indian in North America* by Theodora Kroeber (Berkeley and Los Angeles: University of California Press, 1961), pp. 124–128, 133, 138–139, 144–146, 162, 230, 236. Originally published by the University of California Press. Reprinted by permission of Theodora Kroeber and the Regents of the University of California.

THE UNSPOKEN NAME

The morning after Ishi's arrival at the museum he and Professor A. L. Kroeber, who would become his Big *Chiep* (Ishi pronounced *f* as *p*), met, and a friendship was born of their meeting. Reporters demanded to know his [the Indian's] name, refusing to accept Kroeber's word that the question was in the circumstances unmannerly and futile. Batwi [a "civilized" Yana who acted as interpreter and informant for the anthropologists] intervened, engaging to persuade the wild man to tell his name — a shocking gaucherie on Batwi's part. The wild man, saving his brother Yana's face, said that he had been alone so long that he had had no one to give him a name — a polite fiction, of course. A California Indian almost never speaks his own name, using it but rarely with those who already know it, and he would never tell it in reply to a direct question.

The reporters felt, not unnaturally, that they were being given "the runaround." Kroeber felt more pushed than did his nameless friend who remained relatively detached, not understanding most of what was said and standing quietly by Indian custom so far as he did understand. Said Kroeber, "Very well. He shall be known as *Ishi*." He regretted that he was unable to think of a more distinctive name, but it was not inappropriate, meaning "man" in Yana, and hence not of the private or nickname category. Thus it was that the last of the Yahi was christened Ishi and, in historic fact, *became* Ishi.

He *never* revealed his own, private, Yahi name. It was as though it had been consumed in the funeral pyre of the last of his loved ones. He accepted the new name, answering to it unreluctantly. But once it was bestowed it took on enough of his true name's mystic identification with himself, his soul, whatever inner essence of a man it is which a name shares, that he was never again heard to pronounce it.

Of Ishi then [the morning after his arrival at the museum] and in succeeding days when the ordeal by fear and strangeness was most acute, Kroeber says that the first impression of him was of his gentleness and of a timidity and fear kept under severe control. Ishi started at the slightest sound.

A stranger, the hearty type, burst into the room where Ishi was talking with Kroeber, grabbed Ishi's hand, and pumped hand and arm up and down in vigorous greeting. When released, Ishi stood, his arm frozen in the air for several seconds.

His shyness at first was acute. A blush, coming with a painful intensity, caused his face to mantle and cloud. He continued to blush easily even after he was no longer fearful and tense, covering his blushes with a deprecatory smile or a laugh and the placing of the fingers of one hand over his mouth, in that universal gesture of embarrassment.

A MAN APART

Deeper than shyness and fear was Ishi's awareness that he was alone—not as the unfriendly or too introverted or misanthropic are alone, for he was none of these. To be sure, he would sit, unbored, dreamy, and withdrawn into his own mystic

Ishi, August 29, 1911

A. L. Kroeber and Ishi, 1911

center, but only if there was nothing to do, no one to talk to or to work with. He much preferred companionship, and he smiled readily, his smile beginning in the eyes and traveling from eyes to mouth. He was interested, concerned, amused, or delighted, as the case might be, with everything and everyone he knew and understood.

His aloneness was not that of temperament but of cultural chance, and one early evidence of his sophisticated intelligence was his awareness of this. He felt himself so different, so distinct, that to regard himself or to have others regard him as "one of them" was not to be thought of. "I am one; you are others; this is in the inevitable nature of things," is an English approximation of his judgment on himself. It was a harsh judgment, arousing in his friends compassion, then respect. He was fearful and timid at first, but never unobservant, nor did his fear paralyze his thinking as it paralyzed his gesturing. He faced the disparity of content between Yahi culture and white, and the knowledge that he could not begin from so far behind and come abreast. He would not try to. He would and did adapt as one of goodwill and breeding must adapt to one's host in dress, in the forms of greeting and leave-taking, in the use of knife and fork at table; these and other conventions of simple etiquette.

Meanwhile, he remained himself—a well-born Yahi, never unmindful of the code his mother and uncle had taught him. It might be conjectured that this position of aloofness and aloneness would have driven him into a depression, but such was not the case. Ishi had kept his morale through grief and an absolute solitariness; the impact of civilization could not budge it. Beneath the shyness and reserve he remained possessed of natural, temperamental, and unimpaired outgoingness and interest in people and phenomena, which he was able, day by day, to express ever more spontaneously, as the museum home became more and more *his* home.

His self-respect and pride no doubt prevented Ishi from acquiring a more rapid and facile command of English—he was reluctant to use a word or phrase until he was fairly sure of it—just as they hampered an easy fellowship with people he knew only slightly. But these character traits seemed not to have seriously cut him off from the people and activities he really valued, and they did serve to discourage even the least perceptive white person from the benevolent superiority of the civilized to the primitive, of the first-class citizen to the second-class. Many people, after awhile, laughed with Ishi. He was no king's jester; no one ever laughed *at* him.

CROWDS AND MOUNTAINS

A white man had been, until a few days [before Ishi came to the museum], a signal of mortal danger. He was becoming fairly at ease with his friends in the museum and concealed his sudden fears from them as best he could. But the crowding around of half a dozen people made his limbs become rigid; his first close-up of a group of perhaps 80 or 100 people left his faculties paralyzed. With time, he came to realize that crowds were not intrinsically menacing; his early terrible fear abated, but not his dislike of people in numbers such that the individual becomes lost in the faceless throng. He never liked strangers to come too close or to touch him. He learned to suffer the handshake as a custom universal to the white man and of friendly intent, and to acknowledge a proffered hand promptly and with courtesy. He never himself initiated a handshake.

No dream, no wildest nightmare, prefigured for Ishi a city crowd, its clamor, its endless hurrying past to be endlessly replaced by others of its kind, face indistinguishable from face. It was like a spring salmon run, one fish leaping sightlessly beyond or over another, and he disliked the sweaty smell of people in numbers. It suggested to him the odor of old deer hide.

One Sunday afternoon, Ishi was taken for an automobile ride through Golden Gate Park and to the ocean beach. The ocean is something every inland Indian has heard of, and has some sort of picture of in his mind. They speak of the ocean even when, like Ishi, they have never seen it, and it is likely to figure in myths and tales. Ishi was looking forward to seeing it, but when the car stopped on the bluff above, giving onto a wide view of ocean, surf, and beach, Ishi's breath drew in, not because of the great rolling Pacific, but because of the thousands of people who covered the beach below and spilled over into the surf—a Sunday afternoon crowd on a rare warm September day. He said over and over softly, half-whisperingly, *"Hansi saltu, hansi saltu!* Many white people, many white people!" He had not known so many people could inhabit the earth at one time; the shock of sheer numbers obliterated every other impression. Kroeber thought to distract him by pointing out some of the taller office buildings as a less disturbing wonder to him. Ishi looked at them appraisingly, but without being greatly impressed, since, unlike his inexperience in estimating population figures, he had an adequate measuring rod for the height of a building. He had lived until now in the shadow of Waganupa and in sight of Mount Shasta and between the sheer walls of Deer Creek Canyon. The vertical walls of a city are indeed puny, scarce worthy of comment, by comparison.

RITUALS OF RESPECT

Ishi did not venture off Parnassus Heights [site of the museum] alone until he had been in the city some time, but he went to various places with one person or another. His first such expedition was on the day after his arrival. Waterman took him across the bay to Berkeley where he saw the campus of the university and had dinner with the Watermans and their two children—his first dinner at a white man's table in a white man's home. He was there many times later, and of his first time Waterman reported only that Ishi so closely watched his hostess, imitating her in her choice of fork or spoon, in her use of a napkin, and in the amount of food she put on her plate, that his exactly similar motions appeared to be simultaneous with hers.

Anyone who has had California Indians as house guests will recognize this as very "Indian." Customs differed from tribe to tribe, but a strict etiquette of eating was observed by all of them. The shift to new food and a different way of serving it seems to be adroitly managed when the principle and habit of conventional behavior "at table" is already ingrained.

Getting into and out of a suit coat or topcoat he found unhandy at first, whereas a single demonstration was all he needed to learn to tie a four-in-hand cravat, since he was used to knotting and tying cords of hemp and hide. Pockets he appreciated; within three days of having them he had them filled, and with the usual male miscellany. With the clothes went the code: Ishi, to whom nakedness had been the normal and unmarked state, refused to have his picture taken except when he was fully dressed. Pictures of him in

native undress had to await his return visit to the Lassen foothills.

THE USES OF NUMBERS

[Because of work Ishi did at the museum, he was put on the University payroll at a salary of $25 a month.] He was good with his hands, and there was about this job as about everything he did what Kroeber called a "willing gentleness." He was most grateful for the work, having observed that everyone in the white man's world had a regular job for which he received a regular wage. And he was pleased to have the *mahnee*, which permitted him to pay for his own food and whatever else he wanted instead of having it given to him. He was a proud person, to whom economic independence meant a great deal. Ishi now had a name, an address, and economic status.

[He learned to write his name so he could endorse and cash his paycheck.] Kroeber offered to keep Ishi's money, except for small amounts, in the safe. He showed him how the safe was operated and explained that only he and E. N. Gifford, the new curator, knew the combination and could open it.

Ishi had many times made a cache of valuables of one sort or another—food, arrows, tools, and the like—burying them under a pile of rocks or hanging them high in a tree. He was pleased to learn about the white man's cache and to put his silver there. He saw his money wrapped and stored, his own name plainly written on the outside of the package. The safe was closed. He twirled the combination and, trying to open it, saw that the box would not open. He was immensely satisfied; his treasure was now both well hidden and accessible whenever he wanted to get to it.

All four Yana dialects used a single counting system with almost identical numeral names. Early in their work with Ishi, Waterman and Kroeber asked him to count for them in Yahi, which he did willingly enough: *baiyu, uhmitsi, bulmitsi, daumi, djiman, baimami, uhmami, bulmami, daumima, hadjad;* the same words are in the other Yana dialects except for some consonantal changes. But unlike the others which continued from ten to higher numbers and multiples of higher numbers, Ishi's counting stopped with the numeral *hadjad*, "ten." When he was asked to continue, he would say, "No more. That's all." Here seemed to be an astonishing culture loss, not before encountered in California. The two ethnographers mentioned it in print and on the lecture platform, rationalizing it as owing in all probability to the decades of decimation and hiding; perhaps in the shrunken and meager life there had been little occasion to count or to think in numbers higher than ten.

To make it as easy as possible for Ishi to become familiar with a complex new number system and particularly so that he could learn to make change, the money from his salary check was converted into half dollars for him. The pieces of silver of identical size pleased him, and he soon discovered that an empty canister which had held a film roll was a good container for them. Forty half dollars just filled it, and when it would take no more, Ishi screwed the lid on tight and brought his first cache of the white man's treasure, which he called "twen-y dollar," to be deposited in the safe. There were more empty canisters, because someone was always taking pictures of Ishi; soon a second one was brought, full of treasure, to be laid beside the first, and then a third, for Ishi was saving about half his salary!

From time to time, if it was foggy or rainy out of doors, or after his work was finished, Ishi would come to the office and ask to see his money. Upon being handed it from the safe, he would go to the big table in the center of the room, open the cans, take the half dollars out, and spread them over the table—a king in his counting room.

It was one of the counting-room days. From his desk in the same room Kroeber watched as Ishi absorbedly spread out his money, restacking it in piles, and dividing some of the piles into half stacks which he fingered as if he were counting them. The stacks looked to be the height of the 40 pieces which filled one container. Kroeber joined Ishi at the table. "How much? How much money?" he asked, pointing to a full stack. Ishi answered at once and correctly: *daumistsa*, "forty." "The half stack?" Ishi replied *uhsiwai*, "twenty." Three half stacks he identified as *baimamikab*, "sixty"; and two full stacks as *bulmamikab*, "eighty." The questions and answers went on, but it was already obvious that Ishi's numeral vocabulary and his knowledge of the full Yana counting system were undiminished.

The system was quinary, that is to say there were basic numeral names up to five, and from five to ten there were additions to these, with further additions from ten to 20. When 20 was reached, it became a new unit as 100 is with us, the 20s or scores being given names not built on the smaller numeral names.

Why had Ishi said "No more" at ten? Counting in the abstract was something he was not accustomed to doing. He probably found it trying, and surely he found it pointless. Counting is for counting something tangible such as beads or treasure or the number of quivers in a case, or the number of arrowheads finished, or the number of geese in flight, or salmon in a catch. Abstract numbers did not interest him as such, nor did they figure in philosophy in the Yana world view. Ishi's interrogators knew this, as they knew also that the questionnaire form of putting a query may be expected every so often to yield misinformation, since the presumptions from which it arises may be unknown or meaningless to the person being questioned. They were disconcerted to be caught out using it. That their culpability should have come to light as the wild man was engaged in counting his civilized money in quite the manner of a bank teller was particularly humiliating. Thus, step by step, Ishi began his solitary penetration into the wilds of civilization while his friends made some groping progress into the Yahi world.

ISHI'S DEATH

To survive our civilization, an early and continuing immunization to it is necessary. [Ishi did not have the necessary immunization and died of tuberculosis in 1916.] Now the law reads that when a person dies intestate and without living blood relatives, such monies and property as may have been his at the time of death go to the state. The public administrator who is charged with responsibility to see that this transfer is actually made has, or had in 1916, certain discretionary powers also. Ishi's few personal possessions the administrator left with the museum. There was also Ishi's treasure in the safe in the museum office, his "counting room"—520 half dollars in 13 film cases, each neatly filled to the top. The administrator took half this sum for the state. The other half went where Waterman knew Ishi wished his treasure to go—to the House of the Kuwi. So it was that Doctor Moffitt, dean of the medical school, received 260 half dollars with a covering note from Waterman: "This gift from Ishi is in actual cash, and I hope you will accept it, though of course it is no return for the medical and hospital attention that Ishi received. It will serve perhaps as a recognition of his sense of obligation." Doctor Moffitt acknowledged the gift, thanking Waterman and explaining that he was putting Ishi's money in a special fund rather than taking it as payment of hospital expenses, since there had never been any idea of charging him. In this way, Ishi's treasure continues to contribute its bit to the science of healing, a science for which Ishi himself had so great a curiosity and concern.

A COMMON HUMANITY

A century has passed since Ishi was born, yet he continues to engage the imagination. He was unique, a last man, the last man of his world, and his experience of sudden, lonely, and unmitigated changeover from the Stone Age to the twentieth century was also unique. He was, further, a living affirmation of the credo of the anthropologists that modern man—Homo sapiens—whether contemporary American Indian or Athenian Greek of Pericles' time, is wholly human in his biology, in his capacity to learn new skills and new ways as a changed environment exposes him to them, in his power of abstract thought, and in his moral and ethical discriminations. It is upon this broad base of man's panhumanity that scientists and humanists alike predicate further progress away from the instinctual and primitive and subhuman strata of our natures.

References

American Psychiatric Association
1968 Diagnostic and Statistical Manual of Mental Disorders. Washington, D.C.: American Psychiatric Association.

Aronfreed, Justin
1969 "The concept of internalization." Pp. 263–324 in David A. Goslin (ed.), Handbook of Socialization Theory and Research. Chicago: Rand McNally.

Ausubel, David P. and Pearl Ausubel
1963 "Ego development among segregated Negro children." Pp. 109–141 in A. Harry Passow (ed.), Education in Depressed Areas. New York: Columbia University Press.

Bandura, Albert
1969 "Social-learning theory of identificatory processes." Pp. 213–262 in David A. Goslin (ed.), Handbook of Socialization Theory and Research. Chicago: Rand McNally.

Berger, Bennett
1971 Looking for America. Englewood Cliffs, N.J.: Prentice-Hall.

Berger, Peter L.
1963 Invitation to Sociology, A Humanistic Perspective. New York: Doubleday.

Bernstein, B.
1958 "Some sociological determinants of perception." British Journal of Sociology 9 (June):159–174.

Blake, Judith and Kingsley Davis
1964 "Norms, values, and sanctions." Pp. 456–484 in Robert E. L. Faris (ed.), Handbook of Sociology. Chicago: Rand McNally.

Bronfenbrenner, Urie
1958 "Socialization and social class through time and space." Pp. 400–425 in E. E. Maccoby, J. M. Newcomb, and E. L. Hartley (eds.), Readings in Social Psychology. New York: Holt, Rinehart and Winston.

Brown, Daniel G.
1957 "Masculinity-femininity development in children." Journal of Consulting Psychology 21 (June):197–202.

Capote, Truman
1965 In Cold Blood. New York: Random House.

Chodorkoff, Bernard and Seymour Baxter
1969 "Psychiatric and psychoanalytic theories of violence." Pp. 1117–1162 in National Commission on the Causes and Preventions of Violence, Crimes of Violence. Vol. 13.

Clark, Kenneth B. and Mamie P. Clark
1947 "Racial identification and preference in Negro children." Pp. 169–178 in Theodore M. Newcomb, Eugene L. Hartley, and Guy E. Swanson (eds.), Readings in Social Psychology. New York: Holt, Rinehart and Winston.

Coleman, James S. et al.
1966 Equality of Educational Opportunity. Washington, D.C.: GPO.

Coles, Robert
1967 Children of Crisis. Boston: Little, Brown.

Coopersmith, Stanley
1967 The Antecedents of Self-esteem. San Francisco: Freeman.

Freud, Sigmund
1923 The Ego and the Id. New York: Norton.

Fromm, Erich
1941 Escape from Freedom. New York: Holt, Rinehart and Winston.
1947 Man for Himself. New York: Holt, Rinehart and Winston.

Goff, Regina Mary
1949 Problems and Emotional Difficulties of Negro Children. New York: Columbia University Press.

Golovensky, D. I.
1952 "The marginal man concept, an analysis and critique." Social Forces 30:333–339.

Goslin, David A. (ed.)
1969 Handbook of Socialization Theory and Research. Chicago: Rand McNally.

Harlow, Harry F.
1959 "Love in infant monkeys." Scientific American 200 (June):
68–74.

Harlow, Harry F. and Margaret K. Harlow
1965 "The affectional systems." Pp. 287–334 in Allan M.
Schrier, Harry F. Harlow, and Fred Stollnitz (eds.), Behavior of
Non-human Primates. Vol. II. New York: Academic Press.

Hartley, Ruth E. and Francis P. Hardesty
1964 "Children's perceptions of sex roles in childhood." Journal of Genetic Psychology 105:43–51.

Hartup, Willard W. and Elsie A. Zook
1960 "Sex-role preferences in three- and four-year-old children." Journal of Consulting Psychology 24:420–426.

Hoffman, L. W.
1972 "Early childhood experiences and women's achievement motives." Journal of Social Issues 28 (2):129–155.

Hunt, J. McViker
1969 The Challenge of Incompetence and Poverty. Urbana, Ill.:
University of Illinois Press.

James, William
1891 The Principles of Psychology. Vol. I. New York: Holt,
Rinehart and Winston.

Jensen, Arthur et al.
1969 "Environment, Heredity, and Intelligence." Harvard Reprint Series No. 2. Compiled from the Harvard Educational Review.

Kagan, Jerome
1964 "Acquisition and significance of sex typing and sex role identity." Pp. 137–167 in M. L. Hoffman and L. W. Hoffman (eds.), Child Development Research. Vol. I. New York: Russell Sage.

Kagan, J. and H. A. Moss
1962 Birth to Maturity. New York: Wiley.

Kardiner, A.
1945 The Psychological Frontiers of Society. New York: Columbia University Press.

Kelleher, Roger T.
1965 "Operant conditioning." Pp. 211–247 in Allan M. Schrier, Harry F. Harlow, and Fred Stollnitz (eds.), Behavior of Non-human Primates. New York: Academic Press.

Kellogg, Winthrop N.
1968 "Communication and language in the home-raised chimpanzee." Science (October 25):423–427.

Kohlberg, Lawrence
1966 "A cognitive-developmental analysis of children's sex-role concepts and attitudes." Pp. 82–173 in Eleanor E. Maccoby (ed.), The Development of Sex Differences. Stanford, Calif.: Stanford University Press.

Kohn, Melvin L.
1959 "Social class and parental values." American Journal of Sociology 64 (January):337–351.

Komarovsky, Mirra
1962 Blue-collar Marriage. New York: Random House.

Lifton, Robert Jay
1968 "Protean man." Partisan Review 35:13–27.

Lipsitt, Lewis P.
1971 "Babies: they're a lot smarter than they look." Psychology Today 5 (December):70–72, 88–89.

Maslow, Abraham H.
1965 "Criteria for judging needs to be instinctoid." Pp. 33–48 in Marshall R. Jones (ed.), Human Motivation: A Symposium. Lincoln: University of Nebraska Press.

Mead, George H.
1934 Mind, Self, and Society. Chicago: University of Chicago Press.

Mead, Margaret
1935 Sex and Temperament in Three Primitive Societies. New York: Morrow.

Pavlov, I. P.
1927/1960 Conditioned Reflexes. New York: Dover.

Pfeiffer, John E.
1972 The Emergence of Man. New York: Harper & Row.

Redl, Fritz and David Wineman
1951 Children Who Hate: The Disorganization and Breakdown of Behavior Controls. New York: Free Press.

Riesman, David, in collaboration with Reuel Denney and Nathan Glazer
1950 The Lonely Crowd. New Haven, Conn.: Yale University Press.

Rosenberg, B. G. and B. Sutton-Smith
1960 "A revised conception of masculine-feminine differences in play activities." Journal of Genetic Psychology 96:165–170.

Scott, John Finley
1971 Internalization of Norms: A Sociological Theory of Moral Commitment. Englewood Cliffs, N.J.: Prentice-Hall.

Spitz, Rene A.
1945 and 1947/1964 "Hospitalism." Pp. 399–425 in Rose L. Coser (ed.). The Family: Its Structure and Functions). New York: St. Martin's Press.

Stinchcombe, Arthur
1964 Rebellion in a High School. Chicago: Quadrangle Books.

Stonequist, E. V.
1937 The Marginal Man. New York: Scribner.

U. S. Department of Health, Education, and Welfare
1971 Intellectual Development of Children by Demographic and Socioeconomic Factors, United States. Publication No. (HSM) 72-1012, Series 11, Number 110. Washington, D.C.: GPO.

Wrong, Dennis
1961 "The oversocialized conception of man in modern sociology." American Sociological Review 26 (April):183–193.

Sources and Readings

Aries, Philippe
1962 Centuries of Childhood. New York: Knopf.

Brim, Orvil G., Jr. and S. Wheeler
1966 Socialization After Childhood. New York: Wiley.

Clausen, John A. (ed.)
1968 Socialization and Society. Boston: Little, Brown.

Erikson, Erik H.
1963 Childhood and Society. Second edition, revised and enlarged. New York: Norton.

Field, David (ed.)
1974 Social Psychology for Sociologists. New York: Wiley

Goslin, David A. (ed.)
1969 Handbook of Socialization Theory and Research. Chicago: Rand McNally.

Hoffman, Martin L. and Lois W. Hoffman (eds.)
1969 Review of Child Development Research. New York: Russell Sage.

Maccoby, Eleanor E. and Carol N. Jacklin
1974 The Psychology of Sex Differences. Stanford, Calif.: Stanford University Press.

Mayer, Philip
1970 Socialization: The Approach from Social Anthropology. London: Tavistock.

Mussen, P. H., J. J. Conger, and J. Kagan.
1974 Child Development and Personality. Fourth edition. New York: Harper & Row.

Piaget, Jean
1926 Language and Thought of the Child. New York: Harcourt Brace Jovanovich.
1936 Moral Judgment of the Child. London: Kegan Paul.

Richmond, P. G.
1970 An Introduction to Piaget. New York: Basic Books.

Smelser, Neil J. and William T. Smelser
1963 Personality and Social Systems. New York: Wiley.

Periodicals

Journal of Personality and Social Psychology
Psychological Abstracts
Psychology Today
Sociometry

Primary Groups

Section one introduction

In the preceding chapter (pp. 87–88), some attention is given to the fact that human and other animals need emotionally supportive social contacts. Out of this need arises the phenomenon of *primary bonding*, that is, the establishment of sustained relationships capable of providing the organism reassurance and gratification. There are many forms of primary bonding, including parent–child relations, friendship, love, and membership in a closely knit group or community.

But the social world is not a warm cocoon. The rules and demands of society are often experienced as harsh and threatening; the person is often treated as a thing, an instrument, an abstraction. Hence a major theme of sociological analysis is the tension between a fundamental human need for primary bonding and the individual's inevitable confrontation with an impersonal world. This continuing tension accounts for many of the problems of personal and institutional life.

This chapter examines the nature of primary bonding and shows its significance for the individual, for associations, and for society. The focus is the primary group—the characteristic setting within which intimate, person-centered interaction takes place. The term primary group was first used by Cooley to refer to groups

. . . characterized by intimate face-to-face association and cooperation. They are primary in several senses, but chiefly in that they are fundamental in forming the social nature and ideas of the individual. The result of intimate association, psychologically, is a certain fusion of individualities in a common whole, so that one's very self, for many purposes at least, is the common life and purpose of the group. Perhaps the simplest way of describing this wholeness is by saying that it is a "we"; it involves the sort of sympathy and mutual identification for which "we" is the natural expression. One lives in the feeling of the whole and finds the chief aims of his will in that feeling (Cooley, 1909:23).

For close analysis it is necessary to distinguish between the primary relation and the primary group.

Charles Horton Cooley (1864–1929) is rightly regarded as one of the founders of sociology and is especially associated with the "symbolic interaction" approach (see p. 11) developed by G. H. Mead and John Dewey.

THE PRIMARY RELATION

The chief characteristics of a primary relation are:

1. *Response is to whole persons rather than to segments.* In the primary relation the participants interact as unique and total individuals. Uniqueness means that response is to a particular person and is not transferable to other persons. Wholeness means (1) that one responds to many aspects of another's character and background and (2) that one responds spontaneously and freely, as a unified self, permitting feelings to enter the relationship. The less transferable the response and the more complete the interaction, the more primary is the relation.

Many human relations are not primary (and are therefore often called *secondary*) because they are highly transferable, readily directed and redirected to many persons, and because they are narrowly circumscribed. For example, the relation between clerk and customer is a transferable one; each acts in standardized ways that are applicable to other clerks and other customers. Furthermore, the relation involves only those aspects of each person relevant to conducting a business transaction. To take account of another as a person instead of as a clerk or a customer is to become aware of many facets of the other's personality.

2. *Communication is deep and extensive.* In the primary relation few limits are placed on the range and the mode of communication. In nonprimary relations, communication is limited in more specific ways. In the primary relation, communication is often by nonverbal hints and cues as well as by words; feelings and needs are revealed that are hidden in public situations. Nonprimary relations are not meant to reveal the deeper layers of personality and tend to be restricted to formal and public modes of interaction. The depth of communication in primary relations is important because the expression of feelings and beliefs tends to influence the feelings and beliefs of others. Although communication does not guarantee agreement, it does facilitate and encourage it; and where communication is intimate and extensive, similar attitudes and feelings tend to develop. In nonprimary relations, though there may be agreement or understanding on some matters, it is not often carried over to other matters. In the primary relation, however, increased communication brings with it an increased opportunity for individuals to influence each other. Cooley emphasized the contribution of the primary group to the formation of character—for example, in the influence of parents upon children.

Primary relations do not presume unqualified affection and cordiality. All relationships involve tensions as well as positive responses, although they cannot long subsist

Each of these pictures is a study in personal relations, a blend of behavior defined by social roles and spontaneous person-to-person interaction. Spontaneity and intimacy afford opportunity for personal response and self-expression, but interaction is also governed and constrained by the situation, by the role, and by the past history of interpersonal experience.

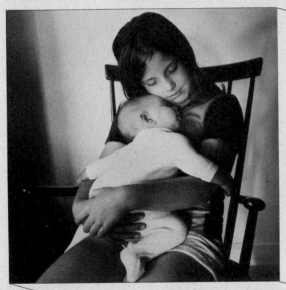

on antagonism alone. The primary relation entails a positive valuing of the other, a sense of belonging together and sharing a common identity. When a personal relation is characterized by antagonism, communication is hampered and response is usually limited to a part of the other's personality.

3. *Personal satisfactions are paramount.* Individuals enter into primary relations because such relations contribute to personal development, security, and well-being. In the primary relation, the individual is accepted for himself and not merely as a means to a practical objective. To the extent that a job gives psychological satisfaction, one may expect to find that primary relations have developed in the work situation.

Primary relations usually, but not necessarily, involve face-to-face interaction. Families, lovers, and friends may be separated physically yet maintain their primary relations. Obviously, many face-to-face settings are impersonal—for example, a courtroom. Hence being face-to-face should not be considered part of the definition of a primary relation (Faris, 1932:41–50). It is a congenial *condition* and a probable accompaniment rather than an essential feature.

The chief characteristics of the primary relation—response to whole persons, deep and extensive communication, and personal satisfactions—are observable when the quality of "primaryness" is most fully developed. In experience, primary groups vary from the ideal type. Most primary relations, even those between close friends, deviate in some ways from the primary-relations model.

THE PRIMARY GROUP

A group is primary insofar as it is based upon and sustains primary relations. Where people live or work together closely for some time, groups based on primary relations usually emerge. Families, play groups, and neighborhood cliques offer congenial conditions for primary-group development.

However, not all small groups are primary.

For example, a committee working together over a considerable time but composed of people of varying backgrounds, ages, and ranks may offer little opportunity for primary-group formation. Small size facilitates primary-group formation but in itself is not a sufficient condition.

On the other hand, largeness, although not a congenial condition, does not necessarily prevent formation of primary groups. Sociologists sometimes speak of whole communities as based on primary relations. The idea of *Gemeinschaft*, or "primary community," is discussed in Section Four.

Such diverse groups as families, soldier groups, boys' gangs, and factory cliques can be classified together because they are based to a significant extent on primary relations and perform functions normally expected of primary groups, such as giving the individual emotional support. Clearly, however, not all these groups protect or gratify the individual in the same way or to the same degree. A primary group within a factory can do some important things for the individual and can affect the factory organization, but it cannot do the family's job. Thus, a primary group can be understood only in the social context within which it has developed and in which it performs its functions.

The primary group is the main link between the individual and society. Because it serves the individual's personal needs, the primary group can fill society's function of getting the individual to want to work, or fight, or exercise self-restraint. Membership in a primary group lends emotional support which binds a person to the group and, through the group, to the aims of the larger society.

That same binding force, however, can weaken the tie between the individual and organized society. If the primary group—a street gang, for example—is not well integrated with the social order, the satisfactions it offers to the member may withdraw loyalty from the larger society. Therefore the contribution of the primary group to social cohesion cannot be taken for granted.

Children and the social bond in two settings: A rural commune and a Navajo family.

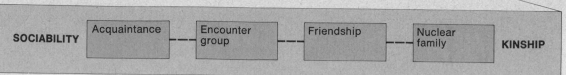

Figure 5:1
The continuum of commitment

The need of the individual for group support has long been recognized, and it is often used as a powerful instrument of social control. The extreme form of control based on this need is banishment, a technique regarded in some societies as equivalent to capital punishment. However, the severity of this punishment varies with the degree of personal isolation forced upon the individual. The individual's distress will be greatest when there is maximum isolation and least opportunity to create new primary relations. A political exile isolated from home ties may experience severe distress, but an exile accompanied by a retinue of followers is supported by continuing primary group ties.

Caution Because of this topic's connection with such experiences as love, friendship, and family life, the reader may mistakenly conclude that primary relations are necessarily good and nonprimary relations are somehow inherently bad. It is true that primary relations bear closely on personal satisfaction. This does not mean, however, that because a relation is primary it is desirable, nor that direct personal satisfaction is the only criterion of social worth.

In many situations, it is advantageous to maintain relatively impersonal, that is, secondary, relations. Much business, military, educational, and legal experience suggests the wisdom of formalizing relations in order, for example, to establish equality of treatment. Formalization permits decisions to be made with reference to the task at hand. Professional standards can be upheld or individuals assigned to hazardous duties without the pressure of personal claims on those in authority.

The relationship between faculty and students is an instance of the problem of formal v. primary relations. Both professors and students value informal and easy contacts; yet such contacts are engaged in with real risks. The professor who is too easily accessible may find it more difficult to make objective judgments about grades, or he or she may be suspected of being influenced by personal attachments. Because of this, many professors sacrifice part of their friendly relations with students rather than jeopardize impartiality and objectivity. The problem arises even more seriously for judges and other government officials. The long historic effort to achieve "a government of laws and not of men" reflects the social value of nonprimary relations in situations where objectivity is paramount.

From sociability to kinship Primary relations vary along a continuum that has pure sociability at one end and kinship at the other. At one extreme is a relatively casual encounter: strangers at a party or on an aircraft who hit it off and are able to respond to each other as persons, communicating easily and expressively. Slightly further to the right (Figure 5:1) is the more enduring group of people who enjoy each other's company and may sustain a friendship over a long period; yet the relationship may have little to support it beyond the immediate satisfactions of companionship. Further along the continuum are groups more securely anchored in personality and social structure. They have a greater psychic investment in the relationship, and the claims people have against each other are supported in law and custom. People who live together and depend upon one another are more likely to know each other intimately and are therefore more capable of responding to one another as whole persons than are mere friends.

These variations suggest that in analyzing primary groups, the context of commitment must always be considered. How much basis is there for an enduring relation? How dependent is the individual on the particular primary group? The primary relation may be undermined at both ends of the scale. Low commitment leads to partial and often superficial interaction. On the other hand, a very high degree of commitment may also weaken the primary relation. People who are locked into an involuntary relationship, because of kinship obligations or personal dependency, may not experience the freedom of response and openness of communication that characterizes the "ideal" primary relation.

Figure 5:1 places the encounter group (see Section Two) toward the low end of the continuum of commitment. The American nuclear family is placed toward the high end: There is a high degree of commitment, but there are strong voluntary elements and high expectations of personal fulfillment.

Figure 5:2 introduces an additional variable: intensity of interaction. The encounter group is marked by high interaction and low commitment. In the nuclear family, interaction and commitment are both high. Ties of kinship among people who do not live together may exhibit high commitment but low interaction. When both variables are low, there is hardly a relationship at all.

Personal networks and the sociogram Like all groups of significant duration, primary groups develop an internal structure, that is, a pattern of relatively stable relations or ways of behaving among the members. To some extent the structure of a group is a reflection of the feelings its members have toward one another as persons. One can imagine lines of attraction and repulsion between various members, holding the group together in some ways and pulling it apart in others. The sociometric test was devised to uncover these attractions and repulsions. It does this by asking the members of a group whom they would choose to play with or work with or to serve as a leader. Based on these responses, a sociogram may be constructed, as described in Adaptation 9. A parallel and somewhat more technical approach to the study of social networks has been developed, primarily by British social anthropologists and sociologists. (See Barnes, 1972.)

The group described in Adaptation 11 is a similar study of interpersonal networks. Whyte did not directly ask the Nortons questions such as "Who are your three best friends in this group?" However, his close observations of group interaction enabled him to plot the informal relations of the members and to relate specific behaviors (for instance, Long John's nightmares) to disruptions of primary-group relations.

Roethlisberger and Dickson (Adaptation 12) directly used sociometric techniques in their study of norms and informal controls in a work group. In mapping the group's

Figure 5:2
Commitment and
intensity of interaction

Intensity of interaction		Commitment	
		Low	High
	Low	Acquaintances Fellow passengers	Kin (dispersed)
	High	Encounter groups	Nuclear family

informal structure, the authors observed patterned conversations, arguments, clique behavior, and the like. They were thus able to describe how group norms emerge and how they are enforced.

Adaptation 9: The technique of the sociogram

Unless a group is very small, it is unlikely that even an astute and experienced observer will have a thorough grasp of the basic relationships without prolonged observation or the aid of objective measures. One technique for the objective presentation and interpretation of relations within groups is the *sociogram*, which shows the informal group structure, such as subgroup and friendship pat-

Procedure

(1) We wrote each chooser's name on the left-hand side of a slip of paper with an arrow pointing to the name of his first choice, which was written on the right-hand side.

(2) After a slip had been made for each choice, we sorted the slips of those who had named the same person as best friend. We found four subgroups, called *sets*, in which the same person had been named as best friend by several persons: William M, chosen by Donald, Skipper, Michael, Clinton, and Alfred; Alfred, chosen by William M and Morgan; Clinton, chosen by William R and Curtis; Robert, chosen by Charles, Herbert (and Sally).

(3) The set with the most slips (William M's) was arranged to converge on his name.

(4) William M chose Alfred, who was a member of another set. Because William M's and Alfred's choices were *mutual*, their slips were placed parallel to each other. The other choice in the second set (in this case Morgan's choice of Alfred) was placed in position with the first set.

(5) Another set which could be attached to the arrangement was Clinton's, and it was put in position.

(6) The fourth set (Robert's) did not attach to the other sets, and it was arranged by itself. Robert's choice was then placed in position.

Sociogram of first choices

(7) The remaining individual slips were fitted into the arrangement, and the sociogram of first choices was completed by sketching the arrangement as a diagram.

Sociogram of first and second choices

(8) The second choices were processed in the same way, but a rearrangement of the diagram was necessary to prevent an undue amount of crossing of choice lines. The completed sociogram of first and second choices is shown opposite.

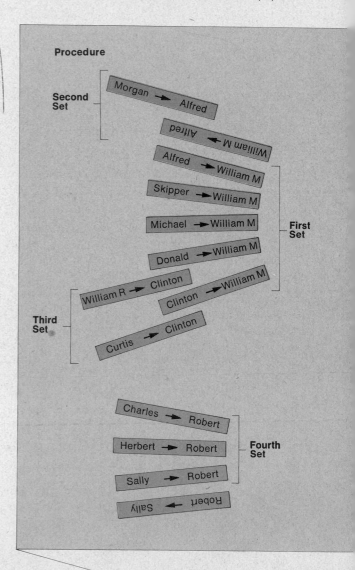

terns, and the position of each individual among his or her fellows. A sociogram is a preliminary step to understanding group action or individual action in a group setting. It may be used to summarize verbal choices, written choices, or the direct observations of a competent observer.

To prepare a sociogram, the student should gather data from a small group, preferably 12 or fewer in number, and follow through the basic steps outlined below. Questions about friendship, leadership, or some other characteristic could be asked. The questions depend entirely upon the problem to be investigated, but they must be phrased clearly and unambiguously. It is ad-

visable to pretest the questions to ensure that they ask what is intended. Students may measure their degree of insight into group relations by predicting the choices the members of the group will make and comparing them with the actual choices that were made.

As an exercise, we asked a third-grade class of 15 boys and 15 girls to "Write the name of the child you like best in this class," and then "the name of the child you like second best." For simplicity we shall explain the processing of the boys' choices only. It is not necessary to show the whole sociogram, because only three boys chose or were chosen by girls.

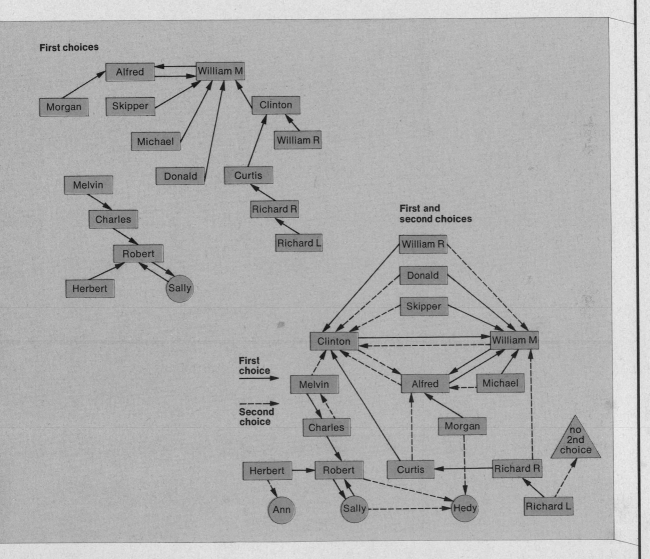

INTERPRETATION

1. The outstanding finding of the first choices is William M's position as the star. He received five first choices from the other 14 boys and two second choices. Clinton received two first choices and five second choices, making him a strong runner-up to William M. Between them they received 14 choices, and their choice of Alfred created a triangle, which dominates the sociogram. The three boys combined received 19 choices.

2. In the first-choice sociogram, there is one mutual choice, or pair, between boys—William M and Alfred—and one between a boy and a girl—Robert and Sally. Additional pairs show when the second choices are counted.

3. There is an island consisting of Melvin, Charles, Herbert, Robert (and Sally) on the first choices. In the second choices a bridge is thrown from the island to the main group of boys by Melvin's choice of Clinton, and there are additional ties between this group and the girls. The island has other girls who do not appear in the figure, and it is interesting that the girls in this group are only weakly integrated with the main group of girls.

4. There are seven isolates: Skipper, Michael, Herbert, Donald, Morgan, Richard L, and William R. These boys received no choices.

5. One error appears in Richard L's failure to make a second choice.

Note that such errors reduce the total number of choices made by the group.

APPLICATIONS AND LIMITATIONS

This example of friendship choices is only one of many possible uses of the sociogram. By comparing the patterning of choices on different criteria (athletic partner, study companion, etc.), the consistency and diversity of ratings in a group can be observed. Like any other research technique, the sociogram has its limitations.

1. Validity Responses are influenced by the subjects' willingness to record their true feelings. If the respondents lack confidence in the investigator or if the investigator shows a preference for certain individuals in the group, the results will probably be influenced. If some individuals resist responding or signing their names, the results are not likely to be valid.

2. Reliability A chart made at any given time is not necessarily a reliable indicator of relations at another time. Especially in groups of young children, there is evidence that relations are unstable. A series of sociograms would be needed to trace changes over a period of time and a retest within a short interval would be a useful reliability check.

3. Cues We have already mentioned the possibility of cues from the investigator's preferences. Other cues should be avoided, too. For example, the students should not be given alphabetical lists of the group members. It is common knowledge that the order in which names appear on a ballot affects the number of votes candidates receive.

4. Privacy The group members should be confident that their choices will be kept secret. If respondents are not assured of privacy, their choices may be clouded by anxiety or may reflect some factor other than the criterion asked for.

5. Applicability The sociogram is especially useful in well-defined and limited groups. A small living group, such as a dormitory or commune, would provide a good experimental setting.

6. Limitation The sociogram is a beginning and not an end. It is usually a first step in the analysis of leadership, morale, popularity, or another aspect of group dynamics.

Section two intimacy and encounter

From the standpoint of the individual, primary groups have a dual significance: (1) They are havens or refuges affording comfort and security and (2) they are settings within which the main dramas of an individual's personal life take place.

THE GROUP AS HAVEN

In the primary relation uniqueness counts. The individual believes that he is accepted and wanted for himself. Ideally, he does not need to be on guard, or prove himself, or put forth his best effort. Therefore primary relations offer a refuge from an outside world that is impersonal, achievement-centered, and universalistic. Primary relations are, in principle, particularistic. What counts is who you are and whom you know.

Adaptation 10 analyzes the quality of friendship in the black ghetto of Washington, D.C., and describes a hunger for enduring ties that offer promise of protection and, perhaps, a feeling of belonging. The account suggests that economic poverty tends to produce impoverished human relations. Friendships are fluid and unreliable when people lack resources and the stability of homes, jobs, and steady incomes.

One way the primary group protects the individual is by modifying goals and rules, adapting them to the person's special capacities and circumstances. For example, parents may blunt the school's effectiveness by requiring only minimum achievement of their children. Or they may support the standards of the school by helping their children to compensate for learning difficulties or to develop special talents. Home is the place where excuses can be arranged to moderate the impact of impersonal rules.

In the case study reported in Adaptation 12, the solidarity of a group of employees limited the effectiveness of management's production standards. In gaining some control over the way rules were administered and standards set, the group could reduce the individual worker's dependence on a distant and impersonal authority.

Peer groups and social control Among children and adolescents, a characteristic group haven is the association of age-mates. Technically, the term *peer group* refers to any collectivity that is homogeneous in some respect, especially age or status. But the concept has special relevance for understanding young people. The youth peer group is a refuge from the adult world, a community which, by virtue of age and dependency, shares a common experience. It is a setting within which strong attachments may be formed, in contrast to adult peer groups, which are more attuned to sociability.

Peer-group solidarity and protection is gained at the price of conformity. This is apparent among children at school (see *EDUCATION*) and is well supported by laboratory studies (Asch, 1956; Sherif, 1936).

The study of gangs and delinquent subcultures (see *CULTURE*, p. 74) shows that to a large extent delinquency is supported by the satisfactions and pressures of peer-group relations. On the basis of these conclusions, some efforts have been made in the correction of delinquency to design programs that build upon the peer group.

One such experiment was carried out in Provo, Utah, where a group of 20 habitual offenders were assigned by the juvenile court to a daytime treatment center instead of being placed on probation or sent to the reformatory. The boys were thus under the control of the court and their participation in the program was mandatory. A unique feature of the program was the deliberate creation of a powerful peer group among the boys.

Attempts to involve a boy with the peer group begin the moment he arrives. Instead of meeting with and receiving an orientation lecture from authorities, he receives no formal instructions. . . . Adults will not orient him in ways that he has grown to expect, nor will they answer any of his questions. He is forced to turn to his peers (Empey and Rabow, 1961:686).

The group was given a great deal of power. Daily group discussions were the core of the program in its first phase, supplemented by work in the community. The group was free to exert strong pressure on the individual; it had a say in deciding when a boy should be released; it participated actively with the staff in solving problems and exercising controls. In the discussions, the boys' values and attitudes were subjected to severe testing. Since the focus was on self-revelation and problem solving, the tendency of the group was to move itself and the boy toward greater realism about the outcome of continued delinquency.

In the Provo experiment, official delinquency rates for boys in the program were considerably lower than for a comparison (control) group of boys placed on probation and almost as low as for boys sent to the reformatory. (Delinquencies occurred among the reformatory boys because some were escapees or were on work leave or furlough.) A follow-up study after four years showed that the experimental group did much better than boys who had been incarcerated, but not much better than boys placed on probation (Empey and Erickson, 1972). Such experiments represent a radical departure from the traditional approach of corrections, which has emphasized the need to protect authority by espousing the norm of "doing your own time" and isolating the prisoner from sustained group interaction (Cloward, 1960).

ENCOUNTER, FULFILLMENT, AND STRESS

The primary relation is the setting for intense interaction. When people respond to one another as whole persons and try to communicate with openness and intimacy, they let down barriers and extend the range of permissible contacts. Openness brings with it opportunity for a growing relationship, for a wider range of deeply felt experiences; but there are also risks of failure and rejection. A common form of rejection occurs when one person is open and vulnerable while the other remains defensive and distant, refusing to become involved.

Since so much may be at stake for the person—especially one who is committed to or dependent upon a particular relationship—signs of stress are not unusual. In Adaptation 11, Long John's psychological difficulties are traced to a change in social relationships. Long John had been identified as Doc's pal until Doc left the Norton Street gang for Spongi's gang. No longer thought of as Doc's pal among the Nortons and unable to establish an identity with Spongi, Long John lost self-confidence and his bowling skill deteriorated. He was unprotected by his old identity and became an object of attack by his old gang. His difficulties persisted until Doc identified Long John as his pal in the new gang.

Encounter groups The psychic costs of interaction lead many people to withdraw and build up barriers, even within the primary group. As a result, they do not experience the full contribution of primary relations to personal fulfillment. In recent years, increasing numbers of people, mostly middle-class, have participated in a deliberate effort to break through interpersonal barriers and find an experience that more nearly approximates the implicit ideal of the primary relation. The form of this effort is the encounter group.

A leader of the encounter-group movement has this to say about what motivates people to join encounter groups:

I believe it is a hunger for something the person does not find in his work environment, in his church, certainly not in his school or college, and sadly enough, not even in modern family life. It is a hunger for relationships which are close and real; in which feelings and emotions can be spontaneously expressed without first being carefully censored or bottled up; where deep experiences—disappointments and joys—can be shared; where new ways of behaving can be risked and tried out; where, in a word, he approaches the state where all is known and all accepted, and thus further growth becomes possible (Rogers, 1970:10–11).

Although encounter groups have spread rapidly, there are no reliable figures on the number of participants. More important, it is not known how significant the experience is for most participants, nor what the effects are of differing styles of group leadership and group interaction (Lieberman et al., 1971).

The encounter group is a form of organized spontaneity. A facilitative leader and general guidelines usually lend pattern to the interaction. Most groups emphasize verbal interchange; some are also interested in sensory awareness. The Synanon "game," developed for drug addicts but extended to the "square" world, is perhaps the most extreme in encouraging verbal assaults on group members. All of the groups try to find devices for breaking through personal defenses.

The word *encounter* has two connotations that convey the spirit of the group experience. One meaning suggests a confrontation, an adversary meeting. The other connotation is that the meeting is casual and unplanned. Together, these meanings imply that the encounter-group experience demands directness and spontaneity. It requires putting aside masks and getting through human defenses. But this is done in a context of informality, as an indirect outcome of open interaction. The encounter is not meant to be an exercise in brainwashing, stripping, or mortification, although some groups come perilously close.

Social research suggests that participation in encounter groups can be hazardous for some people. In a study of 170 students who completed 30 hours in encounter groups under observation, it was found that 16 subjects suffered psychological consequences that were sufficiently negative and enduring to justify classifying them as casualties.

A major finding of the study is that the number and severity of casualties and the manner in which the casualties sustained injury are all highly dependent upon the particular type of encounter group. Some leadership styles result in a high-risk group. Particularly stressful is a leader style which is characterized by intrusive, aggressive stimulation, by high charisma, by high challenging and confrontation of each of the members and by authoritarian control. . . . Individuals who are psychologically vulnerable and who overinvest their hopes in the magic of salvation of encounter groups are particularly vulnerable when they interact with leaders who believe that they can offer deliverance (Yalom and Lieberman, 1971:28, 30).

The encounter group is characteristically a collection of strangers who have little to do with each other outside of the group. In this respect, encounter groups differ markedly from primary groups that presume a wider sharing and a deeper commitment. On the continuum of commitment, from sociability to kinship, the encounter group must be placed toward the sociability end of the scale. In this sense, the encounter group is limited in the contribution it can make to personal well-being. It provides a setting where defenses are down, but it lacks the organic, developmental quality of the more fully realized primary group in which experience dictates that the self will be protected.

Adaptation 10 Liebow: The view from Tally's corner

Tally Jackson was an habitué of the New Deal Carry-out Shop — a neighborhood food store and

Source: Abridged and adapted from *Tally's Corner: A Study of Negro Streetcorner Men* by Elliot Liebow (Boston: Little, Brown, 1967), chap. 6. Published in this form by permission of the author and Little, Brown.

eating place in a blighted section of downtown Washington, D.C. The Carry-out Shop was a point of entry for a participant-observer study of the day-to-day lives of 24 adult black men. The subjects of the study were neither derelicts nor stable partici-

pants in the work force, but casual and unskilled workers, frequently unemployed. The field work was done during 1962 and 1963.

At the Carry-out Shop, food is taken out or eaten standing up because there is no place to sit down. But in the 10-by-12-foot customer area, there are wall space and other leaning facilities where the Carry-out's customers gather for business and pleasure. On top of the cigarette machine, for example, the Carry-out's numbers-man-in-residence conducts his business dealings with the white numbers backer who comes daily to settle accounts with him and with other numbers men from the neighborhood.

Even in a social area characterized by rootlessness and instability, each person has a network of interpersonal relations, and these often assume the character of kinship although no kin ties may be involved. The networks do not add up to a single coherent group, but rather consist of loose and shifting interrelations. Friendships are quickly made, and they are invested with an apparent significance that would take much longer to develop in a more stable social environment. To give their relationships more meaning and depth, the men sometimes create fictional bonds of kinship and sometimes assume imaginary backgrounds and personal ties of long duration. Friendships may dissolve as quickly as they develop. This is an account of the nature and fate of primary relations in a social environment not conducive to stable and prolonged social interactions.

FRIENDS AND NETWORKS

Perhaps more than most other social worlds, the street corner world takes its shape and color from face-to-face relations of the people who live in it. On the street corner, each man has his own network of interpersonal ties: a weblike arrangement of man-to-man and man-to-woman relationships in which he is selectively attached in a particular way to a definite number of persons.

At the edges of this network are those persons with whom his relationship is emotionally neutral, such as area residents whom he has seen around but does not know except to nod or say "Hi" to as they pass on the street. Responses to these persons are limited to simple recognition.

In toward the center are those persons he knows

and likes best, with whom he is "up tight":[1] his "walking buddies," good or best friends, girl friends, and sometimes real or supposed kinsmen. These are the people with whom he is in more or less daily, face-to-face contact and to whom he turns for emergency aid, comfort, or support in time of need or crisis. He gives to them and receives from them goods and services in the name of friendship. Routinely he seeks them out and is sought out by them. They serve his need to be with others of his kind and to be recognized as a unique human being, and he in turn serves them the same way. They are his audience and his fellow actors.

It is with these men and women that he spends his waking, nonworking hours, drinking, dancing, engaging in sex, playing the fool or the wise man, passing the time at the Carry-out or on the street corner, talking about nothing and everything, about epistemology or Cassius Clay, about the nature of numbers or how he would have it made if he could have a steady job that paid him $60 a week with no layoffs.

Friendship is sometimes anchored in kinship, sometimes in long-term associations which may reach back into childhood. Other close friendships are born locally, in the street-corner world itself, rather than brought in by men from the outside. Such friendships are built on neighbor or co-worker relationships, or on a shared experience or other event or situation which brings two people together in a special way.

In general, close friendships tend to develop out of associations with those who are already in one's network of personal relationships: relatives, men and women who live in the area and spend much of their time on the street or in public places, and co-workers. The result is that the street-corner man tends to use the same individuals over and over again: He may make a friend, neighbor, and co-worker of his kinsman, or a friend, co-worker, and kinsman of his neighbor.

THE KINSHIP MODEL

One of the most striking aspects of these overlapping relationships is the blurring of kinship and friendship. Most of the men and women on the

---

[1] This usage deviates from the nonghetto "hip" idiom.

street corner are unrelated to one another and only a few have kinsmen in the immediate area. Nevertheless, kinship ties are frequently manufactured to explain, account for, or even validate friend relationships. One can begin with kinship and build on this, or conversely, begin with friendship and build a kin relationship.

The most common form of the pseudokin relation is known as "going for brothers." This means, simply, that two men agree to present themselves as brothers to the outside world and to deal with one another as brothers. Going for brothers appears as a special case of friendship in which the claims, obligations, expectations, and loyalties of the friend relationship are publicly declared to be at their maximum.

Only the most important members of one's personal network can distinguish between real and pseudokin relationships, partly because the question of whether two men are really brothers or are simply going for brothers is not considered relevant. The important thing for people to know in their interaction with the two men is that they say they are brothers, whether they are or not.

Pseudokinship ties are also invoked in certain man-woman relationships. "Going for cousins" avoids the implication of romantic or sexual connection. Indeed, this seems to be the primary purpose behind going for cousins. It is a way of saying, "This woman (or man) and I are good friends, but we are not lovers." Given the taboo against cousin marriage, going for cousins permits an unrelated man and women to enter into a close-friend relationship without threatening their actual romantic or sexual attachments. It is a public disclaimer of romantic or sexual content in a cross-sex, close-friend relationship.

Sometimes pseudokinship is relied on to sharpen and lend structure to a relationship which is otherwise vague. Occasionally, one hears "He just calls her his sister," or "They just call it brother and sister," or even "They just go for brother and sister." Such was the case of a man whose young daughter was living with a married woman. In caring for his child, the woman was, of course, doing what sisters sometimes do. The assignment of the label *sister* to one performing a function frequently associated with that label was an easy step to take. A vague relationship was rendered specific; it was simplified, and the need

for explanations was reduced. This may also have served to discourage public suspicion about the nature of the relationship. In these respects, perhaps, going for cousins would have served them equally well. And, as in the case of going for brothers, whether they were in fact brother and sister was less important than the fact that they called themselves so. The woman's husband, we must assume, knew they were not related. But because they called themselves brother and sister, the husband's vested interests and public status were not jeopardized.

MUTUAL AID

Most friendships are thus born in propinquity, in relationships or situations in which individuals confront one another day by day and face to face. These friendships are nurtured and supported by an exchange of money, goods, services, and emotional support. Small loans, ranging from a few pennies up to two or three dollars, are constantly being asked for and extended. Although records of debts and credits are not ostensibly made, in fact debts are remembered and claimed in time of need or when friendships break down.

Each person plays an important part in helping and being helped by those in his network. Since much of the cooperation between friends centers around basic daily activities, friends are of special importance to a sense of physical and emotional security. The more friends one has or believes himself to have, and the deeper he holds these friendships to be, the greater his self-esteem and the greater the esteem for himself he thinks he sees in the eyes of others.

The pursuit of security and self-esteem pushes him to romanticize his perception of his friends and friendships. He wants to see acquaintances as friends, and not only as friends but as friends with whom he is up tight, walking buddies, best friends, or even brothers. He prefers to see the movement of money, goods, services, and emotional support between friends as flowing freely out of loyalty and generosity and according to need, rather than as mutual exchange resting on a quid pro quo basis. He wants to believe that his friendships reach back into the distant past and have an unlimited future, that he knows and is known by his friends intimately, that they can trust one another implicitly, and that their loyalties to one another are almost unbounded.

Friendship is at its romantic, flamboyant best when things are going well for the persons involved. But friendship does not often stand up well to the stress of crisis or conflict of interest, when demands tend to be heaviest and most insistent. Everyone knows this. Extravagant pledges of aid and comfort between friends are, at one level, made and received in good faith. But at another level, fully aware of his friends' limited resources and the demands of their self-interest, each person is ultimately prepared to look to himself alone.

The recognition that, at bottom, friendship is not a bigger-than-life relationship is sometimes expressed as a repudiation of all would-be friends. There may be a cynical denial that friendship as a system of mutual aid and support exists at all.

INSTABILITY

A similar attitude leads to the assessment of friendship as a fair-weather phenomenon. Attitudes toward friends and friendships are thus always shifting, frequently ambivalent, and sometimes contradictory. One moment, friendship is an almost sacred covenant; the next, it is the locus of cynical exploitation: "Friends are good only for money."

These shifts and apparent contradictions arise from the fact that, at any given moment, the relationships that comprise an individual's network may be at widely different stages of development or degeneration. They arise, too, from the easy quickness with which a casual encounter can ripen into an intense man–man or man–woman relationship and the equal ease with which these relationships break down under stress.

The overall picture is one of a broad web of interlocking, overlapping networks in which the incumbents are constantly shifting and changing positions relative to one another. This fluidity is reflected in neighbor, kin, family, and household relationships—indeed, in the whole social structure of the street-corner world which rests to so large an extent precisely on the primary, face-to-face relationships of the personal network of the individual.

FICTIONAL HISTORIES

In support of the economic, social, and psychological forces arrayed against the stability of personal networks is the intrinsic weakness of friendship itself. Whether as cause, effect, or both, the fact is that friendships are not often rooted in long-term associations nor do the persons involved necessarily know anything of one another's personal history prior to their association. The man would like to think—and sometimes says—that his friendship with so-and-so goes back several years or even into childhood, but this is not often so. Their relationship rests almost entirely in the present. A man may have detailed knowledge of his friend's present circumstances and connections but little else.

He knows, from looking into himself, the gross characteristic features of the friend's personal history. He knows his friend was raised principally by women and that he holds these women dear, that he was brought up to love and fear God, that he had little formal education, that he has few if any job skills and has worked in different towns and cities, that in one or more of these towns he fathered a child whom he has probably never seen, that he first came here because he has an uncle or aunt here, or because he met this girl, or because he heard about this job, or because he was wanted by the police or someone else. But he does not know the particulars. He does not know whether it was his friend's mother, grandmother, or father's sister who raised him, how far he went in school, which towns and which cities he lived and worked in, and what crucial experiences he had there. Much of this comes out as unsolicited, incidental information in the course of casual talk and hanging around, but much does not. Especially lacking is an exchange of secret thoughts or private hopes and fears.

Friendship thus appears as a relationship between two people who, in an important sense, stand unrevealed to one another. Lacking depth in both past and present, friendship is easily uprooted by the tug of economic or psychological self-interest or by external forces acting against it.

The recognition of this weakness, coupled with the importance of friendship as a source of security and self-esteem, is surely a principal source of the impulse to romanticize relationships, to upgrade them, to elevate to friendship what others see as a casual acquaintanceship, and to upgrade friendship to close friendship. It is this, perhaps, that lies behind the attempt to ascribe a past to a relationship that never had one and to borrow from the bony structure of kinship (going for brothers) to lend support to a relationship sorely in need of it. It is as if friendship is an artifact of desire, a wish relationship, a private agreement between two people to act "as if," rather than a real relationship between persons.

141

*Adaptation 11
Whyte: Stress
and status in
street-corner
society*

Adaptation 11 Whyte: Stress and status in street-corner society

A stable and satisfying pattern of primary relations is of critical importance to self-security. In the following account of street corner groups, psychological difficulties and a breakdown in performance are traced to the disturbance of interpersonal relations.

The account is presented in the first person by the author. It concerns two street corner groups — the Norton Street gang and Spongi's gang — and the difficulties of two of their members, Long John and Doc.

LONG JOHN'S NIGHTMARES

Long John's position in the Norton Street gang was ambiguous. Although he was close friends with the Norton leaders, Doc, Danny, and Mike, and shared some of their prestige, he was not a leader himself and had little influence over the rank and file of the gang.

When Doc and Danny left the Norton Street gang to join Spongi's gang and Mike drifted away, the Nortons regrouped under the leadership of Angelo, a previous follower. Long John divided his time between Spongi's and the Norton Street gang, but the realignment of the two groups placed him in a new and vulnerable position.

Those who hung around Spongi's joint (a local gambling house) were divided into an inner circle and the hangers-on. Danny, Doc, and three others were in the inner circle. When Spongi went for "coffee and," for a drive, or to the movies, he would invite them, but not Long John. Long John was excluded from the inner circle.

Without the support of Doc, Danny, and Mike, Long John lost his old standing among the boys who remained on Norton Street. Long John's bowling soon deteriorated, and he finished next to last in the individual competition that season. The first part of the next season brought no improvement. Doc and Danny, who still occasionally bowled, would say to him, "Well, it looks like you're not the man you used to be. This year maybe you won't be good enough to make the first team."

These remarks were made in a joking manner, but they were symptomatic of the changes in personal relations that had taken place. As if they sensed Long John's defenseless position, the Nortons redoubled their verbal attacks on him. They had always attacked him more than they attacked Doc, Danny, or Mike, but now they subjected him to an unrelenting barrage that was calculated to destroy his self-confidence. When he was bowling poorly, there was little Long John could say to defend himself.

One afternoon Doc came to consult me about Long John. He had confided to Doc that he had not slept well for several weeks. As Doc said, "I talked it over with him. . . . Whenever he gets half-asleep and the sheet comes up over his face, he wakes up thinking he's dead. . . ." I suggested to Doc that he might be able to dispel Long John's anxieties if he took him into Spongi's inner circle

Source: Abridged and adapted from *Street Corner Society* by William Foote Whyte (Chicago: University of Chicago Press, 1943), especially pp. 3–25 and 255–268. Published in this form by permission of William Foote Whyte and University of Chicago Press. The second edition issued in 1955 contains an extended appendix describing the field research methods used in the study.

and if he and Danny began to defend Long John's bowling and encourage him when the others attacked him. Doc was doubtful but agreed to try. Within a short time he had fitted Long John into Spongi's inner circle. As he explained:

I didn't say anything to Spongi, but I already fitted with him. I just made a lot of noise about Long John. If he wasn't around, I would ask the boys where he was. When he came in, I would say to him, "Here's Long John, the dirty bum," and I would ask him where he had been. I gave him so much attention that he moved in there right away. Spongi began asking him to go places with us. Now even when I'm not around John is right in there.

At the same time Doc and Danny began to support him at the bowling alleys. Long John's bowling began to improve. In a short time he was bowling as well as he had in the season of 1937–1938. In the individual competition that climaxed the 1939–1940 season, he won the first prize. He never again consulted Doc about his nightmares.

DOC'S DIZZY SPELLS

Doc's dizzy spells came upon him when he was unemployed and had no spending money. He considered this the cause of his difficulties and, in a sense, it was. But many Cornerville men adjust themselves to being unemployed without serious difficulties. Why was Doc so different? To say that he was particularly sensitive is to name the phenomenon without explaining it. The observation of Doc's changing patterns of primary-group relations provides the explanation.

Doc was accustomed to a high frequency of interaction with the members of his group and to frequent contacts with members of other groups. While he sometimes directly originated action for his group, usually someone would suggest a course of action, and then Doc would get the boys together and organize group activity. In 1938 Doc decided to run for the state legislature (he later withdrew from the campaign). The events of Doc's political campaign indicate that his usual pattern of interactions had broken down. Mike appointed himself Doc's campaign manager and was continually telling Doc what to do about the campaign. At the same time I was telling him what to do about getting a job. However, while we were suggesting action for him with increasing frequency, he himself was unable to originate action in group events. Lacking money, he could

not participate in group activities without accepting the support of others and letting them determine his course of action. Since such a pattern conflicted with Doc's image of himself as a leader, he avoided associating with his friends on many occasions. When he was alone, he did not get dizzy, but when he was with a group of people and unable to act in his customary manner, he fell prey to the dizzy spells.

When Doc finally got a job as the director of a recreation center, the spells disappeared. He was once again able to organize action, first for the boys in his center but also for his own corner boys. Since he had money, he could again associate with his friends and could also broaden his contacts. When the job and money ran out in the winter of 1939–1940, the pattern of interaction on which Doc was dependent was once more upset. The dizzy spells came back, and shortly before Doc got a WPA job in the spring of 1941, he had what his friends called a nervous breakdown. When I visited Cornerville in May 1941, he was once again beginning to overcome the dizzy spells. He discussed his difficulties with me:

When I'm batted out, I'm not on the corner so much. And when I am on the corner, I just stay there. I can't do what I want to do. If the boys want to go to a show or to Jennings or bowling, I have to count my pennies to see if I have enough. If I'm batted out, I have to make some excuse. . . . I don't want to ask anybody for anything. Sometimes I say to Danny or Spongi, "Do you want a cigarette?" They say, "No, we've got some," and then I say, "All right, I'll have one of yours." I make a joke out of it, but still it is humiliating. I never do that except when I'm desperate for a cigarette. Danny is the only one that ever gives me money.

I have thought it all over, and I know I only have these spells when I'm batted out. I'm sorry you didn't know me when I was really active around here. I was a different man then. I was always taking the girls out. I lent plenty of money. I spent my money. I was always thinking of things to do and places to go.

CONCLUSION

Whyte's cases illuminate the importance of primary-group support for individual security. They suggest that individual security is not merely a matter of belonging. Long John and Doc always belonged; neither was ever ostracized, but their old ways of belonging were upset.

The study indicates that even though primary

relations approximate free, personal, and spontaneous conditions, they are nevertheless patterned and structured in definite social ways. Patterning was based on social rank. When Long John and Doc were deprived of their social rank, they were also deprived of those particular interpersonal relations that had been satisfying and supporting.

Whyte's study also suggests that personal maladjustment occurs within a social context and can be aggravated or ameliorated by changes within the individual's social situation. Doc helped to cure Long John's nightmares by changing his social situation. By bringing him into Spongi's inner circle, Doc reestablished the close relationship between Long John, Danny, and himself. In so doing, he protected Long John from the aggressions of Doc's former followers. Then Long John's emotional troubles disappeared, and he again acted with the self-assurance that had previously characterized his behavior.

Doc showed that he was well aware of the nature of his own difficulties, but understanding was not enough to cure him. He needed to act in the manner to which he had grown accustomed. When that was impossible, he was socially maladjusted. A man with low standing in the group, one accustomed to rely on others to initiate group activities, would have experienced far less difficulty in coping with the problem of having no money. The dependence would have fitted in with the pattern of his behavior in the group. Because Doc had been a leader of the corner boys, there was conflict between the behavior appropriate to that position and the behavior necessitated by his penniless condition. Not until this conflict was resolved could Doc master his dizzy spells.

Section three small groups and large organizations

The large, impersonal organization has been called the "representative institution" of modern life. The sociological study of such organizations is discussed in ASSOCIATIONS, where the phrase *informal structure* is used to denote those patterns that arise from the spontaneous interaction of personalities and groups within the organization. This section considers the effect of group dynamics on the capacity of the organization to do its job effectively and meet the needs of employees or members.

When individuals relate to each other as persons rather than according to their assigned roles, they tend to initiate primary relations. A characteristic outcome is the formation of friendships and cliques. The significance of this process is that *new lines of communication and influence* develop that are not provided for in the officially approved patterns. For example, information may be passed among friends even though they are not entitled to it according to the rules. Or an individual in a subordinate position may have personal and informal access to a high official over the head of an immediate superior.

Since the goals of large organizations are impersonal, individual needs tend to be subordinated. On the other hand, because the members are not merely members but persons as well, they want to be treated as unique individuals and not as impersonal instruments. They try to establish personal relations with other participants, and if they fail to do so they may feel uneasy and vulnerable.

An obvious way of overcoming impersonality is to make friends with the boss or with workmates. As described in Adaptation 12, the Hawthorne wiremen banded together informally as a defense against possible arbitrary action by management. Groups of this kind are havens within which the individual's personal needs are taken into account. For example, if a worker is occasionally unable to work effectively, the group will protect him or her. On the other hand, the worker pays a price for protection and must abide by the informal norms set by the group.

DOUBLE-EDGED SIGNIFICANCE OF THE PRIMARY GROUP

Primary groups may either support or undermine the officially approved pattern of communication and command. They may help to mobilize the participants for the achievement of prescribed goals, or, on the other hand, they may have a subversive effect. An illustration of subversion, from the standpoint of management, is the case of the Hawthorne wiremen, whose activities resulted in a self-determined restriction of output. All primary relations and groupings are potentially subversive of large-scale organizations because the special goals or interests of the group, and the effects of group participation on the members tend to take priority, at least some of the time, over the official goals of the organization.

Adaptation 13 discusses the effects of small-group cohesion on high-level policy makers. Decisions in large organizations are often made by committees or task groups. Such groups are no less affected by the dynamics of personal interaction than are small groups of low-level workers. The result is often excessive conformity, game playing, self-protection, wishful thinking, and other distortions of rational decision making.

THE MEDIATING PRIMARY GROUP

Frequently the capacity of a large organization to mobilize and control members is increased if the members belong to it through a primary group. Such primary groups have a mediating function, binding the individual firmly into a larger social structure much as the family mediates between the individual and the larger society. The stronger the mediating primary group, the firmer the bond between the organization and the individual.

It should not be assumed that mediating primary groups are indispensable to the functioning of organizations. Many enterprises do not fully mobilize the energies and loyalties of their employees or members yet accomplish their purposes reasonably well. However, when ordinary incentives are inadequate, the individual's attachment to a mediating primary group may encourage greater participation and even personal sacrifice.

Soldier groups The role of mediating primary groups received special attention in a study of cohesion and disintegration in the Nazi army of World War II (Shils and Janowitz, 1948). Although outnumbered and inferior in equipment, the German soldiers maintained their fighting effectiveness despite the fact that they were being badly beaten. The extraordinary tenacity of the German army during that period had frequently been attributed to the strong Nazi political convictions of the German soldiers. The results of the study indicated, however, that military solidarity was only indirectly and partially based on political convictions. For the ordinary German soldier, the decisive fact was his membership in a squad or section. If he had the necessary weapons, he was likely to go on fighting as long as the group had a leadership with which he could identify and as long as he gave affection to and received affection from the other members of his squad. In other words, where conditions allowed primary-group life to

Individual	Mediating group	Larger organization
Housewife	Family	Church
Employee	Work group	Company
Soldier	Squad	Army
Student	Living group	University

Figure 5:3
Mediating primary groups

Primary groups offer to the individual personal affection and response as well as protection from arbitrary rules. If the primary group is effectively linked to a larger organization, it can heighten participation, but if the link is broken, morale and discipline may suffer.

function and where the primary group developed a high degree of cohesion, morale was maintained regardless of the political attitudes of the soldiers.

The stability and effectiveness of the military primary group depended in large measure on the Nazi hard core, who approximated 10 to 15 percent of the total of enlisted men; the percentage was higher for non-commissioned officers and very much higher among the junior officers. The presence in the group of a few such men provided a model for the less committed men, and threats by the hard core served to check divisive tendencies. Although political ideology was not important to most soldiers, the hard core provided the link between the ordinary soldier in his primary group and the political leadership of the German army and state.

Studies of morale among American soldiers during World War II and the Korean War also stressed the contribution of solidarity at the level of the squad and the platoon (Stouffer et al., 1949:105–191; Shils, 1950:16–39; Little, 1964). A study of combat soldiers in Vietnam, however, concluded that the rotation system, under which military personnel served a definite 12-month tour of duty in Vietnam, tended to limit the development of primary-group ties. The rotation system reinforced a perspective that was "essentially private and self-concerned," especially as the soldier approached the end of his tour in Vietnam (Moskos, 1970:142–143).

The Vietnam study also stressed the significance of self-interest in primary-group solidarity:

At least in Vietnam, the instrumental and self-serving aspects of primary relations in combat units must be more fully appreciated. If the individual soldier is realistically to improve his survival chances, he must necessarily develop and take part in primary-group relations. . . . In other words, under the extreme conditions of ground warfare, an individual's survival is directly related to the support—moral, physical, and technical—he can expect from his fellow soldiers. He gets such support largely to the degree that he reciprocates to the others in his group in general, and to his buddy in particular (Moskos, 1970:145).

The cohesion of the combat primary group is a response to the urgent needs of a specific situation. Characteristically, no lasting commitments are formed. When the soldier leaves his unit, the relationship is ended. "The rupture of communication is mutual despite protestations of lifelong friendship during the shared combat period" (Moskos, 1970:146).

145

Adaptation 12
Roethlisberger
and Dickson:
The bank-wiring
room

Adaptation 12 Roethlisberger and Dickson: The bank-wiring room

Between 1927 and 1932 an extensive program of studies on employee satisfaction was carried out at the Western Electric Company's Hawthorne plant in Chicago.[2] The data for these studies included management records of production, absenteeism, and labor turnover; on-the-spot observation and recordtaking; and an extensive and long-range interview program with management and workers.

The investigation reported here is one part of the famous Hawthorne studies, which had an important influence on industrial sociology. The interpersonal relations and social organization of a small group of factory workers are analyzed. These men wired telephone switchboards in what the company called the "bank-wiring room."

[2] The research was a joint activity of the company and the Harvard Graduate School of Business Administration. The Hawthorne studies have been subject to continuing evaluation and criticism. See Landsberger, 1958; Sykes, 1965; Carey, 1967; Parsons, 1974.

Source: Abridged and adapted from *Management and the Worker* by F. J. Roethlisberger and W. J. Dickson (Cambridge: Harvard University Press, 1939), Part IV. Published in this form by permission of the authors and Harvard University Press.

THE SETTING

For six months, detailed observation was made of a group of 14 men in the bank-wiring room. The work group consisted of nine wiremen, three solderers, and two inspectors. A completed job involved three main types of work: (1) A wireman connected the projecting points of banks, (2) a solderer fixed the connections in place, and (3) an inspector tested the work of both men. The wired banks were assembled into a final product called an "equipment," which was ten or eleven banks long and two or three banks high.

MANAGEMENT'S INCENTIVE SYSTEM

The men worked under a system of group piece-work. Part of their weekly earnings was based upon the number of equipments turned out by the group as a whole during the week. The wage incentive plan had three principal elements:

• Every man was assigned an hourly wage rate based largely upon his own average individual output established by past performance. His basic hourly rate multiplied by the number of hours he worked constituted a worker's basic individual weekly wage. His basic wage was guaranteed by the company irrespective of group output.

• The basic wage was supplemented by a bonus which depended upon the number of equipments the group as a whole had completed during the week. If group output went above a certain level, each man received his share of the increased earnings.

• Since individual hourly wage rates were based upon a man's average output per hour, allowance was made for time lost by stoppages beyond his control. Otherwise the efficiency ratings of men who had been delayed would suffer when compared with ratings of men who had lost little time.

This wage incentive plan assumed that the men wanted to maximize their earnings. Therefore it was expected:

1. Since each individual's total wage was determined to some degree by group output, each worker would try to increase output.

2. If the workers exerted pressure at all, it would be to increase the output of the slower workers.

3. To increase his hourly wage rate, each worker would strive to increase his individual average output.

The plan also assumed a high degree of cooperation between employees and management. Efficiency ratings, for example, were meant to assure a fair distribution of wages. In order to establish efficiency ratings, however, it was necessary to keep detailed records, both of individual output and of time lost. The plan could be fair, therefore, only if the employees did not thwart management's efforts at objective recordkeeping.

Management's wage incentive plan was a workable one, promoting both efficiency and a fair distribution of earnings, only if the men acted in accordance with management's assumptions.

RESTRICTION OF OUTPUT

Actually, the men behaved quite differently. They had their own idea of a proper day's work—about two completed equipments per man—and they felt that no more should be turned out. So far as the company was concerned, total output was satisfactory, and the foreman felt that his "boys" worked hard. Nevertheless, the men had adopted an informal norm setting output below the level it might have reached had each man worked as hard as he could.

If a man worked too fast or produced more than the group thought right, he would be ridiculed as a "rate-buster" or "speed king." On the other hand, if he produced too little, he would be called a "chiseler." Another penalty for nonconformity was a practice the men called "binging." This was a sort of game in which one man might walk up to another and hit him as hard as he could on the upper arm. His victim was then entitled to retaliate with a similar blow. One of the objects of the game was to see who could hit the hardest. But this practice was also used as a penalty and played a role in regulating the output of some of the faster workers. Thus:

First wireman: "Why don't you quit work? Let's see, this is your thirty-fifth row today. What are you going to do with them all?"

Second wireman: "What do you care? It's to your advantage if I work, isn't it?"

First wireman: "Yeah, but the way you're working you'll get stuck with them."

Second wireman: "Don't worry about that. I'll take care of it. You're getting paid by the sets I turn out. That's all you should worry about."

First wireman: "If you don't quit work I'll bing you." (He strikes him and finally chases him around the room.)

Observer, a few minutes later to the man who was binged: "What's the matter, won't he let you work?"

Second wireman: "No, I'm all through though. I've got enough done." (He then went over and helped another wireman.)

The employees believed that their weekly average hourly output should show little change from week to week. They felt that if their output altered much, either from day to day or from week to week, something might happen. An unusually high output might thereafter become the standard their supervisors would expect them to maintain. The men felt it would be a way of confessing that they were capable of doing better. On the other hand, they felt that a low output would afford their supervisors a chance to "bawl them out." If output were kept fairly constant, they thought, neither possibility could happen.

In attempting to keep his production record constant, the worker was repudiating management's assumption that he would try to increase his production and with it his hourly rate. Since average hourly output was calculated by dividing total output by hours of work, the men could keep their output records constant by claiming either more or less than their actual output or more or less than the time actually spent. In practice both methods were used. Most men reported more connections than they completed, but two men who worked quite fast usually reported a little less than their actual count. The men who reported less than their actual output also claimed the least time out.

ATTITUDES TOWARD SUPERVISION

The group felt that no worker should give the supervisor information which could be used to the detriment of his fellow workers. Anyone who did so was branded a squealer and made to feel unwelcome. One inspector was driven from the group with this treatment.

The group also felt that those in authority should not attempt to maintain social distance or act officious. The wage incentive plan provided one of the means by which the group was able in an informal way to decrease the social distance between themselves and their supervisor. To measure individual output the supervisor was supposed to make a daily count of the number of connections made by each wireman. But he did not have time for the job and left it to the wiremen to do themselves. Much the same thing occurred with regard to claims for time lost. The supervisor was responsible for deciding which stoppages were allowable and which were not, but because a clear distinction was often impossible, he approved most of the claims made. In effect, therefore, the workers supervised their own records and, by doing so, were able to hold the supervisor to their own informal work norms.

CONCLUSION

The work norms of the bank wiremen may be summarized as follows:

1. You should not turn out too much work. If you do, you are a rate-buster.

2. You should not turn out too little work. If you do, you are a chiseler.

3. You should not tell a supervisor anything that will be detrimental to an associate. If you do, you are a squealer.

4. You should not attempt to maintain social distance or act officious. For example, if you are an inspector, you should not act like one.

These norms, and the behavior supporting them, were spontaneously elaborated and enforced by the workers themselves and were contrary to management's assumptions.

Adaptation 13 Janis: Groupthink and policy fiascos

How can intelligent people, in positions of high responsibility, come to conclusions that are later seen as grossly mistaken? This question led the author of this adaptation to a careful review of six major foreign policy decisions. Four of these he regarded as disastrous failures, in short, fiascos: President John F. Kennedy's decision in 1961 to support the invasion of Cuba at the Bay of Pigs by about 1,400 Cuban exiles, aided by the U.S. Navy, the Air Force, and the CIA; President Truman's decision to escalate the Korean war in 1950 by authorizing General MacArthur's victorious forces to cross the thirty-eighth parallel in an attempt to occupy North Korea; the lack of vigilance that led to the destruction of the U.S. Pacific Fleet by the Japanese attack at Pearl Harbor in 1941; and President Johnson's decision to escalate the war in Vietnam during the period 1964–1967.

These decisions were compared with two others that seemed to be based on better procedures: the Cuban missile crisis in 1962, created by the fact that within a year of the Bay of Pigs invasion, the Castro regime had worked out an arrangement with the Soviets for the construction of missile sites capable of launching atomic weapons; and the formulation of the Marshall Plan after World War II, which was a comprehensive program for supplying American funds to aid European recovery.

In making these comparisons, the author recognized that policy was formed by groups and not by individual leaders. He concluded that group dynamics had much to do with the quality of the decisions. In particular, the policy fiascos were characterized by a process called groupthink.

WHAT IS GROUPTHINK?

The group dynamics approach is based on the working assumption that the members of policy-making groups, no matter how mindful they may be of their exalted national status and of their heavy responsibilities, are subjected to the pressures widely observed in groups of ordinary citizens. In my earlier research on group dynamics, I was im-

Source: Abridged and adapted from Irving L. Janis, *Victims of Groupthink* (Boston: Houghton Mifflin, 1972). Published in this form by permission of Irving L. Janis and Houghton Mifflin.

pressed by repeated manifestations of the effects — both unfavorable and favorable — of the social pressures that typically develop in cohesive groups — in infantry platoons, air crews, therapy groups, seminars, and self-study or encounter groups of executives receiving leadership training. In all these groups, just as in the industrial work groups described by other investigators, members tend to evolve informal objectives to preserve friendly relations within the group, and this becomes part of the hidden agenda at their meetings.

I use the term "groupthink" as a quick and easy way to refer to a mode of thinking people engage in when they are deeply involved in a cohesive in-group, when the members' strivings for unanimity override their motivation to appraise realistically alternative courses of action. Groupthink is a term on the same order as the words in the Newspeak vocabulary George Orwell presents in his dismaying *1984*—a vocabulary with terms such as "doublethink" and "crimethink." Groupthink refers to a deterioration of mental efficiency, reality testing, and moral judgment that results from in-group pressures.

Caution I do not assume every fiasco must have been the result of groupthink or even that it was the result of defective decision making. Nor do I expect that every defective decision, whether arising from groupthink or from other causes, will produce a fiasco. Defective decisions based on misinformation and poor judgment sometimes lead to successful outcomes. Nevertheless, groupthink is conducive to error in decision making, and such errors increase the likelihood of a poor outcome.

Hardhearted actions by softheaded groups At first I was surprised by the extent to which the groups in the fiascos adhered to group norms and pressures toward uniformity. Just as in groups of ordinary citizens, a dominant characteristic appears to be remaining loyal to the group by sticking with the decisions to which the group has committed itself, even when the policy is working badly and has unintended consequences that disturb the consciences of the members. In a sense, members consider loyalty to the group the highest form of morality, which requires each member to avoid raising controversial issues, questioning weak arguments, or calling a halt to softheaded thinking.

Paradoxically, softheaded groups are likely to be extremely hardhearted toward out-groups and enemies. In dealing with a rival nation, policy makers comprising an amiable group find it relatively easy to authorize dehumanizing solutions such as large-scale bombings. An affable group of government officials is unlikely to pursue the difficult and controversial issues that arise when alternatives to a harsh military solution come up for discussion. Nor are the members inclined to raise ethical issues that imply that this "fine group of ours, with its humanitarianism and its high-minded principles, might be capable of adopting a course of action that is inhumane and immoral."

The concept of groupthink pinpoints a source of trouble that resides neither in the individual nor in the organizational setting. Beyond all the familiar sources of human error is a powerful source of defective judgment that arises in cohesive groups— a concurrence-seeking tendency which fosters overoptimism, lack of vigilance, and sloganistic thinking about the weakness and immorality of out-groups. This tendency can take its toll even when the decision makers are conscientious statesmen trying to make the best possible decisions for their country and for all mankind.

I do not mean to imply that all cohesive groups suffer from groupthink, though all may display its symptoms from time to time. Nor should we infer from the term groupthink that group decisions are typically inefficient or harmful. On the contrary, a group whose members have properly defined roles, with traditions and standard operating procedures that facilitate critical inquiry, is probably capable of making better decisions than any individual in the group who works on the problem alone. And yet the advantages of having decisions made by groups are often lost because of psychological pressures that arise when the members work closely together, share the same values, and above all face a crisis situation in which everyone is subjected to stresses that generate a strong need for affiliation. In these circumstances, as conformity pressures begin to dominate, groupthink and the deterioration of decision making set in.

The central theme of my analysis can be summarized in this generalization, which I offer in the spirit of Parkinson's laws: *The more amiability and esprit de corps among the members of a policy-making in-group, the greater is the danger that independent critical thinking will be replaced by groupthink, which is likely to result in irrational and dehumanizing actions directed against out-groups.*

THE LEADER'S ROLE: FACT VERSUS MYTH

Even in nontotalitarian countries, a powerful leader's advisers may conform with his wishes, thinking "it is not up to me to make this decision." In America, according to traditional political doctrine, the president has sole responsibility for every decision authorized by the executive branch. Thus President Eisenhower was responsible for the erroneous decision to send U-2 spy planes over the Soviet Union even though he was not even informed about them by the Pentagon until after he had publicly denied that the United States had launched any such flights. President Truman, according to the doctrine, had sole responsibility for the Korean War decisions even though he was highly responsive to his advisers' recommendations and on at least one important decision was induced to change his mind completely. John F. Kennedy reinforced the traditional myth by publicly assuming full responsibility for the Bay of Pigs fiasco. Nevertheless, his advisers knew that they shared the responsibility, and some of them acknowledged feeling personally humiliated.

The problem of discerning whether advisers participated as policy makers arises in connection with the major decisions made by business firms, educational institutions, and other large organizations whenever a leader has nominal responsibility for the organization's policies. Only decisions in which the consensus of a stable in-group plays a crucial role in determining the chosen policy are relevant to investigations of the groupthink hypothesis.

WHEN GROUPTHINK OCCURS

The prime condition repeatedly encountered in the case studies of fiascos is group cohesiveness. A second major condition suggested by the case studies is insulation of the decision-making group from the judgments of qualified associates who, as outsiders, are not permitted to know about the new policies under discussion until after a final decision has been made. Hence a second hypothesis is that the more insulated a cohesive group of executives becomes, the greater are the chances that its policy decisions will be products of groupthink. A third hypothesis suggested by the case studies is that the more actively the leader of a cohesive policy-making group promotes his own preferred solution, the greater are the chances of a consensus based on groupthink, even when the leader does not want the members to be yes-men and the individual members try to resist conforming. Thus the hypothetical conditions making for groupthink are (1) group cohesion, (2) group insulation, and (3) leader assertiveness.

The groupthink syndrome In order to test generalizations about the conditions that increase the chances of groupthink, we must describe the symptoms to which it refers. Eight main symptoms run through the case studies of historic fiascos. Each symptom can be identified by a variety of indicators, derived from historical records, observers' accounts of conversations, and participants' memoirs. The eight symptoms of groupthink are:

1. An illusion of invulnerability, shared by most or all the members, which creates excessive optimism and encourages taking extreme risks

2. Collective efforts to rationalize in order to discount warnings which might lead the members to reconsider their assumptions

3. An unquestioned belief in the group's inherent morality, inclining the members to ignore the ethical or moral consequences of their decisions

4. Stereotyped views of enemy leaders as too evil to warrant genuine attempts to negotiate or as too weak and stupid to counter whatever risky attempts are made to defeat their purposes

5. Direct pressure on any member who expresses strong arguments against any of the group's stereotypes, illusions, or commitments, making clear that this type of dissent is contrary to what is expected of all loyal members

6. Self-censorship of deviations from the apparent group consensus, reflecting each member's inclination to minimize to himself the importance of his doubts and counterarguments

7. A shared illusion of unanimity concerning judgments (partly resulting from self-censorship of deviations, augmented by the false assumption that silence means consent)

8. The emergence of self-appointed "mind-guards"—members who protect the group from adverse information that might shatter their shared complacency about the effectiveness and morality of their decisions

When a policy-making group displays most or all of these symptoms, the members perform their collective tasks ineffectively and are likely to fail to attain their collective objectives.

PSYCHOLOGY OF GROUPTHINK

Concurrence seeking and the various symptoms of groupthink to which it gives rise can be best understood as a mutual effort among the members of a group to maintain self-esteem, especially when they share responsibility for making vital decisions that pose threats of social disapproval and self-disapproval.

A shared illusion of invulnerability and shared rationalizations can counteract unnerving feelings of personal inadequacy and pessimism about finding an adequate solution during a crisis. If the threat of failure is salient, the members are likely to convey to each other the attitude that "we needn't worry, everything will go our way." By pooling their intellectual resources to develop rationalizations, the members build up each other's confidence and feel reassured about unfamiliar risks which, if taken seriously, would be dealt with by applying standard operating procedures to obtain additional information and to carry out careful planning.

The members' firm belief in the inherent morality of their group and their use of negative stereotypes of opponents enable them to minimize conflicts between ethical values and expediency, especially when they are inclined to resort to violence. The shared belief that "we are a wise and good group" inclines them to use group concurrence as a major criterion to judge the morality as well as the efficacy of any policy under discussion. "Since our group's objectives are good," the members feel, "any means we decide to use must be good." This shared assumption helps the members avoid feelings of shame or guilt about decisions that may violate their personal code of ethical behavior. Negative stereotypes of the enemy enhance their sense of moral righteousness as well as their pride in the lofty mission of the in-group.

When familiar forms of social pressure are directed against a member who questions the group's wisdom or morality, the members are protecting themselves against anxiety and guilt. If subtle pressures fail, stronger efforts are made to limit the deviation, to create, in effect, a domesticated dissenter. In the case of President Johnson's in-group, one or two of the members disagreed with the majority's position that air attacks against North Vietnam should be increased. A doubter who accepts the role of domesticated dissenter is no longer a problem, because his objections are confined to issues that do not threaten to shake the confidence of the group members in the reasonableness and righteousness of their collective judgments. At the same time, the doubter's tamed presentation of an opposing viewpoint permits the others to think that their group is strong-minded enough to tolerate dissent. If the domestication efforts do not succeed, the dissenter is ultimately ostracized, so that the relatively tranquil emotional atmosphere of a homogeneous group is restored.

When a member is dependent on the group for bolstering his self-confidence, he tends to exercise self-censorship over his misgivings. The greater the dependence, the stronger will be the motivation to adhere to the group's norms. One of the norms that is likely to become dominant during a crisis involves living up to a mutual nonaggression pact. Each individual in the group feels himself to be under an injunction to avoid making penetrating criticisms that might bring on a clash with fellow members and destroy the unity of the group. Adhering to this norm promotes a sense of collective strength and also eliminates the threat of damage to each participant's self-esteem from hearing his own judgments on vital issues criticized by respected associates.

The various devices to enhance self-esteem re-quire an illusion of unanimity about all important judgments. Without it, the sense of group unity would be lost, gnawing doubts would start to grow, confidence in the group's problem-solving capacity would shrink, and soon the full emotional response to all the stresses generated by making a difficult decision would be aroused. Preserving the sense of unity can do more than keep anxiety and guilt to a minimum; it can induce pleasant feelings of elation. Members of a group sometimes enjoy an exhilarating sense of omnipotence from participating in a crisis decision with a group that displays solidarity against an evil enemy and complete unanimity about everything that needs to be done.

Self-appointed mindguards help to preserve the shared sense of complacency by making sure that the leader and other members are not exposed to information that might challenge their self-confidence. If the mindguard were to transmit the potentially distressing information, they might become discouraged by the apparent defects in their cherished policy and find themselves impelled to initiate a painful reevaluation.

CONCLUSION

The greater the threats to the self-esteem of the members of a cohesive decision-making body, the greater will be their inclination to resort to concurrence seeking at the expense of critical thinking. If this hypothesis is correct, symptoms of groupthink will be found often when a decision poses a moral dilemma, especially if the most advantageous course of action requires the policy makers to violate their own standards of humanitarian behavior. Under these conditions, each member is likely to become more dependent than ever on the in-group for maintaining his or her self-image as a decent human being and accordingly will be more strongly motivated to maintain a sense of group unity by striving for concurrence.

Section four the quest for community

The mobility and impersonality of modern life is sometimes exaggerated. Many people, even in large cities, live out their lives within closely confined circles of friends and relatives. But there is enough openness and fluidity, enough anomie and isolation, to create for many a sense of loss—the loss of community. The quest for community is a countertrend to modern mass society. It is an effort to enlarge the primary group, to make affection, communication, and a sense of kinship pervade an entire social world.

GEMEINSCHAFT AND GESELLSCHAFT

A German sociologist, Ferdinand Tönnies (1887) contrasted two types of society, *Gemeinschaft* and *Gesellschaft*. *Gemeinschaft* translates very roughly as "community," but the connotations of the German word are richer, suggesting moral unity, rootedness, intimacy, and kinship. Therefore *Gemeinschaft* is often translated as "primary community" or "communal society." The *Gemeinschaft* is a society characterized by (1) an assignment of status to the whole person so that his job and the rest of his life form a unity, (2) a high degree of cohesion based on the widespread sharing of common attitudes and aims, and (3) a sense of unlimited commitment to the community, which is conceived as an enlarged kinship group, the source of personal identity.

In a *Gemeinschaft*, people feel they belong together because they are of the same kind. Broadly speaking, they are kin, and their membership, which involves emotional meaning for the group as well as for the individual, cannot be freely renounced. People do not decide to join a *Gemeinschaft*; they are born into it or grow into it in the way the bonds of friendship grow. This model of a communal society closely fits the folk or primitive society and the ideal conception of the feudal order. The decline of *Gemeinschaft* is a decline of the sense of kinship with other members of a community.

The *Gemeinschaft* model, however, does not fit all traditional or folk communities. An impoverished peasant village, for example, does not necessarily offer a warm and supportive sense of community, and this is shown in a study of a Calabrian village, in southern Italy:

The peasants of Franza [a pseudonym] are on the whole given to suspicion, quarrels, vituperation, violence, and conflicts of all sorts. . . . The land, which keeps them in the peasant state they

intensely hate, is nevertheless a source of iniquitous quarrels between close relatives almost every time that it comes up for division or revision, which is indeed quite often. By their own standards and admission, the people of Franza are a wretched people (Lopreato, 1967:103–104).

Another study of a town of the same region found that an ethos of "amoral familism" prevailed: "Maximize the material, short-run advantage of the nuclear family; assume that all others will do likewise" (Banfield, 1958:85). This ethos had its roots in, and was supported by, the extreme poverty of the area, excessive centralization of government, and a rigid social structure. The effect was that little energy could be mobilized for community organization.

While the concept of *Gemeinschaft* evokes the image of a humane ideal of communion and belonging, the word also refers specifically to a world of ascription, fixed status, extended kinship, and sacred belief. Such a world may be experienced as oppressive; it may constrain free expression and the full development of some personal potentialities. Moreover, while a *Gemeinschaft* may offer a rich texture of community experience, this may be lacking when everyone is scraping for a bare living and there is little or no economic surplus.

In contrast to a *Gemeinschaft*, a *Gesellschaft* is a voluntary and purposive association. (In German, *Gesellschaft* signifies a special-purpose organization, such as a business association; the word also translates as "society" in the larger sense, but not as "community.") Tönnies designated as a *Gesellschaft* a society in which the major social bonds are voluntary and based upon the rational pursuit of self-interest. People enter into relations with one another not because they must or because it is natural but as a practical way of achieving an objective. The typical relation is the contract, and the typical group is the voluntary special-purpose association. The long historical trend toward societies of large scale and great complexity tends to create the *Gesellschaft*. More and more activities become governed by the voluntary action of individuals who choose freely and keep their options open. Yet the *Gemeinschaft* retains a strong appeal, and there are repeated efforts to recreate the primary community within the framework of a society characterized by voluntary association, mobility, and rational choice. Two such efforts are the contemporary hippie communes and the intentional (utopian) communities which flourished during the nineteenth century.

THE NEW COMMUNES

Beginning in the mid-1960s, a small but significant number of young people began a movement toward communal living. By 1970, there were about 1,000 rural communes and 2,000 urban communes in the United States (Zablocki, 1971:300), and communal groups have been established in many countries. Many communes are quite small, consisting of six to eight members who share a house or farm; others have a population of 25 or more. Most communes include both men and women, adults and children. The rural commune more nearly meets the aspiration that members share a common life than does the urban commune, whose members work at separate jobs or go to school. The rural commune is, in theory, less dependent on the mainstream of society; for that reason too it is closer to the communal ideal.

The commune is partly an expression of alienation from society, partly a way of experimenting with alternative life-styles. The specific impulse toward communal life is the felt need for more satisfying primary relations, and the communes are therefore one response to the impersonality of modern life. They are part of a pattern that includes suburbanization, the ideology of togetherness, and the encounter-group movement. "In this perspective, communes are not nearly so radical a phenomenon as they are commonly thought to be" (Berger, Hackett, and Millar, 1972:279). Nevertheless, forming a commune, or even joining one, is

likely to be experienced by the individual as a radical step. Entering a new and demanding environment, the newcomer is called upon to make commitments and take psychic risks for which there has been no preparation.

Commune and community The hippie communes celebrate spontaneity, love, gentleness, sharing, and communication. They value the wholeness of experience and the attainment of personal fulfillment through group consciousness. In many cases, drugs have been used to enhance apparent openness to these values or to attain the sense of having achieved them. But hippie communes mainly focus on interaction, communication, and a sense of oneness. This perspective is strongly associated with an imagery of kinship. Like the very different people described in Adaptation 10, commune members are thought of as brothers and sisters and the communes as families.

The pure commune, founded on ideals of psychic and physical closeness, is a kind of primary group, but it is not a community. Participants in the movement have stressed this distinction (Houriet, 1971:209, 223).

Typically, communes were made up fairly uniformly of young people who identified with the hip subculture of drugs, rock and voluntary poverty. . . . By contrast, the community embraced a greater diversity of people, not just the hip and the young. Where communes left finances, work and decision to the fickle will of group consciousness, communities leaned more heavily on definite structures: work systems, treasurers, and corporations. Many were united around a single craft or art. . . . The physical, as well as emotional, distance was greater in a community than in a commune. Traditionally, a community was made up of separate houses rather than a large common dwelling (Houriet, 1971:205–206).

The commune is a quest for communion rather than community (Zablocki, 1971: 286). Communion is a psychic unity, whereas community is a form of social organization embracing the entire round of life. The commune is very much a voluntary association, and the members value it only so long as it fulfills their ideals or provides the gratifications they need. The commune is therefore an inherently unstable social form, and when communal groups seek increased stability, they take the road toward community.

The strains of communion In their own way, the communes have rediscovered some of the problems that arise when primary relations are made the focus of social organization:

1. The boundary dilemma The new perspective fostered the idea of an open commune (Houriet, 1971:143). Anyone could come and be welcome; no dividing line of private property — or even group property — could be justified. It was assumed that, in time, things would sort themselves out spontaneously. A balance would be established between the people and the land or the facilities. In fact, a number of communes have faced severe crises because of the failure to establish these boundaries. Some of the difficulties might have been eased if the communes had had more resources, but they would then have had to become larger and ultimately different in character. The apparent lesson is that general ideals of love and brotherhood need to be supplemented by some principle of exclusion. Kinship (or pseudokinship) can serve as such a principle if it is taken seriously and group membership becomes a kind of adoption; by implication, nonkin are excluded. A political or religious doctrine can also be a principle of exclusion, especially if people have to serve for a time as learners or neophytes, proving their understanding and commitment. However, setting such boundaries is not really compatible with the aspiration of many communes to retain maximum flexibility and mobility for members.

2. Decision making The communes have attempted to fuse the person and the group, which means, in part, giving maximum respect to both at the same time. This accounts for a reluctance to accept the principle of majority rule. If the majority decides, the minority may feel "snuffed out," deprived of meaningful participation. One alternative, consistent with democracy, is to strive for as nearly complete a consensus as possible through intense communication and to avoid any action to which there is strong opposition. The result is often a great deal of *inaction*, which may not matter much most of the time but which can render the commune incapable of coping with urgent problems.

Another alternative to majority rule is subordination to charismatic authority. The individual "yields his personal autonomy to a leader, usually authoritarian, whose charisma lies in his command of doctrine which points to The One Correct Way, or in the strength of his personal presence" (Berger, Hackett, and Millar, 1972:297). Through psychic submission, individuals gain a "representative" who can make decisions for them without violating their personalities or their sense of oneness with the group.

3. The quality of relationships If deep and extensive communication among all members is the communal ideal and if group experience is highly valued, then private islands of intimacy are likely to be perceived as anomalous or subversive. In practice, most communities respect certain kinds of privacy — even personal withdrawal or eccentricity. The most common sexual arrangement appears to be serial monogamy. On the other hand, many communes are wary of anything that "privatizes" the individual and thereby makes some particular relationship more important to him than the commune itself. There is therefore resistance to people pairing off and having a life of their own; there is pressure to participate fully in the life of the group. Thus the commune may actually frustrate some primary relations, for within it there is no hiding place.

A study of 120 rural and urban communes during 1965–1975 found that emotional involvement among the members, whether positive or negative, tended to undermine the commune. "The larger the proportion of dyads [pairs] in a commune which are cathected [charged with emotional content], the more unstable the commune will be, both in terms of population turnover and tendency to disintegrate" (Zablocki, forthcoming).

Some observers have noted an "impersonal intimacy" in communal life. People are encouraged to interact and be "up front," but they are not necessarily supported by a sense of closeness and commitment. An ex-member of an urban commune described a lack of genuine intimacy:

Gradually, we began to see a brittleness in the ways Community members dealt with one another, in the set of their faces, in what they said. Compassion was held to be condescending. Favored instead was a sort of brutal honesty that forced distances between people, stressed their apartness (French, 1971:26).

The commune is not necessarily a high road —and certainly not an easy road—to intimacy and self-fulfillment.

INTENTIONAL COMMUNITIES

The new communes invite comparison with older communitarian settlements and experiments—the so-called utopian communities. During the nineteenth century, more than 100 such communities were founded in the United States (Webber, 1959:15). Some, such as the Shakers, the Amana Society, and the Hutterite Brethren, were small Christian sects that hoped to establish a truly godly society in their own small communities. Their activities were a form of religious witness. Other communities were secular experiments in communal, collective life. Among these were the socialist settlements founded in the United States by the British industrialist Robert Owen.

Although such ventures have usually been called utopian, intentional is a more neutral and more accurate designation. An intentional community is a voluntary association of people who share a common life

according to a specific plan of organization and code of conduct. The Israeli kibbutz (Adaptation 24) would properly be considered an intentional community, but not necessarily utopian. By contrast a *natural* community is formed and grows without a plan and without a special set of guiding principles.

The most striking difference between the hippie commune and the intentional community is the commitment of the latter to a tight social structure. If an intentional community endures and is in that sense successful, it is likely to have a fairly elaborate system of social control. The religious communities have the best chance of success, because they can employ religious doctrine to justify subordination of the individual to the group; every sphere of life can be infused with religious meaning and thereby made subject, at least in principle, to the sanctions of the group. The Shakers, for example, prescribed in excruciating detail the routines of daily life: how to get out of bed, how to get dressed, when to eat, when to speak (Webber, 1959:57–59).

The Society of Brothers (the Bruderhof) is a contemporary religious community made up of three colonies located in New York, Pennsylvania, and Connecticut. The community supports itself by manufacturing children's toys, sold to schools under the trade name Community Playthings. About 750 men, women, and children live a highly organized life:

A Bruderhof day is a patterned day, divided into small segments, each with its planned activity. Bells ring for lunch, for supper, for the evening activity, for the morning and afternoon sessions of work and school. But there is none of the frantic rushing to be on time that is so familiar on a city street. A Brother who is late once, or twice, will not be reproved by anyone. A Brother who is late frequently will find himself having a little talk with one of the spiritual leaders of the community, the Servant or a Witness Brother (Zablocki, 1971:45).

A study of 91 utopian communities in the United States between 1780 and 1860 found that 11 lasted for at least 25 years and by that criterion were successful. The successful communities differed from the transitory ones in that they were likely to impose the following requirements:

1. More sacrifices of their members: for example, giving up various personal gratifications as a condition of membership

2. More investment by new members: for example, assignment of property, with contributions treated as nonreturnable

3. More renunciation of the outside world, including family ties and other competing loyalties

4. More group participation (communion), emphasizing joint effort, sharing, and communal activities (In some cases, the shared experience was historical, such as having suffered persecution or having a common religious background, and thus was not necessarily a requirement.)

5. More mortification (see Adaptation 6), such as confession and self-criticism.

6. More surrender of personal autonomy: for example, acceptance of a dominating spiritual leader or detailed rules of conduct (Kanter, 1968:503–516)

References

Asch, Solomon E.
1956 "Studies of independence and conformity: 1. a minority of one against a unanimous majority." Psychological Monographs: General and Applied 70, no. 9, whole no. 416.

Banfield, Edward C.
1958 The Moral Basis of a Backward Society. New York: Free Press.

Barnes, J. A.
1972 Social Networks. Reading, Mass.: Addison-Wesley.

Berger, Bennett, Bruce Hackett, and Mervyn Millar
1972 "Child rearing practices of the communal family." Pp. 271–300 in Hans Peter Dreitzel (ed.), Recent Sociology, no. 4. New York: Macmillan.

Carey, Alex
1967 "The Hawthorne studies: a radical criticism." American Sociological Review 32 (June):403–416.

Cloward, Richard A.
1960 "Social control in the prison." Pp. 24ff. in Richard A. Cloward et al., Theoretical Studies in Social Organization of the Prison. New York: Social Science Research Council.

Cooley, Charles Horton
1909 Social Organization. New York: Scribner.

Empey, Lamar T. and Maynard L. Erickson
1972 The Provo Experiment: Impact and Death of an Innovation. Lexington, Mass.: Heath.

Empey, Lamar T. and Jerome Rabow
1961 "The Provo experiment in delinquency rehabilitation." American Sociological Review 26 (October):679–695.

Faris, Ellsworth
1932 "The primary group: essence and accident." American Journal of Sociology 38 (July):41–50.

French, David
1971 "After the fall." New York Times Magazine (October 3): 20–36.

Houriet, Robert
1971 Getting Back Together. New York: Coward-McCann.

Kanter, Rosabeth Moss
1968 "Commitment and social organization: a study of commitment mechanisms in utopian communities." American Sociological Review 33 (August):499–517.

Landsberger, Henry A.
1958 Hawthorne Revisited. Ithaca, N.Y.: Cornell University.

Lieberman, Morton A., Irvin D. Yalom, Matthew B. Miles, and P. Golde
1971 "The group experience project: a comparison of ten encounter technologies." Pp. 469–497 in L. Blank, G. Gottsegen, and M. Gottsegen (eds.), Encounter Confrontations in Self and Interpersonal Awareness. New York: Macmillan.

Little, Roger W.
1964 "Buddy relations and combat performance." Pp. 195–223 in Morris Janowitz (ed.), The New Military. New York: Russell Sage.

Lopreato, Joseph
1967 Peasants No More. San Francisco: Chandler.

Moskos, Charles C., Jr.
1970 The American Enlisted Man. New York: Russell Sage.

Parsons, H. M.
1974 "What happened at Hawthorne?" Science 183 (March 8): 922–932.

Rogers, Carl R.
1970 Carl Rogers on Encounter Groups. New York: Harper & Row.

Sherif, Muzafer
1936 The Psychology of Social Norms. New York: Harper & Row.

Shils, Edward A.
1950 "Primary groups in the American Army." Pp. 16–39 in Robert K. Merton and Paul F. Lazarsfeld (eds.), Continuities in Social Research. New York: Free Press.

Shils, Edward A. and Morris Janowitz
1948 "Cohesion and disintegration in the Wehrmacht in World War II." Public Opinion Quarterly 12 (summer):280–315.

Stouffer, Samuel A., Arthur A. Lumsdaine, Marion Harper Lumsdaine, Robin M. Williams, Jr., M. Brewster Smith, Irving L. Janis, Shirley A. Star, and Leonard S. Cottrell, Jr.
1949 The American Soldier, Combat and Its Aftermath. Vol. 2. Princeton, N.J.: Princeton University Press.

Sykes, A. J.
1965 "Economic interest and the Hawthorne researches: a comment." Human Relations 18 (August):253–263.

Tönnies, Ferdinand
1887 Gemeinschaft und Gesellschaft. Translated and edited by C. P. Loomis as Community and Society. New York: Harper & Row, 1963.

Webber, Everett
1959 Escape to Utopia. New York: Hastings House.

Yalom, Irvin D. and Morton A. Lieberman
1971 "A Study of Encounter Group Casualties." Archives of General Psychiatry 25 (July):16–30.

Zablocki, Benjamin David
1971 The Joyful Community. Baltimore: Penguin Books.

Forthcoming. Alienation and Charisma: American Communitarian Experiments 1965–1975. New York: Free Press.

Sources and readings

Back, Kurt W.
1972 Beyond Words: The Story of Sensitivity Training and the Encounter Movement. New York: Russell Sage.

Bales, Robert F.
1970 Personality and Interpersonal Behavior. New York: Holt, Rinehart and Winston.

Barnes, J. A.
1972 Social Networks. Reading, Mass.: Addison-Wesley.

Cartwright, Dorwin and Alvin Zander (eds.)
1968 Group Dynamics. Third edition. New York: Harper & Row.

Cooley, Charles Horton
1909/1962 Social Organization. New York: Schocken Books.

Golombiewski, Robert T.
1965 "Small Groups and Large Organizations." Pp. 142–193 in James G. March (ed.), Handbook of Organizations. Skokie, Ill.: Rand McNally.

Hare, A. Paul
1962 Handbook of Small Group Research. New York: Macmillan.

Hare, A. Paul, Robert F. Bales, and Edgar F. Borgatta (eds.)
1965 Small Groups. New York: Knopf.

Homans, George C.
1950 The Human Group. New York: Harcourt Brace Jovanovich.

Jandy, Edward C.
1942 Charles Horton Cooley: His Life and His Social Theory. New York: Dryden Press.

Kanter, Rosabeth Moss
1972 Commitment and Community: Communes and Utopias in Sociological Perspective. Cambridge: Harvard University Press.

Mayo, Elton
1949/1975 The Social Problems of an Industrial Civilization. London: Routledge and Kegan Paul.

Mills, Theodore M.
1967 The Sociology of Small Groups. Englewood Cliffs, N. J.: Prentice-Hall.
1970 Readings on the Sociology of Small Groups. Englewood Cliffs, N. J.: Prentice-Hall.

Shepherd, Clovis R.
1964 Small Groups: Some Sociological Perspectives. New York: Intext.

Slater, Philip E.
1966 Microcosm: Structural, Psychological and Religious Evolution in Groups. New York: Wiley.

Smith, J. H.
1975 "The Significance of Elton Mayo." Pp. ix–xlii in Mayo, 1949/1975.

Periodicals

Human Relations
Sociometry

6 | Social Stratification

Section one introduction

Inequality and social ranking have long been basic preoccupations of sociology because they affect almost all social phenomena: child rearing, husband–wife relations, political preference, and longevity, to mention but a few. This chapter deals with the extent of inequality, the consequences of inequality for life-styles, social mobility, and the formation of social classes.

STRATA AND CLASSES

The major dimensions of stratification are power, prestige, and wealth. However, any unequally distributed reward or resource can be considered a dimension of stratification. For example, in advanced societies, knowledge and skills are increasingly important criteria for the allocation of occupational positions, and occupation largely de-

This chapter draws upon material included in earlier editions written in collaboration with Richard T. Morris and Norval D. Glenn.

termines access to power, prestige, and wealth. In traditional societies, inherited social rank was tied to the privileges and disabilities rooted in law and custom: In feudal Europe, a villein could leave the estate only with the consent of his lord. Many occupations in traditional India were controlled by specific castes, and caste status might govern such details of everyday life as access to a given water supply.

Social strata Individuals, families, or groups that have similar ranks on any of the dimensions of stratification constitute a social stratum, or social level. Thus, there are prestige strata, power strata, wealth strata, and so forth. Families that have incomes within a defined range make up an income stratum, and people who have completed a specified number of years of school make up an education stratum.

In modern industrialized societies, the social strata usually shade into one another. They are more statistical than natural. Identifying strata is therefore a somewhat arbitrary exercise. After studying the statistical distribution of incomes, it might be decided that each $1,000 interval on the scale of annual income or that each 10 percent layer of families should be called a stratum. In some societies, however, especially in pre-industrial ones, there may be sharp divisions in the distribution of individuals according to income, power, or prestige, as was true of the nobility and serfs of medieval Europe.

Some sociologists prefer to restrict the term social stratification to such naturally divided social levels, and they thus refer to *stratified* and *unstratified* groups and societies. However, because the existence of natural strata in modern societies is in doubt, the term social stratification is increasingly used to refer to all forms of inequality, regardless of whether the distribution of rewards and resources is continuous or distinctly divided. In the broader sense, almost all groups are stratified.

Social classes The idea of social classes implies something more than statistically defined strata. In the sense formulated by Marx, class refers to a grouping of people—for example, all wage earners—who share a common situation in the organization of economic production. Marx saw class as rooted in the economic order, which largely determined what happened in society. He expected people to become class conscious, that is, to identify themselves as members of a social class because of their broad economic role. Further, he believed that class membership would be an overriding social identity.

Marx conceived of classes as structural units of society and not arbitrarily delineated strata or statistical categories. (See Section Five). He argued that the members of a class might be drawn from several economic strata and that the members of the same economic stratum might belong to different social classes. For example, small-businessmen differ from industrial workers in their relation to economic organization, but they may have similar incomes and therefore fall in the same income stratum. Factory workers

Table 6:1
Weber's model of stratification

Order	Grouping	Stratifying principle
Economic	Classes	Production/acquisition of goods; life chances
Social	Status groups	Consumption of goods/life-style; honor, esteem
Political	Parties	Power

Source: Weber, in Gerth and Mills, 1946:180–195.

have a wide range of skills and are distributed through several income strata, but in their organization into interest groups (labor unions), they would, according to Marx, have the same class identity.

Weber conceived the system of stratification as made up of three orders—the economic, social and political. (See Table 6:1). Each order is an expression of an underlying stratifying principle and has its characteristic type of grouping (Weber, in Gerth and Mills, 1946:180–195). Like Marx, Weber conceived of *classes* as based on the *economic* order, persons being stratified according to their relation to the production and acquisition of goods. In the *social order*, Weber distinguished *status groups* in which people are stratified by their styles of life, by the way they consume goods rather than how they acquire property. Social esteem (honor) or the contrary is thus recognition of an individual's status and his style of consumption, not simply of his possessions.

Class and status, property and honor are often linked to each other, but not necessarily so. Property as such does not guarantee status or honor, although in the long run it tends to become a status qualification. Men or women who gain property from economic activity may never enjoy the status fruits of their effort, but their children, who have been educated in the life-style of a higher status group, may be accepted.

Weber's third order, the *political*, is concerned with the stratifying principle of *power.* Power is exercised through parties and coalitions in all kinds of groups and forms of political organization, and power is stratified by the amount of access people have to the political and social organization where power resides and where it can be exercised.

STUDYING SOCIAL STRATIFICATION

The principal ways of studying the complex reality of social ranking may be grouped under three headings: *subjective*, *reputational*, and *objective*. In the subjective approach, the analysis of social ranking depends mainly upon the concepts of the social participants or the persons being interviewed. The respondents have ideas about class that have evolved in the course of their own life experience. These class images and schemes determine what is studied in the subjective approach (Davies, 1967; Svalastoga, 1959). Consider the different ways of viewing the system of social rankings in Italy:

Foreigners are delighted . . . because they always find themselves, without knowing it, in a favoured position. The Italian social structure can be compared to the olive tree, that most Italian of all trees, which looks entirely different when seen from above from what it looks when seen from below. The leaves are glossy dark-green on top and powdery grey underneath. The faces of the Italians look flattering, smiling, and kindly from above but overbearing, insolent, pitiless from below. Foreigners are automatically promoted to be honorary members of the ruling class. They occupy a position of vantage. Theirs is the bird's-eye view of the olive tree (Barzini, 1965:350).

In the objective approach, people are grouped into strata such as levels of income as defined by the researcher. The reputational technique lies between the subjective and objective approaches in the extent to which it depends upon the perceptions of the respondent on the one hand and the constructs of the researcher on the other.

The subjective approach The self-rating or subjective approach investigates how individuals perceive their own positions in the pattern of inequality. The investigator may ask people to indicate whether their economic standing in the society or the community is below average, about average, or above average. Or questions may be more specific and ask in what tenth or in what quarter of the population they would place themselves in economic standing, in prestige, or on some other dimension of stratification.

Individuals whose objective ranks are the same may behave very differently in the system of social stratification, because they perceive their ranks differently. People who see themselves standing at about the same ranks may express similar feelings, even though their objective ranks are very different.

How people perceive their position in the system of economic inequality depends in large measure on their *reference groups,* that is, the people with whom they compare themselves. A foreman who lives in a blue-collar suburb may rate himself high because his income exceeds that of most people he knows. However, if he begins to associate with highly paid professional people, his income will seem relatively low. His objective economic position is unchanged, but his perception changes, and so may his reaction to it. Consequently, self-rating studies often try to identify the reference groups of individuals.

In one commonly used subjective technique, persons are asked to name the social class to which they belong, or they are given a list of social classes and asked to indicate to which they belong (Centers, 1949:77). They may be asked to identify themselves as upper, middle, working, or lower class. If there is a high degree of consensus about what class labels mean and if they are familiar to a large part of the population, a class-identification technique can be used to advantage. However, it cannot be assumed that the people who say they are middle class are identifying the same objective entity or that their perceptions of their rankings on the major dimensions of stratification are similar. In fact, many respondents probably do not identify with any social class until they are asked the question.

The reputational approach Since prestige consists of the evaluations people make of one another, it is measured by observing actual social interactions or, more often, by asking people to rank one another. The investigator may go into a small community, select a sample of long-term residents, and ask them to rate the other members of the community on a scale from highest to lowest. In addition, the judges may be asked whether they perceive distinct social levels and if so, to identify the levels and the names of some people in each one. Then to find out what criteria the judges used in defining prestige, the investigator may ask why they rate specific people as they do.

This technique is adequate for measuring the prestige of individuals if the following conditions are met: (1) all raters know, or know the reputations of, most of the people to be rated, and (2) all raters use the same or similar criteria of evaluation. In other words, the method is applicable only in small and culturally homogeneous groups and communities in which there is a commonly accepted and recognized prestige hierarchy.

The reputational technique can be used more generally to determine the relative prestige of groups, occupational categories, and roles. On college campuses, for example, there is usually a recognized prestige hierarchy of clubs or social fraternities, and several studies have shown that there is good agreement regarding the prestige of occupations. (See Section Two.)

The most common deviation from consensus is the assessment of one's own occupation or organization. Almost invariably persons rate their own organizations higher than other individuals do. This common human bias is known as the aggrandizement effect and is most easily avoided by asking judges not to rate anything with which they are affiliated.

The reputational technique is sometimes used in studies of the distribution of power in communities and groups; a panel of judges is asked to identify those persons who can influence important decisions. The technique, however, is less suited to the study of power than of prestige, which consists essentially of reputation, whereas power does not. A person's reputation may overestimate or underestimate his actual power, but reputed power is socially significant regardless of the accuracy of the reputation. Therefore, the reputational technique is best combined with other methods in the study of power.

The objective approach The research strategy of the objective approach uses such indicators as income, years of school completed, occupation, or formal lines of authority. These do not rely on the feelings, evaluations, or perceptions of the individuals studied or of a panel of judges. Objective indicators allow more precise measurement than the reputational and subjective approaches, and most of the measures can be used for studies of entire societies. For these reasons, the objective approach is frequently employed on large populations and as an adjunct to community studies.

The objective method by itself leaves untapped significant aspects of the total reality. When a study has identified all persons whose incomes fall within a certain range, it has not identified a population for whom the social meaning and the social consequences of their incomes is the same. An income of $15,000 a year means one thing to a middle-aged skilled worker near the peak of his earning power, and it means something quite different to a young professional worker just beginning a career. The significance of a given income also varies with such factors as past income, the level of income within one's reference groups, and the security of its source.

Caution The foregoing discussion refers to the self-rating approach as *subjective* and to indicators that do not necessarily involve awareness as *objective*. The distinction as used here refers to types of information, not to standards of evidence. Findings about socioeconomic status based on objective measures are not necessarily superior to data based on attitudes and opinions. Moreover, subjective data (self-ratings and ratings of others) can be the basis of unbiased, scientific conclusions, and in that sense are just as "objective" as conclusions based on census or income data.

Section two inequality

ECONOMIC INEQUALITY

In capitalist countries it appears that property ownership is the source of greater inequality than income, but evidence is not systematic or generally available. In the absence of accurate information regarding possessions and savings, the distribution of income is accepted as the acid test of stratification. By this measure there are no equalitarian countries, for nowhere does everyone receive even approximately the same income.

National variations in record keeping, in what is defined as income, in estimating the income value of fringe benefits, and in the differential impact of taxation make it difficult to compare countries on their degree of inequality. For some countries, such as China, there is little information to compare. Nevertheless, there is much interest in rating countries on economic inequality. A partial answer groups 25 countries into five categories according to the spread of wages and salaries before taxes (Lydall, 1968:156). In the "most equal" category are Czechoslovakia, New Zealand, Hungary, and Australia. In the second category, ten countries are grouped closely together: Denmark, the United Kingdom, Sweden, Yugoslavia, Poland, West Germany, Canada, Belgium, the United States, and Austria. The third category consists of three countries: the Netherlands, Argentina, and Spain. Finland, France, and Japan are fourth. In the fifth category, with the greatest wage and salary spread, are Brazil, Chile, India, Sri Lanka, and Mexico.

The broad picture seems, then, to be that, amongst non-Communist countries, the degree of dispersion of pre-tax employment income is roughly related to the degree of economic development, although Australia and New Zealand are exceptionally equal on this criterion, and France is exceptionally unequal. The Communist countries are, in relation to level of economic development, all more equal than the non-Communist countries, but amongst them the more highly industrialized seem to be more equal than the others. The widest dispersion occurs amongst the very poor and industrially backward countries of Asia and Latin America (Lydall, 1968:157).

It should be emphasized that these groupings are based upon detailed analysis of earned income, but only earned income. Adjustments for other influences, such as unearned income, would probably not change the positions of the countries among the five major groupings. The analysis bears out the generalization that the poorest and industrially least advanced countries have the most economic inequality.

Studies submitted to the 1972 Seventh Asian Regional Conference of the International Labor Organization (ILO) give further evidence of the extreme income disparities in developing countries and suggest that inequality may have increased during the 1960s, the "first development decade" of the United Nations. According to Wilfred Jenks, director of the ILO, "Real incomes of industrial as well as agricultural workers have failed to rise significantly and in some countries have probably declined. Moreover, it is often the incomes of the poorest groups that have suffered most." The per capita annual income for Asia as a whole is estimated at about $100, and in all but seven Asian countries it is less than $200, compared with $1,500 for Japan. Yet there are a number of persons with comfortable incomes and a few families of great wealth in those countries with the lowest average incomes.

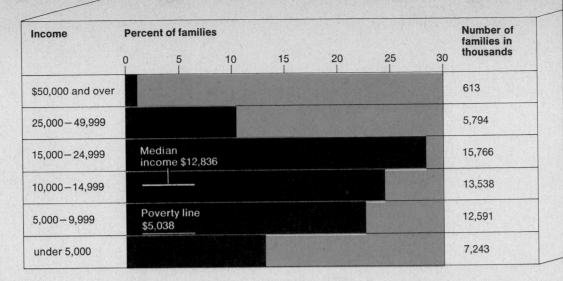

Income	Percent of families						Number of families in thousands
	0	5	10	15	20	25	30	
$50,000 and over								613
25,000 – 49,999								5,794
15,000 – 24,999	Median income $12,836							15,766
10,000 – 14,999								13,538
5,000 – 9,999	Poverty line $5,038							12,591
under 5,000								7,243

Figure 6:1
Stratification of United States families by income groups, 1974

Source: Current Population Reports, Series P–60, No. 101, January 1976: Table 35.

A social worker helps a woman enroll for medicare. Because criteria of eligibility are complex, and poverty is so often associated with a sense of isolation and helplessness, government programs must provide active assistance to potential beneficiaries. This raises a still-unresolved issue: how to alleviate poverty without creating a large and expensive government bureaucracy.

Inequality in U.S. incomes Figure 6:1 is a snapshot of the income distribution at a point in time. It shows in profile the wide disparity in the distribution of incomes in the United States during an economic depression. Slightly more families were below the poverty line than above the $25,000 bracket.

Another way of viewing income is to examine changes over a long period. This is done in Figure 6:2, which reports the trend in the distribution of U.S. family incomes from 1947 to 1974. This information is given in constant 1974 dollars, which signifies that the decline in the purchasing power of the dollar has been taken into account. It thus is possible directly to compare incomes over a long period. If the information had been reported in terms of the number of dollars actually received each year (current dollars), the figures would be hard to interpret, because inflation over the years has drastically reduced the value of the dollar.

Over the 27 years, the median income for

American families, again expressed in 1974 dollars, increased from $6,691 in 1947 to a high of $13,373 in 1973, with a decline to $12,836 in 1974. The percentage of families receiving low incomes declined sharply until around 1968; since then there has been no apparent further improvement. (These facts are discussed further under "Poverty.") The percentage of families with incomes of $10,000 and over, and particularly those with incomes of $15,000 and over, sharply increased. It is clear that since the end of World War II, the economic status of a very large part of the American population has significantly improved, and their consumption styles have changed accordingly. In this sense the socioeconomic condition of the country has been raised.

However, general economic improvement does not necessarily make incomes more equal. To determine whether there is a trend toward greater equality requires a different approach. If American families are divided into fifths according to their rank in income, and if each of these five strata is then examined to see what percentage of the total of all incomes it receives, a fairly direct measure of inequality is given. In a system of perfect equality, each quintile (20 percent) of families would receive 20 percent of all income. Indeed, each 1 percent of families would receive 1 percent of all income. In fact, the lowest 20 percent of families currently receives only slightly more than 5 percent of the aggregate income, and that figure has been quite stable since 1947, the earliest date for which such data are available. The second lowest fifth receives about 12 percent of aggregate income. The middle fifth receives over 17 percent, and the fourth quintile over 24 percent; both thus receive close to the 20 percent they would get in an even distribution. The highest 20 percent of families receives 41 percent, that is, more than twice its proportionate share. Within the very highest category, the *top 5 percent* of families receives more than 15 percent of all income—three times its proportionate share and nearly three times the amount received by the bottom 20 percent of all families. By these measures the United States is far from an equalitarian country. The amount of income going to the top 5 percent of families shows a slight downward drift from a high of 17 percent of all income in 1947. In summary, the evidence points to a general rise in the economic status of the population, but little trend toward equality in income (*Current Population Reports*, Series P-60, No. 101, January 1976:Table 22).

Poverty Data on poverty in the United States have been systematically compiled since 1959, when there were 39.5 million poor persons, making up 24 percent of the population. Throughout the 1960s, the number of persons living in poverty declined by 12 million—an average annual rate of 4.9 percent. Since 1969 the decline has been stopped. The poor population has fluctuated and in 1974 totaled 24.3 million. Since the population as a whole has continued to increase, the *percentage* of the population in poverty has declined and stands at under 12 percent. Whereas whites had an overall poverty rate of 8.9 percent, the rate for blacks was 31.4 percent and for persons of Spanish origin (mostly white) 23.2 percent (*Current Population Reports*, Series P-60, No. 102, January 1976). A further breakdown of income for several populations is given in *RACE AND ETHNICITY*, p. 473–476.

Measures of poverty are prepared by a federal interagency committee, which takes into account studies of the Social Security Administration and the Department of Agriculture and Consumer Price Index data (*Current Population Reports*, Series P-23, No. 28; Series P-60, Nos. 68 and 76). The poverty threshold for a nonfarm family of four in 1974 was income of less than $5,038. Farm families have a lower theoretical poverty threshold, because some of the products they raise can be substituted for what otherwise would have to be purchased.

It is estimated that it would have taken approximately $11.4 billion to raise the income of all poor persons above the poverty line in

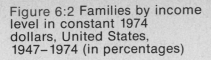

Figure 6:2 Families by income
level in constant 1974
dollars, United States,
1947–1974 (in percentages)

Source: Current Population Reports, Series P–60,
No. 101, January 1976: Table 11.
Prior to 1951 the top bracket refers
to $10,000 and over.

$15,000 and over

$10,000—$14,999

$ 7,000—$ 9,999

$ 5,000—$ 6,999

$ 3,000—$ 4,999

under $3,000

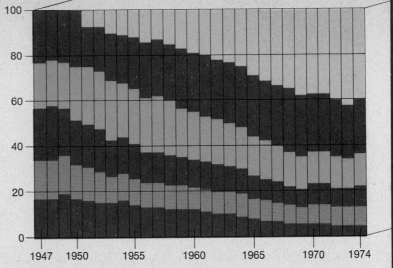

1970 (*Current Population Reports,* Series P-60, No. 77, May 7, 1971:1). Since the gross national product (GNP) of the United States in 1970 was nearly a trillion dollars, the expenditure would have represented a little over 1 percent of the GNP. For comparative purposes, it may be noted that the national expenditure for tobacco was more than $10 billion. Depending upon the values and personal priorities of the statistical interpreter, pointed comparisons can be and are made between the poverty deficit and expenditures for cosmetics, pet food, military hardware, and numerous other goods and services.

As already mentioned, the poverty rate for blacks and persons of Spanish origin is higher than for whites as a whole. The poverty rate for households with a woman as head is higher than for households with a male head. Children under 18 accounted for 36 percent of all white persons below the poverty level, compared to 54 percent of all poor blacks. In contrast, old persons made up a larger proportion of poor whites than of poor blacks.

The provident elderly, who worked at middle-class jobs and saved for the future through retirement plans, often find that the security they earned has been destroyed by inflation. These people, who highly value self-reliance, are caught in the bind of their own values. They have lost the security they bought with savings and often are reluctant to accept the welfare aid for which they might be eligible.

Since a large fraction of the poor are the old, the unskilled, husbandless women with children, and persons with severe mental and physical handicaps, poverty cannot be eliminated by increasing the productivity of the poor. Rather, it can be significantly reduced only by changing the traditional norm that the right to consume beyond a low minimum guaranteed by public relief is tied to the value of the individual's contribution to the economy.

Women The economic status of women is a special case because of their presumed dependency, because their prestige and authority are in large part seen as a by-product of the achievements of their husbands, because their position in the labor force is ambiguous and intermittent, and because their ascribed identity as women is viewed as a governing status.

Relatively fewer women than men participate in the paid labor force, but the difference is narrowing. Despite their lower labor force participation rate, women have a generally higher unemployment rate than men. For instance, in 1975 when the male unemployment rate was running at about 7 percent, the female rate was over 8 percent. (The difference between 7 and 8 percent should be thought of as a difference of nearly 15 percent.) Women are over-represented in relatively low-paying categories, particularly clerical and service occupations. Home obligations and job requirements frequently conflict, resulting in broken careers and part-time work. All of these factors, compounded by declining but real prejudice against women workers, hold down their job seniority and promotion chances. The result is lower income and often less income than men for the same work.

INEQUALITY OF PRESTIGE

Stratification by prestige is a matter of everyday observation and an important source of pain for some and satisfaction for others, but it is difficult to measure. In contrast to economic inequality, for which objective indicators can be readily designed, prestige is stubbornly subjective, changeable, and elusive.

Occupational prestige Studies conducted in the United States since 1927 show a high consistency in the prestige assigned to specific occupations. In the two best-known studies, made by the National Opinion Research Center (NORC) in 1947 and 1963, 90 occupations were rated by national samples. The prestige scores from the two studies are highly correlated, although during the 16 years most scientific occupations increased their standing and most artistic occupations declined.

Ratings from the more recent study are shown in Table 6.2. Viewed as a whole, the prestige scores correlate highly with the income and educational attainments of workers in the occupations (Broom and Maynard, 1969), but there are some interesting deviations. Minister and schoolteacher rank

higher in prestige than in income, but undertaker and singer in a nightclub have less prestige than would have been estimated from their income. A farm owner and operator ranks higher in prestige than predicted by either income or education.

Obviously the prestige of occupations is not a simple function of their economic rewards and educational requirements. Responsibility, independence, aesthetic aspects, and site of work may also influence ratings (Garbin and Bates, 1961). Recent and more complex ratings suggest that what is being measured is not so much prestige as more general values people attach to jobs, a sort of "general goodness" (Goldthorpe and Hope, 1972:31).

The reality of ranking is not argued. What is changing is the detailed interpretation of the differences. Some manual occupations rank above several nonmanual occupations, suggesting that the historic distinction between handwork and headwork is not decisive. The increased importance of, and increased wages for, some kinds of blue-collar work, and perhaps a change in attitudes toward manual labor, may foreshadow further shifting in the relative prestige of some blue-collar and white-collar jobs. Such a reversal has been documented in Poland, where technicians now rate above office employees in certain rewards and styles of consumption, and a similar change may have occurred in other socialist countries (Wesołowski and Słomczynski, 1968:210).

International comparisons of occupational prestige show overall similarities but some variation (Hodge, Treiman, and Rossi, 1966). Between-country correlations average higher for white-collar than for blue-collar occupations; that is, different countries agree more closely on the prestige to be assigned to white-collar work than on the prestige of manual work. Some scholars conclude that an overall similarity of prestige rankings of occupations in countries with dissimilar cultures indicates that prestige reflects the functional importance of the occupation rather than the peculiar values of the society.

Table 6:2 Prestige ratings of occupations

Occupation	Score	Occupation	Score
U.S. Supreme Court justice	94	Policeman	72
Physician	93		
Nuclear physicist	92	*Average*	**71**
Scientist	92		
Government scientist	91	Reporter on a daily newspaper	71
State governor	91	Bookkeeper	70
Cabinet member in the federal government	90	Radio announcer	70
College professor	90	Insurance agent	69
U.S. Representative in Congress	90	Tenant farmer—one who owns livestock and machinery and manages the farm	69
Chemist	89	Local official of a labor union	67
Diplomat in the U.S. Foreign Service	89	Manager of a small store in a city	67
Lawyer	89	Mail carrier	66
Architect	88	Railroad conductor	66
County judge	88	Traveling salesman for a wholesale concern	66
Dentist	88	Plumber	65
Mayor of a large city	87	Barber	63
Member of the board of directors of a large corporation	87	Machine operator in a factory	63
Minister	87	Owner-operator of a lunch stand	63
Psychologist	87	Playground director	63
Airline pilot	86	Corporal in the regular army	62
Civil engineer	86	Garage mechanic	62
Head of a department in a state government	86	Truck driver	59
Priest	86	Fisherman who owns his own boat	58
Banker	85	Clerk in a store	56
Biologist	85	Milk route man	56
Sociologist	83	Streetcar motorman	56
Captain in the regular army	82	Lumberjack	55
Accountant for a large business	81	Restaurant cook	55
Public school teacher	81	Singer in a nightclub	54
Building contractor	80	Filling station attendant	51
Owner of a factory that employs about 100 people	80	Coal miner	50
		Dock worker	50
Artist who paints pictures that are exhibited in galleries	78	Night watchman	50
Author of novels	78	Railroad section hand	50
Economist	78	Restaurant waiter	49
Musician in a symphony orchestra	78	Taxi driver	49
Official of an international labor union	77	Bartender	48
County agricultural agent	76	Farmhand	48
Electrician	76	Janitor	48
Railroad engineer	76	Clothes presser in a laundry	45
Owner-operator of a printing shop	75	Soda fountain clerk	44
Trained machinist	75	Sharecropper—one who owns no livestock or equipment and does not manage farm	42
Farm owner and operator	74	Garbage collector	39
Undertaker	74	Street sweeper	36
Welfare worker for a city government	74	Shoe shiner	34
Newspaper columnist	73		

Source: Hodge et al., 1964:290–292. Used by permission of Robert W. Hodge and the University of Chicago Press.

Prestige in communities Early studies using the reputational technique were conducted by W. L. Warner, his associates, and other workers during the depression years of the 1930s. These studies found that people in small, homogeneous communities tended to use similar criteria in evaluating one another. At the lower economic levels, money is more important, but at the higher levels manners, taste, and family background count for more. Considering the community as a whole, occupation was the most important basis for prestige in Jonesville, a community southwest of Chicago (Warner and Associates, 1949). Size of income, source of income, house type, neighborhood, and amount of education followed occupation in that order. Family background was salient in Yankee City, a city north of Boston (Warner and Lunt, 1941, 1942), and in Old City, a town in the Deep South (Davis, Gardner, and Gardner, 1941), but less important in Jonesville. In Yankee City and Old City, an upper upper class of prominent old families outranked a lower upper class, although, on the average, the latter had more money.

Six prestige levels, ranging from lower lower to upper upper, were identified in Yankee City and five in Jonesville. They are called social classes in the research reports, although they are prestige strata rather than classes in the strict sense. The higher levels, however, do appear to be cohesive social groupings, bound together by ties of friendship and marriage, and they approximate what Weber called status groups. These early studies were an important departure in community research, but they used small static towns located just outside the commuting range of metropolitan centers. They were not representative of the country as a whole or of small communities in general. In most large communities, where prestige criteria are less uniform than in small towns, there is usually no commonly perceived prestige hierarchy. Furthermore, prestige criteria differ among blacks, whites, various ethnic communities, and subcultures.

INEQUALITY OF POWER

If prestige is ephemeral and elusive, power is even harder to study because power understood is power diminished. With only a little exaggeration, Disraeli observed, "The most powerful men are not public men. The public man is responsible and the responsible man is a slave. It is private life that governs the world." The private person who is also powerful tends to guard his privacy, and thus the study of the distribution and use of power at the national level is difficult. It is easier to identify the pattern of influence in local communities.

Elites have been defined as "the few who get the most of any value . . . the rest are the rank and file. An elite preserves its ascendancy by manipulating symbols, controlling supplies, and applying violence" (Lasswell, 1934/1950:3). Thus there are many kinds of elites—business elites, prestige elites, cultural elites, intellectual elites, and power elites. Sometimes elites consolidate into an establishment, as is the case in Britain.

National power—the United States One view represents the American power structure as a cohesive *power elite:* (1) a corporate elite of executives of large companies, (2) a military elite of senior officers, and (3) a small political elite consisting of the president and the most influential members of the executive branch (Mills, 1956:Chap. 12). This power elite makes the most important decisions at the national level. Furthermore, because they resemble each other in social background, values, and interests, its members tend to form similar judgments and act in unison. Plurality of interests and concerns are not balanced off against each other, and power becomes monolithic (cf. Domhoff, 1967).

At the end of his presidency, Eisenhower described a "conjunction of an immense military establishment and a large arms industry" and warned "against the acquisition of unwarranted influence, whether sought or unsought, by the military-industrial complex" (Farewell Address, January 17, 1961). It has been argued that interpenetration of large corporations and government exerts a strong indirect influence on national policies, overriding the traditional separation of public and private sectors (Galbraith, 1967).

An alternative theory of the American power structure is the *pluralist* or *balance* thesis, which holds that major decisions tend to be compromises among the several interest groups, each of which has veto power that obstructs decisions threatening to its fundamental interests (Riesman, 1951: 242–255). In this view, power in the United States has become more widely spread as a result of multiplying interest groups, changes in the capitalist system, and a diversification of business interests. These contrasting perspectives may emphasize important aspects of reality: Various constituencies, interest groups, and power blocs make their influence felt in different ways at different levels of the power structure. Local labor unions are a significant power element in a few communities, but business interests tend to dominate at that level. On the other hand, national labor leaders are a powerful force in national politics and in the formation of broad economic decisions. (On the theory of pluralism, see *POLITICS AND SOCIETY*, pp. 574–576.)

A different kind of national power is exercised by special-interest groups with a small leadership but a broad membership base, which organize effective single-purpose lobbies. The National Rifle Association, for example, has usually been successful in defeating gun control legislation through its ability to concentrate its energies on a specific issue.

Direct participation by the general public in the decision making process is limited in a heterogeneous society because of the enormous diversity of backgrounds and interests. The public rarely plays an active role in such crucial decisions as the making of war, and few would contend that the intervention in Vietnam was endorsed by an in-

formed public. At the time, most people did not have coherent opinions or the information with which to form them. But the peace movement certainly affected the decision to make peace in Vietnam, however gradually the opinion crystallized and however slowly the decision was implemented. A literate population with high exposure to the mass media can develop coherent opinions after the fact, opinions that run contrary to national policy and may redirect it. Perhaps the main effect of the antiwar movement, apart from direct influence on policy in Vietnam, has been to make foreign-policy decisions more visible and less the private province of experts — a development that places limits on the free exercise of elite power.

Community power *Middletown in Transition* (Lynd and Lynd, 1937) is a benchmark of the analysis of community power, but it was more than a decade before the next large-scale study was published (Hunter, 1953). This study of Atlanta reported a monolithic, covert power structure composed of a small group of men, mostly wealthy businessmen, who did not occupy formal political positions but had a determining voice in almost all important community decisions. The members of the power structure were not visible in the sense that they were known to the man in the street, but through the use of the reputational technique, they were identified by a panel of strategically placed informants.

Other studies of American communities show that the distribution of power in Atlanta is only one of a wide variety of power arrangements (Bonjean and Olson, 1964; Spinrad, 1965). Some communities have visible leaders, influential people who are almost universally recognized as such. Others, like Atlanta, have concealed leaders, known to informed members of the community but not to the public. Still others have symbolic leaders with reputed but no real power. Some communities have leaders of each type. Communities also differ in the scope of influence of their leaders; some may exert power on a wide range of issues and others on only a few. Finally, communities vary in the cohesiveness of their leadership, which may form a distinct and unified social group or a collectivity of independently acting persons (Clark, 1974; Hawley and Wirt, 1974).

There is inconclusive evidence that power in American communities is becoming more widely distributed among groups, some of which are in competition but none of which is able or perhaps motivated to influence decisions beyond its special and limited interests (Walton, 1967; Gilbert, 1967; Warren, 1962).

Section three status and life-styles

CORRELATES OF SOCIAL STRATIFICATION

The results of stratification penetrate the details of everyday life and social interaction in a multitude of ways. Some examples are summarized in Table 6:3, reporting differences by strata in life chances and privileges, and in Table 6:4, which reports differences in attitudes and behavior.

In some cases the link between stratification and the correlated variable can be established as one of cause and effect, for example, dental care correlated with income, but in others it remains a matter of statistical association, for example, obesity negatively

Table 6:3   Stratification correlates: life chances and life-styles, United States

Related characteristics		Strata		
		Lower	Middle	Upper
Children ever born per 1,000 women[a]	(E)[b]	Less than 8 years of school: 4,247	High school, 1–3 years: 3,598	College graduates: 2,389
Mortality ratios, white women, aged 25–64[c]	(E)	Less than 5 years of school: 1.60	High school, 1–3 years: 0.91	College graduates: 0.78
Lifetime income[d]	(E)	Less than 8 years of school: $231,000	High school graduates: $393,000	College graduates: $627,000
Annual median family income[e]	(E)	Less than 8 years of school: $7,073	High school graduates: $13,941	College graduates: $20,124
Index of marital instability[f]	(I)	Low income: 23	Middle income: 10	High income: 6
Obesity of women[g]	(I)	Low income: 52%	Middle income: 43%	High income: 9%
Victim of robbery per 100,000 of population[h]	(I)	Income under $3,000: 172	Income $3,000–$6,000: 121	Income $10,000 and over: 34
Own dishwasher[i]	(I)	Income under $5,000: 6%	Income $10,000–$15,000: 23%	Income $25,000 and over: 64%

[a] *Statistical Abstract of the United States,* 1975:Table 75, Women ever married, aged 35–44.
[b] Parenthetical letters indicate the bases for stratification in the studies cited: income (I) or education (E).
[c] Kitagawa, 1972:92.
[d] *Statistical Abstract of the United States,* 1975:Table 200.
[e] *Current Population Reports,* Series P-60, No. 101 (January 1976):Table 36, Family head 25 years and older.
[f] Udry, 1967:673. The index is an estimate of the percentage of white males 25 through 34 years of age who have had one or more broken marriages. The index is higher for nonwhites at all income levels.
[g] Burnight and Marden, 1967:75–92.
[h] *Statistical Abstract of the United States,* 1971:Table 222, Robberies in 1965.
i *Statistical Abstract of the United States,* 1975:Table 665.

Table 6:4   Stratification correlates: attitudes and behavior, United States

Related characteristics		Strata		
		Lower	Middle	Upper
Say they are "very happy"[a]	(I)[b]	Income under $3,000: 29%	Income $5,000–$7,000: 38%	Income $15,000 or more: 56%
Think ideal number of children is three or less[c]	(E)	Less than high school: 67%	High school: 78%	College: 86%
Believe death always comes too soon[d]	(E)	Less than high school: 58%	High school: 50%	College: 24%
Think vasectomy impairs male sexual ability[e]	(E)	Less than 12 years of school: 25%	High school graduates: 14%	College graduates: 6%
Considers self a Democrat[f]	(I)	Income under $5,000: 55%	Income $10,000–$15,000: 43%	Income $20,000 or more: 36%
Voted in 1974 election[g]	(E)	Less than 9 years of school: 34%	High school graduates: 45%	Some college: 55%
Report no close friends[h]	(O)	Unskilled workers: 30%	Skilled, small business, and white-collar workers: 13%	Professionals, top business, and officials: 10%

[a] Gallup survey (1971).
[b] Parenthetical letters indicate the bases for stratification in the studies cited: income (I), occupation (O), or education (E).
[c] Gallup survey (1971).
[d] Riley and Foner, 1968:335. Aged 31–40.
[e] Presser and Bumpass, 1972:525. Women under 45 years (1970).
[f] Gallup survey (1975).
[g] *Statistical Abstract of the United States,* 1975:Table 728.
[h] Kahl, 1957:137–138.

correlated with income. The differences between various levels of the social strata should not obscure the great range of attitudes and behavior within any level. Except where there is high consensus in the whole society, no social stratum shows uniformity of behavior or attitudes. Nevertheless, the correlate approach is a good way of summarizing some effects of stratification and showing that social rank has a pervasive impact on the ways people live, act, and think.

The discussion that follows suggests how the correlates of social stratification produce different life-styles. The interplay of work and life-style is described in Adaptation 14, which contrasts the experience of two women at opposite ends of the occupational scale.

LIFE AT THE TOP

At the top of the social order is a community of mutually aware families, most of whom inherit enough wealth so that they may, if they wish, live without working. But the rich do not always rank at the top of the scale in prestige; some highly esteemed persons are not rich, and some powerful people lack high prestige.

Wealth tends to be achieved before power and often before prestige, at least in the case of status gained in the world of business. On the other hand, the sequence is reversed for many generals and politicians who become rich after their accomplishments gain wide recognition. In a sense, they are financially rewarded as a by-product of their chosen work. Ghostwritten memoirs of famous public figures reflect the pecuniary value of prestige. The attainments of individuals may qualify them for membership in the elite, but their full acceptance in the newly won status in many cases depends on the acceptability of the whole family. There may be doubt about the existence of class consciousness at most levels of society, but there is little question about the self-awareness of the upper class.

Because the rich and powerful can prevent the intrusions into their privacy that systematic study entails, there is little well-documented information about the life-styles of elites. Nevertheless, the following is a plausible characterization of the "old family" upper stratum in large American cities.

They live in one or more exclusive and expensive residential areas in fine old houses in which many of them were born, or in elaborately simple modern ones which they have constructed. In these houses, old or new, there are the correct furnishings and the cherished equipage. Their clothing, even when it is apparently casual and undoubtedly old, is somehow different in cut and hang from the clothes of other men and women. The things they buy are quietly expensive and they use them in an inconspicuous way. They belong to clubs and organizations to which others like themselves are admitted, and they take quite seriously their appearances in these associations.

They have relatives and friends in common, but more than that, they have in common experiences of a carefully selected and family-controlled sort. They have attended the same or similar private and exclusive schools, preferably one of the Episcopal boarding schools of New England. Their men have been to Harvard, Yale, Princeton, or if local pride could not be overcome, to a locally esteemed college to which their families have contributed. And now they frequent the clubs of these schools, as well as leading clubs in their own city, and as often as not, also a club or two in other metropolitan centers.

Their names are not in the chattering, gossiping columns or even the society columns of their local newspapers. . . . For those established at the top are "proud"; those not yet established are merely conceited.

Almost everywhere in America, the metropolitan upper classes have in common, more or less, race, religion, and nativity. . . . In each city, they tend to be Protestant; moreover Protestants of class-church denominations, Episcopalian mainly, or Unitarian, or Presbyterian (Mills 1956:56–60).

In contrast to people at the middle levels, upper-stratum people are oriented to the past rather than the future, they emphasize "being" rather than "doing," and they are less individualistic and more concerned with lineage (Baltzell, 1958:52). Speech differentiates the uppermost stratum from the middle levels, and there is a subtle upper-class accent in the United States that cuts across regional differences. Euphemisms, circumlocutions, and pretentious speech are rarely used among the upper class; their speech is simpler, more straightforward, terser, and by middle-class standards often vulgar. For example:

Upper	*Nonupper*
begin	commence
died	passed away
poor	underprivileged
kin	relative (*Fadiman, 1956:8–10*)

It has been suggested that the social elites in the larger American cities are merging into a national upper class, largely as the result of the rise of national corporate enterprise and rapid communications and transportation (Mills, 1956; Baltzell, 1958). Several institutions seem to have been instrumental in the growth of this class, the most important of which are the New England boarding schools and the fashionable eastern colleges. At these, the rich and well-born from large cities intermingle, intermarry, and form ties that endure after they return to their respective communities. The development of the Episcopal church into a national upper-class institution has both promoted and been a result of the increased solidarity of the intercity moneyed elite in the United States.

BLUE-COLLAR WORLD

In contrast to the dearth of reliable information on upper-stratum life-styles, numerous studies deal with the culture and behavior of lower-class or working-class people (Glenn and Alston, 1967). However, the findings do not give a single, consistent picture, partly because the lower strata are not uniformly defined and partly because lower-stratum values and behavior vary by race, ethnic origin, religion, region, and community size. The description below applies to elements that several lower-class subcultures seem to have in common but excludes the very lowest stratum.

Blue-collar people tend to be politically liberal on welfare and labor issues that involve their economic interests. In almost all other respects, lower-stratum people are more conservative than middle- and upper-stratum people. In religious beliefs, they are often fundamentalists. Even if they are not affiliated with a church or religious organization, they usually believe in a devil, in the virgin birth of Christ, and in a literal interpretation of the Scriptures. On the average, they are less favorable to civil liberties, more ethnocentric, more authoritarian, and more isolationist than people at higher levels.

Relations between husband and wife are frequently lacking in warmth and effective communication (Komarovsky, 1964), and rates of marital dissolution are much greater than in higher strata (Goode, 1962).

Lower-stratum people participate much less in formal organizations than middle-stratum people, they report fewer friends, and much of their visiting and primary interaction is with kin. If relatives do not live nearby, vacations are likely to be spent with them (Miller and Riessman, 1961).

Blue-collar people value education for its vocational and economic utility. Whites from this stratum may sacrifice to send a son to college but think that sending a daughter is a waste of money. If a daughter is sent to college, she is likely to be encouraged to go into elementary education or some other vocational curriculum. Neither a liberal arts education nor training in social skills is considered important (Miller and Riessman, 1961). Blacks, however, do not share the preference for investing in the education of sons rather than daughters.

Many working-class people do not fit the above description, and with increasing education, they seem to be adopting behavior characterized as middle class. However, middle-class life-styles are also in flux.

THE DISREPUTABLE POOR

The antithesis of life at the top of the social order is not the life-style of manual laborers. Blue-collar workers, although stratified below those who have more disposable income, more savings, more education, and more prestigious jobs, can nevertheless be considered part of the same encompassing social structure. They can realistically aspire to improve the lot of their children if not of themselves. But below the lower blue-collar workers is a submerged population marked off by a sharp discontinuity—a natural stratum. It has been termed the disreputable poor (Matza, 1966; cf. Knupfer, 1947) and is made up of several elements:

1. *The dregs* "have been left behind by otherwise mobile ethnic populations. In these families there is at least the beginning of some tradition of disreputable poverty. In America, the primary examples include immobile descendants of Italian and Polish immigrants and of the remnants of even earlier arrivals—Germans, Irish, and Yankees—and Negroes who have already become habituated to the regions in which disreputable poverty flourishes" (Matza, 1966:292).

2. *Newcomers* without funds or marketable skills find their way into depressed neighborhoods. These immigrants are drawn from peasant backgrounds and, unable to cope with an "advanced society," are ex-

ploited, victimized, and indoctrinated by the experienced disreputable poor, often members of their own ethnic group.

3. Skidders, because of alcohol, drugs, psychiatric problems, or a long string of bad luck, hit bottom in the deteriorated parts of the city (cf. Wilensky and Edwards, 1959).

4. The infirm, handicapped by age or some other difficulty beyond their control, drift into disreputable neighborhoods after a conventional life, powerless to help themselves and resentful of their plight and their environment.

Even during periods of prosperity when unemployment is reduced to a relatively low level, the disreputable poor remain unemployed or work irregularly. They are therefore unlike those who become unemployed only during economic depressions and periods of mass unemployment. Thus the disreputable poor cannot be rehabilitated by the simple expedient of providing employment or preparing them to be incorporated into the work force. They are, from the standpoint of the welfare agencies, elusive and hard to reach, and they include among their number a large share of problem families.

They contribute far more than their share to the relief recipients, to crime and delinquency rates, to rates of alcoholism, to the list of unmarried mothers and thus to illegitimate children, to divorces, desertions, and to the mentally ill. [They are] probably the only authentic outsiders, for modern democratic industrial life . . . has had a remarkable capacity for integrating increasingly larger proportions of society (Matza, 1966:290).

Caution Such invidious terms as *disreputable* are frequently and properly regarded as objectionable (cf. Miller and Riessman, 1961). However, the phrase *disreputable poor* refers to the stigma society places on people who live in extreme poverty; it is not a sociologist's evaluation.

Adaptation 14: Life-styles of working women

The long-term trend toward expanded participation of women in the labor force persisted through the economic strains of the 1970s. In 1940 only 27 percent of women were in the labor force. By 1965 the figure had increased to 37 percent and by 1975 to 46 percent. For men the comparable figure in 1975 was 78 percent. In 1975 women made up 39 percent of the labor force, they were entering jobs previously closed to them, and they were moving up the occupational ladder (Statistical Abstract, 1975:Tables 558, 563, 567). Increasingly women are seen in positions of authority in government, business, and industry and are breaking barriers to employment in jobs that have been regarded as the private reserve of men. Nevertheless, on the average their occupational status is inferior to that of men and they are less well paid for the work they do. (See STRATIFICATION, pp. 165–166 and THE FAMILY, pp. 329–333.)

Expanding female employment has altered the division of responsibility in many families and has placed strains on customary family patterns. (See THE FAMILY, p. 329.) This adaptation reports the contrasting life-styles of two working women: one an executive, the other a retail clerk. In both cases, the requirements of their jobs affect their personal life-styles and impinge on the life-styles of other persons.

Ms. McWilliams, an advertising executive, is a woman in command of her job and her domestic situation, adapting clock, calendar, and travel to serve both. Ms. Gray, a Woolworth employee, is largely commanded by the requirements of her job, which fills more of her day and more days in her week. The first case is a woman exercising options to choose a life-style in which she finds movement and satisfaction. The second is a

Source: "Advertising Executive" reprinted from Harriet Lyons, "Found Women," p. 56, Ms magazine (January 1974). "Woolworth Employee" abridged and adapted from Agnes Schipper, "Measuring 30 Years by the Yard," pp. 66ff., Ms magazine (February 1974). Published here by permission of Ms magazine.

woman whose job would seem to exhaust her physical resources and leave few options and little freedom. Nevertheless, she is able to summon up personal reserves to care for aged relatives and gains satisfaction from doing so.

ADVERTISING EXECUTIVE

Gertrude "Jimmy" McWilliams's white colonial house in Pound Ridge, New York, used to belong to Frank Morgan, the actor who played the wizard in *The Wizard of Oz.* The way friends marvel at Jimmy McWilliams makes you wonder if the real wizard isn't now in residence.

A Detroit advertising executive from Monday to Friday, McWilliams flies (in an airplane) to Pound Ridge every Friday night to spend the weekend with her family. This unorthodox commute began in 1969 when General Motors asked her to go to Detroit to help launch the Chevrolet Vega. Her husband and two sons encouraged her to accept the new job and assured her that the logistics could be worked out.

"Our family operates like a square," she explains. "Each has a corner and each believes that the growth of the individual strengthens the group. I feel I have more to offer my family because I have a different life."

Last spring McWilliams became a senior vice-president in charge of special projects at Campbell-Ewald agency, which handles advertising for Chevrolet. "If you can communicate the reasons behind the design decisions," she says, "you'll have the best possible selling information. I have a free range to do anything that contributes to that purpose." She developed the comprehensive kit, distributed to Chevrolet dealers, which explains the operation of the new seat belts in the 1974 models. "The seat belts have to be done up in sequence before the car will start. It took me months to put the procedure into the kind of instructions that wouldn't bedevil the users."

Rather than sapping her energy, the Detroit/Pound Ridge timetable has made Jimmy McWilliams more effective on the job and at home. The weeks seem to shoot by and she and her husband (an automobile sales management executive) try to get as much as possible accomplished before the weekend reunions. "We have targets now which accelerate our productivity," she maintains. "My husband and sons (away at school but frequent weekend visitors) are capable of rising to any domestic challenge. They probably wouldn't be this resourceful had I been around all the time."

A simple but profound fact emerges from the choices Jimmy McWilliams has made. She is a businesswoman and a free agent—and her husband and kids still like her.

WOOLWORTH EMPLOYEE

At 60, Marion Gray has spent more than half her life working for Woolworth's. A certificate commemorating her twenty-fifth anniversary hangs on her wall. On her silver anniversary, the company also gave her artificial flowers and ten shares of stock. Almost everything she owns and wears comes from Woolworth's.

Marion Gray measures her length of service by the age of her son: "He was almost a year old," she said, "when I went back to work to help out the family. I went to work to get us ahead, never thinking I would work this long. But the longer I worked, the more independent I became."

Several years later when her son was in high school, her husband had a stroke. He was hospitalized and she became the sole support of the family. As he was never able to work again, he received small disability payments his last few years, but when he died in 1967, he left nothing.

"We started out with nothing and ended with nothing. My husband had no insurance, no pension, no nothing. He was a peacetime veteran and not entitled to anything, only a grave, and they didn't even give him that. I paid off his funeral at 20 dollars a month and his grave at ten dollars a month. It took me two years.

"I had a pretty rough married life. If I had it to do over again, I wouldn't go through it."

Although she never intended to have any children, within two years of marriage she gave birth to a daughter. They had a second daughter, five years later, and then a son.

At work Marion works from 9:30 to 6:15 P.M. five days a week and from 12 to 5 P.M. on Sundays. Each morning, she catches a 7:15 bus from San Anselmo to San Francisco and usually arrives at least an hour early for work. "Rushing exhausts me," she explains. "I'd rather be at work an hour ahead of time than be late and rush. I'm afraid of traffic tie-ups. I've always been early."

Marion Gray at home

At 9:25 Marion punches in on the time clock and walks down the three flights to the yardage department on the basement floor. She begins her workday by straightening out a mess of half-rolled and displaced fabric bolts left by customers the previous day. A patchwork of colors, textures, and patterns takes order around her. The store opens, and customers begin to stream down the stairs toward the basement.

"Yardage is a real hard department," she says, "because the work is constant. You have to lift heavy bolts and upholstery material. Sometimes you lift several bolts at a time to save footsteps. You do your own cashiering. Your arms are never still. You are constantly on the go."

At home About her living arrangements, she says: "My kids would love to have me live with them, but I'm much too independent for that. I did the best I could for them. They're my children and if they need me, I'm here. They've got their own families and problems and I don't want them to support me. As long as I can take care of myself, I think that's the best way."

If health permits, Marion Gray will work until she is 65 so she can receive a full pension. "Some women would like to work longer than 65 because they don't know what else to do with themselves," she said. She, on the other hand, would like to retire at 62, but then her pension and Social Security payments would be smaller.

In 1963, when her husband was still alive, the Woolworth's branch where she worked in Vallejo closed. She found her current job at a Woolworth's store in San Francisco. That meant giving up 20 years' seniority, which could not be transferred to her new job, and commuting almost four hours a day, leaving on a 6:30 A.M. bus and returning at 8:15 in the evening. Six years later, after her husband died, she finally moved to a small apartment in San Francisco.

A few years later, Marion moved from San Francisco to suburban San Anselmo to "house-sit" for her cousin. Marion now helps take care of her Uncle Cornelius, who is 83, and Aunty Kitty (in her nineties)—both of whom live in the same house. Each evening, she cooks the next day's dinner for them.

"I didn't realize how lonely I was in my little apartment. Now, I have someone waiting for me when I get home, someone who needs me."

Section four social mobility

Vertical mobility is any upward or downward change in the absolute or relative rank of any individual or group. A job promotion or demotion, a change in income, marrying a person of higher or lower status, moving into a better or worse neighborhood—all these are instances of vertical social mobility. An alteration of position with no significant movement up or down in the system of social stratification is called horizontal mobility.

Figure 6:3 shows a few examples of vertical mobility between strata and of horizontal mobility between functional categories called *situses*. The manager of a store in an auto supply chain who is transferred to another store to do the same work, with about the same salary, prestige, and authority, is horizontally mobile, although this horizontal move does not involve a change in situs. But the store manager who takes a similar job in an auto engineering firm has moved from one functional category or situs to another. Some changes entail movement between both strata and situses, for instance, when a junior bank executive joins a manufacturing company at a higher status and salary (Morris and Murphy, 1959).

The strata and situses in Figure 6:3 are only illustrative. They are divided for convenience into broad categories and levels, but the reality is far more complex. Mobility occurs within strata and within situses as well as between them. A change in occupation from accountant to bank manager leaves the individual in the same stratum although probably with a higher salary. Furthermore, according to the occupational prestige scores in Table 6:2 (p. 167), the accountant moves from an occupation with a prestige score of 81 to bank manager with a score of 85—small but measurable upward mobility.

Vertical mobility is often measured by changes in occupation, because the position of the individual in the total pattern of inequality largely depends on his occupation. Furthermore, information on occupation is easy to get. Respondents readily talk about jobs, and, when properly compiled, occupation data are relatively unambiguous.

CAREER MOBILITY

As the term implies, career mobility refers to changes in the social status of individuals. It is usually described by interviewing persons and identifying the jobs held at three or four time points, such as first job, job at the time of interview, and last job, if no longer in the labor force.

The individual's chances of moving up the occupational ladder are strongly influenced

Figure 6:3
Types of mobility

Strata	Functional categories (situses)		
	Finance and records	**Manufacturing**	**Transportation**
High	Bank manager	Industrial engineer	Railroad president
	Accountant	Lithographer	Airline pilot
Middle	Bookkeeper	Bookbinder	Railroad conductor
	Bank teller	Tool and die maker	Mail carrier
Low	File clerk	Forge worker	Bus driver
	Bank messenger	Laborer, steel mill	Section hand

H ◄————————► H

V ↑↓ V

V Vertical mobility, from stratum to stratum

H Horizontal mobility, from situs to situs

by amount of education (Blau and Duncan, 1967:152–161; see also *EDUCATION*, Section Four), but also by less obvious factors such as community size, number of siblings, mother dominance, and late marriage.

1. Community size The probability that children of manual workers in the United States will be upwardly mobile varies with the size of the place in which they spend their childhood and adolescence (Lipset and Bendix, 1959:Chap. 8). Larger cities generally offer better educational facilities and acquaint the manual worker's children with a wider range of occupations. The correlation between community size and upward mobility does not hold for white-collar workers, presumably because middle-class children gain their aspirations within the family.

2. Number of siblings An only child and the child with one sibling have the best chances of being upwardly mobile. The probabilities for upward mobility are reduced with each additional sibling beyond one (Lipset and Bendix, 1959:238–243). Parents with several children must spread their resources or play favorites and are thus less able to provide all their children with the best education or with financial assistance.

3. Mother dominance The strong-mother family seem to be more conducive to upward mobility than the egalitarian or father-dominant family (Warner and Abegglen, 1955:64–107). Possibly mothers are primarily responsible for inculcating ambitions, and dominant mothers are more ambitious for their children. In contrast, the fatherless family, or one with a succession of foster fathers, does not seem to be conducive to upward movement.

4. Late marriage European studies have shown marked differences between the mobility of persons who marry young and those who marry late. In Denmark, males who married before age 25 tended to be downwardly mobile, those who married between 25 and 29 tended to be stable, and those who married at age 30 or older, upwardly mobile (Svalastoga, 1957). There is some evidence

for the same association in the United States. Ambitious males may postpone marriage so that they can more easily complete their education and become established in their careers. Or postponement of marriage may be a sign of a willingness to defer gratifications in order to attain a future goal (Rosen and D'Andrade, 1959:185–217; McClelland, 1961; Straus, 1962:326–335).

INTERGENERATIONAL MOBILITY

The study of career mobility, which examines changes during the working life of an individual, takes in a relatively small slice of time and does not throw much light on the basic issues of class inheritance. A better way to assess the extent to which a society's opportunity structure is open or closed is to compare the positions (usually occupations) of fathers and their sons at paired career points or at specific ages. Because most fathers and sons work for pay at some time, the study of father-to-son mobility is reasonably straightforward.

Mobility of women The same cannot be said of the intergenerational mobility of women; the mothers of many working women were never considered to be in the labor force or worked outside the home only briefly. Although women's work in the home is of significant social and economic value, until recently researchers did not take it into account, possibly because domestic work, whether paid or unpaid, has low prestige value or is mainly a customary, taken-for-granted obligation.

Intergenerational mobility of a woman is often described by comparing the occupational status of her father and her husband (if any) (Rossi, 1971). Thus the daughter of a skilled worker who marries a professional man is considered upwardly mobile. This is indeed vertical social mobility, but it is not the same as occupational mobility between father and son, and it tells nothing about women who do not marry.

The fact that researchers have accepted the

status difference between two men as a measure of female intergenerational mobility is further testimony to the socioeconomic inferiority of women. Occupational studies of women are complicated by the fact that they often have interrupted work careers, and some never join the labor force. However, about 46 percent of U.S. women currently participate in the labor force, and the number is rapidly increasing. The extent of ignorance about the occupational mobility of women is unsatisfactory from the standpoint of sociological knowledge as well as of human values.

The mobility process Although numerous forces and events determine whether mobility will take place, a few conditions and relationships are of major importance. To grasp these influences, it is necessary to winnow out numerous accidental and personal events and concentrate on broad trends. This does not mean that the intimate study of social mobility through the detailed assessment of life histories is not worth doing. Indeed it can throw light on human experience in a way that broad and summary treatments cannot. Nevertheless the account of individual experience can be comprehended most clearly when it is interpreted within a framework of statistical trends and relationships. Such a framework is given in the mobility model (Figure 6:4).

The figure is a simplified version of a path diagram and is based on an American study (Blau and Duncan, 1967:170). The arrows indicate the direct influence of one variable on another, and the weight of the arrows indicates the relative degree of that influence. The figure shows that the idea of

Figure 6:4 A mobility model

The direction of influence is shown by the arrows and the relative degree of influence by the weight of the lines. To facilitate following the basic logic, path coefficients and indications of external influences are omitted.
Caution: The diagram does not exhaust all the variables that determine mobility. One weak link, V–Y, is not shown. The link V–X is also left out because it does not bear on the problem at hand.

Source: After Blau and Duncan, 1967:170.

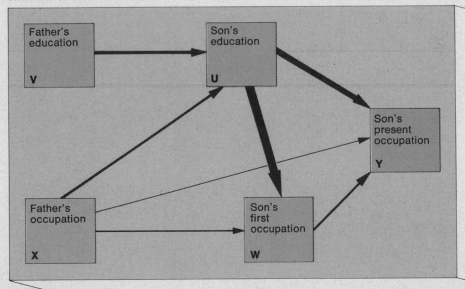

the inheritance of occupational status is more complicated than the term might suggest. The father's condition profoundly affects the son's, but not simply and directly from father's job to son's job. In fact, that direct link (X → Y) is statistically the weakest of all the paths shown, and the path from the father's job to son's first job (X → W) is fairly weak. The weight of paternal background comes from father's occupation and father's education, which together make their impact on son's education (X → U) and (V → U). In turn the son's education strongly influences his first job (U → W) and subsequent job (U → Y).

A more ascriptive kind of society, in which fathers were able to assign jobs to their sons, would show stronger (X → Y) influence. But with modernization and the expansion of jobs calling for high educational qualifications, the U → W and U → Y links would be strengthened even in the face of persistent nepotism.

INTERNATIONAL COMPARISONS

The process of industrialization stimulates social mobility by reshaping the structure of opportunity, reducing jobs in agriculture, and creating a demand for workers in new industries and services. Thus industrial and technological change accompanied by urbanization cause *structural* (or forced) mobility by pushing workers off the land and drawing them into urban and industrial jobs. During periods of rapid industrialization, much of the work force is in flux as it responds to the pressures and opportunities of the labor market. A different kind of mobility, called *circulation* (or free) mobility, can occur even though the total of job opportunities at each level remains the same. Circulation mobility takes place when one person displaces another from a given job.

It has been asserted that once a given level of economic development has been reached, as is the case of most Western industrialized countries, "the overall pattern of social mobility appears to be much the same" (Lipset and Zetterberg, 1959:13). This generalization has been criticized (Miller, 1960; Jones, 1969), but it is widely accepted and frequently cited. A full assessment of the argument would require an extended review, but the problem can be approached directly by comparing the findings from three surveys conducted in the 1960s in Australia, Italy, and the United States (Broom and Jones, 1969). The task of interpretation is simplified because all three are national surveys; they were carried out about the same time; the data are reported in comparable categories; and although the samples differ in size, the sample designs were similar. It is customary in such international comparisons to summarize such data into three categories: nonmanual, manual, and farm, and this has been done in Table 6:5.

The table shows the outflow *from* the fathers' strata *to* the strata currently occupied by their sons. When sons occupy the same stratum as their fathers, they fall in the diagonals of the table, which show the percentage immobile in boldface numbers. An immediate observation is the large proportion immobile in nonmanual and manual occupations in all three countries. In Italy 70 percent, and in the United States 69 percent, of sons from nonmanual backgrounds were themselves in nonmanual jobs at the time of interview. The Australian figure, while less (60 percent), is nevertheless high in absolute terms. In the three countries, between 26 and 35 percent of the sons of nonmanual fathers were downwardly mobile into manual occupations, and a much smaller proportion were downwardly mobile into farm occupations.

The pattern of mobility among sons of manual workers, while similar in all three countries, exhibits greater variety. The figures for upward mobility into nonmanual jobs are particularly interesting. In the American sample, 36 percent of the sons of manual workers were upwardly mobile, compared with only 20 percent in the Italian sample. The Australian figure, 31 percent, is intermediate, but it is closer to the American than to the Italian. If this movement can be taken as indicative of the degree of openness in the stratification system, then the United States has the most open, and Italy the least open, stratification system of the three countries.

Mobility from farm origins varies markedly and throws light on the processes of occupational mobility in societies at different stages and with different rates (perhaps different types) of industrial change. The United States shows by far the highest rate of mobility out of farm occupations: Only 22 percent of the sons from farm origins remained in farm work, 56 percent moved to manual, and 22 percent into nonmanual occupations. In Australia twice as many, proportionately, remained immobile in farm jobs. While farm to nonmanual mobility was comparable with the high U.S. rate, mobility from farm to

manual jobs in Australia was close to two-thirds that of the American figure. The Italian pattern is similar to the Australian, except that it has a larger degree of immobility and very low mobility into nonmanual jobs.

In summary, the United States has the highest rate of mobility among the three, but much of it is caused by the forces of industrial change; that is, much of it is structural mobility. Australia displays less occupational mobility than the United States but more than Italy. A large part of Australian mobility occurs because persons replace each other in given occupations rather than because certain jobs are closing down, as in farming, or opening up in new industries. Australian mobility is therefore of the circulation type rather than structural, and in that sense Australia is more equalitarian. Of the three countries, Italy has the lowest

Table 6:5 **Father-to-son mobility in three countries**

	Father's occupation		Son's occupation in percentages (rows)[a]			
	Number	Percent	Nonmanual	Manual	Farm	Total[c]
Australia, 1965 survey						
Nonmanual	486	26	**60**	35	6	101
Manual	935	51	31	**65**	4	100
Farm	427	23	19	40	**41**	100
Total	1,848	100	35	52	13	100
Italy, 1963–1964 survey						
Nonmanual	209	16	**70**	26	4	100
Manual	526	39	20	**76**	5	101
Farm	603	45	8	39	**53**	100
Total	1,338	100	22	51	26	99
United States, 1962 survey[b]						
Nonmanual	7,517	22	**69**	29	1	99
Manual	15,985	47	36	**62**	2	100
Farm	10,470	31	22	56	**22**	100
Total	33,972	100	39	53	8	100

[a] Cells are to be read as follows: Of Australian workers whose fathers were nonmanual workers, 60 percent were themselves nonmanual workers, 35 percent were manual workers, and 6 percent were farm workers. The boldface numbers appearing in a diagonal pattern for each country are percentage immobile.
[b] The American numbers (in thousands) represent population estimates derived from an initial sample of about 20,700 respondents.
[c] Deviations from 100 percent due to rounding.
Source: Broom and Jones, 1969:Table 1.

overall rate of mobility, and more of it is structural than circulation. Italy is less mobile and apparently less equalitarian than the other two countries. It seems clear that the amount and pattern of occupational mobility differs widely among the three Western industrial countries.

OPEN AND CLOSED MODELS OF MOBILITY

Societies may be classified according to the degree to which they approximate an open model with relatively unhampered mobility or a closed, or caste, model with severe restrictions on such movement. Figure 6:5 depicts the two pure types, as well as a mixed type complicated by color. In the closed model, status is ascribed—that is, based on characteristics over which the individual has little or no control: race, sex, age, and ethnic and family background. Such ascriptive societies are often termed castelike, but there may be no clear case of a true caste system in the sense of absolutely closed social categories with no mobility between them. The caste society is simply one extreme in which ascription predominates.

At the opposite extreme is the open-class society, characterized by achieved status, in which position depends upon the individual's performance: skills, knowledge, education, diligence, and tenacity. This type of society is achievement-oriented rather than ascription-oriented. But all real societies are mixtures of ascription and achievement. Industrial societies tend to demote highly born incompetents and advance capable and ambitious persons from the lower levels. Nevertheless, even the most technologically advanced countries are strongly influenced by ascribed characteristics in allocating rewards and opportunities, and sinecures are found for the mildly incompetent who have the right connections. Family background, sex, race, and ethnicity still count.

The third panel of Figure 6:5 shows a mixed type in which color imposes caste-like restrictions on mobility and limits the operation of achievement criteria. The United States is such a mixed society, and color remains a salient ascriptive mechanism. If sex were substituted for color in the diagram, most societies would have to be classified as mixed societies.

Caste in India Traditional India has long been considered a closed, caste system. The caste order of India before modernization was a complex arrangement of thousands of groupings, governed by rules of descent and marriage, occupation, ritual, and ideas about purity and pollution. Especially in southern India, there were restrictions on touching, approaching, or even seeing an individual of lowest caste. If higher-caste individuals did so, they would be polluted and would have to undergo purification. The lowest groupings (so-called untouchables) were excluded from temples and schools used by higher-caste groupings and were obliged to use separate paths and wells and to live in isolated villages (Leach, 1960; Srinivas, 1962; 1966; Silverberg, 1968).

Recent research, however, has put Indian caste in a different light. Caste is of profound importance, but it "refers only to ranking along the religious and ritual behavior dimension. . . . The religious and ritual rules of behavior prescribed by an individual's caste are an important determinant of his behavior and of how others treat him, perhaps more important a determinant than in other societies. But still they are far from being the only or final determinants" (Barber, 1968:20).

The caste order in India has been put under stress by the forces of modernization. Public transportation, urbanization, and industrialization have broken down many caste rules and interfered with adherence to residential and food taboos. In 1949 the Indian government declared untouchability illegal, but the reforms engendered resistance and deep bitterness, which may have contributed to the assassination of Mahatma Gandhi. Although some caste

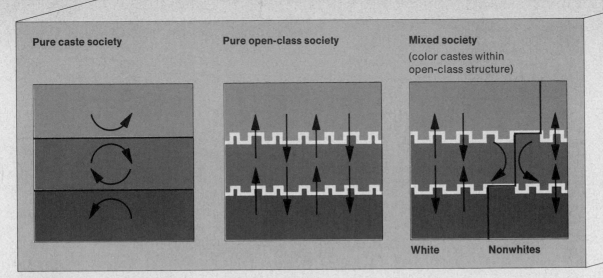

Figure 6:5 Caste, open-class, and mixed societies

practices are under strong pressure, the system persists in altered form throughout Indian society (Srinivas, 1966).

Contrary to popular impressions, the Indian castes are not strata. The numerous castes vary widely on all dimensions of stratification, and several castes may be at the same level. Therefore, a given caste usually does not comprise a complete stratum on any stratification variable but rather shares its standing with other castes.

Despite the elaborate regulations of the system, castes move up and down in prestige, power, and privilege. Members of a caste may improve their collective standing over a period of years by closely adhering to standards of behavior that apply to the high-ranking castes. Furthermore, there is a range of prestige and influence within castes, and individuals and families move within this hierarchy.

Although many traditional occupations are linked to castes, the castes are not strictly occupational categories. Certain castes have a right to engage in certain occupations if they wish to do so, and some occupations, such as agriculture, trade, and military service, are open to all castes.

On the one hand, older caste groups such as the barbers and washermen are breaking down into smaller units because so many of their members no longer follow the traditional occupation and tend to despise those who do. On the other hand, new caste groups are being formed around new occupational specialisms—skilled mechanical work, semiskilled dock and plantation work and so on—because caste affiliations are used, all over India, to facilitate labour recruitment. Once a caste group has attached itself to a particular kind of work it soon increases its hold by bringing into it only fellow members of the same group (Stevenson, 1967:29a).

The survivals of the caste system of India are, therefore, of continuing interest to the student of stratification because of their impact on occupation and because mobility is likely to be by groups rather than individuals.

U.S. mobility channels The chief mobility channels within the mixed class structure of the United States are shown in Figure 6:6.

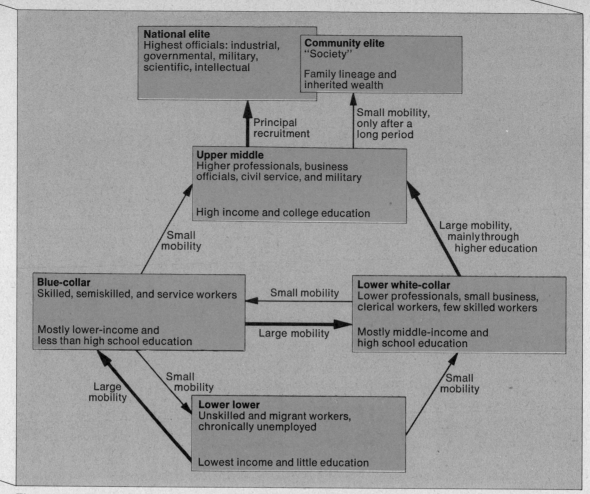

National elite
Highest officials: industrial,
governmental, military,
scientific, intellectual

Community elite
"Society"

Family lineage and
inherited wealth

Principal
recruitment

Small mobility,
only after a
long period

Upper middle
Higher professionals, business
officials, civil service, and military

High income and college education

Small
mobility

Large mobility,
mainly through
higher education

Blue-collar
Skilled, semiskilled, and service workers

Mostly lower-income and
less than high school education

Small mobility

Lower white-collar
Lower professionals, small business,
clerical workers, few skilled workers

Mostly middle-income and
high school education

Large mobility

Large
mobility

Small
mobility

Small
mobility

Lower lower
Unskilled and migrant workers,
chronically unemployed

Lowest income and little education

Figure 6:6 Stratification and generational mobility in the United States

Children born in a lower stratum are as likely to achieve upward mobility as they were a generation or two ago, but they now follow different paths to achievement.

They have little chance of becoming independent farmers or entrepreneurs, and although many manual workers each year quit their jobs to go into business for themselves, few succeed. Because of the difficulty of starting a new business, the government policy of sponsoring the establishment of small businesses among minority communities is a misinterpretation of the present economic scene. It would have been the right

thing to do in 1910, but many such businesses, even with government aid, are doomed to failure in the 1970s. Of those newly established small business enterprises that survive for a number of years, many remain marginal at best, and their owners never attain any more income or economic security than they would have had as wage workers. They may achieve more power or prestige, especially in minority communities, but usually not very much.

Upward mobility from the lowest strata increasingly requires formal education. Even mobility to the lower white-collar and blue-collar levels calls for specialized vocational training or apprenticeship. Therefore, the foundations for upward mobility are laid during adolescence and young adulthood, or not at all. Opportunities for upward movement of poorly educated and unskilled older adults have declined, a consequence of technological change.

Section five class and society

The study of stratification may be approached from either an individual or group perspective. The first looks at the distribution of individuals by income, prestige, or some other dimension, and the consequences of stratification most closely studied are those affecting life-chances and life-styles of individuals. The second perspective examines social classes as group formations and as dynamic forces in history; group interest and power are the major themes. The latter perspective is used in this concluding section.

THE MARXIST MODEL

The discussion of class and society is to a large extent a dialogue between the Marxist view and its critics. Although Marx never developed or set forth a systematic theory of social class, the idea of class was central to his thought, and a reasonably coherent argument can be gleaned from his voluminous writings (Bottomore and Rubel, 1956; Bendix and Lipset, 1966:6–11; Dahrendorf, 1959; Feuer, 1959).

The elements of the Marxist theory may be summarized as follows:

1. Origin of social classes   Social classes arise out of the "relations of production," that is, the way work is organized. Some people own land, others are tenant farmers; some work for wages, others are employers; still others are self-employed. An examination of the social structure of production can disclose who depends on whom, who dominates whom, who controls what re-

Karl Marx (1818–1883). The sociological aspect of the Marxist theory is called historical materialism. See also p. 545.

sources, the group interests that arise, and the potentialities for action based on common concerns. Marx did not identify class with occupation. He saw social class as a more general phenomenon rooted in the key economic roles, such as employer and employee, that cut across most industries and occupations and that characterize a period of economic history.

2. Polarization   In the Marxist model, the major social classes of the modern era, which followed the breakup of feudalism, are the landowners, the owners of capital on the one hand, and those who work for wages on the other. Marx recognized that the system was highly complex, but he foresaw an increasing polarization that would divide society into two great camps: on one side, the capitalists, or *bourgeoisie*, including the commercial farmers, and on the other, the *proletariat*, composed of the large mass of people who owned nothing but their labor power. Under this theory, small farmers, small business owners, and independent professionals would gradually be squeezed out, most of them forced into the proletariat as employees of large business organi-

Curbstone barbers in Calcutta: Services for the poor by the poor

zations owned by a few wealthy capitalists.

3. Objective class and subjective class
Individuals are placed in common circumstances by the organization of production, whether or not they are aware of it. Objective conditions define the individual's class position and his class interests. An employer's interests are opposed to those of the employees irrespective of subjective thoughts or sympathies. A blue-collar worker who identifies as middle class does not thus become a member of the bourgeoisie.

Marx believed that the major classes of society would in time become subjective, self-aware classes as well as objective classes. He noted, however, that some social groups in the system of production, though they share common interests and life situations, do not have the objective potential for becoming a fully developed social class. Thus he wrote of the French peasantry, who were the mainstay of Louis Bonaparte (Napoleon III) in the 1850s:

The small-holding peasants form a vast mass, the members of which live in similar conditions, but . . . their mode of production isolates them from one another, instead of bringing them into mutual intercourse. The isolation is increased by France's bad means of communication and by the poverty of the peasants. . . . Each individual peasant family is almost self-sufficient . . . a small holding, the peasant and his family; alongside them another small holding, another peasant and another family. A few score of these make up a village, and a few score of villages make up a Department. In this way, the great mass of the French nation is formed by simple addition of homologous magnitudes, much as potatoes in a sack form a sack of potatoes. In so far as millions of families live under economic conditions of existence that separate their mode of life, their interests, and their culture from those of the other classes and put them in hostile opposition to the latter, they form a class. In so far as there is merely a local interconnection among these small-holding peasants and the identity of interests begets no community, no national bond, and no political organization among them, they do not form a class. They are consequently incapable of enforcing their class interest in their own name. . . . They cannot represent themselves; they must be represented (Marx, in Feuer, 1959:338–339).

Unlike the French peasants, manual workers would inevitably become an organized and self-conscious class, because the conditions of life in the factory bring the workers together in ways that make them aware of their common interests as well as their common strength.

4. Class rule and class struggle In all past societies, with the exception of primitive communism, a few have ruled and the many have been ruled. But ruling is not best understood in purely political terms. A dominant economic class controls the mainsprings of society, including the government. Modern governments are bourgeois, because in the last analysis they serve the interests of the capitalist class. Thus politics is subordinate to economics, and important social conflicts occur between an ascendant class and a defeated one, or between a ruling social class and an occasionally desperate subordinate one, as in the case of peasant revolts.

5. Progressive and reactionary classes With changes in technology and social organization, new classes arise to challenge the old. The ascendant capitalist class was "progressive" in that it stimulated the development of new forces of production and created the conditions that made a new class—the industrial proletariat—possible and inevitable. The capitalists became reactionary, as did the feudal magnates before them, when they acted to hinder rather than foster social development.

6. The end of the class system The proletariat incorporates most of society and has the widest aspirations. Therefore the victory of the proletariat is a final victory, ushering in a new form of social organization—the classless society. Marx argued that his concept of socialism was scientific in that the conditions for its attainment were prepared for by previous history. He referred especially to the vast increase in productivity under capitalism and the creation of "socialized" property in the form of corporate enterprise.

CRITIQUE

Marx's theories expressed a distinctive intellectual perspective and political impulse, and Marxism is not easily formulated as a set of hypothetical statements subject to the self-corrective method of science. Because it is both a philosophy of history and a political program, Marxism has generated loyalties and responses beyond the realm of scholarship. Nevertheless, the Marxist model is a continuing source of intellectual stimulation and a framework for thoughtful inquiry.

Criticism of Marx's theories centers on the following points:

1. The model overemphasizes the significance of economic class for individual conduct as well as for the explanation of historical trends. Other sources of personal identification and group action are often more important. For example, nationalism and ethnic loyalty are enduring social forces, largely overshadowing class divisions. Other dimensions of stratification, especially prestige, often are compelling influences on human thought and action. While the effect of class interest on politics is at times decisive, there is much evidence that politics goes its own way, independent of class influences (Dahrendorf, 1959:Chaps. 7 and 8).

2. The concept of a ruling class has limited relevance to a complex, industrialized nation. Even the idea of a power elite does not support Marx's contention of rule by the bourgeoisie through its governmental representatives. Although business interests

Niccolò Machiavelli (1469–1527) served the city-state of Florence for 14 years as administrator, politician, and diplomat. Forced out of office, he retired to his study and wrote down his reflections on power and society. His most famous works are *The Prince* and *Discourses on the First Ten Books of Titus Livius*. Machiavelli is one of the fathers of the theory of elites—the view that political life depends on the energy and character of active minorities who have the strength and the will to rule. The rise and fall of elites, and with them the flowering and degeneration of political communities, is in the nature of things; the cycle will be repeated without end. "For, virtue begets peace; peace begets idleness, idleness, mutiny; and mutiny, destruction: and then vice versa: that ruin begets laws; those laws, virtue; and virtue begets honor and good success."

often dominate government policy, at other times these interests are defeated.

3. Marx did not give sufficient weight to the forces that mitigate the class cleavage he observed in the mid-nineteenth century. He thought the advent of universal male suffrage in England would inevitably result in the supremacy of the working class. He assumed that the numerous workers would act politically and vote as a single group, bound together and motivated by their common interests. Nor did Marx rightly gauge the significance for social integration of expanding civic participation and the enlargement of social rights (Marshall, 1950/ 1964).

4. The prediction that workers under capitalism would develop class consciousness and revolutionary aspirations has been borne out only to a very limited extent.

5. Marx's thesis that there would be a polarization of classes has not proven valid, although it is true that modern society has become an "employee society" and that there is great concentration of wealth and power in a relatively small number of corporate entities. But polarization has been offset by the multiplication of strata based on occupation, education, and prestige. The middle classes have not disappeared, but they have changed their character since Marx's time.

6. Perhaps the most important failing of the Marxist model lies in its vision of the postcapitalist future. Marx thought that a proletarian victory would bring an end to exploitation of man by man and that government would be replaced by a benign and rational "administration of things." He did not foresee the rise of totalitarianism as a more likely alternative to capitalist democracy than the humanist socialism he expected.

These criticisms and second guesses after the historical fact qualify but do not discredit the contribution of Marxist thought to sociology, and especially to social history. Although most sociologists do not use the specific categories or adopt the detailed arguments of the Marxist model, they are made alert to the role of class in history, and to some extent they follow lines of thought that Marx began.

CLASS CONSCIOUSNESS IN THE UNITED STATES

The term *class consciousness* is widely used in sociology, but often with a more general meaning than that given it by Marx. Most often it implies little more than a feeling of identification with others in a social class, however class is defined, and a feeling of difference from, and perhaps opposition to, persons in other classes.

Class consciousness in the sense of aware, unified, and opposed class entities is not common in the United States. Public opinion poll data and voting studies show greater unity of opinion and of voting within occupational categories in the countries of western Europe. Broadly defined, occupational categories in the United States contain a wide diversity of opinions and political inclinations. There is little feeling among most occupational groupings that their interests conflict sharply with the interests of other identified groupings.

A number of explanations have been offered for the relatively low level of class consciousness and class solidarity in the United States:

1. Because of widespread belief in opportunities for upward mobility, persons strive to improve their lot by individual rather than collective effort. For some manual workers, opportunities for upward movement may be more illusory than real, but workers who know they will never move to a higher occupation often hope their children will be upwardly mobile, and many have relatives at higher levels.

2. Improvement in the living standards of blue-collar workers reduces discontent and the chance of developing class solidarity. Increasing numbers of wage workers are able to own houses and equipment that were once out of reach. Acquiring consumer goods gives manual workers a feeling of upward mobility (Fallers, 1954).

3. A tendency toward the leveling of differences in the life-styles of manual and nonmanual workers lessens the likelihood of class consciousness.

4. Racial, ethnic, religious, and regional differences in culture and perceived interests cut across classes and inhibit class consciousness and solidarity. Conflict between black and white workers has prevented working-class unity in the South. These differences, not based on class, appear to be persistent, but if they were to diminish, a major obstacle to class consciousness would be removed.

Class consciousness is not entirely absent, however. A Detroit study, for instance, found rather high class consciousness among blacks and recent migrants from rural areas (Leggett, 1964), and surveys indicate political unity of manual workers in the largest cities (Lipset, 1963:265–266). Nor is class conflict absent; strikes and labor disputes are examples of the American version of the class struggle. This conflict, however, is over the conditions of work and the division of spoils. It is a far cry from the proletarian revolution envisioned by Marx. In the words of one observer, the conflict has become institutionalized (Dahrendorf, 1959:Part 2); it proceeds in accordance with established rules and rarely commands the attention or the efforts of more than a minority of the population. It leads to piecemeal changes in social institutions but to no radical changes in social structure. In the institutionalization of class conflict, the democracies of western Europe and the United States are similar.

THE FUNCTIONAL THEORY: IS STRATIFICATION INEVITABLE?

One school of thought holds that social inequality is inevitable and functional (beneficial) to the society as a whole (Davis and Moore, 1945). According to this view, social inequality must exist in all societies with a complex division of labor in order to assure that important and necessary tasks are performed efficiently and conscientiously by well-qualified people. Some tasks are more important, and some require scarce skills and abilities. If a position is relatively important and requires relatively scarce skills, it must be more highly rewarded than many other positions. Skills may be scarce either because they call for unusual talent or because they require long and arduous training.

The idea that people could not be socialized to prepare for and enter important positions requiring scarce skills if they were not relatively highly rewarded has been challenged (Tumin, 1953). The following questions have been raised: (1) Could people who have the potential to become doctors, engineers, scientists, and executives be so socialized that they would feel obliged to enter these occupations even if they anticipated no higher reward than unskilled workers? (2) Would the intrinsic enjoyment of highly skilled work be sufficient to motivate them to prepare for their jobs and perform them diligently? (3) Is the long training undertaken by people in highly rewarded occupations a sacrifice, or is the training itself essentially rewarding? (4) Do high rewards in fact ensure the best performance of responsible tasks? (Broom and Cushing, 1977).

There are no conclusive answers, but there is widespread agreement on the following related points:

1. Even though some inequality in rewards may be necessary, extreme inequalities are not. The salary and fringe benefits of executives in large corporations may be 20 or 100 times that of low-paid employees. The heads of ITT and Ford Motor Company, for example, receive nearly $1 million per year (Cordtz, 1973:290). The fact that the spread is much smaller in publicly controlled organizations that perform similar functions suggests that such a wide difference is not necessary. Apparently, many highly paid people are motivated by the symbolic significance of their income rather than its buying power. Indeed, the rewards need not be monetary at all; prestige and other satisfactions may substitute for money in motivating people to discharge their responsibilities conscientiously. People often make financial sacrifices to accept an appointment with civic importance or to participate in more interesting or challenging work.

2. Many people are rewarded who neither occupy important positions nor apply their skills to socially useful tasks. Indeed, some people are unintentionally rewarded for criminal activities, and others derive large windfalls from legal but unproductive activities.

3. The importance of positions as measured by their rewards is not necessarily determined by their contribution to the survival or improvement of the society. Certain positions that cater to transitory or even damaging popular tastes may be highly rewarded. The production and promotion of cigarettes is an example.

4. If stratification is inevitable and functional, it does not necessarily follow that class inheritance is also functional. Some inequality may be necessary for the development and efficient utilization of talent, but no such claim can be made for inequality transmitted from generation to generation. The latter kind of inequality tends to inhibit rather than foster the discovery and utilization of talent. Inequality in all societies probably exceeds the amount justifiable on the criterion of efficiency.

References

Baltzell, E. Digby
1958 Philadelphia Gentlemen: The Making of a National Upper Class. New York: Free Press.

Barber, Bernard
1968 "Social mobility in Hindu India." Pp. 18–35 in Silverberg.

Barzini, Luigi
1965 The Italians: A Full-Length Portrait Featuring Their Manners and Morals. New York: Bantam.

Bendix, Reinhard and Seymour Martin Lipset (eds.)
1966 Class, Status, and Power. New York: Free Press. Second ed.

Blau, Peter M. and Otis Dudley Duncan
1967 The American Occupational Structure. New York: Wiley.

Bonjean, Charles M. and David M. Olson
1964 "Community leadership: directions of research." Administrative Science Quarterly 9:278–300.

Bottomore, T. B. and Maximilien Rubel (eds.)
1956 Karl Marx: Selected Writings in Sociology and Social Philosophy. New York: McGraw-Hill.

Broom, Leonard and Robert G. Cushing
1977 "A modest test of an immodest theory: the functional theory of stratification." American Sociological Review 42 (February).

Broom, Leonard and F. Lancaster Jones
1969 "Father-to-son mobility: Australia in comparative perspective." American Journal of Sociology 74 (January):333–342.

Broom, Leonard and Betty J. Maynard
1969 "Prestige and socioeconomic ranking of occupations. Social Science Quarterly 50 (September):369–373.

Burnight, Robert G. and Parker G. Marden
1967 "Social correlates of weight in an aging population." Milbank Memorial Fund Quarterly 45:75–92.

Centers, Richard
1949 The Psychology of Social Classes. Princeton, N.J.: Princeton University Press.

Clark, Terry N. (ed.)
1974 Comparative Community Politics. Beverly Hills, Calif.: Sage.

Cordtz, Dan
1973 "Henry Ford, superstar." Fortune 87 (May):290.

Dahrendorf, Ralf
1959 Class and Class Conflict in Industrial Society. Stanford, Calif.: Stanford University Press.

Davies, A. F.
1967 Images of Class: An Australian Study. Sydney: Sydney University Press.

Davis, Allison, B. B. Gardner, and M. R. Gardner
1941 Deep South. Chicago: University of Chicago Press.

Davis, Kingsley and Wilbert E. Moore
1945 "Some principles of stratification." American Sociological Review 10 (April):242–249.

Domhoff, G. William
1967 Who Rules America? Englewood Cliffs, N.J.: Prentice-Hall.

Fadiman, Clifton
1956 "Is there an upper-class American language?" Holiday (October):8–10.

Fallers, Lloyd A.
1954 "A note on the 'trickle effect.'" Public Opinion Quarterly 18:314–321.

Feuer, Lewis S. (ed.)
1959 Marx and Engels: Basic Writings on Politics and Philosophy. Garden City, N.Y.: Doubleday.

Galbraith, John Kenneth
1967 The New Industrial State. Boston: Houghton Mifflin.

Garbin, Albeno P. and Frederick L. Bates
1961 "Occupational prestige: an empirical study of its correlates." Social Forces 40:131–136.

Gerth, H. H. and C. Wright Mills (eds. and trans.)
1946 From Max Weber: Essays in Sociology. New York: Oxford University Press.

Gilbert, Claire W.
1967 "Some trends in community politics: a secondary analysis of power structure data from 166 communities." Southwestern Social Science Quarterly 48 (December):373–381.

Glenn, Norval D. and Jon P. Alston
1967 "Rural-urban differences in reported attitudes and behavior." Southwestern Social Science Quarterly 47:381–400.

Goldthorpe, John and Keith Hope
1972 "Occupational grading and occupational prestige." Pp. 19–79 in Keith Hope (ed.). The Analysis of Social Mobility: Methods and Approaches. Oxford: Clarendon Press.

Goode, William J.
1962 "Marital satisfaction and instability." International Social Science Journal 5:507–526.

Hawley, W. D. and F. M. Wirt (eds.)
1974 The Search for Community Power. 2nd ed. Englewood Cliffs, N.J.: Prentice-Hall.

Hodge, Robert W., Donald J. Treiman, and Petter H. Rossi
1966 "A comparative study of occupational prestige." Pp. 309–321 in Bendix and Lipset.

Hunter, Floyd
1953 Community Power Structure: A Study of Decision-Makers. Chapel Hill: University of North Carolina Press.

Jones, F. Lancaster
1969 "Social mobility and industrial society: a thesis reexamined." Sociological Quarterly (Summer):292–305.

Kahl, Joseph A.
1957 The American Class Structure. New York: Holt, Rinehart and Winston.

Kitagawa, Evelyn M.
1972 "Socioeconomic differences in mortality in the United States and some implications for population policy." Pp. 85–110 in Westoff and Park, 1972.

Knupfer, Genevieve
1947 "Portrait of the underdog." Public Opinion Quarterly 11 (Spring):103–114.

Komarovsky, Mirra
1964 Blue-Collar Marriage. New York: Random House.

Lasswell, Harold D.
1934/1950 A Study of Power: World Politics and Personal Insecurity. New York: Free Press.

Leach, E. R. (ed.)
1960 Aspects of Caste in South India, Ceylon and North-West Pakistan. New York: Cambridge University Press.

Leggett, John C.
1964 "Sources and consequences of working-class consciousness." Pp. 235–247 in Arthur B. Shostak and William Gomberg (eds.), Blue-Collar World: Studies of the American Worker. Englewood Cliffs, N.J.: Prentice-Hall.

Lipset, Seymour Martin
1963 Political Man. Garden City, N.Y.: Doubleday.

Lipset, Seymour Martin and Reinhard Bendix
1959 Social Mobility in Industrial Society. Berkeley and Los Angeles: University of California Press.

Lipset, S. M. and Hans L. Zetterberg
1959 "Social mobility in industrial societies." Pp. 11–75 in Lipset and Bendix.

Lydall, Harold
1968 The Structure of Earnings. London: Oxford University Press.

Lynd, Robert S. and Helen Merrell Lynd
1937 Middletown in Transition: A Study in Cultural Conflicts. New York: Harcourt Brace Jovanovich.

McClelland, David C.
1961 The Achieving Society. Princeton, N.J.: Van Nostrand Reinhold.

Marshall, T. H.
1950/1964 "Citizenship and social class." In Class, Citizenship, and Social Development. Garden City, N.Y.: Doubleday.

Matza, David
1966 "The disreputable poor." Pp. 310–339 in Neil J. Smelser and Seymour Martin Lipset (eds.), Social Structure and Mobility in Economic Development. Chicago: Aldine. Also published in Bendix and Lipset, 1966, pp. 289–302. Citations to latter source.

Miller, S. M.
1960 "Comparative social mobility." Current Sociology 9:1–89.

Miller, S. M. and Frank Riessman
1961 "The working class subculture: a new view." Social Problems 9:86–97.

Mills, C. Wright
1956 The Power Elite. New York: Oxford University Press.

Morris, Richard T. and Raymond J. Murphy
1959 "The situs dimension in occupational structure." American Sociological Review 24 (April):231–239.

Presser, Harriet B. and Larry L. Bumpass
1972 "Demographic and social aspects of contraceptive sterilization in the United States: 1965–1970. Pp. 505–568 in Westoff and Parke, 1972.

Riesman, David
1951 The Lonely Crowd. New Haven, Conn.: Yale University Press.

Riley, Matilda White and Anne Foner
1968 Aging and Society. Vol. I: An Inventory of Research Findings. New York: Russell Sage.

Rosen, Bernard C. and R. D'Andrade
1959 "The psychosocial origins of achievement motivation." Sociometry 22 (September):185–217.

Rossi, A. J.
1971 "Women in science: why so few?" Pp. 110–121 in C. F. Epstein and W. J. Goode (eds.), The Other Half. Englewood Cliffs, N.J.: Prentice-Hall.

Silverberg, James (ed.)
1968 Social Mobility in the Caste System of India. Comparative Studies in Society and History. Supplement III.

Spinrad, William
1965 "Power in local communities." Social Problems 12 (Winter):335–356.

Srinivas, M. N.
1962 Caste in Modern India, and Other Essays. Bombay: Asia Publishing House.
1966 Social Change in Modern India. Berkeley and Los Angeles: University of California Press.

Stevenson, H. N. C.
1967 "Caste (Indian)." Encyclopaedia Britannica 5:24–33.

Straus, Murray A.
1962 "Deferred gratification, social class, and the achievement syndrome." American Sociological Review 27 (June):326–335.

Svalastoga, Kaare
1957 "An empirical analysis of intrasociety mobility determinants." Working Paper No. 9, submitted to the Fourth Working Conference on Social Stratification and Mobility, International Sociological Association (December).
1959 Prestige, Class, and Mobility. Copenhagen: Gyldendal.

Tumin, Melvin M.
1953 "Some principles of stratification: a critical analysis." American Sociological Review 18 (August):387–393.

Udry, J. Richard
1967 "Marital instability by race and income based on 1960 census data." American Journal of Sociology 72:673.

Walton, John
1967 "The vertical axis of community organization and the structure of power." Southwestern Social Science Quarterly 48 (December):353–368.

Warner, W. Lloyd and James C. Abegglen
1955 Big Business Leaders in America. New York: Harper & Row.

Warner, W. L. and Associates
1949 Democracy in Jonesville. New York: Harper & Row.

Warner, W. L. and P. S. Lunt
1941 The Social Life of a Modern Community. New Haven, Conn.: Yale University Press.
1942 The Status System of a Modern Community. New Haven, Conn.: Yale University Press.

Warren, Roland
1962 "Toward a reformulation of community theory." Human Organization 15:8–11.

Wesolowski, Wlodzimierz and Kazimierz Słomczyński
1968 "Social stratification in Polish cities." Pp. 175–211 in J. A. Jackson (ed.), Social Stratification. Cambridge: Cambridge University Press.

Wilensky, Harold and Hugh Edwards
1959 "The skidder: ideological adjustments of downward mobile workers." American Sociological Review 24 (April):215–231.

Westoff, Charles F. and Robert Parke, Jr. (eds.)
1972 Demographic and Social Aspects of Population Growth. Vol. 1 of Research Reports, Commission on Population Growth and the American Future. Washington, D.C.: GPO.

Sources and readings

Barber, Bernard
1957 Social Stratification. New York: Harcourt Brace Jovanovich.

Bendix, R. and S. M. Lipset (eds.)
1966 Class, Status and Power: Social Stratification in Comparative Perspective. Second edition. New York: Free Press.

Blau, Peter M. and Otis Dudley Duncan
1967 The American Occupational Structure. New York: Wiley.

Bottomore, T. B.
1966 Classes in Modern Society. New York: Pantheon Books.

Dahrendorf, Ralf
1959 Class and Class Conflict in Industrial Society. Stanford: Stanford University Press.

Giddens, Anthony
1973 The Class Structure of the Advanced Societies. London: Hutchinson University Library.

Glenn, Norval D., Jon P. Alston and David Weiner
1970 Social Stratification: A Research Bibliography. Berkeley: Glendessary Press.

Heller, Celia S. (ed.)
1969 Structured Social Inequality: A Reader in Comparative Social Stratification. New York: Macmillan.

Kahl, Joseph A. (ed.)
1968 Comparative Perspectives on Stratification: Mexico, Great Britain, Japan. Boston: Little, Brown.

Lane, David
1971 The End of Inequality? Stratification Under State Socialism. Harmondsworth, England: Penguin.

Lopreato, Joseph and Lawrence E. Hazelrigg
1972 Class, Conflict and Mobility: Theories and Studies in Class Structure. New York: Intext.

Lopreato, Joseph and Lionel S. Lewis (eds.)
1974 Social Stratification: A Reader. New York: Harper & Row.

Marshall, T. H.
1963 Class, Citizenship and Social Development. Garden City, N. Y.: Doubleday.

Porter, John
1968 The Vertical Mosaic: An Analysis of Class and Power in Canada. Toronto: University of Toronto Press.

Smelser, Neil J. and Seymour Martin Lipset (eds.)
1966 Social Structure and Mobility in Economic Development. Chicago: Aldine.

Sorokin, Pitirim A.
1959 Social and Cultural Mobility. New York: Free Press.

(Southwestern) Social Science Quarterly 48 (December)
1967 Special issue on community power. Includes a comprehensive bibliography compiled by R. J. Pellegrin.

7 | Associations

Section one introduction

The word *association* is used in this book as a synonym for formal organization or, simply, organization. This chapter is called *ASSOCIATIONS* in order to minimize confusion with the broader idea of social organization. An association is a special-purpose group. The term *formal organization* is often used to emphasize that most such groups have explicit goals and official ways of doing things. An association or formal organization should be distinguished, for example, from a web of friendship or from a system of social stratification. Both are examples of social organization, but they are not associations.

The study of associations touches one of the most sensitive areas of human concern. Without large-scale, complex organizations, the coordination necessary to the operation of modern society would be lacking. The organization is, at the same time, a locus of power and a source of anxiety. A large corporation often has more resources and more direct impact upon its employees and the community than the government of a city or state. For that reason, the large organization is often conceived of as a private government.

Throughout this chapter, two main kinds of organization are treated together. One is the administrative or bureaucratic structure, made up of executives and subordinates brought together to do a job. The chief feature of the administrative organization is its capacity to mobilize human resources for sustained effort. People are hired to devote substantial parts of their lives to the aims of some enterprise. The size, power, and multiplication of administrative organizations have led some writers to call modern society the "organizational society" (Presthus, 1962).

The other major type of organization is the voluntary association (Sills, 1968). Although in a free society most employees can quit their jobs if they wish, we do not usually think of workers or staff personnel as voluntary participants. Employment is usually compelled by economic necessity; it is not the free expression of personal choice.

On the other hand, a voluntary association

is formed by the joining of mutual interests. An interest group, whether religious, economic, political, or recreational, is usually voluntary in that it brings together people who characteristically retain effective freedom to withdraw at will or to vary their contributions. How much one participates in a political party, a club, or a pressure group is usually a matter of choice.

In the United States most adults do not belong to voluntary associations (see Table 7:1), thus contradicting the common belief that Americans are a nation of joiners. In national surveys conducted in 1955 and 1962, more than half the respondents reported no organization membership, but there was a decline in the no-membership response from 64 to 57 percent in the seven-year interval. It has often been observed that the better educated and financially better-off are more apt to belong to organizations and to belong to more of them. For instance, the survey analysis found that in 1962, 44 percent of persons with four or more years of college, but only 11 percent of those with grade school education, belonged to two or more organizations. However, there is evidence of increased association memberships among lower status groups and among blacks (Hyman and Wright, 1971:Tables 4 and 7). (Note that these studies are based on self-reported memberships. Apparently many respondents did not identify their political party affiliations as membership in voluntary associations. Their interpretation was encouraged by the phrasing of the question, which referred specifically to "groups or organizations here in the community.")

Table 7:1
Percent of adults reporting membership in voluntary associations[a]

Number of memberships (excluding trade unions)	1955	1962
None	64	57
One	20	22
Two	9	11
Three	4	6
Four or more	3	4
N	2,379	1,775

Source: Hyman and Wright, 1971:195.

[a] The questions asked were: Do you belong to any groups or organizations here in the community? Which ones? Any others?

a trade union is something more than a voluntary association — in part because membership is often compulsory, but also because the trade union administration (at least on the national level) is large, effective, and self-perpetuating.

Many voluntary associations are formed in order to create an administrative organization for a special purpose, and the members, in effect, tax themselves to support it. For example, members of the National Association for the Advancement of Colored People support a substantial headquarters, including a legal staff that has won celebrated victories for civil rights. Such voluntary associations tend to have relatively low membership participation. (See Section Four.)

CONVERGING TYPES

Under certain conditions, there is a convergence of the two types of organization. A corporation is formed as a voluntary association of investors, but it quickly creates its own administrative organization and work force. The social reality of the corporation shifts as the paid staff becomes the vital part of the organization. Similarly,

SOCIAL PROCESSES

The sociologist views an organization figuratively as a little society. Specialized associations have many of the features of societies, including the processes that bind them together or disrupt them. For example, stratification, socialization, and primary-group formation affect the capacity of the organization to achieve its objectives.

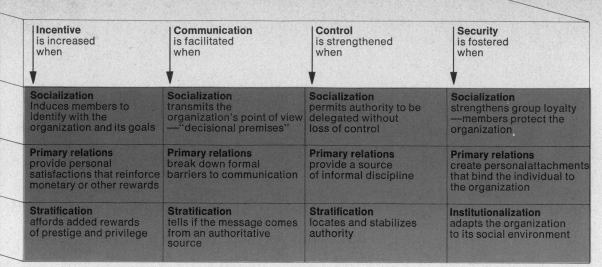

Incentive is increased when	Communication is facilitated when	Control is strengthened when	Security is fostered when
Socialization Induces members to identify with the organization and its goals	**Socialization** transmits the organization's point of view —"decisional premises"	**Socialization** permits authority to be delegated without loss of control	**Socialization** strengthens group loyalty —members protect the organization.
Primary relations provide personal satisfactions that reinforce monetary or other rewards	**Primary relations** break down formal barriers to communication	**Primary relations** provide a source of informal discipline	**Primary relations** create personal attachments that bind the individual to the organization
Stratification affords added rewards of prestige and privilege	**Stratification** tells if the message comes from an authoritative source	**Stratification** locates and stabilizes authority	**Institutionalization** adapts the organization to its social environment

Figure 7:1 Social relations and effective organization

Whatever its special purpose, every organization attempts to coordinate the activities of human beings. Therefore, organizations have a number of common characteristics that claim much of the attention of this chapter. Every association must:

1. Provide *incentives* to its members so as to win and sustain their participation.

2. Set up an effective system of internal *communication*.

3. Exercise *control* so that activities will be directed toward achieving the aims of the organization.

4. Adapt itself to external conditions that may threaten the existence of the organization or its policies—that is, maintain *security*.

If these requirements of effective organization are to be fulfilled, the social relations among the persons involved must be consistent with them. A major task of the sociologist is to explore the ways in which incentive, communication, control, and security depend on the underlying relations among persons and groups. Figure 7:1 outlines how each of these four essential elements of organization are influenced by sociological variables.

Social environments The internal life of an organization is strongly conditioned by external circumstances, that is, by the specific environment within which it operates. The marginal small business, subject to intense competition, has a very different environment from the large corporation; the changing character of the urban environment decisively affects the central-city church. Therefore the idea of viewing organizations as little societies, if taken too literally, may be misleading. Organizations are imbedded in social contexts to which they adapt and which they often influence in important ways. Some aspects of organizational adaptation are considered in Sections Four and Five.

Section two formal and informal structure

A leading theme in the study of organizations is the interplay of formal and informal relations. For a number of years, sociology's distinctive contribution centered largely on the identification of unrecognized, latent, informal processes. It is no longer necessary to prove the existence or the inevitability of informal structure, and these facts are well accepted. Nevertheless, the distinction between formal and informal structure remains a fruitful starting point for the sociological analysis of large-scale organizations.

Elements of formal structure Figure 7:2 is a somewhat simplified chart of the formal structure of a large oil company. It should be referred to throughout this discussion of company organization. The organization chart includes the following four elements:

1. Division of labor The company's operations have four main divisions. One produces the oil, another refines it, still another handles transportation, and a fourth is responsible for marketing. Problems of personnel are also divided. In the division of labor according to a definite plan, *specialization* is the guiding principle. Responsibilities are delegated to particular individuals and groups. This delegation of responsibilities creates new groups, and the

larger association becomes an organization of organizations.

2. Delegation of authority The boxes and lines of the organization chart show the chain of command. Typically, there is a hierarchy, in which some individuals and groups are given the right to issue orders to others. The four main operating divisions are on the same level. Although apparently one step higher, the personnel department does not have the formal right to give orders directly to the operating divisions. Ordinarily, a personnel department is a staff or auxiliary group. (See Adaptation 17.) It receives instructions from the higher administrative and policy levels and makes recommendations to those levels without directly supervising the lower operating divisions.

3. Channeled communication Some complex organizations, notably the military services, go to some pains to insure that indi-

Figure 7:2 **Schematic organization chart of an oil company**

Source: Dale, 1952:28

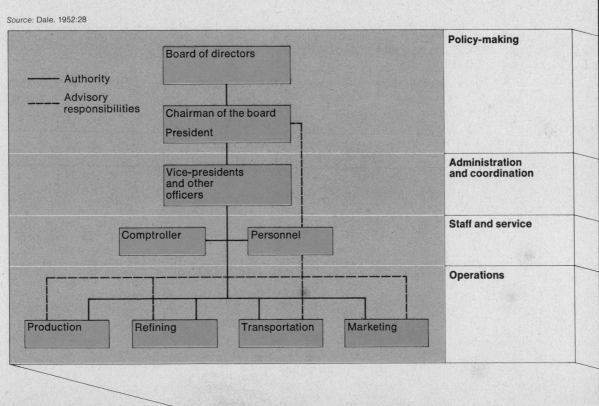

viduals transmit information or requests through channels. For example, according to the organization chart, which shows the officially approved paths for information, requests, and commands, a vice-president who wants to communicate with a member of the board of directors will not bypass the president of the company. Similarly, if the manager of an oil field, who is subordinate to the chief of the production division, wishes to communicate with the manager of an oil refinery on a matter of policy, he is expected to do so through his chief. The latter in turn communicates with subordinates in the refining division through the chief of that division. Rules of this sort are not rigidly held to because they may interfere with the ability of subordinates to solve their problems. But even in the most relaxed organization, the wise subordinate remembers channels when dealing with important matters. Otherwise, his chief will not have the information he needs to make decisions or to defend the actions of his division when questioned by higher authority.

4. Coordination   In order to attain the advantages of specialization, labor is divided, but it is necessary to maintain a united and consistent effort by the organization as a whole. This is the job of the administrative and policy levels, which review the activities and recommendations of the various divisions, consider conflicts that must be resolved, and develop new policies that may be needed. Such coordinating officials often act as judges, weighing the arguments presented by divisions that differ on company policy or that have complaints against each other. Organizations differ in the extent to which top management initiates activity or simply reviews actions initiated at the working level.

Formal structure consists of rules and objectives defining tasks, powers, and procedures according to an officially approved pattern. The pattern specifies how the work of the organization is to be carried on, whether it is producing steel, winning votes, teaching children, or saving souls.

The officially approved pattern is not necessarily codified or written down, nor is it always fully understood by the participants. There may not be an organization chart. Sometimes the official, formal relations are so simple and well understood that there is no need to write them down. On the other hand, the relations may be so complex that a chart of the whole system would be too complicated to be helpful. To find out what patterns of a complex organization will be recognized and enforced as part of official policy is no simple task. Many patterns receive (or are denied) official approval only at the time when they are challenged and must be submitted to the controlling officials for review.

In these respects the formal system of an organization resembles a legal system, and the sociology of law (see *LAW*) has many points in common with the sociology of organizations.

INFORMAL STRUCTURE

The rules of the formal system account for much but not all of the patterned behavior in associations. Beside the formal system and interacting with it is an informal structure based on the spontaneous, problem-solving interaction of persons and groups. Together the formal and informal aspects make up the *social structure* of the organization.

The informal structure is best understood as composed of patterns that develop when people face persistent problems that are not provided for by the formal system. There are four major causes for these problems:

1. Impersonality   The rules and prescribed roles of the formal structure are necessarily impersonal. The individual is treated as a unit in a technical, task-oriented system. In practice, however, it is often necessary to enlist the personal commitments of individuals if their best efforts and highest loyalty are to be gained. Some leeway must be allowed for interpersonal and group relations to supplement the formal patterns of communication and control. The importance of personal contact in organizations, not only for private advantage but to get the job done, is well known. Even in armies, where formal relations predominate, friendship and pride in one's outfit are important ingredients of effective organization.

2. Lag Like any other code of rules or laws, the formal system tends to lag behind changes in actual operations. Those who do the work must solve new problems, some of which may not be officially recognized. For example, a company's rules may have been developed before the organization of a union. The elected shop stewards try to act as spokesmen for the workers on day-to-day grievances. The foreman tries to deal with the union representatives even though the company and the union have not developed formal procedures for negotiating their differences. There may be a temporary informal pattern of consultation between foremen and shop stewards. Eventually the company may recognize the union as the agency representing the workers. Then the informal procedures, usually modified and made consistent throughout the factory, may become formalized.

3. Generality Rules are necessarily abstract and general. There cannot be a separate rule for every possible problem, and some problems cannot be anticipated. Thus a rule deals with a type of problem, but there are limits to reliance on formal rules, and authority must be delegated to the person who does the job, or to an immediate supervisor, so that each decision can be made according to the circumstances.

Moreover, there are usually gaps in a system of general rules. At the operating level there may be a need to regularize behavior and make decisions routine, for example, in determining the use of office equipment or the allocation of responsibility for difficult or unpleasant tasks. These gaps are filled by the development of informal custom or usage. In time some patterns may become formalized, but other patterns may not be officially recognized.

4. Personal problems and interests The foregoing sources of informal structure presume that people care about the organization's aims and do their best to achieve them. It cannot be assumed, however, that individuals are interested solely in helping the organization to reach its goals. Personal needs and private concerns are also important. For example, a new supervisor may cultivate the friendship of an experienced worker, thereby gaining access to valuable information about the work and the employees. The friend may defend the supervisor when things go wrong. This relation, if stabilized, becomes part of the informal structure of the plant. It cannot be officially enforced, yet it is a significant fact that must not be overlooked by anyone who wants to understand or influence that segment of the organization.

The individual may also bring to the job ingrained beliefs, such as negative attitudes toward blacks or foreigners and ties of loyalty to friends or kin. These sentiments and attachments also become part of the organization's social reality. Figure 7:3 summarizes the elements of informal structure and classifies them according to their contribution to three aspects of organizational life: (1) the normative order, (2) the group structure of the organization, and (3) the status system. (See p. 202.)

Roles and the spill-over effect Formal relations coordinate positions and activities, not persons. The rules apply to foremen and machinists, to clerks, sergeants, and vice-presidents. However, no organization of any duration can restrict interaction to formally defined roles. In practice, employees interact as many-faceted persons, adjusting to diverse daily experiences in ways that spill over the boundaries set by their formal roles. The role usually calls for compartmentalization; for keeping in check personal needs, impulses, and orientations. The actor, however, is a unified personality with personal problems and priorities. This tension between person and role is inevitable in organizational life. Some aspects of this tension are explored in Adaptation 15 and in "A Case of Jitters," p. 200.

A case of jitters

Take the case of Bob, foreman in the machine department, when he suddenly discovers that he does not have enough bronze rod on hand to complete the order of part number X37A22 for the end of the week and that it will keep two hand-screw machines going steadily to make delivery on time. So he talks to Charley, the machine operator who came to him asking for the rod:

Bob: "Are you sure there isn't any of that rod over in the rack? When we started on this job, I checked the storeroom records and there was plenty on hand."

Charley: "There sure isn't now. You remember when we first started on this order somebody gave us the wrong specifications and we turned out a lot that had to be junked."

Bob: "That's right. Well, I'll call the stockroom and get some more over right away." (Thinking, I sure did slip up on that. I completely forgot to order more rod.)

(He calls the stockroom.) "I'll need two hundred pounds of that ⅜th bronze rod for part number X37A22. We're in a rush for it, got to get the order out right away and a couple of machines are waiting. Can you get it right over?"

Stockman: "Sorry, we are out of that rod. Won't be able to get it in before Friday. Why didn't you call last week?"

Bob: "Can't you get hold of any before that? If I don't deliver those parts before Monday, the gadget assembly department will be tied up."

Stockman: "We'll do the best we can, but don't expect it before Friday. Why don't you guys give us a little more notice instead of waiting until your machines shut down and then expecting us to do miracles?"

Source: From *Human Relations in Industry* by B. B. Gardner and D. G. Moore (Chicago: Irwin, 1950), pp. 37–38. Revised edition. Reprinted by permission.

Bob: (Thinking: This is a terrible note! I slip up on ordering that rod the one time the stockroom is out of it. Why can't they keep some stock on hand instead of trying to work from hand to mouth. Just trying to make a good showing by keeping down inventory and they tie up production. They ought to realize that they are there to help the shop, not to give us all this trouble. Wonder what I can do now. The boss sure will give me hell when he hears this. Maybe I ought to check with Joe in gadget assembly to see how many parts they have on hand and how long before he will need more. Maybe I better let him know what's happened so he will know what to expect. Maybe he can plan his work so the people on that assembly job can do something else for a few days.

But if I tell him what's happened, he will tell his boss, and his boss will jump on my boss and my boss will jump on me for letting this happen and not letting him know. So before I tell Joe anything I better tell my boss. Maybe if I tell him, he can tell Joe's boss, and I won't have to say anything to Joe. Joe's going to be plenty sore anyway. He got kind of hot the other day when I tried to get him to let me make some changes in the base plate for that Model N job. Seemed like he was just being stubborn. Wonder if he might have enough parts on hand so he could just go along and say nothing about this affair. If I knew he had enough, I just wouldn't say anything and take a chance on getting some to him before he runs out. I'm afraid to risk it, though, without being pretty sure, because if he did have to shut down, my boss sure would raise Cain. Yeah, and Joe called the other day to know how we were coming on that lot we delivered yesterday, said he didn't want to get caught short. But Joe always does that. He starts crowding you for things long before he actually needs them. He seems to think no one *will keep their promises unless he rides them. If I ask Joe how much he has on hand, he will suspect something and I will have to tell him.*

Guess I better not take a chance on Joe. I will have to tell my boss first. But gee, how I hate to tell him! I know just what he will think. I know I should have remembered to order more when we spoiled that first run, but I was so busy getting caught up that I forgot. Anyway, you never would expect the stockroom to be out of a standard item like that. And if they ran this place right, they never would be. But my boss won't care about that. All he'll think is that I must be asleep on the job. He expects me to keep track of everything; and if I have to do the stockroom's job for them to keep my job going, he expects me to do that. What will I tell him, anyway, that won't make me look like a fool who doesn't know his job? Maybe I better not tell him now. It won't hurt to wait till tomorrow, and maybe then the stockroom will know when I can expect the rod. Maybe they will do better than Friday, and I might squeeze by. When I do tell the boss, I want to be able to tell him just when we will be able to start on the job again, and maybe I can plan it so we won't hold up the assembly. Guess I will wait till tomorrow and see what I can figure out.)

And Bob spends the rest of the day in a state of jitters trying to figure a way out of the predicament, or at least a partial solution which he can present to his boss when he finally is forced to tell him. He goes home that night with a terrible grouch, is cross to the children because they are so noisy, gets annoyed with his wife because she seems so cheerful, can hardly eat his supper, sleeps poorly, and hates to go to work the next morning. Such is the human element of communication up the line.

The operating organization is made up of both formal and informal relations. Therefore the sociology of special-purpose associations stresses their interdependence. The following paragraphs, while emphasizing informal processes, show how they relate to more formal devices for attaining organized, concerted effort.

Formal ranks and social strata Most discussions of stratification deal with whole societies or communities, and this is the emphasis in SOCIAL STRATIFICATION. But the basic processes of stratification also occur in special-purpose associations, where they affect communication, incentive, and control.

Stratification in organizations includes both the formal ranking system as revealed in a detailed table of organization and the informally patterned experiences of the persons who occupy the positions. The formal ranking system is readily observed. It is easy to list the official ranks between a five-star general and a lowly private, between the chairman of the board of a corporation and an unskilled worker, between the president of the AFL-CIO and a rank-and-file member of a trade union local.

Formal ranks are associated with distinctive attitudes and interests. The diverse experiences and problems of people at different levels condition (1) how individuals in similar social positions view the world and themselves and (2) the stake they have in the organization. Position in the hierarchy influences manners, outlook, opportunities, and power.

Status is symbolized in many ways. The American office "is a veritable temple of status" (Whyte, 1951). The carpeted office and the privilege of smoking or of first-naming one's colleagues are cues to differential status. The significance attached to names depends on the relative positions of people in the hierarchy. An example of the rank order of address by executives is out-

Values and norms	**Informal group norms** within the organization, e.g., "Don't be a rate-buster"
	Basic attitudes about work, cooperation, loyalty, etc. brought into the organization as a result of prior socialization
	Social control devices, e.g., approval or ridicule
Groups	**Friendships,** either within group or from outside, exert claims on the individual
	Cliques, either friendship groups or merely alliances, show personal loyalty
	Interest groups share a stake in existing social arrangements (may be any groups, including formal units)
Status	**Informal privileges** attached to positions in the formal hierarchy
	Power relations, e.g., balance of power between local and headquarters units, depending on source of funds, locus of membership, etc.
	Dependency patterns, e.g., dependence of staff on line

Figure 7:3 Elements of informal structure

Informal structure refers to patterns that develop during spontaneous interaction of persons and groups within the organization. This structure critically affects communication and power and is indispensable to effective functioning of the organization, but it may also undermine it.

lined by Stephen Potter, a wry student of human relations, in the case of Lumer Farr, a company director who liked to be called "The Guv'nor":

In the science of Christian-naming, Lumer is associated with Farr's Law of Mean Familiarity. This can be expressed by a curve, but is much clearer set down as follows:
The Guv'nor addresses:

Co-director Michael Yates as　　　*Mike*
Assistant director Michael Yates as　*Michael*
Sectional manager Michael
　Yates as　　　　　　　　　　*Mr. Yates*
Sectional assistant Michael
　Yates as　　　　　　　　　　*Yates*
Apprentice Michael Yates as　　*Michael*
Night-watchman Michael Yates as　*Mike*

(Potter, 1952:44)

Organizations are both aided and hindered by the transformation of formal, technical rankings into social strata. People who have feelings of deference toward their superiors more readily accept commands, and the system of authority is thus sustained. On the other hand, exploitation of positions of authority for personal ambition or blind acceptance of commands because they come from a superior may subvert organizational goals. (See Adaptation 16.)

Communication and the chain of command
Adaptation 15 describes how information is filtered as it moves up and down the chain of command. The employees' efforts to protect themselves result in distortions in communication.

Although stratification may distort communication, the formal status system is designed to facilitate it. For example, when an employee receives an order or request, he wants to know if it comes from someone who is in a position to know the facts and who will back up the action taken. Usually knowledge of the sender's place in the formal status system answers his questions. As formal ranking becomes embedded in social relations, more detailed knowledge is necessary to interpret orders. One person at a given formal rank may not need to be taken seriously, but another at the same level might command prompt action. Thus, communications from a "lame duck," a high official who is scheduled to leave office in the near future, are treated more casually than a similar message from an official known to be continuing.

203

*Adaptation 15
Gardner and
Moore: The line
of authority and
communication*

Adaptation 15 Gardner and Moore: The line of authority and communication

The formal line of authority or chain of command in a factory provides a channel of communication extending from top to bottom. But it is not the simple, direct channel it is often thought to be. By its very nature as a linkage of worker–boss relationships, it has a number of peculiarities which affect the quality, accuracy, and speed of communication. In fact, much of the transmission is so difficult that it is rare for a superior who is several steps removed from the work level to have comprehensive knowledge of what goes on in the shop. This adaptation reviews some of the sources of communication difficulties up and down the line.

COMMUNICATION DOWN

Because each person is sensitive to his or her boss's moods, opinions, likes, and dislikes, there is often much confusion and misunderstanding in communication down the line. For example, we see the superintendent passing through the shop, convoyed by the foreman. Being in a jovial mood, he comments, "The girls seem happy this morning, the way they are talking and laughing." The foreman thinks, "Is he hinting that I shouldn't allow them to talk? Does he think I don't keep proper discipline? Those girls ought to have sense enough to stop talking and act busy when he's around. Maybe I better move Mary off by herself because she always gets the others started talking." The boss leaves, quite unaware that his comments have been interpreted as criticism. As soon as he is gone, the foreman bawls out the girls for talking and not paying attention to their work; he moves the Marys around, and it is weeks or even months before the final ripples of disturbance have died down.

DISTORTION UP THE LINE

Because of sensitivity to the boss and dependence on him, there is much distortion in communicating up the line of authority. Along with concern for giving the boss what he wants, there is a tendency to cover up, to keep the boss from knowing about the

Source: Abridged and adapted from *Human Relations in Industry* by B. B. Gardner and D. G. Moore (Chicago: Irwin, 1950). pp. 33–65. Revised Edition. Published in this form by permission of the authors and Richard D. Irwin, Inc.

things that go wrong or the things that do not get done. No one wants to pass bad news up the line, because he feels that it reflects on him and that he should handle his job so there is no bad news. Consequently, he does not tell the boss what a poor job he did or how stupid he was. That is, he does not do so unless he thinks someone else will get to the boss first. (See "A Case of Jitters.") When he does have to break some bad news to the boss, he will probably have the problem fixed or have developed a good excuse. People at each level develop defenses, often complicated and ingenious, to protect themselves from the criticism of those above them in the chain of command.

The subordinate selects what to tell his superior, trying to anticipate what the boss wants to know or what he may want to know later, trying to present things in such a way that the boss will feel that things are not too bad or, even if they have been, that they are now under control, and trying to give him good news to take the sting out of the bad. The boss goes away feeling that he knows what is going on, that he has his finger firmly on the pulse of the shop.

FILTERED INFORMATION

Each individual in the line acts as a filter who sorts the information coming to him and selects what he will pass on to his boss. Because a boss responds most favorably to good news, good news goes up the line quite easily and rapidly. Information about improvements in output, quality, costs, and so on are transmitted readily from level to level. On the other hand, bad news moves more slowly; everyone is reluctant to communicate his mistakes or failures. The what-will-the-boss-think-of-me feeling encourages delays, excuses, and the development of tact in presenting bad news. The filtering of information operates at all levels in the hierarchy.

THE FOREMAN'S ORIENTATION

The foreman, who is usually considered the first level of management, has the most direct and detailed knowledge of the job and the workers. He plans and supervises their work; he checks and judges it; he maintains discipline and enforces the rules. To the workers he is the one who gives orders, who rewards and punishes. It is through him that the downward pressures, the demands and orders, are transmitted to the work group.

The foreman develops an orientation toward the work which is different from that of the rest of the hierarchy. His attention is focused on the everyday details. He sees the immediate difficulties and complexities of getting the work out, and he usually knows the workers and their attitudes. As a result, he tends to be impatient with higher levels or with staff people who try to generalize on the basis of partial knowledge and make decisions which affect his job. He frequently feels that his superiors impose tasks on him and on his group without understanding the difficulties of the job.

Four characteristic orientations of foremen may be identified: (1) worker-oriented, (2) management-oriented, (3) isolated, and (4) integrated.

1. Worker-oriented foremen The foreman who has strong feelings of sympathy with the work group identifies with the workers, acts as though he were one of them, and constantly defends them from his superiors and from outside organizations. Such a foreman generally maintains little social distance between himself and his work group.

There is often a much greater distinction between this foreman and his department chief. In some cases the foreman may actually avoid contacts and force the department chief to come to him. The foreman tries to keep the department chief away from his group, to be present when he is around the job, to cover up mistakes and protect individual workers from his criticism, and otherwise to build strong barriers between them. He resists demands from above for changes, finding reasons for not accepting them or for their failure if they are forced upon him.

2. Management-oriented foremen The opposite type is the foreman who has a strong identification with management and his superiors and who holds his subordinates at a distance. He tends to be critical of the workers and feels that they are not dependable or are not trying to do a good job. They correctly feel that he is aloof, and they hesitate to talk freely to him or to discuss problems with him. He is likely to seek out his superiors, both on the job and outside. He is concerned about his relationship with his department chief and tries to make a good impression.

In this situation, the workers feel forced to be on their guard against their foreman and think of him as someone who is against them rather than for them. They develop various defenses: They watch their behavior whenever he is in sight; they may restrict output without his knowledge; and they may complain about him to the union. Sometimes the tension makes contacts so uncomfortable that even he is aware of it and may withdraw to some extent from the work situation. In extreme cases, he spends most of his time at his desk, talking to his superiors, or when possible entirely out of the department.

3. Isolated foremen Sometimes a foreman is isolated from both his department chief and the work group. In these cases, there is avoidance on the part of all concerned. If the job will run with a minimum of direct supervision, the foreman may stay out of the group most of the time and stay away from his department chief, too. As long as the work goes on, the department chief also avoids the foreman and the group, and all contacts are very formal and uncomfortable. If the job does not go well, the foreman is in difficulties because his boss will be critical of him and may make arbitrary demands. At the same time, the group is defensive and does not respond to the foreman's demands. The foreman is generally critical of them, just as his boss is critical of him. Under these conditions, both the foreman and the workers are uncomfortable, and whenever there is pressure on the foreman from above, he feels isolated and defenseless and takes it out on his subordinates. In other words, such situations may be fairly stable as long as the work is running well, but under pressure a great deal of friction between foreman and workers develops.

4. Integrated foremen Sometimes, on the other hand, we find a situation in which there is strong identification and integration among all three—the workers, the foreman, and the department chief. In such cases we see very easy interaction between workers and department chief, and the department chief is usually in close touch with the details of the job and with the individuals. The foreman is comfortable under these conditions, does not worry about the presence of the department chief, and need not cover up mistakes or try to protect the group. In many instances of this kind, the whole department stands as a unit against outside pressures or against demands from above. These are the most comfortable and satisfactory work situations for the foreman and for the workers.

Section three bureaucracy and authority[1]

Among the master trends of modern history, none has been more widely noted than bureaucratization. Kinship, fealty, and contract were representative modes of social ordering in earlier centuries, but today the principle of rational coordination dominates the scene. (See SOCIAL ORGANIZATION, p. 51.) This principle is congenial to the large, centrally governed administrative organization. While rational coordination is often effective in smaller organizations, it is the effort to run a large enterprise that produces the characteristic social form called bureaucracy.

The term *bureaucracy* carries both positive and negative connotations. In ordinary usage, bureaucracy suggests a certain narrowness and rigidity, a regime of red tape. Bureaucracy is, among other things,

a system of administration marked by constant striving for increased functions and power, by lack of initiative and flexibility, by indifference to human needs or public opinion, and by a tendency to defer decisions to superiors or to impede action with red tape . . . the body of officials that gives effect to such a system.[2]

However, most social scientists define bureaucracy in a more neutral way, as the formal organization of administrative officials. A bureaucrat is simply an official. Bureaucracy does not include the non-supervisory work force in a factory or the members of a trade union. Nor does it usually include the top policy-making leaders or directors who are not involved in the day-to-day operation of the enterprise. *Formal structure*, a more general term, designates the prescribed roles and the rules and procedures applicable to all participants.

For example, the formal structure of a university includes regents (trustees), faculty, administrators, and students. The university bureaucracy is the corps of administrators — president, vice-presidents, registrar, deans, department heads. Many university bureaucrats are also faculty members, most of them senior faculty members; a few may be trustees who serve on committees concerned with managing the university's endowment or some other application of university policy. Although students are almost wholly outside the main bureaucracy, they may have their own bureaucracy in the form of a staff of student officials running the student government and student activities.

In defining bureaucracy as the formal organization of administrative officials, social scientists have tried to avoid prejudgments. A bureaucrat is not necessarily rigid, insensitive, or power-striving. Bureaucracy should be thought of as a *kind* of formal, administrative structure with distinctive characteristics and problems.

BUREAUCRATIZATION

Bureaucracy has a positive connotation when it is considered as a rational way of organizing complex activities. This point of view is associated with the writings of Weber, who saw the rise of modern bureaucracy as part of a larger social process — the rational reconstruction of human institutions. To Weber rationality is the decisive feature of modernity, the key to change in economics, politics, law, and cultural life. In the modern era, more and more aspects of life are instrumental rather than expressive; universalism tends to drive out particularism; achievement becomes, in many spheres, more important than ascription. (See p. 39.) These tendencies are especially evident in military organization, government, and business. Traditional ways of doing things are no longer self-justifying, and merit has increasing weight in the hiring of personnel. Organizations are purged of practices that once made working life more personal but

[1] This section is in part adapted from Selznick, 1969: 75–95.

[2] By permission. From Webster's Third International Dictionary © 1971 by G. & C. Merriam Co., Publishers of the Merriam-Webster Dictionaries.

made business and government less efficient.

Family vs. bureaucratic management The contrast of prebureaucratic and bureaucratic organization is illustrated by the transition from family-based management to professional management in modern industrial organization. Both types still exist, but professional and bureaucratic management are representative of modern society. Family management (sometimes called patrimonial) is characteristic of an earlier era:

Patrimonial management is a common first stage in a country's march toward economic development. In countries where the family is one of the dominating social institutions in the society, the family enterprise is a simple and logical instrument of business activity. Loyalty and trust within the hierarchy are assured. The forces of tradition and religion support the essential integrity of the family dynasty. The enterprise provides the means for safeguarding the security and the reputation of the family (Harbison and Myers, 1959:69).

As the business expands, family management loses ground. Even the extended family is unable to supply enough capital, ideas, or managerial personnel to meet the crises of business growth. For a time, outsiders can be hired without loss of control and without changing the character of the business. But eventually the professionals outnumber the family members and take over more and more responsibility for making business decisions. At last, the family may recognize that its interests are served best by turning over the day-to-day operation of the enterprise, and even the most important policy decisions, to professional managers.

This transition to bureaucracy may be understood by considering (1) managerial authority and (2) rational procedure.

Managerial authority Patrimonial management is typically one-person rule. The boss resists delegation of authority and is inclined to make as many decisions as possible on his own. His relations with his staff are personal, and he expects unreserved loyalty and obedience.

In the bureaucratic setting, authority is more impersonal, more systematic, more limited, and more effectively delegated. Authority is respected primarily for its technical competence, and all officials, including top management, accept a framework of established rules. In this sense, bureaucratic authority is "constitutional."

Rational procedure The prebureaucratic business leader is impatient with formal rules and procedures. He keeps his accounts in his hat and runs the organization from day to day without clear-cut policies. Much is done in accordance with tradition or by improvisation to fit the requirements of the moment. The intuitive understandings derived from one person's experience, often a rich experience, are the foundation of decision making in the enterprise.

The bureaucratic way is directly contrary. Systematic procedure based on principles of sound management is the ideal. Rules and policies are developed to guide decision making in all phases of activity. Employees are hired in accordance with criteria worked out by a personnel department; they are trained, assigned, and supervised according to specified routines. Tradition is never its own justification but is subject to question and revision by specialists in organization planning and human engineering.

Limits to bureaucratization Although the development of a bureaucracy is a long-established fact in most advanced nations, it is still a very lively concern in modernizing countries, and even in Western countries modernization is not complete. One study of a gypsum mining and wallboard manufacturing company, located in a semirural area, found that for many years the company had followed a relaxed, nonbureaucratic policy. Rules were vague and not strictly enforced; absences during hunting season were accepted indulgently; and the employees, who did a lot of handyman work at home and were often part-time farmers, were allowed to appropriate company property for their own use:

An electrician: We can get some nails, a piece of wood, from the storehouse, if we want it. If one of the fellows needs a table fixed, he brings it into the maintenance room and when one of the fellows gets a minute, he fixes it on company time.

A union official: They have a rule that if a worker wants to take home any glass, tin, nails, screws or wood, all he has to do is to get a slip from his foreman and the gateman. . . . They (top management) know that the foreman will have enough brains not to give too much, but just enough to help a fellow out. Why it's the same with the farmers around here. They don't kick about the dust and smoke, but when they want any welding done on their equipment, they bring it in and the Company does it. The Company is like that in other things (Gouldner, 1954:51).

These and other lenient policies made the plant a comfortable place to work for the kind of men who lived in the area. The indulgency pattern was supported by the fact that the plant was "enmeshed in a network of kinship relationships." The management favored local rural people in personnel selection, and in time the plant was filled with friends and relatives. As a result, the spirit of particularism prevailed, as suggested in the remark of a mill foreman: "You can't ride the men very hard when they are your neighbors. Lots of these men grew up together" (Gouldner, 1954:65).

The company's operations were not very efficient, and when a new manager was appointed he set to work breaking down the old informal patterns. Bureaucracy became the order of the day. However, there was substantial resistance to bureaucratization, especially among the gypsum miners. The miners had a long tradition of solidarity, reinforced by their hazardous work conditions, and their attitudes were strongly traditionalistic. The physical danger under which they worked allowed the miners to claim exemption from supervisory authority and from certain work rules (Gouldner 1954:149).

Weber's model According to Weber, three main features identify bureaucracy as a special kind of formal organization (Gerth and Mills, 1946:Chap. 8; Weber, 1922/1947: 329–341):

1. An officialdom The rise of bureaucracy is accompanied by the emergence of the official as a social role. Much of Weber's discussion identifies the distinguishing features of an officialdom: technical expertise, at least in the sense of administrative know-how; a claim to continuity in office; appointment on the basis of merit; definite duties and jurisdiction.

2. Spheres of competence In a bureaucracy, defined spheres of competence are the basic units of the organization. Bureaucratic hierarchy is, therefore, more than a formal chain of command. It is an arrangement of parts—bureaus or offices responsible for some activity or area—that have an integrity and continuity of their own. In this context *competence* means jurisdiction rather than technical knowledge, although the two may be closely connected. A federal bureau—say, the Forest Service—may fight to maintain or extend its jurisdiction, that is, its legal sphere of competence. In doing so, it may argue that it has the technical expertise to regulate logging and protect the forests. The positive significance of this aspect of bureaucracy is discussed in Adaptation 16.

3. Governance by rules Weber considered administration according to "calculable rules . . . of paramount importance for modern bureaucracy (Gerth and Mills, 1946:215)." The bureaucrat's main commitment is to an impersonal order, a system of rules that limits his own discretion and which he must apply in an evenhanded way. In speaking of calculable rules, Weber was emphasizing that modern administration seeks to make decisions as objectively as possible, eliminating whatever is subjective and irrational.

In Weber's model, bureaucracy is a kind of legal system, one that emphasizes fidelity to rules, correct procedure, defined jurisdictions, and the sovereignty of institutional purpose. Therefore Weber called bureaucratic authority "rational-legal." He distin-

Table 7:2   Max Weber on bureaucracy

	Prebureaucratic	Bureaucratic
Purpose	Ad hoc, subjective, reflecting personal aims of political or business leader, military chief, etc.	Explicit, objective, public; normally established by statute or charter to which all are theoretically responsible
Hierarchy	Weak and fluid; subordinate offices held at pleasure of chief; spheres of competence not firmly established	Clear spheres of competence and responsibility; clear channels of communication; authority of each level defined and protected
Rules	Unsystematic, selectively enforced; strongly qualified by particularism	Dependable, related to organizational purpose; rule of law as ideal
Authority	Traditional, charismatic	Rational-legal
Careers	Unstable, nonprofessional; offices available for sale or as part-time prizes for elite	The official as full-time professional; committed to the organization; no personal constituency; appointment on merit
Decision making	Ad hoc, intuitive, subject to whims of one-person rule and to uncontrolled actions by subordinates	Systematic, routinized; assumption of a stable social world, composed of elements classified and made subject to rules

Source: Weber, 1922/1947:328–341; Gerth and Mills, 1946:Chap. 8.

guished this from traditional authority, wherein a leader's claim to personal obedience is sanctioned by custom, and from charismatic authority, which rests on a belief in the special qualities of a spiritual, political, or organizational chief.

Weber's theory is best understood as a contrast between prebureaucratic and bureaucratic forms of organization. In Table 7:2 this contrast is presented as it affects six aspects of organization: purpose, hierarchy, rules, authority, careers, and decision making.

The special attributes of bureaucracy have one thing in common: They tend to reduce the flexibility of administrative action. For that reason, the connection between bureaucracy and rationality must be assessed with caution. For Weber, bureaucratic organization was more rational, in the sense of more efficient, than prebureaucratic organization. Given his historical perspective, it made sense for him to conclude that bureaucracy was a notable achievement compared to the rampant traditionalism and person-centered administration of an earlier era.

On the other hand, Weber was no un-

qualified proponent of bureaucracy or, for that matter, of rationality. He did not look with optimism upon the drift of history, for he believed that a commitment to rational forms would tend to depersonalize the world and that the machinery it created might well crush the spirit. In 1909 he spoke in the following vein:

This passion for bureaucracy . . . is enough to drive one to despair. It is as if in politics the spectre of timidity . . . were to stand alone at the helm; as if we were deliberately to become men who need "order" nothing but order, who become nervous and cowardly if for one moment this order wavers, and helpless if they are torn away from their total incorporation in it. . . . The great question is therefore not how we can promote and hasten it, but what can we oppose to this machinery in order to keep a portion of mankind free from this parcelling-out of the soul, from this supreme mastery of the bureaucratic way of life (Mayer, 1943:127–128).

BEYOND BUREAUCRACY?

The distinctive characteristics of bureaucracy—a career officialdom, defined spheres of competence, governance by rules—create vested interests and a commitment to established routines. Bureaucracy gives great weight to seniority, for example, and to close observance of detailed regulations. The rigidities involved are bearable, and even necessary, when the work of the organization is stable, routine, and heavily dependent on detailed supervision of relatively unskilled personnel.

But bureaucracy as Weber understood it has important limitations from the standpoint of modern management. Many contemporary organizations require greater flexibility than the bureaucratic style allows, and they are more concerned to stimulate initiative than regulate conduct.

The following prophecy is offered by a writer who has emphasized the need for a postbureaucratic perspective:

The social structure of organizations of the future will have some unique characteristics. The key word will be "temporary." There will be adaptive, rapidly changing *temporary* systems. These will be task forces organized around problems to be solved by groups of relative strangers with diverse professional skills. The group will . . . evolve in response to a problem rather than to programmed role expectations. The executive thus becomes coordinator or "linking pin" between various task forces. He must be a man who speaks the polyglot jargon of research, with skills to relay information and to mediate between groups. People will be evaulated not according to rank but according to skill and professional training. Organizational charts will consist of project groups rather than stratified functional groups. (This trend is already visible in the aerospace and construction industries, as well as many professional and consulting firms.) (Bennis, 1968:73–74.)

This vision of an adaptive, problem-centered enterprise has much to commend it. Many students of organization agree that the large enterprise, whether business or government, need not necessarily take on all of the features of bureaucracy. The effective organization is more fully purposive, more flexible, more susceptible to leadership, more congenial to initiative at all levels.

It is not likely, however, that bureaucracy can be wholly transcended. Management will continue to depend on professionalism and will be required to offer security of employment. Authority will have to be delegated, thus creating spheres of competence, and rules of some sort will remain indispensable. If there is a postbureaucratic world, it will not be one in which bureaucracy is eliminated. Rather, bureaucracy will be checked and counterbalanced by other, nonbureaucratic forms of action. Among these are new forms of improvisation, such as the temporary task force cutting across departmental lines; a nonbureaucratic approach to the application of rules, that is, taking account of the purposes the rules are intended to achieve; and techniques for enhancing initiative and morale.

One challenge to bureaucracy is the technical staff group whose job is to innovate and to set new standards. Ideally, such groups are a kind of leaven in the bureaucratic dough. Adaptation 17 analyzes the conflict between line and staff and shows some of the inherent difficulties that beset efforts to change large organizations.

Adaptation 16 **Mosher:** Watergate and bureaucracy

At 2:00 A.M., June 17, 1972, five men were caught in the sixth-floor offices of the Democratic Na-

Source: Abridged and adapted from *Watergate: Implications for Responsible Government* by Frederick C. Mosher and Others (New York: Basic Books, 1974). Published by permission of Frederick C. Mosher and Basic Books.

tional Committee at the Watergate office building in Washington, D.C. This bizarre event turned out to be far more than a routine burglary. Subsequent investigation showed that the break-in was engineered by the Committee to Re-elect the President; White House staff were involved; and an ex-

Reporters Woodward and Bernstein of the Washington Post, who did most to reveal the Watergate coverup, watch President Nixon deliver his resignation speech.

tensive cover-up, reaching to President Nixon himself, was revealed. The national scandal ensued which ultimately destroyed the Nixon presidency. Richard M. Nixon resigned his office on August 8, 1974.

Among the lessons of Watergate was a reassessment of the relation between the presidency and the federal bureaucracy. The president's effort to master the federal agencies at first seemed to many a healthy effort to streamline the government and overcome bureaucratic inertia. As the events unfolded, however, it became clear that Weber's model of bureaucracy, which includes the idea of "spheres of competence," was still relevant and important. It was vividly revealed what might happen if the federal officialdom were treated merely as the president's subordinates, obligated to obey direct orders from the White House. In fact, the heads of federal agencies, such as the Internal Revenue Service and the Department of Justice, are responsible to the Congress as well as to the president. Their authority derives not only from their appointment by the president but also from the statutes that define the programs and appropriate the money for their agencies. The Watergate experience showed that bureaucrats have an obligation to defend their agencies even against pressure from the chief executive or his staff.

The following discussion is adapted from certain sections of a report by the Senate Select Committee on Presidential Campaign Activities, whose

chairman was Senator Sam J. Ervin, Jr. During the fall of 1973 the Ervin committee conducted nationally televised hearings on the events that led to Watergate and the subsequent cover-up.

The Watergate climate may be treated from two perspectives, the political and the administrative. The prime motivating drive behind both political and administrative activities seems to have been presidential power — its enlargement, its exploitation, and its continuation. Power was perhaps sought by some in the presidential entourage for its own sake, but it seems fair to conclude that most sought to impose upon the government the ideological views of the president. Paradoxically, a part of that ideology was to limit the powers of the national government and to return more power to the people and their elected representatives at state and local levels.

THE POLITICAL CLIMATE

The months before the 1972 election were characterized by an obsessive drive for reelection of the president. The drive seems to have colored government plans and decisions even in fields of activity intended to be politically neutral — administration of the revenue laws, antitrust prosecutions, allocation of grants and contracts, clearance of career service appointments and promotions, and many others. It is evident that the imperative to reelect was so great as to override many other considerations, including the public interest and normal ethical and legal constraints.

Following the "mandate" of the 1972 election, the administration acted to remove senior officials in many executive agencies who were considered to be hesitant or doubtful followers of the views and ideology of the president. In terms of top-level political appointees, the transition between the first and second Nixon terms was as extreme as most transitions from one party to the other. Many experienced Republicans in key posts were replaced by others, usually younger, in whom the administration presumably had greater confidence of personal and ideological loyalty and who were innocent of prior allegiances to the agency of their appointment or its associated clienteles. In this and other ways the administration undertook to carry out and enforce its electoral "mandate," even before the inauguration in 1973.

THE ADMINISTRATIVE CLIMATE

As a result of the political climate, aggressive efforts were made to use administrative machinery to carry out political and policy ends, and growing frustration and exasperation developed over alleged bureaucratic impediments. In part, it was a further step in the evolution of a strong presidency—a movement which had begun generations earlier and which students of American government have generally approved.

Taken individually, the majority of changes that the administration instituted or sought were consistent with sound administrative practices; indeed, a good many leaders in public administration had recommended some of them earlier and specifically endorsed them after they were proposed by the president. They included:

• Delegation of federal powers from Washington to the field
• Unconditional grants to state and local governments (called "general revenue sharing")
• Broader categories of, and fewer strings on, functional grants to state and local governments (called "special revenue sharing")
• Strengthening of the managerial role of the Bureau of the Budget (which became the Office of Management and Budget) and vesting of all of its statutory powers in the president
• Consolidation of the activities of most of the domestic departments in four "superdepartments," rationally organized according to subject matter areas
• Formation of a "Federal Executive Service" to encompass all supergrade employees whose qualifications would be approved and whose assignments and salaries would be flexible according to managerial needs
• Encouraging the administrative practices associated with the term "management by objective"
• Interposing generalists with a broader perspective above the specialized, professionalized, "parochial" bureaucracies

But these mostly constructive actions and proposals were accompanied by a number of others which students of government, even those with the strongest commitment to presidential energy and influence, found questionable. These included:

• Usurpation by the White House of powers over both policy and day-to-day operations heretofore carried on in the departments and other established agencies

• Enormous growth of the White House staff, accompanied by the establishment of a tight hierarchy within it
• By-passing of departments and agencies in areas of their assigned responsibilities, first in international and defense matters through the staff director of the National Security Council and later through the staff director of the Domestic Council
• Veiling of White House activities on grounds of national security or executive privilege
• Negating of substantial majorities of both houses of Congress on policy and program matters through accelerating use of the veto power and impoundment of funds
• Interposition of White House aides between the president and the official heads of the executive agencies, such aides having been appointed without confirmation or even public knowledge
• The abortive attempt to give presidential counselors in the White House substantial control over established departments

Considered singly or separately, few of the actions or proposals in the foregoing lists would be cause for great alarm. However, if all of them had been put into effect, the administrative weather could have become very stormy indeed. The American state then would have approached a monocracy, ruled from the top through a strictly disciplined hierarchical system. It would have become difficult to pin responsibility for decisions or actions upon anyone short of the top man, and he was, for the most part, inaccessible and unaccountable. As some of his appointees pointed out, the only ultimate means of holding the president answerable following his election or reelection is impeachment.

THE WHITE HOUSE STAFF

Among the institutions of government on which Watergate has focused attention, none stands out so much as the presidency and those staff and staff organizations surrounding the presidency. Perhaps most controversial has been the revelation that the structure which was designed to provide the president with staff assistance and advice has been gradually fashioned into an instrument of centralized control. Much of this was done in the open, building vigorously upon trends in the organization of the presidency first noted over a decade ago and pursued in the name of efficient, effective, and responsive government. Increasingly, access to the president was restricted. The principal officers of the executive departments and agencies and the leadership (both majority and minority) of the Congress encountered more and more difficulty in seeing him. Equally important, the free flow and competition of ideas and interests were cut off.

What emerges is a picture of the centralization of power in the White House and the concomitant confusion of roles and responsibilities by placing operating authority in the hands of personal and advisory staff who make the key decisions but are shielded from public view and public access. The president needs adequate staff assistance and sufficient flexibility to serve his personal style in meeting his constitutional responsibilities; yet the full bloom of a monocratic presidency cannot fulfill the best interests of the Republic.

ADVISERS AND OFFICERS

The distinction between intimate personal advisers to the president and those exercising executive power on behalf of the president is crucial. Difficulties occur when the privileges and immunities traditionally extended to advisers are assumed to apply to everyone in the White House, regardless of position.

If members of the White House staff are to continue to act in a capacity other than that of personal advisers and staff assistants to the president and are authorized to issue "orders" on the president's behalf or on their own authority, then modifications are called for in present interpretations of executive privilege. Indeed, the question may well be raised as to whether assistants to the president who perform executive functions occupy "offices" subject to Article II, section 2, of the Constitution, which provides that the president

. . . shall nominate, and by and with the advice and consent of the Senate, shall appoint . . . all other officers of the United States, whose appointments are not herein otherwise provided for, and which shall be established by law. But the Congress may by law vest the appointment of such inferior officers as they think proper in the President alone, in the courts of law, or in the heads of departments.

Principal White House assistants with the equivalent of cabinet rank and acting as supercabinet officers would not appear to belong in the category of inferior officers.

The proper relationship between the president

and his office and the departments and agencies which make up the executive branch has been a source of debate as old as the Republic itself. George Washington certainly supposed—and so did the officials of his administration—that he could summon any of them for a review of any pending matter and instruct them as to its disposition. This derived from, among other things, his power to "require the opinion, in writing, of the principal officer in each of the executive departments upon any subject relating to the duties of their respective offices. . . ." But in a contrary direction, Congress, in the Treasury Department Act of 1789, established five distinct offices, each with distinct responsibilities. Subsequent practice, except for emergency legislation, has been to vest statutory powers in bureaus or agencies, or their heads, rather than in the president.

THE CORPORATE STATE

It now appears that recent administrations have been moving toward fundamental changes in the system which, if fully achieved, would have substituted a governmental philosophy foreign to the concepts of the framers of the Constitution and the concepts of most Americans since then. The U.S. government would be run like a corporation—or at least a popular view of the corporate model—with all powers concentrated at the top and exercised through appointees in the president's office and loyal followers placed in crucial positions in the various agencies of the executive branch. This would have effectively destroyed public accountability except for the president himself.

No one can guess how close the American government would be to this closed hierarchical model had not the Watergate exposures halted the trend—at least temporarily.

The panel believes that the Select Committee should emphatically reaffirm the following:

The President is recognized to have general authority and responsibility over the agencies in the Executive Branch, subject to restrictions on such authority in law, and over the nature and direction of public policy within the framework of law.

Virtually all the executive agencies were established by law, duly passed by the Congress subject to Presidential veto, or by Reorganization Plan initiated by the President, subject to Congressional veto; with a few exceptions, all received their powers and responsibilities in the same ways, not by delegation; and, for the most part, their ability to operate is annually renewed through appropriations, passed by Congress, subject to Presidential veto.

The top leaders in almost all the agencies are appointed by the President, subject to confirmation by the Senate.

The heads of the agencies are therefore responsible, in different ways, to both the President and the Congress.

PLURALISTIC BUREAUCRACY

The federal government is necessarily pluralistic, not monocratic. Whereas the president properly exercises overall responsibilities for the operations and policies of the executive branch, the individual departments and agencies must enjoy a degree of independence from the White House, consistent with their dual allegiance to the presidency and to the Congress which participated in creating them and to which they must look for both sustenance and program approval. The intelligence and investigative agencies are particularly subject to criticism resulting from excessive White House direction and must be afforded an even greater degree of freedom from highly centralized control in the executive branch.

Adaptation 17 Dalton: Staff–line conflict in industry

This is a study of social differentiation and its consequences in two major groups of management: the line organization *and the* staff organization. *The line organization consists of the foremen and their superiors who direct the actual work done and who are responsible for production. The staff organization consists of specialists who have a research and advisory function in the plant. Staff groups are relatively new in industry. They provide specialized knowledge and technical advice in such diverse fields as chemistry, statistics, public and industrial relations, personnel, accounting, and engineering.*

Data on staff–line relations in this study were drawn from three industrial plants in related industries. The plants ranged in size from 4,500 to 20,000 employees and from 200 to nearly 1,000 management officials.

THE PROBLEM

The staff has specialized knowledge gained from training and research. In theory it advises the line officers how they can increase production and efficiency. The ideal situation involves two assumptions: (1) that the staff specialists are reasonably content to be advisers without formal

Source: Abridged and adapted from Melville Dalton, "Conflicts Between Staff and Line Managerial Officers," *American Sociological Review* (June 1950), pp. 342–351. Published in this form by permission of Melville Dalton and *American Sociological Review.*

authority, and (2) that their suggestions for improvements are welcomed by the line officers and carried out. This study tests these assumptions in the actual relations of the two groups as they work out their problems.

It must be emphasized that the staff–line conflict discussed here is only one of many frictions in the plants. For instance, there is competition and tension among departments, among individuals, and between union and management.

There are two major sources of friction between the staff and line in the plants considered. One is the *social background* or composition of the two groups, that is, the personal characteristics they bring to the plant. The other source of friction is the differentiation that takes place within the plant, the differences in *social position* they assume once there.

SOURCES OF FRICTION: SOCIAL COMPOSITION

The two groups differ in age, formal education, and social behavior (appearance, manners, etc.).

1. Age The staff members on the average are significantly younger than the line officers. This is a source of friction revealed in the ill-concealed attitude of the older line officers. They resent receiving what they regard as instructions from younger men. The staff officers often attribute to this attitude their lack of success in "selling" ideas to the line. As one assistant staff chief remarked:

"We're always in hot water with these old guys on the line. You can't tell them a damn thing. They're bull-headed as hell! Most of the time we offer a suggestion it's either laughed at or not considered at all. The same idea in the mouth of some old codger on the line'd get a round of applause. They treat us like kids."

2. Education The staff members necessarily have more education than the line officers. Education is part of the qualification for staff jobs; experience is emphasized in the choice of line officers. The staff is in a position to exploit this difference in education, and it probably contributes to a feeling of superiority among them. The line, however, resents the proposals of the staff because of the educational difference involved as well as the age differential. The line often refers to the staff as college punks, slide rules, crackpots, and chair warmers.

3. Social behavior Attention to personal appearance, cosmopolitan recreational tastes, facility in speaking and writing, poise and polish in social intercourse—these also distinguish the staff from the line. The line officers receive occasional snubs from the staff and feel that the staff's emphasis on social prestige is a threat to the line man's own position and not in the best interests of the plant. To quote a line officer on the matter of social intercourse during the working day: "They don't go into the cafeteria to eat and relax while they talk over their problems. They go in there to look around and see how somebody is dressed or to talk over the hot party they had last night. Well, that kind of damn stuff don't go with me. I haven't any time to put on airs and make out I'm something I'm not."

SOURCES OF FRICTION: SOCIAL POSITION WITHIN THE PLANT

The different functions the two groups perform in the plant and the different opportunities they have for advancement, salary, power, prestige, and responsibility are major sources of friction.

1. Chances for advancement Line officers have better chances for advancement than staff personnel for at least three reasons: (a) there are approximately twice as many positions of authority in the line; (b) the line organization reaches higher, for it has six status levels whereas the staff has only three; (c) line salaries for comparable positions are usually higher.

2. The staff is on trial Continuous dispute over the relative worth of the two groups is another source of friction. The line regards the staff as being on trial rather than as a managerial division of equal importance. To the line officer, his authority over production is something sacred, and he resents the implication that after many years in the line he needs the guidance of an inexperienced newcomer. He is ready with charges of crackpot experimentation and costly blunders by the staff. The lower foremen are inclined to suspect that the staff is less an engineering and technical assistance division than a weapon of top management to control the lower line officers.

The staff member is painfully aware of these feelings and of the need of his group to prove its worth. He feels bound to contribute something significant in the form of ideas helpful to management. By virtue of his greater education and knowledge of the latest theories of production, the staff man regards himself as a management consultant, an expert. He feels that he must be, or appear to be, almost infallible once he has committed himself to top management on some point. Whereas in practice adoption of their suggestions depends upon the amount of cooperation that can be won from line officers, the staff prefer to see themselves as agents of top management, independent of the lower line and superior to it.

3. The line resists innovation The different pressures upon the staff officers and the line officers in day-to-day operations create additional tension. As we have seen, the staff must make contributions in the form of suggested changes in order to prove its worth. But it is the line officers who are called on to change work habits. The experienced line officer fears being shown up before his superiors for not having thought of improvements himself. Moreover, changes in methods may bring personnel changes which threaten to break up cliques and other informal arrangements and to reduce the line officer's area of authority. Or such changes may expose forbidden practices and departmental inefficiency and waste. In some cases, these fears have led line officers to strike informal bargains with the staff to postpone the initiation of new practices for a period of time in exchange for some other cooperation from the line officers.

The pressure on staff personnel is to develop new techniques, but they also have to consider how their plans will be received by the line officers. They know from experience that lower line officers may verbally accept a change, but they are in a position to sabotage it in practice. For this reason, there is a tendency for staff members to withhold improved production schemes when they know an attempt to introduce them might fail.

The study found evidence that the accommodation of staff members to demands of the line officers included the manipulation (but not embezzlement) of company funds. Pressures from the lower line organization forced some staff groups to "kick in" some of the funds appropriated for staff use. The line officers were then able to hide inefficiencies and meet the constant pressure from the top to show low operating costs. In return the staff received more cooperation from the line members, and some staff personnel who wished transfer to the line were recommended.

WEAKNESS OF THE STAFF

It is clear that in the plants studied the line organization is the more powerful branch of management. The position of the staff is weak and defensive because of its lack of authority over production and its dependence upon top management for approval and for advancement.

The ultimate authority in the plant rests with top *line* officials. Usually, they have risen to the top by way of the line organization. They understand and sympathize with the daily problems of the line officers in getting the main work done, and their functions as top officials bring them close to the day-to-day pressures and responsibilities of the line. Top line officials also have influence over promotions in the higher staff positions. A staff member knows that if he aspires to one of the higher staff jobs or wishes to transfer to the line he must satisfy the top line officer. The staff member must show his ability to work with the line and to understand its problems. He must make contributions the line will accept and be able to minimize the conflicts occasioned by the social differences in background and role we have described.

CONCLUSION

The ideal conception of staff–line relations assumes that the staff is willing to function in an advisory capacity and that the line organization is willing to accept staff suggestions for improve- *ment. The sources of tension inherent in this situation have been described. One result is a morale problem among new staff members, reflected in disillusionment and high turnover.*

The new staff member, often selected because of his academic record, enters industry prepared to engage in logical, well-formulated relations with other members of management and to carry out the precise, methodical functions for which he has been trained. He believes he has much to contribute and that his efforts will win early recognition and rapid advancement. He soon discovers that his freedom to function is snared in a web of informal commitments, that his academic specialty may not be relevant to his actual assignments, and that he must learn who the informally powerful line officers are and what ideas they welcome.

In the plants studied, ambitious staff men, frustrated by the relatively low hierarchy through which they could move, appeared eager to increase the number of personnel under their authority. And in fact the personnel of staff groups did increase disproportionately to those of the line organization. There was also a trend of personnel movement from staff to line, presumably reflecting the drive, ambition, and qualifications of staff members who were striving for positions of authority, prestige, and higher income.

In general, staff–line friction reduces the distinctive contribution of staff personnel. Their relatively weak position, requiring accommodation to the line organization, tends to restrict their ability to engage in free, experimental innovation. On the other hand, the natural resistance of the line to staff innovations probably usefully restrains over-eager efforts to apply untested procedures on a large scale. The conflicts, however, introduce an uncontrolled element into the managerial system. Under such conditions, it is difficult to know when valuable ideas are being sacrificed.

CAUTION

Dalton's analysis is valuable for the light it casts on the sources of group conflict within administrative organizations. While the specific conclusions are still relevant, the status of staff groups has probably improved, especially in industries that depend on idea people of all sorts. This change is reflected in a tendency in some industries for top officials to be drawn from the staff rather than only from the line:

In the mythology of the modern corporation, "staff" groups are not supposed to have direct influence over line activities; but, in practice, as they gain reputation for their expertise, as they gain control over substantial amounts of company resources, and as they move from ad hoc *advice-giving to long-range, comprehensive research and planning for the organization, they may, in fact, be setting most of the constraints within which "line" managers operate (Dill, 1965:1085).*

Section four participation and control

The analysis of informal structure in Section Two is one way of calling attention to the active human being in the organizational setting. This section considers more directly the nature of participation in large organizations. Two themes are of special importance: the tension between personal aspirations and organizational needs, and the relative power of leaders and members.

MODES OF PARTICIPATION

Participation varies in extent and in quality. Belonging to a book club requires little attention, energy, or interest in its affairs. Such a membership is *segmental*; that is, it affects only a small part, or segment, of the member's life. Most members of most large organizations, including universities, trade unions, and cooperatives, invest only a limited part of themselves in organizational activities. When participation is limited and segmental, the individual is likely to take little responsibility for the affairs of the group. This abdication is the basic social phenomenon that underlies Michels's theory of self-perpetuating leadership. Adaptation 18 reviews his argument and compares it with a closely parallel study of the modern corporation.

The "Michels effect" is important because, although people participate segmentally, they may be seriously affected by the organization's decisions. Members of a trade union may not want to attend meetings or otherwise involve themselves in union affairs, but they have a substantial stake in what the leadership does. Students and faculty may be bored by administrative issues, yet if they opt out they will pay the price of losing control over rules and policies that affect them. Many people are interested in the purposes of an organization and in its policies, but their interest fades when they are faced with the routine chores of participation. To be a member is one thing; to be an active participant is something else.

When segmental participation is accompanied by full freedom of movement from one organization to another, the cost to the individual is minimal. The organization may then be perceived as selling a service or an opportunity. The person who can readily find another job need not depend on a specific employer. The employee is adequately protected by the job market. Ordinary stockholders in a large corporation have the attitude that if the corporation does not do well, they will simply sell their shares. Similarly, in the case of political groups and other voluntary associations, individuals may prefer to participate segmentally and walk out when they no longer like what the organization is doing. They need not concern themselves with choosing new leaders (Olson, 1971).

But freedom of choice and movement are very frequently not available. Most people are dependent on their jobs. Many so-called voluntary organizations (in which members are not employees) are really not so voluntary because they control access to jobs or other opportunities. Trade union membership is the most obvious example, but even lawyers or physicians may find that they must join a professional association in order to practice. Even ideological groups, once they gain influence, tend to limit political alternatives and thus create a kind of dependency. It is not easy to quit a major organization if the alternatives are to join a group that has little influence or to become a loner.

The concept of membership In the discussion above, the word *member* is used rather loosely to designate any participant. However, the term often carries a stronger meaning. In that stronger sense, membership is a special status. One who is a member has rights as well as responsibilities. Minimally, these rights protect a member against arbitrary dismissal or expulsion; but membership also tends to carry with it a claim to participation in the formulation of policy.

For this reason it seems strained to refer to ordinary employees as members of business firms. One is more likely to accord that status to stockholders and to professional or executive personnel. The Berle-Means thesis, in Adaptation 18, raises serious questions about the membership status of stockholders, at least in the large corporation. Legally, an employee has an individual contract of employment, which in most cases means very little because, in the absence of a supplementary trade union contract, the employer can dismiss the employee at will. On the other hand, the expansion of employee rights during the past generation suggests that the concept of membership may be acquiring a greater significance in industrial employment (Selznick, 1969:67–69; 271–273).

Similar questions are raised about the participation of students. Are students members of the university community and therefore entitled to some degree of participation in decision making? Or are students clients receiving a service from the university and therefore less justified in asserting a claim to participation? (Cf. Wolff, 1970:123–126.)

DEMOCRATIC AND AUTHORITARIAN FORMS

Some organizations encourage their members to participate in decision making, while others restrict this privilege. For example,

Parent-Teacher Associations, the League of Women Voters, many political parties, and the United Automobile Workers union are organized so as to permit, at least formally, a degree of membership control. On the other hand, bank tellers, soldiers, pupils, and boy scouts are not expected to participate significantly in the control of their organizations.

Differences in organizational form may reflect the values people hold, but they also develop out of practical necessity. Authoritarian controls are associated with sustained and coordinated activity. If a group does no more than meet occasionally for discussions, democratic forms may be adequate, but groups that carry on extensive and continuous activities usually add authoritarian forms. It is convenient and effective for them to assign to a single individual or small group of executives the responsibility for a job. The executives select others who accept direction, and thus a unified effort is carried out according to a plan. All large organizations follow this procedure, though they vary in the rigidity of discipline, extent of supervision, and autonomy of component units.

The great variety of formal organizations cannot be neatly divided into democratic and authoritarian types. In fact, both forms are found in many large organizations. The United Steelworkers, the Farm Bureau Federation, the National Association of Manufacturers, and a large oil company are alike in their formal provisions for meetings and elections to be held by members or stockholders. They all have large staffs of employees. Democratic forms may control the relations between the members and the top officials. But the officials have an authoritarian relation to the employees of the organization.

Not all organizations controlled from the top are equally authoritarian. Some corporations and agencies permit considerable decision making by committees, wide autonomy for subordinate officials, and action initiated from below. Organizations that encourage these patterns may be thought of as democratic in spirit and to some extent in form, even though final responsibility and authority remain at the top (McGregor, 1960; Likert, 1961).

Sometimes an executive is criticized as authoritarian because he shows a lack of regard for the opinions or feelings of his subordinates. Authoritarian *behavior* of this kind may be found in authoritarian organizations, but the two should not be confused. Some army commanders or corporation officials are authoritarian in their dealings with subordinates; others show tolerance and respect. Some pride themselves on lone-wolf decisions; others consult with subordinates. But in all armies and in most businesses, authoritarian procedures predominate.

The word *authoritarian* has a negative connotation. Indeed, if the kind of discipline and decision making that prevail in an army or even a corporation or government agency were extended to the whole society, self-government could not survive. But authoritarian forms, when limited to specific activities and controlled by law and custom, do not necessarily challenge the cultural ideals of a democratic society. So long as the people at the top, who stand in an authoritarian relation to their subordinates, are themselves responsible to some membership or electorate and are controlled by legal or other norms that restrain arbitrary action, authoritarian forms can readily be accepted. For example, in democratic states there is authoritarian administration within most government agencies, but the head of the agency is responsible to a governor, prime minister, or president who must stand for election.

COOPTATION

In authoritarian contexts, participation often takes the form of cooptation, a concept which has gained increasing currency in recent years. The demand for new forms of participation has arisen within organiza-

tions that are undemocratic in form, for example, universities, government agencies, and such traditionally authoritarian groups as the Catholic church. Rising expectations regarding the extent and quality of participation have led to criticism of "mere" cooptation as a screen behind which old patterns of domination are continued.

In its simplest form, cooptation is a way of enlarging a group, or filling vacancies in it, by decision of the existing members. It is usual for the trustees of foundations and similar organizations to be appointed by cooptation: The incumbent trustees decide for themselves who should be brought in to fill a vacancy.

The idea takes on an expanded meaning when it is said, for example, that the leadership of an organization coopts new leaders by appointing rank-and-file members to committees or junior posts, or by arranging that they be elected to such offices. Robert Michels used the term in that way when he said:

. . . as the chiefs become detached from the mass they show themselves more and more inclined, when gaps in their own ranks are to be filled, to effect this, not by way of popular election, but by cooptation, and also to increase their own effectives wherever possible, by creating new posts on their own initiative (Michels, 1911/1949:126).

Cooptation is more generally defined as "the process of absorbing new elements into the leadership or policy-determining structure of an organization as a means of averting threats to its stability or existence" (Selznick, 1949:13). Thus conceived, cooptation is more than a method of choosing; it is a mode of adaptation and a strategy.

As a strategy, cooptation is characteristically a quest for legitimacy and for greater efficiency in running the organization. If there is discontent among lower participants or clients—students, employees, tenants, hospital patients—it may help if some participation is allowed in a policy-making committee. The coopted participants legitimate the system of authority in the eyes of their fellows, and they can serve as channels of communication and control, thus helping to bridge the gap between rulers and ruled.

The coopting group wants participation, but for its own ends, and usually does not intend to surrender or even weaken its actual power of decision. Nevertheless, cooptation often leads in time to a sharing of power.

The English kings at first tried to use the Parliament as an instrument of cooptation. In American universities faculty power, and later, student power, often began in the same way. Thus cooptation should not be lightly dismissed by those who seek an avenue to power.

Adaptation 18 Michels: The iron law of oligarchy

"Who says organization says oligarchy." With these words the German political sociologist Robert Michels (1876–1936) summed up his famous "iron law of oligarchy." Although his "law" is stated in unqualified form, the argument of Michels's book supports more limited generalizations. His analysis shows that organization as such does not necessarily lead to oligarchy, or self-perpetuating leadership. Rather, certain kinds of organization have that tendency, and then only when certain additional processes are at work. Michels's study was based mainly on the history of socialist and trade-union organizations in Europe before World War I.

His influential book attempts to trace a connection between the basic necessities of organization and the evolution of self-perpetuating oligarchies. Following his argument we shall consider first the general need for organization and then the special circumstances that make for the drift to oligarchy.

THE NEED FOR LEADERSHIP

The importance of leadership depends on the size and complexity of the organization. In a small group, leadership may be but weakly developed; leaders arise spontaneously and serve temporarily, unofficially, and without many rewards. The leaders remain members of the group, sharing its interests and influenced by the same social conditions as the other members. Since the group is small, all or most members may participate in decisions and actions.

On the other hand, no organization of any size

or duration can exist without leaders. Someone has to organize meetings or determine the consensus, represent the group and its decisions to other organizations or the public, and make the countless small and large decisions that are necessary to carry out its aims. Therefore:
• Democratic action, like any action that strives for definite ends, requires organization.
• Organized, concerted action requires the delegation of special tasks, responsibilities, and powers to a few leaders.

Wilma Soss, President of the Federation of Women Shareholders in American Business, has been a perennial gadfly at annual meetings of large corporations. Her activities have dramatized the powerlessness of the small shareholder; yet they may also lead to new forms of public criticism and new restraints on the powers of management.

Source: A summary and interpretation of *Political Parties: A Sociological Study of the Oligarchical Tendencies of Modern Democracy* by Robert Michels (New York: Free Press, 1949). First published in German in 1911 and in English in 1915. Quoted material used by permission of Free Press.

These facts are not enough to justify the view that organization leads to oligarchy. The mere fact of organization, that is, the division of labor and delegation of tasks and powers to leaders, is not in itself undemocratic, so long as the leadership cannot perpetuate itself. Something more is needed to give rise to oligarchy.

CONDITIONS MAKING FOR OLIGARCHY

• The delegation of tasks and powers to leaders results in a concentration of skills and informal prerogatives in their hands. Not all members can perform the tasks of leadership in complex organizations. The jobs become specialized and require experience, knowledge, and individual aptitude.

Administrative skills are required to keep the organization functioning and to get things done. Relations with the outside world, such as diplomacy, collective bargaining, or public relations, require technical skills that the leaders alone possess. Their skills set them apart from the rank and file, and social differentiation begins. This specialization makes the members dependent on the leaders in office, because they are the ones who can keep things going and get things done that further the aims of the group. The dependency of the rank and file—a central theme in Michels's work—makes the leaders indispensable and hence gives them increased power.

Leadership carries prerogatives. In choosing the organization's staff, the leader can select people whose first loyalty is to him, thus personal machines are built. Leaders also control the channels of information within an organization, and their control gives them special access to and influence over the opinions of the members. These prerogatives and similar opportunities that characterize the social position of leadership tend to make leaders independent of the rank and file, and the power inherent in the concentration of skills is consolidated.

• The position of leaders is strengthened by the members' political indifference and by their sense of obligation to those who guide them and do the main work. Ordinary members do not have the inclination or time to participate in the demanding, complex tasks of an organization, and they are glad to have the work done by someone else. Moreover, they recognize their own incompetence compared with the skills of their leaders. The rank and file then submit willingly rather than reluctantly to the widening power of the officials.

• The concentration of skills and prerogatives in the leaders' hands and the willing submission of the rank and file create opportunities for the self-perpetuation of the leaders. It is not surprising that they take advantage of the situation and try to stay in office. Michels held that leaders try to keep their power because it is inherent in human nature to seek power and retain it. "The desire to dominate, for good or evil, is universal" (1911/1949: 206). This is a dubious and unnecessary assumption, and perhaps Michels's weakest point.

He gave other more defensible reasons for the self-perpetuation of leaders. Certainly leaders have a desire for personal security, and the prerogatives of leadership give them social status distinct from the ordinary members. They wish to retain their status and prerogatives, including their accustomed way of living and type of employment. The union official resists returning to the shop. Leaders may also believe sincerely that they are serving the best interests of the organization and that a threat to them is a threat to the group as a whole.

CONSEQUENCES OF OLIGARCHY

• Self-perpetuation of leaders tends toward subversion of the aims of the organization. If leaders are independent of rank-and-file control, there is a temptation to use the organizational machinery and power to further personal aims. There is a divergence of interest between the leaders and the led, and in the absence of effective democratic control, leaders follow policies that may not serve the aims for which the group was organized.

Because he studied social reform movements, Michels was especially interested in the subversion that comes from the conservatism of an oligarchic leadership that places stability and security for the organization (and for the leaders) above all other action aims. Action is slow and cautious, risks are minimized, powerful enemies are placated, and aims are modified to assure stability. There was a strong tendency among the trade unions of Europe to move from revolutionary to more conservative aims once they had achieved extensive membership, financial security, and discipline. Organization was necessary for the achievement of the original goals, and it introduced new interests that modified group aims.

• Oligarchy is inherent in democracy and cannot be eliminated. Michels held that the social differentiation between leaders and led is universal. This does not mean that tyranny abounds everywhere but that there is a predisposition to oligarchy which requires definite social checks. "Nothing but a serene and frank examination of the oligarchical dangers of democracy will enable us to minimize these dangers, even though they can never be entirely avoided" (1911/1949:408).

COUNTERVAILING FORCES

To minimize the dangers, it is necessary to capitalize on a countertendency of democracy to stimulate and strengthen the individual's aptitude for criticism and control.

This predisposition towards free inquiry, in which we cannot fail to recognize one of the most precious factors of civilization, will gradually increase in proportion as the economic status of the masses undergoes improvement and becomes more stable, and in proportion as they are admitted more effectively to the advantages of civilization. A wider education involves an increasing capacity for exercising control. Can we not observe every day that among the well-to-do the authority of the leaders over the led, extensive though it be, is never so unrestricted as in the case of the leaders of the poor? . . . It is, consequently, the great task of social education to raise the intellectual level of the masses, so that they may be enabled, within the limits of what is possible, to counteract the oligarchical tendencies of the working-class movement (1911/1949:406f.).

COMMENTARY

An argument similar to Michels's thesis was put forward by Berle and Means in their study of the modern corporation (1933). In the very large company, there is wide dispersion of stock ownership: No individual or group owns more than a small fraction of the total shares. Even as early as 1929, no one owned more than 1 percent of the stock of the Pennsylvania Railroad, American Telephone and Telegraph, or United States Steel. Spreading ownership and risk among many shareholders permits the massing of large quantities of capital for industrial development, but the individual stockholder has only a small voice in the company's affairs, and ownership is separated from control.

Power is concentrated in the hands of management, which often becomes self-perpetuating.

Thus, self-perpetuating leadership is a general phenomenon, by no means restricted to the political organizations studied by Michels. The following points should be considered.

1. The members of many organizations abdicate their formal right to make decisions, even important ones. They are willing that someone else take over the task so long as their own special interests (for example, the continued flow of reasonable dividends) are not seriously affected. When members abdicate their powers in normal periods, the incumbent leaders are able to consolidate their positions, and the members find it hard to assert themselves in times of crises.

2. The weakness of members can be ameliorated if they band together in organized factions. If alternative centers of power are created in the organization, the leaders may be called to account for their actions. This is what happens in the organization of pressure groups and parties in a political democracy. In special-purpose organizations, however, the narrowness of member interests less readily sustains permanent opposition groups that can mobilize opinion and supply alternative leadership.

For a study of a deviant case—a trade union within which an institutionalized opposition developed—see Lipset, Trow, and Coleman, 1956.

3. The analyses of Michels and of Berle and Means indicate a basic trend toward self-perpetuating leadership in large-scale organizations. However, leaders of corporations and labor organizations are occasionally challenged or ousted, and the business pages of newspapers report contests for internal control of large corporations and unions.

Discussions of shareholder expectations have been largely colored by the model of American Telephone and Telegraph, with over 3 million shareholders, and General Motors, with over 1.4 million. Only a few of the giants are so large and so fragmented. A recent study has pointed out that "corporations whose stock is so distributed that shareholders would not expect to participate in structural decisions are atypical" (Eisenberg, 1969:34).

Section five organizations and institutions

In the language of sociology, an institution may be a group or a social practice, the Republican party or the secret ballot. This is not as confusing and ambiguous as it may seem at first glance. Whether it is a group or a practice, a social form becomes an institution when it takes on a fixed and distinctive character, when it is charged with meaning as a vehicle of group identity, or when it serves as a receptacle of vested interests. The Republican party qualifies as an institution on all of these counts. It is more than a technical instrument for mobilizing votes and contesting elections. It has a distinctive character, conservative in orientation and related to the business community and upper-income groups. Many people have a stake in its continuity. For those who believe in its principles or whose families are traditionally Republican, the party is a vehicle of group identity. Similarly, the secret ballot is an institution, valued as a part of constitutional democracy.

Thus institutions serve broad rather than narrow interests and do so in accepted and enduring ways. That is why, in common speech, the word *institution* is reserved for public or quasi-public groups or practices. A list of American institutions would include constitutional democracy, Harvard University, private enterprise, and Thanksgiving dinner. But the formation of institutions is a pervasive process, and the results are not necessarily so highly visible; therefore the sociological concept of institutions must be more general and inclusive.

Institutionalization may be defined as the development of orderly, stable, socially integrating forms and structures out of unstable, loosely patterned, or merely technical types of action. The key phrase is "socially integrating." As a group or practice is institutionalized, two outcomes are observed: (1) loosely patterned activities become stabilized, as when a coffee break becomes both a right and a ritual, and (2) action that is merely instrumental becomes valued for its own sake or otherwise contributes to group solidarity. Technical procedures in science and industry, such as those governing the shipment of freight or the assembly of a complicated machine, do not necessarily contribute to the formation or maintenance of a social group and are, therefore, not institutional. On the other hand, some technical procedures, such as piloting a ship, may symbolize an occupation or profession for its members and take on an institutional meaning.

Organizations and institutions may be usefully distinguished:

The term "organization" suggests a certain bareness, a lean no-nonsense system of consciously coordinated activities. It refers to an *expendable tool*, a rational instrument engineered to do a job. An "institution," on the other hand, is more nearly a natural product of social needs and pressures—a responsive, adaptive organism. This distinction . . . does not mean that any given enterprise must be either one or the other. While an extreme case may closely approach either an "ideal" organization or an "ideal" institution, most living associations . . . are complex mixtures of both designed and responsive behavior (Selznick, 1957:5–6).

The existence of an institution is inescapably a matter of degree. Groups and practices are more or less institutionalized, that is, more or less transformed from expendable tools into more textured social realities.

The social processes discussed in this chapter—the development of informal structure, bureaucratization, cooptation—have an institutionalizing effect. They build into the organization habits, values, vested interests. Each organization is a creature of its own history, the kind of people who have made up its membership, the groups they formed, and the way the organization adapted to its environment. The outcome may be beneficial if the organization has a stable and distinctive competence, an established reputation, and a network of long-nurtured alliances. Well-established organizations have a head start over later rivals.

On the other hand, the process of settling down, of becoming established and stabilized, can be costly. What began as a vigorous, purposeful group may end up institutionalized, fat, secure, and useful, but without its former energy or idealism.

Four institutionalizing processes, important in the life history of associations, are: (1) formalization, (2) self-maintenance and conservatism, (3) infusion with value, and (4) development of a distinctive social composition and social base.

Formalization The most obvious type of institutionalization in associations is the development of formal systems, which often emerge out of trial-and-error informal practices, as discussed in Section Two. Social integration is directly and explicitly promoted by formal devices of coordination and communication. The transformation of informal groups and practices into legally recognized and formally established institutions occurs continuously, not only within associations but in the larger society as well. For example, many preexisting practices and duties regarding marriage and family life are formalized in the law of domestic relations. Similarly, zoning ordinances in a city often give formal approval to patterns of land use that have already developed in an unplanned way.

Formalization is a way of increasing control. Practices hitherto spontaneous, governed only by tradition or the give-and-take of personal and group interaction, become subject to explicit rules and limitations. For example, labor-management legislation formalized some practices that were already worked out, but at the same time it made collective bargaining subject to greater public scrutiny and control. To take a simpler case, when the informal coffee break in an office is formalized, the practice is made legal, but it is also more readily controlled.

Self-maintenance and conservatism The quest for permanence and stability also makes for institutionalization. The demand for security usually occurs rather early in the life history of an organization because many people, and especially the leaders, have a stake in its continued existence. Therefore, priority is given to (1) maintaining the organization as a going concern, (2) avoiding risks, and (3) achieving long-run rather than short-run objectives. The leaders become willing to sacrifice quick returns for organizational security.

Adaptation 18 summarizes Michels's study of the conservative tendencies in certain types of political organization. The conservative influence is traced to the emergence of self-perpetuating leadership, an oligarchy whose main concern is to protect its vested interests.

The history of labor is largely dominated by efforts to win union security through provisions for compulsory membership (the closed shop and its variants), for automatic deduction of dues payments from wages (the checkoff), and for joint consultation with management. These objectives may bring immediate gains for the members, but they also serve the long-run interests of the union as an institution. They have a strong stabilizing effect.

Large corporations are also concerned with institutional security and in recent years have been particularly sensitive to the need for a favorable climate of public opinion. Institutional advertising reflects this trend. Expensive newspaper and magazine space is bought not to promote sales, at least in the short run, but to build a favorable image of the corporation and of business in general.

Infusion with value When an individual identifies with an organization, becomes habituated to its methods, or otherwise mixes his personality with it, the organization becomes for him a valued source of personal satisfaction. Administrative changes are difficult when individuals are habituated to and identified with long-established procedures. For example, the shifting of personnel is inhibited when individuals resist changes that threaten personalities. Infusion with value helps to institutionalize the organization, giving it a greater stability and social integration, transforming it from a mere tool into something that is valued for itself.

From the standpoint of the national community, most of the many thousands of organizations are not highly valued for themselves, although certain principles on which they are based, such as free speech or competition, may have deep cultural roots. With some very important exceptions, such as the Supreme Court, when any particular organization is threatened, there is no national outcry. On the other hand, special groups or localities are often urged to help keep an organization from dying for lack of support. For example, public appeals are often made to keep major league teams in their "home" cities, but commerce rather than local pride usually determines what happens.

Development of a distinctive social composition and social base In its day-to-day activities, an organization makes many kinds of decisions. Most are easily revised and have no permanent effect. Other decisions, however, are more binding and impart to the organization a particular character, especially when the social composition of the organization is affected. For example, private schools or colleges may attempt to preserve tradition by giving preference for admission to students with "appropriate" family backgrounds. More often the development of a distinctive social composition is gradual and accidental, resulting from the unplanned selectivity that takes place because of the tendency to bring in people who share the backgrounds and perspectives of existing members or leaders. Deliberate or not, the result is a membership or personnel characterized by similar attitudes and habits of work.

The social base of an organization is closely related to its social composition. Many organizations, such as political pressure groups, are connected to a particular clientele or constituency upon whose support they are dependent. Because of this dependency the personnel and methods of the organization tend to reflect the social characteristics of the constituency. Even in business, adaptation to a particular market (by locality or quality of goods) may affect the habits and outlook of the sales and production departments.

Analysis of an organization's social base can reveal the pressures that play upon it and can help one understand its historical evolution and the role it plays in the community. The social base of the American Federation of Labor lay in the craft-organized skilled workers, and the split that led to the formation of the Committee for Industrial Organization (later the Congress of Industrial Organizations) in 1935 reflected the effort to shift the base so as to include semi-skilled workers in mass-production industries. New social forces in the American electorate, particularly the labor and minority vote, have changed the social base of the Democratic party with significant consequences for its program and its chances of victory. The Anti-Saloon League was based on rural Protestant churches, from which it drew heavy support, but whose influence in American life was waning. The structure and policies of the National Association for the Advancement of Colored People, especially at the outset, were affected by the paucity of leadership in the black population and an orientation toward the black middle class. Similarly, Adaptation 31 discusses the social base of Canadian Methodism and the consequent limitation of the church's appeal to the urban working class.

References

Bennis, Warren G.
1968 "Beyond bureaucracy." Pp. 53–76 in Warren G. Bennis and Philip E. Slater, The Temporary Society. New York: Harper & Row.

Berle, A. A. and G. C. Means
1933 The Modern Corporation and Private Property. New York: Macmillan.

Dale, Ernest
1952 Planning and Developing the Company Organization. New York: American Management Association.

Dill, William R.
1965 "Business organizations." Pp. 1071–1114 in James G. March (ed.), Handbook of Organizations. Chicago: Rand McNally.

Eisenberg, Melvin A.
1969 "The legal roles of shareholders and management in corporate decision-making." California Law Review 57 (January): 1–181.

Gerth, H. H. and C. Wright Mills (eds.)
1946 From Max Weber: Essays in Sociology. New York: Oxford University Press.

Gouldner, Alvin W.
1954 Patterns of Industrial Bureaucracy. New York: Free Press.

Harbison, Frederick and C. A. Myers
1959 Management in the Industrial World. New York: McGraw-Hill.

Hyman, Herbert and Charles R. Wright
1971 "Trends in voluntary association memberships of American adults: replication based on secondary analysis of national sample surveys." American Sociological Review 36 (April):191–206.

Likert, Rensis
1961 New Patterns of Management. New York: McGraw-Hill.

Lipset, S. M., M. A. Trow, and J. S. Coleman
1956 Union Democracy: The Internal Politics of the International Typographical Union. New York: Free Press.

Mayer, J. P.
1943 Max Weber and German Politics. London: Faber.

McGregor, Douglas M.
1960 The Human Side of Enterprise. New York: McGraw-Hill.

Michels, Robert
1911/1949 Political Parties: A Sociological Study of the Oligarchical Tendencies of Modern Democracy. New York: Free Press.

Olson, Mancur, Jr.
1971 The Logic of Collective Action: Public Goods and the Theory of Groups. Cambridge: Harvard University Press.

Potter, Stephen
1952 One-upmanship. New York: Holt, Rinehart and Winston.

Presthus, Robert
1962 The Organizational Society. New York: Knopf.

Selznick, Philip
1949 TVA and the Grass Roots. Berkeley: University of California Press. Harper Torchbook Edition, 1966.
1957 Leadership in Administration. New York: Harper & Row.
1969 Law, Society and Industrial Justice. New York: Russell Sage.

Sills, David L.
1968 "Voluntary associations: sociological aspects." Pp. 362–376 in International Encyclopedia of the Social Sciences. Vol. 16.

Weber, Max
1922/1947 The Theory of Social and Economic Organization. New York: Oxford University Press.

Whyte, W. H.
1951 "Status in the American office." Fortune (May).

Wolff, Robert Paul
1970 The Ideal of the University. Boston: Beacon Press.

Sources and readings

Blau, Peter M. and W. Richard Scott
1962 Formal Organizations: A Comparative Approach. San Francisco: Chandler.

Blau, Peter M. and Richard A. Schoenherr
1971 The Structure of Organizations. New York: Basic Books.

Brinkerhoff, Merlin B. and Phillip R. Kunz (eds.)
1972 Complex Organizations and their Environments. Dubuque, Iowa: Brown.

Caplow, Theodore
1964 Principles of Organization. New York: Harcourt Brace Jovanovich.

Downs, Anthony
1967 Inside Bureaucracy. Boston: Little, Brown.

Emery, F. E. (ed.)
1969 Systems Thinking. Baltimore, Md.: Penguin.

Etzioni, Amitai
1961 A Comparative Analysis of Complex Organizations. New York: Free Press.
1969 A Sociological Reader in Complex Organizations. New York: Holt, Rinehart and Winston.

Galbraith, J.
1973 Designing Complex Organizations. Reading, Mass.: Addison-Wesley.

Hydebrand, W. V. (ed.)
1973 Comparative Organizations. Englewood Cliffs, N.J.: Prentice-Hall.

Katz, Daniel and Robert L. Kahn (eds.)
1966 The Social Psychology of Organizations. New York: Wiley.

Likert, Rensis
1961 New Patterns of Management. New York: McGraw-Hill.

March, James G. and Herbert A. Simon
1958 Organizations. New York: Wiley.

March, James G. (ed.)
1965 Handbook of Organizations. Chicago: Rand McNally.

Perrow, Charles
1970 Organizational Analysis: A Sociological View. Belmont, Calif.: Wadsworth.
1972 Complex Organizations: A Critical Essay. Glenview, Ill.: Scott, Foresman.

Presthus, Robert
1962 The Organizational Society. New York: Knopf.

Thompson, James D.
1967 Organizations in Action. New York: McGraw-Hill.

Wilensky, Harold L.
1967 Organizational Intelligence: Knowledge and Policy in Government and Industry. New York: Basic Books.

Periodicals

Administrative Science Quarterly

Fortune

Harvard Business Review

Public Administration Review

8 | Collective Behavior

Section one introduction

Much of sociology deals with the structured aspects of social life. The term *collective behavior*, on the other hand, designates the study of relatively unstructured social situations and their products, such as crowds, riots, revivals, rumor, public opinion, fads, and social movements. These phenomena are not fully controlled by cultural norms and ordered social relations. They are characteristically open to the free play of emotions, a high degree of personal interaction and influence, the give-and-take of political competition, and the emergence of transitory opinions and allegiances.

Collective behavior includes not only events that make headlines and sometimes change history, but also spontaneous activities that may be little noticed yet give rise to new norms and values. The early phases of social change are usually marked by unstructured forms of action. The organization of workers often begins in spontaneous protests against some immediate threat to jobs or wages. Many of the respectable religious denominations of today originated in movements that excited crowd behavior. (See Adaptation 31.)

Through collective behavior, new ways of acting and new groups are created in response to felt needs, pressures, and excitements, rather than as a result of consciously coordinated activity. The development of informal structure in associations is a product of collective behavior. (See ASSOCIATIONS, p. 198.) Spontaneous actions also occur in conjunction with concerted and organized behavior, in such dramatic episodes as mass protests and insurrections.

Collective behavior is a part of everyday life and does not always take dramatic form. The study of collective behavior views the social world from the standpoint of action, of constant regrouping and continuously changing perspectives. There is always some degree of unstructuredness in human situations if only because no two events are exactly alike, and established structures cannot make allowances for all possible variations in situations or the diversity of human response.

Symbolism and action for political solidarity: An I.R.A. parade through a Belfast cemetery on Easter Sunday.

Collective behavior is one of the fields of sociology most closely related to social psychology. A complete grasp of some collective behavior topics depends in part on knowledge about human motivation, emotion, perception, and communication. The sociological contribution specifies the social conditions that produce collective behavior and the effect it has on group conflict, morale, consensus, and changing patterns of social organization.

CONDITIONS OF COLLECTIVE BEHAVIOR

Three conditions characterize relatively unstructured and unstable situations:

1. Absence or weakness of social forms Where existing social arrangements do not prescribe what is proper and acceptable behavior, people improvise. A crisis or disaster, such as a flood or famine, a revolution or an invasion, is something for which people are usually unprepared. Action is called for, yet routines to cope with the emergency are lacking or inadequate. The ordinary processes of orderly communication break down, and rumors, perhaps exaggerated and fear-provoking, take their place.

2. Ambiguous and open decisions Especially in a democratic society, much government policy is deliberately left open, to be determined by expressions of public opinion. While a broad framework of orderly rules is maintained, decisions are not reached by accepting the pronouncements of a traditional authority but are worked out in the interplay of competing interest groups. Public opinion is not predetermined but subject to the pressures of competing interests.

3. Changed perspectives and values Innovations, such as the growth of factory technology, bring about changes in goals and outlooks. Old practices are questioned, and pressure is exerted on custom and tradition. A period of fluidity ensues. When the prevailing patterns cannot be readily changed in prescribed ways, individuals often band together outside the official framework. Such conditions make for social movements, often with radical ideologies and a high degree of emotional involvement. If the movement is successful, its new perspectives become accepted and institutionalized. Then collective behavior aspects diminish in importance.

These conditions, widespread in modern society, lend importance to the study of spontaneous and temporary social relations and groups. Section Two discusses crowds and collective excitement. Section Three deals with publics, public opinion, and propaganda. Section Four reviews social movements and social change.

Section two crowds and collective excitement

The fragility of authority and of social routines is often dramatically revealed under conditions of collective excitement. "There is nothing more surprising to the holders of power, or perhaps to its subjects, than the frailty of their commands in certain types of crises" (Merriam, 1934:156). Collective excitement is sustained by emotional contagion, which occurs in a wide range of phenomena, including panics, political demonstrations, riots, cheering sections, and *esprit de corps*. These phenomena show a common mood, a shared state of mind affected by emotion. A mood influences the thought and action of the participants by facilitating some acts and inhibiting others. This is most apparent in the protest of an angry mob, but it is also true of more conventional situations. In a solemn religious ceremony, for example, there is no place for levity, and even unbelievers share the common mood.

ELEMENTS OF EMOTIONAL CONTAGION

The processes that induce or sustain emotional contagion are not fully understood, but they include suggestibility and stimulation.

Heightened suggestibility In unstructured situations people tend to look to others for cues on how they should behave. The readiness to take cues can be heightened by emotional tension, which narrows the field of awareness and attention. A fearful person, alert to signs of danger, responds to cues that promise relief from anxiety. At the same time, he or she is apt to ignore other stimuli in the environment. An important consequence of heightened suggestibility is the loss of critical ability. When tension dominates consciousness, the weighing of alternative courses of action and the costs of action recede into the background.

It is heightened suggestibility that makes rumor so important in situations of collective excitement. A rumor is an unconfirmed, but not necessarily false, communication, usually transmitted by word of mouth in a situation of anxiety or stress. Rumors spring up in unstructured situations when information is needed but reliable channels do not exist (Shibutani, 1966:17).

Because they are so often colored by emotions, rumors tend to be rapidly disseminated and to distort or falsify the facts. A rumor may begin as an inaccurate report because of the narrowing of perception in an emotionally charged situation. It may become progressively more distorted, because all oral communication is subject to distortion. Even when emotional elements are lacking, factual reports tend to become shorter and simpler as they are passed on, with distortion of details in accordance with personal and cultural predispositions or "sets" (Allport, 1947).

Heightened stimulation Different personalities show different degrees of suggestibility. However, suggestibility can be induced and the range of awareness narrowed when there is an increase in the volume and intensity of stimuli from other persons who are excited. In large crowds where there is close physical proximity, stimulation takes the form of *circular response*. A stimulates B to fear. B's fear not only stimulates C in turn but is reflected back to A and reinforces his fear. Being close to others also calls attention to such physical manifestations of emotion as heavy breathing, perspiration, and muscular tension. If emotion is present in one participant, others are likely to be aware of it and to react to it.

Caution To sustain emotional contagion, there must be shared dispositions and background. Crowd stimuli are not strong enough to make a guard join a prison riot, but may cause him to lose self-control and behave in an undisciplined way. Fads and crazes are often limited to a particular age, class, or ethnic group whose members share emotional needs and attitudes. A crowd composed of people from different ethnic, age, and educational backgrounds is less likely to develop emotional contagion than a more homogeneous crowd.

CROWDS

In common usage any large number of people gathered in one place is called a crowd, but crowds differ in the extent to which interaction occurs or leads to unity of feeling and behavior. The "sidewalk superintendents" around a building under construction form a *casual* crowd in which interpersonal relations are at a minimum. What captures attention is of no great emotional import. Nevertheless, a crowd is a potential medium for arousing and expressing emotion. Large gatherings provide congenial conditions for emotional contagion. Stimulation and suggestibility are heightened; the presence of others gives the indi-

vidual a sense of security and approval; and crowds convey a feeling of anonymity.

In times of social unrest or tension, street crowds may be transformed into *acting crowds* or *mobs* when the event that attracts attention stimulates underlying hostilities. A mob is a crowd bent upon an aggressive act such as lynching, looting, or the destruction of property. The term refers to a crowd that is fairly unified and single-minded in its aggressive intent. Mob action is not usually randomly destructive but tends to be focused on a single target.

By their very nature casual crowds and mobs are not part of an organized and controlled system of social relations. They arise spontaneously without orderly preparation. There is no etiquette of crowd behavior. If feelings of hostility, anger, or resentment are aroused, the socially uncontrolled interaction of the crowd may have serious consequences. (See Adaptation 19.)

In recent history, especially in Europe, the calling of general strikes has often been a prelude to revolutionary attacks upon governments. The effect of a general strike, in addition to raising the level of tension and excitement, is to draw people away from stable institutionalized activities at work and home, conditions that may lead to the formation of street crowds. One of the first moves of an insecure government is to break up gatherings of more than a few people, because even small knots of excited people might expand into uncontrollable street crowds.

Integrative crowd behavior Not all crowd behavior is spontaneous and unguided, and controlled emotional contagion can serve a useful social function. It may allow release of emotions and tensions that ordinarily find no expression, and it may stimulate feelings that enhance group solidarity. Organized gatherings of many kinds provide settings that integrate crowd behavior into the social structure.

1. Expressive crowds Parties, dances, and some spectator sports are gatherings in which certain emotions and tensions can find a degree of orderly release. In parties and dances emotional contagion makes for freer interpersonal relations. Sports contests, especially contact sports, stimulate shouting, singing, and aggressiveness in the audience. Without the unity of the crowd, people would not feel so free to engage in emotional or boisterous behavior.

2. Audiences Many audiences are similar to casual crowds in their passivity and low degree of emotional unity. Nevertheless they may be susceptible to emotional contagion. In some audience situations, like lectures or concerts, the presence of others encourages expressions of enthusiasm. Performers or their agents who understand this fact have been known to occasionally employ claques, people hired to cheer and stimulate the spread of approval. Cued and prerecorded applause and laughter at TV shows operate from the same understanding of emotional contagion and with the same objective—to stimulate a desired response.

3. Religious services Services that arouse contagious emotions of humility and piety may support deep religious feelings. In some religious sects, emotional contagion results in relatively uncontrolled and predominantly expressive behavior. As institutionalization develops, more restrained services appear.

4. Mass meetings and deliberative assemblies Meetings of voluntary associations usually have two functions. As deliberating bodies they hear and pass upon reports from leaders and choose new leaders. They are also designed to stimulate feelings of solidarity. Meetings in a political campaign are largely of the latter kind, and people go as they do to a football game, expecting to cheer and otherwise express their feelings. When large numbers are involved, it is common for deliberative meetings to become subject to emotional contagion. Although conventions of unions, veterans, and political parties are usually highly organized, the leaders are aware of the danger that the meeting may get out of hand. An unimpor-

tant individual may gain the attention of the meeting and develop influence he might not otherwise have.

Assemblies become mass meetings when the solidarity aspect is predominant, and emotional demonstrations are expected and encouraged. The emotions displayed are often stereotyped, however, and need not reflect real feelings. The "demonstrations" at national political conventions are often calculated efforts to put on a show of enthusiasm for a candidate and the television audience.

In "The House of Commons and Parliamentary Psychology," p. 232, Churchill takes account of the crowd potential even in the highly institutionalized British Parliament. The small rectangular chamber has two effects. At ordinary meetings, it encourages a conversational style. At historically significant sessions when all members are present and the chamber is packed, there is "a sense of crowd and urgency." However, the semicircular seating arrangement, which Churchill objected to, is the form adopted in many countries where party systems prevail. Whether they would work better in the setting of the rectangular chamber is open to argument.

COLLECTIVE VIOLENCE

Crowd behavior is most significant when it involves danger and violence. Panic, for example, is a form of action in which a crowd, excited by a belief in some imminent threat, may engage in uncontrolled and therefore dangerous collective flight. This does not mean that the action of the panicky crowd is wholly irrational. As individuals, participants may act to escape a genuine threat. But uncoordinated and uncontrolled action and the response based on emotional contagion give panic an irrational character.

A riot is a form of civil disorder marked by violent mob action. It is a "hostile outburst" (Smelser, 1963) of resentment or rebelliousness. Although a riot may have an objective and may be selective in its targets, it characteristically involves turbulent and undisciplined conduct. An organized insurrection or guerrilla action is distinguished from a riot by internal discipline and clarity of objective.

Race riots: a changing pattern Until the recent past most American race riots were initiated by whites, although during the course of a riot blacks sometimes attacked whites. In some cases, neither whites nor blacks were clearly the initiators. The scenes of violence were usually black ghettos, the downtown business districts, or white neighborhoods where white mobs attacked individual blacks. White marauders frequently invaded black ghettos, and black mobs attacked individual whites in black neighborhoods (Grimshaw, 1959; 1960; Rudwick, 1966; Lee and Humphrey, 1943).

The Civil War draft riots have been called "the archetype of most of the racial clashes that took place before the summer of 1964" (President's Commission, 1967:117). For four days in 1863, white mobs controlled much of New York City, looted stores, burned Negro[1] dwellings, and beat or lynched Negroes. Occurring during a time of national tension and anxiety, the draft riots were a reaction by predominantly working-class whites to a requirement that they assist Negro emancipation by military service. The rioting went on throughout the city with attacks and counterattacks between whites and Negroes. In one incident, a white mob attacked, looted, and burned a Negro orphan asylum. The violence was prolonged because officials were reluctant to invoke military measures and because the troops and police sympathized with the rioters (Lader, 1959).

Several patterns of race riots are identifiable (Grimshaw, 1969). During the first

[1] Although this text adheres to the preferred usage of *black* in discussing the contemporary scene, in certain historical contexts the then current word *Negro* is sometimes employed. Quoted matter follows the original source. For a discussion of the vocabulary of race, see RACE AND ETHNICITY, pp. 443–446.

third of the twentieth century, race riots took the form of punitive white action against blacks. In "Southern-style" riots, whites charged blacks with threatening white supremacy, and allegations of assaults by black men on white women were usually involved. The Southern pattern was one of overwhelming repression, the blacks offering little resistance, receiving little or no protection from the police, and fleeing from white attacks. "Northern-style" race riots, such as the Chicago riot of 1919 (Chicago Commission, 1922; Broom and Selznick, 1963:267–274), were also triggered by alleged black threats to white superiority, but they were more closely connected to practical issues, such as competition over jobs and the use of public facilities. The Chicago riot was precipitated when a young black drowned after being stoned by whites who saw him enter "their" side of the water at a segregated beach. In the Northern-style riots, blacks fought back, and both sides engaged in violent mob action.

An important feature of race riots in the early twentieth century was attack upon persons. The conflicts centered on the relations between blacks and whites, with whites insisting that blacks show deference and maintain distance. The violence took the form of beatings and killings.

The race riots of the 1960s had a different pattern: (1) They tended to be initiated by blacks, often in response to what were perceived as provocations by white police; (2) the new riots were directed mainly against property rather than against persons; and (3) grievances centered on poverty, discrimination, and repressive police action. "While the civil disorders of 1967 were racial in character, they were not *inter-racial*" (Kerner Report, 1968:110). Insofar as there was group conflict, it involved clashes between black citizens and white police. Adaptation 19 is a case study of a riot of the 1960s.

The riot as protest Upheavals in black ghettos during 1964–1968 brought a searching

The House of Commons and parliamentary psychology

On October 28 [1943], there was the rebuilding of the House of Commons to consider. One unlucky bomb had blown to fragments the Chamber in which I had passed so much of my life. I was determined to have it rebuilt at the earliest moment that our struggle would allow. I had the power at this moment to shape things in a way that would last. Supported by my colleagues, mostly old Parliamentarians, and with Mr. Attlee's cordial aid, I sought to re-establish for what may well be a long period the two great principles on which the British House of Commons stands in its physical aspect. . . . The first is that its shape should be oblong and not semicircular. Here is a very potent factor in our political life. The semicircular assembly, which appeals to political theorists, enables every individual or every group to move round the centre, adopting various shades of pink according as the weather changes. I am a convinced supporter of the party system in preference to the group system. The party system is much favoured by the oblong form of chamber. It is easy for an individual to move through these insensible gradations from Left to Right, but the act of crossing the Floor is one which requires serious consideration. I am well informed on this matter, for I have accomplished that difficult process, not only once, but twice. Logic is a poor guide compared with custom. Logic, which has created in so many countries semicircular assemblies with buildings that give to every member not only a seat to sit in, but often a desk to write at, with a lid to bang, has proved fatal to Parliamentary government as we know it here in its home and in the land of its birth.

The second characteristic of a chamber formed on the lines of the House of Commons is that it should not be big enough to contain all its Members at once without overcrowding, and there should be no question of every Member having a separate seat reserved for him. The reason for this has long been a puzzle to uninstructed outsiders, and has frequently excited the curiosity and even the criticism of new Members. Yet it is not so difficult to understand if you look at it from a practical point of view. If the House is big enough to contain all its Members, nine-tenths of its debates will be conducted in the depressing atmosphere of an almost empty or half-empty chamber. The essence of good House of Commons speaking is the conversational style, the facility for quick, informal interruptions and interchanges. Harangues from a rostrum would be a bad substitute for the conversational style in which so much of our business is done. But the conversational style requires a fairly small space, and there should be on great occasions a sense of crowd and urgency. There should be a sense of the importance of much that is said, and a sense that great matters are being decided, there and then, by the House.

Source: Abridged from *Closing the Ring* by Winston S. Churchill (Boston: Houghton Mifflin, 1951), pp. 168–169. Reprinted by permission of Houghton Mifflin Company.

reexamination of the nature of race riots. It became evident that the Watts type of riot could not be dismissed as an eruption of "senseless" or merely destructive mob action. The riots were a kind of social protest, a way of expressing urgent demands for social change.

Research on recent riots has tended to undermine official claims that riots were sparked by outside agitators or were carried out by "riffraff." The riffraff theory holds that (1) only a small percentage of ghetto residents take part in riots; (2) the participants are criminals, drug addicts, drifters, leaders of youth gangs, and welfare cheaters and are therefore not representative of the community; and (3) the riot is an isolated event and receives little or no support from the community. In fact, none of these propositions is supported by the evidence on Watts (Sears and McConahay, 1969). Research on other riots of the 1960s has led to similar conclusions. For example, surveys conducted for the Kerner Commission covering the riots of 1967 showed that participation in the riots involved a substantial minority of ghetto residents, ranging from 10 to 20 percent of randomly selected respondents; many more were sympathetic bystanders; and still larger percentages believed that the riots were helpful to the black struggle (Fogelson and Hill, 1968).

The riot as a form of social protest is not new to history. Outbursts against oppressive taxation, rising food prices, threats to jobs, and similar issues have occurred over many centuries. The grievances themselves do not necessarily produce riots, for much is borne in silence, especially under repressive conditions. But when other avenues of public participation are blocked, the riot is a characteristic form of public protest. A study of European riots during the period 1732–1848 showed that many riots had limited objectives and very often displayed a "remarkable single-mindedness":

The study of the pre-industrial crowd suggests that it rioted for precise objects and rarely engaged in indiscriminate attacks on either properties or persons. Equally, though riots might spread by contagion or other means, beyond the rural or urban boundaries within which they started, they rarely spread to areas untouched by the grievances that gave them birth. . . . This merely shows, once more, the need to study the behavior of crowds, like the leaders and the crowds themselves, in its social and historical context. Such illustrations suggest, too, that the crowd was by no means "irrational" in the wider meaning of the term. It might be diverted or provoked by panic, as it might be stirred by Utopian pipe dreams or millenarial fantasies; but its purposes were generally rational enough and often led it, as we have seen, to choose not only the targets but the means most appropriate to the occasion (Rudé, 1964:254).

This analysis interprets a type of riot as a rational form of protest. If the interpretation is accepted, the actions of individual rioters cannot be dismissed as the product of mental disturbance or criminality but must be assessed for underlying grievances. On the other hand, as a form of purposeful activity, riots have serious limitations. Although riots may call attention to grievances, not all participants engage in rioting with such a clear purpose, and they may be distracted by fantasy, false rumors, or anger. Moreover, riots may be self-defeating if they provoke repression or result in destruction of resources the rioters themselves need. In other words, the riotous protest is a desperate form of action, and as such may exact heavy costs from the rioters as well as from their targets.

Adaptation 19 Riot in Watts: Los Angeles, 1965

The Watts riot in the late summer of 1965 lasted six days, from August 11 to 17. During the worst days, from Thursday through Saturday, thousands of blacks took to the streets. They beat up white passersby whom they pulled from their cars, overturned and burned cars, looted stores, set buildings afire, stoned and shot at firemen, and exchanged shots with law-enforcement officers. A total of 3,927 people were arrested. The disorder spread through an area of 46.5 square miles and was ultimately controlled only with the aid of military authority and a curfew.

Thirty blacks were killed and four whites, including a fireman and two law-enforcement officers. Of the 1,032 reported injured, there were 90 Los Angeles police officers, 136 firemen, 10 National Guardsmen, 23 persons from other governmental agencies—almost all whites; and 773 civilians—the great majority of whom were blacks.

Property loss was estimated at over $40 million. More than 700 buildings were damaged by burning and looting. Of this number, more than 200 were totally destroyed by fire. The rioters concentrated primarily on food markets, pawnshops, and liquor, furniture, clothing, and department stores. Service stations and automobile dealers were for the most part unharmed. No residences were deliberately burned, and damage to schools, libraries, churches, and public buildings was minimal.

THE SETTING

The South Los Angeles area, the scene of the 1965 riot, contains the largest concentration of blacks in the city. It includes Watts, for which the riot was named. In November 1965, three months after the riot, a special 10 percent sample census survey was conducted, and the report of the survey permits comparisons with the findings of the 1960 census (*Current Population Reports*, Series P-23,

Source: Based on "Violence in the City—An End or a Beginning?" (The McCone Report) by the Governor's Commission on the Los Angeles Riots, 1965; *Rivers of Blood, Years of Darkness* by Robert Conot (New York: Bantam, 1967); *Burn, Baby, Burn!* by Jerry Cohen and William S. Murphy (New York: Avon Books, 1966); *Task Force Report: Crime and Its Impact—An Assessment* by The President's Commission on Law Enforcement and Administration of Justice (Washington, D.C.: GPO, 1967), Chap. 9; and press and periodical reports.

No. 18, June 28, 1966). Interpretations should be made cautiously, because part of the observed changes between 1960 and 1965, but certainly not all, may be consequences of the riot.

The South Los Angeles area roughly corresponds with the curfew zone established during the riot. The total population of 321,000 in 1965 had declined from 355,000 enumerated in the 1960 census, but the number of blacks had increased from 248,000 to 260,000, or from 70 percent of the population to 81 percent. At the same time, whites with Spanish surnames (largely of Mexican ancestry) had declined from 43,000 to 32,000 and other whites from 56,000 to only 24,000.

In other words, South Los Angeles was a large, highly homogeneous segregated area—in current vocabulary, a ghetto. Its segregation was compounded by the lack of an efficient public transportation system so that residents who needed access to governmental offices or clinical facilities had to use slow and costly buses. The area was not a ghetto in the sense of being a slum made up of old tenements with a high density per acre and per room and with most dwelling units in dilapidated condition. However, about 5 percent of the dwelling units occupied by blacks were classified as dilapidated, not suitable for habitation, and 26 percent as deteriorating. The statistics show a decline in the quality of housing compared with 1960, but despite that fact property values had risen and median rentals had increased from $69 to $78 per month.

Of the 260,000 black residents, about 80,000, or 31 percent—the same percentage as in 1960—were living below the poverty line, which is defined as expenditure of a third or more of income on food. Approximately 24 percent of the total population received public assistance. The median annual income of families was $4,669, hardly changed from the 1959 figures. At the time of the riot the poverty level was $3,223 (*Current Population Reports*, Series P-60, No. 102, January 1976: 143).

Only 16 percent of male workers held white-collar jobs, and 11 percent of the male labor force was unemployed. In sum, the black population of South Los Angeles lived in a predominantly black environment under poor and sometimes severely

Police and firemen were helpless as stores burned in the riot area.

depressed conditions, highly isolated from the dominant population. Those with the means to move elsewhere found it difficult or impossible to do so.

Initial episode (Wednesday) The first incident was the arrest of a black youth for drunken driving on the complaint of another black. A white motorcycle officer made the arrest under rather ordinary circumstances in a predominantly black neighborhood near Watts on a hot evening, August 11. What had begun as a routine arrest, with 25 to 50 curious spectators, escalated as the youth's mother and brother became involved and the youth became physically resistant, eliciting forceful action by the several officers who were called for assistance. The hostility of the youth's family, the bystanders' belligerence, the resistance to arrest, and the use of force by the police drew a crowd of 1,000 per-

sons within half an hour. Before the officers withdrew, five arrests had been made: the driver, his brother, his mother, a young black woman for spitting on an officer, and a young black man for inciting the crowd to violence. As the last police car left, it was stoned by the now irate mob.

The crowd did not disperse but ranged in small groups within a few blocks of the arrest scene. Until midnight they stoned automobiles, pulled white motorists out of their cars and beat them, and menaced a police command post that had been set up in the area. Although the outbreak seemed to be under control by 1:00 A.M., there were sporadic reports of unruly mobs, vandalism, and rock throwing until nearly daylight.

Atmosphere of trouble (Thursday) The next morning there was an uneasy calm, and a strong expectancy of further trouble kept the atmosphere tense. A meeting called by the Los Angeles County Human Relations Commission at the request of county officials failed to lower the tension. The meeting was held in the early afternoon 12 blocks from the scene of the first arrests, with every available representative of neighborhood groups, black leaders, elected officials, and members of law-enforcement agencies present, as well as about 100 unexpected teen-agers, and representatives of press, radio, and television, with cameras focused on the microphone.

The meeting began with discussions of how to restore law and order. Even the mother arrested the night before asked the crowd to "help me and others calm this situation down so that we will not have a riot tonight." But the tone and conduct of the meeting shifted to a discussion of grievances, especially about police conduct. A black high school boy grabbed the microphone and shouted: "It's like this, the way the policemens treat you round here. . . . It ain't going to be lovely tonight whether you like it or not! [Shouts of disapproval.] I was down on Avalon last night and we the Negro people have got completely fed up! They going out to Inglewood and everywhere else the white man supposed to stay. They going to do the white man in tonight!"

Catcalls and jeers from the audience drowned him out, and he was dragged away from the microphone. Other youths began to pummel him, and only the intercession of adults saved him from a beating. A youth leader returned to the microphone, declaring that the boy did not represent the consensus and that the majority of people wanted only a fair hearing. A group led by a black woman police sergeant pleaded with TV camermen not to show the boy who had made the threatening speech. It was pointed out that there might be an unfortunate reaction if his isolated opinion were broadcast. The television newsmen were noncommittal. "Everybody has it. We can't say we won't use it, and then have some other station put it on the air." The inflammatory language was broadcast to television sets throughout the nation, and the boy's utterance was seldom balanced by less emotional statements made at the meeting. Some reports indicate that during the riot, crowd behavior was deliberately manipulated for newsmaking purposes. Cameramen encouraged youths to throw stones so they could be photographed as "stars" (Conot, 1967:43, 51).

Community proposals After the main meeting, a smaller group of leaders and representatives of youth gangs met to decide upon a course of action. Early in the evening, they proposed to the police: (1) that they withdraw uniformed officers from the troubled neighborhood and allow selected community leaders to undertake the responsibility for law and order; (2) if police found the first proposal unacceptable, that they substitute for white officers black officers in civilian clothes and unmarked cars. Both proposals were rejected, and the meeting at the Seventy-seventh Street Police Station generated ill feeling on both sides. Using only black officers was contrary to the Los Angeles Police Department policy of deploying black officers throughout the city and not concentrating them in the black area.

There were only about 200 blacks on the force, a number far below parity, and they were scattered throughout the city, with only seven in the Seventy-seventh Street station. Police officials asserted that it would be too difficult to assemble the necessary number of black officers. They rejected the proposals as untested methods of handling a rapidly deteriorating situation. The police set up a perimeter to contain the trouble and to keep all others out.

About 5:00 P.M. on Thursday, Police Chief Parker alerted Adjutant General Hill of the California National Guard. A guard colonel was sent to Los Angeles as a liaison officer, and the Fortieth Armored Division in southern California was alerted. In the absence of Governor Brown, Lieutenant Governor Anderson was informed of the situation.

Late in the afternoon, inflammatory handbills were distributed, and around 7:00 P.M. crowds at the scene of the previous night's trouble had grown to more than 1,000. Firemen who came into the area to fight fires in three overturned automobiles were shot at and bombarded with rocks. The first fire in a commercial establishment was set only one block away, and police had to hold back rioters as firemen fought the blaze. Shortly before midnight, rock-throwing and looting crowds for the first time ranged outside the perimeter.

Lull (Friday) By 4:00 A.M. the police department felt that the situation was, at least for the moment, under control. At 5:00 officers were withdrawn from emergency perimeter control. Before 7:00

the intelligence officer on duty reported to the lieutenant governor that "the situation is rather well in hand," and the lieutenant governor left the city for a meeting.

Official indecision Around 8:00 A.M. crowds formed again and looting resumed. About 9:00 A.M. Mayor Yorty and Chief of Police Parker agreed by telephone to call out the national guard, but the mayor then left the city to keep a speaking engagement in San Francisco. The mayor told the McCone Commission: "By about 10:00 or so, I have to decide whether I am going to disappoint that audience in San Francisco and maybe make my city look rather ridiculous if the rioting doesn't start again, and the mayor has disappointed that crowd." The mayor returned to Los Angeles at 3:35 P.M.

By late morning, ambulance drivers and firemen were refusing to go into the riot area without armed escort. About the same time, Chief of Police Parker thought he would need approximately 1,000 men and formally requested the governor's executive secretary in Sacramento to send the national guard. The lieutenant governor received the request at 11:00 A.M. in Berkeley but did not act on it until 5:00 P.M. in Los Angeles, although in the meantime he was in consultation with national guard officers who agreed to assemble 2,000 men at the armories by 5:00 P.M., which was said to be the earliest feasible hour.

Approximately 850 guardsmen were available, outfitted with weapons in Long Beach (12 miles from the riot) enroute to summer camp. The McCone report criticizes the lieutenant governor's delay: "He hesitated when he should have acted. . . . Further escalation of the riots might have been averted if these Guardsmen had been deployed on station throughout the riot area by early or mid-afternoon Friday."

Meanwhile, Governor Brown was reached by telephone in Athens and briefed on the situation. He said he felt the guard should be called immediately, that the possibility of a curfew should be explored, and that he would return to California as fast as possible.

Early Friday afternoon, rioters drove off firemen by sniper fire and by throwing missiles. By late afternoon, gang activity had spread as far as 60 blocks to the north.

Although assembled in armories as early as 6:00 P.M., the guard was not deployed until shortly after 10:00 P.M.

The first death occurred between 6:00 and 7:00 P.M. Friday when a black bystander, trapped between police and rioters, was shot and killed.

Peak of the riot On Friday night, burning and looting were widespread, and the riot was out of control. At 1:00 A.M. Saturday, 100 engine companies were fighting fires—all of which were arson. Snipers shot at firemen. A fireman was killed on the fire line by a falling wall, and a deputy sheriff was killed when another sheriff's shotgun discharged in a struggle with rioters.

The law-enforcement officials tried a different tactic. Police made sweeps on foot, moving en masse along streets to control activity and enable firemen to fight fires. By midnight Friday another 1,000 national guard troops were marching shoulder to shoulder clearing the streets. By 3:00 A.M. Saturday, 3,356 guardsmen were on the streets. Throughout the morning hours of Saturday and during the long day, the crowds of looters and arsonists spread out and increased until an 8:00 P.M. curfew was imposed on Saturday.

Beginning of control (Saturday) Again using sweep tactics, the guardsmen and police were able to clear a major riot area by Saturday afternoon. Guardsmen rode "shotgun" on the fire engines and stopped the sniping and rock throwing at firemen. Saturday evening, roadblocks were set up in anticipation of the curfew.

When the curfew began at 8:00 P.M., police and guardsmen were able to deal with the riot area as a whole. Compared with the holocaust of Friday evening, the streets were relatively quiet, with the only major exception the burning of a block of stores. Snipers again prevented firemen from entering the area, and while buildings burned there was a gun battle between law-enforcement officers, the guard, and the snipers. By midnight Saturday, 13,900 guardsmen were committed.

During the day Sunday the curfew area was relatively quiet. Because many markets had been destroyed, food distribution was started by churches, community groups, and government agencies. Governor Brown, who had returned Saturday night, personally toured the area and talked to residents. Major fires were under control, but there were new fires and some rekindling of old ones. On Tuesday Governor Brown was able to lift the curfew.

SUMMARY

1. Watts is an isolated, predominantly black ghetto but not a uniformly high-density slum.

2. The black population includes many low-income families and has a high unemployment rate.

3. The precipitating incident was a routine encounter with the police, of a sort that occurs many times every day throughout the country.

4. Officials were slow to take decisive action in calling out the national guard and in declaring a curfew.

5. The mass media gave preferential exposure to the more intemperate behavior and in some cases stimulated such behavior to make a good picture. After the riot was under way, the saturated coverage by the media may have contributed to sustaining a high level of tension.

6. The loss of life and the number of gunshot injuries were low considering the amount of gunfire and the heavy property damage. Of 1,032 reported injuries, 118 were gunshot wounds.

7. No evidence has been reported that the riot was planned, but criminal elements and extremists used the riot after it began.

CONCLUSIONS

1. Community initiative failed. Tentative efforts to extemporize cooperative action were rebuffed by the police. The abortive effort to establish a dialogue confirmed poor relations between police and the community. Community organization and leadership were weak, and civil rights leaders were unable to establish effective communication with the rioters.

2. Rumor dissemination was facilitated by hot weather, which kept people out of doors, and by ecological segregation and cultural homogeneity. Inflated and distorted rumors about the first arrests spread quickly. For example, the young woman arrested was wearing a barber's smock, and the false rumor circulated that she was pregnant and had been abused by police.

3. The police were distant from the community and perceived as abrasive. The Los Angeles Police Department is regarded as efficient and incorrupt. It is a small force for the large area and population it serves, and it depends on advanced technology for crime control and detection. It is highly motorized and mobile. The department has integrated slowly and with reluctance. In 1965 only 200 of 5,000 officers were black. Little attention is given to community relations. Police officials had little interest in communicating with civilians. The department encounters the citizenry in the line of duty, but otherwise hardly at all.

The subordinate populations, both blacks and Mexican Americans, had frequently complained of the harsh and abrasive attitudes of the police. Of 586 blacks interviewed after the riot by UCLA researchers, 90 percent thought the police were insulting and used unnecessary force in the area, and about 50 percent claimed to have seen such police behavior. Nearly 30 percent said they had been insulted by police, and more than 5 percent said the police had used unnecessary force on them (*President's Commission, 1967: 121*).

4. There was wide participation. One estimate places the total number of participants at about 15 percent of the adult black community, or over 30,000 persons. They were predominantly young men, and their riotous behavior was viewed sympathetically by older men and young women who made up the bulk of the large number of spectators, perhaps 30 percent of the area's residents (*Sears and McConahay, 1969:19*).

Of the 3,927 people arrested, most were blacks, but only 556 were legally juveniles (under 18), while 2,111 were over 25; 602 were over 40. The riot was participated in by those who had a stake in the community as well as those who did not. For example, 10 percent of those convicted of various offenses were homeowners.

More than half the blacks interviewed by the UCLA survey thought the riot had "a purpose." Expression of "hostility, resentment and revenge" and "gaining attention" were the most commonly mentioned purposes. In the words of the Task Force Report: "The implication is evident that many Negroes believe that if only the white community realized what the ghetto was like and how its residents felt, the ghetto would not be permitted to exist" (*President's Commission, 1967: 122*).

Section three public opinion and propaganda

In emotional contagion, individuals are united by temporary psychological bonds and by the compelling influence of an immediate situation. But emotional contagion is not the only source of temporary and shifting unities. A shared political belief may be temporary, or people may find themselves united by a transitory common interest, for example, antibusing or automobile safety.

PUBLICS

A public consists of people who (1) regard themselves as affected by an event or condition, (2) can in some way register their concern, and (3) are consequently taken into account by business executives, political leaders, or government officials. *Public* is a general term that may apply to groupings of widely varying significance: magazine subscribers, stockholders, voters, or consumers.

Like crowds, publics develop in unstructured situations. But in the public, a free play of interest rather than emotion is released. In its "pure" form, political competition occurs without the excitement found in crowds. Whereas crowd behavior leads to a loss of self-consciousness, in political publics there is more explicit recognition of personal interests and intensification of group self-consciousness. Publics provide the social base out of which organized groups grow and on which such groups depend. (See *ASSOCIATIONS*, p. 224.)

VALUES, ATTITUDES, AND OPINIONS

Personal integrity is highly prized in American culture, and it is felt persons should be secure in their bodies, ideas, and families. This underlying *value* affects a wide range of thought and behavior and is expressed in specific *attitudes*. For example, valuing personal integrity may dispose people to react negatively to the use of informers (who violate personal confidences), wiretapping, or other ways of securing evidence against suspected criminals. "An individual's attitude toward something is his predisposition to perform, perceive, think, and feel in relation to it" (Newcomb, 1950:118). Attitudes are in turn reflected in *opinions*, which are specific judgments on particular issues. The conceptual sequence from value to attitude to opinion can be thought of as a series of steps from the general to the specific, from a broad mental set or disposition (a value) to a narrower one (an attitude) and finally to a specific and concrete expression (an opinion).

Opinions are situational and therefore are not direct expressions of values. An opinion may run counter to what a person is predisposed to believe because of pressures in the immediate situation. An opinion is often the complex resultant of many attitudes. For example, attitudes derived from the value of personal integrity would logically call for rejection of wiretapping. But a belief that the community is in danger may bring other attitudes into play. The resultant opinion may accept wiretapping, perhaps with some reservations.

GROUP BASIS OF PUBLIC OPINION

Public opinion fluctuates with changes in immediate situations. Even topics on which near-consensus has been reached may become issues again in the swift movement of events. There is a large degree of unpredictability in the ebb and flow of public opinion. The more general a judgment—for example, "The English people are our natural allies"—the more likely it is to endure. But opinions on specific policies and persons—such as, "Do you approve or disapprove of the way Nixon is handling his job as president?"—tend to reflect immediate pressures.

Variation in popular approval for former president Nixon is shown in Figure 8:1. Responding to transitory events, major trends, and the ultimate debacle, Nixon's

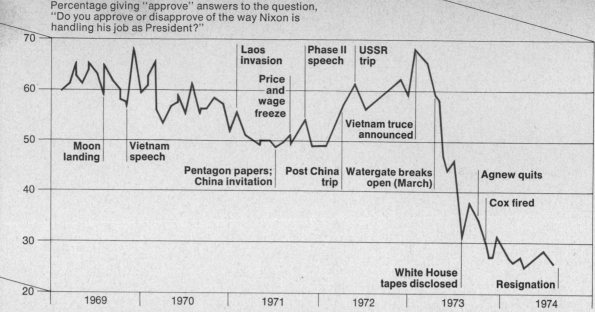

Percentage giving "approve" answers to the question, "Do you approve or disapprove of the way Nixon is handling his job as President?"

Figure 8:1 Popularity of President Nixon, 1969–1974

Source: Compiled from Gallup Opinion Index, various dates.

popularity fluctuated between a high of 68 percent in November 1969 and 24 percent at his August 1974 resignation. But for a year beginning with February 1971 there was slight variation from 50 percent. For ten of those months the range was only four percentage points. Such stability was unprecedented in three decades of polling presidential popularity. Ordinarily presidential popularity is highly volatile and responds to fluctuating economic, international, and political events—not to mention dramatic scandals.

Level of popularity while in office is not a good measure of a politician's prospects for reelection. The attrition of popularity of an incumbent during his tenure in office is commonly observed; all discontents tend to be focused on him. In an election, however, the public estimates the candidate against a real opponent. Furthermore, an incumbent has a unique opportunity to influence events and determine the timing of actions that can reflect credit upon him.

Despite its instability, public opinion develops within a *social setting.* The better the

setting is understood, the less arbitrary the shifts in opinion appear. Though opinion emerges from day-to-day interaction, people have social backgrounds and group affiliations; they are not separate atoms moving about at random (Blumer, 1948).

1. Social background Social backgrounds affect the way individuals respond to events and, consequently, the opinions they form. Although each population segment varies from time to time in its attitudes, the pattern of response tends to be consistent. In recent elections, Democratic candidates have been relatively favored by men, manual workers, Catholics, Easterners, and large-city people.

Because the categories listed are overlapping, a more precise analysis is necessary. For instance, Catholics are heavily concentrated in urban areas, and Catholics and big-city people favor Democrats. But is the preference a general, large-city phenomenon or merely the consequence of a large Catholic population? To answer this question, big-city non-Catholics and big-city Catholics would have to be tabulated separately. It would then be possible to tell how much of the large-city approval is the result of heavy urban representation of Catholics and how much is a large-city phenomenon without respect to religion. The statistical problem of which this is an example is called the *confounding effect.*

2. Reference groups Differences in social background affect perspectives and therefore opinions because they make people sensitive to different things, provide experiences that give them feelings of weakness or strength, make them more or less verbal more or less tradition-centered, and more or less prone to join organized groups. In addition, people tend to see themselves and the world through the framework provided by the groups in which they participate. However, a person's reference group (that group whose perspectives are assumed) is not always derived from an occupational role or economic position. For example, many low-income people identify with and accept the standards of middle-class life. In modern society, with open communication channels, people may assume the perspectives of groups they aspire to or to which their parents belonged instead of those to which they actually belong.

Reference groups (Shibutani, 1961:257–260) should be distinguished from social categories, for example, people in the same income level, or from membership groups, for example, trade unions. Social categories and membership groups, however, often become reference groups. In studying opinion it is important to know to what extent social categories and membership groups have been transformed into reference groups. It is also necessary to know which of many reference groups influence the individual on a given issue.

3. Strong and weak groups The many groups that influence public sentiment differ in their effectiveness. There are wide variations in group prestige, size, and re-

sources and in the significance they have for the individual. To the extent that people think of themselves as belonging to a given class, regardless of income, this reference group plays a significant role in the formation of their opinions. Middle-class values and attitudes are widely held, but organization among white-collar workers and consumers is still relatively weak, although it is increasing. On such specific issues as legislation on the environment, tariffs, and labor, well-organized labor and business groups have greater weight. Even strongly held opinions may not influence decisions unless they have an organizational base that gives them focused expression. On most subjects no popular vote is taken, and differences in organizational and financial resources determine the final outcome.

Overlapping or multiple membership accounts in part for the relatively unstable and shifting character of public opinion. The individual is constantly pulled in different directions by various memberships and roles. A member of a labor union is also a consumer, but concern about income is likely to exceed concern about the rising cost of living or the quality and even the wholesomeness of purchases. The ascendancy of employment and income considerations over less immediate matters, such as health, is illustrated by the argument that more people make their living from cigarettes than have died from them. Multiple membership tends to limit the influence of particular groups. The demands upon the members, to support a policy or to give funds, compete with similar demands by other groups. Group strength is not to be judged by mere size. The influence of even a large group depends on its significance for the member. A physician may be a member of many groups, some of which play a greater role in his or her life than the medical association. An interest group of considerable size may have little influence. Another of the same size may include a core of devoted workers who effectively mobilize the opinions of numerous less committed members.

4. Active and passive groups People who are most concerned with controversial issues join or form interest groups. Others make up a large spectatorlike body, interested enough to follow developments but not sufficiently concerned to participate directly. The passive elements are not necessarily without importance. As an audience whose reactions must be taken into account, they are arbiters in the struggle among interest groups. The pursuit of interests is limited not only by law and custom but also by the other members of the public whose approval is required. Interest groups try to show that their interests are tied to the general welfare, and active groups bid for the support of spectators who judge whether private and public interests are truly related. Therefore, trade unions, business associations, and professional organizations like the American Medical Association devote much effort to public relations.

Table 8:1
Gallup poll accuracy in eleven presidential elections, 1936–1976, in percentages

Year	Winner	Final survey[a]	Election result	Error
1936	Roosevelt	55.7	62.5	−6.8
1940	Roosevelt	52.0	55.0	−3.0
1944	Roosevelt	51.5	53.3[b]	−1.8
1948	Truman[c]	44.5	49.9[d]	−5.4
1952	Eisenhower	51.0	55.4	−4.4
1956	Eisenhower	59.5	57.8	1.7
1960	Kennedy	51.0	50.1	0.9
1964	Johnson	64.0	61.3	2.7
1968	Nixon	43.0	43.5[d]	−0.5
1972	Nixon	62.0	61.8	0.2
1976	Carter	48.0	50.6	−2.6

Source: Compiled from Gallup Opinion Index.

[a] Released to the press on the Sunday before the Tuesday election
[b] Civilian vote only
[c] Dewey election predicted
[d] Winner with less than 50 percent of popular vote

Knowledge of the group structure of society is indispensable to a proper understanding of public opinion. Opinions are affected by social experience, social background, and identification. The interaction of groups that vary in strength and activity determines the weight and direction of public sentiment.

ASCERTAINING OPINION

In a free society, people "vote" in many ways. They speak out at home and among their friends and associates, write letters to newspapers and legislators, join or quit organizations, and go to the polls. Because opinion is variously expressed, a number of different research methods have been devised to ascertain and evaluate opinion. One approach is to study the organizational context of opinion and to examine the rise and decline of organizations—for example, the organizational basis of Prohibition sentiment leading to the passage of the Eighteenth Amendment to the U.S. Constitution. Another approach is to find out what the most active people, the opinion leaders, in a community think and to assess opinion in influential business, professional, and government circles. Finally, public opinion polling is used to try to discover what the public believes, how people are likely to vote, and what their votes mean.

The prediction of election returns is an important achievement of modern social science, and the surveys have helped to demonstrate that the behavior of large populations can be studied through the sophisticated use of sampling techniques. It has been repeatedly shown that a small nationwide sample can accurately reveal certain characteristics and opinions of the population as a whole. (See Table 8:1.)

Election polls are designed to predict a single, highly complex event. This is an exacting task, for it requires not merely one prediction but a whole chain of subordinate ones. The polls must be able to analyze the "don't know" or undecided responses and predict how the respondents will vote on election day. The pollsters must also predict how many people will actually vote and from what groups in society they will come, because many who state their preferences when asked do not take the trouble to vote. When the 1948 election polls were analyzed by a committee of the Social Science Research Council, it became evident that inadequate treatment of the "don't know" responses and the nonvoters probably caused the failure to predict President Truman's reelection.

By the mid-1950s, a number of improvements in polling techniques were well established, and since then the errors in forecasting national elections have been kept within narrow limits. As shown in Table 8:1, surveys since 1956 have been very close to the election results. The 1944 prediction was also very close, but the average error from 1936 to 1952 exceeded 4 percent and consistently underestimated the winner's vote.

The election poll and the election itself have built-in limitations as ways to ascertain public opinion, because of the following factors:

1. Intensity Persons who express their preference to an interviewer may or may not take their vote seriously; they may be very unhappy or quite undisturbed if their preferred candidate loses. Strength of opinion affects the chances that citizens will actually vote.

2. Meaning A vote may mean quite different things to different people, and many questions remain unanswered by an election. Was the election merely a popularity contest? Did the voters mean to give the new administration a mandate on specific issues? Which issues were central and which peripheral? There is room for several interpretations after an election is over, especially when the results are very close, as they were in the Kennedy–Nixon contest of 1960 and the Humphrey–Nixon contest of 1968.

3. Action As a result of variation in intensity and meaning, it is difficult to say whether an expressed preference will lead to any action. This applies most immediately to whether a person votes at all, but beyond that it is important to know whether voting leads to other forms of political action. The mere expression of preference does not tell.

Modern and sophisticated public opinion surveys that go beyond the simple expressions of preference attempt to overcome these limitations. Intensity can be gauged by avoiding simple yes–no answers and providing graded alternatives from which to choose. People may be asked directly whether they strongly approve, approve, don't care, etc., or a more carefully worked-out series of alternatives may be used. The problem of meaning can be dealt with by asking a series of increasingly specific questions on the same topic. Each succeeding question requires a more precise answer about what the words mean or what the implications of the point of view are. Superficial responses are filtered out in this way, as shown in Table 8:2. (See Moser and Kalton, 1971:325.)

As it becomes more sophisticated, public

Figure 8:2 The format of a survey question

The boxed instruction means: If respondent is black, skip to question 48. Thus the interviewer restricts certain questions to the appropriate persons in the sample. One code number (1, 2, or 8 in question 40) will be circled by the interviewer. The key-punch operator will punch the circled number in column 57, which is indicated in the margin as the column assigned for this question. If more than one card is needed for an interview, the deck number is also shown. Usually the information is transferred from punch cards to computer tape.

Source: Question from an NORC interview schedule.

IF R. IS BLACK, SKIP TO Q. 48. Q's. 40 THROUGH 47 ARE FOR NON-BLACKS ONLY.

40. Do you think Negroes should have as good a chance as white people to get any kind of job, or do you think white people should have the first chance at any kind of job?

As good a chance 1   57
White people first 2
Don't know 8

Table 8:2
Filtering conventional responses

Question	Answer	Percentage
Do you believe in freedom of speech?	Yes	97
	No	1
	Don't know	2
If "Yes": Do you believe in it to the extent of allowing Fascists and Communists to hold meetings and express their views in this community?	Yes	23
	No	72
	No opinion	5

Source: Cantril, 1944:22.

opinion analysis places less emphasis on specific predictions and more on understanding underlying trends. It is more important to know whether the coalition of social groups that contributed to a party's majority is basically intact than to predict a given election. An election may result in part from accidental circumstances, whereas a trend may be related to more enduring changes in population composition, such as the assimilation or isolation of ethnic minorities, the improvement of the economic condition of some groups, or the development of new values.

The public opinion poll is an application of the sample interview survey, one of the research tools of the social sciences. It is used to study such widely different problems as the behavior of consumers, the distribution of income, the plans of management, religious participation, and many other topics. It is one of the chief methods enabling social science to deal with large-scale problems in a quantitative way.

INFLUENCING OPINION

Propaganda may be defined as the calculated dissemination of partisan ideas with the intent of influencing group attitudes and opinions. It is a form of special pleading in which truth is often subordinated to effectiveness. Some regard propaganda as morally neutral, justified or not according to the ends it

serves. Others feel it is inherently manipulative and tends to corrupt the free formation of considered judgments, whether in choosing a toothpaste or a foreign policy. This debate turns largely on a matter of degree. Most propaganda operates within limits, foregoing the barefaced lie and the more strident emotional appeal.

In an older and more restricted usage, propaganda is the dissemination of a systematic doctrine, such as Catholicism. The Communists hold to this usage, distinguishing *propaganda* from *agitation*. The former refers to intensive work among small groups, with emphasis on communicating fundamental ideas, for example, Marxist economic and political theories. Agitation is the spreading of a few ideas, usually with a heavy emotional content, to a great many people. In its restricted sense, propaganda is closer to indoctrination and does not have many of the characteristics associated with the use of mass communications. The discussion in this section uses the term propaganda in the more general sense, as defined above, without distinguishing it from agitation.

Propaganda usually refers to writings, speeches, and other symbolic behavior. *Propaganda of the deed* is used to refer to the dramatic actions of nineteenth-century anarchists who attempted to call attention to purported evils by assassinations or other acts of violence. In more recent history, the most notable and persistent acts of terror—murder, bombing, hijacking—for propaganda purposes have been carried on by Palestinians seeking world attention for their national aspirations and their grievances against Israel.

There are also many examples of government action taken with a view to influencing attitudes. The Soviet action in constructing the Aswan Dam in Egypt was part of a propaganda effort comparable to U.S. activities in the field of foreign aid. Both are efforts to win the "hearts and minds of the people." Any act or event can have a symbolic meaning, communicating the intentions as well as the strength or weakness of the actor.

The nature and effectiveness of propaganda depend on objectives and on the characteristics of the target population. If the aim is to sell cigarettes, attention-getting techniques may suffice. But if the objective is to win support for a political belief or economic doctrine, the methods must be adapted to the experiences of the listener, and this usually requires a selective approach to various types of audiences. The following discussion considers some characteristics of propaganda aims and methods.

Aims As a mass-communications activity, propaganda tends to have short-run aims that appeal to a diverse population on the basis of immediate interests, fears, or desires. The propaganda of advertisers, interest groups, and political parties is largely of this kind. The objective is not so much to influence the individual deeply as to gain support for some immediate issue, candidate, or product. The more short-run and superficial the aims, the easier it is to use propaganda tricks and gadgets. (See "The Tricks of the Trade," p. 246.) Long-run aims, which attempt to change basic attitudes, are more difficult to achieve.

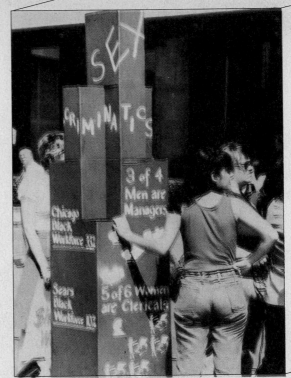

Militancy on the job front: NOW members picket Sears stockholders meeting with a mockup of the Sears Tower.

Methods In the study of propaganda, most attention has been given to techniques and relatively little to aims or targets. A number of characteristic propaganda methods have been identified:

1. Gaining attention Many and varied techniques have been used, from luminous paint to the "big lie." The effectiveness of attention-getting techniques depends on the nature of the medium used as well as the disposition of the audience. Accusations against an individual often receive wide publicity in the press, whereas answers to these charges seem inherently less interesting and are given less prominent display.

2. Associating a partisan cause with existing values, attitudes, and symbols The propagandist, pleading for a special interest, tries to identify the cause with a wider community by transferring to the cause symbols that are known to elicit favorable responses.

Smear tactics or guilt by association are the opposite of the same mechanism, transferring to an opponent the negative feelings attached to some despised symbol. It is also very common to employ prestigious figures, sometimes merely to grace a letterhead, as a way of legitimizing propaganda. (This is not necessarily to be deplored, because if the members of a public know the views of prestigious figures who are actually involved, the device can help to identify the appeal and its source.)

In modern history the struggle for valued symbols has been a common feature of propaganda contests. Adolf Hitler took advantage of the fact that *socialist* was a high-prestige word for many Europeans when he called his party the National Socialist German Labor Party.

3. Concealing identity and aims The attempt to associate a cause with existing com-

The tricks of the trade

Some of the devices now so subtly and effectively used by good and bad propagandists are as old as language. All have been used in one form or another by all of us in our daily dealings with each other. Propagandists have seized upon these methods we ordinarily use to convince each other, have analyzed and refined them, and have experimented with them until these homely devices of folk origin have been developed into tremendously powerful weapons for the swaying of popular opinions and actions.

The chief devices used in popular argument and by professional propagandists—together with our symbols for them—are:

 Name calling—giving an idea a bad label—is used to make us reject and condemn the idea without examining the evidence.

 Glittering generality—associating something with a "virtue word"—is used to make us accept and approve the thing without examining the evidence.

 Transfer carries the authority, sanction, and prestige of something respected and revered over to something else in order to make the latter acceptable; or it carries authority, sanction, and disapproval to cause us to reject and disapprove something the propagandist would have us reject and disapprove.

Source: Abridged by permission from *The Fine Art of Propaganda* by Alfred McClung Lee and Elizabeth Briant Lee. Copyright © by the authors 1939, 1967. (New York: Octagon Books, 1972.) The propaganda symbols were designed by Lee and Lee.

 Testimonial consists in having some respected or hated person say that a given idea or program or person is good or bad.

 Plain folks is the method by which a speaker attempts to convince his audience that he and his ideas are good because they are "of the people," the "plain folks."

 Card stacking involves the selection and use of facts or falsehoods, illustrations or distractions, and logical or illogical statements in order to give the best or the worst possible case for an idea, program, person, or product.

 Band wagon has as its theme "Everybody—at least all of us—is doing it"; with it, the propagandist attempts to convince us that all members of a group to which we belong are accepting his program and that we must therefore follow our crowd and "jump on the band wagon."

Once we know that a speaker or writer is using one of these propaganda devices in an attempt to convince us of an idea, we can separate the device from the idea and see what the idea amounts to on its own merits.

munity sentiment is often jeopardized when the true aims and special interests of the sponsors are known. An evasive technique is the use of "front" organizations that have innocuous names and objectives but are controlled and manipulated by covert interests. The use of front organizations by extremists of various kinds has greatly increased the sophistication needed for effective political participation.

4. Raising anxieties The critical ability of an audience may be impaired by techniques that induce anxiety and fear. This is widely practiced in advertising that plays on anxieties about health, love, and appearance. In political propaganda conspiratorial enemies are commonly emphasized.

5. Showing strength Propagandists are fully aware of the reluctance of people to support a weak cause, and they devote much effort to putting on displays of strength. Sometimes this consists of propagating an ideology that history is necessarily moving in a particular direction and that the cause represents the "wave of the future." Parades, meetings, strikes, and similar demonstrations are also effective, but if the turnout is not impressive, the effort will boomerang. Propaganda by itself does not last long. Effective organizational work is necessary to supplement propaganda and to sustain its effects.

FEARS AND PROSPECTS

When many publics exist, each able to weigh conflicting views according to the criterion of self-interest, the multigroup character of society is preserved. However, modern mass communication makes many millions available to similar and simultaneous influences. The danger that emotional contagion, based upon common fears of war or subversion, will lead to excessive and irresponsible reactions has been referred to as the degeneration of publics into crowds. It has been said that the "mass-state," built upon the eradication of groups, replaces reason with propaganda and enslaves man by delivering him to his emotions (Lederer,

1940). In such a society, public opinion is not the result of the slowly working interplay of interests and ideas but is the crowd-like response of an amorphous population.

A similar view has been expressed by Neumann (1942:115):

Mob psychology, when it seizes a whole nation, destroys the web of its complex structure. Like the individual differentiation of its members, so the innumerable associations of the living community are melted into one gray mass. This process of "massification"—the dissolution of free organizations, the flattening of the social pyramid—in a way preceded the rise of modern dictators. They were the product of this disintegration of society which in turn became the basis of their established rule.

Views of this kind, which emphasize the extension of crowd behavior to many aspects of social life, have been common during the past century (Le Bon, 1917; Ross, 1908). They are usually stated in exaggerated terms, but they probably point to an authentic underlying hazard.

A graphic depiction of an imaginary society dominated by the calculated manipulation of symbols is found in George Orwell's novel *1984.* Orwell describes a totalitarian society ruled by Big Brother and his Ministry of Truth. The Ministry systematically rewrites history and has for its slogans WAR IS PEACE, FREEDOM IS SLAVERY, IGNORANCE IS STRENGTH. The machinery of propaganda and intimidation is highly developed, including an official language, Newspeak, deliberately constructed for political purposes. (See "Newspeak and Expressive Symbolism," p. 58.) Orwell's account is a projection of some of the features of the totalitarian societies of Nazi Germany and Stalinist Russia.

Anxiety about the future of public opinion is based on the strong pressures toward conformity in the mass-communications industries. Since profit making is the criterion of successful operation, the tendency is to try to please as many people as possible and to avoid antagonizing highly vocal groups. The industries are fearful of divergent views and tastes and try to avoid sensitive or controversial issues. The forums that should be available to differing opinion if the public is to be well informed may be closed. A dead level of uniformity in taste, stirring no antagonism and raising no new issues, may stultify creativity. On the other hand, new technological developments may change the situation drastically by opening more channels of communication to experiment and education.

Section four social movements and social change

The fluid conditions of a rapidly changing society are conducive to collective behavior. Active protests sometimes leading to violence occur when rising aspirations are not met by speedy and visible fulfillment. Religious sects emerge when established churches fail to respond to the needs of new life situations. Swift alternations of war and peace bring widespread shifts in public opinion. Collective behavior reflects underlying changes, and in responding to them it creates new perspectives, new lines of action, and new institutions.

PERSPECTIVES AND IDEOLOGIES

A perspective is a complex pattern of attitudes, values, and perceptions that together make up an ordered view of the world. It includes what one sees as foreground and as background, a hierarchy of values, and specific conceptions about persons, groups, and oneself. People in similar situations tend to have shared perspectives: They see the world alike and have the same assessments of what is good, what is likely, and what is possible. When circumstances change, a period of uncertainty and exploratory behavior occurs until a new perspective or "definition of the situation" is adopted that seems to fit the world as it is experienced by people in like circumstances.

In the study of social change, nothing is more fundamental than an understanding of altered perspectives. Every epoch has its distinctive evaluations of the role of the individual and the meaning of history. The nineteenth century was a period of great industrial expansion and self-confidence. Ideas that stressed the power of the individual and hailed change as progress were widely held. The twentieth century is an age of wars and revolutions, of pessimism and anxiety, and the idea of progress is questioned. The development of vast resources and the expansion of productivity have raised hopes of a better life. These changes in perspective have, for better or worse, made possible and perhaps inevitable many of the movements and institutions that characterize the times, such as collectivism, bureaucratization, and increased state control.

Two types of perspectives are often associated with fundamental historical change:

1. Perspectives affecting group identity Perhaps the most potent force in history is the sense of common belonging felt by many people. New perspectives may lead to the alteration of established groupings, as in the rise of nationhood or the attempt to preserve a racial, religious, or linguistic identity.

2. Perspectives that initiate change In the perspectives of rulers and merchants, the position of England in the fifteenth and sixteenth centuries shifted from the perimeter to the center of the maritime world. The result was an epoch of trade and conquest that has only recently run its course. Religious and political ideas have also broadened perspectives and sent people out as missionaries, colonists, and warriors.

Ideologies When self-conceptions and world views are in flux, people grope uncertainly for some way to interpret their emergent perceptions. The time is ripe for ideologies, which are relatively systematic doctrines that articulate group perspectives and provide a basis for collective action (Mannheim, 1936). Ideologies tend to be "organized around one or a few pre-eminent values, such as salvation, equality, or ethnic purity" (Shils, 1968:66).

Many ideologies claim to formulate the interests and aspirations of major social groups. For example, the ideology of women's liberation purports to speak for women, nationalist or ethnic ideologies for people who have a common language or history, Marxist socialism for the working class. Ideologies therefore play an important part in efforts to raise the consciousness of such groups, that is, encourage them to feel a sense of shared identity or fate.

Some ideologies are defensive, serving mainly to rationalize or justify a social order. For example, ideologies of management have sought "to justify the subordination of large masses of men to the discipline of factory work and to the authority of employers" (Bendix, 1956:xix). Other ideologies, such as socialism, are critical and future-oriented, formulated as alternative perspectives for group life.

All ideologies profess to be true not only in upholding certain values but in giving a picture of what the world is like. Some go far in attempting to provide detailed formulations of group perspectives. In an epoch of change, active ideologues propose many different systems of belief. However, only a few ever gain wide acceptance, because to be effective the beliefs must fit the shared perspectives of many people and must make sense in terms of their backgrounds and experience.

SOCIAL MOVEMENTS

For the most part, social change occurs gradually and without design. However, new perspectives and aspirations often generate collective action to combat presumed evils and to institute new ways of life. Sometimes the action is sporadic and temporary, as in the case of isolated uprisings against oppressive conditions. Collective action is called a social movement when it is unified, lasting, and has:

1. A distinctive perspective and ideology The women's suffrage movement arose out of redefined perspectives about the place of women, and these were formulated in a doc-

trine that was widely accepted. The ideology of a movement provides direction and self-justification; it offers weapons of attack and defense; and it holds out inspiration and hope (Blumer, 1951:210–211). Social movements place great emphasis on ideology, particularly when other sources of orientation and cohesion are lacking.

2. A strong sense of solidarity and idealism Membership in a movement typically means more to the individual than other affiliations. The person is dedicated and feels part of an idealistic and active enterprise. Especially in the early stages, idealism plays a role in all movements, political or religious, progressive or conservative.

3. An orientation toward action The very word *movement* suggests unconventional methods of appeal, such as street meetings and the sale of propaganda tracts. Small movements can sometimes gain wide attention by dramatic actions, particularly if they involve violence. The stress on action in part reflects the problem of maintaining interest and solidarity. There is a constant need to give the members something to do to keep them from slipping away to other interests and involvements.

Movements and organizations A movement is usually made up of a variety of forms and groupings. For example, the Prohibition movement included the Anti-Saloon League, the Prohibition party, the Women's Christian Temperance Union, and many church groups. The socialist movement in England has included a number of different political parties, trade unions, newspapers, and groups of intellectuals such as the Fabian Society. Thus a movement tends to have a somewhat amorphous character; there is usually no official leadership for the movement as a whole, and its boundaries are vague.

Research on social movements tends to focus on ideologies and on specific organizations, which are the most tangible and enduring elements of social movements. But the role of collective excitement and public opinion cannot be ignored (Cantril, 1941). The distinctive character of movements is found in the ebb and flow of public opinion and the occasional upsurge of collective excitement. The peace movement opposing the war in Vietnam was supported by a wide array of organizations, many of which were very short-lived. Their task was to create and mobilize antiwar sentiment. Mass parades and rallies were the chief vehicles of collective action, although mobilization could not have been accomplished without the organized effort of small groups of dedicated activists. To some extent, the activist core of the movement was sustained by coalitions with more permanent pacifist and socialist organizations. As the antiwar movement became more effectively organized, (1) the demonstrations decreased in number but increased in size and (2) more effective organization tended to reduce the level of violence (Horowitz, 1970:8).

On the other hand, the anti-Vietnam war movement and, more generally, the early years of the New Left were strongly anti-organizational. The very name—The Movement—symbolized the spirit of many young adherents who resisted identification with any particular organization and grudgingly accepted the need for leadership (Skolnick, 1969:Chaps. 2, 3; Jacobs and Landau, 1966).

Women's liberation Abigail Adams's letter to her husband John, who was attending the Constitutional Convention in 1787, is often cited as a benchmark of American feminism. She wrote, "If particular care and attention is not paid to the ladies, we are determined to foment a rebellion, and will not hold ourselves bound by any laws in which we have no voice and representation." But her protest was not heeded by the men who wrote the Constitution.

Like the prohibition movement, nineteenth century American feminism had one main purpose—to win the vote for women. When the efforts were finally rewarded in 1920 with the passage of the Nineteenth Amendment, which granted suffrage, the women's movement lost its momentum. Not until the 1960s did pressures build up again to improve the status of women.

The contemporary movement differs in form and breadth of objectives from both the women's suffrage efforts and the prohibition movement. (See Adaptation 20.) Women's suffrage and the Anti-Saloon League were essentially single-purpose movements, but the women's liberation movement has many purposes. Sponsorship of the Equal Rights Amendment is only one manifestation of activist women's objectives, and the passage of the amendment is not likely to bring the women's movement to a halt.

There are two major factions in the contemporary feminist movement: The women's rights faction is concerned primarily with legislative reform through traditional pressure-group politics. The women's liberation faction is concerned with changing the broader cultural definition of women's roles and is hostile to traditional political forms (Carden, 1974). Thus there is a division of labor between the more radical women's liberation groups, which are a source of new ideas, and the more reformist women's rights branch, which supplies direction and political clout.

The prohibition movement had a clearly defined base in the Protestant and rural population; the feminist movement base is less clearly defined, but it is largely white, urban, middle-class, and college educated. Within the women's movement the two main factions differ in organizational form as well as in political and social objectives. The legislatively oriented women's rights faction is characterized by the National Organization for Women (NOW), the best known and perhaps the most important of the formal women's rights organizations.

Adherents of the liberation branch tend to be younger than members of NOW and other women's rights groups. To a great extent the younger women mistrust organization and organizations.

The thousands of sister chapters around the country are virtually independent of each other, linked only by journals, newsletters, and cross-country travelers. . . . One result of this style is a very broadly based, creative movement, to which individuals can relate as they desire, with no concern for orthodoxy or doctrine (Freeman, 1975: 450).

In contrast to organizations such as NOW that coordinate the energies of its members for direct political action, the loosely structured liberation branch of the movement is nearly apolitical. Its participants have "rap" sessions to raise feminist awareness and, like the black power attitude that excludes whites, these sessions are closed to men.

Whereas the older reformist elements have settled down to pursue political objectives, the younger liberation branch is organizationally unstable and harder to predict. Some younger women turn to one of the conventional women's rights organizations, others continue to find personal rewards in participating in liberation groups, and still others drift away from any active role in the movement.

Types of movements Social movements might be classified according to their distinctive purposes and constituencies. For example, the woman's suffrage movement had the *goal* of achieving the vote for women, and its *constituency*, that is, its members and supporters, consisted mainly of middle-class women. Similarly, one may identify the goals and constituencies of student movements, religious movements, or any other social movement.

A different approach to classification is summarized in Table 8:3. The analytic strategy is as follows. First, a broad distinction in goals is made between value-oriented and norm-oriented movements (Smelser, 1963: Chaps. 9, 10). A *value-oriented* movement speaks to a rather general social concern, such as democracy, peace, nationalism, or godliness. A *norm-oriented* movement has a narrower focus: It strives to establish or change a specific social form or practice, such as women's suffrage, child labor, or separation of church and state.

This initial classification according to the kind of goal a movement has — value-oriented or norm-oriented — is related to another set of variables: the nature of the means used in pursuit of those goals (Turner and Killian, 1957:Chaps. 16–19).

Three kinds of means are identified: power, persuasion, and participation. The two kinds of goals and the three kinds of means yield a sixfold classification, and examples are given for each.

A *power-centered* movement is an instrument for exercising political muscle and winning victory in the political arena. Usually a single organization becomes the focal point of such a movement. In the table, revolutionary socialism, embodied in the Leninist type of "combat party" (Selznick, 1960), exemplifies the power-centered, value-oriented type of movement. The Prohibition movement, as focused in the activities of the Anti-Saloon League, was also power-centered, though norm-oriented. Power-centered movements tend to use illegitimate means, ranging from undue pressure on legislators to open violence, their members believing that the end justifies the means.

A *persuasion-centered* movement looks to

Table 8:3   Social movements classified by means and goals

| Means orientation | Goal orientation | |
	Values	Norms
Power	Revolutionary socialism	Prohibition (Anti-Saloon League)
Persuasion	Social democracy Pacifism	Birth control Women's suffrage
Participation	Utopian communities Sects	Labor movement

education, including propaganda and legitimate political action, to forward its aims. The women's suffrage movement is so classified. Other examples are democratic socialism (sometimes called social democracy) and pacifism, both of which are persuasion-centered and value-oriented. Persuasion-centered movements tend to be gradualist and accommodative. They emphasize education, believe that people must be reached "where they are," and try to approach people in terms they can understand and accept. As a result, such movements often appear timid and self-restrained but, in contrast to power-centered movements, they are more likely to respect the rights of others.

A *participation-centered* movement is mainly interested in its members and potential members; it is less concerned to change social policy or the social order, except indirectly. Such a movement characteristically finds its success in the creation of a cohesive group of committed members. Utopian communities and many religious sects illustrate the participation-centered, value-oriented movement. The hallmark of the movement is a fellowship of true believers. A norm-oriented movement may also be participation-centered when people are enlisted in the movement as a way of influencing them as individuals. This is characteristic of the labor movement, whose success is measured more by numbers of members than by the effect it has on the social order. Movements for self-help and self-improvement, such as Alcoholics Anonymous and the encounter-group movement are also participation-centered and norm-oriented. Probably most participation-centered movements tend to be value-oriented, because a commitment to values creates a moral identity and thus justifies and sustains participation. The participation-centered movement has an isolating effect, for it tends to withdraw its members into a subsociety.

Cautions (1) The distinctions suggested in Table 8:3 are not hard and fast. In the real world, any given social movement stands somewhere on a continuum between an orientation to values and an orientation to norms, and where it stands on the continuum is different at different stages of the movement's history.

(2) The sixfold classification is not intended merely for tagging social movements and placing them into appropriate boxes; it is a way to help analysis. Once the tentative classification has been made, a movement's distinctive traits can be considered, including, for example, the problems that arise when a movement narrows its focus from values to norms or tries to combine power and persuasion.

Reformers and radicals In most important social movements, struggles occur over means and ends. A militant, uncompromising extreme faction is pitted against gradualist reformers. The gradualists believe that the movement can be most effective if it is willing to compromise, give their energies to immediate and attainable goals, and participate in the political process. The extremists resist any dilution of the movement's ultimate goals and argue that militant confrontation is more effective than reform and education.

Internal conflict between radicals and reformers, who ostensibly share the same aims, can be bitter and violent—a fact often puzzling to outsiders. But when the stakes are recognized, the life-or-death quality of the conflict can be better understood. First, the factions are in direct competition for the loyalty of an activist core that is small in numbers but of great strategic importance. Second, the conflict affects the "soul" of the movement itself—what goals it should pursue and by what means—and people who feel strongly about the moral significance of a movement cannot look with tranquility at the possibility that the movement will be subverted or betrayed.

Reformers and radicals can live together in the same movement with mutual benefit if all are accepted as belonging to the same moral community. Thus the civil rights movement of the 1960s embraced a combination of moderate and radical groupings, some espousing legal change and negotiation for more jobs for blacks, others demanding rejection of white society. To some extent, the strategy of the moderates depended on radical "threats" which gave the moderates some leverage in negotiating with the white community. On the other hand, the more extreme militants risked alienating white support.

The Michels effect Many social movements follow a roughly discernible "career" or natural history, from an early stage of unrest and conflict to a later stage of settling down. This Michels effect, manifested in narrowed goals, accommodative strategies, and self-perpetuating leadership, has been widely noted. (See Adaptation 18, p. 219, and Adaptation 31, p. 390.)

253

Adaptation 20
Odegard:
The
Anti-Saloon
League

Adaptation 20 Odegard: The Anti-Saloon League

In 1920 the Eighteenth Amendment to the U.S. Constitution was ratified, prohibiting "the manufacture, sale, or transportation of intoxicating liquors." Passage of the Eighteenth Amendment can largely be attributed to the national Anti-Saloon League, formed in 1895. This organization transformed the existing temperance movement from a moral appeal directed at individuals into a political power, with its strength based on Protestant churches (Gusfield, 1963). The following account describes the nature and strategy of the Anti-Saloon League.

The social base of the prohibitionist movement Although in theory the Anti-Saloon League was a nonsectarian organization, in fact it was almost entirely an instrument of the Protestant churches, principally the Methodist, Baptist, Presbyterian, and Congregational denominations. Prohibitionist sentiment was strong among these groups, and the Anti-Saloon League was organized to give them effective political organization. In theory it was open to anyone; in practice it was controlled by the Protestant churches from whom it drew both its leadership and its principal membership support. The churches opened their pulpits to Anti-Saloon League speakers and provided the league with an extraordinary access to church membership. According to one account, pastors in more than 2,000 churches in Illinois discussed a pending temperance measure on a single Sunday.

Source: Abridged and adapted from *Pressure Politics: The Story of the Anti-Saloon League* by Peter H. Odegard (New York: Columbia University Press, 1928). Published in this form by permission of Peter H. Odegard and Columbia University Press.

During the prohibitionist heyday, Protestant church members were predominantly rural and native born. Even in the cities, Protestant churches were composed largely of people born in rural areas. Where Protestants were in the majority, as in the South, prohibitionist sentiment was strong: Nine of the southern states adopted Prohibition prior to 1916. Connecticut and Rhode Island never ratified the Eighteenth Amendment; Catholics made up 67 percent and 76 percent, respectively, of the total church population in these states.

The Anti-Saloon League did not have to create prohibitionist sentiment; the sentiment already existed in the rural native-born Protestant areas. Nor did it have to organize prohibitionist sentiment; it was already organized in the Protestant churches. But with singular success, the league *mobilized* the organized sentiment and directed it toward a political purpose, the passage of prohibitionist legislation.

Moral sentiment into political action The Anti-Saloon League, formed as a national organization in 1895, was, as its name suggests, a league of already-established temperance organizations. Behind it lay almost a century of temperance agitation and largely unsuccessful efforts to pass Prohibition legislation. One local organization, however, the Oberlin Temperance Alliance, had secured the passage of such legislation in Ohio. In 1887 the Oberlin Temperance Alliance circulated petitions demanding the passage of a statewide Township Option Bill, by which individual municipalities might vote to outlaw the sale of liquor. The bill was put through the lower house and went to the state senate where, according to a preliminary poll, it had a majority of one. Two days before the vote was to be taken, Senator Crook of Dayton, one of the bill's supporters, announced that after having been visited by three committees of Dayton brewers, distillers, and saloon-keepers, he had been persuaded to vote against the measure.

Senator Crook's frankness was his own undoing. The prohibitionists reasoned that if he could be influenced by pressure from the liquor interests, he could be encouraged to return to the straight and narrow by greater pressure from the other side. That afternoon, the Reverend H. H. Russell, employed by the Alliance to push the bill, went to Dayton. Soon letters, telegrams, and petitions from citizens of that city poured in upon the recalcitrant Crook demanding that he support local option. The senator did vote for it, and the measure was passed by a majority of one.

Senator Crook and his three committees of brewers, distillers, and saloon-keepers provided the Anti-Saloon League with a lesson in politics. Thereafter the temperance movement diverted its efforts from appealing to conscience to applying pressure, especially on legislators.

Single-purpose politics With the Ohio experience as a model, the national Anti-Saloon League organized itself into a legislative pressure group. It set itself up as a single-purpose organization, concentrating solely on the passage of Prohibition legislation. Some prohibitionists had earlier formed themselves into a Prohibition party, arguing that the existing parties would not and could not institute Prohibition. But it had never won significant electoral support, and in 1896 it split on the silver and gold issue, each side putting its own presidential candidate into the field. The Anti-Saloon League avoided all side issues upon which disagreement and factional splits could occur, and which might alienate potential supporters. Advocates of silver or of gold, of free trade or of a high tariff could all join in the Anti-Saloon League's drive for Prohibition legislation without compromising their other loyalties.

Instead of entering politics as another party, the league worked through the Republican and Democratic parties, supporting whatever dry candidates were nominated. It did not care what else a candidate stood for, so long as he stood for Prohibi-

tion. It frequently supported both Republicans and Democrats in the same election, provided both candidates were dry. Nor did the Anti-Saloon League insist that a candidate be a personal abstainer. The league's theory was that it is better to have a drunkard who will "vote right, than to have a saint who will vote wrong."

The league's objective was to hold the balance of power. With virtual control of a large block of voters, the league frequently forced the major parties to nominate candidates friendly to its interests, since the dry vote often spelled the difference between victory and defeat.

Direct action Having decided on a satisfactory candidate, the league did all it could to see that he was elected. Women and children were urged to gather near the polls to act as reminders of the evil of the saloon. They often paraded before polling places wearing badges: "Vote Against Whiskey and For Me," or "Vote Against the Saloon—I Can't Vote" (the Nineteenth Amendment to the Constitution, guaranteeing the right of women to vote, was not ratified until 1920). The following report in the *New York World* of May 13, 1919, described a North Carolina election scene:

When a voter came within range he was immediately surrounded by . . . ministers . . . women and children. The clergymen employed words of advice and confined their activities to the proprieties. But the women and children were less tactful. They clutched at the coats of the voter. They importuned him to vote the dry ticket. A phrase constantly employed was "Mister, for God's sake don't vote for whiskey," repeated with parrot-like accuracy that results from thorough coaching. . . . A few of the wets ran the gauntlet of the women and children . . . but the greater majority of the voters viewed the conflict from afar and returned to their offices and homes. The drys won the day.

The league provided funds and personnel for more routine campaign activities, often employing organizers to canvass voters in their homes. In 1906 in New York it promised aid in his current campaign to any state assembly member who had voted dry and was being opposed on that account. Thirty-six dry members requested such assistance, and all were reelected.

When Prohibition legislation was pending, the Anti-Saloon League employed many kinds of direct action techniques designed to impress recalcitrant legislators with the size and strength of dry opinion. As in the campaign of the Oberlin Temperance Alliance, local league organizations saw to it that legislators received letters and telegrams from dry voters. Petitions were also effective. When national Prohibition was up for debate in the House of Representatives in 1913, long slips of paper listing the names of over 6 million petitioners hung from the balconies filled with Prohibition supporters. One congressman suggested that the House move out of Washington to avoid pressure from the drys. That same year Congress had been petitioned to submit Prohibition to the states by a parade of 4,000 men and women, many of them grown gray and infirm in the long campaign, wearing the white ribbon of temperance and marching to the strains of "Onward, Christian Soldiers."

Rural power The threat of defeat for wets and the promise of victory for drys was, however, the principal political weapon of the Anti-Saloon League. In 1917, just before the House passed the resolution to submit Prohibition to the states, the *Washington Times* asserted, "If the ballot on the constitutional amendment were a secret ballot, making it impossible for the Anti-Saloon League bosses to punish disobedience, the Amendment would not pass." The newspaper implied that national Prohibition was about to be passed not out

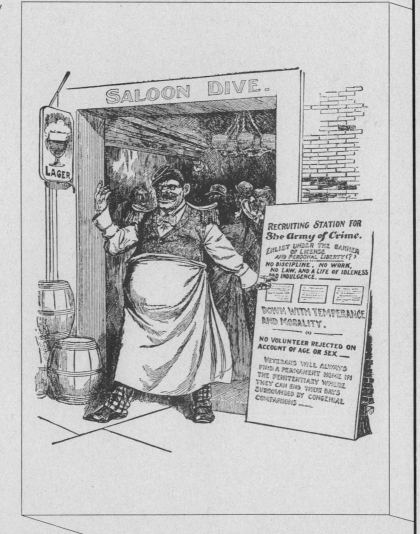

The Recruiting Sergeant for the Army of Crime: This cartoon, depicting the saloon as a natural center for vice and crime, was widely used in Anti-Saloon League publications.

of conviction but out of fear of political reprisal. The league's electoral effectiveness depended on two things: (1) its control of the rural vote and (2) the dependence at that time of both the state and national legislatures on rural areas. If the rural vote had not been very nearly a solid block firmly committed on the dry issue, the league's promise to deliver votes would have been far less effective than it actually was. If the legislatures had been as dependent on the cities as they were on the rural areas, the league's hold over the rural voters would have been a less potent political weapon.

When the Anti-Saloon League turned its energies from reforming the individual to pressing for the passage of Prohibition, it sought to exert its influence where the rural population had its political power. This was in the chambers of the state legislatures which tend to overrepresent rural and small-town areas by basing representation on geographical area rather than population, as in the U.S. Senate where a sparsely settled rural state like North Dakota has as many senators as a densely populated state like New York. In addition, the movement toward the cities tends to weight legislative bodies toward rural overrepresentation, since reapportionment lags behind actual population changes. In 1917, when the league put on its strongest drive for national Prohibition, one of its leaders pointed out, "We have got to win it now because when 1920 comes and reapportionment is here, forty new Congressmen will come from the great wet centers with their rapidly increasing population."

In most cases the Anti-Saloon League opposed submitting the Prohibition issue to direct popular vote, trusting rather to its influence in the state legislatures. In the debate on national Prohibition, it was proposed that ratification be by state conventions elected by popular vote for that purpose. To this the league spokesmen objected. They insisted that the more usual procedure of ratification by state legislatures be followed. They argued that since state conventions would be chosen by the same electorate that had chosen the state legislatures, the proposal to submit ratification to a more direct vote was merely a delaying tactic. Although the league had pressed for a seven-year ratification period in case ratification in some states would prove difficult, three-fourths of the

states ratified within 14 months. The speed with which the amendment was ratified surprised the wets as well as the drys.

The grip held by the Anti-Saloon League over the state legislatures was never better illustrated than in the manner in which these bodies obeyed the command to ratify. In vain were suggestions made that the lawmaking bodies were without instructions from the people on this most important question. In vain were efforts made to have the sentiment of the electorate tested by referendum voting (*Yearbook of the United States Brewers' Association,* 1919:18).

Propaganda strategy National Prohibition was first written into the law as an aspect of food conservation during World War I. Legislation was passed under the pressure of the drys prohibiting the manufacture of foodstuffs into distilled spirits, and giving the president authority to extend the restriction to beer and wine. The war gave considerable impetus to dry propaganda, Prohibition being presented as part of the war effort. Nor did the league hesitate to play upon anti-German attitudes prevalent at the time. According to *American Issue*, the national organ of the Anti-Saloon League, "German brewers in this country have rendered thousands of men inefficient and are thus crippling the Republic in its war on Prussian militarism (*American Issue,* Ohio Edition, August 3, 1917).

The league directed its propaganda not so much *for* Prohibition as *against* the saloon and its evils. This was an effective device because even drinkers who balked at the idea of absolute Prohibition were willing to admit that the American saloon had become a noisome thing. The United States Brewers' Association itself had recognized the need for reform. Reform, however, would not satisfy the league, and it pictured the saloon as hopeless beyond redemption.

The saloon is the storm center of crime; the devil's headquarters on earth; the schoolmaster of a broken decalogue; the defiler of youth; the enemy of the home; the foe of peace; the deceiver of nations; the beast of sensuality; the past master of intrigue; the vagabond of proverty; the social vulture; the rendezvous of demagogues; the enlisting office of sin; the serpent of Eden; a ponderous second edition of hell, revised, enlarged and illuminated (*American Issue,* Kentucky Edition, April, 1912).

The anti-saloon propaganda of the league tried

to induce a favorable attitude toward Prohibition by attaching it to an already-existing attitude, a negative attitude toward the saloon. It used the same strategy when it attached its fight for local option to democratic values. Local option, by which any political unit—county, city, town, or even ward—could vote to ban the saloon, was presented as an extension of self-government and home rule. Many people who personally disliked Prohibition felt obliged to support the drive for local option as consonant with democracy. Woodrow Wilson, then governor of New Jersey and no partisan of Prohibition, wrote,

I am in favor of local option. I am a thorough believer in local self-government and believe that every self-governing community which constitutes a social unit should have the right to control the matter of the regulation or the withholding of licenses (*American Issue*, Vermont Edition, March, 1912).

CONCLUSION

The success of the Anti-Saloon League, and the subsequent history of Prohibition, suggest two points concerning the relation of means and ends:

1. Through the activities of the Anti-Saloon League, the temperance movement decided to pursue its larger aims by means of a high-pressure political strategy designed to make the most of rural Protestant power. But the social base of the movement was already beginning to lose its political strength, and in any case did not include the emerging big-city populations. The movement thus took the risk that the new constitutional amendment would be based on a temporary and unstable majority.

2. As the temperance movement became a Prohibition movement, a decision was made to achieve the aims of temperance by means of repressive legislation. But that legislation, when enacted on a national scale, resulted in widespread lawlessness and an upsurge of organized crime. After 13 years it was decided that the social costs of Prohibition were too high, and the Eighteenth Amendment was repealed.

The moral ideal of temperance was compromised by undemocratic pressure politics and by "coercion to virtue." (See LAW, p. 421.)

References

Allport, Gordon W.
1947 The Psychology of Rumor. New York: Holt, Rinehart and Winston.

Bendix, Reinhard
1956 Work and Authority in Industry. New York: Wiley.

Blumer, Herbert
1948 "Public opinion and public opinion polling." American Sociological Review 13 (October):542–549.
1951 "Social Movements." Pp. 199–220 in A. M. Lee (ed.), New Outline of the Principles of Sociology. New York: Barnes & Noble Books.

Broom, Leonard and Philip Selznick
1963 Sociology: A Text with Adapted Readings. New York: Harper & Row. Third edition.

Cantril, Hadley
1941 The Psychology of Social Movements. New York: Wiley.
1944 Gauging Public Opinion. Princeton, N. J.: Princeton University Press.

Carden, Mary Lockwood
1974 The New Feminist Movement. New York: Russell Sage Foundation.

Chicago Commission on Race Relations
1922 The Negro in Chicago. Chicago: University of Chicago Press.

Conot, Robert
1967 Rivers of Blood, Years of Darkness. New York: Bantam.

Fogelson, Robert M. and Robert B. Hill
1968 "Who riots? A study of participation in the 1967 riots." Pp. 221–243 in Supplemental Studies for the National Advisory Commission on Civil Disorders. Washington, D.C.: GPO.

Freeman, Jo
1975 "The women's liberation movement: its origins, structures, impact, and ideas." Pp. 448–460 in Women: A Feminist Perspective, edited by Jo Freeman. New York: Mayfield.

Grimshaw, Allen D.
1959 "Lawlessness and violence in America and their manifestations in changing Negro-white relationships." Journal of Negro History 44 (January):52–72.
1960 "Urban racial violence in the United States: Changing ecological considerations." American Journal of Sociology 64 (September):109–119.

Grimshaw, Allen D. (ed.)
1969 Racial Violence in the United States. Chicago: Aldine.

Horowitz, Irving
1970 The Struggle Is the Message. Berkeley, Calif.: Glendessary Press.

Jacobs, Paul and Saul Landau
1966 The New Radicals. New York: Random House.

Lader, Lawrence
1959 "New York's bloodiest week." American Heritage 10 (June):44–49.

Le Bon, Gustave
1917 The Crowd. London: Allen and Unwin. First published in French in 1895.

Lederer, Emil
1940 The State of the Masses. New York: Norton.

Lee, A. M. and N. D. Humphrey
1943 Race Riot. New York: Holt, Rinehart and Winston.

Mannheim, Karl
1936 Ideology and Utopia. New York: Harcourt Brace Jovanovich.

Merriam, Charles E.
1934 Political Power. Chicago: University of Chicago Press.

Moser, C. A. and G. Kalton
1971 Survey Methods in Social Investigation. London: Heinemann.

National Advisory Commission on Civil Disorders
1968 Kerner Report. New York: Bantam.

Neumann, Sigmund
1942 Permanent Revolution. New York: Harper & Row.

Newcomb, Theodore
1950 Social Psychology. New York: Holt Rinehart and Winston.

President's Commission on Law Enforcement and Administration of Justice
1967 Task Force Report: Crime and Its Impact — An Assessment. Washington, D.C.: GPO.

Ross, E. A.
1908 Social Psychology. New York: Macmillan.

Rudé, George
1964 The Crowd in History, 1730–1848. New York: Wiley.

Rudwick, Elliott M.
1966 Race Riot at East St. Louis, July 2, 1917. Cleveland: Meridian.

Sears, David O. and John B. McConahay
1969 "Participation in the Los Angeles riot." Social Problems 17 (Summer):3–20.

Selznick, Philip
1952/1960 The Organizational Weapon. New York: Free Press.

Shibutani, Tamotsu
1961 Society and Personality. Englewood Cliffs, N. J.: Prentice-Hall.
1966 Improvised News: A Sociological Study of Rumor. Indianapolis: Bobbs-Merrill.

Shils, Edward A.
1968 "Ideology." Pp. 66–75 in International Encyclopedia of the Social Sciences. Vol. 7. New York: Macmillan and Free Press.

Skolnick, Jerome
1969 The Politics of Protest. New York: Simon & Schuster.

Smelser, Neil J.
1963 Theory of Collective Behavior. New York: Free Press.

Turner, Ralph H. and Lewis M. Killian
1957 Collective Behavior. Englewood Cliffs, N. J.: Prentice-Hall.

Sources and readings

General works

Blumer, Herbert
1951 "Collective behavior." Pp. 167–222 in A. M. Lee (ed.), New Outline of the Principles of Sociology. New York: Barnes & Noble.

Brown, Michael and Amy Goldin
1973 Collective Behavior: A Review and Interpretation of the Literature. Pacific Palisades, Calif.: Goodyear.

Lang, Kurt and Gladys E. Lang
1961 Collective Dynamics. New York: Crowell.

Smelser, Neil J.
1963 Theory of Collective Behavior. New York: Free Press.

Turner, Ralph H. and Lewis M. Killian
1972 Collective Behavior. Englewood Cliffs, N. J.: Prentice-Hall. Revised edition.

On collective violence

Grimshaw, Allen D. (ed.)
1969 Racial Violence in the United States. Chicago: Aldine.

Kerner Report: National Advisory Commission on Civil Disorders
1968 New York: Bantam Books.

Skolnick, Jerome H.
1969 The Politics of Protest. New York: Simon & Schuster.

On social movements

Ash, R.
1972 Social Movements in America. Chicago: Markham.

Banks, J. A.
1975 The Sociology of Social Movements. London: Macmillan.

Evans, Robert R. (ed.)
1972 Social Movements: A Reader and Sourcebook. Skokie, Ill.: Rand McNally.

Gamson, W. A.
1975 The Strategy of Social Protest. Homewood, Ill.: Dorsey Press.

Gusfield, Joseph R. (ed.)
1970 Protest, Reform, and Revolt: A Reader in Social Movements. New York: Wiley.

On public opinion and propaganda

Berelson, Bernard and Morris Janowitz (eds.)
1966 Reader in Public Opinion and Communication. New York: Free Press.

Ellul, Jacques
1969 Propaganda. New York: Knopf.

Erikson, Robert S. and Norman R. Luttbeg
1973 American Public Opinion: Its Origins, Content, and Impact. New York: Wiley.

Key, V. O., Jr.
1961 Public Opinion and American Democracy. New York: Knopf.

On surveys and polling

Hyman, Herbert
1955 Survey Design and Analysis: Principles, Cases, and Procedures. New York: Free Press.

Kisch, Leslie
1967 Survey Sampling. New York: Wiley.

Moser, C. A. and G. Kalton
1971 Survey Methods in Social Investigation. London: Heinemann.

Oppenheim, A. N.
1966 Questionnaire Design and Attitude Measurement. New York: Basic Books.

Roll, Charles W., Jr. and Albert H. Cantril
1972 Polls: Their Use and Misuse in Politics. New York: Basic Books.

Periodicals

Journal of Communications

Public Opinion Quarterly

9 | Population

Section one introduction

A population is the total number of human beings in a society or community. They may be counted and classified by age, sex, occupation, or any other meaningful characteristic. Such data are used to explore the underlying causes and significance of major social trends, such as a declining birth rate, or to interpret the meaning of a preponderance of one sex or a shortage of individuals in their productive years.

The technical study of human populations — *demography* (from the Greek *demos*, meaning "people") — is made possible by the collection of statistics either from official records like birth, death, and marriage registrations or from periodic censuses and sample surveys. As records and censuses become more exact and detailed, demographers are able to consider the interrelations of a larger number of population characteristics. It is simple enough to add up the number of registered births and deaths in a state. It is more complicated but more important to relate maternal and infant mortality rates to the age, income, and race of the mother. Information collected in such a socially relevant form can be used to guide social policy, for example, by identifying populations that are not getting the benefits of public resources.

Since much of the knowledge about population is interpreted by considering social or economic factors, demography is closely related to sociology and economics as well as to statistics. Most university courses on population are given in sociology departments, though there are a few independent demography departments and research institutes (Population Association of America, 1971; Macleod, 1974).

An understanding of population phenomena offers clues to underlying forces in the society that would be difficult or impossible to perceive by compiling people's opinions or studying their social interactions. One of the most serious contemporary problems is the explosive growth of population. Although the increase has tapered off in developed countries, the populations of developing countries will maintain a high rate of growth for many years. Consequent pressures on land and irreplaceable resources will continue to have profound effects on the organization of societies and on relations among nations, particularly between rich and poor countries. A sudden appreciation of the seriousness of the population problem is generating anxiety and the beginnings of worldwide action, but population pressure will not be eased merely by advances in the techniques of birth control. The future population of the world will be determined by such distinctively social considerations as the willingness and ability of people to change deeply ingrained attitudes toward family size and by the capacity of political leaders to communicate the urgent need for action that may be perceived dimly or not at all by most citizens. (See Section Five.)

No state can develop wise, long-term plans for the training and effective use of its human resources without the sort of information compiled by sophisticated census taking. The most important single source of information on population is the census, periodically conducted in most countries. Adaptation 21 briefly reviews the history and operations of the U.S. census, which has become a continuing, year-round activity as well as a population count conducted each decade. The large geographic area and population size and the diversity of the United States make census taking a more difficult task than in countries with relatively small and homogeneous populations. Consequently, the U.S. census may not be as precise as, say, Sweden's. On the other hand, the U.S. Bureau of the Census does not have to cope with populations in remote and inaccessible regions or with a high rate of illiteracy. In these respects it has an easier task than the census departments of some developing countries.

Section Two discusses population characteristics and outlines a few elementary techniques used to present and interpret data on age and sex composition. Section Three describes frequently used measures of fertility and mortality, assesses trends in birth and death rates, makes some worldwide comparisons, and comments on the chances for longevity. Section Four examines the history of international migration, touches upon the consequences of migration for the countries of origin and for the countries of destination, and briefly treats migration within the United States. Section Five outlines the predicament of world population growth, considers some factors affecting success or failure in restraining growth, and discusses the implications of zero population growth.

Adaptation 21: The United States census

BACKGROUND

The United States was the first modern nation to make a legal provision for regular census taking. A census is called for in the apportionment clause, Article I, Section 2, of the Constitution, which reads in part as follows:

Source: Based in part on *Bureau of the Census, Factfinder for the Nation, 1948: The Story of the Census, 1790–1916; U.S. Census of Population and Housing, 1960, Principal Data-Collection Forms and Procedures* (1961); *1970 Census User's Guide,* and other publications of the Census Bureau, Washington, D.C.

Representatives and direct Taxes shall be apportioned among the several States . . . according to their respective Numbers, which shall be determined by adding to the whole Number of free Persons, including those bound to Service for a Term of Years, and excluding Indians not taxed, three-fifths of all other Persons. The actual Enumeration shall be made within three Years after the first Meeting of the Congress of the United States, and within every subsequent Term of ten Years.

The scope of the first census in 1790 was somewhat greater than required by the Constitution because James Madison recognized the potential

SCHEDULE of the whole Number of PERSONS within the several Districts of the UNITED STATES, taken according to "An Act providing for the Enumeration of the Inhabitants of the United States;" passed March the 1st, 1790.

DISTRICTS.	Free white Males of sixteen years and upwards, including heads of families.	Free white Males under sixteen years.	Free white Females including heads of families.	All other free persons.	Slaves.	Total.
* Vermont	22,135	22,328	40,505	255	16	85,539
New-Hampshire	36,086	34,851	70,160	630	158	141,885
Maine	24,384	24,748	46,870	538	NONE	96,540
Massachusetts	95,453	87,289	190,582	5,463	NONE	378,787
Rhode-Island	16,019	15,799	32,652	3,407	948	68,825
Connecticut	60,523	54,403	117,448	2,808	2,764	237,946
New-York	83,700	78,122	152,320	4,654	21,324	340,120
New-Jersey	45,251	41,416	83,287	2,762	11,423	184,139
Pennsylvania	110,788	106,948	206,363	6,537	3,787	434,373
Delaware	11,783	12,143	22,384	3,899	8,887	59,094
Maryland	55,915	51,339	101,395	8,043	103,036	319,728
Virginia	110,936	116,135	215,046	12,866	292,627	747,610
Kentucky	15,154	17,057	28,922	114	12,430	73,677
North-Carolina	69,988	77,506	140,710	4,975	100,572	393,751
South-Carolina	-	-	-	-	-	-
Georgia	13,103	14,044	25,739	398	29,264	82,548
	Free white Males of twenty-one years and upwards, including heads of families.	Free Males under twenty-one years of age.	Free white Females, including heads of families.	All other Persons.	Slaves.	Total.
S. Western Territory	6,271	10,277	15,365	361	3,417	35,691
N. Do.	-	-	-	-	-	-

Truly stated from the original Returns deposited in the Office of the Secretary of State.

TH: JEFFERSON.

October 24, 1791.

* This return was not signed by the marshal, but was enclosed and referred to in a letter written and signed by him.

under 16 years of age. Slaves were "other Persons" in the Constitution, and 60 percent of their number counted in the apportionment. The report of the first census is contained in a pamphlet of 56 pages without the explanatory text, percentages, and detailed analyses that now accompany census statistics.

Not until the fifth census (1830) were printed schedules used. Before that marshals' assistants had used such paper as they happened to have, ruling it, writing in the headings, and binding the sheets together themselves.

Beginning with the seventh census in 1850, a number of important improvements were made. The individual replaced the family as the unit of enumeration, and additional data such as age, sex, race, and occupation were reported. The change of unit increased the analytic usefulness of the census by improving the accuracy of enumeration, by permitting detailed tabulations of the additional data, and by facilitating cross-tabulations. The ninth census (1870) made the first use of machine tabulation. Another innovation was the use of maps, charts, and diagrams to present graphically the more significant facts. These were published in a separate volume called *The Statistical Atlas of the United States*.

In 1880 field operations were reorganized. Specially qualified supervisors were appointed, and they were able to give closer supervision to the work of enumeration.

The number and types of inquiries were greatly increased in the censuses of 1880 and 1890 and resulted in reports on a wide variety of subjects, but in spite of new techniques of more rapid enumeration and tabulation, publication was delayed. Two things became apparent. First, the decennial census had become burdened with fields of investigation that might better be subjects of continuous inquiry throughout the decade.

Consequently the 1900 decennial census was limited to four subjects: population, manufactures, agriculture, and mortality. Second, the process of building a completely new temporary organization for each census was no longer economical, and in 1902 the Bureau of the Census was established as a permanent agency.

In 1940, sampling for some items was adopted, and the 1960 census introduced further innovations: It gathered more information on a sample basis than in previous years; for the first time it

value of the census for rational policy making. Congress accepted his recommendation that it

had now an opportunity of obtaining the most useful information for those who should hereafter be called upon to legislate for their country, if this bill was extended to embrace some other objects besides the bare enumeration of the inhabitants; it would enable them to adapt the public measures to the particular circumstances of the community.

The name of the head of each family was recorded and the total number of persons in the family, classified as free or slave. Free persons were further classified as white or other, free whites as male or female, and free white males as over or

asked householders to fill out questionnaires instead of only responding to enumerators' questions; and it made extensive use of high-speed, electronic data-processing equipment. The census has been a leader in experimentation with statistical processing since Herman Hollerith, a census employee, devised a punch-card machine which was used in tabulating the 1890 census.

In 1960 and 1970 the information was entered on a schedule designed for FOSDIC (Film Optical Sensing Device for Input to Computers). FOSDIC scanned microfilm of completed schedules and from the position of marks on the schedules converted the information into magnetic impressions on tape. The tape was then processed by electronic computers. The use of FOSDIC eliminated the card-punching operation and, thus, one important source of clerical error. The enormous capacity of the electronic computer made it possible to do much more uniform editing and coding than in earlier censuses and to insure consistency among a larger number of interrelated items.

ACCURACY

The management of the census must consider basic social attitudes as well as the improvement of such techniques as enumeration, computing, and tabulating. Essentially a vast reporting procedure, the census can be only as accurate as its reporters and respondents. Many countries have difficulty in conducting censuses because the people mistrust the intentions of the government and elude the enumerator or give incomplete and faulty information. Although some people in the United States mistrust the census and regard it as an invasion of privacy, it has been remarkably, but not entirely, free of this kind of impediment. A survey to assess public reaction to the 1970 census found broad acceptance and cooperation from a sample of Wisconsin respondents in regard to the census in general and to the use of mailed forms in particular (Sharp and Schnore, 1971).

However, a competitive spirit has occasionally affected the interpretation of census statistics. In 1960 and again in 1970 some cities with aspirations to be as large as possible questioned the accuracy of census figures. The census reported in many areas that a central city had not grown very much or had even declined in population, an expected fact in view of the movement to the sub-urbs. This news was received with angry protests from municipal officials and local patriots, and some cities incurred considerable expense to check on the accuracy of published figures. (In addition to local pride, some cities stood to lose federal funds that are allocated on the basis of population.)

Checking census accuracy To check on the accuracy of the census a number of techniques are used. For instance, birth and death statistics for the period between censuses are examined, and an estimate of expected population is made. This is done for the country as a whole and for regions and cities. Then the actual count is compared with the expected population. Where a significant difference exists, careful analysis is made to determine possible error.

Toward the end of the enumeration period in 1960, many newspapers published "Were You Counted?" forms, which contained the questions asked of 100 percent of the population. Readers were urged to fill in forms and send them to the census district office if they believed they or members of their household had been missed in the enumeration.

In 1950 and 1960, specially trained and supervised enumerators did Post-Enumeration Surveys (Taeuber and Hansen, 1964:1–14; U.S. Bureau of the Census, 1960). The sample recounts found that many people had been erroneously enumerated or omitted from enumeration. The techniques of such surveys are far too costly to be used for the whole census, but they provide a check on its methods and accuracy. Estimates of enumeration errors in the two censuses expressed as percentages of the census-enumerated population are as follows:

Enumeration errors	*1950*	*1960*
Omissions	2.3%	3.0%
Inclusions	0.9	1.3
Net undercount	1.4	1.7

The percentages seem small, but the 1.7 percent undercount in 1960 represents about 3 million people, and the 1.4 percent in 1950 about 2 million. It might appear from the figures that the 1950 census was more accurate than the 1960 census, but probably it was not. Rather, the 1950 Post-Enumeration Survey and the methods of analysis associated with it were less precise than the survey conducted in 1960.

Probably all censuses undercount the population. The sociological usefulness of the census is somewhat impaired by this fact but even more by the fact that different parts of the population are counted more accurately than others. The young, old, mobile, poor, and racial minorities are likely to be underenumerated. Young, mobile black, Puerto Rican, or Chicano men are the ones most often missed by the census. Inasmuch as the undercounted parts of the population include many persons who need special social services, the errors can result in shortchanging some groups.

Minority leaders are thus caught in a value conflict between the conviction that public records should be color-blind, that is, should not record ethnic origin, and the practical fact that getting a fair share of resources involves being accurately counted. The balance of opinion seems to be falling on the pragmatic side; leaders of several ethnic communities, particularly blacks and Mexican-Americans, have claimed that their members were undercounted in the 1970 census.

Although poor people are among the ones most often missed by the census, a study in Baltimore showed that users of public facilities are fully counted by welfare agencies. Therefore, the "social pathology" rates are inflated in the following way: The numerator (agency clients in an area) is complete, the denominator (total population in that area) is too small (Chaiklin and Lewis, 1964:43–47; Chaiklin, 1966:7–8).

SAMPLING IN THE CENSUS

It would be impossible for the bureau to gather the amount of data that it does during the regular decennial census or to conduct current surveys if it did not use sampling techniques. Since 1950 much population information has been based on samples—20 percent for 1950 and 25 percent for 1960—which are so identified in the census reports.

Figure 9:1 **1970 census questionnaire**
(Separate identical lines for recording information on persons ②–⑦ have been deleted.)

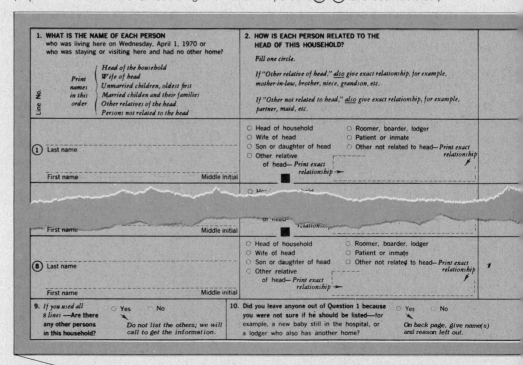

In 1970, four households in five received a census form containing seven questions relating to each individual, three to make sure everyone was counted, and 13 relating to the house. For one household in five there were additional items. One household in 20 received a form which could total 89 questions, but these included inquiries about the house. Not all questions applied to every family (1970 Census User's Guide, 1970:4).

The basic population questionnaire for the 1970 census is given in Figure 9:1. Figure 9:2 shows some of the questions asked of the 15 percent and 5 percent sample populations. Questions 13a, 21, 22, 23, and 25 were put to both sample populations and are thus asked of a 20 percent sample.

Estimates of the total number of persons with specified characteristics are obtained by multiplying by five the number of persons with these characteristics in the 20 percent sample, and by multiplying by four the number in the 25 percent sample. This procedure of deriving overall figures from sample figures is a matter of probability. For example, the 1950 census shows that 17.6 percent of males 25 years and over *in a 20 percent sample* had completed four years of high school. On the basis of this sample, the census reports that 7.5 million, or 17.6 percent of all males *in the total population* 25 years and over, completed high school, but it does not mean that the national figure is exactly 7.5 million. The figure is used with the following understanding: The chances are approximately two out of three that the figure for the total population lies between 7.5 million plus 5,440 and 7.5 million minus 5,440. (The degree of probability and the range of accuracy claimed are derived from the mathematics of statistics.) 7.5 million falls at the midpoint of a fairly narrow range within which the actual figure probably lies.

In one sense, total census figures based on sampling, like all such figures, are never precise. They are presented and must be used with the understanding that the actual figures are probably close to the computed figures. In another sense, however, they are very precise, because once the acceptable range of accuracy is specified, the de-

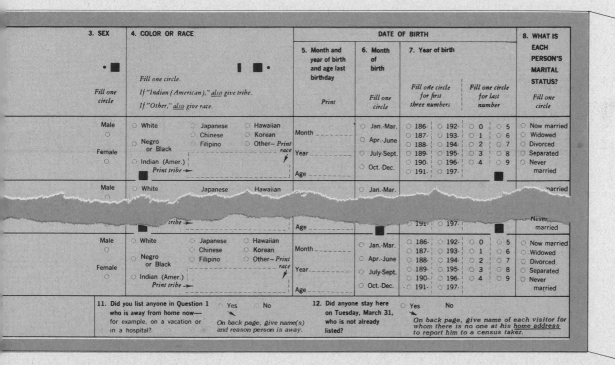

Name of person on line ① of page 2

Last name   First name   Initial

15 and 5 percent

13a. Where was this person born? *If born in hospital, give State or country where mother lived. If born outside U.S., see instruction sheet; distinguish Northern Ireland from Ireland (Eire).*

○ This State

OR

(Name of State or foreign country; or Puerto Rico, Guam, etc.)

5 percent

b. Is this person's origin or descent— *(Fill one circle)*

○ Mexican   ○ Central or South American
○ Puerto Rican   ○ Other Spanish
○ Cuban   ○ No, none of these

15 percent

14. What country was his father born in?

○ United States

OR

(Name of foreign country; or Puerto Rico, Guam, etc.)

15. What country was his mother born in?

○ United States

OR

(Name of foreign country; or Puerto Rico, Guam, etc.)

5 percent

16. *For persons born in a foreign country—*

a. Is this person naturalized?

○ Yes, naturalized
○ No, alien ■
○ Born abroad of American parents

b. When did he come to the United States to stay?

○ 1965 to 70   ○ 1950 to 54   ○ 1925 to 34
○ 1960 to 64   ○ 1945 to 49   ○ 1915 to 24
○ 1955 to 59   ○ 1935 to 44   ○ Before 1915

15 percent

17. What language, other than English, was spoken in this person's home when he was a child? *Fill one circle.*

○ Spanish ■   ○ Other—
○ French   *Specify*
○ German   ○ None, English only

18. When did this person move into this house (or apartment)? *Fill circle for date of last move.*

○ 1969 or 70   ○ 1965 or 66   ○ 1949 or earlier
○ 1968   ○ 1960 to 64   ○ Always lived in
○ 1967 ■   ○ 1950 to 59   this house or apartment

19a. Did he live in this house on April 1, 1965? *If in college or Armed Forces in April 1965, report place of residence there.*

○ Born April 1965 or later
○ Yes, this house .... *Skip to 20*
○ No, different house

b. Where did he live on April 1, 1965?

(1) State, foreign country, U.S. possession, etc.

(2) County

(3) Inside the limits of a city, town, village, etc.?
○ Yes   ○ No

(4) If "Yes," name of city, town, village, etc.

15 percent

20. Since February 1, 1970, has this person attended regular school or college at any time? *Count nursery school, kindergarten, and schooling which leads to an elementary school certificate, high school diploma, or college degree.*

○ No ■
○ Yes, public
○ Yes, parochial
○ Yes, other private

15 and 5 percent

21. What is the highest grade (or year) of regular school he has ever attended?
Fill one circle. If now attending, mark grade he is in.

○ Never attended school— *Skip to 23*
○ Nursery school
○ Kindergarten ■

Elementary through high school (grade or year)
1 2 3 4 5 6   7 8   9 10 11 12
○ ○ ○ ○ ○ ○ ○ ○ ○ ○ ○ ○

College (academic year)
1 2 3 4 5 6 or more
○ ○ ○ ○ ○ ○

22. Did he finish the highest grade (or year) he attended?

○ Now attending this grade (or year)
○ Finished this grade (or year)
○ Did not finish this grade (or year)

23. When was this person born?

○ Born before April 1956— *Please go on with questions 24 through 41.*

○ Born April 1956 or later— *Please omit questions 24 through 41 and go to the next page for the next person.*
● ■

5 percent

24. *If this person has ever been married—*

a. Has this person been married more than once?

○ Once   ○ More than once

b. When did he get married?   When did he get married for the first time?

Month   Year   Month   Year

c. *If married more than once—* Did the first marriage end because of the death of the husband (or wife)?

○ Yes   ○ No ■

15 and 5 percent

25. *If this is a girl or a woman—*
How many babies has she ever had, not counting stillbirths?
1 2 3 4   5 6 7 8
○ ○ ○ ○   ○ ○ ○ ○
Do not count her stepchildren or children she has adopted.
9 10 11 12 or more   None
○ ○ ○ ○   ○

15 percent

26. *If this is a man—*

a. Has he ever served in the Army, Navy, or other Armed Forces of the United States? ■

○ Yes
○ No

b. Was it during— *(Fill the circle for each period of service.)*

Vietnam Conflict *(Since Aug. 1964)* .... ○
Korean War *(June 1950 to Jan. 1955)* .... ○
World War II *(Sept. 1940 to July 1947)* .... ○
World War I *(April 1917 to Nov. 1918)* .... ○
Any other time .... ○

Figure 9:2 1970 census questionnaire: sample population questions

gree of probability that it has been attained (e.g., odds of 2:1) can also be specified.

    Although sample statistics for the United States as a whole may be accepted as approximating very closely the results that would have been ob-tained from a complete enumeration of the population, this is not true of smaller populations. Generally speaking, the smaller the sample and/or the smaller the total population, the less reliable are the results of a sample.

U.S. GOVERNMENT SOURCES

Statistical Abstract of the United States (Washington, D.C.: GPO), a summary of statistics on population, social, political, and economic characteristics and trends. This annual publication can be used as a direct source and as a convenient way to locate more detailed information, both from official and unofficial sources. To use the *Statistical Abstract* most efficiently, (1) examine the information reported in the appropriate tables, (2) note the sources cited in the tables, and (3) refer to the appendix, "Guide to Sources of Statistics."

Historical Statistics of the United States: Colonial Times to 1957 (Washington, D.C.: GPO, 1960), and *Historical Statistics of the United States: Continuation to 1962 and Revisions* (Washington, D.C.: GPO, 1965). These two volumes, which should be used together with the latest *Statistical Abstract,* contain a compilation of statistical time series on social and economic changes going back as early as 1610. The volumes are reference guides as well as direct sources of information.

Bureau of the Census Catalog of Publications: 1790–1972. (Washington, D.C.: GPO, 1973) includes a reprint of the *Catalog of U.S. Census Publications, 1790–1945.*

Bureau of the Census Catalog, issued quarterly, cumulative to the annual (fourth) issue. First published in 1946. Part I is a classified and annotated bibliography of all bureau publications issued during the year to date. Geographic and subject indexes, selected publications of other agencies, and technical papers by bureau staff are cataloged. Subject divisions include population and housing, agriculture, business, fishing, government, manufactures, mining, and transportation. Part II lists data files and special tabulations, computer tapes, punched cards, maps, and computer programs.

Immigration and Naturalization Service: *Annual Report; I & N Reporter,* quarterly.

Bureau of Labor Statistics: *Handbook of Labor Statistics,* annual; *Monthly Labor Review.*

Women's Bureau: *Handbook on Women Workers.*

Public Health Service: *Monthly Vital Statistics Report; Vital Statistics of the United States,* annual; *Vital and Health Statistics* (Publication No. 1000), which includes several series on a range of health-related topics.

Current Population Reports The *Current Population Reports* series provides an almost continuous record of the population, housing, and social and economic characteristics of the United States between censuses and covers many topics not enumerated by the census. Reports are based on the monthly Current Population Survey samples in 449 areas throughout the 50 states and the District of Columbia. In 1975 nearly 50,000 housing units containing about 105,000 persons 16 years and older were eligible for interview and about 95 percent of the eligible households were interviewed in a given month. From time to time the sample construction for the surveys is changed, and a major revision, involving an increase in sample size and alterations in computer procedures, was undertaken in 1976.

Section two population composition

The term composition refers to significant biological or social characteristics of a population such as sex, age, race, birthplace, occupation, and dependency. Population figures may be presented in different ways to answer the needs of government, science, and industry. For example, the number unemployed suggests the economic health of a country; the numbers at various income levels indicate the society's affluence and degree of equality; and the numbers with specialized higher education reveal the skills available in the labor force.

Population composition gives a cross-sectional view of a population at a given time. It contains clues to what has happened in the past as well as hints about changes to come. To assess the significance of population composition, it is necessary to (1) compare different populations or (2) compare a time series of cross sections and thus evaluate trends and changes in the same population.

Table 9:1 is a simplified summary of the population composition of the United States by age, sex, and major activity. Even this capsule treatment suggests how the population may be broken down into socially meaningful clusters. To take one example, the majority of women identified as not in the labor force are in the housekeeping category. But note that relatively few women, compared with men, are classified as retired. When women reach retirement age, they continue their responsibilities. Such statistics do not reveal changes in the household division of labor among old couples, a topic that deserves more study (Riley and Foner, 1968: 352). Men who perform or share housekeeping duties during retirement are rarely called housekeepers.

Table 9:1
Population^{*a*} **of the United States by activity, age, and sex, 1975**

Activity type and age	Males	Females
	(in thousands)	
In labor force, aged 16 and over		
In armed forces	2,100	100
Employed civilians	50,400	33,100
Unemployed civilians	4,600	3,200
Not in labor force, aged 16 and over		
In school	3,600	3,600
Keeping house	200	33,100
Retired	6,200	1,300
Ill and other	5,000	5,200
In school, aged 5–15	21,300	20,600
Not in school, aged 5–15	400	400
Under 5 years of age	8,300	7,900

a Excludes institutional population. Figures rounded to the nearest 100,000 and adjusted to the 1975 population.

Source: Compiled from Statistical Abstract of the United States, 1975:Tables 183, 558, and 562.

THE SEX RATIO

The proportion of males to females within a population is called its sex ratio (SR) and is stated as the number of males per 100 females. A sex ratio of 100 means that the population is evenly divided between males and females, a figure greater than 100 means there are more males than females, a figure less than 100 that there are fewer males than females. At birth the sex ratio for whites in the United States approximates 106, but at successively older ages the proportion of males diminishes; that is, the sex ratio declines with increasing age. The life expectancy for American females is higher than for males. In some countries this is not the case, and it was not so at some earlier periods in the United States.

Unbalanced ratios A sex ratio that deviates markedly from 100 in either direction is thought in Western cultures to be biased or out of balance (cf. von Hentig, 1952:443). This attitude probably expresses the values of a monogamous marital system. A polygynous family system (one with plural wives) would not be concerned about an excess of females, and a polyandrous system (one with plural husbands) might welcome an excess of males.

An unbalanced ratio might have sinister significance in some societies. For example, in traditional China, sons were a form of old-age insurance and were essential to continue the family line and to perform religious rituals for the ancestors. Daughters, on the contrary, had no part in perpetuating the family line, did not play a part in ancestor worship, and were a financial burden when marriage was contemplated and dowries and gifts had to be provided. The cultural solution was female infanticide, which persisted into the present century and was sufficiently widespread to be revealed in a sex ratio with a preponderance of males (Orleans, 1972: 36–37).

The overall sex ratio of the United States now stands at an all-time low of 95. In the last hundred years it fluctuated between about 102 and 105 and reached a high of 106 in 1910. Until the 1940s the number of males had always exceeded the number of females in the country as a whole. The sex ratio of Canada is also at a low point of about 100. It too has varied widely, reaching a peak of 113 at the census of 1911 (Norland [Yam], 1974:Table 3:1). The relatively high sex ratio through much of American and Canadian history resulted from a disproportionately heavy immigration of males. The high proportion of males of marriageable age among immigrants created competition for spouses and interfered with family building, especially in the early stages of immigrant communities. In adapting to these problems, many men remained single, others married at a later age, and still others sent to the home country for brides or married outside the ethnic group. In contrast to "new" countries like Canada and the United States, which have had sustained masculine immigration that has kept the sex ratio high, Great Britain, an "old" country, for the most part has been a net exporter of people. For this reason and because of heavy war casualties, Britain's sex ratio has held in the middle and low 90s throughout this century.

The sex ratio for blacks in the United States has been lower than for whites, but the reasons are obscure. Allowing for the fact that significant numbers of young black men are missed by the census, there is still a significant difference between the black and white sex ratios. For all age groups in 1975, blacks had a sex ratio of 91, whites of 96. Under age 15, the ratios were about 101 for blacks and 104 for whites. The most important difference was for the category between ages 25 and 44, where blacks have a ratio of 85 and whites 99 (*Current Population Reports*, Series P-25, No. 614, November 1975, computed from Table 1). Whatever the underlying causes, the low sex ratios of blacks create social complications. Low ratios at the ages of maximum work force participation and family building aggravate personal problems and impose strains on many black families and persons.

AGE COMPOSITION

The industrial, military, and reproductive potentials of a nation depend on its age as well as its sex composition. A population with heavy concentrations in the productive years has a relatively large labor force and a larger potential for mobilization in time of emergency. A country with a small population in the productive years may be less able to respond flexibly to threats against its security and may be less adaptable to technological change.

Dependency ratio When a population is concentrated at the extremes of the age distribution, it has a high dependency ratio, that is, the number of nonproductive individuals is large compared with the working population. Ordinarily the dependency ratio is calculated by summing the age groups under 15 years plus those age 65 and over and dividing that total by the population age 15–64. This calculation, like similar ratios, requires a number of assumptions. It assumes that persons enter the labor force at age 15 and leave it at age 65, that everyone in the 15–64 bracket works, and that everyone outside that bracket does not. These assumptions are obviously false in detail and are keyed more to a rural or other labor-intensive economy than to an advanced technology that relies on a highly skilled work force. For industrialized countries, a dependency ratio calculated on the real facts would place the cutting point for youthful dependence at 18 years or even later and for persons leaving the work force at 67 or so and would make realistic adjustments for actual participation in the work force. The age bracket 15–64 is, however, frequently used as the yardstick in comparing nations, and on that criterion the United States in 1975 had a dependency ratio of about 55, lower than Canada's ratio of 60 at about the same time but higher than Japan's, to take a culturally different but highly industrialized country. As a matter of fact, Japanese scholars favor a productive age bracket of 15–59 rather than 15–64. (For a discussion of past

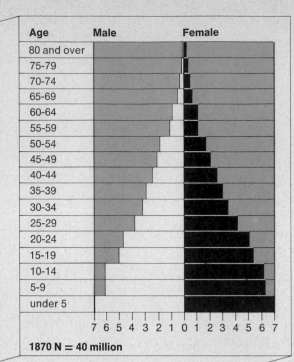

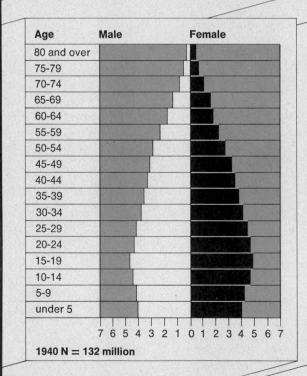

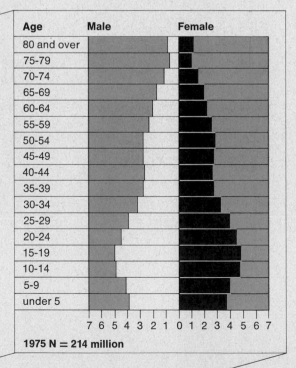

Figure 9:3 Population pyramids, United States: 1870, 1940, and 1975 (in percentages)

and projected dependency ratios in Japan, see Kuroda, 1973:79–92.)

Population pyramid Sometimes called the "tree of ages," the population pyramid summarizes age and sex characteristics at a given time. (See Figure 9:3.) A vertical line divides the percentages of males (on the left) and females (on the right). The percentages on the scale are calculated from population figures compiled by age categories, that is, males under five, between five and nine, and so on. The distributions are expressed in percentage terms, but pyramids can also be constructed with absolute numbers instead of percentages.

Figure 9:3 shows the age–sex pyramids of the United States at three points in the past century. The diagram for 1870 is shaped like a true pyramid, typical of populations with high birthrates but also high death rates. It has a very broad base and a narrow top with less than 5 percent of the population aged 60 years and over. "Each year's crop of babies was larger than that of the year before, and the older birth classes, besides being smaller to begin with, had tended to die at a relatively early age" (Notestein, 1951:30).

The 1940 figure describes a much different population. Both birth and death rates had declined, and the population was more highly concentrated in the productive years between ages 20 and 50. The proportion in older dependent ages also increased, but the proportion of children had decreased sharply because of the lower birthrates of the depression years of the 1930s.

The pyramid for 1975 shows an increase in the population under 35 years of age, the result of the so-called baby boom in the 1940s and 1950s. This increase was a reversal, probably temporary, of a long-term trend toward a lower birthrate. (See Section Three.) The short age bars, which were at the base of the pyramid in 1940, moved up in 1975 to become a notch at ages 35–44. Thus the pyramid graphically reveals the earlier history of the population.

Thomas Malthus (1766–1834). Modern work in population began with Thomas Malthus, whose "Essay on the Principle of Population, etc." was first published in 1798. Malthus posed the problem of the unchecked growth of human population versus the slower growth of the means of subsistence. He held that population tends to increase up to the limit of the food supply, thus preventing any considerable rise in the standard of living. In later editions of his work, he brought together empirical data and developed the idea of positive checks on population growth: (1) hunger, (2) disease, (3) war, and (4) vice. He also recognized preventive checks which might depress the birth rate: (1) deferred marriage and (2) celibacy. He regarded the use of contraception as a "vice."

Demographic disaster: the USSR Depressions, wars, epidemics, and famines leave scars on the demographic structure of a country, not only directly by deaths that reduce specific cohorts, but indirectly through the effects of such losses on subsequent generations. Such impacts are shown, sometimes with extraordinary vividness, as in the population pyramid for the USSR

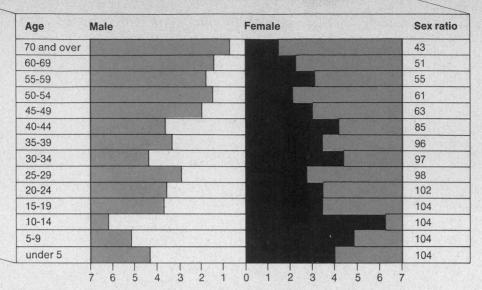

Figure 9:4 Population pyramid, USSR, 1970 (in percentages)

Source: The Current Digest of the Soviet Press, vol. 23 (May 18, 1971):14. Reported by the USSR Council of Ministers' Central Statistical Administration.

(Figure 9:4), which still reveals the direct losses of World War I as well as World War II and the indirect effects in the reduction in births owing to the depletion of potential fathers.

The figure thus displays the ravages of two wars, a revolution, a depression, an influenza epidemic, and a famine. A population expert could make some plausible guesses about what was going on even without knowing anything about Russian history. The narrowing of this pyramid toward the top is much more exaggerated than would have occurred without catastrophe, and the very low sex ratio beginning with middle ages suggests that a highly selective catastrophe had occurred, namely World War I and the Russian Revolution.

The cohorts aged 35 to 39 in 1970 were reduced by the low birthrates of the worldwide depression of the 1930s, and the cohorts aged 15 to 29 are relatively small for several reasons: (1) the loss of potential fathers in World War I and the revolution, (2) the reduction in the number of potential fathers and mothers in the worldwide influ-

enza epidemic and a famine, and (3) deaths directly attributable to World War II, which struck the same cohorts.

At the right-hand margin of the pyramid the sex ratio for each age bracket is presented. Note the sharp drop-off beginning with age 40. Above age 44, the sex ratio averages a remarkably low 55 males per 100 females. At younger ages, the sex ratio is approximately normal (100). By comparison, the sex ratio in the United States is also close to parity at age 44 and below, while it declines to about 92 for ages 45 to 64 and close to 70 for ages 65 and over.

In terms of the sex ratio, World War I had a far greater impact than did World War II, when a large part of Soviet territory was repeatedly a field of battle, and an estimated 17 million Soviet men, women, and children were casualties (Frumkin, 1951:162–164; Borrie, 1970:92, 138). As a consequence of World War II, the pyramid narrows on both sides, whereas the direct attrition from World War I is primarily on the male side, owing to battle deaths.

The size of the youngest cohorts is affected

by what happened to the cohorts of their great-grandparents and grandparents. Both World War I and World War II reduced the number of potential parents of the present generation of young children.

Section three fertility and mortality

In population literature, *fertility* refers to actual reproduction and *fecundity* to potential reproduction, that is, the biological maximum number of births. In modern urbanized and industrial nations, fertility is only a fraction of the possible number of births. Even in predominantly rural countries with high birthrates, fertility does not approach the biological maximum (Bongaarts, 1975).

MEASURING FERTILITY

A simple way to measure fertility is to compare the number of births with the size of the population. This *crude birthrate* (CBR)

Table 9:2 Crude birth and death rates, natural increase and years to double population, selected countries, 1974

Country	Rates per 1,000 of population			Years to double population[b]
	Births	Deaths	Natural increase[a]	
World	30	12	18	39
Australia	19	8	11	64
Brazil	37	9	28	26
Canada	15	8	7	95
China	24	10	14	50
France	15	10	5	175
West Germany	10	12	−2	—
India	38	16	22	32
Ireland	22	11	11	64
Italy	16	10	6	128
Japan	19	7	12	59
Mexico	44	9	35	20
New Zealand	19	8	11	64
Sri Lanka	28	8	20	35
USSR	18	9	9	69
United Kingdom	15	9	6	128
United States	15	9	6	128

[a] Natural increase is crude birthrate minus crude death rate.
[b] Estimated number of years to double the population, assuming that natural increase continues at the rate reported.

Source: Basic data courtesy of International Statistical Programs Center, U.S. Bureau of the Census; to be published in *World Population, 1975* (forthcoming).

is expressed as a rate per 1,000 of population, calculated as follows:

$$\frac{\text{births in a year}}{\text{midyear population}} \times 1,000 = \text{CBR}$$

Substituting 1975 figures for the United States in the formula:

$$\frac{3,149,000}{213,631,000} \times 1,000 = \text{CBR } 14.7$$

The crude birthrate is most commonly used in popular writing about population problems and in widely published statistics about various countries. (See Table 9:2.) It is therefore important to understand the limitations of the measure. The discussion of age and sex composition in Section Two indicates why the crude birthrate should be interpreted with caution. A given population could have an apparently low crude birthrate but be composed disproportionately of males, or it could be weighted with young or old persons. Under such circumstances, a low crude birthrate might turn out to be a high fertility rate by a more precise measure.

Whether a given birthrate should be interpreted as high or low depends on the number of women of childbearing age in the population. In fact, the current fertility of U. S. women, compared with earlier periods in American history or compared with the fertility of women in Asia or Latin America, is lower than is indicated by the crude birthrate because of the different age characteristics of these populations. A relatively large proportion of the U. S. population is composed of females of childbearing age, whereas at earlier stages in American demographic history (see Figure 9:3, p. 270) the population was highly concentrated in ages below puberty, as is true in developing countries.

Age-specific fertility Demographers have designed more refined measures based on what is called "the population at risk." In the case of fertility the population at risk consists of women of childbearing age — approximately 15 to 44 years old. Sometimes demographers calculate birthrates for married women of childbearing age or for women ever-married. Because a large fraction of births, especially in Western countries, occur to women in a fairly narrow age band, say 20 to 29, population analysts also calculate *age-specific birthrates*. The age-specific birthrate is obtained by dividing the number of births to mothers of a specific age group by the number of women of that age group and multiplying by 1,000. The rounded age-specific birthrates for U.S. and Canadian women for comparable years were as follows:

	United States		Canada	
Ages	**1955**	**1973**	**1959**	**1971**
15–19	90	60	60	40
20–24	242	121	234	135
25–29	190	114	227	142
30–34	116	56	148	77
35–39	59	22	87	34
40–44	16	5	28	1

Source: Statistical Abstract of the United States, 1975:Table 70; George, 1974:Table 2.4.

Births per 1,000 women in the age group 15 to 44 — the whole span of childbearing ages — is referred to as a *general fertility rate*. For the United States in 1973 this stood at 69, compared with 118 in 1955. "The Case of the G.E. Babies," p. 276, demonstrates the importance of using a measure of fertility appropriate to the age and sex characteristics of the specific population.

Net reproduction rate An important measure utilizing age-specific birthrates eliminates uncertainties of varying age and sex composition in measuring fertility: The *net reproduction rate* (NRR) describes the extent to which a given group of women are reproducing themselves with daughters. NRR is defined as the total number of female children born per woman to a cohort of women passing through the childbearing period. If

Figure 9:5
**Fertility ratio for the
United States, 1800–1975**

Children under 5 years of age
per 1,000 women 16–44

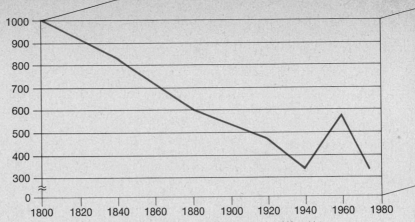

Source: Adapted from *Population Problems* by Warren S. Thompson (New York: McGraw-Hill, 1953), p. 175. Data added for 1960 and later.

NRR equals 1.0, it means that each woman on the average produces one daughter to "replace" herself. In fact, the average woman would have to produce slightly more than one daughter to compensate for women who die before reaching the end of their potential reproductives lives, and the NRR builds this correction into the calculations. NRR is used in Section Five in connection with a discussion of zero population growth.

In 1975 the NRR for the world was estimated at about 1.7. Figures for Canada, West Germany, Japan, the United Kingdom, and the United States in the early 1970s were 1.0 or lower. By contrast China stood at 1.4, India at 1.9, Sri Lanka at 2.1, and Mexico at a very high 2.8 (estimates courtesy International Statistical Programs Center, U.S. Bureau of the Census).

Fertility ratio Age-specific birthrates cannot be calculated without accurate age and birth registration data, which are lacking or unreliable in many countries. It is therefore desirable to have a simple measure that can be calculated directly from census data on age and sex without using birth records. To calculate the *fertility ratio*, the only data needed are the number of children under five years of age and the total number of women between ages 15 and 44. The formula for the fertility ratio (FR) is as follows:

$$\frac{\text{children under 5}}{\text{women ages 15–44}} \times 1,000 = FR$$

Substituting estimated U.S. resident figures for 1975:

$$\frac{15,896,000}{47,165,000} \times 1,000 = FR \ 337$$

Figure 9:5 depicts the fertility ratios of the United States since 1800. From about 1,000 in 1800 the fertility ratio declined to 342 in 1942, increased to 563 in 1960, and dropped to a low of 337 in 1975. The increase in fertility following World War II may have been a temporary deviation from a long-term declining trend, and the recent decline in fertility may be a reassertion of that trend.

Assuming equally good enumeration of the young and the mature, fertility ratios make it easy to compare the fertility of different countries or trends within the same country. However, if comparisons are made between areas of migration, it is necessary to know if children live with their mothers. When rural mothers migrate to the city but leave their children to be cared for in rural areas, as they do in many developing countries, the comparison of fertility ratios for country and city would be misleading. The rural fertility ratio would be too high because of the extra children, and the urban fertility ratio would be too low because of the extra mothers.

Fertility differentials Groups within a population reproduce at different rates, although

The case of the G.E. babies

On January 14, 1953, General Electric announced that it would award five shares of its common stock to any employee who had a baby on October 15 — the company's seventy-fifth anniversary. Originally the company said it expected about 13 winners. It arrived at this figure by applying a daily U.S. birthrate to its own 226,000 employees. This computation actually yielded a prediction of 15 births; but a G.E. public relations man thought it might be nice to trim the figure to 13, the number of original G.E. investors. The mathematics suffered from more than public relations, however. G.E. employees, since they include no children and no one over 65, are obviously a much more fertile group than the population as a whole. When this fact sank in, a company statistician made a new assault on the problem. He estimated that the size of an average G.E. family was 4.2. This meant that the total number of people in the G.E. families was close to a million. Applying the crude annual birthrate to this group and dividing by 365, he came up with a new prediction of 72 births on the big day.

As it turned out, there were not 13, 15, or 72 babies born to G.E. employees on October 15. There were 189.

Subtracting the company's highest expectation of 72 from 189 gives 117 "extra" babies. Where did G.E. go wrong? Well, among other things, the company made no allowance for the incentive provided by its own stock. This oversight, remarkable in a company that has had a lot to say about capitalist incentives, was apparently rectified by the employees. The latter not only enjoy having children, but, it appears, they rather enjoy the idea of becoming capitalists. And they seem to have known a good thing. In a generally declining stock market, G.E. common stock rose during the pregnant months from 69⅛ to 78⅞.

Source: The foregoing is reprinted from *Fortune*, January 1954. Reprinted by special permission of the editors. Copyright Time, Inc.

HOW G.E. WENT WRONG

They applied the wrong rate to the wrong group. They applied the crude birthrate to G.E. employees, assuming that only the employees would have babies. If the crude birthrate were used, it should have been applied to the whole population of G.E. families, not just the workers. They finally did this when they included families in their calculations of the crude birthrate. But the crude birthrate requires a cross section of the total population, and they did not have one. Even the whole population of G.E. families is not representative of the whole population of the United States. For instance, G.E. families contain an abnormally large proportion of individuals in the productive (and reproductive) years and few aged persons. The G.E. statistician also failed to consider (1) the section of the country, (2) the size of the communities where the employees lived, (3) their income, (4) their education, and (5) their race, all of which affect the birthrate.

COULD G.E. HAVE DONE BETTER?

They could have made a closer approximation to the true number by applying age-specific birthrates to the women of childbearing ages in G.E. employee families. This number could have been further refined by correcting for seasonal fluctuations in births. Corrections for the characteristics G.E. failed to consider would be far more difficult to make and, under the conditions noted below, pointless.

Because figures for the characteristics of the G.E. population are not available, a more refined estimate cannot be calculated. Probably, but not certainly (as Fortune assumed), the announcement of the award was an incentive. The influence of incentive could have been estimated and the quality of the prediction further improved by interviewing a sample of G.E. wives and female employees. Of course, G.E. could have eliminated the incentive entirely by announcing the award eight instead of nine months before October 15. The anniversary announcement was made about one week less than the 280 days of a full-term pregnancy, and a number of births may have been induced (hastened) by physicians.

There is at least one additional complication. Any estimate of a daily birthrate, even for a rather large population like the G.E. families, is subject to an additional source of error. Daily birthrates vary even more widely than seasonal or monthly birthrates. In 1950, U.S. registered crude birthrates ranged from 20.9 for the month of April to 25.5 for September. The shorter the time period, the greater the range of variation in birthrates (and the smaller the population, the greater the range of variation of birthrates). The chances of getting close to the mark on any particular day for any particular group are, therefore, not very good.

the amount of difference seems to be diminishing. Some fertility differentials that have been fairly well established for the United States are as follows:

1. Rural farm areas have higher fertility than rural nonfarm areas.
2. Rural areas have higher fertility than urban areas.
3. The larger the city, the lower the fertility; that is, size of city is inversely related to fertility.
4. In general, blue-collar families have more children than white-collar families.
5. Catholic fertility tends to be higher than Protestant fertility, but Catholic fertility is also declining, and the Catholic–Protestant difference is lessening.
6. Black fertility is higher than white fertility, but it follows white trends.

In the Western world in recent decades, lower income groups and those with relatively low education have shown higher birthrates than the middle and upper classes and the relatively well educated. (For further discussion of trends see Section Five.)

MORTALITY

The calculation of death rates is subject to the same problems as the calculation of fertility. The best-known death rate, the *crude death rate* (CDR), states the number of deaths per 1,000 of population and is calculated as follows:

$$\frac{\text{deaths in a year}}{\text{midyear population}} \times 1,000 = \text{CDR}$$

Substituting 1975 U.S. values:

$$\frac{1,910,000}{213,631,000} \times 1,000 = \text{CDR } 9.0$$

This was roughly half the average CDR of 17.2 recorded in 1900 in the death registration states. If the U.S. crude death rate of 9.0 is subtracted from the crude birthrate, calculated above as 14.7, the result is a natural increase of 5.7 per thousand of population in 1975.

Table 9:2 (see p. 273) reports estimates of

crude death rates for several countries. As in the measurement of fertility, it is necessary to relate crude death rates to age structure in order to make meaningful interpretations. The CDRs in the United States, Canada, and Europe are low in absolute terms despite the fact that the populations include relatively large numbers of old persons. The fairly high CDRs in India and China are in relative terms even higher because these countries have predominantly young populations. Even the low CDR in Sri Lanka is not as favorable as it seems because the age composition of that country is very young.

Age-specific death rates are expressed as the number of deaths per 1,000 persons of specified ages. In 1974 the U.S. age-specific death rates ranged from 0.4 for ages 5–14 to 165 for persons 85 years and over (U.S. HEW, 1975:Table D). The preoccupation of the public health profession with the mortality of certain groups has led to the development of special measures. Three of these are the following:

1. Infant mortality rate Considered to be an acid test of a country's welfare status, the infant mortality rate reports for 1,000 live births how many infants die in their first year. Infant mortality ranges from rates exceeding 100 or even 150 per thousand in some developing countries of Latin America, Africa, and Asia to values as low as 10 to 13 in Scandinavia and the Netherlands. The United States, Canada, Australia, New Zealand, and most countries of Western Europe have rates around 20 or a little lower. The U.S. rate in 1975 was 16; in 1950 it was 29.

2. Neonatal mortality rate As the infant mortality rate has been brought under control, more attention has been given to the large proportion of infant deaths occurring during the first month after birth, when nearly three-fourths of all infant mortality occurs (U.S. HEW, 1975:Table F). The neonatal mortality rate is an age-specific death rate for the age group, birth to one month. Such vital statistics tell medical scientists and practitioners where problems lie and

where their efforts might be expected to produce immediate benefits.

3. Maternal mortality rate This rate states the number of mothers dying per 10,000 live births. The current U.S. rate is under 3 maternal deaths per 10,000 live births, a decline from 58 in 1935. Maternal mortality statistics bear out the popular belief that, holding age constant, the first birth is relatively the most hazardous for the mother. By age, the risk of childbirth is greatest for older mothers, and the most favorable period for childbearing is the early twenties.

Life expectancy and life span The place and year of birth to a great extent govern life expectations. Being a recently born female in an advanced industrial country is the best assurance for longevity.

In the early 1970s the countries with low infant mortality rates were the same as those with the longest expectations of life at birth. (Infant survival of course figures into the expectation of life at birth.) Western Europe in general, but especially the Scandinavian countries, and Canada and the United States have favorable figures. Sweden scores high (75 years) as do Norway (74) and Japan (73). Expectations in Canada are 73 and in the United States 72. Mexico and Brazil (61) have made significant progress in improving life expectancy in recent years. China (53) and India (46) lag far behind.

There are real survival advantages to being a female in an industrialized country. Typical patterns are the following: Canada, 69 years for males v. 76 years for females; United States, 68 v. 75; England and Wales, 69 v. 75; Australia, 68 v. 75. But the situation is reversed in India: 47 years for males v. 46 for females (*Statistical Bulletin*, Metropolitan Life Insurance Company, Oct. 1974: 9–11 and Oct. 1975:5–9; U.S. HEW, May 30, 1975:8).

The chances of survival Figure 9:6 shows a dramatic improvement in the chances of survival between 1850 and 1969 but forecasts only a slight continued improvement.

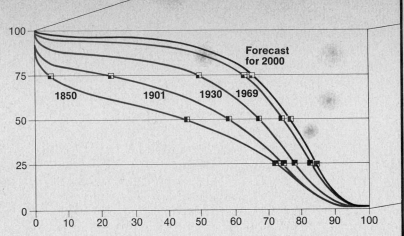

Figure 9:6 Survivors from
birth to successive ages,
United States, 1850–2000

Source: For 1850, 1901, and 1930, *Statistical Bulletin*, Metropolitan Life Insurance Company, March 1952. For 1969, compiled from *Monthly Vital Statistics Report, Annual Summary for the United States, 1969*, vol. 18, no. 13, October 21, 1970: Table 3. For 2000, compiled and computed from unpublished data supplied by the U.S. Bureau of the Census, National Population Estimates and Projections Branch.

Age at which survivors are reduced by

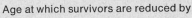 1/4   1/2   3/4

In 1850 only three-fourths of the newborn in the United States reached the age of five; in 1901 the same proportion reached age 24; and in 1969 the same proportion survived more than 60 years. The age to which one-half of the newborn survived increased from 45 years in 1850 to more than 74 years in 1969. Advances in medical care and in public health practice along with improvements in nutrition and the standard of living are responsible for the gains. Some consequences of these changes are the following:

1. Large numbers of persons live through their working years, thus contributing to the productivity of the nation.

2. A larger number of persons reach old age, thus creating a significant dependency problem and a need for institutional innovation.

3. The marked reduction in deaths of the young enables the population to sustain or increase its numbers with relatively fewer births.

4. "Premature" deaths have been reduced and may be reduced somewhat further, but there is no clear evidence that the upper age limits of human existence will be significantly raised. To assume so is to misinterpret improved average longevity as an extension in the limits of the human life span. Note in Figure 9:6 that the gain in survivors at the three-fourths point and beyond is not nearly so impressive as at one-half and one-fourth.

Indeed, beyond the one-half level, the 1969 curve is close to the curve forecast for 2000, suggesting relatively little anticipated improvement (cf. *Statistical Bulletin*, Metropolitan Life Insurance Company, Aug. 1965 and Sept. 1975). It would take a major breakthrough in control of the disorders of age to extend significantly the human life span. Whereas a further significant increase in the number of persons surviving to old age may not take place in the developed countries, continuing progress is still probable in modernizing societies where large numbers of premature deaths occur from causes susceptible to control by public health measures and improved nutrition.

Section four migration

INTERNATIONAL MIGRATION

The chief sources of data on international migrations are immigration records, which are usually better than emigration records. Intake and outflow statistics never match because most countries pay more attention to who comes in than to who goes out. The United States has not compiled information on emigrants since the late 1950s. Travelers can be classified as tourists, transients, temporary residents, returning residents, or permanent residents. They can be classified according to their dependency or occupational status. They are counted or ignored according to their means of travel by sea, land, or air and the distance traveled. Unfortunately for social science, there is less than unanimity in different countries about what constitutes a migrant, but careful assessment of available data can lead to worthwhile generalizations, at least about large-scale migration.

Push and pull The influences underlying migration are often classified as push and pull factors (Lee, 1966; Ravenstein, 1885; 1889). Among the push factors are unemployment and economic hardship, food shortages, racial or religious discrimination, political repression, deteriorated environments, and crowding. The pull factors include the availability of jobs, cheap land, political and religious freedom, and education. The push and pull factors work selectively on different potential migrants: Feelings of deprivation and discouragement about the home situation motivate individuals to seek ways to improve their lot elsewhere, but sentiment and habit inhibit people from moving. Furthermore, one person's push is another's pull. A bachelor may be pushed by burdensome school taxes from which he thinks he does not benefit. A family may be pulled by the good schools the taxes support. Most mass migration occurs when there is a perceptible difference in the levels of economic development or employment opportunity between countries. The same forces that affect between-country movements influence geographic mobility between regions of a country or between countryside and city.

MIGRATION HISTORY

The largest intercontinental migration before 1800 was the forced movement of slaves from Africa, mainly to the New World. Estimates of the number of Africans transported are unreliable and range between 10 and 20 million (Curtin, 1969). Most of them were carried across the Atlantic during the eighteenth century. (See Adaptation 34.) Migrants from Europe to the New World prior to 1800 were probably not half as numerous as slaves from Africa.

Beginning in the nineteenth century, a massive movement from Europe to the Western Hemisphere took place, and perhaps 75 million people entered the Americas after 1800. This spread of European peoples is the largest sustained intercontinental population movement in history. The opening of the New World came at an opportune time for Europe. Migration relieved population pressure during a period of explosive increase and provided employment for excess workers as well as new sources of food and other commodities. But countries under no population pressure also participated in colonization. For instance, small Portugal drained her population in attempting to people her far-flung colonies from Asia to Brazil.

Although the early data are hardly more than educated guesses, estimates of migration for the nineteenth and twentieth centuries merit closer interpretation. Table 9:3 presents the sources and destinations of migrants during the period of maximum intercontinental migration. All but 2 million of the 53 million intercontinental emigrants between 1846 and 1932 were from Europe, and more than three-quarters of all migrants originated in the British Isles, Italy, Austria-Hungary, Germany, and Spain.

The figures for the countries of destination exceed the reported emigration by about 6 million. This discrepancy is owing to the difference in time spans—111 years for immigration compared with 86 years for the emigration data—and to the fact already mentioned that immigration records are better than emigration records. Both statistical summaries are incomplete, but the broad outlines would not be significantly altered by incorporating later data. The chief donor countries were European, the chief receiving countries were in the Americas; the United States alone received three-fifths of the total.

It is not known how many transocean migrants were temporary residents. Carr-Saunders estimates that about 30 percent of those entering the United States between 1821 and 1924 and 47 percent of the migrants to Argentina returned to their homelands (1936:49). Some adjusted poorly or failed to find useful employment, but many immigrants never intended to remain. Others who planned to be sojourners became permanent settlers contrary to their expectations. Even temporary migrants play a significant part in developing new countries. Between 1901 and 1930 Australia had an immigration of 2,773,000 but a net gain (immigration minus emigration) of only 536,000. Yet the transient labor contributed to the nation's economic development.

The view from the village The perspective on migration tends to emphasize the receiving countries, but migrants can profoundly alter life in their native communities. Nowhere has the influence of change agents been more apparent than in southern Italy.

Just before the turn of the present century, the almost complete isolation of the village broke down. The principal factor involved was a great wave of emigration which reached its peak at the dawn of World War I. Hundreds of local young men traveled in search of work to several countries in North and South America. Those who went to the United States, where economic conditions were better, eventually turned out to be the agents of the most significant form of social change in the history of the village. Some eventually came back to Franza to find wives, then returned abroad to settle permanently and raise American children. Others worked a few years or even a few months and then returned, discouraged, to their home community. While abroad, however, most kept in more or less close contact with their home town—at least for the first few years. Many sent money and new ideas and customs from their place of work. Some who settled

abroad are still doing so today. Many who returned to settle in the village bought land and had a relatively comfortable new house built. In a few cases they sent their sons to the higher grades of school and their daughters to learn a trade at the seamstress shop. More important still, in their conception and emulation of a "better life," they became the symbols of a new style of life and the token of a new class. The ranks of the leisurely professionals expanded, and so did those of the less leisurely but still

Table 9:3
The great intercontinental migration

Country of origin[a]	Percent of emigrants
British Isles	34
Italy	19
Austria-Hungary	10
Germany	9
Spain	9
Scandinavia	5
Russia	4
Portugal	3
Other Europe	4
Non-Europe	3
Total emigrants	53,450,000

Country of destination[b]	Percent of immigrants
United States	58
Argentina	11
Canada and Newfoundland	9
Brazil	7
Other America	6
Australia and New Zealand	6
Other Non-America	3
Total immigrants	59,167,000

[a] Emigrants for the period 1846–1932.
[b] Immigrants to the United States, Canada, and Brazil for the period 1821–1932. Various dates apply for all other countries.

Source: Computed from Carr-Saunders, 1936:49.

respectable artisans and shopkeepers. The desire to improve one's condition now had a concrete and visible stimulus for the general population. In short, the emigrants ushered in the modern era (Lopreato, 1967:153–154).

Migration to the United States As the chief receiving country for intercontinental migrants, the United States has had an immigration marked by duration, size, and variety. It gained a population to match its resources, a work force for its farmlands and industries, and an internal consumer market large enough for economies of scale. Many migrants brought with them knowledge and skills that made lasting contributions to the New World.

Until World War II, immigration to the United States was disproportionately composed of males in their productive years. Although this was a gain for an agricultural economy turning industrial, the unbalanced sex ratio complicated the adjustment of the immigrants and placed strains upon the society. The successive introduction of migrants from many countries with different languages and cultures generated additional stress, but it also led to cosmopolitan diversity. The complicated ethnic composition of the United States crosscut the socioeconomic structure and inhibited the formation of self-conscious social classes.

U.S. immigration policy The peak number of foreign-born in the United States in a census year, over 14 million, was reported in 1930. Since then the ratio of foreign-born to the total population has declined. The 1970 census counted about 11 million for the 50 states, which was close to the number in 1900. From 1860 to 1920 foreign-born ranged between 13 and 15 percent of the population, but in 1970 they were only 5 percent of the total. The decline in the percentage of foreign-born is in part a consequence of a restrictive immigration policy. During the 1950s and 1960s, the reported rate of immigration recovered from the low levels of the 1930s and 1940s. Some of the increase was "statistical" rather than real in that immigration, especially from Mexico and Canada, was more accurately reported than in earlier periods. Nevertheless, immigrants from countries in the Western Hemisphere are not fully counted, and the entry of many thousands of persons into the United States, especially from Mexico, is "unauthorized" and does not appear in the immigration statistics.

Immigration after 1921 was limited by annual quotas depending on the population of foreign-born or foreign stock already living in the United States. Western Hemisphere countries were excepted. Although quotas for western and northern Europe often were not filled, quotas from southern and eastern Europe were quickly oversubscribed. The quota laws were exceedingly complex in their provisions, but the essential impact was nearly to eliminate immigrants from Asia, to restrain immigration from southern and eastern Europe, and to encourage immigration from western and northern Europe.

This stringent policy, which prevailed for a generation after 1921, was criticized as discriminatory, and it has been somewhat relaxed. The Immigration Act of 1965 continued the quota principle but allowed unfilled quotas to be used by "preference" immigrants whose national quotas had been exhausted. Preference immigrants are those who want to be reunited with their families and those who have desired skills and talents. The special provision for skilled persons has been criticized on the grounds that it encourages a brain drain from countries that have a greater need for the trained talent. Admission to the United States of many medical practitioners and scientists from Asian countries as well as from Europe gives force to the brain drain argument (Keely, 1974).

In 1968 the discriminatory or "selective" provisions were further relaxed. A limit of 170,000 is now set for immigrants who are natives of the Eastern Hemisphere, with a 20,000 maximum on natives of any one country. Provisions are also made for admitting immediate relatives of U.S. citizens, categories of special immigrants, Western Hemisphere natives, displaced persons, and refugees from Cuba. As a consequence of changed laws, in 1974 legal immigrants were chiefly from the West Indies, Mexico, the Philippines, and Korea. In 1960 the chief contributing countries were Mexico, West Germany, Canada, and Great Britain (*Statistical Abstract of the United States*, 1971: 87–94; and 1975:Table 161).

Emergent policy Until recently, in many countries opposition to immigration was largely due to ethnocentrism and prejudice directed at culturally different peoples, although concern about job competition played its part. Opposition has now begun to come from a different impulse and with different reasoning. Scepticism about the merits of indefinite growth of population and industrial production and concern about the depletion of resources have prompted questioning of immigration policy. Even in Australia, where since World War II there has been a strong consensus that immigration should be fostered and subsidized, a debate about continuing the policy has emerged.

Anti-immigration forces in the traditional receiving countries emphasize that added population imposes strains and costs even though it may provide labor and expand markets. If there are to be more people, there must be more schools, more roads, more public utilities, more housing—all of which must be paid for. These costs are a burden to the taxpayer and an ecological burden upon land and resources. Such considerations were not so important in largely rural economies, but advanced urban societies must make a much larger investment for each citizen to maintain a high standard of living.

The propensity to migrate Gallup surveys conducted in polling organizations in nine countries asked their samples the following questions: "If you were free to do so, would you like to go and settle in another country? What country?" Table 9:4 reports the percentage of respondents expressing a wish to migrate and their preferred countries of destination. Note the relatively large percentage who want to migrate and the reiteration of preferred countries. The United States appears in eight preferred destinations, Australia in four, and New Zealand in three.

Although the percentage of U.S. respondents wanting to migrate is the smallest of the countries listed, the 12 percent figure for 1971 is twice that in a 1959 poll and three times that recorded after World War II. In the United States an expressed wish to emigrate was highest among young adults with college training, one-third of whom responded affirmatively.

Whether the wish to migrate is a response to push or pull factors cannot be learned from these figures. The fact that young U.S. respondents had a higher reported preference to move has invited the conclusion that they were expressing the discontent of the young, but the fact is that young adults, discontented or not, are always overrepresented among free-choosing migrants.

A more useful interpretation flows from the list of target countries. They are for the most part countries in the forefront of industrial development, none is a communist state, and they include the richest nations. The increase in the number of countries with a high standard of living suggests that there may be an increasing flow among the industrial countries.

A related trend is the periodic movement of workers from the less developed nations of the Mediterranean to the highly industrialized labor-short countries of Western Europe. The temporary migration of workers across national boundaries in Europe has been a major feature of the postwar world. (See *TECHNOLOGY AND CIVILIZATION*, p. 520.)

Table 9:4 Percent who want to emigrate, and where

Nation	Percent who want to leave		Preferred destinations
	1971	1974	
Australia	–	13	Great Britain, New Zealand
Brazil[a]	17	–	United States, Italy
Canada	–	15	United States
Finland	19	–	Sweden, United States
Germany (West)	27	–	United States, Switzerland
Great Britain	41	39	New Zealand, Australia
Greece[a]	22	–	United States, Great Britain
Netherlands	16	–	Australia, New Zealand
Spain	–	13	West Germany, France
Sweden	18	–	Spain, United States
Switzerland	–	21	United States, Australia
Uruguay[a]	32	41	United States, Canada, West Germany
United States	12	10	Australia, Canada, Great Britain, Switzerland

[a] Metropolitan residents only. Not strictly comparable with national samples.

Source: Gallup Opinion Index, March 1971 and April 1974.

INTERNAL MIGRATION

Data on migration within the United States are gathered by the Current Population Survey annually, by the census every ten years, and by special surveys occasionally. The census compiles data on changed residence for the five previous years. The annual survey asks the following questions (*Current Population Reports*, P-20, No. 210, January 15, 1971):

"Was [the subject] living in this house March 1 a year ago?" If the answer was "no," the enumerator asked:

"Was [the subject] living in this same county on March 1 a year ago?"

If the answer was "no" again, the enumerator asked:

"What state (or foreign country) was [the subject] living in a year ago?"

The responses can be classified as follows:
1. Nonmovers

2. Persons who moved within the same county

3. Migrants between counties in the same state

4. Migrants between states

5. Persons abroad

Because of the question format, conclusions can be drawn about the number of movers but not about the total number of moves, because some people may have moved more than once. Furthermore, someone who moved away and then returned to the same address before March 1 would have been classified and counted as a nonmover although in fact she or he would have moved twice.

The percentage of the population changing residence in a year has shown little variation since such surveys began in 1948, ranging from 18 to 21 percent. Of the 199 million persons one year old and over living in the United States in March 1970, an estimated 161 million, or 81 percent, had been living at the same address a year earlier. (Babies under one year were excluded from the survey because they were not part of the population at risk.)

Of the 36.5 million who moved within the U.S. borders, 64 percent remained in the same county, 17 percent moved between counties in the same state, and 19 percent moved between states. In addition, 1.5 million persons, or nearly 1 percent of the population, were abroad at the beginning of the period.

Blacks have a higher total movement rate than whites, but they are more likely to move within counties. Whites have higher migration rates between counties and between states. White-collar workers with a college education have a higher rate of moves over long distances, a fact which suggests that they operate in a wider labor market.

A comparison of internal migration in Canada, England and Wales, Japan, and the United States found that .(1) in all four countries blue-collar workers had higher rates of short-distance moving; (2) except for Japan, white-collar workers had higher rates of movement over greater distances than blue-collar workers, and (3) in all four countries professional and technical workers had higher migration rates than other white-collar workers (Long, 1973:255 and Tab. 5).

Lifetime migration A few findings from a national survey that included data on residence histories can be briefly summarized (*Current Population Reports*, P-23, No. 25, March 8, 1968; Taeuber, Chiazze, and Haenszel, 1968:esp. pp. 93–96):

Two-thirds of the adult population lived at their current residence for ten years or more, and nearly 90 percent of the population reported a lifetime total of five residences or less. Frequent migrants manifest their migration tendencies early: Persons who do not make frequent moves before age 35 do not do so after age 35 either. Perhaps there are two kinds of people—those who

are easily detached from their homes and those who are not attracted by opportunities elsewhere.

For most persons, place of birth and current residence account for all, or nearly all, of their residential histories. More than one-fourth of the adult native population have always lived in the place where they were born, and many others live for a longer period in their birthplace than anywhere else. Close study of residential mobility thus challenges a popular image of Americans as rootless. The impression of a generally high rate of geographic mobility is conveyed by a visible minority of frequent movers.

Section five world population trends

Change in the population size of any country or locality is the consequence of four interacting forces—births and deaths, discussed in Section Three, and immigration and emigration, discussed in Section Four.

THE COMPONENTS OF POPULATION CHANGE

It is useful to show the determinants of population in a single graph. This is done in Figure 9:7, which presents the components of population change expressed as rates per 1,000 of population for the United States, including armed forces overseas, over the past generation. Births minus deaths gives the net natural increase (or decrease). Immigrants minus emigrants gives the net immigration (or emigration). Net natural increase plus net immigration gives the net growth. Separate curves for immigration and emigration are not presented but are summarized in the net immigration rate. The curve showing the net change due to natural causes is also left out because that curve looks very much like the net growth rate, which combines the results of all the contributing factors.

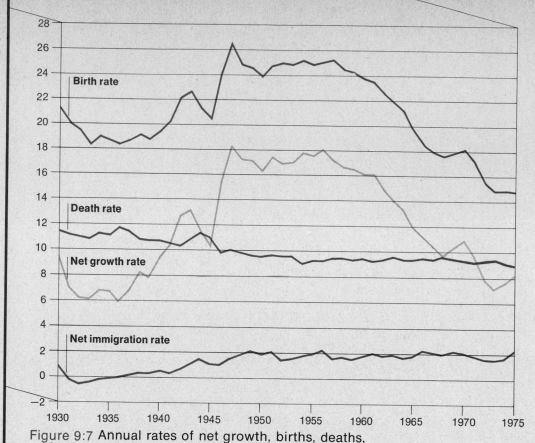

Figure 9:7 Annual rates of net growth, births, deaths, and net immigration, United States, 1935–1975

Source: U.S. Bureau of the Census, *Current Population Reports*, Series P–25, no. 545 April, 1975 and Series P–25 monthly estimates.

The figure shows that the net growth rate has largely been governed by changes in the birthrate, and the other components of change have played a much smaller part. The death rate has drifted down to a fairly stable level from which it fluctuates little except during major catastrophes. Net immigration has been more volatile and is understated, but it is a relatively small component. The birthrate, on the other hand, has fluctuated widely.

Each component of population change has a different relationship to the individual's freedom to act and to the agencies of social control. To a large extent, governments can regulate immigration and emigration through an elaborate network of passports, visas, and border checks. Although the regulations work imperfectly, there is little doubt that the total of worldwide migration is much less than it would be if international movements were uncontrolled.

The death rate can also be affected significantly. It can be lowered

. . . without individual or family intelligence, knowledge, or inclination. . . . Deaths can be greatly reduced by governmental control of water supply and waste disposal, by the control of noxious and infectious insects, bacteria, or animals which cause or transmit disease, and by governmental action in the improvement of transportation and the distribution of food to areas threatened with famine (Hertzler, 1956:45).

Unlike migration and death, however, the birthrate is to a greater extent determined by the personal decisions of hundreds of millions of people. In industrialized countries, modern birth control methods effectively place decisions in the hands of individuals, and when this is so they appear to choose smaller families. Countries concerned with ensuring military strength may oppose birth control. In developing countries, suitable contraceptive methods may not be readily available, and when available, their use may clash with traditional values that favor large families. Countries struggling to modernize thus find their objectives in collision with established tradition.

Governmental intervention
Governments, especially totalitarian ones, can intervene decisively for or against fertility. Nazi Germany and fascist Italy were instances of governments with pronatalist policies. China and more recently India have shown that they are prepared to use the same kind of administrative muscle to limit reproduction.

China In the first years of the communist regime (after 1949) the new Chinese leaders were unconcerned about overpopulation.

Marxist ideology attributed human misery not to excessive population growth but to the maldistribution of income and other supposed defects in the existing social order. Since under the new society the productivity of the people was supposed to increase more rapidly than their number, the Communist leaders were reluctant to admit that the size of China's population could, in any sense, present a problem. They held that the wealth of the country was in the hands of the workers and peasants—and the larger number of hands could only create greater wealth. As late as April 1952, the *People's Daily* denounced birth control as "a means of killing off the Chinese people without shedding blood" and as quite unnecessary since China was a country with vast unsettled lands and unexploited natural resources, and people were "the most precious of all categories of capital" (Orleans, 1972:39).

Soon afterward, birth control was encouraged, and since then policy has shifted with the political winds. The present policy is definitely to limit fertility by postponing marriage and disseminating intrauterine devices, pills, and other contraceptive materials.

The young people of China have been saturated with government policies that denigrate family, cultural traditions and domesticity, but uphold service and sacrifice for motherland and socialist conformity—conformity so traditional in Chinese society. Because early marriage and numerous children are un-Maoist and reactionary, there now seems to be a stigma attached to having large families. Given the climate of opinion wherein small families are part of a patriotic duty, the youth might well be willing to postpone marriage and to accept and practise some form of birth control within the marriage relationship.

Relevant here are the activities (or inactivities) of the Red Guards during the Cultural Revolution. Despite some speculation to the contrary, China is one of the few countries in which millions of teenaged boys and girls can travel, demonstrate and sleep under the same roof without affecting the country's birth rate. In pre-Communist China, premarital sexual intercourse was regarded as extremely reprehensible, and chastity held a high place on the list of womanly virtues. This is one of the traditions of old China accepted and nurtured by the Communists and the "liberation" of Chinese women does not extend to the endorsement of free love. All evidence suggests that China's youth continue to pursue the puritanical sexual mores of the past. There was truly little need for the slogan: "Making love is a mental disease which wastes time and energy" [It is estimated that the crude birth rate had been reduced from 43 per thousand before 1949 to about 32 by 1970 and that a rate of 20–25 by 1980] "would probably be doing extremely well" (Orleans, 1972:46, 49–50).

Mother India India's shift to a hard-line restrictive policy is only beginning to take shape. It had been clear for many years that ingrained tradition, especially in rural areas, would not quickly respond to gradual dissemination of birth control information and small-family propaganda. With a youthful age structure favorable to a very high crude birthrate, the explosive growth of the Indian population consumes any increase in economic productivity. Therefore the country is exposed to grave hazards in time of crop failure.

Experiments in the distribution of birth control measures, educational efforts, and sterilization campaigns had some local successes, but they were not of a scale to interrupt the pattern of rapid increase. Nevertheless, a country that considers itself a democracy is understandably reluctant to use compulsion. The new policy designed to break the large-family system by mass (and, if necessary, compulsory) sterilization as well as less drastic means sets three children as the limit in some states. But even if the measures are adopted throughout the country and strictly enforced, the population of India will continue to grow rapidly for a long time because of its youthful age composition and declining death rate. Furthermore, it is one thing to interrupt a traditional practice and temporarily to lessen its grip on the people. It is quite another matter to alter those traditions permanently and to substitute in their place small-family norms that could eventually lead to a stationary population. Present measures should be understood as a belated effort to moderate the rate of increase of a rapidly growing population, and there is no reason to think that the legislation already passed is the final word. Indeed there is good reason to expect that government intervention will become more coercive. The target of a three-child family may only be an intermediate objective.

FERTILITY TRENDS

As already stated, in the United States and other rich Western countries of high literacy, control of the timing and number of births is within the capacity of the great majority of people. To a considerable extent, in such countries fertility can be described as *self-controlled*.

In the nature of the case, self-controlled fertility may increase or decrease in response to historical events, economic changes, and shifting social values (Dorn, 1950:332). A sharp increase in first births, probably deferred fertility, produced the baby boom after World War II. The rate for first births peaked immediately after the war; the rate for second births remained high until the mid-1950s, when a steady decline appeared; and the declines in subsequent births seem to have occurred in sequence.

A large-scale survey conducted in 1965 in the United States found that desired family size averaged 2.7 children, but the families were actually having an average of about 3.1 children (Ryder and Westoff, 1971). This is about 0.4 child in excess of the number desired and almost 1.0 more than is required to achieve a stationary population. Whether an excess of 0.4 (or 1.0) is a near miss or a large error is a matter of statistical interpretation.

Keeping the number down to about 3.1 when the collective goal is 2.7 means that in the aggregate, families are about 90 percent of the way to matching desires with performance. On a scale which runs from zero to seven, the difference between 2.7 and 3.1 is rather small in historical perspective. . . . For couples wanting two children, three is a 50 percent error rate, although a statistician might view three as a major reduction from a potential six or seven (Freedman, 1971:89). [In the nineteenth century, families with six or seven children were not unusual.]

A second survey covering the period 1966–1970 found that desired fertility was 2.4, projected completed fertility 2.9, and unwanted births 0.45 (Westoff and Ryder, in press; c.f., Ryder and Westoff, 1972).

Caution The foregoing figures are rounded from estimates that assume a continuation of fertility rates then current for women in the survey still of child-bearing age. The actual completed fertility of all the women in the survey and of the population of American women from which the sample was drawn could end up higher or lower than 2.9 births. Although short-run trend data and sample survey evidence should always be considered with care, the change reported between the two surveys must be regarded as further confirmation of observations from vital statistics studies.

Shrinking differentials In the United States the period since 1965 is notable both for a sharp decline in fertility and for narrowing differences between social and economic groups (Ryder, 1973; for observations on Canada, see Long, 1970; Henripin and Légaré, 1971). Differentials between whites and blacks and between Catholics and non-Catholics in number of births wanted and in actual births has diminished. This generalization also holds for high versus low socio-economic groups in their fertility desired and achieved.

WORLD POPULATION GROWTH

The population of the world increased sevenfold in 325 years. Improvements in production and transportation, advances in agriculture and medicine, and the effects of the Industrial Revolution have combined to reduce death rates and to prolong life and in some places to raise the standard of living. In 1650 the world population was 500 million. Two centuries later the population had more than doubled; by 1850 the total was about 1.25 billion (Carr-Saunders, 1936:42). In the last century it has again more than doubled: The 1975 estimate was over 4 billion. (See Figure 9:8, p. 292.)

Demographic transition The sequence of demographic changes that accompanied the industrial and urban development of Europe have been summarized in the idea of demographic transition. There are three stages.

Stage one is the hypothetical condition that has characterized almost the entire span of human existence: a high death rate, especially high infant mortality, balanced by a high birthrate.

Stage two was a period of explosive growth which began in Europe about the middle of the seventeenth century. The death rate gradually declined, but the birthrate remained high. It should be noted that European birthrates before the demographic transition were not as high as the rates in most contemporary developing countries. For example, the birthrate in Britain in the early 1800s is estimated at less than 35 per thousand, but in such countries as Tanzania and Iran it is over 45, and in some countries it may be over 50 per thousand (Teitelbaum, 1975).

Stage three occurs when fertility control takes effect. The birthrate declines, the age

March, 1976: Chicago's Museum of Science and Industry pays its respects to the world population problem.

composition changes, and there is a trend toward a balance of births and deaths.

The demographic transition is thus a model based on European experience. A complete demographic transition, in the sense that the birthrate is ultimately reduced to a level close to the death rate, has only been approached in technologically advanced, literate, essentially modern societies.[1] Not only do developing countries start with higher birthrates, their death rates have been brought down with great rapidity largely by measures introduced from industrial countries.

Prospects for control Some demographers claim that effective population control is within reach [e.g., Bogue (1967), confidently, and Kirk (1971), with more reservations], but it may be too soon for such claims. Detailed and rigorous evidence on desired family size comparable to the U.S., Canadian, and European fertility studies is not available for developing countries, where growth rates are very high. But the steps (or obstacles) to controlled fertility are the same in all societies:

1. The desire for small families
2. The availability of effective (traditional or innovative) means of contraception
3. Awareness of the availability of the methods
4. Acceptance of the methods as a way to achieve small families

All of the steps must occur if fertility is to be brought under control in developing countries as has been done in some developed countries.

Although it is reasonable to contemplate the prospect of stationary populations in the advanced countries of North America, Western Europe, and Japan, the possibility is remote in developing countries. Stationary populations are still not in view even for

[1] In Japan a modified form of the demographic transition occurred around 1920 when both birth and death rates began to decline at about the same time without the lag in the birthrate observed in Europe and North America (Muramatsu, 1971:1).

Taiwan, South Korea, and Hong Kong, which have been successful in reducing fertility rates to relatively moderate levels. In such countries rising education and standards of living began to reduce fertility even before family planning programs were introduced. Family planning accelerated trends already under way. But from the standpoint of population control it is claimed that family planning has not led to a quick decline in fertility "in a population still mired in illiteracy and poverty and characterized by traditional behavior" (Hauser, 1971:453).

Sri Lanka is far from the most illiterate and poorest of nations, but it is a society with strong traditions that foster high fertility. In 1871 the population was 2.4 million. In the 60 years to 1931, it more than doubled to 5.3 million, and at the census of 1963 it had doubled again (*Statistical Abstract of Ceylon* [Sri Lanka] 1969:22–24). By the mid-1970s it had reached 14 million. Adaptation 22 discusses some of the factors influencing Sri Lanka's high fertility: the family pattern, the value placed upon relations between the sexes and upon women and children, the location of authority in the family and community, and the relationship between the family and larger kin and locality groups. The analysis shows the limitations of biological and technical approaches to the restriction of population growth. To be successful, the techniques of population control must be designed and administered so that they take into account cultural differences and where possible build upon traditional practices of birth limitation.

ZERO POPULATION GROWTH

Because the term *zero population growth* (ZPG) has become a slogan for proponents of population control, it is important to be clear about its meaning. In popular discussion it is often implied that a stationary population would be achieved as soon as all families on the average had about two children. However, we have seen that population growth depends on age and sex composition as well as on birth and death rates. For that reason, a population with a large proportion of women of childbearing age, even with a fairly low net reproduction rate, could produce a high crude birthrate and continued population growth for many years. (See p. 274.)

The arithmetic of ZPG If in the United States NRR = 1 in the years 1980–1985, the population would continue to grow until about the year 2030 because of the age composition of the country. In other words, ZPG in the sense of a stationary population would not occur for 45 to 50 years after the birthrate reached a level when the cohort of mothers would just replace themselves with daughters. To achieve a stationary population with a shorter time lag would require an NRR of less than one.

The relationship between the NRR and a stationary population is shown in two graphic examples. In Figure 9:9 the populations of the United States and China are pro-

Education for infertility: The woman

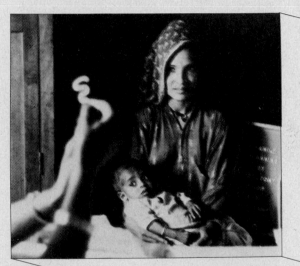

Education for infertility: The men

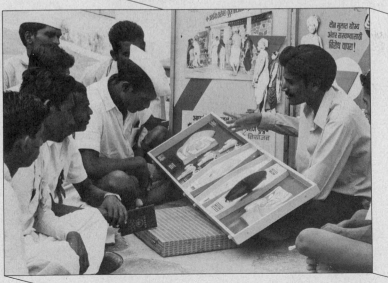

jected according to four different sets of assumptions, labeled Series A, B, C, and D. Series A assumes that the fertility rates will remain constant at present levels. Series B assumes that fertility will decline until it reaches an equivalent of NRR = 1 around 1980–1985. Series C assumes that NRR = 1 around 1990–1995, and Series D that NRR = 1 about 2000–2005. The dates when NRR = 1 are marked on the curves as BX, CX, and DX.

The dates when the populations would become stationary according to the different assumptions are shown as BY, CY, and DY. For the United States, BY is reached in 2030 with a stationary population of 271 million, CY in 2035 with a population of 279 million, and DY in 2055 with a population of 288 million. These statistical projections are not forecasts of future population sizes because they cannot take into account possible changes in age-specific mortality rates, migration, or natural disasters. Nevertheless

they are realistic in that they demonstrate the time lag between a given change in fertility behavior and the probabilities of a stationary population.

The information on China is presented for comparison and to suggest the enormous increase in absolute numbers when a replacement level of fertility is postponed for various lengths of time. Perhaps the best way to comprehend the magnitudes of the populations involved in these projections is to take the population of the world as the unit of interpretation. The world's population in the mid-1970s was around 4 billion, and the population of China was more than 800 million, or about 20 percent of the world total. If China should continue to grow at the constant rate represented by curve A, it would reach 4 billion, the magnitude of the world's 1975 population, in about 50 years. For a comparison, in 100 years the United States at constant fertility (curve A) would equal

Figure 9:8 World population growth, 1800–1970 (projected to 2000)

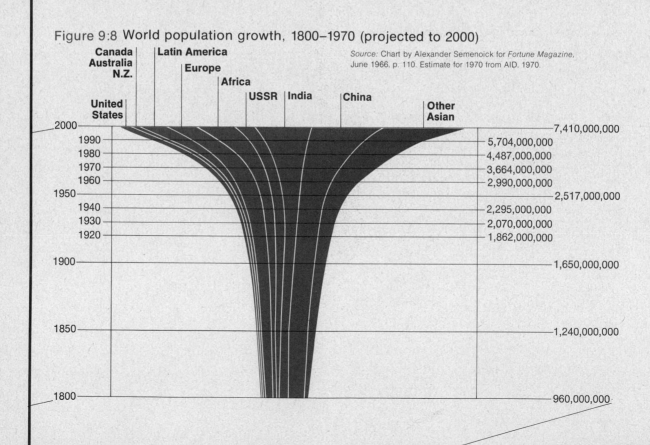

Source: Chart by Alexander Semenoick for *Fortune Magazine,* June 1966, p. 110. Estimate for 1970 from AID, 1970.

Figure 9:9
Projected population under
varying fertility assumptions,
1970–2070

Source: Bureau of the Census, 1971: Table 2.

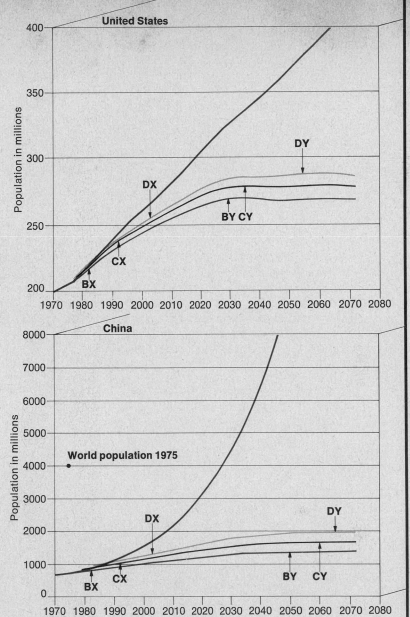

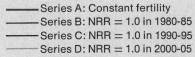

Series A: Constant fertility
Series B: NRR = 1.0 in 1980-85
Series C: NRR = 1.0 in 1990-95
Series D: NRR = 1.0 in 2000-05

400 million, or half the present population of China. China, however, is not the most rapidly growing large country. India has a smaller population than China, but it has a higher rate of natural increase. Consequently, at constant fertility India would reach the 1975 world size in roughly 50 years, about the same time as China, and would surpass China to become the world's largest population soon after. Even Indonesia, which has somewhat over half the population of the United States, would exceed 4 billion in less than a century at constant fertility and would reach the current size of China in half that time. Mexico at constant fertility would equal the present population of the United States in 35 to 40 years and of China in about 75 years.

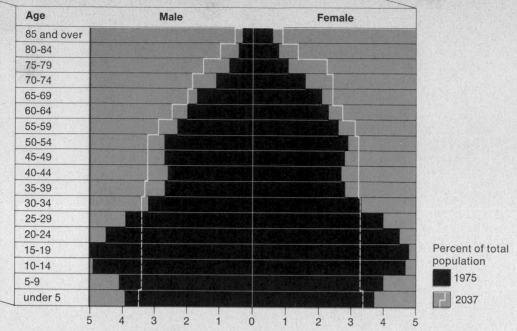

Figure 9:10 Age and sex of 1975 population and stationary population (2037), United States

Source: *Current Population Reports*, Series P–25, no. 448, August 6, 1970. Data for 1975 added.

Such statistical comparisons dramatize the decision-making task of political leaders and especially of those in developing countries who fear that proposals to control population are made merely for the benefit and convenience of rich countries (Stycos, 1968). Emigration can play only a minor role in relieving population pressure. Even if the less densely populated parts of the world, such as the USSR, North America, and Australia, were willing to lower their standard of living to accommodate many immigrants from countries with burgeoning populations, it would give only transitory relief. Clearly the population problem must be solved within the confines of all but the smallest countries.

Living in a stationary population The consequences of ZPG are viewed with concern by people who fear that with a declining proportion of youth the yeast would go out of society. A static population, they reason, would resist innovation and experiment,

would have a large dependency burden, and would cause the economy to lose the impulse of continued growth. The differences in the shapes of the 1975 population and a stationary population for the United States are shown in Figure 9:10. The latter approximates the stationary model of a population with a long expectancy of life.

A stationary population would have a higher average age, about 37 years, compared with about 29 years in 1975. It would also have a larger percentage of retired people; perhaps 16 percent of the population would be over 64, compared with about 10 percent in 1975. But the dependency ratio would be reduced by the smaller proportion of population of school age. In 1975 approximately 25 percent of the population was under 15 years of age, or (to take an older cutting point) about 35 percent was under 20 years of age. The stationary population described in the figure would have about 20 percent under 15 years of age, or about 27 percent under 20 years. Counting all persons under age 15 and over 64, the dependency ratio in 1975 was 55, or just about that for a stationary population. However, taking age 65 as an arbitrary date for dependency may not be realistic in an era of improved living conditions and better average health. It is reasonable to expect that the span of working life as well as of life expectancy might increase. Thus a stationary population would have a higher productive potential.

A stationary population with a stable age composition might have more open options and more opportunity for long-term planning because fewer decisions would be forced upon it by continuous growth in numbers. With a stationary population, housing and civic facilities could catch up with the backlog of demand from the era of incessant growth, and more of the resources of the society could be devoted to improving the quality of residences and public facilities rather than increasing their quantity. Obviously it would be a long time before housing and other institutional facilities became adjusted to the new population structure (Enke, 1973).

Although the demographic factor would become predictable, the development of new tastes and life-styles would be no more predictable. Indeed, a society less constrained by demographic forces and with a smaller dependency task might be more congenial to innovative personal styles. Such conjectures are as plausible as the assumption that an economy that does not have an ever-expanding population will become moribund.

Adaptation 22 Ryan: Fertility and family in Sri Lanka

The populations in many Asian areas are rapidly increasing, but there is no assurance that birth limitation will be practiced as it has been in Western Europe and North America. This adaptation examines social and cultural factors that may contribute to maintaining high birth rates in Sri Lanka, formerly called Ceylon.

It cannot be assumed that Sri Lanka will follow the Western pattern of persistent diffusion of the small-family system. It is overwhelmingly a rural country, and the difference between city and village is much greater than in most Western nations. It is unrealistic to expect the rapid diffusion of new values and new techniques from the urban to the rural population. A revolutionary development is even less likely to appear spontaneously in the countryside. Controlled fertility is typically associated with individualistic and romantic marital unions. No such social climate exists in Sri Lanka, nor is it likely soon to exist. If the small-family pattern and birth limitation are to be introduced, they must be imposed upon a society now tied to large-family values.

THE MARRIAGE PATTERN

In Sri Lanka marriage is a calculated and rational extension of kinship; as a relation between two persons dominated by thoughts of each other, it is immoral and atypical. The individual is subordinated to the family. Evidence of social change may be found in the frequency of romantic suicides, which are protests against the control of the kin group, but these also show the continuing power of community and kin. The individual has a lifelong involvement with his relatives, and this is true even among urban sophisticates.

The old system is sacred, and the accepted scope of individualism simply does not provide for personal preferences in marriage. Previous acquaintance is usually of little concern to the parties involved, and there is virtually no comprehension of the concept of romance and seldom even a hint of rebellion. There is a potent and intricate interdependence of individual and kin. The arranged match is crucial, and romantic marriage is abhorrent and socially disorganizing. Rigid cri-

Source: Abridged and adapted from "Institutional Factors in Sinhalese Fertility" by Bryce Ryan. *The Milbank Memorial Fund Quarterly 30* (October 1952), 359–381. Published in this form by permission of Bryce Ryan and The Milbank Memorial Fund.

teria are applied in spouse selection: (1) membership in the same ethnic community, e.g., Sinhalese; (2) identity of caste; (3) bride younger than groom; (4) bride a virgin; (5) horoscopes of each closely matched. In addition, the dowry power of the girl's people, security and occupational prestige of the boy, and the status of family lines are considered in matchmaking.

A number of factors support familism and are inconsistent with the romantic ideal. The greatest moral duty of a father is a good marriage for his daughter, and this duty falls on a son at the father's death. These are responsibilities to blood kin, fully as much as to the daughter. Desire for family prestige may press the father or brother toward almost impossible financial sacrifices.

In marriage the individual is both imprisoned and sheltered by his kinship group. The son helps with his sister's dowry and in so doing protects his own status, which in turn is rewarded in dowry. A challenge to the arranged match is a challenge to the prerogatives of kin. The lineal family as a status-bearing entity in the community has its most critical time in the period approaching marriage. Every relative has his funds or status at stake. Romantic marriage is not consistent with the rigid dictates of caste, prestige, and house honor. It threatens not merely the father's rightful authority but the honor of the generations, past and future, of which the father is the legitimate guardian. Marriage by choice has no claim upon kin for dowry, no claim for help in harvest, and no claim for cooperation in marrying some ultimate daughter of the union. Although the infrequent romantic marriages in villages do not necessarily meet with ostracism if caste propriety and other rigid matters have been observed, there is partial or complete estrangement from kinfolk. In the closely knit affairs of the village, life for such a couple may be far from pleasant.

The requirement of astrological suitability deserves special mention. Almost universally the Sinhalese, young and old, educated and uneducated, believe that suitably matched mates are perfectly revealed in the horoscopes.

DOMINANCE OF THE MALE

The Sinhalese family is usually patrilineal, descent following the male line, and patrilocal in the limited sense that the couple settles in the husband's village. A new marital unit is dominated by the husband's kin through their very proximity. The father-husband is the social authority. Except toward small children, he avoids overt expressions of affection and gives much evidence of his dignity and prerogatives. This patriarchalism is not harsh; few relations among Sinhalese are that.

From early childhood the male is schooled in his superiority. A family of many males is a "fortunate one"; one of many daughters is "burdened." To the father's position services are due and deference is paid. There is a deeply seated belief that in marriage the wife must give complete loyalty and subservience to her husband. He stands in the place of her father as well as in the role of her husband. On the other hand, it is generally agreed that the husband owes his first allegiance to his own parents rather than to his wife. Rarely a rigid disciplinarian, the father is still *master* in a society where that concept has a living feudal history.

MARRIAGE AND FERTILITY

The village studied is in the Low Country, six miles from a market town. The mean age at marriage for village women (based on a one-fourth sample of existing marital units) was 21.9 years, and for men, 28.4 years.[2] There is some reason to believe that the age of women at marriage is rising, but there is no evidence of such a change among men. It is probable that the relatively high ages at marriage are influenced by the difficulties of dowry. About one-fourth of the marriages had no dowry, owing to poverty, a few romantic marriages, and other reasons. The proportion of dowryless matches has not changed with passing years. Marriages by personal choice but with parental approval account for 13 percent of marriages and show no increase. Only 4 percent claim to have married in spite of their parents' wishes. More than 80 percent of all marriages and more than two-thirds of recent marriages were arranged by the parents. Most marriages conform closely to traditional patterns.

Children are viewed by all as products of destiny. When women say "All children are a blessing," they are expressing the mores of the com-

[2] The mean age at marriage for women in the United States is about the same, and for men it is considerably younger. Compare the trends in age at marriage for this village with those for the whole country, as reported on p. 298.

munity; but for a substantial proportion of mothers, it might be said that *many* children are *imposed* as a blessing. Many mothers accept only reluctantly a pattern of childbearing that approaches fecundity, that is, the biological limit. Women do not face continuous pregnancies without misgivings, although most accept them with fatalistic composure.

ATTITUDES TOWARD BIRTH CONTROL

To wish that destiny might be kind is one matter; to seek actively the prevention of birth is another. In response to this suggestion a woman said: "If a dead 'soul' wishes to be born into your family, it would be a terrible sin to prevent its birth. We will pay for such acts in our next life. Children that are to be born to you must be allowed to be born. That is how life goes on. We cannot and should not prevent this." Here speaks the voice of the community, echoed by men and women alike. A rebirth in the great cycle must not be denied to any being. (The belief in reincarnation is a basic tenet of Sinhalese culture.) A former prime minister supported this village interpretation, a position not held, however, by several other prominent Buddhist political leaders. In spite of verbal conformity by the villagers, the interviewers agree that a majority of the mothers would welcome some morally suitable relief from the imminent arrival of the next baby. They also agree that the fathers see no cause for worry and have nothing ill to say of the most fertile marriage.

The attitudes of men toward family size and birth control are not modified by the burden of childbearing and child care. Men sincerely want large families, and especially many sons: "Children are prosperity." Not once in the extensive discussions with village men was there a mention of the difficulties of child care. The personal trials and burdens of parenthood are almost wholly the mother's. Father is proud parent toward his neighbors, a caresser of infants in the home, and contributor to his kin status through well-calculated marriages. He is served by his household, and the larger his small kingdom, the greater his dignity and glory. Through children, especially sons, he gains status as a man and is assured that his responsibilities will be inherited by others and that he himself will have security in his old age. The wife has no avenue of escape from the increasing demands upon her made by the growing family. The father works no harder to provide for a large family. He merely lives less well until the youth begin earning.

The husband's sexual authority is the most important single element for an understanding of fertility. Time and again the word *property* appears describing the wife, and frequent allusions are made to the transfer of paternal authority from the wife's father to the husband. The woman's lot is cast with an unknown male prepared for the role of patriarch. Economic dependence supports this pattern. Once a woman is given in marriage, she is expected to stick to her husband regardless of how trying married life with him may be. Her parents cannot afford to maintain grandchildren or meet the expense of a second marriage.

Only with respect to age at marriage is the Sinhalese pattern inconsistent with high reproductivity. (In the more remote districts, however, girls are frequently married soon after puberty.) For the most part family structure and mores are consistent with high reproduction, and the economic cost of children is slight. The village girl fears spinsterhood or being a childless wife; infertility is treated with contempt. However, the stigma of infertility is relieved with the birth of even a single child, and the difficulties of childbearing and child care increase in at least arithmetical ratio to numbers. With these difficulties the husband has no part and rarely much concern, for they are the natural functions of his wife and her god-given means of pleasing him. The husband is also motivated by something the wife can never fully share. Children are contributions to *his* family, not to hers; the wife is an agent for the husband's kin; he is of its very substance. To her, children may be assets of the conjugal union, but to him they are also assets in the community to which his first loyalties belong.

Undoubtedly a substantial minority of village women are today trying to reduce the frequency of pregnancies. Lack of technical knowledge is perhaps no greater a handicap than the unsympathetic attitudes of dominant males. It seems fair to conclude that *if* women were provided with simple contraceptive techniques which were made consistent with moral precepts, and *if* the techniques were used without their husbands' knowlege, the more youthful mothers of several children would use them. The "moral rationalization" of contraception should present no great difficulties, for the Buddhist position is not doctrinaire, and the people are skilled in adapting and compromising even rigid precepts. However, the secret use of contraceptive devices is improbable. The combined effects of male sex dominance and the distinctive male rewards for numerous progeny may retard a small-family movement more than might be expected from Western experience.

COMMENTARY

Since this research was done, the crude death rate in Sri Lanka has declined to a low eight per thousand. The birth rate has also declined, although it probably did not meet the government target of 25 per thousand set for 1975. Reduction in the birth rate was achieved in part by a concerted effort in family planning in which the Sri Lanka government, the Swedish international development authority, various agencies of the United Nations and UNESCO, and private foundations have all been involved. Urban, middle-class people have been more responsive than the less educated and culturally conservative populations. Christians and Moslems, who make up only 15 percent of the population, have been more receptive than the rural Buddhist and Hindu majority (Statistical Abstract of Ceylon, 1969:33).

In some respects the age structure of the country is now conducive to a high birth rate (AID, 1970:151–153). A countervailing effect, however, is an imbalance in the sex ratio at marriageable ages leading to the postponement of marriage or spinsterhood for many women. So long as this so-called marriage squeeze lasts, it will be a significant brake on the birth rate. Currently a high rate of unemployment for young men complicates and reinforces the marriage squeeze. The average age at marriage increased from 25 to 28 for males and from 18 to 24 for females between 1900 and 1971. Such delays postpone births and reduce the total fertility rate. The percentage of women who had ever married also declined. In 1901, 52 percent of women between the ages of 15 and 19 had ever been married; by 1971 the figure was only 10 percent. For ages 20 to 24 the decline was from 70 percent in 1901 to 47 percent in 1971, and for ages 25 to 29, the decline was from 85 to 75 percent (Fernando, 1975). These demographic forces relieve some of the pressure on the planners, but at a personal cost to Sri Lanka men and women, many of whom will not enjoy the rewards of family life.

In the longer run, the control of Sri Lanka population growth will be determined by a complex set of social and demographic factors. This adaptation describes the underlying social forces at the village level that must be taken into account by government and planning agencies concerned with reducing the growth rate of the country. The local problems described, although not the specific Sinhalese values and customs, confront many countries struggling with rapidly increasing populations.

References

AID (Agency for International Development)
1970 Population Program Assistance. Aid to developing countries by the United States, other nations, international and private agencies. Washington, D.C.

Bogue, Donald J.
1967 "The end of the population explosion." Public Interest, No. 7 (Spring):11–20.

Bongaarts, John
1975 "Why high birth rates are so low." Population and Development Review 1 (December):289–296.

Borrie, W. D.
1970 The Growth and Control of World Population. London: Weidenfeld and Nicolson.

Carr-Saunders, A. M.
1936 World Population. Oxford: Clarendon.

Chaiklin, Harris
1966 "Motivating the poor." Pp. 3–13 in Benjamin Schlesinger, Poverty in Canada and the United States: Overview and Annotated Bibliography. Toronto: University of Toronto Press.

Chaiklin, Harris and Verl S. Lewis
1964 A Census Tract Analysis of Crime in Baltimore City. Baltimore: University of Maryland School of Social Work.

Curtin, Philip D.
1969 The Atlantic Slave Trade: A Census. Madison: University of Wisconsin Press.

Dorn, Harold F.
1950 "Pitfalls in population forecasts and projections." Journal of the American Statistical Association 45 (September): 311–334.

Enke, Stephen
1973 "The impact of population growth on the national economy." Pp. 97–108 in Westoff et al., 1973.

Fernando, Dallas F. S.
1975 "Changing nuptiality patterns in Sri Lanka, 1901–1971." Population Studies 29 (July):179–189.

Freedman, Ronald
1971 "U.S. birth trends analyzed." Perspectives 3 (October): 88–90. (Review of Ryder and Westoff, 1971.)

Frumkin, Gregory
1951 Population Changes in Europe Since 1939. London: Allen & Unwin.

George, M. V.
1974 Chapter 2. Pp. 9–29 in Leroy O. Stone and Andrew J.
Siggner (eds.), The Population of Canada. Ottawa: Statistics
Canada.

Hauser, Philip M.
1971 "World population: retrospect and prospect." Pp. 103–122
in National Academy of Sciences, Rapid Population Growth:
Consequences and Policy Implications. Baltimore: Johns Hopkins Press.

Henripin, Jacques and Jacques Légaré
1971 "Recent trends in Canadian fertility." Canadian Review of
Sociology and Anthropology 8 (May):106–118.

Hertzler, Joyce O.
1956 The Crisis in World Population. Lincoln: University of
Nebraska Press.

Keely, Charles B.
1974 "Immigration composition and population policy." Science 184 (August 16):587–593.

Kirk, Dudley
1971 "A new demographic transition?" Pp. 123–147 in National
Academy of Sciences, Rapid Population Growth: Consequences
and Policy Implications. Baltimore: Johns Hopkins Press.

Kuroda, Toshio
1973 Japan's Changing Population Structure. Japan: Ministry of
Foreign Affairs.

Lee, Everett S.
1966 "A theory of migration." Demography 3(1):47–57.

Long, Larry H.
1970 "Fertility patterns among religious groups in Canada."
Demography 7 (May):135–149.
1973 "Migration differentials by education and occupation:
trends and variations." Demography 10 (May):243–258.

Lopreato, Joseph
1967 Peasants No More: Social Class and Social Change in an
Underdeveloped Society. San Francisco: Chandler.

Macleod, Betty
1974 "History and background of population activities in Canada." Canadian Studies in Population 1:147–152.

Muramatsu, Minoru
1971 "Japan." Country Profiles. New York: Population Council.

Norland (Yam), Joseph
1974 "Population composition: age and sex." Pp. 31–39 in
Leroy O. Stone and Andrew J. Siggner (eds.), The Population of
Canada. Ottawa: Statistics of Canada.

Notestein, Frank W.
1951 "Population." Scientific American 185, 3(September):30.

Orleans, Leo A.
1972 Every Fifth Child: The Population of China. London: Eyre
Methuen.

Population Association of America
1971 Directory of Population Study Centers. Washington, D.C.

Ravenstein, E. G.
1885 "The laws of migration." Journal of the Royal Statistical
Society 48, Part 2 (June):167–227.
1889 "The laws of migration." Journal of the Royal Statistical
Society 52 (June):241–301.

Riley, Matilda White and Anne Foner
1968 Aging and Society. Vol. 1. An Inventory of Research Findings. New York: Russell Sage.

Ryder, Norman B.
1973 "Recent trends and group differences in fertility." Pp.
57–68 in Westoff et al., 1973.

Ryder, Norman B. and Charles F. Westoff
1971 Reproduction in the United States, 1965. Princeton, N. J.:
Princeton University Press.
1972 "Wanted and unwanted fertility in the United States,
1965–1970." Pp. 467–487 in Westoff and Parke, 1972.

Sharp, Harry and Leo F. Schnore
1971 "Public response to the 1970 census: a Wisconsin survey."
Demography 8 (August):297–305.

Stycos, J. Mayone
1968 "American goals and family planning." Pp. 19–44 in
Franklin T. Brayer (ed.), World Population and U.S. Government Policy and Programs. Washington, D.C.: Georgetown University Press.

Taeuber, Conrad and Morris H. Hansen
1964 "A preliminary evaluation of the 1960 census of population and housing." Demography 1:1–14.

Taeuber, Karl E., Leonard Chiazze, Jr., and William Haenszel
1968 Migration in the United States: An Analysis of Residence
Histories. Public Health Monograph No. 77. Washington, D.C.:
GPO.

Teitelbaum, Michael S.
1975 "Population theory and the LDCs." Science 188 (May 2):
420–425.

Thompson, Warren S.
1953 Population Problems. New York: McGraw-Hill.

U.S. Bureau of the Census
1960 "The post-enumeration survey: 1950." Technical Paper
No. 4. Washington, D.C.: GPO.
1970 Census Users' Guide. Washington, D.C.: GPO.
1971 The Two-Child Family and Population Growth: An International View. Washington, D.C.: GPO.

U.S. HEW (Department of Health, Education and Welfare)
1975 Monthly Vital Statistics Report. (Provisional Statistics)
Annual Summary for the United States, 1974: Births, Deaths,
Marriages, and Divorces. Vol. 23 (May).

von Hentig, Hans
1952 "The sex ratio." Social Forces 30 (May).

Westoff, Charles F. et al.
1973 Toward the End of Growth: Population in America. Englewood Cliffs, N.J.: Prentice Hall.

Westoff, Charles F. and Robert Parke, Jr. (eds.)
1972 Demographic and Social Aspects of Population Growth.
U.S. Commission on Population Growth and the American Future. Research Reports, Vol. 1. Washington, D.C.: GPO.

Westoff, Charles F. and N. B. Ryder
In press. The Contraceptive Revolution. Princeton, N. J.: Princeton University Press.

Sources and readings

Borrie, W. D.
1970 The Growth and Control of World Population. London:
Weidenfeld and Nicolson.

Commission on Population Growth and the American Future.
1972 Population and the American Future. Washington, D.C.:
GPO. (See also the detailed Commission Research Reports in
seven volumes, especially Vol. 1. Demographic and Social Aspects of Population Growth.

Ford, Thomas R. and Gordon F. DeJong (eds.)
1970 Social Demography. Englewood Cliffs, N. J.: Prentice-Hall.

Heer, David M.
1975 Society and Population. Second edition. Englewood Cliffs, N. J.: Prentice-Hall.

Kalbach, Warren E. and Wayne W. McVey
1971 The Demographic Bases of Canadian Society. Toronto: McGraw-Hill of Canada.

Kammeyer, Kenneth C. W.
1971 An Introduction to Population. New York: Chandler.

Kuroda, Toshio
1973 Japan's Changing Population Structure. Japan: Ministry of Foreign Affairs.

Nam, Charles B. and Susan O. Gustavus
1976 Population: The Dynamics of Demographic Change. Boston: Houghton Mifflin.

National Academy of Sciences
1971 Rapid Population Growth: Consequences and Policy Implications. Baltimore: Johns Hopkins Press.

Orleans, Leo A.
1972 Every Fifth Child: The Population of China. London: Eyre Methuen.

Population Reference Bureau
1976 World Population Growth and Response, 1965–1975: A Decade of Global Action. Washington, D.C.: Population Reference Bureau, Inc.

Shryock, Henry S., Jacob S. Siegel, and associates
1971 The Methods and Materials of Demography. Two volumes. Washington, D.C.: Bureau of the Census. (Technical.)

Stone, Leroy O. and Andrew J. Siggner (eds.)
1974 The Population of Canada. Ottawa: Statistics Canada.

Thomlinson, Ralph
1976 Population Dynamics. Second edition. New York: Random House.

U.S. Bureau of the Census
1970 Census Users' Guide. Washington, D.C.: GPO.
1974 Population of the United States, Trends and Prospects: 1950–1990. Current Population Reports, Series P-23, No. 49. Washington, D.C.: GPO.

Westoff, Charles F. et al.
1973 Toward the End of Growth: Population in America. Englewood Cliffs, N. J.: Prentice-Hall.

Periodicals

Canadian Studies in Population
Demography
International Migration Review
Population and Development Review
Population Index, chiefly devoted to a classified and annotated bibliography
Population Studies
Statistical Bulletin of the Metropolitan Life Insurance Company
Demographic Yearbook of the United Nations

Part Two
Analysis
of Major
Institutions

10 | The Family

Section one family and kinship

The family as an institution is in some disarray. It appears that values long associated with family life in the Western world—permanent union, kinship loyalty, motherhood—are losing their unquestioned and absolute character; the very necessity for family organization is sometimes challenged. Furthermore, the family is weakened as an institution as it loses some of its historic functions. As a unit of production and a way of life, the farm family had a strong claim on the community. The authority of the parent made sense to a child who could see before his eyes what his father did and why what he did was important. In this chapter the fate of the modern family and the problems of the contemporary Western nuclear family are given special attention.

The terms *family* and *kinship* are often used interchangeably, but it is important to distinguish the two ideas. Kinship is a more inclusive idea than family, for kinship does not necessarily define a functioning group. Kin refers to a network of relatives who may or may not live together; the family is a kin-based cooperative unit. Broadly speaking, kinship is a relationship that is close and enduring enough to sustain a sense of common origin or commitment. Theoretically, kinship can be founded in long association and shared tradition, with only a vague biological reference. But a more definite way of recognizing relatives is helpful in fixing specific rights and responsibilities. Hence a common ancestry is the usual basis of kinship, supplemented by other recognized ties, such as affinity through marriage or adoption.

The essential point is that there is a social definition of who is counted as kin. The biological basis is a convenient starting point, but it is not the sole determinant. Kinship may be closely defined—for example, tracing ancestry only in the father's line—or every imaginable relative may be counted. The *consanguine* family is based on biological relatedness; it is the family of blood relatives and is the main basis of kinship. The *conjugal* family is the group formed by marriage. The children have blood (consanguineal) ties to their siblings, parents, and parents' relatives, but the married partners or conjugal pair may or may not be counted as kin. Although every marriage creates a network of in-laws, the latter may have few or many responsibilities to each other, or they may not be recognized as kin at all.

UNIVERSALITY OF THE NUCLEAR FAMILY

In contemporary discussions of the family a major issue is: How universal is the nuclear family? Are there societies that do without it? The interest in these questions is partly a matter of intellectual curiosity, but it is also stimulated by a concern for what the answers might imply. If the nuclear family is universal, it may also be considered inevitable, thus making any quest for alternatives pointless.

The nuclear family consists of a conjugal pair and their offspring. From the standpoint of husband and wife, the nuclear family is the conjugal family; from the standpoint of the children, it is part of the

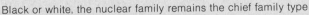
Black or white, the nuclear family remains the chief family type

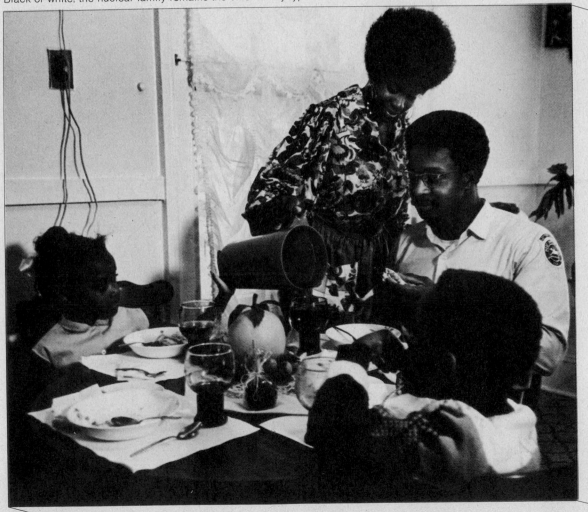

Commerce and childcare: The marketplace in
Agwarra, northern Nigeria

study of 250 societies, that some form of
nuclear family is found in every society
(Murdock, 1949:2).

Murdock's conclusion that the nuclear
family is universal is widely accepted, but it
has been questioned (Levy and Fallers,
1959:647–651). The sticking point is whether
the nuclear family always has "the distinctive and vital functions" of the family—
sexual, reproductive, economic, educational
(Murdock, 1949:3). But not all of these functions are necessarily performed by the nuclear family, and under some circumstances
the nuclear family may lose functions or
even disappear altogether. Adaptation 24
discusses the family in the Israeli kibbutz at
an early stage of its history, a setting not
sympathetic to the nuclear family.

Another apparent exception to the universality of the nuclear family was the social
system of the Nayar caste in India during the
nineteenth century, before British rule. The
Nayar husband owed most of his responsibilities to his sister's children but had minimal obligations to his conjugal family and
was usually absent as a mercenary soldier.
Although there was a concept of marriage
and paternity, the nuclear family, defined
as including the husband, hardly existed
(Mencher, 1965; Gough, 1960).

The matrifocal family An important source
of doubt and controversy regarding the universality of the nuclear family is the fact that
in many cases, the elementary family unit
consists of a mother and her children. This is
a commonly observed pattern among lower-
stratum populations in many parts of the
world. The debate centers on whether such
family units are really incomplete families
or whether they should be considered viable
adaptations to social and cultural circumstances.

Some anthropologists argue that the
mother-child unit is the true social atom:

The conjugal family . . . is often stated by anthropologists to be the "basic" and "universal" unit
of human society, and certainly of kinship systems. This is, however, an assertion of dubious

consanguine family. It has been argued that
the conjugal family is a more basic social
unit than the consanguine family, because
the conjugal family reflects the biological
facts of sexuality and the need for security
and satisfaction in personal relationships.
According to Linton, the consanguine family "is a social artifact whereas the conjugal
family is a biological unit differing little, in
its essential qualities, from similar units to
be observed in a great variety of mammalian
species" (Linton, 1959:34). This point of
view is supported by a finding, based on a

truth and utility. . . . The basic unit is the mother and her child, however the mother came to be impregnated. Whether or not a mate becomes attached to the mother on some more or less permanent basis is a variable matter. This attachment varies from nonexistent through highly doubtful to fairly stable. The mother-child tie is inevitable and given. The "conjugal" tie is variable (Fox, 1967:37, 39–40).

This controversy can be tentatively resolved if emphasis is placed on probabilities rather than on universal propositions. The matrifocal, fatherless family is an observable pattern (although seldom the preferred one) in human societies. It is likely to occur under conditions that are uncongenial to male responsibility, for example, when men do not have steady jobs or must be highly mobile in order to earn a living.

The extended family The kin-based unit that most often supplements the nuclear family—and theoretically may displace it—is the extended family. In one form of extended family, three generations live together under the same roof or in a family compound. Several married siblings, their spouses and offspring, and the grandparents together form a residential, economic, and educational unit. In such a setting, where perhaps 20 closely related people live together, the nuclear family, as such, is less important and less sharply defined. The economic unit is the extended family, and aunts, uncles, and cousins have a part in child rearing. Nevertheless, in nearly all societies most nuclear families retain their identity and some of their distinctive functions, despite being embedded in an extended family system (Zelditch, 1964:478–479).

Variations in the nuclear family Although some form of nuclear family is virtually universal, the variations may be as important as the similarities. It makes a great deal of difference whether the nuclear family is off on its own, relatively isolated, or part of a larger household or closely knit collection of fam-

ilies. In the latter case, relatives are always close at hand, a fact which may be liberating and supportive in some respects and stifling in others.

Furthermore, even when nuclear families are similar in form and in their relation to the kinship group, there may be great variations in internal structure and in the way life is experienced by family members. A historian has called attention to changes in perceptions of the family and especially in conceptions of childhood:

In medieval society, the idea of childhood did not exist; this is not to suggest that children were neglected, forsaken, or despised. The idea of childhood corresponds to an awareness of the particular nature of childhood, that particular nature which distinguishes the child from the adult, even the young adult. In medieval society this awareness was lacking. That is why, as soon as the child could live without the constant solicitude of his mother, his nanny, his cradle-rocker, he belonged to adult society. The infant who was too fragile as yet to take part in the life of adults "did not count" (Aries, 1962:9).

The great changes that have taken place in this respect, as in so many others, suggest that the *kind* of nuclear family a society develops is of crucial importance to human well-being. The possibility of eliminating the nuclear family entirely is theoretically interesting, but the actual choice, for most people, is between one kind of nuclear family and another.

KINSHIP TERMS

A technical vocabulary is necessary to describe precisely the intricate web of kinship. Some of this vocabulary has already been introduced; more is discussed in Adaptation 23. In addition, the following terms should be noted:

Choice of marriage partners
    Exogamy: the partner must be chosen from outside a defined group (e.g., members of the same extended family lineage may not marry)

Endogamy: the partners must be members of the same group (e.g., a religious community)

Number of marriage partners
Monogamy: one man to one woman
Polygamy: two or more partners
Polygyny: one man to two or more women
Polyandry: one woman to two or more men

Residence
Patrilocal: husband and wife live with or near the husband's parents
Matrilocal: husband and wife live with or near the wife's parents
Neolocal: husband and wife live by themselves

Authority and dominance
Patriarchal: father dominant
Matriarchal: mother dominant

Adaptation 23 Kitaoji: Family, descent, and kinship

The specialist in kinship analysis uses a set of conventional symbols to designate relationships and persons:

△ male

○ female

= affinity (marital tie)

| filiation (parent-child tie)

▲
● } persons who transmit descent

□ sibling tie

Source: Prepared especially for this book by Yuriko Kitaoji.

F father	D daughter
M mother	B brother
S son	Z̷ sister

FAMILY TYPES

Four major types of family are shown in Figure 10:1:

(a) Extended family After marriage two or more siblings (either brothers or sisters) may live together with their parents. Extended families vary according to descent rules, as follows:

The patrilineal extended family is composed of the parents, their sons, and the sons' wives and children. Brothers are the core dyad. The whole of Figure 10:1 shows the basic pattern of a patrilineal extended family.

The matrilineal extended family, not shown in the figure, is composed of the parents, their daughters, and the daughters' husbands and children. Sisters are the core dyad.

(b) Stem family (Le Play, 1884) Only one child continues to live with the parents after marriage (Figure 10:1b). His or her siblings must leave the family after they marry (Kitaoji, 1971). This family, therefore, consists of the parents, a son or daughter, and his or her spouse and children. The core dyad is the father and son, or father and son-in-law.

(c) Nuclear family (Murdock, 1949:Chap. 1) A married couple and their unmarried children live

Figure 10:1 Types of family

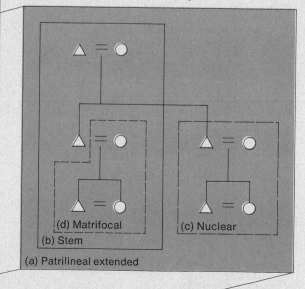

(d) Matrifocal
(b) Stem
(c) Nuclear
(a) Patrilineal extended

together (Figure 10:1c). This is also called the elementary family (Radcliffe-Brown, 1950:4–5). The core dyad is the husband and wife.

(d) Matrifocal family Typically this family consists of a mother and her children without the husband-father (Figure 10:1d). This family is also called the maternal family (Frazier, 1939), or simply the mother–child unit (Fox, 1967:Chap. 1). The core dyad is the mother and daughter. In some cases the matrifocal family includes the mother's mother (Buchler and Selby, 1968:26–27).

PRINCIPLES OF DESCENT

Descent may be unilineal or nonunilineal. About two-thirds of the 564 societies in the World Ethnographic Sample adhere to unilineal descent principles (Murdock, 1957:686–687).

Unilineal descent The two principal forms of unilineal descent are patrilineal and matrilineal. In the *patrilineal* system (Figure 10:2a) descent is traced through males only. Ego (the person whose descent is being reckoned) and his siblings belong to ego's father's descent group (Radcliffe-Brown, 1950).

The *matrilineal* system traces descent through females only (Figure 10:2b). Ego and her siblings belong to ego's mother's descent group. However, the authority of the descent group may reside in males, despite the fact that descent is determined through the female line. Usually the mother's eldest brother is the authority figure (Mair, 1965: Chap. 5).

Nonunilineal descent The main type of nonunilineal descent is *bilateral,* in which descent is traced through both males and females at the same time, and in principle both sides are equally important. Ego and his siblings belong to both their paternal and maternal kin groups (Murdock, 1960:6).

Lineal and collateral kinship Collateral relatives belong to the same ancestral stock as ego, but they are not in the direct line of descent. For example, mother, daughter, and grandmother are *lineal* kin, but sisters, cousins, nieces, and aunts are *collateral* kin. Collateral distance from ego (see Figure 10:3) is often referred to as "degree

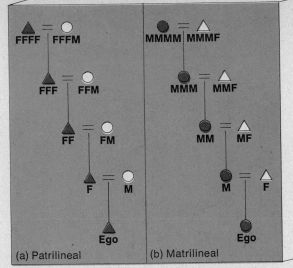

Figure 10:2 **Principles of lineal descent**

of consanguinity," or blood relationship, which may be important in determining inheritance or eligibility for marriage.

THE AMERICAN KINSHIP SYSTEM

In the American kinship system descent is traced bilaterally through ego's father and mother. No distinction is made between the father's and mother's sides in reference terms. For example, both father's and mother's brothers are referred to by the term *uncle.* However, the distinction between lineal kin and collateral kin is important; ego's father is clearly distinguished from father's brother (uncle) and mother from mother's sister (aunt).

The modal type of kin reckoning in the contemporary United States is shown in Figure 10:3. Although there are regional and ethnic variations, the scheme diagrammed from the perspective of ego covers most of the recognized consanguineal (blood) kin for most Americans. Note that the diagram does not cover ego's kin by marriage, although some of the same terms are used to refer to them; for example, a wife's aunt is referred to as *aunt.*

The basic criteria for distinguishing consanguineal kin in this system are sex (except for cousins), generation distance, and collateral distance. Seven generations are shown in the figure:

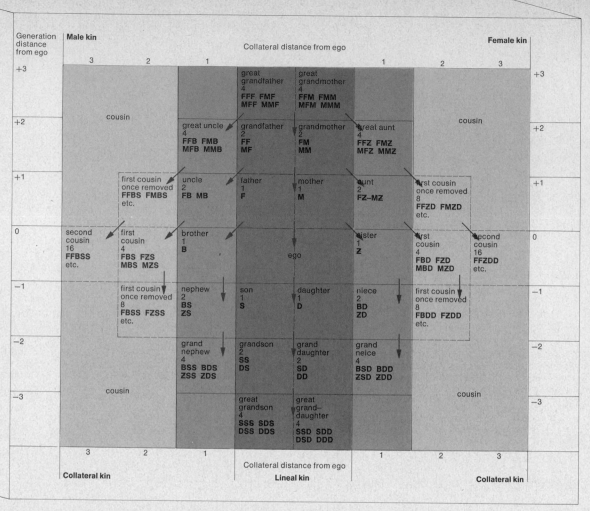

Figure 10:3 The universe of blood kin, United States

Source: Suggested by Arensberg, 1939:Fig. 10.

three above and three below ego. Ego and his lineal kin are in the main trunk of the diagram, labeled 0. Three degrees of collateral distance on each side of the trunk show ego's collateral kin, including brother and sister.

This universe of kin is made up of *kin categories* (each cell) into which *kin types,* as they are related to ego, are grouped, male kin on the left, female kin on the right. Each kin category has a reference term, such as *aunt.* The numeral in each cell indicates the number of kin types in each kin category. In the case of *aunt,* there are two possible: father's sister (FZ) and mother's sister (MZ). Arrows show the filial relationship between cells, that is, aunt's

mother is ego's grandmother, and aunt's children are ego's first cousins.

Compared with some other kinship systems the range of recognized kin is rather limited. It rarely extends from ego lineally beyond three generations or collaterally beyond the third degree, that is, beyond second cousin on ego's generation level. In this system the term cousin covers a wide range of ego's consanguineal kin, not all of which are shown in the diagram. Cousin refers to all collateral kin beyond the first degree from ego. The terms first cousin and second cousin refer to the second and third degrees of collateral distance. First cousin once removed refers to the second degree of collateral kin who are one generation older or younger than ego. For discussion of American kinship terminology, see Goodenough (1965), Schneider and Homans (1955).

309

Section two social organization and the nuclear family

Section two social organization and the nuclear family

For most people, group affiliation begins with membership in a family. The family mediates between the individual and society, helping him to take his place in the larger world and at the same time providing an island of protection and privacy. In every society, at some point in its history, kinship has been the key unit of social organization, asserting its influence in the economy, political life, and religion.

Sometimes kinship *is* social organization:

There are cultures with little or no economic organization beyond division of labor, by sex, within the family. This is true of the Polar Eskimo who live in the bleak environment of the shores of Smith Sound, N. W. Greenland, the furthermost northern settlement. Without agriculture and with few wild vegetable foods, they depend for meager subsistence upon hunting, fishing, and collecting. To survive, they must live in small groups, which (during the summer) usually consist of one or two primary families who hunt caribou and fish. Even in winter, when they live in villages, the community rarely exceeds seven or eight families. The village is transitory and has no head. Since hunting bands may include members who are not kin, there is some economic organization apart from the family, but not much (Nimkoff, 1965:33).

THE DETACHED NUCLEAR FAMILY

A basic fact of modern history is the decline of extended kin groups and the emergence of the detached nuclear family as the representative form of family life (Goode, 1963). This trend is associated with (1) free choice of mates, in the sense that marriages are contracted without reference to the larger kin group; (2) more divorce; (3) increased residential mobility, with accompanying weakening of kinship ties; (4) emancipation of women and their entry in large numbers into the labor force; and (5) diminished responsibility of children for their parents and grandparents.

The detached nuclear family maximizes freedom, but it also takes on a heavy burden of responsibility and is subject to severe internal strains. Although there is less responsibility for kin who are not members of the nuclear family, there is greater responsibility for children and for the psychic well-being of husband and wife. When divorce occurs in the American system, there are necessary extensive readjustments in economic arrangements, care of children, social participation, and emotional involvements.

In sharp contrast, in the Hopi pattern the married couple lives with the wife's parents and her sisters and their husbands, sharing in many communal activities (Queen and Adams, 1952:23–43). Loss of an adult from the Hopi extended family requires only minor readjustments. Children are already part of the larger kin group, and all the adults have served to some degree as parents. Because intimacy between husband and wife is only slightly greater than among all the adults in the extended unit, the suffering over loss of a spouse is minimized. There is little disruption in the life of a divorced woman who has a regular pattern of sociability and close cooperation with kin.

Recent appraisals of the contemporary conjugal family (Skolnick and Skolnick, 1971:16–26) have emphasized both the burden placed on women, who have the main responsibility for child care and domestic chores, and the great power of the nuclear family over the child:

There is a minimal *social regulation* of parent-child relations in our culture; this is, above all, what makes lethal child-care practices possible.

In a primitive culture, where many relatives are around to take an active interest in one's baby, where life is open, or in large households, where many people can see what a mother is doing and where deviation looses critical, interested tongues, it is impossible for a parent to do as he or she pleases with his children. In a literal sense, the baby is often not even one's own in such societies, but belongs to a lineage, clan, or household—a community—having a real investment in the baby. It is not private enterprise (Henry, 1963:332).

These and similar comparisons stress the human costs of the detached nuclear family.

In considering the emergence of the detached nuclear family, two points should be remembered: (1) the isolation of the detached nuclear family from the larger kinship group is uneven and sometimes exaggerated; and (2) the human costs of the extended family system should not be ignored.

Persistence of kinship Although the detached nuclear family is the dominant form in modern life, it is not the exclusive form. Kinship ties remain important, especially in the working class but among middle-class people too. A study of Bethnal Green, a community in East London, showed an extensive kinship network, with important effects in economic life (father-son succession in occupations, helping relatives to get jobs), as well as in personal relationships. However, the same study shows the importance of residence, of staying in the same immediate community, for the nurturing of kinship ties. Families that moved to a new housing "estate" less than 20 miles from Bethnal Green tended to become more isolated (Young and Willmott, 1962; compare Gans, 1962). On the other hand,

several recent studies have shown that, even in those societies where family mobility is great, the kindred form a functional group. Families spend their vacations with kinsfolk. The parents help the new couple establish themselves with loans and gifts. At every emergency of the family life cycle—birth, marriage, sickness, divorce, death—

kinsfolk are invoked or offer assistance (Mogey, 1964:516).

There is, of course, a considerable difference between long-distance or occasional support and the sharing of a day-to-day life. Nevertheless, the importance of continuing support to the detached nuclear family, especially from the parental family during the early years of marriage, should not be overlooked. Furthermore, for many people, social life consists mainly of visiting among relatives.

Human costs of the extended family The usual corollary of social support is social control. Where the extended family is powerful, the freedom of individuals is restricted. They are dependent on others, including whoever has authority in the group, and they are subject to stresses and demands that may make life something less than idyllic. A study of kinship in Africa south of the Sahara points out that extended families make corporate decisions affecting property and economic cooperation and that such decisions are often made by people who have known each other since childhood:

This affords opportunities to base group solidarity on early affective ties, which may be very close, but it also means that the resentments and rivalries engendered in the early years may affect performance in adult relationships within the group. The emotional intensity of such long-standing hostilities may be greater than that characterizing the competition of strangers. While suppressed in everyday behavior, these grudges formed in childhood may flare into the open when a crisis occurs, pitting brother against brother, son against father, or nephew against uncle (Le Vine, 1965:191–192).

In some cases of patrilocal residence, as in India, a daughter-in-law may have a hard time of it. She must live her life among strangers and may have to suffer the domination of her husband's mother.

For these reasons, critics of the detached nuclear family do not favor the reinstatement of the old kin-based extended family but rather are searching for new forms which may offer a more acceptable combination of freedom and constraint. "The functional problem of the family today is the re-creation of extended family relationships without kinship" (Skolnick and Skolnick, 1971:29).

Adaptation 24 discusses the fate of the nuclear family in three settings of modern Israel.

Adaptation 24 Talmon-Garber: Family and society in Israel

This study analyzes the impact of radical and rapid social change on patterns of family organization and on the relation between the family and the community. Three types of Israeli families are considered: (1) the family in collective settlements (kibbutzim), (2) the family in cooperative settlements (moshavim), and (3) the family among European refugees in the Israeli cities. Three distinct modes of interaction between family and community are portrayed. In the kibbutz the community is supreme and the family is subordinated to it. The traditional family in the moshav is kin-centered: The nuclear family is subordinated to wider kin groupings that mediate between it and the community. The isolated refugee family in urban centers is cut off from kin and estranged from the community.

THE COLLECTIVIZED FAMILY

The *kibbutz* (plural: *kibbutzim*) is a form of collective settlement, first founded in 1910, long before the establishment of the state of Israel in 1948. The early settlers of the kibbutzim were young and unattached migrants from Eastern and central Europe, who were not accompanied by parents or other relatives.

In the kibbutz, which may range from less than 100 to 2,000 members, there is common ownership of property, except for a few personal belongings. The members agree to subordinate their personal interests to the attainment of communal goals and

to seek self-expression only through service to the community. In theory, and to a large extent in practice, devotion to communal ideals takes precedence over kinship obligations. Feeling for fellow members and for the community is more significant than family loyalty. Relatives who are not members are by definition outsiders, almost strangers.

The revolutionary phase From its inception the collective movement realized the risk of conflicting loyalties and set out to redefine and curtail family obligations. The community took over most of the traditional functions of the family. Many ingenious devices were developed to prevent the consolidation of the family as a distinct and independent unit. Members of the same family were not assigned to the same place of work. All meals were taken in the common dining room. Families looked after their own rooms but had few other household responsibilities.

At this stage the family was not even relied on to maintain the community's population or to rear its children. The kibbutzim ensured their continuity and growth by recruiting volunteers rather than by depending on natural increase. The care and rearing of children were basically the responsibility of the kibbutz, not of the parents. In most kibbutzim, children lived apart from their mothers and fathers. Instead they slept, ate, and studied in special children's houses.

Children met their parents and siblings in off-hours and spent the afternoons and early evenings with them. On Saturdays and holidays they stayed with their parents. There were thus frequent and intensive relations between parents and children; but mainly the child was in the hands of community agencies.

Source: Abridged and adapted from Y. Talmon-Garber, "Social Change and Family Structure," *International Social Science Journal 14*, No. 3 (1962), 468–487. Published in this form by permission of the UNESCO publication, *International Social Science Journal.* At the time of her death in 1966, Dr. Talmon-Garber was associate professor of sociology at the Hebrew University, Jerusalem.

Persistence of the family Even during the earliest phases, when antifamilism was strongest, the family remained a distinct unit. Although premarital sexual relations were permitted, there was a clearcut distinction between casual sexual experimentation, love affairs, and more durable and publicly sanctioned unions. By asking for a room of their own, a couple made public their wish to have permanent relations and eventually to have children. Residence in a common bedroom-living room allocated by the kibbutz conferred legitimacy on the couple. While children did not share a common domicile with their parents, they visited the parents' room every day, and it was their home by reference. The parents could exert influence on the trained personnel in charge of their children. Interaction among family members, though less frequent than contacts with friends and work associates, was often more meaningful and intense. The emotional ties that bound husband and wife and parents and children were much more intimate and exclusive than their ties with other members of the community. The family's unconditional love and loyalty insulated its members from communal pressures and enhanced their security.

Changes in the kibbutz As the kibbutz became better established and its work more routine, as it accepted new groups of settlers, and as a new generation grew up within it, the community became more heterogeneous and less cohesive. There were more different types of people with diverse interests and perspectives. New settlers, who joined the founders at different stages of the community's development, contributed to the process of differentiation. In time the collectives became more tolerant of the existence of subgroups, and hostility toward the family abated. It was assigned a place among other subgroups.

The coming of the second generation gradually transformed the relations between the generations. Whereas the first settlers broke away from their own parents, the children of the kibbutz are expected to continue their life work in the kibbutz. Parents and children are now members of the same community. They live in close proximity and share, at least to a degree, the same ideals; identification with one's family reinforces identification with the collective.

Restoration of family functions The new empha-sis on continuity between the generations is expressed in a partial emancipation of the family. As the family regains some of its lost housekeeping functions, more meals are eaten at home, rooms become flats, and more of the couple's personal allowance is spent on the flat. The flat is an important symbol of family solidarity and a physical manifestation of its separateness.

At the same time, the family increases in importance as an agency of reproduction and child rearing. There is a considerable increase in the fertility of the women of the kibbutz. The difficulties experienced by the kibbutzim in recruiting and absorbing new immigrants underscore the importance of natural increase. Emphasis has shifted from recruitment of volunteers to expansion from within. The family is now called upon to help the kibbutz ensure its continuity and growth. As a corollary, the parents take a more active role in the care and education of the child. There is more parental supervision of behavior and parental involvement in choice of friends, reading habits, and future occupations. In some kibbutzim which have introduced a more radical reorganization, children no longer sleep in the separate children's houses. They stay with their peers during the day but return home every afternoon.

The tendency toward a more familistic pattern may be discerned in many ways. Marriage now normally precedes the establishment of a family. Husbands help in household duties, but in most families women are mainly responsible for domestic work. In spite of a blurring of the roles of father and mother, there are signs of differentiation.

There is also a subtle transformation of informal relations and leisure-time activities. Free time spent in public has diminished. Members of the kibbutz are less eager to attend public meetings. Husband and wife spend most of their free time together, and it is now considered impolite to invite only one spouse.

The resurgence of familism has brought with it a gradual development and renewal of wider kinship ties. In the early days most members did not have any kin except their own nuclear family living in the same community. However, when the kibbutz embraces three generations, relatives who live in the same community establish close contacts through frequent visiting and mutual help. Wider kinship ties serve as connecting links with

Children of a kibbutz in the
Jordan valley: Bomb-sheltered
sleeping quarters

the outside world, and members tend to renew their contacts with relatives who live outside the kibbutz.

Persisting tension In spite of the changed position of the family, the kibbutzim remain basically nonfamilistic. The kibbutzim make far-reaching demands on their members. Because the proper functioning of the kibbutz depends on whole-hearted identification with its aims and ideals, the collectives cannot allow the family to become independent and self-sufficient. They still fear that the family may become the main focus of loyalty and satisfaction, with kinship ties more important than ties among members.

The militant antifamilism of the revolutionary phase has abated but not disappeared. It is superseded by a moderate collectivism which regards the family as a useful though uneasy ally. The kibbutzim control and limit the family and employ it for the attainment of collective goals.

THE TRADITIONAL FAMILY

A second important pattern of immigration and settlement in Israel is illustrated by North African Jews who migrated to Israel later than the founders of the kibbutzim and after the establishment of the state of Israel.

Historically, Jews in North Africa lived in small communities composed of large patriarchal families of three or four generations. The father directed his married and unmarried sons in work and maintained discipline within a common residence. There were close kinship ties. Males customarily held dominant positions, and female roles were limited to home and family. The synagogue was an important place of male gathering. Allegiance to Jewish ritual and observance centered around the synagogue and religious schools.

This traditional pattern remained more or less intact in the villages and small towns, but it was undermined in the cities of North Africa. Rapid urbanization dispersed relatives and splintered the kinship group. Young men became independent, and their ways were secularized.

The traditionalist North African Jews went to Israel with a deep sense of Jewish solidarity and a vague messianic striving. The more urbanized among them were mainly interested in security and economic advancement. But neither the rural nor the urban North Africans, shared the basic values and dynamic aspirations of the new Israeli society. They took their old life with them and hoped to continue their former ways unmolested. Families, neighborhoods, and sometimes even whole communities migrated together.

The moshav Some of the North Africans were settled in cooperative communities known as *moshavim*. The moshav presumes a semiindependent family working on a family farm. In the moshav a familistic division of labor is combined with mechanized farming and centralized management of cooperative institutions. Land and machinery are publicly owned. There is rough equality in size of farm and basic investment; marketing and purchasing are cooperative; and there is a ban on hired labor.

The kibbutzim were formed by volunteer pioneering groups that sought to realize both personal and national ideals. The moshavim are administered communities, planned and managed by governmental and quasi-governmental agencies. State planners, guided by defense considerations and by a desire to disperse the Israeli population, ordered the construction of 274 cooperative settlements and directed new immigrants to these villages.

The settling agency regarded the traditional kin-centered social organization of the immigrants as detrimental to the development of modern cooperative villages, and the planners intentionally disregarded the settlers' former attachments and loyalties. In organizing the settlements, kinship groups were dispersed.

Reassertion of kinship The traditional kinship structure soon reasserted itself. Settlers sought out their relatives and encouraged them to settle in the same village. After a period of reshuffling, most villages emerged with two or three major kinship groups. Although the moshav economy is based on the nuclear family, and each nuclear family has a separate household and a separate farm, there is much cooperation among kin.

Reunion of kinsmen occurred more easily and rapidly in traditional families which maintained wider kin ties and arrived in the country in family or neighborhood groups. However, even relatives who were separated before they left North Africa and had not seen each other for years sought each other out. In the unfamiliar and unstructured social setting, kinship ties regained their lost significance and served as a major basis of spontaneous organization. The settlers found psychological support in relationships that had been long neglected.

Kinship and social structure In this setting kinship pervades the social structure of the village. It is the keynote of the social system. Village politics center on control of community institutions, especially the central committee, which brings practical advantages as well as prestige to the family. The kin groups become rival factions, each struggling with the other for power. The political history of each village involves a continuous struggle among the kinship groups, and politics reinforces the ties of kinship. Paradoxically, in this context, radical modernization has strengthened and revived the kin-dominated traditional order.

Yet the growing dominance of the kinship group is troublesome to the village community. Village officers, elected on the basis of kinship ties, discriminate against nonrelatives, and the nepotism of officeholders breeds inefficiency and suspicion, as well as bitter feuds. Deadlocked factions may immobilize the management of cooperative institutions for many months. It sometimes becomes necessary to transfer one of the warring factions to another village. The solidarity of the kinship group develops at the expense of the solidarity of the village community.

The planners have come to realize that the kinship groups are vitally important units in the absorption of traditional immigrants, but they understand the risks. They therefore accept the kinship groups but try to limit their influence on central cooperative institutions. In some of the villages, there is a growing tendency to replace officeholders by hired experts who have no kin in the village, are not involved in the village feuds, and are better trained. Because they are more objective and more efficient, management is partly disentangled from the kinship network, and cooperative institutions can continue to function even when there is conflict among the families.

THE ISOLATED FAMILY

European Jewish refugees who settled in Israel after World War II did so under conditions of great stress and suffering. In many centers of Jewish population only a few people managed to escape the Nazi annihilation, and few families remained intact. Uprooted and isolated, they arrived with few, if any, relatives. Their former lives were destroyed, and most had spent long periods of compulsory collective living in concentration camps.

The refugees were unprepared for the difficult conditions of settlement in the new country. Many remembered their shattered prewar past with nostalgic yearning and tended to idealize it. They had diffuse positive attitudes toward Israel but no strong identification with its aims and values. The experience of concentration camp life had left them with a deep desire for privacy and undisturbed personal development. This preoccupation with personal aspirations ran counter to the ideological and collectivist orientations of the absorbing society.

The family turns inward The reaction to isolation and alienation is a wholehearted attachment to the nuclear family, which withdraws to its small and isolated private world. The immigrants seek solace and security in the intimacy of family life. They defend the independence of the family against the demands of the absorbing society. In the family they are their own masters and need not constantly accommodate to outside influences. They can continue to cultivate their former ways of life.

The immigrants work indefatigably to benefit the family but are unconcerned with purely occupational problems and uninterested in the wider implications of their work. Isolated families develop few significant contacts outside the family circle. Informal relations and recreation are family-centered. The members refrain from joining organizations, distrust authorities at any level, and hold political parties in cynical contempt. They keep aloof from political or social activities and are apathetic to the goals of the society as a whole.

Costs of isolation The isolated family protects the uprooted individual and supports him, but eventually the self-imposed isolation adversely affects family unity. The outside world does have its effect as the children gradually adopt the values of the surrounding society. However, the parents cannot help their children find a place in the Israeli society, and the children become ambivalent and frustrated. Isolation of the family thus weakens its own solidarity on which it has staked so much.

CONCLUSION

Immigration to Israel deepened the solidarity of the traditional and isolated families. Moshav and refugee families segregated their members from the larger society, which was perceived as threatening and hostile.

In the early kibbutz, on the other hand, the youth of the settlers, their pioneering spirit, their socialist ideology, and an intense communal life made the family irrelevant—for a time.

Each situation had its distinctive problem:

* *The kibbutz faced the problem of allowing family units more privacy and independence without harming the cohesion of the community.*
* *The moshav had to preserve the unity of the kinship group while limiting its influence on village management.*
* *The communities containing a considerable number of isolated families had to preserve the internal solidarity of the nuclear families and, at the same time, find ways of extending their participation and identification.*

Section three love and marriage

In contemporary America the union of love and marriage is taken for granted as a cultural ideal. Most people understand that the ideal does not govern all decisions to marry or to stay married. But it strongly influences the expectations people have and therefore what they experience as success or failure.

PREVALENCE AND CONTROL OF LOVE

Love as a general phenomenon—the experience of warm affection, attachment, and sympathy—is hardly unique to Western society. Furthermore, sex-based love, which combines sexual attraction with feelings of affection and tenderness, occurs among many peoples, although the exact prevalence is in doubt. In some societies, however, and perhaps in many, the union of sex and love is neither experienced nor appreciated (Stephens, 1963:204–205):

> For the Lepchas of Zongu sexual activity is practically divorced from emotion; it is a pleasant and amusing experience, and as much a necessity as food and drink; and like food and drink it does not matter from whom you receive it, as long as you get it; though you are naturally grateful to the people who provide you with either regularly (Gorer, 1938:170).

Whatever its prevalence, sex-based love is not necessarily valued, encouraged, or permitted to determine important decisions. On the contrary, many societies have fairly elaborate social mechanisms for the control of love, which is potentially disruptive of social hierarchies and family alliances. In these societies, the idea of marrying for love is a social absurdity, an affront to common sense, and a threat to the fabric of community life. This is especially true where kinship dominates social organization, for then the distribution of property and the protection of social status or group identity may be at stake. Under such circumstances a marriage has serious consequences for a network of relatives. To control these consequences, rules and procedures for the selection of mates emerge. Usually these are among the most salient and coercive of customs. In Sumner's language (see *CULTURE*, p. 60), they are mores, not folkways.

The variety of patterns controlling marriage is suggested in Figure 10:4. Two variables are considered: *specification of mates by social norms* and *external intervention*, that is, arrangement of marriages by third

parties. Two preliterate cultures are compared with feudal Japan and the present-day United States according to the interplay of these variables (Freeman, 1958:27–39):

1. The Yaruros of Venezuela are a nomadic tribe of fishermen and hunters. Marriage is both arranged and highly specified. The marriage is arranged by a shaman who knows exactly what he must do—find an eligible cross-cousin. A boy's cross-cousin is his mother's brother's daughter or his father's sister's daughter. The daughters of his mother's sister or of his father's brother do not qualify. The boy's uncle determines which of the eligible cross-cousins will be selected.

2. In eighteenth-century feudal Japan, the patriarchal household was the individual's center of existence. The welfare of the family as a corporate group was accepted as the touchstone for all decisions. Marriages were carefully arranged, using go-betweens to avoid humiliating rejections. But the family could range widely in its search for eligible marriage partners. There was no strict specification as among the Yaruros.

3. The Hottentots of southwest Africa resemble the Yaruros in that cross-cousin marriage is required. Hence the field of eligibles is narrowly prescribed. Unlike the Yaruros, however, the Hottentots are free to choose for themselves who to marry so long as a cross-cousin is selected.

4. In American society, individual choice prevails, limited by pressures toward racial, class, and age-group endogamy. Within these limits, a wide range of eligibles is available, and third parties have little control

		Specification by social norms	
		High	Low
External intervention	High	**Yaruros**	**Feudal Japan**
	Low	**Hottentots**	**United States**

Figure 10:4
Specification of mates and marriage arrangement

Source: Adapted from Freeman, 1958:39.

over the matter. They may have a lot to say, but in the end it is the prospective spouses themselves who make the decision.

In addition to the control mechanisms discussed above—arrangement of marriages and specification of eligible spouses—others include (1) child marriage; (2) isolation of potential mates, for example, a system which requires marriage to someone from another village; and (3) close supervision, especially of adolescent girls (Goode, 1959).

Caution Except for close supervision, these mechanisms may not have originated for the purpose of controlling love, but they do have that effect, as well as other effects. Furthermore, the mechanisms do not foreclose the emergence of love. Indeed, they may encourage it by creating appropriate expectations. Although love may be controlled and channeled, it is not necessarily eliminated.

ROMANTIC LOVE

The Western ideal of romantic love includes the following components: (1) idealization of the loved one; (2) feelings of euphoria and excitement; (3) exclusive attachment to a single person, with associated attitudes of fidelity and jealousy; and (4) salience of love's moral claim over other social responsibilities. Taken together, these elements constitute a culturally defined *sentiment*, that is, a special constellation of feeling, evaluation, and perception.

It is useful to distinguish the related ideas of emotion and sentiment. An emotion is a tension-laden physiological state, such as rage, anger, or fear. A sentiment is a *culturally elaborated* emotion:

The emotion of rage or anger can be compared with the sentiment of indignation. The infant registers a state of arousal that the observer identifies as rage, especially if the observer can connect the state to some frustration. But indignation comes only after the child has learned the social concept of justice and therefore is able to experience anger under the special circumstance of being the victim of someone's deliberate injus-

tice. . . . In order to be indignant, one must learn how to appear outraged, to maintain a stance and tone of voice that distinguish the manifestation from another less socially acceptable sentiment often called temper (Turner, 1970:225–226).

Much the same may be said of romantic love, mother love, compassion, and many other sentiments. To have a sentiment is to have learned both an accepted *way* of feeling and a proper *object* of feeling.

The Christian background Early Christian spokesmen adopted a strongly ascetic morality. They reacted against the frank sexuality, widespread adultery, easy divorce, and feminine independence of the later Roman era. Saint Paul set the tone when he said:

It is good for a man not to touch a woman. Nevertheless, to avoid fornication, let every man have his own wife, and let every woman have her own husband. . . . I would that all men were even as I myself. . . . I say therefore to the unmarried and widows, it is good for them if they abide even as I. But if they cannot contain, let them marry: for it is better to marry than to burn (1 Cor. 7:9).

The church fathers took up the battle for continence and chastity. The story of Adam's temptation and fall was given a new and harsh interpretation: Sex was inherently shameful and evil; women were lesser beings who deserved subordination and were best left alone. "He who too ardently loves his own wife," said St. Jerome, "is an adulterer." The proper office of sex in marriage was procreation. (See *RELIGION*, p. 402.)

The Christian morality divorced sex and love. The new ideal was a spiritual union, a continent marriage in the service of God. Gradually the concept of marriage as a sacrament—permanent and indissoluble—gained acceptance. At the same time, "sexual self-denial stood above all else as the ethical way of life" (Hunt, 1959:113). The effect was to elevate marriage and debase sex.

Courtly love Among the upper classes of feudal Europe a new conception of ideal love emerged. This sentiment flourished in the world of chivalry and found its home in the courts of dukes and princes. It was communicated and celebrated by the troubadors of France and by their counterparts, the minnesingers of Germany. Courtly love built upon the Christian heritage but was also a dramatic reaction against it. For this new romanticism glorified chastity, idealized women, and encouraged adultery. The romantic ideal envisioned a pure and ennobling passion—not within marriage, but outside of it.

The ideal of courtly love was in time denounced as heretical and ridiculed as absurd. However, it gave a new legitimacy to sex-based love. Although it treasured a fantasy of unconsummated desire—Tristan and Isolde lying side by side, a sword between—there was a strong emphasis on erotic pleasure. Love requited would include the opportunity to undress the lady and caress her. The very effort to achieve a chaste sexuality contributed to a potential union of love and sex which requires self-restraint and concern for the other. Furthermore, what began as a quest for love outside marriage fostered attitudes that would ultimately make romantic love within marriage a cultural ideal.

Adaptation 25 describes a famous love affair whose themes reveal the essence of courtly love.

Adaptation 25 Hunt: The gentle agony of courtly love

Ulrich von Lichtenstein, knight-errant, jouster of great prowess, minnesinger of some talent, was born about 1200 in Austria. His father must have been a member of the lesser nobility, for he grew up within castle walls and was knighted after a suitable apprenticeship. At the height of his fortune he owned not only the castle of Lichtenstein, from which he took his name, but two other castles and considerable land.

When he grew old, Ulrich prepared an autobiography in narrative verse. Its title is the story of his life: Frauendienst, *the service of woman.* Frauendienst *is not a work of fiction, even though the aging man-at-arms may have yielded to the delights of exaggeration or been tricked by the distortions of memory. Nor is it a work of satire. It is one man's personal testimony—the actual record of his life as he lived it under the domination of courtly love.*

LOVE'S ONSET

When he was a mere lad of five, says Ulrich, he first heard older boys saying that true honor and

Source: Abridged from *The Natural History of Love* by Morton M. Hunt (New York: Knopf, 1959), pp. 133–138.

happiness could come only through serving a noble and lovely woman. He was deeply impressed and began to shape his childish thoughts in that direction. Even at that tender age, he clearly understood that such service, the keystone of courtly love, could be undertaken only for a woman one could never marry. True love had to be clandestine, bittersweet, and beset by endless difficulties and frustrations: By virtue of all this, it was spiritually uplifting and made a knight a better man and a greater warrior.

The subject evidently dominated the boy's thoughts, for by the age of 12 he put away childish things and consciously chose as the lady of his heart a princess. In every way, it was a perfect choice: She was far too highborn for him, considerably older than he, and, of course, already married. He became a page in her court and conscientiously cultivated his feelings of love until they commanded his whole being. He adored her in total secrecy and trembled (inconspicuously) in her presence. When he saw her hands touch the petals of flowers he had secretly placed where she could see them, he was all but in a faint. And when she washed her hands before dinner, young Ulrich would sometimes filch the basin, smuggle it off to his room, and there reverently drink the dirty water.

THE VOW

Five years of this went by, but his love affair progressed no further since, being totally unworthy of the lady, he dared not even tell her of his feelings. At the age of 17 he therefore took himself off to the court of the Margrave Henry of Austria to raise his status; there he studied knightly skills for five more years, and at last in 1222, during the wedding festival of the Duke of Saxony, he was made a knight. By a marvelous coincidence, his ladylove, whom he had not seen but had religiously dreamed of during those years, was one of the guests at the wedding. The very sight of her so moved him that he immediately took a secret vow to devote his newly won knighthood to serving her. This decision filled him with melancholy and with painful longings, a condition which apparently made him very happy.

That summer, feverish and flushed with his infatuation, he roamed the countryside fighting in numerous tourneys and winning many victories, all of which he ascribed to the mighty force of love within him. At last, having compiled an impressive record and feeling worthy to offer the lady the tribute of his devotion, he persuaded a niece of his to call on her and privately tell her of his desire to be an acknowledged but distant, respectful admirer of hers. He even got his niece to learn and sing for the princess a song he had written.

RESPONSE AND SELF-RENEWAL

The heartless lady, unmoved by his ten years of silent devotion and his recent feats of valor, sent back a cruel and pointed reply: She considered him presumptuous, was scornfully critical of the high-flown language of his quite inappropriate offer, and, for good measure, took the trouble to let him know he was too ugly to be considered even in the role of a very distant admirer. For it seems (and the lady was specific) that the unhappy young knight had a harelip. Undaunted—perhaps even inspired by this obvious proof that she had actually noticed him—Ulrich promptly undertook a journey to a famous surgeon and had his lip repaired. Considering the techniques of medieval surgery, this must have been both excruciatingly painful and quite dangerous; indeed, he lay feverish on a sickbed for six weeks. News of this, plus a new song he wrote for her, softened the lady's heart, and she sent word that he might attend a riding party and enjoy the rare privilege of speaking with her for a moment, if the opportunity should arise. And it did, once, when he had the chance to help her down from her horse. He could have uttered a sentence or two of devotion, but unfortunately he was tongue-tied by her nearness and could say nothing. The lovely lady, considerably put out, whispered to him that he was a fraud and gracefully indicated her displeasure by ripping out a forelock of his hair as she dismounted.

LOVE'S LABOR SCORNED

Not in the least angered by this, Ulrich reappeared the next day, this time found his voice, and humbly begged her to permit him to be her secret knight and to allow him to fight for her and love her. She accepted his service, but under the very minimum conditions, granting him no "favor" whatever—neither embrace, kiss, nor word of promise and not so much as a ribbon to carry in his bosom. Ulrich, nevertheless, was filled with joy and thankfulness for her kindness, and sallied forth, tilting about the countryside with anyone who would break a lance with him and composing many a song to his ladylove, which his secretary set down for him, since writing was not a knightly accomplishment. The messages and letters that passed between him and the princess at this time conveyed, in the one direction, her condescension, coldness, and criticism. But this was exactly what was expected of her in the situation, and he found each new blow a delicious pain; a large part of his pleasure lay in observing his own noble constancy under duress.

At the end of that period, Ulrich petitioned her forthrightly through a go-between to grant him her love, at least verbally, in return for his faithful adoration and service. The princess not only sharply rebuked the go-between for Ulrich's unseemly persistency but expressed her scorn that Ulrich had falsely spoken of losing a finger fighting for love of her. Actually, he had suffered a finger wound which healed, but an incorrect report had reached her. When the go-between related her scornful message, Ulrich paled for a moment, then resolutely drew out a sharp knife and ordered his friend to hack off the finger at one blow. This done, the knight had an artisan make a green velvet case in which the finger was held by gold clasps. He sent her the mounted digit as a keepsake, together with a special poem about the matter. Deeply impressed by this evidence of her power over him, she returned word that she would look at the finger every day from thenceforth, a message which, incidentally, he received as he did all other communiqués from her—on his knees, with bowed head and folded hands.

AN ULTIMATE EFFORT

Determined now to earn her love by some stupendous feat, Ulrich conceived the scheme of a jousting trip from Venice to Bohemia in the disguise of Venus. He went to Venice and there had seamstresses make a dozen white gowns to his own measurements; meanwhile he sent off a messenger with an open letter announcing the event. The northward march began on schedule on April 25, 1227, and concluded five weeks later, during which time Ulrich shattered an average of eight lances every day and acquired great glory and honor, all in the cause of love and for the sake of the princess he so faithfully adored.

ULRICH'S MARRIAGE

It comes as something of a shock when one reads Ulrich's own statement that in the midst of his triumphal journey he stopped off for three days to visit his wife and children. For the fact is that this lovesick Galahad had long had a wife to lie with when he had the urge and a family to live with when he felt lonely. He himself speaks of his affection (but not his love) for his wife; to love her would have been improper and almost unthinkable. Like other men of his class and time, Ulrich considered marriage a phase of feudal business management, since it consisted basically of the joining of lands, the cementing of loyalties, and the production of heirs and future defenders. But the purifying, ennobling rapture of love for an ideal woman—what had that to do with details of crops and cattle, with fleas and fireplaces, with serfs and swamp drainage?

THE REWARD

Having completed his epochal feat of love service, Ulrich waited for his reward, and at long last it came: The princess sent word that he might visit her. Yet he was to expect no warm welcome; she specified that he must come in the disguise of a leper and take his place among the lepers who would be visiting her to beg for alms. But of course this monstrous indignity fazed the faithful Ulrich not in the least. Nor did he falter when she knowingly let him, disguised in his rags, spend that night in a ditch in the rain. Nor was he outraged when, the next night, he was finally allowed to climb a rope up the castle wall to her chamber, only to find it lit by a hundred tapers and staffed by eight maids-in-waiting who hovered about her where she lay in bed.

Even such torments could not go on forever. The cruel princess next ordered Ulrich to go on a crusade in her service, but when she learned that he joyfully and obediently received the direct command from her, she suddenly relented, bade him rather stay at home near to her, and finally granted him her love. What an outpouring of thankful verses then! What a spate of shattered lances, dented helmets, broken blades, humbled opponents! For having won her love, Ulrich was puissant, magnificent, impregnable; this was the height of his career as a knight. Regrettably, it is not clear in the *Frauendienst* just which of her favors she so tardily vouchsafed after nearly a decade and a half, but in the light of other contemporary documents concerning the customs of courtly love, one can be fairly sure that she permitted him the kiss and the embrace, and perhaps even the right to caress her, naked in bed. If she gave him the final reward at all, it was probably on extremely rare occasions. For sexual outlet was not really the point of all this. Ulrich had not been laboring nearly 15 years for so ordinary a commodity; his real reward had always been in his suffering, striving, and yearning.

Section four family dynamics

More than most groups, the family is built upon and sustains primary relations. Affection, intimacy, openness, mutual commitment, and personal satisfaction are legitimate expectations.

But the family is more than a setting for primary relations. It is also a unit of social organization and as such has requirements that set limits on participation and interaction. For example, family membership is not necessarily voluntary, and members who feel trapped may withdraw from free communication or otherwise undermine the primary-group ideal. Furthermore, patterns of inequality and authority are inevitable if only because of the dependency of children.

Members of the family have personality traits, goals, and outside involvements that affect how they act and respond. In Western societies adolescents often reject family intimacy; they may have much closer relations with their peers outside the family than with their parents; within the family a pseudo-intimacy may be maintained out of a sense of duty and propriety. Thus the primary-relations model cannot account for the complexity of interaction in the family setting. The family is a kind of primary group, not a pure example or prototype.

FAMILY SYSTEMS

Two groups are no more alike than any two individuals. In some there are permanent cliques and coalitions, rivalry and conflict; others are characterized by shifting coalitions, flexibility, and harmony; still others have no cliques or coalitions, maintaining a loose integration. Some groups are more or less isolated from the larger community; others are involved in it and susceptible to external influences.

The family as an example of a small social system can be described with reference to three features: (1) the group boundary, (2) the role system, and (3) the pattern of coalitions.

The closed-family system A closed family is turned inward. It tends to be isolated from the larger community: Parents have relatively few contacts outside the family, and children have few friends. The members tend to draw a sharp distinction between the family in-group and the outside world. (See the case of the Israeli urban refugee family discussed in Adaptation 24.) In an extreme case the outside world is viewed with apprehension, while the internal life of the family is idealized.

High levels of commitment and cooperation are required by the closed family. The

wife who does not look to outsiders for help and sociability expects more from her husband and children. The husband, having few outside involvements, is free to participate in household chores. One result may be a blurring of sex roles. A study in London found that relatively isolated families tended to turn inward and in doing so broke down the sharp segregation between the duties of husband and wife:

Such continuity as they possess lies in their relationship with each other rather than in their external relationships. In facing the external world they draw on each other, for their strongest emotional investment is made where there is continuity. Hence their high standards of conjugal compatibility, their stress on shared interests, on joint organization, on equality between husband and wife. They must get along well together, they must help one another in carrying out familial tasks, for there is no sure external source of material and emotional help (Bott, 1971:95).

The desegregation of sex roles in closed families is less likely to occur where the family is more than a consumption and child-rearing unit. If the family is an economic unit and runs a family farm or business enterprise, there is a practical basis for close cooperation linked to a clear division of labor.

There is some evidence, based on clinical studies of troubled families and families of schizophrenics, that the closed family is vulnerable to the formation of permanent coalitions (Vogel and Bell, 1960:382–397; Lennard et al., 1965:166–183). A typical pattern is the coalition of a mother and one child. Mother and child form a deep, though frequently ambivalent, emotional attachment, creating a split between themselves and the rest of the family, sometimes resulting in painful isolation of another member, "scapegoating," or pathological dependency.

The open-family system The classic case of the open-family system is the nuclear family embedded in a homogeneous, kin-based community. In such a setting the boundaries of the nuclear family are permeable, and the members have sustained outside relations.

Family reunion in North Carolina

Thus "nuclear families are open in closed societies" (Farber, 1966:79). The tightly organized community fully involves its members in participation, and obligations extend to the whole community.

The closely knit community fosters role segregation within the open family:

Close-knit networks are most likely to develop when husband and wife, together with their friends, neighbours, and relatives, have grown up in the same local area and have continued to live there after marriage. Many people know one another and have known one another since childhood. Women tend to associate with women and men with men. . . . The marriage is superimposed on these pre-existing relationships. . . . Because old relationships can be continued after marriage, both husband and wife can satisfy some personal needs outside the marriage, so that their emotional investment in the conjugal relationship need not be as intense as it is in other types of family. The wife, particularly, can get outside help with domestic tasks and with child care. A rigid division of labour between husband and wife is therefore possible (Bott, 1971:92, 94).

A fluid and amorphous environment, however, provides little support for open families. As a result, the modern middle-class urban family has the task of balancing openness and withdrawal. To accomplish this it must create a semipermeable boundary, sufficiently closed to maintain the integrity of the family yet open enough to draw upon the uncertain resources of the outside world and adapt to changing circumstances.

The adaptive family is characterized by shifting rather than permanent coalitions. In the American middle-class family the wife often accepts responsibility for managing internal relations in the family:

Insofar as this division of roles occurs, the wife

is in the position of balancing the demands of the husband with those of the children. Successful mediation by the wife of the husband's and children's demands and needs is necessary for the smooth coordination of activities within the family (Farber, 1964:321).

Effective mediation requires a sensitivity to the need for shifting coalitions. If the mother sides consistently with one family member to the exclusion of another, the family may become polarized and degenerate into conflict and permanent coalitions.

COMMUNICATION AND INTERACTION

In the contemporary middle-class family communication is expected to be deep and extensive. Husband and wife are companions who confide in each other on the basis of mutual trust and openness. In a more limited way, the same ideal applies to the relations between parents and children.

However, there is probably a substantial gap between ideal and reality in all sections of the population. Recent research has shown that this gap is especially apparent among working-class couples. Moreover, many couples do not aspire to the ideal; they do not expect or even want to have full communication.

A study of 58 blue-collar marriages (Komarovsky, 1964) gave special attention to the "marriage dialogue." Following is a summary of the study's main findings:

1. The couples were sharply divided in their conceptions of the ideal marriage. By one measure (responses to the complaint of a wife that her husband "doesn't talk to her"), 37 percent showed they valued communication, but an equal percentage denied that the wife had a legitimate grievance.

2. In practice, meager communication was fairly common. About one-third of the couples rated low on a measure of self-disclosure, although "almost one-half of the respondents share their feelings and thoughts 'fully" and even 'very fully' with their mates" (Komarovsky, 1964:140).

3. There were significant differences between the less educated and the better educated respondents, even within this working-class sample. The high school graduates were more likely to share middle-class ideals of companionship and marital privacy and to emphasize the importance of psychic congeniality in marriage.

The less-educated couples tend to be more traditional in their ideas about sex-linked interests and about "rights" of men to silence and protection from tiresome children and women's trivia. They tend to think that friendship is more likely to exist between members of the same sex, whereas they see the principal marital ties as sexual union, complementary tasks and mutual devotion (Komarovsky, 1964:132).

4. There were several barriers to communication:

(a) Sharp differences in the interests of men and women "Women's talk" is considered trivial and irrelevant by the husbands, and the wives have little interest in such male preoccupations as sports, carpentry, motorcycles, and the like.

(b) Separation of work and home life The men perceive their jobs as uninteresting, something to get away from rather than to share. Moreover, talk about the job tends to take the form of griping, which is seen as unmanly.

(c) A general impoverishment of life, few leisure-time activities, and limited interaction with other couples The following comment on one marriage is suggestive:

The strains put upon this marriage are all the greater because life contains so little else for the pair. They are almost completely isolated from meaningful social contact and their low income restricts recreation activities. In a more affluent situation, Mrs. J.'s needs for reassurance would remain, but a pleasanter life would provide some diversions and would siphon off some discontent — she spoke with warmth about a bus trip to Florida she and her husband once made together to visit relatives (Komarovsky, 1964:170).

5. The equilibrium of marriages based on role segregation depended on "the availability of close relatives and friends who fulfill for both, but especially for the wife, func-

The invalidated self

A 38-year-old woman came for therapy following what was apparently a suicide attempt with an overdose of barbiturates and alcohol. She had remnants of former attractiveness but was now quite plump and puffy. In high school she had been chosen queen of the state fair and was most popular. An only child whose middle-class parents gave her "everything," she remained gracious and temperate and was never thought of as "spoiled." After high school she matriculated at a school of nursing where again dates were plentiful and she excelled in her work.

She met and subsequently fell in love with a young law student, quite handsome, with a promising future. There were no religious or ethnic disparities; both sets of parents looked on approvingly. They were married while he was attending law school and she was completing her nursing training. Completing her education first, she was able to obtain immediate work at the university hospital, where again she was both accepted and praised. She was there for two years. When her husband completed law school, they moved to another city, where he was appointed a junior partner in a prominent and prestigious law firm.

She, meanwhile, became pregnant, much to the satisfaction of the entire family. Thereafter she was to attend to her new family. As a specialist in a new field in great demand, her husband made meteoric progress in the new city. His prestige, social status, and income were quite unique for a young man. She was contented at home; in a short time there were two children.

When she openly wondered about the possibility of "keeping her hand in" nursing, her husband, as well as her parents, indicated that there was really no need for it, and it might be an embarrassment to the husband. After all, the wife of a successful man should not be handling bedpans. She offered no resistance—there was too much going for them.

She made friends easily and in her own right ascended the social ladder. She became president of the garden club, was the star of local dramatic productions, and became a leader in the Junior League. They complemented each other in success—the couple everyone envied. And a romantic spirit persisted. Yes, there were rounds of country club dances and parties, wild and otherwise, with ubiquitous drinking, but intemperance was at the time more of a problem for him than for her. She was known not only as the wife of a successful young man but also as a person in her own right.

In this setting and circumstance he was sought out to become a full partner in a metropolitan law firm in another city. The offer held forth both a large income and unique political opportunities. He was elated.

The good news, however, met, for the first time in their marriage, with a sense of doubt on her part. He overcame this with reassurances of how great it would be for everyone. She was unconvinced but was hardly in a position to veto such an advantage. Her parents convinced her that she should not obstruct her husband. He was disappointed in her slight resistance, interpreting it as a breach of loyalty—something new in their relationship.

The move was made, a new home purchased, children placed in the right schools, proper country club and church joined. However, while he

Source: Abridged from Robert Seidenberg, "Dear Mr. Success: Consider Your Wife," *Wall Street Journal*, February 7, 1972. Dr. Seidenberg is a practicing psychiatrist in Syracuse, N. Y. The original article is the nucleus of the book *Corporate Wives—Corporate Casualties*, published by the American Management Association, 1973.

continued climbing, she seemed to have lost her former zest. She tried to make the social contacts expected of her, but she was now new — low person on the totem pole. The social climate was kindest to old established families; women were alumnae of exclusive Eastern schools. Although she was accepted into membership of various organizations, it was quite apparent to her that unlike his, her credentials were specious; she would be tolerated but would receive none of the adulation that she had known.

She became increasingly withdrawn. Her children were now grown and away at school and seemed to do very well without her. Predictably, as she withdrew she used alcohol and barbiturates increasingly, which made social and service organizations more difficult to attend. She became determined to return to nursing despite the feelings of her husband. But then the problem of licensing in a different state arose. Refresher courses became a requirement, but her drinking made this impossible.

When she appeared for therapy she had been drinking for three years. Cajoling, threats, and abusiveness by her husband had had no salutary effect. She had been sent out of town for three months for residential therapy. Her husband preferred that she be treated out of the city "to try to keep the whole thing as hidden as possible." She was referred to me from the hospital. The husband, however, had grave reservations about having his family affairs known to any psychiatrist locally. "Allowing" her to come to me for help was a concession on his part that he made with great misgivings.

What came out in treatment? A docile, timid, fear- and guilt-ridden person presented herself, for she had "let everyone down." She had been a disappointment to her parents and a burden to her husband. Everyone makes moves; why couldn't she?

Wasn't she weak and ungrateful? All the women she knew would give anything to have such a loving and successful husband. Her parents, in their less generous moments, called her selfish and spoiled; when they felt charitable, they called her mentally ill.

As therapy continued it became increasingly apparent that this woman had had excessive demands placed on her more-than-adequate resources. She was indeed responding to the impossible task of rebuilding an identity for the second or third time. She had simply run out of gas. No one around her either understood or could perceive the social and psychological burden imposed on her.

The irony of the situation was compounded by the fact that neither husband, parents, nor friends would concede that she even suffered a loss by the move, which made her feel that she was all the more unreasonable. A timid person, she had never known the tactics of rebellion or social action. Her role was one of submission and obeisance, of which alcoholism, drug taking, and suicide are the conventional derivatives.

Since therapy was not producing the results that he was hoping for, the husband forbade her to come any more. On her own, she sought help from a social agency and joined Alcoholics Anonymous. Two years after the termination of therapy with me, she called. She volunteered the information that she was doing fairly well, attributing gains through her work with AA — real anonymity. And she was living apart from her husband. There is no indication that she has been active in the community other than in Alcoholics Anonymous.

Nothing fails like success. It is quite likely that this woman would not have suffered "culture shock" if she had not attained heightened status before the move.

If one must discover the tragic flaw in this patient, she must be faulted for *leaving her profession in the beginning, thus depriving herself of residual power for changes that had to be made later. She was entirely too docile and submissive here, sadly responding, of course, to the normal upbringing of every woman of her class by placing love of husband before any personal ambitions and strivings.*

tions lacking in marriage'' (Komarovsky, 1964:176). This finding bears out the point made above regarding role segregation in open-family systems. Although communication with her husband may be meager, a wife may have extensive contact with her mother or women friends, thus reducing her need for marital companionship. Her contentment is increased if she believes that role segregation is right and proper:

The case of Mr. and Mrs. K. illustrates how close and satisfying marriage can be despite a very specialized pattern of sharing. Even within the strictly personal sphere (her hurts, enthusiasms and problems) Mrs. K. makes a sharp distinction between what is appropriate to share with her husband, on the one hand, and with her girl friends and female relatives, on the other. Deeply satisfied in their emotional needs, Mr. and Mrs. K. live large segments of their lives apart from one another (Komarovsky, 1964:176).

Thus marriage may be successful, in the sense of creating a deep emotional bond, without conforming to the ideal of companionship. However, without a supportive environment, the psychic burdens may be very great.

FAMILY PRESSURE AND MENTAL DISORDER

Under some circumstances the family exerts extreme pressure on one or more members by an insistent demand for conformity to role expectations. Some psychiatrists and sociologists have argued that family demands are often so stressful that they result in mental breakdowns. "The Invalidated Self," p. 324, is a psychiatrist's case study of psychic overload.

An important feature of this case is that the wife is perceived as "unreasonable." The fact that she expresses her needs is taken as evidence of character deficiency or mental illness. In effect, her own needs and perceptions are not taken seriously. This theme has been developed by R. D. Laing, an English psychiatrist who views the mentally ill as having their own rationality, responding in understandable ways to oppressive family situations. (See Laing and Esterson, 1964; also Sampson et al., 1964.)

SATISFACTION WITH MARRIAGE

Crudely measured as the number of divorces per 1,000 persons, the divorce rate has increased from 0.9 in 1910 to 4.6 in 1974. Over the same period, the marriage rate fluctuated between 8.5 and 12.2, and in 1974 it was 10.5. Thus the divorce rate approaches half the marriage rate. Despite this high and increasing divorce rate, 74 percent of males aged 18 and over and 68 percent of females of the same age are currently married, and most of those are still in their first marriage (*Statistical Abstract of the United States*, 1975: Tables 67 and 94). A happy marriage and good health are rated as the two most important values in American life (Campbell et al., 1976:Chap. 3).

A sample of currently married persons was asked three broad questions intended to evaluate the quality of their marriages. The questions and responses are given in Table 10:1. The third question in the table is presented in a seven-point scale from "completely dissatisfied" to "completely satisfied." Such scales are frequently used to grade verbal answers. Not surprisingly, married people described their marriages in favorable terms. The very fact that divorce occurs widely as a solution to marital discord contributes to that finding, because the favorable responses were given by people whose marriages remained intact after the most dissatisfied ones had been sifted out.

At the beginning of married life, there is a high level of satisfaction, which appears to decline "to nearly the twentieth year of marriage. After this point reports of marriage satisfaction sweep upward into very old age"

Table 10:1   Measures of marriage satisfaction (in percentages)

	Yes, often	Some-times	Once in a while	Hardly ever	Never	Total	N
"Have you ever wished you had married someone else?"							
Women	1	5	6	18	70	100	763
Men	*	4	7	17	72	100	684
"Has the thought of getting a divorce ever crossed your mind?"							
Women	1	4	8	23	64	100	763
Men	1	3	5	20	71	100	685

	Completely dissatisfied				Completely satisfied				
"All things considered, how satisfied are you with your marriage? Which number comes closest to how satisfied or dissatisfied you feel?"									
	1	2	3	4	5	6	7		
Women	1	1	2	9	8	23	56	100	763
Men	0	*	1	6	6	27	60	100	685

* Not a meaningful percentage

Source: Campbell et al., 1976:324, sample survey.

(Campbell et al., 1976:325). Families with no children in the home express the highest level of satisfaction, and satisfaction among both women and men declines with increased number of children in the home. The burden of external pressures, such as financial responsibilities, may explain this finding.

In general, men seem to be somewhat more satisfied with marriage, and there is a negative relationship between amount of education and marital satisfaction. "Men with only a grade school education seem especially well satisfied with their marriages, but their wives (assuming that these men marry women of similar educational status) are considerably less enthusiastic and are the most likely of all the educational groups to describe their marriages in neutral or negative terms" (Campbell et al., 1976:327–328).

Among college graduates, 50 percent of the men and a little less than 40 percent of the women describe themselves as completely satisfied with their marriage, but only 10 percent are neutral or dissatisfied. There is, indeed, a high divorce rate and much questioning and experimentation, but the findings of this study hardly suggest a universal disenchantment that would soon lead to the end of marriage as a basic social institution.

Section five social policy and social change

In a period of rapid social change, the family is both the pressure point and the shock absorber. As an institution, it is pushed to adapt to numerous external demands. As a personal resource for individuals adjusting to situations of stress, the family is the institution of last resort. Among the problems that call for institutional innovation and for new perceptions of family life are (1) the growing participation of women in the work force, (2) the role of the family in the economic and social attainment of its members,

and (3) increasing interest in alternative, nontraditional forms of marriage.

LONGEVITY AND THE FAMILY CYCLE

The growing expectation of life in industrialized countries means that many people complete an entire life cycle from dependent infancy to dependent, or at least economically unproductive, old age. In 1973 the average future life for American males at birth was 68 years and for females, 75 years. As recently as 1920 the respective figures were 54 and 55 years (*Statistical Abstract of the United States*, 1975:59). (See Figure 9:6, p. 279.) Thus until recently, relatively few married couples lived out long lives together. Most of those who survived beyond middle age would have been widowed and would have sought a second spouse. The fact that both husband and wife are now likely to survive beyond middle age presents both opportunities for extension of the conjugal relationship and, frequently, a need to reassess a relationship formed to create a family and raise children. There are few precedents for dealing with these problems, because the traditional family was geared to reproduction and child care rather than adaptation to an "empty nest." Older couples now often face the difficult task of reevaluating the personal worth of a relationship that might have been established four decades earlier.

In the United States six well-defined stages of the family cycle can be identified (Collver, 1963):

1. Marriage to birth of first child (short interval)

2. Childbearing (completed within a short time)

3. Child rearing (prolonged)

4. First child married to last child married (short time)

5. Empty nest (long period)

6. Widowhood (fairly long)

Although most people are not do-it-yourself demographers or sociologists, many

Figure 10:5
Percentage of married women
in the labor force,
United States, 1890, 1949,
1961, 1970, and 1975

^a For 1970 and 1975, ages are 16–24.

Source: Data for 1890 and 1949, Jaffe and
Stewart, 1951:172. Data for 1961,
Monthly Labor Review, January 1962:Table B.
Data for 1970,
Statistical Abstract of the United States, 1971:
Table 333. Data for 1975 extracted from unpublished
tabulations, courtesy of the
Bureau of Labor Statistics.

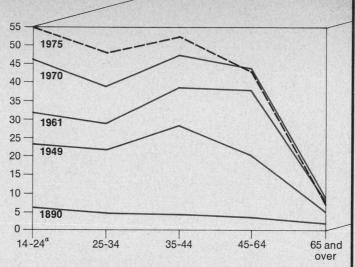

do accurately perceive that they will pass through stages of a family cycle and they plan accordingly. The movement of married women into and out of the labor force at the different points in the family cycle is an important example of personal adaptations that raise questions of social policy.

By providing day-care facilities for small children, and by encouraging part-time employment and flexible hours, industrialized countries can make it easier for married women to leave the labor force during childbearing and early child-rearing. These innovations are at an early stage and remain controversial.

Married women at work In 1900 only 18 percent of workers were female. In 1965 the figure was 34 percent, and in 1975, about 40 percent. There is every likelihood that a larger proportion of women will be employed and that they will make up a larger proportion of the total work force. Changes in family structure and changed participation of women in the work force have gone hand in hand. Traditionally the major economic contribution of women to the family was not in earnings but in the production of goods for household consumption and the provision of numerous services. As women have lost some of their more obvious eco-

nomically productive roles in the household and as rising consumption standards require more money income, women have gone outside the home for employment in increasing numbers. This trend has been spurred by the decline in family size and changing attitudes toward the propriety of married women working. Figure 10:5 shows the increasing percentage of married women in the labor force by age groups since 1890.

The curves show a dip in labor force participation at ages when child-care responsibilites are most demanding. However, the rapid decline in family size means that this period of withdrawal from the labor force is becoming brief. Women now complete their childbearing and child caring when they are relatively young and have long potential working lives before them.

The fact that there is no recent increase in participation among older women is somewhat puzzling. It may be that the age limits to work force participation have been defined or that enough women have been working long enough to be eligible for retirement benefits.

The foregoing statistical discussion does not imply that the movement of women into and out of the work force is a smooth matter facilitated by employers, government, and unions. When, at the time of marriage or at the birth of the first child, they leave the labor force to become full-time homemakers, they lose occupational momentum that is rarely recovered. The acquisition of job experience is interrupted, and their bargaining power when they wish to return to work is reduced because by that time, their qualifications may be obsolete. It is said that women tend to have jobs, not careers (Poloma and Garland, 1971:536). Surviving sanctions against women who work when they have young children complicate the difficulties of combining home and job responsibilities. However, the dual career is increasingly recognized as a legitimate domestic arrangement, and researchers are beginning to investigate "the enabling process," the family arrangements and expectations that encourage women in their careers (Rapoport and Rapoport, 1971:531).

WEALTH, POVERTY, AND THE FAMILY

An old adage says that the rich get richer and the poor get children. This folk sociology has a basis in fact. Above a certain level of accumulated capital, it takes exceedingly bad luck, inept management, or spendthrift behavior to dissipate resources faster than they accumulate. The family may not be the most efficient wealth-concentrating ma-

chine, but the mechanism of inheritance enables it to bind together the efforts of its members over several generations.

Countries differ in the extent to which they tax a person's capital resources rather than merely tax income, although high and progressive rates of income tax retard capital accumulation. The U.S. federal estate tax allows a specific exemption of $60,000, plus deductions for debts, expenses, charities, and the spouse, before a tax is assessed. Beyond the exemption and deductions, the estate tax starts at a quite moderate level, although the rate of taxation gets progressively larger. A taxable estate of $100,000 pays a tax of about $21,000; an estate of $500,000, a tax of $146,000; an estate of $1 million, a tax of $326,000; and an estate of $10 million, a tax of $6,088,000 (*1976 World Almanac*:61). Certain states assess additional inheritance taxes but at relatively modest rates. In summary, the wealth-concentrating ability of American families is not seriously impaired by death taxes. Although such taxes are a potentially powerful means of redistributing wealth and restructuring the economic strata, they have a relatively weak impact in the United States.

Poverty and the family The family is the chief vehicle for ensuring a smooth or a

Table 10:2 Percentage of persons in poverty by family, sex, and ethnic status, United States, 1974[a]

Persons in family	White	Black	Spanish origin
Male head	5	14	15
Related children under 18	7	22	20
Other family members	4	13	13
Female head	25	53	50
Related children under 18	43	66	64
Other family members	8	33	24

[a] Each figure is the percentage of the total in that category below the poverty line in 1974. For instance, the top of the left column indicates that 5 percent of all white male family heads are in poverty, and the bottom of the third column says that 24 percent of other family members of Spanish origin are in poverty.

Source: Current Population Reports, Series P-60, No. 102, January 1976, extracted from Tables 1 and 42.

rough start in life. A child has a fair chance for economic security if the head of the family is a male, especially a white male. Just 7 percent of children in such families were in poverty in 1974. (Row 2, Table 10:2.) But 43 percent of children in white families with female heads were in poverty (Row 5). Because the fertility rate is relatively high for poor families, their resources are spread over more people, reducing the training and other opportunities available to poor children. Black families offer much less economic security than white ones. While 22 percent of related children in black families with male heads (Row 2) were poor, 66 percent of children were in poverty if the head was a black woman (Row 5). Such families reflect the inferior occupational status of women, the inferior occupational status of blacks, and the combined tasks of wage earning, housekeeping, and parental obligations.

The poor fatherless family has long been recognized as one of the black family types (Frazier, 1939). Two cautions should be kept in mind: (1) Blacks do not have a monopoly of fatherless families and (2) the fatherless family is not the "typical" black family.

A dubious policy affecting fatherless families has been applied in the administration of social welfare benefits. The Aid to Dependent Children program has restricted benefits for families with fathers or father surrogates. Therefore in many cases it has been in the interests of the family for the "man in the house" to disappear. As an unintended consequence, the program increased the number of fatherless families.

The predicament of fatherless families is a current topic of public debate. Some feel that the fatherless family is nearly by definition a deviant type and that the only solution is to increase the relative number of mother-father families. However, even though the responsibilities of being the sole parent are a burden to the mother, many fatherless families are effective primary groups that rear well-adjusted and self-reliant children.

E. Franklin Frazier (1894–1962). In *Negro Family in the United States* (1939) he identified the major family types and traced their historical influence. Although later research has questioned some details of Frazier's assessment, his work remains the foundation for the study of black families.

MARRIAGE AND DIVORCE

In traditional legal doctrine, marriage combines both the idea of contract and the idea of status. Marriages are formed voluntarily, by mutual assent. On the other hand, marriage is more than a contract; once established it takes on a new dimension. Marriage contemplates a permanent union and the creation of a new status. To be a husband or wife is to be endowed with rights and obligations by operation of law. Moreover, the relation differs from a contract in that the partners cannot dissolve it by mutual consent.

Freedom *to* marry is limited mainly by rules against marrying near relatives, forbidding bigamy, and limiting marriages of young people. Until recently, in the United States there were laws against interracial marriages. In addition, some states prohibit marriages by habitual drunkards, narcotics addicts, insane people, parolees, and even paupers.

On the whole, however, the law has been less concerned with the opportunity to marry than with the problem of divorce. Here the social origins of the law and the problem of adapting law to social reality are plainly revealed.

The religious influence The traditional Anglo-American law of divorce shows the strong influence of Christian doctrine. "Wherefore they are no more twain, but one flesh. What therefore God hath joined together, let not man put asunder" (Matt. 19:6). At an early date marriage was proclaimed a holy sacrament. A valid marriage, consummated by sexual intercourse, was considered indissoluble.

The impossibility of divorce, somewhat eased by the law of annulment, has remained the doctrine of the Roman Catholic church. The Protestant reformers of the sixteenth and seventeenth centuries rejected this absolute prohibition, and most Western countries permit divorce. However, the Christian influence makes itself felt in the legal policy of most states that divorce may be granted only when one of the parties is guilty of a grievous fault, such as adultery, desertion, or extreme cruelty. This has come to be known as the fault principle.

Under Catholic church (canon) law, it is the duty of husbands and wives to live together, but they may appeal to church courts for permission to separate. Canon law has developed rules on separation, not divorce. Adultery is the only basis for permanent separation, but temporary separations are allowed for other causes. Divorce law in the United States took over the canon law philosophy. Roughly speaking, what were grounds for separation under canon law became grounds for divorce in the civil courts.

Secular policy The persistence of the fault principle can be explained in part by the continuity of religious and secular perspectives. The concept of indissoluble marriage was a way of affirming the community's stake in family life. Modern secular communities value the family for the contribution it makes to social life, especially in socialization and social control. Therefore secular policy begins with the premise that marriages should be preserved. The fault doctrine, with its deep historical roots and wide, almost automatic acceptance, was useful to the secular state as a way of placing barriers in the way of divorce.

A purely contractual view of marriage would (1) allow the parties to decide what their rights and obligations should be during the marriage, (2) permit dissolution by mutual consent, and (3) insist that the contract be for some definite term of years, after which even one of the partners could dissolve the marriage. This approach has not been accepted, although it was tried in an even more radical form by the Soviet Union, which in 1917 established the principle of free divorce, without reasons and available on request of one or both parties. However, by 1936 divorce was made somewhat more difficult, and in 1944 the basic Soviet policy was changed, requiring an attempt at reconciliation and the granting of divorce only for good reasons (Hazard and Shapiro, 1962: 100–101).

The alternative to fault is the "breakdown" principle, which holds that a divorce should be granted if the marriage is in fact irretrievably disrupted. There is a trend toward accepting the breakdown principle in the United States: At least ten states, including California, Iowa, Florida, and Colorado, have passed such laws, and the National Conference of Commissioners on Uniform State Laws (1970:7) has recommended for enactment in all the states a Uniform Marriage and Divorce Act making "irretrievable breakdown of the marriage relationship the sole basis for its dissolution." It remains to be seen how many state legislatures will follow the recommendation, but the consensus of the commissioners tends to support the trend. Other Western countries are also questioning the fault principle.

ALTERNATIVE FORMS OF MARRIAGE

With the movement toward divorce by mutual consent, or even at the request of one of the partners, a major change in social policy is occurring. But divorce is only one aspect of the legal regulation of marriage. In addition there have been long-standing assumptions regarding the roles and responsibilities of husbands and wives. Traditionally, the husband was considered the head of the family, and the wife lost much of her independent identity. She took her husband's name and was required to accept his decision about where they should live. The husband was responsible for supporting the family and the wife for providing domestic and child-care services.

These and other assumptions of the law are being challenged today because they are inconsistent with much of sociological reality. The law of marriage has been largely based on a single model of the marital bond — lifelong commitment, a first and only marriage, the expectation of children, conventional division of labor, monogamy, and heterosexual union. This model may still be dominant in American society, but it is far from universal.

In fact, many marriages end in divorce, remarriage is frequent, and new life-styles are altering what people expect from marriage and what arrangements they prefer. Diversity is rampant, but law and social policy have done little to support the opportunity of individuals to decide for themselves what the terms of their marriage should be. Some changes have occurred. For example, in 1965 the Supreme Court upheld a right of "marital privacy" when it struck down a Connecticut statute forbidding the use of contraceptives (*Griswold* v. *Connecticut*, 381 U.S. 479 [1965]). And if the Equal Rights Amendment is adopted, many of the laws discriminating against married women will be nullified. But for the most part little attention has been given to overhauling the law of marriage to take account of diversity in fact and in aspiration.

Adaptation 26 suggests a new and different approach. It proposes that rules of marriage be established by the partners themselves, by voluntary agreement, rather than by operation of law. This would make possible a wide variety of marital forms determined by the interests of the prospective partners rather than by a public policy supporting a particular pattern of married life.

This "modest proposal" is clearly at odds with the traditional view that there is a public interest in protecting a historic form of the family. It is possible, however, that more realistic voluntary arrangements may increase rather than decrease the stability of marriages, especially if provision is made for orderly settlement of disputes, for example, by referring them to an arbitrator.

At the present time, such contracts are not enforceable in the courts. The courts have resisted upholding contracts that alter the elements of the marital relationship, for example, those affecting sexual relations or the obligation of the husband to support his family. "A bargain between married persons or persons contemplating marriage to change the essential incidents of marriage is illegal" (Weitzman, 1974:1259). A contract in place of marriage rather than within marriage would also be a legal novelty and subject to many obstacles, for example, the fact that extramarital intercourse is contemplated. It is apparent, however, that the legal structure of marriage is subject to considerable strain and imaginative new forms may be accepted in a not-too-distant future.

Adaptation 26 Weitzman: The conjugal contract

Two novel forms of "marriage" contract are presented below. The first presumes a traditional marriage but spells out in detail the expectations of the partners and their mutual promises. However, a number of provisions in that contract deviate from usual public policy, for example, agreements about birth control and abortion and provision for dissolution of the marriage at will by either party.

The second example is more unconventional, for it contemplates a form of marriage quite different from the traditional and legal model. Equality is the keynote, and the contract is designed to facilitate the maintaining of two professional careers as well as a conjugal union, including child rearing. This second model may be considered a contract in lieu of marriage.

TRADITIONAL MARRIAGE—PARTNERSHIP OF DOCTOR AND HOUSEWIFE

David is a first-year medical student who may have to drop out of medical school for lack of financial support. Nancy wants to be a professional dancer. She is planning to enroll in a special training program in Paris for the following two years. Although David and Nancy have known each other only two months, they are deeply in love. David wants Nancy to give up her dancing and Paris, and to stay in New York and marry him. In return he promises her a comfortable life as a doctor's wife. He asks Nancy to get a job to support him through medical school and internship. He assures her of lavish support in return, once he becomes a doctor. Nancy decides that she could be happy as the wife of a successful doctor, and she agrees to accept David's proposal on the condition that they have an explicit agreement giving her a future share in his career and making adequate provision for her in the event of dissolution. Nancy feels that she is giving up her potential career to become a partner in David's career. She knows her expectations will be drastically altered in the event of a divorce, and she will then be too

Source: Abridged from Lenore J. Weitzman, "Legal Regulation of Marriage: Tradition and Change," *California Law Review* 72 (July–September), 1974: 1169–1288. Published in this form by permission of Lenore J. Weitzman.

old to pursue her dancing career. David realizes that Nancy is making a great sacrifice for the relationship, and for him personally, and he wants to assure her of future compensation. David and Nancy write a contract to make their relationship an equal partnership in which everything will be community property. Their contract also provides compensation for Nancy's psychological, educational, and financial loss if the marriage dissolves.

a. Aims and expectations   Both parties want to state their goals and future expectations at the time this contract is signed. Nancy is entering into the relationship with the expectation that she will enjoy the usual benefits of being a doctor's wife. In return for the assurance of a future in which she will be supported in comfort, she is willing to give up her dancing career and to support David until he completes his internship. While she supports David she realizes that she will have to work hard and make do with very little money. Further, she realizes that David's studies will be very time-consuming and that he will be less than an ideal companion. Since she will be making a very significant contribution toward David's career, she expects to have a future interest in it. Once David becomes a doctor, she will enjoy the social benefits of being a doctor's wife. Nancy expects to have a beautiful home and summer home, expensive clothing, vacations in Europe, child care and private schools for her children, and a housekeeper.

David understands that Nancy's efforts will make it possible for him to obtain his medical education in a fairly comfortable fashion. Her support will ensure that he will not have to drop out of school to earn money and he will not have to spend any time on part-time jobs or housework. He will be able to devote all his time to his studies. In return, he wants to guarantee Nancy a share in his future career.

Both parties feel that they are making a lifetime contract and are building a community from which they will both benefit. Both parties feel that they are equal partners in this community and that income, property, and other gains that may accrue to the income-earning partner are the result of the joint efforts of both parties and therefore belong equally to both parties.

b. Property   Any property of the parties shall be

jointly owned as community property. Nancy will manage and control the community property and will take care of all other household business matters.

c. Support Nancy will work as a secretary in order to support David until he has finished medical school and an internship. David will support the family from then on; he will take a (paying) residency or begin to practice medicine. Nancy will not work outside the home after David's career has commenced.

d. Domicile The location of the family domicile will be decided by David; the main consideration in making such a decision will be the best interests of David's career.

e. Name Both parties will use David's surname.

f. Housekeeping responsibilities Nancy will be responsible for maintaining the household with the assistance of a full-time housekeeper.

g. Birth control Since the most efficient contraceptives currently available are female contraceptives, Nancy will assume the responsibility for birth control for the present. However, if a male oral contraceptive or other safe and effective male contraceptive is perfected, David agrees that he will use it.

h. Other responsibilities Nancy agrees to further David's career by entertaining, serving on medical auxiliary committees, and maintaining good social relations with other doctors' wives. She will also participate in church and country club activities to enhance contacts with potential patients. David agrees to accompany Nancy to the ballet at least once a month. He also agrees to schedule at least two two-week vacations with her each year, at least one of them in Europe.

i. Children Children will be postponed until David's education is completed. If Nancy should become pregnant prior to that time, she will have an abortion. Nancy will have full responsibility for the care of the children; financial responsibility will be assumed by David.

j. Termination This partnership may be dissolved by either party, at will, upon six months' notice to the other party.

If this partnership is terminated by either party prior to the completion of David's education, Nancy's obligation to support him will cease. Moreover, once David's career has begun, he will have the obligation of supporting Nancy at the rate of $12,000 a year (1974 rate to be adjusted for in-

flation and cost of living) for as many years as she supported him. If necessary, David will secure a loan to repay Nancy for her support. If Nancy prefers a lump-sum settlement equal to the value of this support, David will arrange a loan to provide it. Both parties agree to treat Nancy's original support of David as a loan of the value specified above. David's obligation to repay this loan has the standing of any other legal debt.

If the partnership is terminated after David's career has begun, Nancy will be entitled to one-fourth of his net income for as many years as their partnership lasted. David will purchase insurance or a bond to guarantee this payment. It is agreed that this payment is not alimony and that it shall be continued unmodified regardless of her earning capacity or remarriage. The parties consider this Nancy's reimbursement for helping David's career. It is agreed that her efforts will have helped to make his success possible, and he will therefore owe her this compensation.

David also agrees to pay Nancy the fixed sum of $15,000 if their marriage terminates within 15 years, as liquidated damages for the pain and suffering she will experience from the change in her expectations and life plans.

David also agrees to pay for Nancy's medical expenses or to provide her with adequate insurance at the rate of one year of coverage for every year of marriage. It is explicitly agreed that psychiatric and dental bills be included in the above.

Community property will be divided equally upon termination. If there are children, Nancy will have custody of the children. David will have full responsibility for their support, as well as the responsibility for compensating Nancy for her services in caring for them (at the current rate for private nurses). Suitable visiting arrangements will be made.

k. Death Both parties agree to make wills stipulating the other partner the sole legatee. After termination of this agreement this obligation will not continue; however, David is obliged to make sure any continuing support obligations toward Nancy and the children are reflected in his will.

YOUNG, DUAL-CAREER, PROFESSIONAL COUPLE

Susan and Peter will be graduating from college in June and both want to continue their education. Susan wants to obtain a law degree, and Peter wants to obtain a master's degree in social work. Although they want to share their future lives, both are deeply committed to their work and feel that their careers need not be sacrificed for their personal relationship. They want a contract in lieu of marriage that will assure both of them a professional education and an equal opportunity to pursue their careers. The contract they write focuses heavily on equality of career opportunity.

a. Educational and living expenses Susan and Peter decide that they will take turns going to school, so that the nonstudent partner can support the other until he or she receives a degree. Because Susan will earn more money as an attorney, they decide that they will maximize their joint income if Susan goes to school first. They therefore agree that Peter will be solely responsible for Susan's educational expenses and support for three full years. Susan will assume these same responsibilities for the following two years. If their partnership should dissolve at any time during these first five years, their contract stipulates that each shall have the following financial obligations to the other: (1) If dissolution occurs during the first three years, Peter will pay Susan's remaining tuition (which may be up to three full years' tuition in graduate school) and pay her $4,200 a year for living expenses. (2) Thereafter, Susan will pay Peter's remaining tuition (up to two full years of tuition in a school of social work) and pay him $4,200 a year in living expenses. All living expenses will be paid at the rate of $350 a month. This amount will be tied to the cost-of-living index to allow for automatic increases.

b. Domicile Susan and Peter agree to maintain a joint domicile for the first five years of their relationship, location to be determined by the student partner to maximize educational opportunity.

After the first five years, Susan and Peter will make decisions regarding domicile jointly, with no presumption that the career of either is of greater importance in making the decision. However, if they cannot agree on where to live, the decision will be Susan's, for a period of three years. Peter will then have the right to choose the location for the following three years. They will continue to rotate the domicile decision on a three-year basis. As both parties realize that their career opportunities may not coincide with this prearranged schedule, they may decide to exchange the right of decision for any given period or make

another equitable agreement which would then be incorporated into this contract. Further, both parties will always retain the option of establishing a temporary separate residence, at their own expense, if this is necessary for their careers.

c. Property During the first five years all income and property, excluding gifts and inheritances, shall be considered community property. The income-earning partner shall have sole responsibility for its management and control.

After the first five years an inventory will be taken of all community property. Thereafter each party's earnings, as well as any gifts or bequests or the income from any property held, shall be his or her separate property. Neither party will have any rights in any present or future property of the other. A list will be kept of all household items in order to keep track of their ownership; in the event Susan and Peter decide to make a joint purchase, this will be noted on the list. Any joint purchases of items of value over $100 will be covered by a separate agreement concerning its ownership. Each party will manage and control her or his separate property and will maintain a separate bank account.

d. Household expenses (This part of the agreement shall go into effect five years hence.) Household expenses will consist of rent, utilities, food, and housekeeping expenses. Susan and Peter will each contribute 50 percent of her or his gross income to household expenses. Their contributions will be made in monthly installments of equal amounts and placed in a joint checking account. Responsibility for the joint account and for paying the above expenses will be rotated, with each having this responsibility for a three-month period. Each partner will be responsible for his or her own cleaning expenses and for food and entertainment outside of the household. Each will maintain a separate car and a separate phone and will take care of these expenses separately. If money in the joint account is not exhausted by household expenses, it may be used for joint leisure activities.

Both parties recognize that Susan's income is likely to be higher than Peter's and that 50 percent of her income will allow her more money for separate expenses. The parties therefore agree to review this arrangement six months after it goes into effect. If it seems that the arrangement places an unfair burden on Peter, they will change the second line above to read: Each party's contribution to household expenses shall be as follows: Susan shall contribute 55 percent of her gross income; Peter shall contribute 40 percent of his gross income.

e. Housekeeping responsibilities Housework will be shared equally. All necessary tasks will be divided into two categories. On even-numbered months Susan will be responsible for category one and Peter for category two, and vice versa on odd-numbered months. Each party will do his or her own cooking and clean up afterward for breakfast and lunch, as well as keeping his or her own study clean. Dinner cooking and cleaning up will be considered part of the housework to be rotated as specified above. In the event that one party neglects to perform any task, the other party can perform it and charge the nonperforming partner $15 per hour for his or her labor, or agree to be repaid in kind.

f. Sexual relations Sexual relations are subject to the consent of both parties. Responsibility for birth control will be shared equally. Susan will have this responsibility for the first six months of the year, Peter for the second six months.

g. Surname Both parties will retain their own surnames.

h. Children While the parties have decided to have two children at some time in the future, birth control will be practiced until a decision to have a child has been reached. Since the parties believe that a woman should have control over her own body, the decision of whether or not to terminate an accidental pregnancy before then shall be Susan's alone. If Susan decides to have an abortion, the party who had responsibility for birth control the month that conception occurred will bear the cost of the abortion. This will include medical expenses not covered by insurance and any other expenses or loss of pay incurred by Susan. However, if Susan decides to have the child and Peter does not agree, Susan will bear full financial and social responsibility for the child. In that event, Susan also agrees to compensate Peter should he be required to support the child. If the parties agree to have a child and Susan changes her mind after conception has occurred, she will pay for the abortion. If Peter changes his mind after conception has occurred and Susan agrees to an abortion, he will pay for it. If she does not agree, Peter will share the social and financial responsibility for the

child, just as if he had not changed his mind.

When the parties decide to have a child, the following provisions will apply: Susan and Peter will assume equal financial responsibility for the child. This will include the medical expenses connected with the birth of the child as well as any other expenses incurred in preparation for the child. If it is necessary for Susan to take time off from work in connection with her pregnancy or with the birth of the child, Peter will pay her one-half of his salary to compensate for the loss. If either party has to take time off from work to care for the child, the other party will repay that party with one-half of his or her salary. All child-care, medical, and educational expenses will be shared equally.

Since Peter expects to become a psychiatric social worker specializing in preschool children, he will have the primary child-care responsibility. He will take a paternity leave after the birth in order to care for the child full-time, until day-care arrangements can be made. Susan will compensate him at the rate of one-half of her salary. Responsibility for caring for the child on evenings and weekends will be divided equally.

Any children will take the hyphenated surnames of both parties.

i. Dissolution If there are children, both parties agree to submit to at least one conciliation session prior to termination. In addition, if a decision to dissolve the partnership is made, both parties agree to submit to binding arbitration if they are unable to reach a mutual decision regarding the issues of child custody, child support, and property division. A list of mutually agreeable arbitrators is attached to this agreement. While both agree that custody should be determined according to the best interests of the child, a presumption exists in favor of Peter, since he will have had superior training in the rearing of children. Each party agrees to assume half of the financial burden of caring for the child.

If there are no children, this household agreement can be terminated by either party for any reason upon giving the other party 60 days' notice in writing. Upon separation, each party will take his or her separate property and any jointly owned property will be divided equally. Neither party will have any financial or other responsibility toward the other after separation and division of property.

References

Arensberg, Conrad M. and Solon T. Kimball
1939 Family and Community in Ireland. Cambridge, Mass.: Harvard University Press.

Aries, Philippe
1962 Centuries of Childhood. New York: Knopf.

Bott, Elizabeth
1971 Family and Social Network. London: Tavistock. Second edition.

Buchler, Ira and Henry Selby
1968 Kinship and Social Organization: An Introduction to Theory and Method. New York: Macmillan.

Campbell, Angus, Philip E. Converse, and Willard L. Rodgers
1976 The Quality of American Life: Perceptions, Evaluations, and Satisfactions. New York: Russell Sage.

Collver, Andrew
1963 "The family cycle in India and the United States." American Sociological Review 28 (February):86–96.

Farber, Bernard
1964 Family: Organization and Interaction. New York: Chandler.

Farber, Bernard (ed.)
1966 Kinship and Family Organization. New York: Wiley.

Fox, Robin
1967 Kinship and Marriage. Harmondsworth, England: Penguin.

Frazier, E. Franklin
1939 The Negro Family in the United States. Chicago: University of Chicago Press.
1957 Black Bourgeoisie. New York: Free Press and Falcon's Wing Press. First published in 1955 in French.

Freeman, Linton C.
1958 "Marriage without love: mate-selection in non-western societies." Pp. 19–39 in Robert F. Winch, Mate Selection. New York: Harper & Row.

Gans, Herbert J.
1962 The Urban Villagers: Group and Class in the Life of Italian-Americans. New York: Free Press.

Goode, William J.
1959 "The theoretical importance of love." American Sociological Review 1 (February):38–47.
1963 World Revolution and Family Patterns. New York: Free Press.

Goodenough, Ward H.
1965 "Yankee kinship terminology: a problem in componential analysis. Pp. 259–287 in E. A. Hammel (ed.), Formal Semantic Analysis. Special Publication of American Anthropologist 67 (5):Part 2.

Gorer, Geoffrey
1938 Himalayan Village. London: Michael Joseph.

Gough, E. Kathleen
1960 "Is the family universal?—the Nayar case." Pp. 76–92 in Norman W. Bell and Ezra F. Vogel (eds.), A Modern Introduction to the Family. New York: Free Press.

Hazard, John N. and Isaac Shapiro
1962 The Soviet Legal System. Dobbs Ferry; N.Y.: Oceania.

Henry, Jules
1963 Culture Against Man. New York: Random House.

Hunt, Morton M.
1959 The Natural History of Love. New York: Knopf.

Jaffe, A. J. and Charles D. Stewart
1951 Manpower Resources and Utilization. New York: Wiley.

Kitaoji, Hironobu
1971 "The structure of the Japanese family." American Anthropologist 73 (October):1036–1057.

Komarovsky, Mirra
1964 Blue-Collar Marriage. New York: Random House.

Laing, R. D. and Aaron Esterson
1964 Sanity, Madness and the Family. Baltimore: Penguin.

Lennard, H., M. R. Beaulieu, and N. G. Embrey
1965 "Interaction in families with a schizophrenic child." Archives of General Psychiatry 12 (February):166–183.

Le Play, F.
1884 L'Organisation de la Famille. Paris: Dentu Libre.

Le Vine, Robert A.
1965 "Intergenerational tensions and extended family structures in Africa." Pp. 188–204 in Ethel Shanas and Gordon F. Streib (eds.), Social Structure and the Family. Englewood Cliffs, N.J.: Prentice-Hall.

Levy, Marion J. and Lloyd A. Fallers
1959 "The family: some comparative considerations." American Anthropologist 61 (August):647–651.

Linton, Ralph
1959 "The natural history of the family," Pp. 30–52 in Ruth Nanda Anshen (ed.), The Family: Its Function and Destiny. New York: Harper & Row.

Mair, Lucy
1965 An Introduction to Social Anthropology. New York: Oxford University Press (Clarendon Press).

Mencher, Joan P.
1965 "The Nayars of South Malabar." Pp. 163–191 in M. F. Nimkoff (ed.), Comparative Family Systems. Boston: Houghton Mifflin.

Mogey, John
1964 "Family and community in urban-industrial societies." Pp. 501–534 in Harold T. Christensen, Handbook of Marriage and the Family. Chicago: Rand McNally.

Murdock, George Peter
1949 Social Structure. New York: Macmillan.
1957 "World ethnographic sample." American Anthropologist 59 (August):664–687.
1960 "Cognitive forms of social organization." Pp. 1–14 in George Peter Murdock (ed.), Social Structure in Southeast Asia. Viking Fund Publication in Anthropology, No. 29. New York: Wenner-Gren.

Nimkoff, M. F. (ed.)
1965 Comparative Family Systems. Boston: Houghton Mifflin.

Poloma, Margaret M. and T. Neal Garland
1971 "The married professional women: a study in the tolerance of domestication." Journal of Marriage and the Family 33 (August):531–540.

Queen, Stuart A. and John B. Adams
1952 The Family in Various Cultures. Philadelphia: Lippincott.

Radcliffe-Brown, A. R.
1950 "Introduction." Pp. 1–85 in Radcliffe-Brown, A. R. and C. Daryll Forde (eds.). African System of Kinship and Marriage. London: Oxford University Press.

Rapoport, Rhona and Robert N. Rapoport
1971 "Further considerations on the dual career family." Human Relations 24 (December):519–533.

Sampson, Harold, Sheldon L. Messinger, and Robert D. Towne
1964 Schizophrenic Women: Studies in Marital Crisis. New York: Atherton.

Schneider, David M. and George C. Homans
1955 "Kinship terminology and the American kinship system." American Anthropologist 57 (December):1194–1208.

Skolnick, Arlene S. and Jerome H. Skolnick
1971 The Family in Transition. Boston: Little, Brown.

Stephens, William N.
1963 The Family in Cross-Cultural Perspective. New York: Holt, Rinehart and Winston.

Turner, Ralph H.
1970 Family Interaction. New York: Wiley.

Vogel, Ezra F. and Norman W. Bell
1960 "The emotionally disturbed child as the family scapegoat." Pp. 382–397 in Norman W. Bell and Ezra F. Vogel (eds.), A Modern Introduction to the Family. New York: Free Press.

Weitzman, Lenore J.
1974 "Legal regulation of marriage: tradition and change." California Law Review 62 (July–September):1169–1288.

Young, Michael and Peter Willmott
1962 Family and Kinship in East London. Baltimore: Penguin Books.

Zelditch, Morris, Jr.
1964 "Cross-cultural analyses of family structure." Pp. 462–500 in Harold T. Christensen (ed.), Handbook of Marriage and the Family. Chicago: Rand McNally.

Sources and readings

Handbooks

Christensen, Harold T. (ed.)
1964 Handbook of Marriage and the Family. Chicago: Rand McNally.

Goode, William J., Elizabeth Hopkins, and Helen M. McClure
1971 Social Systems and Family Patterns: A Propositional Inventory. Indianapolis: Bobbs-Merrill.

Anthologies

Coser, Rose Laub
1964 The Family: Its Structure and Functions. New York: St. Martin's.

Hadden, Jeffrey K. and Marie L. Borgatta
1969 Marriage and the Family: A Comprehensive Reader. Itasca, Ill.: Peacock.

Skolnick, Arlene S. and Jerome H. Skolnick
1971 The Family in Transition. Boston: Little, Brown.

Sussman, Marvin B.
1963 Sourcebook in Marriage and the Family. Boston: Houghton Mifflin.

Comparative perspectives

Anshen, Ruth Nanda (ed.)
1959 The Family: Its Function and Destiny. New York: Harper & Row.

Arensberg, Conrad M. and Solon T. Kimball
1939/1968 Family and Community in Ireland. Cambridge: Harvard University Press.

Barash, Meyer and Alice Scourby (eds.)
1970 Marriage and the Family: A Comparative Analysis of Contemporary Problems. New York: Random House.

Elkin, Frederick
1964 The Family in Canada. Ottawa: Canadian Conference on the Family.

Goode, William J.
1963 World Revolution and Family Patterns. New York: Free Press.

Hill, Reuben and Rene Konig (eds.)
1970 Families in East and West: Socialization Process and Kinship Ties. The Hague: Mouton.

Nimkoff, M. F. (ed.)
1965 Comparative Family Systems. Boston: Houghton Mifflin.

Queen, Stuart A., Robert W. Habenstein, and John B. Adams
1961 The Family in Various Cultures. Phila.: Lippincott.

Stephens, William N.
1963 The Family in Cross-cultural Perspective. New York: Holt, Rinehart and Winston.

Representative texts

Burgess, Ernest W., Harvey J. Locke, and Mary Margaret Thomes
1971 The Family: From Traditional to Companionship. Fourth edition. New York: Van Nostrand Reinhold.

Farber, Bernard
1964 Family: Organization and Interaction. New York: Chandler.

Kephart, William M.
1972 The Family, Society and the Individual. Boston: Houghton Mifflin.

Scanzoni, Letha and John Scanzoni
1976 Men, Women, and Change: A Sociology of Marriage and the Family. New York: McGraw-Hill.

Turner, Ralph H.
1970 Family Interaction. New York: Wiley.

Waller, Willard and Reuben Hill
1951 The Family: A Dynamic Interpretation. New York: Dryden Press.

Williamson, Robert C.
1972 Marriage and Family Relations. New York: Wiley.

Periodicals

Family Law Quarterly
International Journal of Sociology of the Family
Journal of Comparative Family Studies
Journal of Marriage and the Family

11 | Education

Section one introduction

Most socialization is informal and occurs in the course of spontaneous interaction. However, institutionalized agencies for deliberate socialization are a universal feature of complex societies. There were schools in Egypt and China by at least 2000 B.C. The first schools trained priests and officials, and until recent times formal education was a device for maintaining a small "establishment," that is, a unified political, religious, military, and economic elite.

Today education is more important in scope than ever before in human history. In earlier times the educated person was economically unproductive; today productivity depends on wide distribution of specialized skills. Modern political systems, too, call for mass education.

Like the broader process of socialization, formal education has a dual significance. It is person-centered and society-centered. Education enhances the capabilities of the individual and contributes to self-realization; at the same time, education does symbolic and practical work for the social system. The need to balance these functions, personal and social, poses the perennial issues of education.

FUNCTIONS OF EDUCATION

Cultural transmission Formal education is especially relied on in societies that are culturally self-conscious. Awareness of a cultural heritage is usually associated with concern that traditional values and cultural "mysteries" will be lost if no one has special knowledge of them. While cultural transmission tends to emphasize respect for tradition, values of criticism and inquiry may be passed on as well as conservative values. The function of cultural transmission encourages humanist scholarship and teaching in order to preserve and perhaps critically examine a society's history, language, religion, and philosophy.

Social integration Formal education is a major agency for transforming a heterogeneous and potentially divided community into one bound together by a common language and a sense of common identity. The rise of national states in Europe, for example, was aided by the creation of systems of public education. The schools taught an official language, which they helped to standardize, and thereby fostered the consciousness of being French or German rather than Burgundian or Bavarian. In the United States, educational institutions have carried a major share of the task of integrating millions of immigrants; they are now expected to bring into the mainstream of American life many other millions who have been disadvantaged. Until quite recently public education paid little regard to the cultural diversity of immigrant or ethnic children. In some cases the effort to achieve a culturally homogeneous community has turned education into a system of coercive assimilation. (See Section Four.)

Selection and allocation In traditional society, when only a few were educated, the school played a smaller part than family membership in determining the student's ultimate role and status. But under conditions of mass education, the school system takes over the job of screening and allocating. How the individual performs in school, how far he pursues his education, and the course of study he chooses often determine his future occupation, income, and prestige. The school becomes the central mechanism for facilitating social mobility.

The allocating function tends to bring the educational system into coordination with government and industry. However, a close fit is not guaranteed. In a period of rapidly changing technology, the school system runs the risk of turning out students who are ready for yesterday's jobs rather than today's or tomorrow's.

Personal development Formal education communicates skills and perspectives that cannot readily be gained in other social settings. The school is often a place of transition from a highly personal to a more impersonal world; new habits are learned, such as the punctuality necessary in a time-conscious society. (See Adaptation 27.) But schooling can have psychic costs as well; if the school unduly prolongs dependency, instills feelings of inferiority, or exaggerates the worth of intellectuality, it may have negative effects on personal growth and well-being.

BASIC DILEMMAS

Two broad issues affecting the aims of education are (1) education versus training and (2) elite versus mass education.

Education v. training The question of "genuine" education as distinguished from technical training was raised by Socrates in the fifth century B.C., and the issue remains lively today. Three ideas shaped the classic Greek view of knowledge and education. First, education is the development of the power to think, not the acquisition of information. The educated person lives "the examined life," and education is the enlargement of understanding through the social process of questioning and being questioned. Second, education is a quest for "virtue" rather than technical proficiency. Third, education looks to lasting truth, based on reason, and not to mere opinion or to practical knowledge that depends on changing utilities and circumstances.

Two thousand years later, in his book *Emile*, the French-Swiss social philosopher Jean-Jacques Rousseau (1712–1778) argued for a less intellectualized, more person-centered, more experience-based concept of education. He held that education should posit the uniqueness and worth of the individual, provide a setting within which the individual's distinctive potential might develop, and allow opportunity for learning through experience. Rousseau thought that the practical arts could contribute to education, not as narrow training but as resources for moral development.

In this century, the American philosopher

John Dewey carried forward with greater sophistication Rousseau's emphasis on education as the reconstruction of experience. Like most of his predecessors, Dewey also believed that virtue could be taught, but he stressed the active role of the individual and the need to cultivate personal freedom and autonomy. This ideal could be attained, he thought, only if the school provided a democratic environment.

These themes are counterposed to the view that the chief business of the schools is to train people in specific disciplines. The conflict between education and training takes place at all levels in the educational system. At lower levels it is a conflict between child development and the three Rs; at higher levels liberal, general education is pitted against professional specialization.

The development of programmed and computer-assisted instruction in recent years has posed in a new way the old dilemma of training versus education. The new techniques are remarkably efficient for some kinds of instruction, but by that very fact they are seductive. Makers of educational policy may be induced to give a disproportionately large place in the curriculum to instructional materials that efficiently use the new technology.

To program a computer . . . one must define the instructional objectives in precise, measurable, "behavioral" terms; one must be able to specify the "behavior" to be produced with far greater precision than is needed in the conventional classroom. [But] behavioral objectives are easier to define in some curriculum areas than in others. It is not coincidental, for example, that most of the applications of programmed instruction have been in training courses for industry and the armed forces, where it is relatively easy to define the knowledge or skills to be taught in precise behavioral terms, and where the motivation to learn is quite strong. . . . It is a lot harder, however, to specify the behavior to be produced, say, by a course in Shakespeare or music or American History (Silberman, 1970:196–197).

These reflections place on the advocates of the new educational technology the burden of showing that technology will not dictate curriculum and that education will not be reduced to training.

Elite v. mass education Historically, the conflict between education and training has been an aspect of the struggle of high-status groups to maintain their prestige. The ideal of a cultivated person, as distinguished from a specialist, has been the basis of social esteem in a number of historical settings, notably the Chinese imperial government manned by "literati" described by Weber (Gerth and Mills, 1946:Chap. 17) and the English system of administration by "gentlemen."

Advancing technology and the spread of democracy have resulted in the extension of some form of education to virtually the entire population. In the nineteenth century it became apparent that a literate labor force was needed in a modern economy, and the demand for wider participation in government added strength to the cause of universal education.

ILLITERACY

Enrollment statistics show the progressive democratization of education. Through the expansion of primary education, illiteracy in the United States has been reduced to a low level for the whole population, including blacks, who were late to participate in the broadening of educational opportunity.

Defining literacy as the ability to read and write, or, indirectly, by at least five or six years of schooling, less than 1 percent of Americans—approximately 1.4 million—are now illiterate. (See Figure 1:1, p. 17.) Surveys by the Department of Health, Education and Welfare, using stricter definitions of literacy, such as the ability to read at a base fourth-grade level, show that nearly 5 percent of all youths 12–14 years of age— nearly 1 million out of 23 million—could not be classed as literate. The present-day bureaucratic world runs on paper, and true

Figure 11:1 Population 25 years
and older with indicated number of
years of school completed or more,
1910–1970 (in percentages)

Source: Data for 1910–1950, Folger and Nam, 1967:133;
data for 1970 computed from *Statistical
Abstract of the United States,* 1975:Table 197.

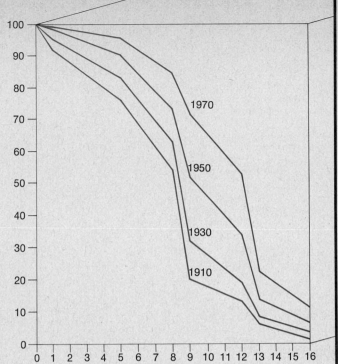

literacy is best measured by the ability to
cope with forms and printed instructions.

A 1970 Louis Harris Poll showed 18.5 million
Americans 16 years or older to be functionally
illiterate—in the sense of being unable to fill out
such basic forms as these:

Three per cent of those tested were unable to
fill out a public-assistance form.

Seven per cent could not make out the equivalent of an application for a Social Security
number.

Eight per cent failed at completing an application for a driver's license.

Eleven per cent were stumped by an application for a personal bank account.

Thirty-four per cent found it too much to fill
out an application for medical aid (*U.S. News
& World Report,* August 19, 1974:37).

This does not imply that official forms are
models of communication (Weightman,
1975). They often seem to be written by
lawyers for lawyers. Nevertheless, there is
no escaping the fact that a higher level of
literacy is required in industrial society in
the last quarter of the twentieth century

than in a world that ran more nearly by
word-of-mouth, and illiteracy is a much
greater personal handicap than it used to be.

EDUCATIONAL ATTAINMENT

The educational status of the American
population has decidedly improved since
the last century, but reliable estimates for
the period before 1910 are not available.
Data on the elderly recorded in the 1960
census indicates that the population born in
the 1870s and 1880s had an average of eight
years of schooling. More detailed and more
reliable evidence reconstructed from the
1950 census for the years 1910 and 1930
is combined with more recent data and
shown in Figure 11:1. Note that in 1910
nearly a quarter of the population aged 25
and older had completed less than five years
of school, about 14 percent had four or more
years of high school, and only 3 percent had
graduated from college (Folger and Nam,
1967:131–133). By 1970 the respective fig-

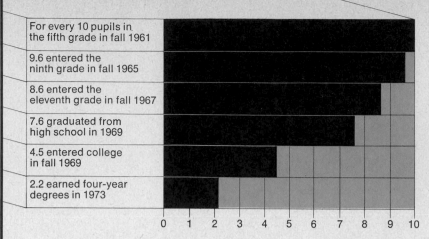

For every 10 pupils in
the fifth grade in fall 1961

9.6 entered the
ninth grade in fall 1965

8.6 entered the
eleventh grade in fall 1967

7.6 graduated from
high school in 1969

4.5 entered college
in fall 1969

2.2 earned four-year
degrees in 1973

0 1 2 3 4 5 6 7 8 9 10

Figure 11:2
Estimated retention rates,
fifth grade through
college graduation:
United States, 1961–1973

Source: Simon and Grant, 1970:
Table 10, p. 9.

ures were 5 percent, 53 percent, and 11 percent. The 53 percent who graduated from high school includes the 11 percent who graduated from college and an additional 11 percent who attended college but did not graduate. The numbers with relatively little education include many older persons who went to school in earlier periods.

The figure also depicts the shift away from a school system organized to impart the basic skills of literacy to most people and some advanced schooling to an elite toward a system of mass education. The latter offers at least a secondary education to almost everyone and some college experience to a large segment of the population.

The consequence of expanding educational opportunities is graphically shown in the retention rates by cohorts. Figure 11:2 shows the pattern of school retention (and depletion) for the cohort graduating from college in 1973. The major break-off point is now at high school graduation; a generation ago it was at high school entrance.

The question presented by mass education is whether high standards can be maintained when large numbers participate. Attempts to deal with the problem center on the diversification of educational institutions, that is, the creation of a variety of schools and colleges—some highly select, others oriented to mass participation.

Section two schooling and the micro-order

The frustrations of teaching and learning have rekindled interest in the micro-order of the schools. Inspired in part by popular critics of education (Holt, 1970; Dennison, 1969; Friedenberg, 1965), there is a growing concern about the patterns of interaction that develop in the schools and the ways such patterns are related to the broader goals of education.

The following discussion treats two important aspects of the micro-order of the schools: (1) face-to-face interaction in the classroom and (2) the role of peer groups. The underlying theme is that the micro-order of the schools betrays a "hidden curriculum" which is often at cross-purposes with genuine education, and if educational reform is to be successful, it must involve changes not only in the formal organization and facilities of schools but, more basically, in the daily patterns of face-to-face interaction between students and teachers.

THE MICRO-ORDER OF THE CLASSROOM

The social organization of the classroom, described in Adaptation 27, is a focal point for inquiry and innovation in contemporary education. Typical classroom interaction is dominated by the requirements of people processing. The situation is defined, for both teachers and pupils, as one of constraint and subordination. And the hidden curriculum is "education for docility."

The prevalence of fear Many, if not most, children live in fear during school hours. They are afraid of being called on; when called on they are afraid of giving the wrong answer and appearing foolish before the teacher or their classmates.

What is most surprising of all is how much fear there is in school. Why is so little said about it? Perhaps most people do not recognize fear in children when they see it. They can read the grossest signs of fear; they know what the trouble is when a child clings howling to his mother; but the subtler signs of fear escape them. It is these signs, in children's faces, voices, and gestures, in their movements and ways of working, that tell me plainly that most children in school are scared most of the time, many of them are very scared (Holt, 1970:75).

That the conventional organization of classroom activities should create such fears is an obvious barrier to learning. If it is assumed that learning should be a pleasurable and rewarding activity, it is doubly important. The negative effect of such fears on the learning strategies of children may generate "rituals of interaction," as discussed in *SOCIAL ORGANIZATION*, pp. 32–33. The child learns how to avoid embarrassment and disapproval, how to disappear in the crowd, and how to minimize risks. The school-induced fear of failure forces the child to come up with the "right" answers—to be a producer rather than a thinker.

Teachers and administrators have taken for granted that a repressive atmosphere is an inevitable, if unfortunate, accompaniment of learning in groups. A certain kind of order—the teacher talking and the children listening—has been presumed to be the first requirement of organized instruction.

Beyond repression These assumptions, however, are once again under attack. In the 1920s and 1930s a "progressive education" movement led by John Dewey, Harold Rugg, and others called for the creation of new schools that would allow students more personal freedom and more involvement in their own education. The movement may have been historically premature in potential public acceptance as well as in the development of adequate educational theory and technique. But today, in the face of widespread public anxiety about the effectiveness of the schools, new impetus has been given to what is variously called informal education, the open classroom, or the free school. A report prepared for the Carnegie Corporation (Silberman, 1970) details the new practices and their educational foundations and includes an extensive description of informal education in English primary schools.

Informal education would transform the

John Dewey (1859–1952) was a close associate of G. H. Mead. He believed that ideas should be guides to action and that true learning takes place only when the individual can freely explore the social world.

micro-order by (1) freeing the children from the discipline of sitting quietly while the teacher attempts to instruct the whole class; (2) creating opportunities for a flow of students among various activity centers, all of which are equipped with materials for attracting and sustaining the child's interest; (3) freeing the teacher to respond to individual needs without being bound to a set lesson plan; and (4) adapting administrative arrangements to the needs of the children rather than adapting the children to administrative arrangements.

A major assumption of informal education is that a different kind of order emerges from the pattern of multiple, freely chosen activities. The alternative to formal, discipline-centered schooling is not chaos but organization based upon the child's involvement

in tasks that engage him or her as a person— tasks that satisfy the child's need for concreteness, for physical motion, and for relatedness to other children. Informal education presumes toleration of what appears to be disorder as children interact: moving about the room talking, and spreading out their "props" and materials. However,

. . . informal education can be as mindless in its own sweet, well-intentioned way as the arid formalism it replaces. Certainly there is danger evident in a few of the classrooms visited in England and the United States, and perhaps inherent in the approach itself, that the pendulum of informality and child-centeredness may swing too far, thereby embracing the flabbiness and anti-intellectualism that characterized so many of the progressive schools of the 1920s, '30s, and '40s. "You have to be careful not to let this new kind of teaching become a 'cop-out,'" a teacher in

Time out for fingerpainting

Lore Rasmussen's Philadelphia program warns. "The kids are happy, the discipline problem is nil, and it's awfully easy for a teacher to convince herself that the kids are having a 'learning experience' or some damned thing, no matter what they're doing" (Silberman, 1970:321–322).

Continuing controversy centers on the informal school's ability to meet standards of instruction, especially in the three Rs. Success will depend on the ability of the teacher to maintain an open classroom without abandoning responsibility for maximizing the educational worth of informal activities. The child may then spend the compulsory academic hours in a world that is not organized to stifle the spirit.

STUDENT PEER GROUPS

The age-graded peer group is familiar to anyone who has grown up in twentieth-century America, but it is a recent phenomenon. Prior to the advent of formal schooling, after the age of about seven or eight, children often served as apprentices and domestics in households where they came into daily contact with people of all ages. With the first "grammar" schools, children began to be segregated from adults but still associated with other children of different ages. In many nineteenth-century schools, it was common to find seven- and eight-year-olds being taught in the same classroom as 14- and 15-year-olds. Today, however, the process of age segregation in the schools has proceeded to an extreme.

If the spread of public schools has encouraged the emergence of age-graded peer groups, the peer groups in turn have profoundly affected the character and experience of schooling. For the young child in school, participation in a peer group is the key to recognition and social identity.

The friendship game Observations of classroom behavior show that for many children the schoolroom is a setting within which they build a world of their own—a world in which friendship "transactions" are para-

mount. To have a friend, and preferably many friends, is to be counted in.

Making friends is serious business, and the child uses whatever resources are at hand. Among these is the teacher. If the child can show, even if only for a short time, exclusive "possession" of the teacher, he or she has something of value to offer:

It is after recess and Mrs. B. announces it is time for math. Most of the children are allocated to the bingo game, puzzles, or simple counting games. Heidi, a first-grader, selects one of the lotto games and then asks Mrs. B. if she will play with her. As they are getting ready to play, Regina and Lisa, confirmed friends that day, run over and ask if they may play, too. Heidi, before Mrs. B. can respond: No. You said I wasn't your friend. Lisa: Will you be our friend now? Heidi: Okay, you can play (Levin, 1971).

In such transactions the coinage is social acceptance. The friendships thus created may be fleeting and wanting in quality, but for the child they are a matter of day-to-day survival.

Student groups and social status Peer relations among adolescent students are intimately involved with the status system. They strengthen the prestige of some persons and weaken that of others. The network of cliques in a high school is a status system; the student finds a high or low status according to clique membership or lack of it. Some students confer prestige on a clique: a star athlete, a socially prominent or wealthy child, or a brilliant student may raise the status of a circle of friends. A student group may collectively move up or down as a result of its own actions; for example, it may lower (or raise) its position in the school by defiant or delinquent behavior.

Teachers help determine which activities are rewarded with high status. When teachers in three schools were asked, "If you could see any of three boys elected president of the senior class, which would you rather it would be—brilliant student, athletic star, or a leader in extracurricular activities?" they preferred the activities leader to the brilliant student 73 to 19 percent, and only 8 percent chose the athlete (Coleman, 1961: 193). The teachers avoided naming the brilliant student because they thought he would not have leadership ability, be close to students, or command attention.

Peer groups and the student subcultures they breed present both challenges and opportunities to the school. On the one hand, the values of the peer group may run counter to the values of the school, thereby dampening the students' concern for academic achievement. On the other hand, if the energies of the peer group can be harnessed toward educational goals, the incentive to learn can be greatly increased.

In the Soviet Union, "socialist competition" has been a way of bringing peer-group pressure to bear in the interests of schooling:

This competition involves all phases of activity and behavior: sports, shop work, service projects, housekeeping, personal grooming, moral conduct, etc. The over-all status of each pupil is evaluated weekly by his peers, following standards and procedures taught by the upbringers. Since each child's status depends in part on the standing of the collective of which he is a member, it is to each pupil's enlightened self-interest to watch over his neighbor, encourage the other's good performance and behavior, and help him when he is in difficulty. In this system the children's collective becomes the agent of adult society and the major source of reward and punishment (Bronfenbrenner, 1970:49–50).

This approach is mentioned to illustrate the potential power of the student peer group when organized by adult society. As a description of Soviet education, it may already be outdated. In the American context, such group discipline would run counter to ideals of individuality and spontaneity.

Adaptation 27 Jackson: Life in classrooms

On a typical weekday morning between September and June, some 35 million Americans kiss their loved ones good-by, pick up their lunch pails and books, and leave to spend their day in that collection of enclosures (totaling about 1 million) known as elementary school classrooms. This massive exodus of children from home is such a common experience in our society that we hardly pause to consider what happens to them when they get there. In the six or seven years before he or she is ready for junior high school, the average child spends about 7,000 hours in school — 7,000 hours that he must spend whether he wants to or not.

School is a place where tests are failed and passed, where amusing things happen, where new insights are stumbled upon and skills acquired. But it is also a place in which people sit, and listen, and wait, and raise their hands, and pass out

paper, and stand in line, and sharpen pencils. School is where we encounter both friends and foes, where imagination is unleashed and misunderstanding is overcome. It is also a place in which yawns are stifled and initials scratched on desk tops, where milk money is collected and recess lines are formed. Both aspects of school life, the celebrated and the unnoticed, are familiar to all of us, but the latter, if only because of its characteristic neglect, seems to deserve more attention than it has received to date from those who are interested in education.

The characteristics of school life to which we now turn our attention are not commonly mentioned by students, at least not directly, nor are they apparent to the casual observer. Yet they are as real, in a sense, as the unfinished portrait of Washington above the cloakroom door. They comprise three facts of life with which even the youngest student must learn to deal and may be introduced by the key words crowds, praise, *and* power.

THE PRESS OF NUMBERS

Learning to live in a classroom involves, among other things, learning to live in a crowd. Most of the things that are done in school are done with others, or at least in the presence of others, and this fact has profound implications for determining the quality of a student's life.

Teacher roles A study of elementary classrooms found that the teacher engages in as many as 1,000 interpersonal interchanges each day. The seemingly placid classroom is more like the proverbial beehive of activity. The teacher channels the social traffic of the classroom:

1. As the manager of the classroom dialogue. When a student wishes to say something during a discussion it is usually the teacher's job to recognize his wish and to invite his comment. When more than one person wishes to enter the discussion or answer a question at the same time (a most common event), it is the teacher who decides who will speak and in what order. Or who will not speak: If Jenny is called on first, Billy may find himself with nothing to say because Jenny has already said it.

2. As supply sergeant, because space and materials are limited. Therefore, the number of students desiring to use various classroom resources at any given moment is often greater than the number that can use them. This explains the lines of students that form in front of the pencil sharpener, the drinking fountain, the microscope, and the washroom door.

3. As an official timekeeper who sees to it that things begin and end on time, more or less, and determines the proper moment to switch from discussion to workbooks or from spelling to arithmetic.

All of the teacher's actions described so far are bound together by a common theme. They are all responsive, in one way or another, to the crowded condition of the classroom. It is, in part, the press of numbers and of time that keeps the teacher so busy. The things the teacher does as he/she works within the physical, temporal, and social limits of the classroom have a constraining effect upon the events that might occur there if individual impulse were allowed free reign. If everyone who so desired tried to speak at once, or offered help in threading the movie projector, classroom life would be much more hectic than it commonly is.

There are three unpublicized features of school life with which the child must learn to cope: delay, denial, and social distraction. Each is produced in part by the crowded conditions of the classroom, and in most instances they are inevitable.

Delay (waiting) In most elementary schools students stand in line several times a day. The entire class typically lines up during recess, lunch, and dismissal, and there are smaller lines that form sporadically in front of drinking fountains, pencil sharpeners, and the like.

Nor does the waiting end when the line has disappeared. Even when the students are sitting in their seats they are often in the same position, psychologically, as if they were members of a line. When teachers move down rows asking questions, or calling for recitations, or examining seatwork, students interact with the teacher in a fixed order, with each student waiting until his turn arrives, speaking his piece, and then waiting for the teacher to get to him again in the next round. Even in rooms where teachers do not operate "by the numbers," the idea of taking turns during discussion and recitation periods is still present.

The line-up: a part of the hidden curriculum

Denial (frustration) The denial of desire is the ultimate outcome of many of the delays occurring in the classroom. Not everyone who wants to speak can be heard, not all of the students' queries can be answered to their satisfaction, not all of their requests can be granted. Most of these denials are probably psychologically trivial when considered individually. But when considered cumulatively their significance increases. Regardless of whether or not these denials are justified, they make it clear that part of learning how to live in school involves learning how to give up desire as well as how to wait for its fulfillment.

Distraction Interruptions of many sorts create a third feature of classroom life that results, at least in part, from the crowded social conditions. During group sessions, irrelevant comments, misbehavior, delivery of messages from outside, and other students coming to the teacher for advice are common—petty interruptions which are the rule rather than the exception.

Typically, things happen on time in school, and this fact creates interruptions of another sort. Adherence to a time schedule requires that activities often begin before interest is aroused and terminate before interest disappears. Thus students are required to put away their arithmetic books and take out their spellers even though they want to continue with arithmetic and ignore spelling. In the classroom, work is often stopped before it is finished. Questions are often left dangling when the bell rings.

Another aspect of school life, related to the general phenomena of distractions and interruptions, is the recurring demand that the student ignore those around him. In a sense, students must try to behave as if they were in solitude, when in point of fact they are not. These young people, if they are to become successful students, must learn how to be alone in a crowd.

THE INTRUSION OF JUDGMENT

All children experience the pain of failure and the joy of success long before they reach school age, but their achievements, or lack of them, do not really become official until they enter the classroom. From then on, a semipublic record of their progress gradually accumulates, and as students, they must learn to adapt to the continued and pervasive spirit of evaluation that will dominate their school years. Evaluation, then, is another important fact of life in the elementary classroom.

The chief *source* of evaluation in the classroom is obviously the teacher. He is called upon continuously to make judgments of students' work and behavior and to communicate that judgment to the students in question and to others. But the teacher is not the only one who passes judgment. Classmates frequently join in the act. Sometimes the class as a whole is invited to participate in the evaluation of a student's work, as when the teacher asks, "Who can correct Billy?" or "How many believe that Shirley read that poem with a lot of expression?" An anthropologist has witnessed signs of what he terms "a witch-hunt syndrome" in several elementary classrooms. A chief component of this syndrome is the destructive criticism of each other by the students, egged on, as it were, by the teacher.

A third source of evaluation entails self-judgment. When a student is unable to spell any of the words on a spelling test, he has been apprised of his failure even if the teacher never sees his paper. As students respond to test questions or complete exercises in their workbooks, they inevitably obtain some information about the quality of their performance.

Secret evaluations Students soon come to realize that some of the most important judgments of them and their work are not made known to them at all. Some of these "secret" judgments are communicated to their parents; others, such as IQ scores and the results of personality tests, are reserved for the scrutiny of school officials only. Judgments made by peers often circulate in the form of gossip or are reported to persons of authority by tattletales. Before they have gone very far in school, students must come to terms with the fact that many things are said about them behind their backs.

Logically, evaluation might be expected to be limited chiefly to the student's attainment of educational objectives. But there are at least two other types of evaluation quite common in elementary classrooms. One has to do with the student's adjustment to institutional expectations; the other, with his possession of specific character traits. Indeed, the smiles and frowns of teachers and classmates often provide more information about these seemingly peripheral aspects of the student's behavior than they do about his academic progress.

Moreover, even when the student's mastery of certain knowledge or skills is allegedly the object of evaluation, other aspects of his behavior are commonly being judged at the same time.

As every schoolchild knows, teachers can become quite angry on occasion, but more likely for a breach of institutional expectations, such as a giggle during arithmetic period, than for academic shortcomings when he fails to grasp the intricacies of long division. When students are praised for correctly responding to a teacher's question, it may look as though they are simply being rewarded for having the right answer. But obviously there is more to it than that. If the teacher discovered that students had obtained the answer a few seconds before by reading from a neighbor's paper, they would have been punished rather than praised. Similarly, if they had blurted out the answer rather than waiting to be called on, they might have received a very different response from the teacher. Thus, it is not just the possession of the right answer but also the way in which it was obtained that is being rewarded. In other words, students are being praised for having achieved and demonstrated intellectual mastery in a prescribed, legitimate way. They are being praised, albeit indirectly, for knowing something, for having done what the teacher told them to do, for being good listeners, for being cooperative group members, and so on.

Because both the teacher and his fellow classmates may evaluate a student's behavior, contradictory judgments are possible. A given act may be praised by the teacher and criticized by peers, or vice versa: A second-grade boy was complimented by the teacher for his gracefulness during a period of creative dancing and teased by his male classmates for acting like a sissy. Students are often concerned with the approval of two audiences whose tastes may differ. The problem, for some, is how to become a good student while remaining a good guy, how to be at the head of the class while still being in the center of the group.

The conflict between teacher and peer approval may be greater for boys than for girls. Many of the behaviors that the teacher smiles upon, especially those that have to do with compliance to institutional expectations (e.g., neatness, passivity, and cleanliness), are more closely linked in North American society with feminine than with masculine ideals.

Learning how to live in a classroom involves not only learning how to handle situations in which one's own work or behavior is evaluated, but also learning how to witness, and occasionally participate in, the evaluation of others. In addition to getting used to a life in which their strengths and weaknesses are often exposed to public scrutiny, students also have to accustom themselves to viewing the strengths and weaknesses of their fellow students.

THE AWARENESS OF POWER

The fact of unequal power is a third feature of classroom life to which students must become accustomed. Unlike the relations between parent and child, the relative impersonality and narrowness of the teacher–student relationship affect the way authority is handled in the classroom. It is there that students must learn to take orders from adults who do not know them very well and whom they do not themselves know intimately. For the first time in the child's life, power that has personal consequences for him is wielded by a relative stranger.

A parent's authority is chiefly concerned, at least during the early years, with prohibiting action, with telling the child what *not* to do. The teacher's authority, in contrast, is as much prescriptive as restrictive, characterized as much by "do" as by "don't," especially in commanding the child's attention. At home the child must learn to stop; at school the child must learn to look and listen.

The school as total institution Any worker, if he doesn't like his job, can throw down his tools and walk away. He may live to regret his decision, but the decision to leave is his. But if a third grader should refuse to obey the bells that tell him when to enter and when to leave the classroom, the wheels of retributive justice would begin to grind. And the teacher would sound the alarm. This fact calls attention to an important aspect of the teacher's authority. Schools resemble so-called total institutions (see *SOCIALIZATION*, p. 97), such as prisons, mental hospitals, and the like, in that one subgroup (the inmates) is involuntarily committed to the institution, whereas another subgroup (the staff) has greater freedom of movement and, most important, has the ultimate freedom to leave the institution entirely. Under these circumstances, it is common for the more privileged group to guard the exits, either figuratively or literally. In progressive prisons, as in most class-rooms, the inhabitants are allowed certain free-doms, but there are real limits. In both institutions, the inmates might be allowed to plan a Christmas party, but in neither place are they allowed to plan a "break."

Because the oppressive use of power is anti-thetical to our democratic ideals, we typically play down or fail to recognize the extent to which stu-dents are expected to conform to the expectations of others. Yet the habits of obedience and docility engendered in the classroom have a high payoff for other settings. So far as their power structure is concerned, classrooms are not too dissimilar to factories or offices. Thus, school might really be called a preparation for life, but not in the sense in which educators usually employ that slogan. Power may be abused in school as elsewhere, but

its existence is a fact of life to which we must adapt. The process of adaptation begins during the first few years of life, but it is significantly ac-celerated, for most of us, on the day we enter kindergarten.

THE HIDDEN CURRICULUM

The crowds, the praise, and the power that com-bine to give a distinctive flavor to classroom life collectively form a hidden curriculum which each student (and teacher) must master if he is to make his way satisfactorily through the school. The de-mands created by these features of classroom life may be contrasted with the academic demands— the "official" curriculum—to which educators tra-ditionally have paid the most attention. The reward system of the schools is linked to success in both curriculums.

Section three bureaucracy and education

Like most other modern institutions, edu-cation is increasingly managed by complex bureaucratic organizations. The rise of a corps of full-time administrators at all levels of the educational system is a striking phe-nomenon of recent history. The administra-tion does not teach, but it decisively affects what is taught, by whom, and to whom. The educational bureaucracy is a center of power within the community and of authority over teachers and students. It also represents a spirit and style that is often at odds with educational ideals. The bureaucracy can sometimes be an effective source of innova-tion and change, but more often it is incapa-ble of initiating positive actions.

THE GOVERNANCE OF EDUCATION

The control of most schools and colleges in the United States is officially vested in an elected or appointed board of laymen—a board of education (see Figure 11:4) or, in the case of colleges or universities, a board

of trustees or board of regents. The practice of locating authority in the hands of laymen goes back to the origin of schools and col-leges in the United States and is based on the belief that schools should be directed by "the community" rather than by the regular government or by professional personnel. In tax-supported schools, board members are considered representatives of the commu-nity, and especially of parents. In private institutions the members of the board often represent a sponsoring constituency. Many American schools and colleges were estab-lished by church groups. For example, the Quaker community founded Haverford Col-lege. There is a tendency for private boards of trustees to become independent of the founding constituency and for the college to evolve into an independent organization.

In the public sector, authority is placed in the hands of a lay board to insulate the school from political influence. In many cases local school districts have their own taxing authority and are therefore not de-pendent on the regular municipal budget, which is subject to the control of the mayor or city council.

PUBLIC SCHOOL SYSTEMS

Although the separation of politics and education is an often-expressed ideal, in fact there is variation in the extent to which school policy is influenced by local mayors. In large cities such as New York, Boston, and Chicago the school boards have considerable independence, but some matters are more subject to outside control than others. The independence of school systems is greatest on matters of curriculum and least in determining teachers' salaries.

These variations in part reflect the formal authority of the mayor. In New York City and Boston, for example, the mayor has more responsibility for the school budget than in Chicago, San Francisco, or Atlanta. Furthermore, an atmosphere of crisis, such as a teachers' strike or racial tension, may lead to political intervention. Mayor John Lindsay of New York adopted a strongly interventionist stance during his administration in the late 1960s. He assumed that it was up to him to provide leadership in public education despite the independence of the board of education, and he moved to limit the board's power over the school budget (Rosenthal, 1969:139). Similarly, in the early 1970s Mayor John Alioto of San Francisco took an active part in attempting to resolve controversies over school integration and busing.

Figure 11:3 Influences which convert school boards into legitimating agencies

Source: Kerr, 1964:59.

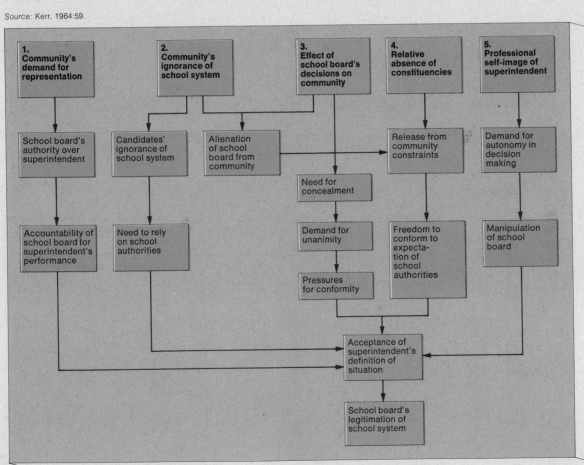

School boards and administrators Local school boards are often dependent on school superintendents, and this limits their effectiveness as representatives of the community. In normal times the boards tend to support the policies and perspectives of the school administration. A study of two suburban school districts (Kerr, 1964) analyzed some of the reasons for this outcome, and the argument is summarized in Figure 11:3. School board members become dependent on the bureaucracy because they usually do not have clear-cut views on educational matters, are relatively unfamiliar with board activities and the school program, and do not represent definite interest groups. They are susceptible to indoctrination by the administration, which tends to divert them from discussion of educational issues. As the school board members develop experience and realize how little the public knows, they become somewhat cynical about representing the public's wishes:

The board's alienation from the community developed from the members' greater understanding of the needs of the system, combined with the community's unwillingness to grant them superior knowledge. As a consequence, the board members in the larger district were further released from community restraints and more exposed to the values of the administration. They therefore became preoccupied with the task of explaining and justifying the needs of the system to the community (Kerr, 1964:55).

In confronting the community, the board seeks to bolster its position by presenting a united front. Controversial issues are hidden behind a screen of unanimity. As a result, the visibility of decision making is reduced, and the community has less leverage to affect educational policy.

This pattern is another example of the "Michels effect." (See ASSOCIATIONS, p. 216.) The process is not inevitable, however. Many school boards do maintain their independence and do engage in public controversies. In recent years, the cozy relation between school boards and administrators has been upset by two factors: the emergence of divisive issues within the community, such as busing for racial integration, and a decline in the prestige of educational administrators, who have not had much luck in meeting unprecedented crises within the schools.

The bureaucracy, the principal, and the teacher Figure 11:4 is a somewhat simplified organization chart of the San Francisco Unified School District. The chart shows a large headquarters composed of many divisions, but note that the elementary and secondary school principals have no intermediate organization between them and their respective assistant superintendents. The 95 elementary school principals in San Francisco report directly to the assistant superintendent, Elementary Division, who has a small staff. As a result, there is little direct contact between the headquarters and the school principals. The principals are largely on their own except for a steady flow of written memoranda and directives that arrive from headquarters. Moreover, in many school districts the authority of the principal is very limited. He or she is mainly in the business of handling day-to-day needs and crises, such as disciplining recalcitrant students, dealing with parents, coaxing supplies from headquarters, maintaining the physical plant, and organizing special programs within the school. The relative isolation of the school principal modifies the bureaucratic character of the school system. In some cases, for example, the school principal may develop a special relation with parent groups and thus have an independent constituency. On the other hand, the principal may be subject to the kind of "bureaucratic centralism" described in Adaptation 28.

In smaller school districts a rather different pattern is to be expected, involving more frequent and informal visits to headquarters, more productive principals' meetings, and a general atmosphere of shared knowledge regarding the objectives and programs of the school district.

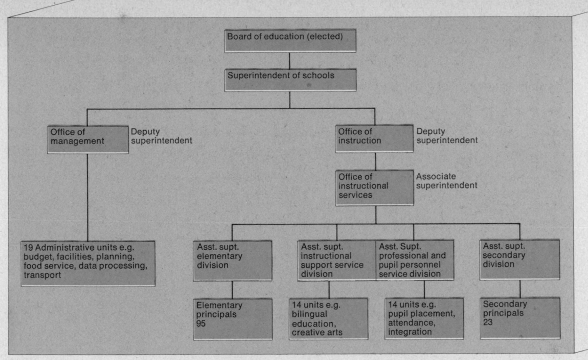

Figure 11:4 Organization Chart: San Francisco Unified School District, 1975

Historically, the classroom teacher has been even more isolated than the principal, despite the demand for lesson plans and for conformity to other rules handed down from above. In fact, teaching tends to be largely self-directed. Close supervision is not easily maintained, and administrative rules have little relevance to classroom experience. Instruction and class management are more strongly influenced by the requirements of the immediate situation than by general rules. Each teacher tends to develop a style or "bag of tricks" to deal with fluid and often unpredictable classroom events (Jackson, 1968; Smith and Geoffrey, 1968; Goodlad and Klein, 1974). Thus, from the standpoint of the teacher, the school is not so much a disciplined bureaucratic system as an organizational eggcrate within whose compartments relatively independent (and sometimes strange) activities are carried on.

Where new government programs have been instituted, especially in the field of compensatory education for disadvantaged children, the character of the classroom tends to be transformed. The employment of a teacher's aide, for example, adds another adult to the classroom, and some programs have made substantial use of parent volunteers. These new participants reduce the social isolation of the teacher. There is also more active supervision by headquarters personnel, who are responsible for the administration of the government-financed program. The classroom is then more firmly attached to a system of bureaucratic control. The result may be helpful to the educational process or stifling, depending on the character of the bureaucracy.

A comparative study of 21 school systems in the Los Angeles area found that bureaucratization increased the likelihood that reforms would be accepted. It appears that the more bureaucratic school systems were the ones better able to adjust to change (Bishop, 1970).

BUREAUCRACY AND ALLOCATION

The school as people-processor The public school serves as a distribution center for society (Goffman, 1961:74 ff.). As students pass through the schools, they are sorted and classified. They are routed into one of a number of possible student careers or tracks, for example, college preparatory, vocational, or even deviant careers, as a result of being classified by administrators as conduct problems. The student's educational career in large part determines the place he will occupy in the social order.

The growing complexity of occupations has put pressure on the schools to identify more closely the capability of each child and help him or her make an appropriate choice of occupation and course of study. Schools and colleges try to do this job at minimum cost in time and effort. They need to measure ability and progress and to maintain a cumulative record of performance, which leads to the development of extensive programs of testing and record keeping. Many public school systems begin a file on the pupil in the lower elementary grades, and the records accumulate and pass along through channels as the child moves up the grades.

While the student is in theory free to choose a career and field of study, in practice such decisions are frequently made on the basis of aptitude and achievement test scores (Brim et al., 1965). The "objective" records must be interpreted, and teachers and counselors are the custodians and interpreters of the students' files. The interpretation of any given case is the outcome of a complicated process of social typing or labeling, which is subject to the policies, perceptions, and stereotypes of school personnel. Consequently, the distribution of students among various educational careers is in many cases less the result of students' decisions than of administrative activity.

Role of the school counselor The "bureaucratization of the search for talent" has brought with it the professionalization of counseling in the schools and has given the counselors a growing influence over the student's educational career (Cicourel and Kitsuse, 1963). Though performing an advisory function, the counselor makes many important decisions. For example, a counselor who thinks a student has low ability may assign courses that do not carry college entrance credit, and the student may not realize what has happened until he or she tries to get into college. The counselor's influence may extend to certifying students for extracurricular activities (which may also affect admission to college) and exercising direct influence through letters of recommendation to colleges and employers. Thus counselors occupy a strategic position in determining student opportunities.

The most important counseling activity is the interpretation of student records and test scores. In this process the counselor considers (1) academic achievement, (2) school conduct or "citizenship," and (3) emotional adjustment. Within each of these categories there is social typing of the student: academically, as an underachiever or overachiever; as a conduct problem or as part of a group that is labeled serious or rowdy on the basis of demeanor and style of dress; psychologically, as well adjusted or disturbed. These labels become part of the record and may affect responses to the student for many years.

Cooling out The allocative function of the educational system requires the school to develop techniques for directing less competent students away from academic curriculums and into vocational programs. The necessity of guiding students into less prestigious (and financially less rewarding) careers creates a potentially explosive problem, because students must come to grips with the task of redefining their self-conceptions. The procedures developed to cope with this problem make up the cooling-out function of education (Clark, 1960:71–76, 160–165). "Cooling the mark out" is a phrase used by confidence men to refer to

357

Adaptation 28
Rogers:
Bureaucratic
pathology in the
New York City
school system

the ways they manage a "mark" (victim) so as to prevent him from calling the police; when the mark realizes he has been "taken," the confidence men try to cool him out gradually, that is, get him to accept his disappointment (Goffman, 1952:451–563).

In the eyes of the general public and many students, the junior college is simply the first two years of college. But educators and administrators, knowing that relatively few junior college students actually complete a four-year program, emphasize the terminal and vocational role of the junior college.

The junior college usually admits all students regardless of qualification. It has an open-door admission policy to provide equal opportunity for higher education consistent with popular democratic ideals. However, many students fail. In one junior college studied, fewer than one-sixth of those entering completed junior college; only 24 percent of those in the transfer program later transferred to a four-year college, where, as a group, they did poorly. (Many students who transfer to four-year programs do well, however.)

Most students enter junior college hoping to transfer to a four-year college. Caught between these expectations and knowledge of what actually happens, the junior college faces the task of redirecting students and changing their outlook, of persuading transfer-oriented students to accept a terminal program. First, if the student's pre-entrance tests are low, he or she is assigned to remedial classes—such as "Sub-Freshman English"—which cast doubt on academic ability and slow the student's progress through the course of study. A second step is an interview with a counselor.

A common case is the student who wants to be an engineer but whose test scores and school grades indicate that he is a nearly hopeless candidate. Said one counselor, "I never openly countermand his choice, but edge him toward a terminal program by gradually laying out the facts of life." Counselors can become more severe later in the sequence when they have grades as a talking point and the student is in trouble (Clark, 1960:71).

Third, the college may require courses that are especially devised to lead students toward a reassessment of their capabilities. For example, "Psychology 5, Orientation to College" may cover aptitude testing and evaluation of vocational choices. These courses give the teacher-counselor an opportunity to talk about the disparity between unrealistic goals and personal capacity.

Finally, the student may be placed on probation. The function of probation is not so much to push students out of school as to direct them to the terminal program. In some junior colleges, it is possible to receive the A.A. (Associate in Arts) degree even while on probation. However, in such cases the students must agree beforehand to accept terminal status.

Adaptation 28 Rogers: Bureaucratic pathology in the New York City school system

The New York City school system is typical of what social scientists call a "sick" bureaucracy—a term for organizations whose traditions, structure, and operations subvert their stated missions and prevent any flexible accommodation to changing client demands. It has all the characteristics of any large bureaucratic organization, but they have been followed to such a degree that they no longer serve their original purpose. As a result, the system is characterized by (1) overcentralization, the development of many levels in the chain of command, and an upward orientation of anxious sub-

Source: Abridged and adapted from *110 Livingston Street: Politics and Bureaucracy in the New York City School System* by David Rogers (New York: Random House [Vintage Books], 1969), pp. 267–283. Published in this form by permission of David Rogers.

ordinates; (2) vertical and horizontal fragmentation, isolating units from one another and limiting communication and coordination of function; (3) the development of vested interests within particular units, reflected in actions to protect and expand their power; (4) strong, informal pressure to conform for the purpose of bureaucratic self-protection, ignoring the organization's wider goals; (5) compulsive rule following and rule enforcing; (6) rebellion of lower-level supervisors against headquarters directives, at times alternating with overconformity, as the supervisors become anxious about ratings and promotions; (7) increasing insulation from clients, as internal politics and personal careerism override the interest in serving the public; and (8) the tendency to make decisions in committees, with the result that it is difficult to pinpoint responsibility and authority.

These characteristics are exaggerations of administrative patterns that are not bad in themselves if not carried too far. In the New York City school system, however, they are carried to the point where they paralyze the system in the face of rapid social changes that demand new administrative arrangements and programs.

Though the term *bureaucracy* usually has negative connotations in popular usage, I am using it here in a neutral sense, referring simply to social patterns associated with large-scale organizations. There can be "good" and "bad" bureaucracy, and much of my analysis of the New York City school system, using the social science model of bureaucratic pathology, will include examples of "bad" bureaucracy.

BUREAUCRATIC CENTRALISM

Many of the pathologies of the New York City school system can be traced to the overcentralization of decisions, combined with the proliferation of specialized administrative units. Most decisions on curriculum, staffing, budgeting, supplies, construction, and maintenance are made by professionals at central headquarters, several layers removed from the schools themselves. The headquarters personnel who make decisions do not know the problems directly, while district superintendents, principals, and teachers, who do have some direct knowledge, have never had the authority to adjust, experiment, and innovate, though

a few adventurous types have taken it upon themselves to run their schools or classrooms as they see fit, without reference to headquarters.

Like any large bureaucracy that must establish rules for the operation of its field units, the Board of Education has a system of formulas for applying programs to schools as the schools fit into particular classifications—special service, transitional, segregated Negro–Puerto Rican, mid-range, segregated white. The system does not take into account gradations within each category at the school level, which limits flexibility for effective use and distribution of supplies and personnel. While it may be important for large bureaucracies to classify operating units and generalize about situations, they do so here with disastrous results. The categories are too gross, and many local variations and problems are overlooked.

The New York City Board of Education is thus the prototype of what students of administration call "top down" rather than "bottom up" management. Instead of looking at the particular school and community (with particular ethnic and socioeconomic groups, local resources, and institutions) and saying "Here is a school and community; now let's work with parent and community groups to set up an appropriate program," they say "Here is a program; now let's see where it can go." Too many schools and communities have their own particular problems that do not fit into standard formulas and programs.

Originally there were valid administrative reasons for centralization—to guarantee uniform standards across the city, to preserve professional autonomy from outside political interference at the local level, to prevent ethnic separatism, and to maintain headquarters control over field officials. Also, the sheer size and geographic spread of the system contributed to centralization.

OUT-OF-TOUCH ADMINISTRATION

Decisions on curriculum and instruction are made by headquarters officials who are often removed from local conditions, insulated from national developments, and not in a position to implement new ideas. Field supervisors have become so used to their limited authority that many won't assume responsibility for innovating and thus subjecting themselves to questions and criticism from curriculum and instruction officials at headquarters. "What's wrong with the system," says one principal, "is the teachers who won't take any responsibility for trying anything new. The reason they won't do so is that assistant principals, principals, and district superintendents won't either, and this goes all the way up the chain of command."

The problem is that the professionals are concerned about their careers and do not want to alienate their bureaucratic superiors by instituting new programs; and at the same time, headquarters does not always provide support for school officials who want to attack the problems of limited services and low reading levels. "It is known by everyone," said a school official with many years of experience, "that headquarters doesn't know what's going on. Information does not get back from the field and they don't even care. To some extent, field people don't even know what policy actually is. They get no help from headquarters, only a mass of paper directives. It is set up like a machine, and the basic set throughout the system is not in any way toward experimenting or even pushing at a rule. A coherent plan has to aim at loosening up the central bureaucracy to begin with, and you have to build in rewards to innovate."

SUPERVISION AND SUPPORT

Overcentralization has contributed to what headquarters officials themselves refer to as a pattern of "overadministration" and "undersupervision." Headquarters officials are preoccupied with forcing field personnel to conform to numerous rules and directives. "There is pressure from the top down in this system," reported a board member who had made visits to ghetto schools before being discouraged from doing so, "and by the time it reaches the teacher it gets pretty strong, and the teacher sometimes takes it out on the kids."

Authoritarian and paternalistic supervision are as prevalent in principal–teacher relations as at higher levels. Many teachers and union spokesmen report that ghetto principals run their schools in a custodial way. By custodial I mean that the principals seem content just to keep the pupils off the streets and devote little time and resources to education. Teachers may be subjected to such administrative sanctions as extra chores, assignment to special classes, or continued visits to their classes by the principal. There are also informal sanctions from one's peers, such as those imposed on the former Harlem junior high school teacher whose colleagues resented his "overstimulating" the pupils.

The pattern of tight supervision rather than professional support is perhaps most acute in principal–teacher relations. Teachers feel that principals are often authoritarian, coercive, and paternalistic, and union spokesmen describe principals as similar to old-line foremen, who talk of "my" school and "my" teachers. The teachers want a more egalitarian and professional relationship, suggesting that decisions about school policy and procedures should be made jointly with teacher representatives rather than unilaterally by the principal.

Principals are in a difficult position, too. They are the middlemen in the system, and they feel they are increasingly ignored in headquarters policy decisions. They see the powerful union and headquarters encroaching on their authority through collective bargaining, they bear the brunt of community protests, and they have the major responsibility for the operation of the schools. They can't hire or fire regular teachers, either. Their desire to control their staff in the ways they can is at least partly a reflection of these pressures.

If principals had more professional assistance from field superintendents, they might be under less pressure and perform better. A recent study of the New York City schools concluded, however, that "individual conferences with principals were rare, evaluation scanty, and services to principals limited." Superintendents are also ground down by the system. They have insufficient staff and limited authority to direct and organize their staff according to the needs of the schools. The headquarters bureaucracy retains the real authority, but it is out of touch with local situations.

359

Adaptation 28
Rogers:
Bureaucratic
pathology in the
New York City
school system

Section four social policy and social change

Traditionally, Americans have placed great hope in education as an instrument of public policy and social change—to create a literate and informed citizenry, provide for social mobility and equality, and assimilate successive waves of immigrants. The public schools have been relied on as prime vehicles of national integration and social betterment. During the first decades of the twentieth century, millions of immigrants learned English and the rudiments of the American political system to qualify for citizenship and for jobs. Their children filled the urban schools. "Assimilation" was the keynote—for the most part eagerly accepted by the new Americans.

The history of public education has not been completely benign, however, and the high hopes of earlier generations have not been entirely fulfilled. This section reviews three aspects of educational policy—the treatment of American Indians, racial integration in the schools, and the contribution of schooling to social equality.

EDUCATION FOR COERCIVE ASSIMILATION

The conquest of native Americans, a process that took almost 300 years, aimed to "civilize the barbarian" and divest him of his lands. Between 1778 and 1871 Indian tribes ceded almost a billion acres by "treaties." During the nineteenth century, the government tried to transform Indians into small farmers, thus binding them to specific pieces of land. They would then be easier to control, and millions more acres could be released for white exploitation and settlement. In 1887 a major piece of federal legislation—the Dawes Severalty Act—provided for allotments of land to individual Indians and struck a devastating blow against tribal organization based on communal ownership. In the 46 years until the law was changed in 1934, Indian tribal lands were reduced from 140 million acres to about 50 million acres.

The boarding schools A system of off-reservation boarding schools conducted by the Bureau of Indian Affairs was a major instrument of cultural domination. The first of these schools was the Carlisle Indian School in Pennsylvania, established in 1879 in an abandoned army barracks by General H. R. Pratt, a former Indian fighter.

The school was run in a rigid military fashion, with heavy emphasis on rustic vocational education. The goal was to provide a maximum of rapid coercive assimilation into white society. It was designed to separate a child from his reservation and family, strip him of his tribal lore and mores, force the complete abandonment of his native language, and prepare him in such a way that he would never return to his people (U.S. Senate Committee on Labor and Public Welfare, 1969:148).

Carlisle became a model for similar schools, many of which were set up in old army posts. For 50 years, this was the characteristic pattern of Indian education. Children were transported long distances and placed in total institutions that tried, with some success, to "strip the self." (See Adaptation 6.) The children were not prepared for life on the reservation, yet "more than 95 per cent of the Navajo children went home, rather than to white communities, after leaving school, only to find themselves handicapped for taking part in Navajo life because they did not know the techniques and customs of their own people" (Kluckhohn and Leighton, 1962:141).

The off-reservation boarding school program was cut back sharply under the Roosevelt administration, following passage of the Indian Reorganization Act of 1934.

Continuing cultural insensitivity Responsibility for the education of some 160,000 Indian children is now shared by local public school systems, private schools, and federal schools. A survey by a U.S. Senate committee concluded that the system is a failure in many respects. For example, the dropout rates of Indian children are twice the national average. Achievement levels and self-confidence are low. "Indian children, more than any other minority, believe themselves to be 'below average' in intelligence" (U.S. Senate Committee on Labor and Public Welfare, 1969:ix).

The survey report emphasized that many teachers remain insensitive to the special need of Indian children for a self-affirming cultural identity. The teachers and administrators are often mainly interested in education for citizenship and conformity rather than academic achievement. They appear to believe that the Indian must choose between complete assimilation to the American culture and an isolated, poverty-stricken life on the reservation.

Beyond paternalism Stimulated by the federal antipoverty and community-action programs, some new possibilities have been explored for finding a middle way. The Rough Rock Demonstration School, established in 1966 on the Navajo reservation, is based on a new perspective for Indian. education (Conklin, 1967). The school is a center of community life and is controlled by a Navajo board of education. While Rough Rock is a boarding school, the maintenance of close ties between parents and children is encouraged, and some parents work in the dormitories. The policies of the school contrast dramatically with the traditional assumptions of the Bureau of Indian Affairs, especially the belief that the children must break away from their backgrounds. Incorporation of Indian values and tradition into the school curriculum is no longer rejected on the grounds that it might impede assimilation. On the contrary, at Rough Rock educators hold that the student should participate in both worlds and that an Indian-oriented education will promote rather than undermine the child's ultimate capacity to achieve full citizenship in the larger society.

RACIAL INTEGRATION AND THE SCHOOLS

A glaring exception to the national policy of using the schools to unify the nation was the widespread segregation of black and white

Self-confidence and racial pride can foster educational achievement and in the long run support racial integration of the schools.

children. In the South, school segregation was, for the most part, official policy; in the North and West segregation was largely de facto, that is, based on patterns of residential segregation and the practice of sending children to neighborhood schools. For many years, the policy of segregating children by race was thought to be constitutional, for in *Plessy* v. *Ferguson* (1896) the Supreme Court held that "separate but equal" public facilities would meet the requirement of the Fourteenth Amendment that all persons be afforded "equal protection of the laws."

In 1954 the Supreme Court rejected the "separate but equal" doctrine. State laws establishing separate schools for blacks and whites were declared unconstitutional because, under such laws, black children have unequal educational opportunity. In overturning the *Plessy* decision (which had dealt with public transportation rather than schools) the court reasoned as follows:

In approaching this problem, we cannot turn the clock back to 1868 when the [Fourteenth] Amendment was adopted, or even to 1896 when *Plessy* v. *Ferguson* was written. . . .

Today, education is perhaps the most important function of state and local governments. Compulsory attendance laws and the great expenditures for education demonstrate our recognition of the importance of education to our democratic society. . . . It is the very foundation of good citizenship. . . . In these days, it is doubtful that any child may reasonably be expected to succeed in life if he is denied the opportunity of an education. Such an opportunity, where the state has undertaken to provide it, is a right which must be made available to all on equal terms. . . . To separate [children] from others of similar age and qualifications solely because of their race generates a feeling of inferiority as to their status in the community that may affect their hearts and minds in a way unlikely ever to be undone. . . . We conclude that in the field of public education the doctrine of "separate but equal" has no place. Separate educational facilities are inherently unequal (*Brown* v. *Board of Education,* 347 U.S. 483, 1954). (For an explanation of legal citations, see *LAW,* p. 411.)

The *Brown* decision set the stage for a broad attack on unequal educational opportunity. Moreover, opportunity was to be measured by results, by what pupils got out of schooling, and not merely by school attendance or even by the quality of educational facilities. The concept of "compensatory education" emerged, and the Elementary and Secondary Act of 1965 initiated a broad range of programs to enrich the educational opportunities of poorer children. In this way a transition was made from a concern for race to a concern for poverty. This made sociological sense, because children whose disadvantage arose from racial prejudice were mostly poor. It also made political sense, because it was easier to mount a war on poverty than provide special benefits to blacks or other minorities.

These efforts have raised searching questions regarding the effectiveness of public education. Despite the money and effort poured into compensatory education, school desegregation, and other programs, the gap between disadvantaged and advantaged students has remained and even widened, both in short-term effects (school achievement scores) and long-term effects (later earnings). Because expectations have not been quickly matched by results, education has become perhaps the most controversial institution in American society today.

Recent sociological research suggests that many expectations of what the schools can do are unrealistic. The thrust of this work is to call into question the idea that education is the key to social and economic equality. An era of "lowered expectations" is indicated.

The Coleman report The Civil Rights Act of 1964 directed the commissioner of education to investigate inequalities in educational opportunities for the major racial and ethnic categories of the population. Consequently a national sample survey was conducted of nearly 600,000 public school students in grades one, three, six, nine, and twelve, along with their teachers, principals, and superintendents. Questionnaires were submitted to the students inquiring about their home backgrounds and their educational aspirations, and the students were tested on ability and educational achievement. The teachers were questioned concerning their own training, backgrounds, attitudes, and verbal skills. Principals and superintendents supplied information on their backgrounds and training as well as on school facilities, curriculums, supervision, and administration. Approximately 30 percent of the schools selected for the survey did not participate, but the evidence indicates that the findings were not significantly biased by that fact (Coleman et al., 1966:550–568).

The report documented many inequalities in educational opportunity and achievement that had long been known or suspected:

1. Most black and white Americans attended different schools. A decade after the Supreme Court's famous desegregation decision, the vast majority—about 80 percent—of all white children attended schools that were 90 to 100 percent white. For black students, about 65 percent attended schools in which over 90 percent of the students were black.

2. A comparison of the scores on several standardized achievement tests which were used indicated that on the average black students scored significantly below whites. Roughly 84 percent of the blacks scored below the median level achieved by the whites. In other words, 34 percent more blacks scored below a specified level than did whites. Since these differences held for both grade school and high school students—and were actually most pronounced at the twelfth grade—it appears that, under present conditions, school experience does not enable blacks to overcome the deficiencies with which they begin school (Coleman et al., 1966:20–23).

3. Blacks performed better in schools where they had white, relatively affluent classmates. This finding was to provide a rationale for the use of busing as a means of achieving equal educational opportunity.

Other findings surprised and even shocked many people in educational circles. Despite popular impressions to the contrary, the physical facilities, formal curricula, and most of the measurable characteristics of teachers in black and white schools were similar. More important, the study showed that differences found in such measures as physical facilities, formal curricula, and teacher characteristics had very little effect on either black or white students' performances on standardized tests (Coleman et al., 1966:21–22).

The evidence indicated that family background (i.e., class background) explained more of the variation in test scores than differences between schools. Earlier findings that integrated schools have an important effect on educational outcomes refer not to the quality of schools per se but to the composition of the student bodies, which in turn reflects family and class backgrounds. And this contradicted the assumptions on which the administration in Washington and urban school boards were expending large funds on compensatory education programs.

How does family background affect educational outcomes? One line of reasoning is that a great deal of the child's learning occurs out of school. The child raised in an environment of poverty has less exposure to books, libraries, museums, and other educational experiences. Although children raised in an environment of poverty may learn as much as children raised in a middle-class family, they learn quite different things. Since the tests or measures of educational outcomes are oriented to the middle-class experience, the poor child is penalized. Another view stresses motivation and attitudes. Disadvantaged children are not encouraged, either directly (for example, by parental pressure) or indirectly (for example, by observation of the "payoff" of education to others like themselves) to seek success in schools.

Whatever the precise reasons, the fact remains that there is a strong and consistent relationship between family background and educational outcome. Minority children have a serious educational deficiency at the start of school, and this initial disparity between advantaged and disadvantaged children only widens as children proceed through the first to the twelfth grades. The policy implications are summarized as follows:

Taking all these results together, one implication stands out above all: That schools bring little influence to bear on a child's achievement that is independent of his background and general social context; and that this very lack of independent effect means that the inequalities imposed on children by their home, neighborhood, and peer environment are carried along to become the inequalities with which they confront adult life at the end of school. For equality of educational opportunity through the schools must imply a strong effect of schools that is independent of the child's immediate social environment, and that strong independent effect is not present in American schools (Coleman et al., 1966:325).

HOW SCHOOLS MAKE A DIFFERENCE

The Coleman report stimulated a continuing reexamination of a much broader issue — the effectiveness of schooling as a means of reducing economic inequality. Traditionally,

Americans have viewed education as a means of social advancement: By providing equal educational opportunity to all, schooling could serve as a progressive force for eliminating poverty and promoting economic equality. Yet the report called this traditional belief into question. If schooling has only a marginal influence in reducing short-run differences between blacks and whites as measured by achievement tests, its effectiveness in reducing long-term economic differences between the advantaged and disadvantaged is doubtful. On the other hand, the connection between education and occupational mobility does lend support to the traditional belief.

Father-to-son mobility Figure 11:5 (which should be followed closely in this discussion) reports both the direction and extent of the difference between sons' and fathers' occupational achievement according to the amount of sons' education (Blau and Duncan, 1967:152–171).

Upward mobility (*a* and *b* in the figure), particularly long-distance upward movement (*a*), from fathers' occupational status is clearly related to sons' higher education.

Figure 11:5 Direction and distance of intergenerational mobility for men (in percentages)

Source: Based on Blau and Duncan, 1967:Fig. 4.5, p. 157, and Table J 4.1, p. 499.

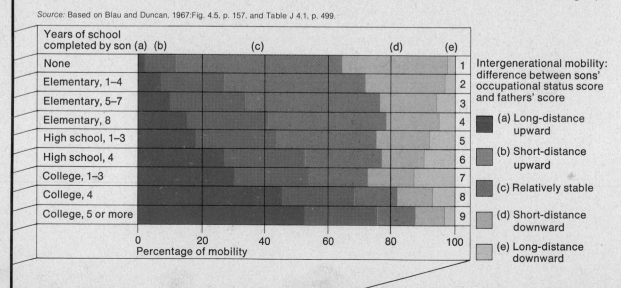

More than half the men with five or more years of college (bar 9) showed long-distance upward mobility, and 76 percent had some upward movement, that is, long-distance or short-distance. The corresponding figures for four years of college (bar 8) are 46 percent and 69 percent.

Relative stability, that is, little or no change between fathers' and sons' occupational status, is associated with low education. Almost half of those with less than five years of school (bars 1 and 2) showed little change from their fathers' occupational status. But the percentage occupationally stable (c) diminishes with higher education, and only 13 percent of those with four or more years of college (bars 8 and 9) were occupationally stable.

Downward mobility is not quite so easy to interpret. Nearly one-third of men with the smallest amount of education (bars 1 and 2) were downwardly mobile. Although a large percentage of these low-educational categories show status loss compared with their fathers, the amount of loss is not great (compare d and e). The predominantly short downward movement is owing to the fact that their fathers were already near the bottom, and the sons did not have far to go. This phenomenon is sometimes called "the floor effect."

The downward mobility pattern is confused at the intermediate levels of education. More than one-fourth of those who started but did not complete college were downwardly mobile, and this educational category (bar 7) has the highest rate for extreme downward mobility. Perhaps the same kinds of people who are downwardly mobile drop out of college: those who do not persevere at tasks or unrealistically take on tasks for which they lack the required talents. Or it may be that college education without the credential of a degree has little more occupational value in some cases than a high school diploma. Some men who do not get a degree, perhaps for reasons beyond their control, lose ground compared with high school graduates who immediately enter the job market full-time.

Income The average annual income in 1974 for Americans age 25 and over was $4,642 for women and $11,474 for men. The relation between amount of education and mean annual income was as follows:

	Women	Men
Some elementary schooling	$2,625	$ 5,758
Completed elementary school	3,114	7,676
Some high school	3,883	9,626
Completed high school	4,777	11,770
Some college	5,576	13,275
Completed college	6,873	16,191
Five or more years of college	9,075	18,404

Source: Current Population Reports, Series P-60, No. 101, January 1976:Table 58.

These figures include persons who work part-time or not at all. When the figures are restricted to year-round full-time workers, the incomes are considerably higher for both sexes, but the relative advantage of men over women remains. Women are rewarded for educational effort at a far lower rate than are men. Nevertheless, the educational ladder clearly leads to higher-paid occupations for both sexes. Without education one has lower horizons occupationally, socially, and in life-styles.

Credentialism Often it is assumed that education contributes to mobility because it produces skilled and more productive workers who therefore gain better jobs and better pay. Other explanations are possible. The correlation between education and higher-paying jobs may not be so much the result of the increased skills and productivity of educated workers but rather a consequence of the redefinition of job qualifications. In many cases employers have raised the educational requirements for workers, especially for higher-status occupations, but the education called for may have little or nothing to do with the work to be performed.

A study summarizing evidence on the contribution of education to worker produc-

In an era of financial stringency university administrators must reckon with student opinions about priorities.

tivity found that better-educated employees are not generally more productive and in many cases are less productive among samples of factory workers, maintenance men, department store clerks, technicians, secretaries, bank tellers, engineers, industrial research scientists, military personnel, and federal civil service employees (Berg, 1970; see also Harrison, 1972; Collins, 1971).

These conclusions focus on credentialism —the use of educational requirements to screen out potential employees irrespective of the relationship between education and job performance. From the standpoint of social policy, the critique of credentialism suggests that there should be a greater investment in elementary and secondary education and less investment in mass higher education. "America should be doing a far better job in assuring that *all* of her people reach adult life with twelve years of quality training and education" (Berg, 1970:189).

Schools and schooling The question, Do schools make a difference? may obscure an important distinction. The Coleman report, discussed above, studied the effects of differences among schools and found that the differences measured had relatively little effect on educational achievement. But even if it does not matter very much which school one attends, it does not follow that schooling is unimportant.

If every school taught children to read, for example, but each did so in a relatively uniform fashion, the differences between schools might well be miniscule. One would not wish to argue, however, that schooling has no impact on reading. (Heyns, 1977:Chap. 4)

To test the effects of schooling compared with family influence, a study was undertaken of what happened to a sample of Atlanta schoolchildren during the summer of 1972. The summer is a time of minimum school attendance and maximum family influence on children of school age. The results showed a dramatic decline in the relative achievement of the least advantaged students. "The gap between black and white children, and between high and low income children widens disproportionately when schools are not in session" (Heyns, 1977: Chap. 9). When school is in session, the effect of family background is offset, but it is reasserted when school is not in session. Children who come from more affluent families experience less loss in achievement. It follows that properly organized school programs may significantly benefit disadvantaged children, but such programs are not likely to produce equality in educational achievement.

Conclusion Although schools cannot accomplish as much as was previously thought, schooling does make a difference. Whether or not there are gains in social equality, education remains a major avenue of individual opportunity. Even if schools cannot do the whole job, for the disadvantaged they are still the main potential resource for communicating basic skills, improving health, and making children feel part of a welcoming world. These are attainable objectives, and to achieve them there is no substitute for educational investment and educational reform.

References

Berg, Ivan
1970 Education and Jobs: The Great Training Robbery. New York: Praeger.

Bishop, Lloyd
1970 "Bureaucracy and educational change." The Clearing House 44 (January):305–309.

Blau, Peter M. and Otis Dudley Duncan, with the collaboration of Andrea Tyree
1967 The American Occupational Structure. New York: Wiley.

Brim, Orville G., Jr., David C. Glass, Isadore Goldberg, and David A. Goslin
1965 The Use of Standardized Ability Tests in American Secondary Schools and Their Impact on Students, Teachers, and Administrators. New York: Russell Sage.

Bronfenbrenner, Urie
1970 Two Worlds of Childhood: U.S. and U.S.S.R. New York: Russell Sage.

Cicourel, Aaron V. and John I. Kitsuse
1963 The Educational Decision-Makers. Indianapolis: Bobbs-Merrill.

Clark, Burton R.
1960 The Open Door College. New York: McGraw-Hill.

Coleman, James S.
1961 The Adolescent Society. New York: Free Press.

Coleman, James S., Ernest Q. Campbell, Carol J. Hobson, James McPartland, Alexander M. Mood, Frederic D. Weinfeld, and Robert L. York
1966 Equality of Educational Opportunity. Washington, D.C.: GPO.

Collins, Randall
1971 "Functional and conflict theories of educational stratification." American Sociological Review 36 (December):1002–1019.

Conklin, Paul
1967 "Good day at Rough Rock: they're giving education back to the Indians." American Education 3 (February):4–9.

Dennison, George
1969 The Lives of Children: The Story of the First Street School. New York: Random House (Vintage Books).

Folger, John K. and Charles B. Nam
1967 Education of the American People. Washington, D.C.:GPO.

Friedenberg, Edgar Z.
1965 Coming of Age in America: Growth and Acquiescence. New York: Random House.

Gerth, H. H. and C. Wright Mills (eds.)
1946 From Max Weber: Essays in Sociology. New York: Oxford University Press.

Goffman, Erving
1952 "On cooling the mark out: some aspects of adaptation to failure." Psychiatry 15 (November):541–563.
1961 Asylums. New York: Doubleday.

Goodlad, John I. and M. Frances Klein
1974 Looking Behind the Classroom Door. Belmont, Calif.: Charles A. Jones. Second edition.

Harrison, Bennett
1972 Education, Training, and the Urban Ghetto. Baltimore: Johns Hopkins University Press.

Heyns, Barbara
1977 Summer Learning: The Effects of Schooling and Social Inequality Reexamined. New York: Academic Press. In press.

Holt, John
1970 How Children Fail. New York: Dell.

Jackson, Philip W.
1968 Life in Classrooms. New York: Holt, Rinehart and Winston.

Kerr, Clark
1964 The Uses of the University. Cambridge: Harvard University Press.

Kluckhohn, Clyde and Dorothea Leighton
1962 The Navaho. Garden City, N.Y.: Doubleday.

Levin, Sue Ann
1971 "The friendship game." Unpublished.

Rosenthal, Alan
1969 Pedagogues and Power: Teacher Groups in School Politics. Syracuse, N.Y.: Syracuse University Press.

Silberman, Charles E.
1970 Crisis in the Classroom: The Remaking of American Education. New York: Random House (Vintage Books).

Simon, Kenneth A. and W. Vance Grant
1970 Digest of Educational Statistics. Washington, D.C.: U.S. Department of Health, Education and Welfare, National Center for Educational Statistics.

Smith, Louis M. and William Geoffrey
1968 Complexities of an Urban Classroom: An Analysis Toward a General Theory of Teaching. New York: Holt, Rinehart and Winston.

U.S. Senate Committee on Labor and Public Welfare
1969 Indian Education: A National Tragedy — A National Challenge. Report No. 91-501. Washington, D.C.: GPO.

Weightman, Gavin
1975 "Unravelling red tape." New Society (November 13):365–366.

Sources and Readings

Banks, Olive
1971 The Sociology of Education. London: Batsford.

Cave, William M. and Mark A. Chester (eds.)
1974 Sociology of Education: An Anthology of Issues and Problems. New York: Macmillan.

Clark, Burton R.
1962 Educating the Expert Society. New York: Chandler.

Clifford, Geraldine J.
1975 The Shape of American Education. Englewood Cliffs, N. J.: Prentice-Hall.

Corsin, B. R., I. R. Dale, G. M. Esland, and D. R. Swift
1971 School and Society: A Sociological Reader. Cambridge: Massachusetts Institute of Technology Press.

Dewey, John
1916/1966 Democracy and Education. New York: Free Press.

Halsey, A. H., Jean Floud, and C. Arnold Anderson
1961 Education, Economy, and Society. New York: Free Press.

Havighurst, Robert J. and Bernice L. Neugarten
1975 Society and Education. Fourth Edition. Boston: Allyn Bacon.

Jencks, Christopher and David Riesman
1968 The Academic Revolution. New York: Doubleday.

Katz, Michael B.
1975 Class, Bureaucracy and Schools: The Illusion of Educational Change in America. New York: Praeger.

Liegle, Ludwig
1970 The Family's Role in Soviet Education. New York: Springer-Verlag.

Simon, Kenneth A. and Marie G. Fullam
1971 Projections of Education Statistics to 1979–80. Washington, D.C.: U.S. Department of Health, Education, and Welfare, National Center for Educational Statistics.

Swift, D. F. (ed.)
1970 Basic Readings in the Sociology of Education. London: Routledge and Kegan Paul.

Veblen, Thorstein
1918/1954 The Higher Learning in America. Stanford, Calif.: Academic Reprints.

Young, Michael
1958 The Rise of the Meritocracy, 1870–2033. London: Thames and Hudson.

Periodicals

Change: The Magazine of Higher Education
Harvard Educational Review
Journal of Negro Education
School Review
Sociology of Education

Section one foundations of religion

Religious beliefs and practices exist in every known society, from the most simple to the most complex. The universality of religion is no more remarkable than its diversity. Some religions worship a single supreme being; others are polytheistic. In Buddhism the central figure is a great teacher, and the idea of god is elusive. In some preliterate societies, religion centers around capricious and sometimes malevolent spirits and forces.

Religious rituals and prescriptions are no less varied than religious beliefs. A ritual may be a ceremony of adoration and supplication addressed to an all-wise and merciful god; it may propitiate a being who would otherwise bring evil upon the community; it may be solemn and dignified or include dancing, sexual rites, and the release of feeling. Religious emotions run the gamut from reverence to terror, joy to self-abasement, ecstasy to peace of mind.

This chapter was prepared with the collaboration of Gertrude Jaeger.

Early efforts by social science to account for the universality of religion tended to see it as a prescientific relic of the primitive past. Religious belief was often interpreted as a kind of error or fantasy characteristic of uninformed minds. For example, a century ago Tylor traced the concepts of a soul and of spirits to primitive attempts to account for dreams and death (Tylor, 1873:Chap. 11).

Modern social science takes a different approach. The universality of religion is traced not to the human propensity to make false inferences, but to traits of the human condition that persist even in an age of science. The explanation of human religiosity is sought in the basic functions religion performs for the individual and for society.

FUNCTIONS OF RELIGION

Religion arises as a response to individual psychic needs and to the requirements of social solidarity.

1. Overcoming fear and anxiety To the extent that the world is dangerous and unpredictable, people suffer and face both specific fears and more general anxiety. Unease

Religious devotion in a public place

powers of nature, appease them, or seek their cooperation. One may also look to a supernatural realm in which, after death, the individual will be safe from the frustrations of human existence.

2. Making the world comprehensible Religious symbolism is drawn on to explain the environment and interpret the place of human beings within it. This may take the form of a cosmology explaining the origins of the earth and the heavens; various animals may be seen as mysterious beings whose qualities of swiftness or cunning need special explanation; the fruitfulness or barrenness of the land, the cycles of birth and death, winter and summer, can all be represented in a more or less elaborate mythology. This process of interpretation reflects an impulse to make the world more comprehensible, usually by attributing familiar, human motives to supernatural beings and forces.

3. The quest for ultimate meaning In all societies there is evidence of a search for moral meaning. Human beings seek an organizing principle that will validate their most important strivings and make sense of their sufferings. If they can believe in a God-given scheme of things, individuals can exercise power or accept frustration with greater equanimity. They can turn potential chaos and meaninglessness into an orderly world view.

4. The search for self-transcendence Most human experiences are routine and do not evoke strong emotions or extraordinary feelings, but there are circumstances that transcend the routine. Great natural events may accomplish this by casting people into a state of wonder and awe. In addition, certain individuals are able to enter into psychological states that appear to enlarge their vision and bring them into mystic union with the world. Many religions foster this kind of experience through incantation, dance, and similar practices. A sense of self-transcendence may also be induced by drugs, as in the Peyote cult among North American Indians (Lanternari, 1965:Chap. 2).

may stem from fear of natural forces and the sense of human weakness and dependency. Social circumstances, too, can be cruel and capricious, and there is always the uncertain certainty of death. Some human responses to such fears and anxieties are to revere the

5. The celebration of human powers and achievements Many religious beliefs and activities reflect pride and exultation rather than humility and despair. A victory dance, the divinity of kings, a belief in being specially chosen for a divine mission—these and many other acts and symbols celebrate the special relation of a human being or a group to the ultimate source of power and meaning.

6. Supporting social norms and values Societies depend on the willing cooperation of their members. For the most part, cooperation is won through ordinary processes of socialization. But the socializers need all the help they can get, particularly when a large amount of self-discipline is required. By adding divine sanction to human values, religion buttresses social norms and creates a moral community. The members feel a common bond because they share a belief in an unobservable or transcendent reality.

This list of personal and social needs and desires is not exhaustive. Obviously, not all individuals or groups have the same religious needs and motives. In some societies or historical periods, religion may be largely a way of handling fears; at another time or place the significant source of religion might be the quest for a moral identity, the celebration of human achievement, or the effort to make the world comprehensible. An understanding of the variety of problems that tend to produce religious responses leads us away from trying to locate the origin of religion in some single factor. Religion is not a response to a unique problem. It is a way of meeting many different problems.

Nor is religion the only way of overcoming anxiety, integrating personality, supporting social norms, or satisfying the other conditions mentioned above. Other social institutions, such as politics, education, science, the arts, and psychotherapy, serve many of the same ends. Religion sometimes supplements these other social devices, sometimes competes with them, and often fills the breach when they are absent or inadequate. Many religionists and some social scientists argue that even where alternative belief systems are available, only religion can meet the deepest human and social needs.

The basic response The defining characteristic of religion is the creation of the sacred. When something is made sacred, it is invested with a special meaning or worth and treated with reverence, awe, and respect. Anything can be made sacred: a mountain, a part of the human body, a belief, a meeting place, an animal, a cup of oil or water. But if it is sacred, it is perceived as different from the everyday world. What is sacred is not a mere means or instrument. Though it may be used in a ceremony, it is itself a thing apart toward which proper respect is due.

Sometimes the sacred is created by endowing parts of the world with a special and mysterious power. This does not necessarily involve a belief in particular gods or spirits. Thus the idea of *mana*, associated with the peoples of Polynesia and Melanesia, refers to an impersonal power that may be located in any object—a song, a man, a plant, a stone. The essential point is that mana is extraordinary power and produces extraordinary results.

Street scene in the holy city of Benares, India. A woman offers a cow cakes prepared and sold to pilgrims for this purpose. The cow is worshipped by the Hindus and its slaughter is forbidden.

If a man's pigs multiply and his gardens are productive, it is not because he is industrious and looks after his property, but because of the stones full of mana for pigs and yams that he possesses. Of course a yam naturally grows when planted, that is well known, but it will not be very large unless mana comes into play: a canoe will not be swift unless mana be brought to bear upon it, a net will not catch many fish, nor an arrow inflict a mortal wound (Codrington, 1965:257).

Mana sets things apart and gives them a unique significance. It transcends the ordinary. Therefore the principle of mana is a long step toward the creation of a sacred realm, even though all the attitudes usually associated with sacredness may not be present.

The recognition or creation of sacredness lays a foundation for faith and moral commitment. What is sacred has its own claim to respect and obedience. Because it is a special realm, the sacred may offer a new vision and a new truth unlimited by the criteria of the common-sense world.

To recognize, create, elaborate, and protect the sacred is the distinctive competence of religion. But this is not solely the province of specialized religious institutions. The political community also creates sacred documents and symbols, such as the constitution, the flag, and founding fathers like Thomas Jefferson, Mao Tse-tung, and Simon Bolivar (Warner, 1962:Chap. 1). In that case we may speak of a "civil religion" (Bellah, 1970:

Reading the Torah in Frankfurt-am-Main: Judaism survives in contemporary Germany.

168–186). Similarly, the culture can lend an air of sacredness to basic values ranging from the profit motive to the preservation of human life. The more sacred any act or belief, the more likely it is to take on a religious quality. Religious institutions specialize in the sacred. But other institutions frequently engage in the creation of sacredness in order to evoke attitudes of reverence and commitment.

ELEMENTS OF RELIGION

Following Durkheim, "a religion" may be defined as a unified system of beliefs and practices relative to sacred things, uniting into a single moral community all who adhere to those beliefs and practices (1912/1947:47). In the study of religion, it is necessary to distinguish the following elements or components (Glock and Stark, 1965:18–38):

1. Ritual All religions observe ceremonial practices or rituals. Religious rituals are prescribed acts that are sacred in themselves and also symbolize the sacred. In Christianity the communion service is sacred and also symbolizes the sacrifice of Christ.

The ritualization of behavior is a mechanism by which sacredness is created and sustained. A way of making baskets, a family gathering, or any other socially important practice may, by being ritualized, become set apart as inviolate and of special significance. In its origin, a ritual practice may be simply a way of coordinating activity and creating respect for the group and its traditions. But as the practice takes on more symbolic meaning and is connected with other religious acts and symbols, people come to think of it, and act toward it, as a religious ceremony.

2. Emotion One function of ritual is to evoke appropriate feelings. The religious emotion depends on the nature of the ceremony and what it symbolizes. Humility, reverence, and awe are common religious feelings, but ecstasy or terror may also be displayed. Whatever the feeling, it is prescribed as appropriate, it is expected, and it is stimulated and supported by the resources and techniques of the religion. Religious emotions are also appropriate to whatever is most sacred in the society. The patriotic rite brings forth loyalty, pride, and a sense of closeness to one's fellow citizens. In this way the sacredness of the nation and of civic identity is affirmed.

3. Belief Religious ritual and feeling may occur prior to, and independently of, specifically religious ideas (Kluckhohn, 1942: 45–79). However, in almost all known societies, there are beliefs that justify and support religious rituals and feelings. Moreover, beliefs have their own powerful role to play in the creation of sacredness and in meeting the human problems to which religion responds.

In the past, religious beliefs have almost always involved the supernatural. Divine beings are not of this world but outside it or above it and not subject to the ordinary limitations of man and beast. In theory, however, religion can exist without a belief in supernatural beings. A set of great truths or principles may be given a sacred status around which a system of auxiliary beliefs and practices is organized.

The ways of believing are variable and problematic. Some individuals are literal and dedicated believers; others believe in a routine way; others "believe" in an ambiguous or highly qualified way. Some try to reinterpret religious doctrines to make them compatible with other beliefs, such as the findings of science. They may emphasize the symbolic significance of beliefs and thus avoid a literal acceptance of conventional views about an afterlife or the origins of the universe.

Protestant laymen as well as theologians hold a diversity of opinions even on the basic question of belief in God. Among Protestant denominations a wide range of attitudes exists and in some denominations there is a significant internal division of opinion. Congregationalists are hardly of one mind, whereas the fundamentalist Southern Baptists hold strikingly uniform

Table 12:1 Belief in God, by church members, in percentages

Which of the following statements comes closest to what you believe?	Congregationalists	Presbyterians	Southern Baptists
"I know God really exists and I have no doubts about it."	41	75	99
"While I have doubts, I feel that I do believe in God."	34	16	1
"I don't believe in a personal God, but I do believe in a higher power of some kind."	16	7	0
Other responses	9	2	0
Total percentage	100	100	100
Number of respondents	151	495	79

Source: Abstracted from Glock and Stark, 1965:Table 1, which reports additional details and responses of other denominations. Based on a random sample of church members in northern California.

beliefs. Presbyterians occupy a middle position. (See Table 12:1.)

In 1976 94 percent of a national sample of Americans reported that they believed "in God or a universal spirit." Among those who answered yes to that question, 68 percent said they believed "that this God or univer-

Table 12:2 Religion reported, United States, 1957 and 1975

	1957[a]	1975[b]
Protestant	66.2	61
Baptist	19.7	20
Lutheran	7.1	7
Methodist	14.0	11
Presbyterian	5.6	5
Other Protestant	19.8	18[c]
Roman Catholic	25.7	27
Jewish	3.2	2
Other religion	1.3	4
No religion	2.7	6

[a] Source: *Current Population Reports,* Series P-20, No. 70 (February, 1958). Based on a national sample survey.
[b] Source: *Gallup Opinion Index,* 1976:34–37. Based on a national sample survey.
[c] This includes 3 percent Episcopalians.

sal spirit observes your actions and rewards or punishes you for them" (Gallup Opinion Index, 1976:12).

4. Organization The organization of religion is needed to conduct religious assemblies where belief and feeling are reinforced, to recruit and train specialists in religious ritual and doctrine, and to deal with the relations between the religious group and the rest of society. In undifferentiated societies, there may be no separate religious organization; the religious group is coextensive with the community.

Any given religion is made up of a combination of the components mentioned above—ritual, emotion, belief, and organization. Some religions may be strong on organization but make few demands on feeling; others may emphasize ritual but not belief. In comparing religions one must specify what components, or combination of them, are being considered.

The same caution applies when asking: "Who is more religious?" "Are people becoming more or less religious?" "Is religion declining or gaining strength?" Unless the basis of comparison is specified, incorrect conclusions may be drawn. For example, an observed strengthening of religious *organization,* measured by increased membership, funds, or number of buildings, may or may not be associated with a strengthening of religious *belief*.

Religions of the United States Table 12:2 shows the pattern of religious affiliation in the United States as estimated from a Current Population Survey in 1957 and a Gallup survey in 1975. There is considerable stability in the percentages, but note the decline of Methodists and Jews, and the increase of those reporting other religions and no religion. It is evident that at least nominal religious commitment is widespread in the United States.

VARIETIES OF RELIGIOUS CONSCIOUSNESS

There are many different ways of experiencing religion. For most people, religion is mainly a vehicle of social participation—a way of belonging to a community, affirming a social identity, and cementing social bonds. "The family that prays together stays together." For others religion is a source of comfort, such as reassurance in the face of inevitable death. Still others seek a vague moral uplift and a sense of righteousness. And then there are those who desire a personal renewal—to be "born again"—or a feeling of ecstatic unity with the source of religious power or truth.

These motivations combine with, and in part demand, different orientations toward the world of spirit and the mundane world of ordinary life. Religious *dualism* makes a sharp distinction between what is this-worldly and what is otherworldly, and finds "reality" in the realm of spirit. To sustain religious dualism and commune with that reality, some form of withdrawal from the world is sought. This may take the form of sustained meditation or enthusiastic participation in a highly demanding sect or cult.

Adaptation 29 describes the religious consciousness of the Hare Krishna movement. Note especially the "world view" of the movement and the continuities of this world view with the perspectives and experiences of the young people who participated in the San Francisco drug culture of the 1960s.

Adaptation 29 Johnson: Hare Krishna and the counterculture

On a street bordering Golden Gate Park in the Haight-Ashbury section of San Francisco stood the Krishna Consciousness temple. The sounds of chanting and music filled the street. Inside there were dozens of brightly colored paintings on the wall, thick red rugs on the floor, and a smoky haze in the air. This smoke was incense, an element of the ceremony in progress. The people in the room were chanting barely audible Sanskrit words. The room was nearly full, with about 50 people, all of whom appeared to be young, sitting on the floor. Assembled in front were about 20 persons with white paint on their noses wearing long, loose-fitting saffron robes. Many of the men had shaved their heads except for a ponytail. The women with them also had white paint on their noses and small red marks on their foreheads.

The chanting ceremony (mantra) increased in tempo and in volume. Two girls in long saffron robes were now dancing to the chant. The leader of the chant began to cry the words *Hare Krishna, Hare Krishna, Krishna, Krishna, Hare, Hare; Hare Rama, Hare Rama, Rama, Rama, Hare, Hare*. The entire group repeated the words and attempted to maintain the leader's intonation and rhythm. Many of the participants played musical instruments.

The music and chanting grew very loud and became very fast. The drum was ceaselessly pounding. Many of the devotees started personal shouts, hands upstretched, amid the general chant. The leader knelt in front of a picture of the group's

Source: Abridged and adapted from "The Hare Krishna in San Francisco" by Gregory Johnson, in Charles Y. Glock and Robert N. Bellah (eds.), *The New Religious Consciousness* (Berkeley and Los Angeles: University of California Press, 1976), pp. 31–51. Published in this form by permission of Gregory Johnson and the University of California Press.

Krishna Consciousness in New York

"spiritual master" on a small shrine near the front of the room. The chanting culminated in a crescendo, and the room became silent. The celebrants knelt with their heads to the floor as the leader said a short prayer in Sanskrit. Then he shouted five times, "All glories to the assembled devotees," which the others repeated before they sat up.

After the chanting concluded, three female initiates went to a room behind the altar and returned with large containers of food and paper plates. They proceeded to serve the meal. Each plate was passed back hand-to-hand to the people in the rear of the room until everybody had been served. The food was rich, spicy, and strictly vegetarian, without meat, fish, or eggs. After the meal one of the devotees began to explain the objectives of the temple. He outlined the development of the movement and the reasons it had come to San Francisco.

ORIGINS OF THE MOVEMENT

The Krishna Consciousness movement was founded in New York in 1966 by a 70-year-old Indian expatriate, A. C. Bhaktivedanta, who was believed to be the direct link to the deity Krishna. He had been a successful businessman in India, and he relinquished his job and family to move into the East Village section of New York City in 1965 to establish an American version of an Indian religious discipline that has existed since the fifth century.

Early in 1967, Bhaktivedanta relocated himself and about half of the 30 members of the New York temple to San Francisco, for two significant reasons: to continue as a city organization rather than retreat to the country in order to become contemplative and nature-oriented, like many similar groups, and to make a conscious effort to recruit young persons, whom the swami was convinced were open to the particular message of Krishna.

The group moved into a remodeled laundromat near the center of the Haight-Ashbury area in early 1967. Coinciding with a large migration of young people to the area, the move proved to be a windfall for the movement. The migrants acted as a vast reservoir of potential recruits. By July 1974 the movement had grown to 54 temples throughout the world.

WORLD VIEW OF THE MOVEMENT

The stated beliefs of the movement were based on the *Bhagavad-Gita* as translated by its founder, A. C. Bhaktivedanta. At all times, the devotees attempted to reduce the sacred text to simple yet comprehensive directives that would apply to the lives of persons in the Haight-Ashbury. For the residents, the ideology became especially sensible once one granted a crucial assumption, which seemingly corresponded to experiences within Haight-Ashbury: The present age was undergoing a decisive transformation, characterized by unprecedented confusion and turmoil. Events had shown that previous beliefs did not work; people were searching for a spiritual absolute that would lead them beyond war, strife, and chaos. In articulating these positions, the devotees claimed that the world was near the end of the materialistic age of Kali-Yuga, the last cycle of a four-cycle millennium. If the populace could be aroused, this age of Kali-Yuga would be concluded, and a new age of peace, love, and unity would be discovered.

Furthermore, this new age would arrive through the transformed consciousness of millions of people. Most important, this transformation would be a psychological one, within the minds of individuals, rather than through changed institutions. This position held that if each person practiced the Bhakti yoga discipline, he would be eternally blissful as well as protected by Krishna. "Someday there will be only one political party," one member predicted. "People will not vote, they will chant." Within this scheme, what were called "social problems" would automatically disappear, because people would be unified by Krishna Consciousness.

The material world (*maya* in Hindu scriptures) was portrayed as superficial and unreal. Advertising, supermarkets, movies, and newspapers were all senseless diversions. Every person had a potential for both tranquility and ecstasy, which would be achieved only through renunciation of superficial distractions. This renunciation would lead man to his natural state of being; he would be able to breathe better, work better, sleep better, eat better, love better, and be a happier person.

The devotee's rejection of the world is applied to the entire physical environment. When I asked why the temple does not move to a mountain retreat in the country, away from the materialism of the city, one devotee replied:

The city is better, because it is so ugly. One can appreciate the ugliness of the temporal world much easier in the city, so it is easier to escape it and find Krishna. The country deceives you, because its beauty and serenity make one think that he achieved liberation when he really hasn't. His head is still the same. They are all the same; country and city are material worlds.

The absolute insight experienced by a devotee could not be interpreted by words or logic. It was something that each person "knows" when he "feels" it. The devotees stressed that all logical, rational arguments about truth are worthless; logic will lead only to disagreement, never to one path as the answer, but to many paths. The end of learning was not questioning and communicating with others, but self-realization.

The movement's espousal of personal enlightenment was given a specific emphasis, directed to the residents of the Haight-Ashbury; a most important interest at that time was the use of hallucinogenic drugs—mescaline, lysergic acid diethylamide (LSD), and psilocybin. The temple's appeal to persons who had experimented with these drugs was indicated by a four-foot-high multicolored poster on the wall of the temple:

Stay high forever. No more coming down. Practice Krishna Consciousness. Expand your consciousness by practicing the Transcendental Sound Vibration. Hare Krishna, Hare Krishna, Krishna, Krishna, Hare Hare, Hare Rama, Hare Rama, Rama Rama, Hare Hare. The chanting will cleanse the dust from the mirror of the mind and free you from all material contamination. It is practical, self-evident, and requires no artificial aid. Try it and be blissful all the time. *Turn on* through music, dance, philosophy, science, religion and prasadam (spiritual food). *Tune in.* Awaken your Transcendental Nature! Rejoice in the Ocean of Bliss! The process of Sandirtan brings about transcendental ecstasy. *Drop out* of movements employing artificially induced states of self-realization and expanded consciousness. Such methods only lead to spiritual laziness and chaos. *End all bring-downs,* flip out and stay for eternity. Bhakti yoga has been practiced for many centuries and is authorized by India's great acharyas. Swami Bhaktivedanta is in the bonafide line of Krishna's discipline succession. He has especially come to this country to spiritually guide young Americans.

The above statement indicates how the movement made a sophisticated effort to translate its appeals into contemporary form. A centuries-old belief system was revised to appeal to the alleged concerns of the youthful residents of the Haight-Ashbury.

It would be a mistake, however, to emphasize the values and doctrines of the movement as the sole reason for its growth. In attracting adherents, its chanting ceremonies seemed to be much more significant than its doctrines. On many occasions I observed visitors who had been fully absorbed in chanting and dancing leave the temple quietly when the post-mantra doctrinal discussions began. It seemed apparent that the chanting ceremonies were the movement's distinctive contribution to the residents of the Haight-Ashbury. Three times daily the mantras provided a freely accessible opportunity for collective emotional release. Moreover, it was an activity that demanded complete involvement, in contrast to the passive, audiencelike participation in most events in the area, such as rock music concerts.

SELF-SURRENDER AND THE QUEST FOR ORDEAL

On entering Hare Krishna, all aspects of the convert's prior identity were surrendered. The hair of a male was shaved. Clothes, money, and personal effects were given to the temple. Initiates gave up their previous names and were assigned Sanskrit names from the scriptures of the temple. The initiate was given a set of Hindu robes (usually orange, sometimes yellow), which were worn at all times. This alteration of appearance was fortified by a rigorous set of prohibitions on conduct: strictly forbidden was the eating of meat, illicit sex (outside marriage), gambling, all intoxicants, cigarettes, and drugs. These proscriptions were based on A. C. Bhaktivedanta's interpretation of the Vedic texts and were crucial to the Bhakti yoga discipline.

This life of self-imposed poverty and ascetic denial seemed especially dramatic in contrast with the origins of most devotees. The best available indications are that most devotees came from prosperous homes: A questionnaire study of

the life histories of 31 devotees conducted in 1971 disclosed that the annual incomes of the fathers of the respondents averaged over $20,000.

Conversion to Krishna seemed to be an emphatic rejection of conventional affluent America. In contrast with the solely ideological rejection characteristic of youthful political radicals, many of whom retained the trappings of middle-class life, such as televisions, automobiles, and stereo equipment, Hare Krishna converts completely changed the course of their lives. This was a rejection expressed through actions rather than words. The roots of this decisive transformation of identity were expressed by a recent convert when he explained why he believed that so many young persons were discovering spiritual enlightenment:

Like most everybody else, we were given everything when growing up. Our parents thought that material possessions meant spiritual satisfaction. But we knew it was false. Even then, we knew that true spiritual happiness was in an energy of a higher form. Many other young people have come to understand this principle. Material gain is illusory. It brings nothing but unhappiness.

Many young persons seemed to pursue vigorously the hardships and obstacles denied by affluence. In the process, they hoped to attain precisely the rewards that had escaped their parents: community, self-insight, and a rich and varied experience.

THE APPEAL OF NONCHEMICAL TRANSCENDENCE

When I asked a convert how many of the other devotees had used hallucinogenic drugs prior to conversion, he replied:

Almost all of us, I suppose. . . . Maybe 95 percent or more. . . . Such experiences affected me and I was much different afterwards. This is true of others too. But these experiences were unsatisfying because they were temporary. . . . Drugs provided temporary knowledge, perhaps, but not wisdom. . . . Nothing like the wisdom from Krishna.

Although drugs were strictly forbidden in devotional service, many devotees freely discussed their past drug experiences. Several described drugs as a necessary but insufficient precondition to achieving a psychological state permanently sustained by the Bhakti yoga discipline (its chanting and food especially). "It opened the door, but Krishna let me step through," said one devotee. "It freed my mind, it washed out the old structures," claimed another. Rather than the pleasurable or sensual aspects of drug use, the devotees stressed the use of psychedelics as a means to internal discovery. The sense of ordeal so prevalent in the discipline of devotion to Krishna seemed also essential to drug-induced enlightenment. In criticizing the extensive proliferation of the use of LSD and mescaline in the Haight-Ashbury, a convert said,

most of the people in the Haight are destroying their minds on drugs because they don't realize the powers they are dealing with. They have to be dedicated. It is like becoming a devotee of Krishna almost—you must be dedicated to the correct ways to spiritual knowledge. Also you must listen to those who have gone before. Like the spiritual master is to us. . . . When I first took acid I was guided by a friend who had taken it many times before. Many people now do not do this. They don't realize that acid is not just for sense gratification. It is a serious matter. They find this out too late and many of them end up crazy.

A central theme underlying commitment to the movement was the rejection of the pursuit of personal pleasure, of which drugs were an integral part. This placed the movement in fundamental opposition to the larger counterculture. If the counterculture was unified, it was unified in its obsession with personal experience; within it, an individual was not subordinate to a social role, an ideology, or a group; existing legal and normative controls were largely rejected; each individual was urged to pursue freely a personal state of ecstasy. The discipline of Krishna Consciousness represented a conservative reaction to this passionate assertion of self.

For many devotees, the hypnotic quality of the mantra seemed to be an experience equivalent to hallucinogenic drug use. Not only did the mantra generate feelings of ecstasy or transcendence, but it also involved a community—something lacking in the drug experience. The hallucinogenic drug experience is by its very nature a solitary one; the users confront their innermost feelings of fear, awe, and fantasy.

In contrast, the individual's experience of transcendance within the temple became regularized and predictable. The group's daily chanting rituals (mantras) became the expression of feelings previously reserved for the drug experience. The drug culture was one of resignation and passivity, whereas the Krishna movement stressed participation and affirmation.

CONCLUSIONS

The Hare Krishna movement initially emerged because it effectively translated its ancient rituals and doctrines to meet contemporary needs. Two specific features seem especially significant:

1. An apocalyptic ideology   The world was portrayed as being in danger of imminent collapse, which would render meaningless any previous desires for personal achievement or material acquisition. The movement's selective emphasis on these elements of its doctrine represented a deliberate effort to resonate with the attitudes of its neighbors in the Haight-Ashbury.

2. Participatory rituals   The movement's chanting ceremonies were perhaps more significant than its ideology in generating involvement; unlike the audiencelike behavior at episodic musical events, the mantra allowed full personal participation within a collective.

For its recruits, the movement seemed to embody many of the aspirations for an alternative community not fulfilled by the Haight-Ashbury. Conversion to Krishna served to sustain the promise of "psychedelic utopianism" within narrowly defined (and legally immune) limits. Perhaps the most significant aspect of hallucinogenic drug use was its redefinition of the possible pathways to knowledge. In a similar fashion, the ceremonies of the Krishna temple offered direct, unmediated communion with supernatural, transcendent forces. The experience became regularized, controllable, and predictable within the Bhakti yoga discipline. Transcendence became a routine state of being.

Section two religion and social cohesion

During most of human history, religion has been more than just another institution. It has been the sanctifier of important activities, the protector of group continuity, the builder of morale and solidarity, the bridge between person and person, group and group.

FUSION OF RELIGION AND GROUP LIFE

In ancient Greece and Rome, religious practices and beliefs were an inseparable part of family and civic life. Religion was, at first, a religion of family and hearth. A sacred fire burned at an altar in every house, and care was taken that it not be extinguished. Family ancestors were venerated, and the head of the household was its priest. The family was a religious unit with its own gods.

Religion has been called the "constituent principle" of the family in early Greece and Rome (Coulanges, 1864/1956:40). Common worship was the foundation of family life and the criterion of family membership. A son was no longer counted part of the family if he renounced the worship.

The special character of this domestic religion influenced other aspects of social life. The hearth was perceived as permanent, remaining forever on the same site, establishing an intimate and mysterious connection with the soil. The gods thereby "owned" the soil; but since the family "owned" its gods, there was a strong identification between a particular family and its land.

The enlargement of religious identity If each family has its own god or gods, then there are many gods. Such extreme polytheism is inconsistent with the enlargement of the group beyond the boundaries of the family. In early Greece and Rome, this problem was eased in two ways. First, family religion began to include *gods of nature*—representations of the sea, the sun, the forest, and so on—as well as deified ancestors, and

the gods of nature, being universal, could be shared with other families. Second, the multiplicity of family gods was modified when one family and its nature god attained greater influence.

As families united into tribes and tribes into a city, religion remained both symbol and bond of the new association. The union was marked by appropriate ceremonies, such as the lighting of a sacred fire, and by adoption of a common religion. Unification was strengthened when the image of the divine transcended the particularity of family and place. Ultimately, universal religions were founded on principles and symbols common to all mankind.

When religious identity and social identity are fused, we speak of *communal* religion. In a communal religion, a person is considered a believer, or member of the religious community, by virtue of membership in a family, clan, city, or state. A person is born into the religion, and to renounce one's religion is to renounce one's social group. It is said that in the communal religion of ancient China,

there was no choice in religious beliefs, but neither did it occur to the common man to make any other choice. Religious values were imbedded in the traditional moral order, and religion was an integral part of communal existence, inseparable from the individual's existence (Yang, 1961:111).

One mark of communal religion is the combination of religious and secular roles. In a family-based communal and patriarchal religion, the father is the priest and the home is the temple. In the broader city-based communal religion, political and religious authority are combined. High priest, judge, and political chief are often one.

DURKHEIM'S THEORY

As the foregoing discussion has suggested, one of the great potential capabilities of religion is the promotion of group cohesion. Durkheim was so impressed by this that he built his theory of religion on it. "The idea of society," he wrote, "is the soul of religion" 1912/1947:419).

He tried to find behind the variety of religious rites, symbols, and beliefs the fundamental characteristic of all religions.

There is something eternal in religion which is destined to survive all the particular symbols in which religious thought has successively enveloped itself. There can be no society which does not feel the need of upholding and reaffirming at regular intervals the collective sentiments and the collective ideas which make its unity and its personality. Now this moral remaking cannot be achieved except by the means of reunions, assemblies and meetings where the individuals, being closely united to one another, reaffirm in common their common sentiments. . . . What essential difference is there between an assembly of Christians celebrating the principal dates of the life of Christ, or of Jews remembering the exodus from Egypt or the promulgation of the decalogue, and a reunion of citizens commemorating the promulgation of a new moral or legal system or some great event in the national life? (Durkheim, 1912/1947:427).

In all these activities Durkheim saw one basic function: the celebration of the social group, whether a clan or a larger community. By such celebrations individuals are bound into a group which they need and which needs them. The symbols of religion, he thought, really represent society. "The god of the clan, the totemic principle, can therefore be nothing else than the clan itself, personified and represented to the imagination under the visible form of the animal or vegetable which serves as totem" (Durkheim, 1912/1947:206). Religious worship is, in effect, worship of society.

Limitations of Durkheim's theory Durkheim based his analysis on anthropological reports of religion in preliterate societies, especially in Australia. However, he did not restrict his conclusions to those or similar societies. He thought he had found the fundamental significance of all religion.

As a generalization, Durkheim's view needs the following qualifications:

1. It is wrong to ignore the varied *content* of religious beliefs and symbols. Divine ancestors or totems may indeed be interpreted as standing for the family or clan. In such cases, it may be correct to say that the group itself is worshiped. However, many religious ideas go beyond representation of the group. They may foster distinctive moral principles, such as the Christian idea of self-sacrificing love.

2. Not all religious experience can be understood from the standpoint of its contribution to social solidarity. The quest for salvation may be an individual act and may lead to a weakening of group ties. Religion can be a *divisive* force when a number of different religious groups compete for communicants or when religion struggles with other institutions, such as the government, for preeminence.

RELIGION AND SOCIAL TABUS

A great many conventional attitudes and practices are supported by religion. In most societies the mores (see p. 60) are intimately bound up with religious belief and authority. This is especially true of customs that touch closely on the sanctity of life and the symbolic meaning of the human body. In Western society people are revolted by the idea of eating human flesh, yet this tabu is not necessarily supported by religious doctrine. A clear distinction is made between killing a person for food and, in cases of necessity, eating the flesh of one who is already dead. Adaptation 30 describes (1) the tension between tabu and religion and (2) religion as a resource for overcoming a deeply felt repugnance.

Adaptation 30 Read: Cannibalism and religion: The case of the Andes survivors

In October 1972, 15 members of a Uruguayan rugby team and 25 of their relatives and friends set out for Chile, over the Andes, in a chartered aircraft with a crew of five. All of the passengers were Catholics. The rugby players were alumni of the Christian Brothers school, where their parents had sent them because of the order's "traditional methods and old-fashioned objectives" (19). The weather was bad, the pilot miscalculated his position, and the plane crashed in snow in the treacherous cordillera at an altitude of 11,500 feet. Some of the passengers and crew were killed in the crash, others were seriously injured and lived only a short time, and many of the survivors had broken bones and other injuries.

Although the team members were young and in good physical condition at the beginning of the trip, in the arduous conditions of the crash site they suffered many hardships: frostbite, altitude sickness, gangrene from injuries, exhaustion, diarrhea, severe constipation—and starvation. They huddled together in the fuselage of the plane dressed in lightweight clothing and punched each other to keep from freezing. There were no facilities for treating the injured and only two premedical students to help them. The terrain was extremely precipitous and subject to avalanches, with sheer mountain walls on three sides. It was above the tree line, and the weather was bitterly cold. No food had been put aboard because the flight was to be a short one, and there were only a few snacks carried by the passengers to be found in the wreckage.

Search planes failed to locate the crash. As hopes for a quick rescue faded, some of the survivors realized that they were faced with starvation and began to assess their situation.

THE POSSIBILITY OF CANNIBALISM

While most of his companions only thought of being rescued, Parrado considered the active option of somehow getting back to civilization by his own

Source: Abridged and adapted from *Alive: The Story of the Andes Survivors* by Piers Paul Read (New York: Avon, 1975). Quoted passages used by permission of Piers Paul Read.

efforts, and he confided this determination to Carlitos Páez, who also wanted to leave.

"Impossible," said Carlitos. "You'd freeze to death in the snow."

"Not if I wore enough clothes."

"Then you'd starve to death. You can't climb mountains on a little piece of chocolate and a sip of wine."

"Then I'll cut meat from one of the pilots," said Parrado. "After all, they got us into this mess."

Carlitos was not shocked by this because he did not take it seriously (60).

However, by the tenth day several of the boys realized that if they were to survive they would have to eat the bodies of those who had died in the crash. It was a ghastly prospect. The corpses lay around the plane in the snow, preserved by the intense cold in the state in which they had died. While the thought of cutting flesh from those who had been their friends was deeply repugnant to them all, a lucid appreciation of their predicament led them to consider it.

Gradually the discussion spread as these boys cautiously mentioned it to their friends or to those they thought would be sympathetic. Finally, Canessa brought it out into the open. He argued forcefully that they were not going to be rescued, that they would have to escape themselves, but that nothing could be done without food, and that the only food was human flesh. He used his knowledge of medicine to describe, in his penetrating, high-pitched voice, how their bodies were using up their reserves. "Every time you move," he said, "you use up part of your own body. Soon we shall be so weak that we won't have the strength even to cut the meat that is lying there before our eyes."

Canessa did not argue just from expediency. He insisted that they had a moral duty to stay alive by any means at their disposal, and because Canessa was earnest about his religious belief, great weight was given to what he said by the more pious among the survivors.

"It is meat," he said. "That's all it is. The souls have left their bodies and are in heaven with God. All that is left here are the carcasses, which are no more human beings than the dead flesh of the cattle we eat at home" (76).

A meeting was called, and for the first time all twenty-seven survivors discussed whether or not to eat the bodies of the dead. To allay their own doubts about what their dead friends would have thought, the boys made a pact that if any more of them were to die, their bodies were to be used for food (77).

A 35-year old woman was among the survivors. Her instinct to survive was strong, her longing to see her children was acute, but the thought of eating human flesh horrified her. She did not think it wrong; she could distinguish between sin and physical revulsion, and a social taboo was not a law of God. "But," she said, "as long as there is a chance of rescue, as long as there is *something* left to eat, even if it is only a morsel of chocolate, then I can't do it" (78).

Her husband agreed but would not deter others from doing what they felt must be done. No one suggested that God might want them to choose to die. They all believed that virtue lay in survival and that eating their dead friends would in no way endanger their souls, but it was one thing to decide and another to act.

Their discussions had continued most of the day, and by midafternoon they knew that they must act now or not at all, yet they sat inside the plane in total silence. At last a group of four rose and went out into the snow. Few followed them. No one wished to know who was going to cut the meat or from which body it was to be taken.

THE ACT

Most of the bodies were covered by snow, but the buttocks of one protruded a few yards from the plane. With no exchange of words, Canessa knelt, bared the skin, and cut into the flesh with a piece of broken glass. It was frozen hard and difficult to cut, but he persisted until he had cut away twenty slivers the size of matchsticks (78).

Revulsion was strong, but the will to survive stronger, and over a period of several days, first one and then another of the boys forced themselves to eat the raw flesh. A small amount of meat was roasted, which helped three boys to overcome their repugnance. But fuel was extremely scarce, and some argued against cooking because it shrank the amount of food to be consumed and destroyed food value as well.

As the days passed and the twenty-five young men grew stronger on their new diet, the married couple, living on what remained of the wine, chocolate, and jam, grew thinner and more feeble.

The boys watched their growing debility with alarm. Marcelo begged them over and over again to overcome their reluctance and eat the meat. He used every argument, above all those words of Pedro Algorta. "Think of it as Communion. Think of it as the body and blood of Christ, because this is food that God has given us because He wants us to live."

Liliana listened to what he said, but time and again she gently shook her head. "There's nothing wrong with you doing it, Marcelo, but I can't, I just can't" (90–91).

Although she grew weaker, life ebbing from her body, she continued to refuse until the group heard on a transistor radio that the search had been called off. Then her husband was able to convince her to eat the meat.

THE PRACTICE OF CANNIBALISM

In spite of the persistent inner conflict about eating human flesh, the survivors finally came to accept the realities of their situation. A number of considerations were taken into account in regulating the order in which the bodies were to be eaten. Out of respect for the sensibilities of the survivors, the eating of relatives or close friends was postponed as long as possible. Similarly the women's bodies were left untouched. The bodies of the crew, who had been strangers, were the first to be used. As the plane had broken apart when it crashed, bodies were widely scattered and many could not be reached. On the seventeenth day an avalanche killed eight more of their number, but these victims were already emaciated and therefore offered less food value than did those who had died in the crash.

Cutting meat off the bodies of friends was a task that only a few boys had the determination to perform. However, after large pieces of meat were cut from a body these would then be passed to another team, which would divide the chunks into smaller pieces with razor blades. This work was not so unpopular, for once the meat was separated from the bodies it was easier to forget what it was (124). It was more difficult to eat what was recognizably human—a hand, say, or a foot, but they did so all the same (215).

383

Adaptation 30
Read:
Cannibalism
and religion:
The case of the
Andes survivors

RATIONING

The meat was strictly rationed, but it was agreed that those who worked would have more, because they used up energy through their exertions, and that the expeditionaries could have almost as much as they liked. One corpse was always finished before another was started (124).

They had, from necessity, come to eat almost every part of the body. Canessa knew that the liver contained the reserve of vitamins; for that reason he ate it himself and encouraged others to do so until it was set aside for the expeditionaries, the only ones who ever ate their fill of meat. The others felt a continuous craving for more to eat, yet realized how important it was that what they had should be rationed. Only the lungs, the skin, the head, and the genitals of the corpses were thrown aside (125).

Eventually, when supplies grew short, they learned to accept or even seek out parts that had previously been discarded.

Some of the boys continued to find it difficult to eat raw human flesh. While the others extended the limit of what they could stomach to the liver, heart, kidneys, and intestines of the dead, three still balked at the red meat of the muscles. The only occasions on which they found it easy to eat was when the meat was cooked; and every morning one of them would ask, "Are we cooking today?"

Cooking was allowed once or twice a week as the weather permitted, and on those occasions the less fastidious would hold back so that the others could eat more (126–127). Marrow was more easily accepted by everyone.

ESCAPE

After about a month, expeditionaries were chosen to climb the mountain to seek help, but to improve their chance, they postponed their departure, hoping for warmer weather. Two earlier parties had been unsuccessful because of the harsh conditions, and the group decided they must plan and prepare more carefully. Although there were signs of the spring thaw, the weather did not improve as much as they had hoped, but when another boy died they felt they could delay no longer, and the expedition set out on December 11—60 days after the crash. After an awful ten-day trek through mountains later measured at 13,500 feet, two boys reached a peasant's hut. A few days before Christ-mas the other 14 were rescued alive—a "Christmas Miracle." The peasant gave the two some bread and cheese and left them alone to see to his cows. They ate the cheese and rested. Then, before he returned, they took what remained of the human flesh they had brought with them and buried it under a stone, for no sooner had the bread and cheese passed their lips than some of the early revulsion they had felt returned to them (246).

Most of the survivors were hospitalized briefly and their wounds and illnesses treated. They were all severely underweight, having lost from 30 to 80 pounds. This enormous difference showed not only how thin they had become but how heavy they had been before (277). At first the hospital allowed them no visitors except a young priest.

VOICE OF THE CHURCH

In permitting Father Andrés to visit the survivors, the doctors had chosen a most healing therapy. The decision to eat the bodies of their friends had been a severe trial for the consciences of many of the boys on the mountain. They were all Roman Catholics and were open to the judgment of their church on what they had done. Since it is the teaching of the Catholic Church that anthropophagy *in extremis* is permissible, this young priest was able not so much to forgive them as to tell them that they had done nothing wrong. This judgment, backed with all the authority of the church, assured the peace of mind at least of those who felt uncertain (280).

Later, a Uruguayan Jesuit who taught theology at the Catholic University in Santiago came to the hotel to talk to some of the survivors, in preparation for the mass that was to be held for them the next day. They told him that they had eaten the bodies of their friends to stay alive, and, like Father Andrés, Father Rodríguez did not hesitate to endorse the decision they had made. Whatever doubts there might have been about the morality of what they had done were dissipated in his mind by the sober and religious spirit in which they had made their decision. The two boys told him what Algorta had said when they had cut meat from the first body, and while the Jesuit discounted any strict correlation between cannibalism and communion, he was moved as so many others had been by the pious spirit which was manifest in the dictum.

The Christmas mass was held at the Catholic University at twelve the next day, and the sermon delivered by Father Rodríguez, though it made no mention of anthropophagy, was an unequivocal affirmation of what the young men had done to stay alive. The boys and their parents all believed in the authority of the Catholic Church and were profoundly reassured by what was said (299).

PARENTAL DISMAY

Unaccountably, the waiting families of the crash victims had not anticipated that cannibalism was the only possible expedient for survival, and the happy reunions were clouded by their reactions on learning of the anthropophagous aspect of the Christmas Miracle. Unprepared for the news, they had been shocked and for the most part never alluded to it again. They also quite clearly dreaded that the news would break on the outside world, and though some of the survivors conceded to themselves that their parents' reaction was only to be expected, they were all decidedly upset and injured that anyone should be appalled at what they had done. They read into those involuntary expressions of shock and disgust a preference for the alternative—which was that all of them should have died.

Their peace of mind was not assisted by the presence in the hotel of a mass of journalists and photographers asking incessant questions and taking pictures of them whenever they moved, ate, or kissed their parents. And more agonizing still were the equally persistent questions of the relatives of the boys who had not returned, relatives who wanted to know the exact circumstances of the death of their brothers and children. It was not something which, at that moment, the survivors wished to remember and discuss (296).

They were bombarded by the press with questions which they would not answer. Indeed, they became increasingly disgusted with the journalists, who showed no reticence or tact in what they asked. There were even persistent suggestions by an Argentine journalist that the avalanche had not occurred but had been invented to conceal the fact that the stronger boys had killed the weaker ones to provide themselves with food.

The survivors were still exceedingly vulnerable, and these assaults upset them. Moreover, a Chilean magazine published photographs of limbs and bones which had lain around the crashed plane. Another Chilean newspaper printed the story under the headline: "May God Forgive Them" (300).

NOTHING TO FORGIVE

When the argument was put forward that the survivors should have died rather than eat human flesh, the Catholic Church was quick to dismiss this primitive reaction. "You cannot condemn what they did," said Monsignor Andrés Rubio, Auxiliary Bishop of Montevideo, "when it was the only possibility of survival. . . . Flesh survives when assimilated by someone in extreme need, just as it does when an eye or heart of a dead man is grafted onto a living man. . . . What would we have done in a similar situation? . . . What would you say to someone if he revealed in confession a secret like that? Only one thing: not to be tormented by it . . . not to blame himself for something he would not blame in someone else and which no one blames in him."

And finally the theologian of *L'Osservatore Romano*, Gino Concetti, wrote that he who has received from the community has also the duty to give to the community or its individual members when they are in extreme need of help to survive. Such an imperative extends especially to the body, which is otherwise consigned to dissolution, to uselessness. "Considering these facts . . . it is legitimate to resort to lifeless human bodies in order to survive."

On the other hand, the church did not concur with the view that eating flesh of friends was equivalent to Holy Communion. When Monsignor Rubio was asked whether a refusal to eat the flesh of a dead human being could be interpreted as a form of suicide, and the opposite as an act of communion, he replied, "In no way can it be understood as suicide, but the use of the term communion is not correct either. At most it is possible to say that it is correct to use this term as a source of inspiration. But it is not communion" (308–309).

It was clear, therefore, that the survivors were to be regarded neither as saints nor as sinners, but a role was increasingly sought for them as national heroes. The newspapers and radio and television stations began to take an understandable pride in what these young fellow countrymen had achieved. There were many articles describing their courage, endurance, and resourcefulness. The survivors, on

385

Adaptation 30
Read:
Cannibalism
and religion:
The case of the
Andes survivors

the whole, rose to the occasion. Many of them kept their beards and long hair and were not ill pleased to be recognized wherever they went in Montevideo and Punta del Este (309).

Twenty-nine of those who had left in the aircraft had not returned, and for the families of those twenty-nine, the return of the sixteen meant the confirmation of their death. It was, moreover, a confirmation of a disturbing nature. To hearts already brimful with sorrow, however noble and rational the mind may have been in contemplation of this end, there was a primitive and irrepressible horror at the idea that the body of their beloved should have been used in this way. For the most part, however, they mastered their repugnance. The parents showed the same selflessness and courage as their sons had done and rallied around the sixteen survivors. One father went with his family to the press conference and afterward spoke to the newspaper *El País*. "I came here with my family," he said, "because we wanted to see all those who were the friends of my son and because we are sincerely happy to have them back among us. We are glad, what is more, that there were forty-five of them, because this helped at least sixteen to return" (313–314).

Section three church, sect, and cult

The varieties of religious consciousness (p. 375) tend to create distinct forms of religious association. People who are mainly interested in social participation or in spiritual comfort will be content with a sedate and unchallenging religious organization; people who want a deeper or more exciting experience will seek out or form a sect or cult. This sorting-out process is seldom precise or complete. Most people are born into a religious community, and it is not easy to break old ties and choose another identity. Therefore the same religious organization may include many different kinds of people who have quite different religious aspirations.

These differences produce internal stress and conflict. A perennial theme is the contradiction between religious purity and institutional stability. The quest for purity pushes the organization in one direction; the desire for stability tends to compromise the faith but also makes possible an easy bridge between the mundane world and the spiritual world.

THE CHURCH AND THE SECT

The church The word *church* is commonly used to designate any organized religious group. However, sociologists use the term in a more strict sense as a religious association characterized by (1) a relatively high degree of institutionalization (see ASSOCIATIONS, pp. 222–224), (2) integration with the social and economic order, (3) a membership recruited on the basis of residence or family, and (4) relatively restrained and routinized participation.

Within this broad category may be distinguished the *ecclesia* and the *denomination*. The ecclesia is a church that strives for fullest integration with the rest of society and for universal membership embracing an entire community. Unity of church and state is welcomed, and in the ideal case the ecclesia is an "established" church that counts as members all residents or citizens of a given area.

The denomination has more limited aspirations and a more restricted membership. For the most part, it is assumed that children will, in the normal course of events, be inducted into the church. Therefore family membership is the main basis of recruitment, and the family is the main support of religious participation. As in the case of the ecclesia, no great demands are made upon the individual for high levels of religious commitment. Denominations are the churches of a pluralist society and are compatible with a belief in the separation of church and state.

Table 12:3 Sect and church

Sect	Church
Relation to the social and economic order	
Membership composed chiefly of the propertyless	Membership composed chiefly of property owners
Economic poverty in church property and salaries	Economic wealth
Cultural periphery of the community	Cultural center of the community
Renunciation of or indifference to prevailing culture and social organization, including established churches	Acceptance of prevailing values and of political and economic order
Self-centered religion based on personal experience	Culture-centered religion based on affirmation of citizenship in an existing community
A moral community excluding unworthy members	A social institution embracing all who are socially compatible
Many religious services regardless of interference with other aspects of life	Regular services at stated intervals
Adherence to strict biblical standards, such as tithing or pacifism	Acceptance of general cultural standards as practical definition of religious obligation
Participation and internal control	
Unspecialized, unprofessionalized, part-time ministry	Specialized, professional, full-time ministry
Voluntary, confessional bases of membership	Ritual or social prerequisites only
Principal concern with adult membership	Equal concern for children of members
Emphasis on evangelism and conversion	Emphasis on religious education
High degree of congregational participation in services and administration	Delegation of responsibility to a small percentage of the members
Fervor and positive action in worship	Restraint and passive listening

Source: Adapted from Pope, 1942:122–124.

The sect The chief features of a religious sect have been summarized as follows:

It is a voluntary association; membership is by proof to sect authorities of some claim to personal merit — such as knowledge of doctrine, affirmation of a conversion experience, or recommendation of members in good standing; exclusiveness is emphasized, and explusion exercised against those who contravene doctrinal, moral, or organizational precepts; its self-conception is of an elect, a gathered remnant, possessing special enlightenment; personal perfection is the expected standard of aspiration, in whatever terms this is judged; it accepts, at least as an ideal, the priesthood of all believers; there is a high level of lay participation; there is opportunity for the member spontaneously to express his commitment; the sect is hostile or indifferent to the secular order and to the state (Wilson, 1959:4).

Sects are concerned with purity of doctrine and with the depth and genuineness of religious feeling. As a result, demands are

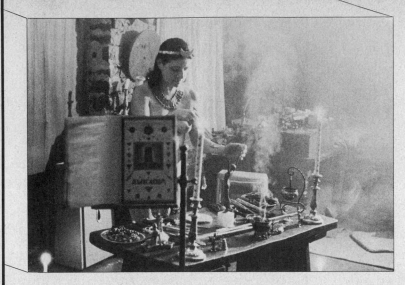

English occultist at work

made upon the member to be an active participant, even a leader or missionary, as a warrant of faith. The emphasis on the need for purity of belief tends to create intolerance toward other groups and moves the members of the sect toward a more critical assessment of the secular world in accordance with the ideals of the gospel.

Within a church, the impulse toward deeper religious commitment may be taken care of by the creation of special religious groups having selective memberships and distinctive practices. The religious orders of the Roman Catholic church, such as the Benedictines, Dominicans, Franciscans, and Jesuits, are good examples. The partial autonomy of these groups enables them to serve a sectlike function, but they remain within the church and contribute to its work.

Interplay of sect and church Two major conclusions may be drawn from sociological studies of the relation between sect and church (Troeltsch, 1912/1949:331–341; Pope, 1942:118 ff.; Niebuhr, 1957; Wilson, 1961):

1. Some sects develop into denominations. If a sect is strongly interested in seeking new members, it may tend to water down its beliefs and take in people who are not truly committed. If in addition the sect's demands are simple, asking only that members affirm that they feel converted, it will not be effectively insulated from the world and in time may adapt to it. Other institutionalizing processes, such as concern for a stable ministry, religious education, respectable quarters, benefit funds, seminaries, and "good works," help this evolution along. But not all sects become denominations. One important criterion is whether the sect is *conversionist*, reaching out into the world rather than withdrawing from it (Wilson, 1959:14).

2. There is also a reverse movement, from church to sect. This comes about mainly by a process of schism. The watered-down belief and practice, the respectability and accommodation of the church, may become unacceptable to some of its members. Thus the poor may leave middle-class churches to form religious groups of their own, characterized by greater purity of belief, emotional fervor, a lay ministry, and an all-encompassing communal life. However, as the founders of the sect become more prosperous and respectable, they become more receptive to churchlike organization and behavior. They in turn neglect the special religious needs of the poor. "This pattern recurs with remarkable regularity in the history of Christianity. Anabaptists, Quakers, Methodists, Salvation Army, and more recent sects of like type illustrate this rise and progress of the churches of the disinherited" (Niebuhr, 1957:28).

Adaptation 31 describes some of these processes as it analyzes the relation of church and sect in Canada.

Caution Like all typologies, the church-sect distinction should be applied with the understanding that in the real world these distinctions are blurred. Many churches have some sect characteristics, and, conversely, a pure sect may be hard to find. The categories are starting points for analysis.

CULTS

The word *cult* derives from the Latin *cultus*, which means both cultivation and worship. Thus cult connotes a certain kind of religious practice or ritual:

The way to be right with the god . . . is to cultivate him; that is, to assume the attitudes, to perform the acts and to pronounce the words which are pleasing in his sight and which move him therefore to provide in return what man's heart desires. Such cultivation is worship (Kallen, 1930:619).

A cultic practice is not any form of worship but one that has a special focus or mystery — veneration of a saint, living or dead; a snake dance; or belief in some esoteric doctrine, such as the imminent coming of a messiah or the doom of the world. Cultic practices or groups are often found within larger church communities, such as the Catholic church. The Protestant sects, which emphasized salvation through faith, tried to minimize ritual and they vigorously attacked the cult aspects of Catholicism, such as the sacraments, the veneration of Mary, and the worship of images.

As more commonly understood, a cult is a separate religious group or movement whose main preoccupation is an esoteric belief or

form of worship. Thus the Peyote cult centered on a ritual all-night meeting which "largely consisted of singing, prayer, and the consumption of peyote" (Wilson, 1973: 420).

When a particular form of worship is at the center of religious experience, other aspects of religion, such as doctrine and organization, tend to be absent, attenuated, or

Jesus people in a soundproof cellar

given a special and mysterious form. Thus cult beliefs often include an element of secrecy, and outsiders are excluded from the cult's esoteric knowledge.

Because of its special emphasis, the cult attracts people who are isolated from the community; it is relatively structureless; its unity stems from participation in ritual or in intensive communication of the special doctrine; and it often depends upon a leader who can win the personal commitment of the cult members. The term cult, therefore, usually suggests "small size, search for a mystical experience, lack of an organizational structure, and presence of a charismatic leader" (Yinger, 1957:154).

Adaptation 29 (pp. 375–379) describes a more or less typical modern cult. A number of similar cults of Eastern origin have arisen in the United States, such as the Divine Light Mission (Guru Maharaj Ji) and the Healthy-Happy-Holy Organization (Glock and Bellah, 1976). Some faith healing cults engage in dramatic and dangerous rituals, such as the handling of poisonous snakes (Mathison, 1960).

As these illustrations suggest, there is a tendency for the cult to be exotic, that is, to involve rites and beliefs that seem strange and even alien to the rest of the community. The exotic character of a cult adds a sense of excitement, as well as confidence that one has gained a special "way" to spiritual salvation.

Although the line between them is often unclear, the cult may be distinguished from the sect in that sects place a greater emphasis on purification of existing doctrine and usually arise as splits from established churches. Cults, on the other hand, are more random and accidental in origin and tend to "draw their inspiration from other than the primary religion of the culture" (Glock and Stark, 1965:245). When a proliferation of cults occurs, a special sociological and historical explanation is required, such as a cultural crisis which erodes confidence in traditional systems of belief (Eister, 1972).

Adaptation 31 Clark: The Methodist church and the Salvation Army

This study is concerned with the conflict between church and sect forms of religious organization in relation to the changing community structure of Canada. The view set forth is that the church requires social stability and that when such a condition is not present the church gives way to the sect form of religious organization. The church seeks to accommodate religious organization to the community. The sect emphasizes the exclusiveness of religious organization: It thinks of the worldly society as something evil, to be withdrawn from, or to be won over by missionary zeal. Within the church,

the spirit of accommodation tends to dominate, and within the sect, the spirit of separation.

This adaptation deals with the Methodist church and the Salvation Army as they met the challenge of the Canadian city toward the end of the nineteenth century.

After about 1885, many migrants swelled the size of the Canadian city. The chief task and opportunity of religious organization became one of gaining the support of people who found themselves in a new social setting, in many cases far from their old home community and past associates. Traditional religious attachments broke down, and new ones had to be formed if religion were to maintain its hold. Established churches

Source: Abridged and adapted from *Church and Sect in Canada* by S. D. Clark (Toronto: University of Toronto Press, 1948), pp. 381–429. Published in this form by permission of the University of Toronto Press and S. D. Clark.

such as the Methodist church experienced their greatest losses to such religious movements as the Salvation Army. The army also brought its teaching to those who had no religion. Its success came largely from its influence on the urban poor.

THE SOCIAL BASE OF METHODISM

The limitations of traditional religious denominationalism, which largely accounted for the rapid growth of new sectarian religious movements, can be most clearly seen in the case of the Methodist church. The failure of the Methodist church after 1885 was not a failure to grow with the city, nor was it a failure to gain influence in the social life of the urban community. The building of handsome places of worship, the employment of learned and in some cases highly paid ministers, the increasing reliance upon prominent citizens in the organization of Sunday school and missionary work, and the growing participation of the pulpit in political discussion strengthened the position of the church in the Canadian city. The church gained support in the better residential areas of the city, and its influence declined among the poorer classes.

Methodist leaders strenuously tried to avoid placing the church in opposition to labor. Methodist religious publications expressed their sympathy for the cause of the workingman and appealed to employers to improve working conditions. But such an appeal had little relation to reality as seen by the workingman concerned with strengthening his bargaining position through the organization of trade unions. The Methodist appeal, which expressed the individualist philosophy of a natural harmony of interests of social classes, attacked the economic and social assumptions of working-class philosophy.

The predominantly rural background of the membership and the long rural history of the church in Canada had much to do with the failure of Methodism to appeal effectively to labor. The conception of work as a virtue and of leisure as a temptation to sin persisted strongly in Methodist thought. The puritan outlook of persons of rural background was little different from the individualistic outlook of capitalist employers, and whereas Methodist membership continued to be largely of rural origin, leadership passed to the capitalist elements of the urban community. The increasing influence of employers within the councils of the church made it more difficult to develop a positive appeal to the working-class population of the cities.

Mobility of the urban workers Only a small proportion of the working population of the city, however, was being drawn into trade union organization. The bulk of urban workers, unskilled and transient, lacked a working-class philosophy or a consciousness of being a part of a distinct working class. Without permanent jobs, homes, or neighborhood attachments, they had few strong loyalties and little sense of social responsibility. These elements of the population participated little in the group life of the community. They withdrew into transitory forms of association—gangs, associations of the saloon, and ephemeral groupings based upon the casual contacts of the street, rooming house, or street-corner store.

Abandonment of the practice of street preaching, as employed by the early Methodist preachers, and reliance upon services held in imposing places of worship cut the church off from the floating population of the urban community. The problem faced by the Methodist church in the latter decades of the nineteenth century did not grow only out of social differences between the rich and poor of the city. It resulted from a new kind of social mobility in the community for which the machinery of the church was not adapted.

Limitations of church appeal to the lower classes Mobility imposed demands upon the church organization that could be met only by new techniques. Methodism had abandoned the sectarian policy of recruiting members by religious conversion. It had come to rely upon the techniques of the church, seeking to perpetuate itself from generation to generation. The Sunday school developed as the chief means of keeping the new generation within the church, but mobility was greatest among the younger people, and there was an increasing gap between the membership of the Sunday school and the membership of the church. Many who had grown up in the Sunday schools were lost to the church through the development of new interests outside religion.

The house of worship was designed to meet the needs of a settled population; it did not effectively serve a floating population which had no strong local community attachments. For the masses of

391

Adaptation 31
Clark: The
Methodist
church and the
Salvation Army

the urban community, the street became the center of social life. Religious organization had to adapt itself to urban ecology. In failing to do so, Methodism lost the support of the more mobile elements of the population.

The churches had to do more than reach the urban population; they had to attract support through their religious appeal. A half century of effort to build itself into a denomination had led Methodism to emphasize a wordly pulpit appeal. By 1885 the church had lost much of its evangelical drive. The polished and studied sermon took the place of the passionate exhortation calling on people to repent and seek forgiveness. The pulpit lost some of its force as a spiritually reorganizing agency among those of the city who were looking for direction and comfort and a means of securing new ties.

If churches were to be filled with people financially able to maintain them, the pulpit appeal had to be directed toward the higher social levels of the population. Evangelism and the large church edifice were incompatible. The former attracted the support of the poor, the latter required the support of the rich. In becoming a religion of the church, Methodism increasingly depended on the settled residents of the community, on people who enjoyed a sense of status and security.

Church-sponsored evangelism Despite this incompatibility, an effort was made by the church to maintain a revivalist atmosphere, in part by the use of professional evangelists who appeared in the United States around the 1870s and soon became a powerful force. Though not connected with any church and unordained, the professional evangelist worked within rather than outside the regular churches. He gained his influence not by building up a following of his own or by developing a set of doctrinal teachings, but by making a special appeal to regular church followings. In this way, the more successful evangelists were able to gain a hearing among hundreds of thousands of people without interfering with the work of the church.

When the evangelists preached to people who were faithful churchgoers, they strengthened the churches, especially by getting more financial contributions. On the other hand, the value of the professional evangelist to the regular churches was limited by the fact that the churches were unable to maintain the religious interest aroused by

the evangelist. The nonchurchgoer who took part in revivalist services in a tent or public hall did not usually attend regular religious services. Revivalism was seldom successful in establishing enduring religious attachments except where it led directly to the formation of a new religious sect.

What was needed, if the church were to reach the highly mobile elements in the city, was a body of workers prepared to go onto the city streets, into the homes of the poor, and into the public meeting places of ordinary people. The need of maintaining his professional dignity made it difficult for the minister to do this. Even if the evangelist had been prepared to do such work, they were too few. It required an army of workers, and such an army could only be built by drawing upon lay volunteers. In this the Salvation Army succeeded.

THE SALVATION ARMY

In 1883, the first Canadian branch of the Salvation Army was organized in London, Ontario—the beginnings of what was to become a dominant religious force in urban Canada during the next 15 years. The army capitalized on the great evangelical revival of 1885–1900. With its sensational methods, the Salvation Army came into sharp conflict with the traditional order of Canadian society. Deeply entrenched institutions, both secular and religious, encountered a formidable challenge in its teachings. The saloon was an obvious point of attack, but the saloon was not the only institution subjected to onslaught. Nothing opposed to evangelical religion escaped. Army workers made no nice distinction between what was considered the province of religious interest and what was not. There was no place—saloon, billiard parlor, or brothel—where the individual could take shelter from the scrutiny of Salvationists concerned about the state of his soul.

Challenge to the regular churches The established churches relied on stated places of worship, a professional ministry, and a ritual, however simple, to maintain a sense of dignity and decorum. The professional status of the minister and the social standing of the congregation in the community depended upon ridding religion of any appearance of being strange or irrational.

The emphasis in Salvation Army teachings on free expression of religious feelings and the willingness of army workers to resort to any method, however spectacular, to attract attention, threatened to destroy the good name of religion. The army's teachings tended to shift the prerogative of judging spiritual worth from the institution to the convert. Religion was made popular in the sense that the understanding of its mysteries was not confined to the select few. Like all religious sects, the army attacked directly the claims and pretensions of a professional ministry. It thus attacked the whole system of ecclesiastical control and struck at the basis of authority within the church. The church could not meet the army on its own ground. More was involved than religious rivalry; there was a fundamental conflict between types of religious organization: the church and the sect. The loss of members by the churches to the Salvation Army represented not a shift of denominational attachments but a strengthening of a spirit of religious fellowship hostile to the whole position of denominationalism.

The Methodist church felt most strongly the effects of Salvation Army influence. The army originated from a split within the Methodist church in Great Britain, and its doctrines and teachings were very similar to those of Methodism. Therefore the army tended to draw many recruits from the Methodist congregations, which were proportionately weakened.

Army methods and organization The methods employed by the Salvation Army won the support of footloose elements of the urban population. Street preaching was revived as a regular feature of religious work, and the combination of street preaching with parades led by brass bands attracted attention. Crowds gathered on street corners, in public parks, and in other open spaces, and when a sufficient state of religious enthusiasm had been aroused, they paraded to the barracks where a revivalist meeting took place. At no point did the army impose any serious obstacle to the participation of the individual in religious service. He could easily join the crowds on the street

393

Adaptation 31
Clark: The
Methodist
church and the
Salvation Army

Street evangelism, new style

and as easily depart. The army carried on religious services in barracks and public halls, where people unaccustomed to churchgoing would feel at home. The service itself was informal and encouraged the free movement of individuals. The lack of decorum in army meetings had a quality of homeliness and ease, in contrast to the stiff formality of the church.

The centralized organization of the army, like that of Methodism a century earlier, was highly effective for evangelical work. Military discipline became a central feature of army organization, and while the autocratic character of the leadership led eventually to internal dispute and schism, it was an element of strength in the early years of the army's growth.

The movement was a religious order. The property rights of recruits were surrendered to the organization: They lived in army residences, were clothed and fed by the army, and earnings were turned over to army headquarters. The recruits tended to be down-and-outs, the social outcasts of the community, who welcomed the economic as well as the emotional security provided by the army. Their enthusiasm for the cause substituted for any desire for individual gain. The discipline of the soldier and the devoutness of the ascetic combined to build up among workers a strong feeling of group loyalty and attachment to the leaders.

The emphasis placed by the army upon the reclamation of the individual—the drunkard, criminal, prostitute, and wastrel—led to practical results which could be demonstrated and dramatized. The sudden reformation of the individual assumed something of the character of a religious miracle, and colorful reports of such reformation provided effective advertising. The work of the army among the down-and-outs of the city won for it the affection of those who did not feel welcome in the houses of worship of the more richly endowed denominations and the sympathy of those who had a philanthropic interest in the welfare of less fortunate elements of the population. The army worker had no hesitation in stopping to minister to the drunkard, ex-criminal, or prostitute on the street; the army hostel was open to those who needed food and clothing. Philanthropic activities became an important part of the army's work. Primarily, however, the force of its appeal lay in its emphasis upon the simple message of the gospel. The army grew with all the enthusiasm of the new religious

sect. It was prepared to encourage extravagant forms of religious expression if converts to the cause were gained.

Efforts of the older churches to adopt some of the methods of the Salvation Army were an indication of their effectiveness. But the success of the army, in the end, was not due to any particular method. The strength of the army lay in the fact that it was an exclusive religious sect. It expanded through its appeal to a particular class in the community. However much the older churches may have employed its methods, they were unable to make the sort of single appeal characteristic of the army. No matter what the traditional churches did for the urban masses, the fact of social distinction was emphasized. In the army, social differentiation disappeared in the emphasis upon spiritual worth.

Institutionalization of the army Barracks that are still standing in many towns and villages provide an indication of the rapid growth of the movement. The same buildings, long since abandoned or converted to other uses, suggest an equally rapid decline. The high peak was reached about the turn of the century. Subsequent development was in the direction of limiting the field of evangelical work and strengthening the organization. Like other religious movements before it, the army was forced away from the role of religious sect in seeking a closer accommodation with the community.

The Salvation Army's evangelism had been dominated by the consciousness of souls still to be saved, and this restless search for the wicked and the damned gave their work its distinctive character. But the urge to spread ever further the message of religious salvation led inevitably to an impatience with the slow and laborious task of building up a permanent organization. Consequently many who were drawn into the army were later lost through failure to follow up the early work of evangelization.

In the interests of the larger movement, army headquarters decided to withdraw from areas where there was insufficient support to maintain a strong local organization. The decision reflected the viewpoint of a leadership concerned with problems of administration and finance rather than the evangelist's main concern for saving souls. Necessarily, as the army grew, greater attention had to be paid to building up a following loyal to the movement as a whole. Those served by the army had to be taxed for its support. This meant an increasing emphasis on organization and a reduction in evangelical work.

The shift in emphasis did not come about without bitter internal conflict, which on a number of occasions led to open division and the organization of rival armies. The differences were fundamental. The international leadership was concerned with building the movement into a permanent religious organization with its own following. The dissident evangelists were concerned with saving souls wherever they might be found, with little regard to denominational lines. The one view reflected the spirit of the church, the other the spirit of the religious sect. Although the army suffered a serious loss of support from these defections, in the end it built up a strong organization. If it were to survive, it had to rid itself of some of the very attributes which had accounted for its early success.

By 1914 the Salvation Army in Canada had ceased to be a movement of the lower class. The typical army worker who had been a reformed drunkard, ex-prostitute, or ex-criminal was now a person of some social standing with a particular competence as a religious teacher and social welfare worker. A division developed between the army personnel and those being saved. Greater attention was paid to the educational qualifications, social position, and personality of those in officer rank. Establishment of a training school to equip young men and women for positions of responsibility and leadership marked the passing of the old type of salvationist and the emergence of the professional Salvation Army worker.

The change in the character of the army leadership was closely related to change in the general position of the army within the community. The movement developed into a social welfare organization. Rescue work among such groups as ex-convicts, drunkards, prostitutes, and unmarried mothers led to the establishment of special homes

and institutions, and the management of these claimed a greater share of the attention of army leaders. Recognition of the value of its good work won for the army a larger measure of public goodwill, while the increasing financial costs of the work, in turn, forced the army to seek support from the public. World War I hastened a development already under way before 1914. Its war work secured the reputation of the army as a patriotic organization and strengthened its ties with the community. Once the support of the community had been secured, it could not easily be abandoned. Vested interests operated to check any shift back to the separatist position of the religious sect.

CONCLUSION

1. Rapid urbanization, accompanied by increased mobility, rootlessness, and class cleavage, affected the social basis of religious participation in late nineteenth-century Canada.

2. Institutionalization of the Methodist church tied it to the more well-to-do elements of the community. Comfortable affluence was reflected in the leadership of the church, its social doctrine, its methods, and the nature and location of its churches. These characteristics limited the access and appeal of Methodism.

3. Church-sponsored evangelism, an effort to reach a broader population, was unsuccessful because it failed to provide a new channel for religious participation and was unable to use an aggressive corps of lay workers.

4. The Salvation Army, an offshoot of Methodism, operated as a religious sect, with unconventional methods and organization. It was thus able to gain access to the mobile city poor.

5. In time the Salvation Army itself became institutionalized, with an increasingly professional ministry, limited evangelism, and an emphasis on regularized social welfare activity.

Section four religious participation and social class

The Christianity of the Gospels is directed toward the poor and exalts the poor. It promises them a status in heaven denied them on earth, a place unlikely to be gained by the rich and mighty.

And, behold, one came and said unto him, Good Master, what good thing shall I do that I may have eternal life? . . . Jesus said unto him, if thou wilt be perfect, go and sell that thou hast, and give to the poor, and thou shalt have treasure in heaven: and come and follow me. But when the young man heard that saying, he went away sorrowful: for he had great possessions. Then said Jesus unto his disciples, Verily I say unto you . . . It is easier for a camel to go through the eye of a needle, than for a rich man to enter into the kingdom of God (Matt. 19:16; 21–23; 24).

In theory, the churches are open to all, regardless of wealth and status, and are especially hospitable toward those least favored by society. In practice, they reflect the realities of secular life.

SOCIAL COMPOSITION OF THE CHURCHES

Viewed as a whole, the Christian community includes all economic strata. Its denominational divisions, on the other hand, reflect the class and ethnic divisions of the larger society. For example, a study of several national sample surveys conducted in 1956 reported that 46 percent of Episcopalians had family incomes of at least $7,500 compared with 26 percent of Presbyterians and 11 percent of white Baptists. The comparable figure for black Baptists was only 2 percent (Lazerwitz, 1964:429).

The greatest impact of social class is at the level of the local congregation. Especially in urban areas, income is one of the most important determinants of neighborhood residence. The result is that individual churches tend to be more homogeneous in socioeconomic characteristics than the denominations to which they belong.

Social class and religious involvement The extent and character of religious participation differs with socioeconomic status (Glock and Stark, 1965:187; Goode, 1966). The poor are less likely to be members of a congregation, to attend church regularly, or to take part in organized church activities. They are also less likely to be informed about religious matters. However, the poor who go to church tend to be both more believing and more emotionally involved in their religion than persons who are better off (Demerath, 1965).

A study of 4,000 members of 12 Congregational Christian urban churches measured the religious involvement of members along four "dimensions": (1) knowledge of the Bible and religious matters in general, (2) participation in the church, (3) belief in church doctrine, and (4) religious "feeling" as indicated by faith in prayer, daily Bible reading, and belief in the necessity of a conversion experience (Fukuyama, 1961). Religious knowledge and participation were associated with higher socioeconomic status, intensity of religious feeling with lower status.

The financially well-off tend to be religious in a more intellectual, formal, and organizational way. They attend church regularly, they are active in the church, and they are informed about their religion. But, compared with poor churchgoers, they are apt to be less believing, less expressive, and less emotionally dependent on their religious faith. The poor attend church less regularly, their knowledge is scantier, and they participate less in church activities. But when they are religiously involved, they are apt to be more unquestioning in their faith and more reliant on it.

CAPITALISM AND THE PROTESTANT ETHIC

Early capitalism depended on the enterprise and work of individuals rather than on complicated and impersonal large-scale organizations. The development of capitalism needed businessmen and manufacturers who were motivated to work hard, save, compete for markets, expand their enterprises, and accumulate capital. For both the entrepreneur and his subordinates, self-discipline and industriousness were essential to fulfilling the requirements of business. For the workers, regular attendance in the factory and continuous operation of the machines were necessary. "Grass may grow and sheep may graze if the peasant lies drunk under the hedge occasionally, but the wheels of mills cannot turn steadily if boiler stokers must have frequent debauches" (Beard, 1930:149).

Weber's theory In *The Protestant Ethic and the Spirit of Capitalism,* Max Weber argued that Protestant doctrine shaped the personalities of the rising class of entrepreneurs in which capitalism had its origins (Weber, 1904/1930; Tawney, 1926/1947; Gerth and Mills, 1953:234–236, 360–363). The connections between early Protestant doctrine and the psychology of entrepreneurship may be summarized as follows:

1. Self-discipline and work The Calvinist doctrine of predestination held that people were either condemned by God to everlasting hell or chosen to "live in the House of the Lord forever." Because believers in this doctrine were uncertain whether they were among the elect, they were anxious and insecure. Strict self-discipline, rejection of worldly pleasures, and righteous success in this world through hard work came to be regarded as signs of grace—evidence that one was in God's favor. Relief from religious anxiety was thus sought in disciplined effort. To work was to pray, and work was regarded as a personal mission or calling.

2. Initiative and acquisition Hard work and self-discipline won economic advantage over competitors and led to the acquisition of wealth. Since the Calvinists were supposed to avoid worldly pleasure, be thrifty, and abhor waste, they could not use wealth in traditional ways. They could, however, use their capital to expand their business activities. Individual initiative was rewarded, since success in work was interpreted as a sign of God's blessing. Furthermore, continual work in one's calling alleviated constant anxiety about salvation. No matter what a Calvinist accomplished in this world, he had no guarantee of salvation. Therefore, he could not relax.

3. Individualism and competition Calvinists believed that man is alone before his Maker, that he should not trust the friendship of other people, that only God should be his confidant because even those closest to him might be among the damned. Each individual could seek success as the sign of grace, and this striving was consistent with economic competition. He should deal honestly and righteously with other people, but he could take advantage of his opportunities even if that meant outdoing his competitors.

The capitalist spirit did not flow directly from the religious revolution of Luther and Calvin. But the revolution did go beyond religion to influence more general cultural attitudes toward work, poverty, individual obligation, and the worth of trade and industry. The rising merchant and industrial classes of the seventeenth and eighteenth centuries embraced the new values, were strengthened by them, and in turn helped mold religion to the requirements of a commercial age (Tawney, 1926/1947:Chap. 4).

Religion and mature capitalism As the new economic order became more formalized and institutionalized, and as accounting systems and other controls developed, capitalism depended less on religious reinforcement of thrift and economic prudence. However, many of the ideas earlier associated with Protestantism continue to support modern industry. Self-discipline and the ability to defer gratification are valued, as are initiative, hard work, and success. These values have become part of the culture, and in industrialized societies there is little difference among Catholics, Protestants, and Jews with respect to attitudes toward work and achievement (Greeley, 1964).

Poverty and salvation The exaltation of middle-class virtues and middle-class success led to a new approach to poverty and social responsibility. Though by no means universal among Protestants, the following attitudes characterized much Protestant activity and social policy for several centuries and in some measure continue to do so.

1. Poverty, no longer seen as inevitable and necessary, became something to censure. The poor evoked blame rather than compassion. Poverty, singled out by the Gospels as a blessed state because it was a guarantee against the sin of pride, was now associated with personal vices and weakness of character.

2. A missionary rather than a charitable

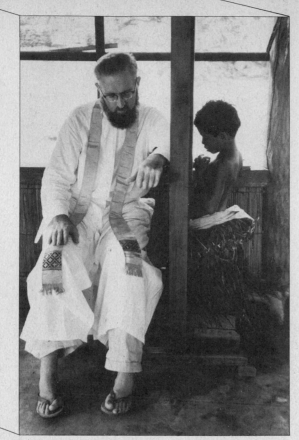

In the confessional two cultures are bridged.

approach was taken toward the poor. Since secular society was no longer regarded as a divine community into which all are born and in which all participate, Protestantism was faced with the task of gathering in the unchurched and of "converting" the nominal Christian. It would be inaccurate to say that the evangelical efforts of Protestantism were restricted to the poor. Nevertheless, the poor were regarded as most in need of salvation, since they were most in need of being saved from their personal failings.

THE MARXIST CRITIQUE

In 1844 religion was described by Karl Marx in the following words, of which only the last sentence is generally remembered today: "Religion is the sigh of the oppressed creature, the heart of the heartless world, just as it is the spirit of a spiritless situation. It is the opium of the people" (Marx, 1844/1964:42). Whatever the intention of religious innovators or leaders, Marx thought their effect or function was to create a docile and subordinate population.

From its earliest beginnings, Marxism attacked the otherworldly promises of Christianity as serving to deflect the economically oppressed from bettering their conditions in the present. Marxism saw that the effect of Christian teaching was to create a docile laboring class to protect the rich from threats to their wealth and power, and to perpetuate social inequality.

Many facts support the Marxist critique, but there are aspects of Christian doctrine and of church history that point the other way. Medieval Catholicism emphasized the social obligations of all classes in society. More recent Catholic thought has expanded the doctrine of social justice. Most notable is Pope Leo XIII's encyclical *Rerum Novarum* (Of New Things), which as early as 1891 supported the formation of trade unions (Fremantle, 1956:166–195; see also John XXIII, 1961; Paul VI, 1963). During the last century there grew up within Protestantism the concept of the Social Gospel, according to which Christianity is required to work for social justice and the salvation of society, not merely for the salvation of individual souls.

The Gospels hold forth no promise of material progress, but their high valuation of the individual, rich or poor, and the assertion of man's spiritual brotherhood laid an ethical foundation for secular movements toward social equality. While the church as an institution may be a buttress of status and privilege, its doctrines have often inspired social idealism and economic reform. In many respects Western civilization lives on the spiritual capital of the Judeo-Christian tradition.

Section five social policy and social change

CHURCH AND STATE

"Render therefore unto Caesar the things that are Caesar's, and unto God the things that are God's." This well-known biblical injunction reflects the tension between religious and political authority, between church and state. Because both religious and political institutions lay claim to fundamental loyalties of people, the relation between the two has been historically a source of conflict and tension.

The early American experience To a large extent, the American colonies were settled by those seeking religious freedom from the established churches of Europe. It is therefore ironic that so little religious freedom was allowed in the early settlements and colonies.

Two prime examples are the Massachusetts Bay Colony and Virginia. Massachusetts' Puritan settlers established what for all intents and purposes was a state church. The colonial government was expected, as part of its service to its citizens, to support public worship and suppress heresy. Taxes were used to support the Congregational Church and its clergy. The Congregationalist meeting house was used for both governmental and religious activities. Colonial law compelled all people to attend church services regardless of their personal beliefs and denied equal rights to the "unorthodox." Citizens were subject to trial by the colonial government for what the church called sins but the government called crimes— heresy, blasphemy, and idolatry. People like Roger Williams, Anne Hutchinson, and various Presbyterians, Quakers, and Catholics quickly found out what the laws meant as they were fined, imprisoned, and even banished.

In Virginia, Anglicanism was established as the official church, but in a somewhat different form than in Massachusetts. Whereas in Massachusetts the church tended to control the government, in Virginia the government tended to control the church. In Virginia all citizens were required to attend Anglican services and were taxed to support the Anglican church, no non-

Anglican clergymen were allowed to perform the clergy role, no non-Anglican religious group could hold services, specifically no Catholic or Quaker could hold public office, and no one who didn't believe in infant baptism could even become a citizen of the colony (Johnstone, 1975: 179–180).

After the founding of the United States, however, the First Amendment to the Constitution repudiated the concept of an "established" church: "Congress shall make no law respecting an establishment of religion, or prohibiting the free exercise thereof." Thus emerged the principle of the separation of church and state. Religious bodies were to be voluntary associations unsupported by the power of government.

Yet, despite the First Amendment, separation of church and state was far from complete. In saying that Congress could pass no laws respecting the establishment of religion, the amendment left the door open for individual states to favor one church or another as an official religion. Massachusetts, in 1833, was the last state to abandon its state–church commitments, and it was not until the passage of the Fourteenth Amendment, in 1868, that the constitutional limitation was officially extended to the states.

Church, state, and schools As a public policy issue, the problem of the relation of church and state remains alive, particularly in the area of education. Part of the problem lies with the First Amendment itself:

The First Amendment in its attractive brevity leaves much unstated and seems to take much for granted. Even its spirit is elusive. Is it a practical expression of "a religious people"? Or is it a tolerant statement of commitment to a secular experiment? Does it indeed put us "under God"? What is "establishment" and what is an "exercise" of religion? The Amendment does not explain itself (Tussman, 1962:xiii).

In its role as interpreter of the Constitution, the Supreme Court has played a major part in shaping church–state relations in contemporary society. The Court has been asked to decide a number of controversial issues: How much state support, if any, can be given to parochial schools? To what extent is the exercise of religion allowable in public schools?

Parochial schools The right of parents to send their children to religious (parochial) schools was first affirmed in 1925. Oregon had passed legislation requiring every child to attend its public schools, but the Court declared parochial schools a valid alternative. Since then, controversy has centered on the issue of how much public support for parochial schools is permissible without breaching "the wall of separation between church and state." The Supreme Court has approved as constitutional the supply of free textbooks for all children, whether they attend a public or a private school, as well as tax-supported bus transportation for children attending parochial schools:

The establishment of religion clause of the First Amendment means at least this: Neither a state nor the federal government can set up a church. Neither can pass laws which aid one religion, aid all religions, or prefer one religion over another. Neither can force nor influence a person to go to or to remain away from church against his will or force him to profess a belief or disbelief in any religion. No person can be punished for entertaining or professing religious beliefs or disbeliefs, for church attendance or non-attendance. No tax in any amount, large or small, can be levied to support any religious activity or institution, whatever they may be called, or whatever form they may adopt to teach or practice religion. Neither a state nor the federal government can, openly or secretly, participate in the affairs of any religious organizations or groups and vice versa. Measured by these standards, we cannot say that the First Amendment prohibits New Jersey from spending tax-raised funds to pay the bus fares of parochial school pupils as part of a general program under which it pays the fares of pupils attending public and other schools. It is undoubtedly true that children are helped to get to church schools. There is even a possibility that some of the children might not be sent to the church schools if the parents were compelled to pay their children's bus fares out of their own

pockets. Cutting off church schools from these services would make it far more difficult for the schools to operate. But such is obviously not the purpose of the First Amendment. That amendment requires the state to be a neutral in its relations with groups of religious believers and nonbelievers; it does not require the state to be their adversary. State power is no more to be used so as to handicap religions, than it is to favor them. . . . The First Amendment has erected a wall between church and state. That wall must be kept high and impregnable. We could not approve the slightest breach. New Jersey has not breached it here (*Everson* v. *New Jersey*, 330 U.S. 1, 1947).

The pattern of Court decisions reflects the conviction that parochial schools serve an important social function that would be lost in a completely public educational system.

Religion in public schools While the policy of limited public support for parochial schools has gained tentative acceptance, the debate over religion remains controversial. The early 1960s saw a flurry of decisions concerning Bible reading and prayer in public schools. Perhaps the most dramatic of these was *Abington School District* v. *Schempp* (1963). At issue was a Pennsylvania law requiring daily Bible readings in the schools. Although the law had been amended so that any child could be excused from the readings, a Unitarian family, the Schempps, nevertheless challenged the practice on First Amendment grounds:

Mr. Schempp contended that the noncompulsory provision in the revised law was not a satisfactory resolution in that his children, should they be excused, would be labeled as "oddballs" by fellow students and teachers alike, that they would likely be branded atheists, with the "un-American-atheistic-Communist" connotation that atheism implies for many people (Johnstone, 1975:188).

The district court supported the Schempps, and its decision was upheld by the Supreme Court in 1963.

The continuing dilemma The *Schempp* and subsequent Court rulings limiting religious practices in public schools met considerable resistance (Dolbeare and Hammond, 1971). On the one hand, many religiously committed people felt that the Court had gone too far and that prayer, on a voluntary basis, had a proper place in the schools. Fearing that society was losing its religious and moral bearings, some attempted to build a grass-roots movement aimed at passing a constitutional amendment permitting voluntary prayer and Bible reading in schools. One such proposal, however, twice failed to pass the Senate. On the other hand, opponents of religion in the schools were emboldened by the Court's rulings to press for even further restrictions on school practices, such as the observance of religious holidays.

Controversy over the proper relation between church and state is not likely to disappear. It is inherent in the First Amendment itself, which affirms two values that are often in conflict when applied to specific cases: "nonestablishment" and "free exercise." People who feel strongly about religion are not content to limit "free exercise" to regular church services or other private occasions. They want religious commitment to infuse social life, and that means, perhaps above all, the education of children. On the other hand, almost any intrusion of religion into public institutions, especially where public funds are used, can be interpreted as a form of "establishment." The historical solution, which created a consensus of sorts for at least a century, was to allow certain forms of public support, such as official expressions of belief in God and tax exemption for church properties, so long as no particular church was favored. That consensus is being challenged today because a significant minority resists traditional religious symbolism and demands a completely secular state.

AMERICAN CHURCHES IN TRANSITION

Following World War II, the United States experienced an unprecedented upswing of interest in religion. Between 1940 and 1950 membership in churches rose from 49 to 57 percent of the population and by 1959 peaked at 63.6 percent (Landis, 1964:290). Thousands of new congregations were established, and the rate of new church construction showed a dramatic rise. The "religious revival" was also reflected in the popular culture: many books, movies, and songs reflected religious themes. Postage stamps and money began to bear the legend "In God We Trust"; the phrase "under God" was inserted into the Pledge of Allegiance.

Despite the apparent success of the churches, many were concerned about whether the upswing actually indicated a deeper religiosity on the part of the American people or a more superficial and transient interest in church activity merely because it had become fashionable. Much of the rise in church membership and construction took place in newly emerging suburban, middle-class congregations, where it appeared that the social and entertainment function of the church was perhaps as important as the religious.

The 1960s was a decade of doubt and conflict—about politics and war, about education, about race—and religion was not exempt. From outside the churches, criticisms were voiced about the alleged "irrelevance" of the church to contemporary problems; the churches were accused of encouraging Americans to "consume" religion in much the same way that they consumed Coca-Cola or new automobiles. But inside the churches, too, voices of discontent were evident. Some Protestant theologians proclaimed the "death of God"; young, activist clergy began to challenge church policies and practices; Roman Catholic priests and nuns left the church with disturbing frequency. After the upswing of the 1950s, church attendance showed a gradual decline, from 49 percent attending church during an average week in 1955 to 42 percent in 1970. The decline has apparently halted, however. During 1971–1975 the percentage reporting church or synagogue attendance leveled off at 40 percent (Gallup Opinion Index, 1976:26).

The following discussion treats two underlying aspects of unrest in the churches: the crisis of authority and the conflict over the purpose of religion.

The challenge to authority The 1960s saw the emergence of numerous disputes within the churches which seriously undermined the authority of their leadership. The underlying issue in many of these disputes was the conflict between religious "liberalism" and "conservatism," between a more flexible approach to religious doctrine on the one hand and the maintenance of traditional orthodoxy on the other.

Among Protestant denominations clergy are generally somewhat more liberal than laity; moreover, younger clergy as well as those in colleges and seminaries are often far more liberal than older, parish ministers (Hadden, 1969:51, 196, 201–203). This sets the stage for conflict, not only between laity and clergy but among divergent factions of the clergy itself. For example, in the Lutheran Church-Missouri Synod, there was a long-standing dispute between the denomination's major seminary on the one hand and the leadership and laity of the denomination on the other. The faculty of Concordia Seminary in St. Louis pressed for a more liberal interpretation of scriptural language but were opposed by conservative church officials as well as many laymen; in the end, many faculty members were dismissed from the seminary. In other Protestant denominations, similar disputes have arisen between laity and parish ministers, the latter taking more liberal stands than their parishioners were willing to accept; frequently this has resulted in a decline in attendance and financial support. As the modern church has become increasingly a voluntary association, its authority has become more vulnerable to lay challenge in the form of withdrawal of support. In an earlier age, when established churches held the ultimate key to heaven and hell, such challenges would have been unthinkable.

This is not to say that American churches lack support. On the contrary, in a 1975 survey 44 percent of Americans expressed a "great deal" of confidence in organized religion compared to much lower high-confidence ratings for other institutions. Moreover, 39 percent thought religion was gaining in influence on American life, up from fourteen percent in 1970. Nevertheless, doubt and dissension persist; the same survey showed that 51 percent believed religious influence to be declining (Gallup Opinion Index, 1976:58, 62).

Because the Protestant denominations are so decentralized, it is difficult to assess how widespread the challenge to authority is. The Roman Catholic church, in contrast, is highly centralized and thus offers a striking illustration of the present crisis of religious authority.

The crisis in Catholicism: sex, love, and birth control Historically, the Roman Catholic church has forbidden its members to use contraceptive methods of birth control. Procreation was held to be the only lawful purpose of intercourse and abstinence the only permissible way to limit births. Though some nineteenth-century Catholic theologians had come, with some hesitation, to accept the fostering of love as a legitimate purpose of sexual intercourse, the church hierarchy continued to distinguish between primary and secondary ends and held to the position that the primary objective of marriage was the production of children. Barring artificial birth control, Catholics had either to forego sex or use the unreliable "rhythm method" if they were to stay within the bounds of church doctrine.

Modern American Catholics, however, have tended to disregard church doctrine on this matter. Analysis of data compiled over a period of 15 years (see Table 12:4) shows a rapid decline in the percentages of Catholic women who follow the church's instruction to use no form of contraception or the rhythm method. If the "other" row is taken as a measure of nonconformity to church teach-

Table 12:4   Percentage of white, married Catholic women, age 18 to 39, by contraceptive usage, United States, 1955–1970

Most recent method	1955[b] (N = 787)	1960[b] (N = 668)	1965 (N = 846)	1970 (N = 1035)
None[a]	43	30	21	18
Rhythm	27	31	28	14
Other	30	38	51	68

Source: Westoff and Bumpass, 1973:Table 1.

[a] The percentages indicated for the row labeled "None" identify women who have never used any method of contraception.
[b] Data for 1955 and 1960 do not include sterilization.

ing, it can be seen that the percentage of those not conforming more than doubled during the 15-year period. Apparently the trend accelerated after 1960.

Because sterilization is strongly condemned by the Catholic church, one would expect Catholics to be among those most opposed to its use. Table 12:5 shows that in the short span of five years there was a sharp increase of approval of sterilization among married women of child-bearing ages. Both Protestant and Catholic women participated in this attitude shift. Although a smaller percentage of Catholics approved in both years, the differences between Protestants and Catholics diminished, and a large minority of Catholic women rejected the church's teaching in this respect.

The Vatican Council of 1965 (see below, p. 405) was thus welcomed by many Catholics, since it seemed to foreshadow a liberalization of church policy on birth control. The council did not deal directly with contraception, but it decisively and self-consciously affirmed that sexual intercourse in marriage was to be given positive value, not only as a means of procreation but as a vital ingredient of marital love. It rejected the terminology of primary and secondary ends while continuing to stress the importance of children.

In 1968, however, Pope Paul VI issued the encyclical *Humanae Vitae* ("On Human Life"), restating the Church's opposition to contraception: "The Church . . . teaches that each and every marriage must remain open to the transmission of life" (Callahan, 1969: 213–214, 220). The encyclical came as a shock to many Catholics who had expected a further liberalization of church policy. An American sociologist and Catholic priest analyzed a national sample of Catholic opinion in order to assess the impact of Pope Paul's pronouncement. He concluded that

Table 12:5
Percentage of women approving sterilization, by couples' religion, United States, 1965 and 1970[a]

	1965	1970
Approve male sterilization		
Protestant	40	55
Catholic	17	41
Approve female sterilization		
Protestant	44	59
Catholic	20	39

Source: Presser and Bumpass, 1973:Table 17 (sample survey).

[a] Data in the table are restricted to women under 45 years of age currently living with husbands of the same faith. Wives of mixed Protestant-Catholic marriages show approval rates intermediate between those for Protestants and Catholics.

its effect was to create a broad decline in American Catholics' acceptance of ecclesiastical authority—a decline that went far beyond the specific issue of birth control (Greeley et al., 1976:Chap. 5).

Personal salvation versus social activism A second major issue that surfaced during the 1960s was the conflict over the purpose and mission of the church. Was its primary purpose to provide personal benefit and salvation for its members? Or was its larger mandate to challenge social injustice and actively to promote social and political change? Religious conservatives generally held that the church had no place "meddling" in secular affairs; social and spiritual concerns should be sharply separated:

I go to church to hear heralded the mind of Christ, not the mind of man. I want to hear expounded the timeless truth contained in the Scripture. . . . To commit the church as a corporate body to controversial positions on which its members differ sharply is to divide the church into warring camps, stirring dissension into one place where spiritual unity should prevail (Pew, 1966:3–4).

Religious liberals, on the other hand, held that a genuine commitment to religious values necessarily implied a commitment to social change; in compartmentalizing the spiritual and secular realms, they argued, contemporary religion indirectly bolstered the status quo:

It has all but been forgotten that Christianity began as a revolutionary religion whose followers embraced an entirely different set of values from those held by other members of society. Those original values are still in conflict with the values of contemporary society; yet religion today has become as conservative a force as the original Christians were in conflict with (Berton, 1965:80).

The issue is an old one. There has long been an activist minority among American Protestants that challenged the more conservative majority. In the past, however, the conflict was largely contained by the institution of "special ministries," missions, or-

phanages, and the like, into which the energies of the activist minority could be channeled. Liberal clergy were often assigned to campus ministries or administrative positions in denominational bureaucracies where their contact with rank-and-file laity was minimized (Hammond and Mitchell, 1965:133–143).

The issue of personal salvation versus social activism reemerged with special force during the 1960s primarily because of the increasing involvement of American clergy in the civil rights and antiwar movements. A national survey of Protestant clergy in 1965 showed that they were overwhelmingly sympathetic to the general principle of achieving social justice for blacks in America. Though there were differences between denominations, fundamentalist clergy being somewhat more conservative on the issue, the vast majority agreed that "the churches have been woefully inadequate in facing up to the civil rights issue" and were "in basic sympathy with Northern ministers and students who have gone to the South to work for civil rights" (Hadden, 1969:105, 109). Statistics on actual participation are sketchy, but the evidence suggests that involvement by the clergy was more widespread than commonly believed. A 1969 survey of Protestant clergy in California that investigated their reactions to the war in Vietnam classified 29 percent as "hawks" and 35 percent as "doves." Of the doves, 85 percent believed it was appropriate to express one's opinions in a protest march and 19 percent had actually done so. Eighty percent of the doves had delivered sermons on the war, half had attended protest meetings, and a third had joined peace organizations. Almost three-quarters approved of civil disobedience, and 7 percent had actually committed illegal acts of protest (Quinley, 1969:10–13).

Clergy involvement in and support for civil rights and antiwar protest received much publicity and provoked a storm of controversy within the churches. The reason for the controversy becomes evident when the attitudes of laity and clergy are compared. A national sample of the American public in 1967 found that 44 percent "basically disapproved" of the movement for black civil rights; this contrasts with the less than 10 percent of the clergy who gave a similar response. Regarding actual protest behavior, only 37 percent of the laity, as compared to 64 percent of the clergy, expressed sympathy for those who went to the South to work for civil rights. And 72 percent indicated they would be "upset" if their minister were to participate in a picket line or demonstration (Hadden, 1969:127, 141, 136).

The conflict over the mission of the church is unlikely ever to be finally resolved though it appears, at least in the short run, that the pendulum is now swinging back in a conservative direction. The more conservative attitudes of the laity combined with the halt in the growth of church membership and resultant financial pressures have tightened the job market for clergy, especially those with an activist orientation; many have chosen or been forced to leave the ministry. Nevertheless, a study of 18,000 Protestant seminary students indicates that the seminaries are producing activist-oriented clergy at a greater rate than at any time in the past (Bridston and Culver, 1965:227). The long-run direction of church policy is thus likely to depend significantly on whether the new generation of clergy chooses to continue the struggle from within or to pursue their activist concerns outside the framework of institutionalized religion.

The Catholic aggiornamento The Roman Catholic church offers an outstanding example of the movement for renewal. For many years the Catholic church has been a prototype of the highly institutionalized church—the ecclesia. Catholicism gathered in whole communities and often became the established church. It has had a powerful hierarchy and a clergy largely independent of lay control; an entrenched and conservative bureaucracy, the Roman Curia, became a symbol of tradition-bound organization; an elaborate system of forms, rituals, and church laws was associated with an emphasis on authority and obedience.

In 1959 Pope John XXIII decided to convene a general (ecumenical) council, which would be an assembly of all the Catholic bishops throughout the world and other major church officials, such as the heads of religious orders.

The keynote of the council was set by Pope John when he used the Italian word *aggiornamento* ("renewal" or "updating") to characterize its mission. From the outset it was clear that many bishops favored change. Although many compromises were made to achieve maximum consensus, in the end a large majority voted for a new spirit within the church. The conservative Curia, which had the main role in preparing the draft documents for consideration of the council, lost control.

When the council completed its final session in 1965, it had taken a number of steps to change the direction of the church: The power of the bishops relative to the pope was increased, thus opening the way to a greater democratization; Catholic laymen were accorded a greater dignity and freedom; a more open attitude toward Protestantism was expressed, and anti-Semitism was condemned; reform of Catholic ritual was ordained, allowing much greater variety, more use of the vernacular, and increased participation by the congregation in religious services.

The significance of the council went beyond the specific changes adopted. New attitudes were fostered, perhaps most important, a questioning of received authority and of tradition.

Pope Paul VI, who succeeded John XXIII in 1963, has tended to restrain some of the liberalizing impulses set in motion by the council. He has been critical of rebellious priests and has warned against the erosion of church authority and tradition. Nevertheless, there are many signs of both renewal and disarray in the Catholic church. To some extent the process of institutionalization is being reversed.

References

Beard, Charles A.
1930 "Individualism and capitalism." Pp. 145–163 in Encyclopaedia of the Social Sciences. New York: Macmillan.

Bellah, Robert N.
1970 Beyond Belief. New York: Harper & Row.

Berton, Pierre
1965 The Comfortable Pew. Philadelphia: Lippincott.

Bridston, Keith and Dwight W. Culver
1965 Pre-Seminary Education. Minneapolis: Augsburg Publishing House.

Bumpass, Larry L. and Harriet B. Presser
1973 "The increasing acceptance of sterilization and abortion." Pp. 33–46 in Charles F. Westoff et al., Toward the End of Growth. Englewood Cliffs, N.J.: Prentice-Hall.

Callahan, Daniel (ed.)
1969 The Catholic Case for Contraception. London: Macmillan.

Codrington, R. H.
1965 "Mana." P. 275 in W. A. Lessa and E. Z. Vogt, Reader in Comparative Religion. Second edition. New York: Harper & Row.

Coulanges, Fustel de
1956 The Ancient City: A Study on the Religion, Laws, and Institutions of Greece and Rome. Garden City, N. Y.: Doubleday.

Demerath, Nicholas J., III
1965 Social Class in American Protestantism. Chicago: Rand McNally.

Dolbeare, Kenneth M. and Phillip E. Hammond
1971 The School Prayer Decisions. Chicago: University of Chicago Press.

Durkheim, Emile
1947 The Elementary Forms of the Religious Life. New York: Free Press. First published in 1912.

Eister, Allan W.
1972 "An outline of a structural theory of cults." Journal for the Scientific Study of Religion 11 (December):319–333.

Fremantle, Anne
1956 The Papal Encyclicals in Their Historical Context. New York: New American Library (Mentor Books).

Fukuyama, Yoshio
1961 "The major dimensions of church membership." Review of Religious Research 2 (Spring):154–161.

Gallup Opinion Index
1976 Report No. 130. Princeton, N.J.: American Institute of Public Opinion.

Gerth, Hans and C. Wright Mills
1953 Character and Social Structure. New York: Harcourt Brace Jovanovich.

Glock, Charles Y. and Robert N. Bellah (eds.)
1976 The New Religious Consciousness. Berkeley: University of California Press.

Glock, Charles Y. and Rodney Stark
1965 Religion and Society in Tension. Chicago: Rand McNally.

Goode, Erich
1966 "Social class and church participation." American Journal of Sociology 72 (July):102–111.

Greeley, Andrew
1964 "The Protestant ethic: time for a moratorium." Sociological Analysis 25 (Spring):20–33.

Greeley, Andrew M., William C. McCready, and Kathleen Mc-Court
1976 Catholic Schools in a Declining Church. Kansas City: Sheed & Ward.

Hadden, Jeffrey K.
1969 The Gathering Storm in the Churches. Garden City, N. Y.: Doubleday.

Hammond, Phillip E. and Robert E. Mitchell
1965 "Segmentation of radicalism: the case of the Protestant campus ministers." American Journal of Sociology 71 (September):133–143.

John XXIII
1961 Mater et Magister (Mother and Teacher).

Johnstone, Ronald L.
1975 Religion and Society in Interaction. Englewood Cliffs, N. J.: Prentice-Hall.

Kallen, Horace M.
1930 "Cults." Pp. 618–621 in Encyclopaedia of the Social Sciences. New York: Macmillan.

Kluckhohn, Clyde
1942 "Myths and rituals: a general theory." Harvard Theological Review 35 (January):45–79.

Landis, Bensen Y.
1964 Yearbook of American Churches. New York: National Council of Churches.

Lanternari, Vittorio
1965 The Religions of the Oppressed. New York: New American Library (Mentor Books).

Lazerwitz, Bernard
1964 "Religion and social structure in the United States." In Louis Schneider (ed.), Religion, Culture and Society. New York: Wiley.

Marx, Karl
1844/1964 "Contribution to the critique of Hegel's philosophy of right." Pp. 41–58 in Karl Marx and Friedrich Engels, On Religion. New York: Schocken Books.

Mathison, Richard
1960 Faiths, Cults and Sects of America. Indianapolis: Bobbs-Merrill.

Niebuhr, H. Richard
1957 The Social Sources of Denominationalism. New York: New American Library (Meridian Books).
1966 "Contraception and the council." Commonweal (March 11):657–662.

Paul VI
1963 Pacem in Terris (Peace on Earth).

Pew, J. Howard
1966 "Should the church 'meddle' in civil affairs?" Reader's Digest (May):49–54.

Pope, Liston
1942 Millhands and Preachers. New Haven, Conn.: Yale University Press.

Presser, Harriet B. and Larry L. Bumpass
1973 "Demographic and social aspects of contraceptive sterilization in the United States: 1965–1970." In Charles F. Westoff and Robert Parke, Jr. (eds.). Demographic and Social Aspects of Population Growth. U.S. Commission on Population Growth and the American Future. Research Reports. Vol. 1. Washington, D.C.: GPO.

Quinley, Harold E.
1969 "Hawks and doves among the clergy: Protestant reaction to the war in Vietnam." Ministry Studies 3:5–20.

Tawney, R. H.
1926/1947 Religion and the Rise of Capitalism. Baltimore: Penguin Books.

Troeltsch, Ernst
1912/1949 The Social Teachings of the Christian Churches. Vol. 1. New York: The Free Press of Glencoe. First published in German.

Tussman, Joseph
1962 The Supreme Court on Church and State. New York: Oxford University Press.

Tylor, Edward B.
1873 Primitive Culture. London: Murray.

Warner, W. Lloyd
1962 American Life: Dream and Reality. Chicago: University of Chicago Press.

Weber, Max
1904/1930 The Protestant Ethic and the Spirit of Capitalism. Trans. by Talcott Parsons. London: Allen and Unwin. First published in German.

Westoff, Charles F. and Larry Bumpass
1973 "The revolution in birth control practices of U.S. Roman Catholics." Science 179 (January):41–44.

Wilson, Bryan R.
1959 "An analysis of sect development." American Sociological Review 24 (February):3–15.
1961 Sects and Society. Berkeley and Los Angeles: University of California Press.
1973 Religion in Secular Society. Baltimore: Penguin Books.

Yang, C. K.
1961 Religion in Chinese Society. Berkeley and Los Angeles: University of California Press.

Yinger, Milton J.
1957 Religion, Society and the Individual. New York: Macmillan.

Sources and readings

Birnbaum, Norman and Gertrud Lenzer (eds.)
1969 Sociology and Religion: A Book of Readings. Englewood Cliffs, N. J.: Prentice-Hall.

Durkheim, Emile
1947 The Elementary Forms of the Religious Life. New York: Free Press.

Eister, Allan W. (ed.)
1974 Changing Perspectives in the Scientific Study of Religion. New York: Wiley.

Freud, Sigmund
1928 The Future of an Illusion. London: Hogarth.

Glock, Charles Y. and Phillip E. Hammond (eds.)
1973 Beyond the Classics? Essays in the Scientific Study of Religion. New York: Harper & Row.

Hammond, Phillip E. and Benton Johnson
1970 American Mosaic: Social Patterns of Religion in the United States. New York: Random House.

Hargrove, Barbara W.
1971 Reformation of the Holy: A Sociology of Religion. Philadelphia: F. A. Davis.

Johnstone, Ronald L.
1975 Religion and Society in Interaction. Englewood Cliffs, N.J.: Prentice-Hall.

Lessa, William A. and Evon Z. Vogt
1972 Reader in Comparative Religion. New York: Harper & Row. Third edition.

McNamara, Patrick H. (ed.)
1974 Religion American Style. New York: Harper & Row.

Newman, William M. (ed.)
1974 The Social Meanings of Religion. Chicago: Rand McNally.

O'Dea, Thomas F.
1966 The Sociology of Religion. Englewood Cliffs, N. J.: Prentice-Hall.

Robertson, Roland
1970 The Sociological Interpretation of Religion. Oxford: Blackwell.

Schneider, Louis
1970 Sociological Approach to Religion. New York: Wiley.

Weber, Max
1904/1930 The Protestant Ethic and the Spirit of Capitalism. London: Allen and Unwin.
1915/1951 The Religion of China. New York: Free Press.
1917/1958 Ancient Judaism. New York: Free Press.
1916/1958 The Religion of India. New York: Free Press.

Yinger, J. Milton
1970 The Scientific Study of Religion. New York: Macmillan.

Periodicals

Journal for the Scientific Study of Religion
Review of Religious Research
Sociological Analysis

13 | Law

Section one introduction

Every society has some machinery for upholding norms, settling disputes, and dispensing justice. In simple societies law shades into custom and is upheld through informal procedures and sanctions. In a complex society the legal order is more clearly distinguished and carries a heavy burden of social integration. Legal recognition lends coherence, regularity, and acceptance to social forms and codes of conduct.

Law in society is best understood as an activity or enterprise—a living institution performing social tasks. The legal order is more than a system of norms or rules. It is also a set of agencies responding to social needs, pressures, and aspirations.

The legal system is an arena of conflict as well as a source of stability. Courts, lawyers, and police are preoccupied with disputes and offenses. Law is therefore a public, institutionalized mechanism for resolving controversies. Its contribution to social integration is active, not passive.

FUNCTIONS OF LAW

The major social functions of a legal system are:

1. Maintaining public order Law offers an alternative to private warfare and vengeance. Legal machinery for the settlement of disputes supplements the more informal social process by which individuals and groups adapt to each other and accommodate their interests. A legal resolution of controversy makes two contributions to public order: (a) it provides a basis for conclusive settlement, so that the same controversy will not be repeatedly reopened, and (b) if the legal process is fair to the parties concerned they may be content with the outcome.

The order-maintaining function of law is also apparent in the suppression of deviance. Although an encounter between an armed robber and his victim might be thought of as a "dispute," it is not so conceived in law or custom. In the usual case, the robber is treated as someone to be suppressed, not as one who needs a legal alternative to dangerous private action.

2. Upholding rights and duties In most

Doing justice is often a routine activity, without high drama, without robes, without much ceremony.

human interaction, people have to accept the risk that others will not do what is expected of them. Being courteous, showing up for meetings, lending a neighborly hand, and many other expectations are important to orderly social life, but for the most part they receive no legal recognition. Some expectations, however, are formally recognized and can be the basis of *claims of right*. Such a claim, if it stems from a person's status as a human being or a citizen, is usually formulated as a basic or constitutional right—for example, the right to a fair trial or to be secure in one's home. Other rights and duties pertain to a particular role or status, such as the duty of a manufacturer to avoid harmful negligence or the rights of children to be sup-

ported by their parents. Still other claims and obligations arise out of agreement. A modern industrial society is especially dependent on legal protection of rights, because there is so much cooperation between strangers who cannot rely on kinship ties or other informal social controls for the protection of their interests.

3. Facilitating cooperative action   Law encourages joint effort by determining what people can rely on in the conduct of others. Business transactions depend on the law of contracts, which enforces mutual promises, and on the law of property, which establishes rights in land and goods. In addition, a modern legal system creates a wide range of opportunities for cooperative action, such as the right to form corporations, partnerships, trusts, and nonprofit associations. In this respect, the law often lags behind social organization. Trade unions were first organized with only very limited legal recognition and in the face of much hostility from the courts, but in 1935 a new labor law (the Wagner Act) facilitated the organization of American unions.

4. Conferring legitimacy Law moderates the struggle for power by providing criteria of legitimate succession and by saying *who* has a right to exercise *what kind* of power. The legitimating function of constitutional law is the clearest example, for it sets out the conditions for becoming a president, premier, king, or chief. But the problem of legitimacy arises in other contexts too. For example, it has long been assumed that an employer may legitimately give orders to employees; but the nature and scope of the employer's authority have not always been clearly established in law. Similarly, the right of college administrators to govern the conduct of students has been questioned in recent years, especially where authority is presumed to be based on the principle of *in loco parentis* (in the place of a parent).

5. Communicating moral standards When the law defines rights and responsibilities and backs up its definitions with the threat of coercion, it becomes a powerful agency of communication. Every act of enforcement is at the same time an act of communication. Therefore, it is important that there be close coordination of legal purpose and legal administration. Fairness at a trial may not offset the effect on public opinion of brutal or even disrespectful conduct by police at the time of arrest.

The educational significance of law accounts for the reluctance to change laws that embody moral standards. For example, many people may question the wisdom of attempting to regulate sexual conduct through law but want to keep the law on the books as an expression of what they believe is right and proper. They fear that removal of the ban on, say, homosexual relations would be taken as public approval. By the same token, proponents of new values may be content for a while with a law that has no "teeth." They hope that having the law on the books will educate the public to the new values, in part by drawing upon the reservoir of respect for law.

Just as religion is only one way of overcoming anxiety and supporting social norms (see *RELIGION*, p. 371), so the functions noted above are not the exclusive province of law. Other institutions contribute in their own ways to the same ends.

TWO FACES OF JUSTICE

The variety of social functions performed by law tends to create a double image. On the one hand, justice is the judgment of authority, a commanding presence, and a system of duties. The Ten Commandments present this face of justice. "Thou shalt not" is the idiom of Mosaic law. And for many people in contemporary society, the law is personified by police and zealous prosecutors.

On the other hand, justice is the protector of rights. Law offers a forum to which people can appeal when they feel aggrieved or victimized. Such appeals may be compatible with a repressive "Thou shalt not" kind of law. The cry for justice may be a victim's demand that someone be punished who has violated a rule and intruded on the rights of others.

There is a broader implication, however. When justice is perceived as the protection of rights, a door is opened to the enlargement of those rights. If a legal system contains general principles as well as specific rules, the principle can be appealed to as a kind of promise that justice will be done even if the current rules allow no legal claim. The U.S. Constitution embodies principles of this sort, guaranteeing freedom of speech, equal protection of the laws, and due process. These abstract phrases are, in effect, constitutional promises. They provide a basis for criticizing particular laws. For example, the Supreme Court decision on school segregation (see *EDUCATION*, p. 362) enlarged the rights of blacks by invoking a constitutional principle. The court held that state laws establishing separate schools for blacks and whites were unconstitutional because, under such laws, black children had unequal educational opportunity and therefore were denied "equal protection of the laws" (*Brown* v. *Board of Education*, 347 U.S. 483, 1954).[1]

SOCIAL ADVOCACY

In recent decades there has been a substantial increase in efforts to achieve social change through law and especially to win from the courts an enlargement of the rights of citizenship. This activity has taken the form of group legal action; its targets have been allegedly unjust laws and government practices; its main strategy has been to invoke constitutional principles on behalf of whole classes of citizens, such as blacks, Mexican Americans, welfare recipients, children, and others who are relatively weak politically.

The most prominent participants in this activity are the Legal Defense Fund of the National Association for the Advancement of Colored People, the American Civil Liberties Union, and some of the local offices set up by the federal government's "war on poverty" agency, the Office of Economic Opportunity (OEO). The OEO program is especially noteworthy because a deliberate decision was made to enlarge the concept of legal assistance to the poor. Some legal assistance programs have been active in speaking for low-income people threatened with eviction because their homes are to be torn down to

Louis Dembitz Brandeis (1856–1941) began his career as a corporation lawyer but became a spokesman against monopoly and in favor of social reform. In 1908, defending the constitutionality of an Oregon statute "that no female (shall) be employed in any mechanical establishment, or factory, or laundry in this State more than ten hours during any one day," he introduced the "Brandeis brief," which marshalled economic and sociological evidence on the condition of women in industrial employment. Thus Brandeis set a pattern that opened legal issues to social inquiry.

make way for government-sponsored urban renewal projects.

Another example of social advocacy is the work of Ralph Nader in the field of consumer protection. Nader has a kind of "public interest" law firm—the Center for Responsive Law—but his main strategy has been to issue timely reports for public information rather than to sponsor lawsuits (*Yale Law Journal*, 1970:1069–1152, esp. 1103–1105, 1130).

Persistence of the double image The recent successes of social advocacy are evidence that law can be used to enlarge rights and challenge injustices. But legal institutions also serve the status quo, especially in maintaining order and in protecting such established interests as property rights. More-

[1] The decisions and opinions of appellate courts are published in law reports and cited as follows: The volume number appears first; next there is an abbreviation indicating the court (state or federal); and then the page reference follows. Thus, 347 U.S. 483, 1954, reads as Volume 347 of *United States Reports* (official reports of the Supreme Court) at page 483. The year of the decision is 1954.

Dispute and compromise in North India

This is a simplified description of the actual processes of intracaste disputes among the Chamars. The distinctions between the types of meetings are not explicitly made by the Chamars, and one type meeting can easily flow into another. In general, the processes of settlement are similar in all types of meetings.

LEADERS AND AUDIENCE

The general rule is that the leaders of the units of the persons involved will act in some sense as mediators, since by social definition the position of each leader depends on his ability to function not only as a leader of one unit but to lead in the next larger unit and take a wider role and more active part in it; hence, he would endanger his role of leader in the wider circle if he were to push the claims of his immediate followers too much . . . it is the role of the leader to bridge the gaps between the rings of the social "onion," by balancing between advocacy of the rights of his immediate followers and the demands of the wider social group. All interested parties, whether they be leaders or directly concerned with the dispute, are free to attend meetings, to comment, and to take part in the proceedings. The people attending form the "public opinion," and part of the leader's function is to sense, as well as direct, "public opinion" as it develops at the meeting.

TALK AND TIME

Essentially, a dispute among the Chamars seems to get settled through talking it out. The act of talking seems to relieve some of the aggression built up in the dispute. No one is cut off, and a person can raise any issue or

Source: Bernard S. Cohn, "Some Notes on Law and Change in North India," *Economic Development and Cultural Change* 8, No. 1 (October 1959), pp. 85–86. Used by permission.

problem he wants. On several occasions . . . what appeared to be completely irrelevant issues were discussed for hours. The Chamars do not expect to settle the dispute in any specified number of meetings. A meeting will last three or four hours and then be adjourned for a week; meanwhile, mediators will talk to the parties in the dispute. The meeting will be reconvened, and there will be more talk. Eventually a "compromise" will be suggested, and even though it may be more favorable to one party, as long as it can be defined as a compromise in a rhetorical sense, both parties seem to be satisfied.

THE RELEVANT DISPUTE

Very often a meeting will be held ostensibly to hear one dispute, and people will then discuss and adjudicate another dispute which lies behind the antagonism and comes to the surface as a side issue. They feel no necessity of "sticking to the point." The Chamars do not lead a segmented life in which behavior or situations can be compartmentalized easily, and they see no point in trying to decide matters only on the basis of an immediate situation.

THE PERSONAL CHARACTERISTICS OF THE DISPUTANTS

The Chamars in their daily lives have clear ideas about the relative worth of their fellow Chamars. When it comes to settling a dispute, the Chamar sees no reason why he should not include his knowledge of the disputants in his evaluation of the dispute. Some men's promises are worth more than others, some are known to be quarrelsome, some are relatively rich, well-connected, or dependents of important Thakurs. Some come from honorable Chamar families, some are educated, some have traveled, some are loose morally, some are stupid, some lazy—all these personal characteristics are known, enter into the adjudicative process, and need not be made explicit.

over, the system includes prosecutors as well as judges, vice squads as well as poverty lawyers. The legal order has many different commitments, some of which tend to give it a repressive and punitive cast. The image one has of the law depends on where one stands on the social ladder. For the affluent, law is usually helpful and protective; for the poor, it is more often alien and oppressive.

SOCIOLOGY AND LAW

Sociology views the legal order in *context* and in *action*. The context of law is studied by exploring the social sources of legal change, especially the response of law to altered values and to new forms of social organization; by examining the relation of law to other institutions, such as medicine, or to social movements, such as the labor movement or the civil rights movement; and by considering the social environment within which lawyers, judges, police, and other legal officials do their jobs. For example, public apathy toward certain types of crimes is part of the context of police work, as is the enthusiasm of some groups for getting rid of deviants.

The social context sets problems for legal agencies, limits their resources, and sometimes transforms their purposes. Thus the objective of *suppressing* crime may become one of merely *regulating* it. A sensitivity to law-in-context leads to a concern for law-in-action, that is, for understanding how decisions are made. Such understanding must take account of all the social forces that play upon official agencies, those that come from outside as well as those that arise from within.

The major theme of legal sociology is the interplay of formal and informal processes. As in the study of formal organizations (see ASSOCIATIONS, pp. 197–198), sociological inquiry tends to emphasize informal structure and the informal influences on decision. This emphasis, however, does not detract from the importance of the formal or legal system.

Section two law and culture

In any society, the various functions of law are not equally developed or valued. One society may emphasize the dispute-settling function, with a complex machinery of adjudication, frequent recourse to the courts, and high status of judges; law in another society may mainly serve to justify authority. Law may be thought of as a necessary evil and lawyers a plague on the body politic; alternatively, law may be associated with the divine. Cultural conceptions of law determine whether the legal order will help create people who are submissive to authority or critical of it, jealous of their rights or only dimly aware of them.

Adaptation 32 is a study of how conceptions of justice develop in the course of childhood experience. This is one way of appreciating how culture, through socialization, affects fundamental notions of fairness.

CULTURE CONFLICT AND DIVERSITY

Cultural differences affecting law are sharply revealed when a colonial power attempts to impose its legal system. When the British governed India, they tried to reform the Indian courts on the English model. The British assumed that their own ideas about fair procedure were inherently just. The result was a continuing conflict between the assumptions of the British judicial system and the value premises of the Indian peasant society that they ruled.

The [English] common law proceeds on the basis of equality before the law while indigenous dispute-settling finds it unthinkable to separate the parties from their statuses and relations. The common law gives a clear-cut "all or none" decision, while indigenous processes seek a face-saving solution agreeable to all parties; the common law deals only with a single isolated offense or transaction, while the indigenous system sees this as arbitrarily leaving out the underlying dispute of which this may be one aspect; the common law has seemingly arbitrary rules of evidence, which do not permit that which is well-known to be proved and that which is not can be proved; the common law then seems abrupt and overly decisive, distant, expensive, and arbitrary (Galanter, 1964:25).

Two basic characteristics of such a peasant society contradict the assumptions of English (and American) law. First, fixed status pervades all of life. A court that ignores ethnic or status identity, treating the person as merely a plaintiff or defendant, seems detached from social reality. Second, in peasant society ties of kinship and locality have an overriding importance. They provide the indispensable context within which a dispute takes place and which should govern the settlement. To treat a dispute as an isolated event according to abstract principles makes no sense to the peasant community. See "Dispute and compromise in North India" (p. 412).

British policy in India also shows how law can *create* conflict. A study of a locality in North India reported that the British tax laws tended to disrupt the solidarity of the local high-caste group by making *individuals* responsible for land taxes and recognizing individual rather than group interests in land. This policy ran counter to the traditional social organization and had the effect of loosening the dependence of the individual on other members of the community. He could more freely use the British courts as a battleground.

Moreover, the alien character of the courts made them easier to use for harassing enemies and ruining competitors.

Since British procedure and justice appeared capricious to the Indians, someone with a bad case was as prone to go to court as someone with a good case. The standard was not the justice of his case, but his ability to outlast his opponents (Cohn, 1959:93).

Law and mediation in China In Anglo-American law, the parties to a private dispute (for example, arising from an automobile accident) are encouraged to compromise and settle out of court (Coons, 1964). But this aspect of the legal system is less visible than the "adversary principle" in which two contending parties square off before an impartial court which then returns an authoritative decision.

Adjudication and the adversary principle are not so highly regarded in other cultures. For example, students of Chinese law have noted that mediation rather than adjudication was the preferred mode of dispute settlement in traditional China (Cohen, 1966; Lubman, 1967). In mediation, a third party uses persuasion and negotiation to encourage a settlement; no decision is imposed.

The Chinese preference for mediation is grounded in the Confucian attitude toward law and morality. The followers of Confucius (551–479 B.C.) had a low regard for law, in part because they perceived it as made up of rigid and narrow rules.

The Confucian perspective, which remained dominant in China until recent times, was incompatible with the adversary principle. Self-criticism and compromise were moral imperatives, and a person was not supposed to insist on his "rights." A lawsuit was an embarrassment to both sides: The victor displayed a lack of moderation; the loser showed that he was unable to win an indispensable, face-saving concession (Cohen, 1966:1208). The sensed impropriety of going to law was supported by practical experience. In traditional China, the administration of justice was harsh, expensive, and corrupt. There was little public confidence in courts that were often geographically distant and manned by an insensitive bureaucracy. Emperor K'ang-hsi, who reigned from 1662 to 1722, justified the situation in his own way:

Law suits would tend to increase to a frightful amount, if people were not afraid of the tribunals, and if they felt confident of always finding in them ready and perfect justice. As man is apt to delude himself concerning his own interests, contests would then be interminable, and the half of the Empire would not suffice to settle the lawsuits of the other half. I desire, therefore, that those who have recourse to the tribunals should be treated without any pity and in such a manner that they shall be disgusted with law, and tremble to appear before a magistrate (quoted in Cohen, 1966:1215).

Adaptation 32 Piaget: The child's conception of justice

415

*Adaptation 32
Piaget: The
child's
conception of
justice*

Jean Piaget (1896–   ) is a Swiss psychologist who has strongly influenced the study of intellectual and moral development. His work has important continuities with Durkheim and G. H. Mead and shows the interaction of philosophical, psychological, and sociological perspectives. As a student of philosophy, he directed his attention to the structure of mind and the nature of moral judgment. A sensitivity to the importance of social settings led him to conclusions similar to Mead's, especially the view that genuine socialization fosters an appreciation of cooperative living as well as the development of personal competence.

In his research on children, Piaget first undertook studies of language and thought, judgment and reasoning. He then turned to the question of morality, particularly the development of a sense of justice. In this study Piaget and seven collaborators observed and interviewed a total of 382 children who were pupils at various schools in Switzerland. Different groups of children participated in different phases of the research. A characteristic technique was to tell the child a brief story and elicit a response.

MORALITY AND RULES

Piaget began with the premise that "all morality consists in a system of rules, and the essence of morality is to be sought for in the respect which the individual acquires for these rules" (p. 13). He used the game of marbles to study the child's conception of rules. By observing the children and asking them to explain the game and respond to possible variations, he uncovered an intricate system of rules governing nearly every contingency that might arise in the course of play. However, Piaget was primarily interested not in the content of the rules but in how children perceived their obligations. Two kinds of rules were identified:

1. Coercive rules based on respect for authority, in which children's feelings of obligation stem from their respect for the person who enunciates

the rule—an adult or an older child. Such a rule is a divine law, the meaning of which is incomprehensible but which must be blindly obeyed. Children do not understand that there is a purpose to a rule; instead, compliance is secured by punishment.

2. Rational rules based on mutual respect among peers. In this context the child understands that rules are necessary to ensure fair and open competition in the game. Cheating is wrong because it is unfair to others, not simply because it invites punishment.

THE MORALITY OF CONSTRAINT

Having formulated his basic concepts—coercive v. rational rules, respect for authority v. mutual respect, constraint v. cooperation—Piaget applied them in the study of developmental differences. He concluded that there are two major stages in the development of moral judgment in children, the first (ages 3 to 8) characterized by respect for authority and the morality of constraint, the second (ages 9 to 12) by the gradual ascendancy of mutual respect and the morality of cooperation.

Piaget in the lecture hall

Source: A summary and interpretation of Jean Piaget, *The Moral Judgment of the Child* (New York: Free Press, 1965). First published in 1932. Quoted material cited to pages in the 1965 edition is published in the United States by permission of The Macmillan Company and of The Free Press, a Corporation. All other world rights granted by permission of Routledge & Kegan Paul, Ltd., London. This adaptation was prepared by Saul Geiser.

Until the age of about seven or eight (Piaget cautions against overemphasizing specific ages), children tend to perceive rules as fixed, externally imposed laws. They interpret them literally and do not understand that the spirit of the rules must at times override the letter if the purpose for which the rules were set up is to be achieved.

For the young child, good is defined in absolute terms: Any act that conforms to the literal rule is good; any act that does not so conform, regardless of circumstances, is bad. In spite of this rigid adherence to the letter of rules, there is little inward acceptance of them. Like physical laws, rules are perceived as external realities which influence behavior by force of nature, not force of principle or purpose. This orientation Piaget called "moral realism."

Piaget asked children to compare two stories, the first about a boy who accidentally broke 15 teacups that had been left out of sight behind a door, the second about a boy who broke a single cup while in the act of stealing jam from a cupboard. Here are two characteristic responses:

G., age six: Have you understood these stories? —*Yes.*—What did the first boy do?—*He broke eleven cups.*—And the second one?—*He broke a cup by moving roughly.*—Why did the first one break the cups?—*Because the door knocked them.*—And the second?—*He was clumsy. When he was getting the jam the cup fell down.*—Is one of the boys naughtier than the other?—*The first is because he knocked over twelve cups.*—If you were the daddy, which one would you punish most?—*The one who broke twelve cups.*—Why did he break them?—*The door shut too hard and knocked them. He didn't do it on purpose.*—And why did the other boy break the cup?—*He wanted to get the jam. He moved too far. The cup got broken.*—Have you got a brother? *No, a little sister.*—Well, if it was you who had broken the twelve cups when you went into the room and your little sister who had broken one cup while she was trying to get the jam, which of you would be punished most severely?—*Me, because I broke more than one cup.*

S., age six: Have you understood the stories? Let's hear you tell them.—*A little child was called in to dinner. There were fifteen plates on a tray. He didn't know. He opens the door and he breaks the fifteen plates.*—That's very good. And now the second story?—*There was a child. And then this child wanted to go home and get some jam. He gets on to a chair, his arm catches on to a cup, and it gets broken.*—Are these children both naughty, or is one not so naughty as the other?—*Both just as naughty.*—Would you punish them the same?—*No. The one who broke fifteen plates.*—And would you punish the other one more, or less?—*The first broke lots of things, the other one fewer.*—How would you punish them? *The one who broke the fifteen cups: Two slaps. The other one, one slap.*

The striking fact about these responses is that both children ignore the intentions of the boys. It is the number of cups broken, not the intent, that defines the moral quality of the act. Beyond age eight the reverse is true: Older children hold the thief responsible. Piaget saw the failure of the younger children to take intent into consideration as resulting from their conception that rules have nothing to do with the "insides" of people.

The externality of rules is both a cause and consequence of adult constraint. Because the child is not yet able to comprehend that rules have a purpose, that they are a means to achieve order and cooperation, it is difficult for parents to control the child's behavior without exercising constraint. The child of four or five cannot be persuaded that obedience to rules is good because it promotes solidarity and mutual respect. At the same time, adult constraint serves to reinforce the young child's restricted conception of rules.

THREE CONCEPTS OF JUSTICE

After about age eight, the morality of cooperation gradually replaces the morality of constraint. Piaget studied this development by examining the child's conception of justice. Among the aspects of justice considered were: (1) fairness in punishment (retributive justice), (2) fairness in the distribution of benefits (distributive justice), and (3) attitudes toward authority.

Retributive justice Piaget queried his young subjects about the justness of various punishments for rule violations, using stories such as the following:

Story I. A boy has broken a toy belonging to his little brother. What should be done? Should he (1) give the little fellow one of his own toys? (2) pay for having it mended? (3) not be allowed to play with any of his toys for a whole week?

Story II. A child is looking at a picture book belonging

to his father. Instead of being careful, he makes spots on several of the pages. What shall the father do? (1) The child will not go to the cinema that evening. (2) The father will not lend him the book any more. (3) The child often lends his stamp album to the father; the father will not take care of it as he has always done up till then.

Piaget found a clear difference between older and younger children with respect to the kinds of punishment they thought were fair. Younger children (ages 6 to 7) were more likely to choose severe punishments, whatever the rule violation, while older children (ages 8 to 12) favored milder punishments. For the younger group, justice was associated with severity of punishment.

In contrast to the notion of retributive justice, the older children develop a more advanced conception of justice, based on the principle of *reciprocity*.

B., age nine, responding to Story II: *I would dirty his album for him, because that would be the fairest punishment. It would be doing the same thing to him as he did.*—And of the other two, which is the fairest?—*I wouldn't have lent him the book again because he would have made spots on it again.*—And how about the first punishment to stop him going to the cinema?—*That one is the least fair. It does nothing to the album, the book. It has nothing to do with the book.*

R., age ten: Which punishment do you think the fairest?—*Not the one of the cinema, because that's rather too strict for having made spots.*—And which of the other two?—*The one of making spots on his album . . . it was right to do to him what he had done.*

B., age twelve-and-a-half, responding to Story I: [*The fairest statement is that he*] *should give one of his toys to the little boy.*—Did you choose that one just because it came into your head, or because it seems to you more just?—*He took a toy away from the little boy, so it is right that he should give one back to him.*

Invoking the principle of reciprocity, the child conceives of just punishment as one that causes offenders to suffer the same consequences as they cause others to suffer. In this way, they are made to realize the significance of their misdeeds. They are persuaded that the rule should be obeyed, not merely because they might be punished, or simply because the rule exists, but because to disobey the rule is to destroy mutual respect and reciprocity among one's peers. Piaget argued that

this represents a radical shift from the idea of coercive punishment to a concept of punishment aimed at restoring the bonds of solidarity.

Distributive justice The problem of distributive justice was approached by eliciting the children's attitudes toward favoritism.

A mother had two little girls, one obedient, the other disobedient. The mother liked the obedient one best and gave her the biggest piece of cake. What do you think of that?

In one group of 167 children, 70 percent of the young children (age 6 to 9) but only 40 percent of the older children (age 10 to 13) approved of the mother's action. Piaget concluded that "the children's reactions evolve according to a relatively constant law. With the little ones punishment outweighs equality, whereas with the older ones the opposite is the case" (p. 264). He also noted a difference in the quality of the responses that the children gave:

[The younger children] do not attempt to understand the psychological context; deeds and punishments are for them simply so much material to be brought into some sort of balance, and this kind of moral mechanics, this materialism of retributive justice, so closely akin to the moral realism studied before, makes them insensible to the human side of the problem. Whereas [the older children show] a singularly delicate moral sense—the mother's preference for the obedient child will discourage the other, will make it jealous, lead it to revolt, and so on. . . . Children who put retributive justice above distributive are those who adopt the point of view of adult constraint, while those who put equality of treatment above punishment are those who, in their relations with other children, or more rarely, in the relations between themselves and adults, have learnt better to understand psychological situations and to judge according to norms of a new moral type (pp. 267 f.).

Piaget recognized that the desire for distributive justice, for fairness in allocation, may stem from adult example and tutelage. But he clearly preferred the hypothesis, without being able to prove it, that

the idea of equality develops essentially through children's reactions to each other and sometimes at the adult's expense. . . . The relation between child and adult as such does not allow for equality. And since equalitarianism is born of the contact of children with one another, its development must at least keep pace with the progress of cooperation between them (p. 275).

Attitudes toward authority In their early years, children are unable to distinguish between a just rule and an authoritative rule. Until about age seven, justice and authority are one.

Once there was a camp of Boy Scouts (or Girl Guides). Each one had to do his bit to help with the work and leave things tidy. One had to do the shopping, another washed up, another brought in wood or swept the floor. One day there was no bread and the one who did the shopping had already gone. So the Scoutmaster asked one of the Scouts who had already done his job to go and fetch the bread. What should he do?

B., a girl, age six-and-a-half: *She ought to have gone to get the bread.* — Why? — *Because she had been told to.* — Was it fair or not fair to have told her to go? — *Yes, it was fair, because she had been told to.*

Z., a boy, age six-and-a-half: *He ought to have gone.* — Why? — *To obey.* — Was it fair, what he had been asked to do? — *Yes. It was his boss, his chief.*

Compare these responses, which associate justice with submission to authority, to those of children only slightly older:

L., a boy, age seven: *He shouldn't have done it because it wasn't his job.* — Was it fair or not to ask him to do it? — *Not fair.*

C., a girl, age nine: *She oughtn't to have done it. It was not her job to do it.* — Was it fair to do it? — *No, it was not fair.*

Now the child distinguishes sharply between justice and authority; the question of the fairness of the rule is separated from the fact that the rule originated with adult authority.

Piaget contended that an essential feature of the child's idea of justice is the growing sense of equality that emerges during the seventh and eighth years. This sense of equality explains, in great part, the child's new capacity to discriminate between what is just and what is merely authoritative. The idea of equal treatment for all provides an independent standard against which the child may evaluate the commands of adults. To the extent that adult rules are compatible with equality, the child judges them fair and just; but where adult rules are opposed to equality, the child rejects adult authority.

A DEVELOPMENTAL MODEL

Figure 13:1 shows the major variables studied by Piaget. Each stage of moral evolution is the result of three interdependent influences: (1) the level of development of the child's personality — egocentric or autonomous, (2) the nature of rules — coercive or rational, (3) the kind of social relations to which the child is exposed — constraining or cooperative.

Stage one relates egocentricity, coercive rules, and the morality of constraint. The egocentricity of young children has two aspects: They are basically loners, unable to engage in genuine cooperation, and their play is characteristically imitative; at the same time, they are dominated by respect for adult wishes. At this stage children do not distinguish their own perspectives from the perspectives of others.

In order to become conscious of one's ego, it is necessary to liberate oneself from the thought and will of others.

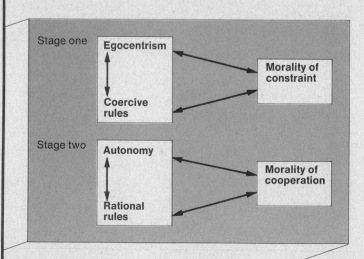

Figure 13:1
Piaget's two stages
of moral development

The coercion exercised by the adult or the older child is therefore inseparable from the unconscious egocentrism of the very young child (p. 93).

The morality of constraint is a morality of punitive rules and subordination to authority. The psychological bases for criticism of authority have not been laid.

The transition to stage two is marked by the child's increasing freedom from adult constraint. In the peer group, cooperation takes hold. Cooperation involves communication by way of shared meanings. Group participation encourages a more generalized, less egocentric approach to the world and helps children discover the boundaries that separate them from others. As their own autonomy grows, they have increasing respect for the autonomy of others. Cooperation presumes the participation of independent individuals.

So long as the child does not dissociate his ego from the suggestions coming from the physical and social world, he cannot cooperate, for in order to cooperate one must be conscious of one's ego and situate it in relation to thought in general (p. 94).

Rational rules go together with autonomy and cooperation. In contrast to coercive rules, rational rules gain force from the child's understanding of them, not from fear of punishment. Rational rules therefore presuppose an autonomous individual, capable of consenting or withdrawing consent.

LATER RESEARCH

A recent review of studies conducted to test Piaget's hypotheses concluded that many of his findings have been confirmed, especially his theory that "the child's earliest morality is oriented to obedience, punishment, and impersonal forces, and that it progresses toward more internal and subjective values" (Kohlberg, 1964:399). Some more specific conclusions, such as the importance he gave to the peer group in producing the morality of cooperation, have not been supported.

Section three crime and society

A modern legal system includes a great variety of rules and procedures covering almost every aspect of organized group life. Constitutional law, contract law, property law, the law of negligence, administrative law, family law, corporation law, tax law, environmental law—all these contribute to the complex reality of a modern legal system.

The criminal law has a special significance for most people because it is the most visible part of the legal system. Especially if they are poor or have little property, it is the part of the law they are most likely to experience. Moreover, this is the law that touches most closely on ordinary conduct and social conformity. The criminal law is a way of suppressing deviance and carries with it the threat of social stigma, imprisonment, or worse.

THE MEANING OF CRIME

Crime is properly understood as part of the broader phenomenon of deviance. To understand criminal behavior and rates of crime it is necessary to understand the dynamics of conformity and deviation, including the processes of social disorganization, differential association, and labeling discussed in *SOCIAL ORGANIZATION*, pp. 41–45.

At the same time, the norms that define a crime are special norms. They are part of the legal order. Not everything forbidden by custom is a crime. It may be a violation of custom to engage in homosexual conduct and the practice may induce shame and secrecy, but it is not a crime unless the law says it is.

A crime is conduct forbidden by law for which punishment is prescribed. Thus, the ideas of crime and punishment are intimately connected. To commit a crime is to run the risk that punishment will be imposed. It may be said, indeed, that the law defines conduct as criminal in order to justify the use of the criminal sanction, that is, some form of punishment.

The precise meaning of punishment has troubled students of law, as well as legislators and judges, for a long time. However,

Ratero en accion: A pickpocket exploits a distracting crowd situation.

court-room; a prisoner of war camp may well provide a harsher environment than a state prison; death on the field of battle has the same physical characteristics as death by sentence of law. It is the expression of the community's hatred, fear, or contempt for the convict which alone characterizes physical hardship as punishment (Gardner, quoted in Hart, 1958:405).

It follows from this perspective that only what is truly perceived as blameworthy should be treated as a crime. When the legislature treats other wrongs as crimes, it does so at the risk of diluting the special function of the criminal law and overextending its reach. This is the problem of "criminalization," some aspects of which are discussed below. (See p. 422.)

the following definition is an acceptable starting point for most discussion: Punishment is the infliction of pain by official authorities as a form of condemnation or for the purpose of preventing offenses against legal rules.

Thus there are two main reasons for treating conduct as criminal and thereby justifying the use of punishment. First, the aim of the law may be to say that murder, theft, or bigamy are reprehensible forms of deviance and as such should be condemned and suppressed. Punishment is a way of communicating the gravity of the offense and the moral outrage of the community. Second, even when there is no great sense of moral outrage or a desire to condemn, conduct may be defined as criminal because punishment is thought to be the only practical way of controlling the undesired conduct. For example, there are criminal penalties for driving without a license, selling liquor to minors, filing false financial statements, and violating corporate antitrust statutes.

It has been argued that the distinctive function of the criminal law is to express the moral condemnation of the community:

The essence of punishment for moral delinquency lies in the criminal conviction itself. One may lose more money on the stock market than in a

Crimes and private wrongs Much legal activity is devoted to the settlement of private disputes, such as controversies over contracts and claims resulting from automobile accidents. In such cases, the community is essentially neutral, and the objective of the law is to reestablish social equilibrium. In these "civil" actions damages are assessed, property is restored, and rights and obligations are determined. Although "punitive damages" are sometimes granted (if the harm has been done with great malice), normally the question of punishment does not arise. A crime, however, is an offense against the community. When a crime is committed, the community takes over the job of investigating and prosecuting the case, and the objective is to suppress such offenses.

Crimes and private wrongs often overlap. For example, a *tort* is a private wrong other than a breach of contract, such as harm produced by negligence, slander, assault, or stealing. Some torts are also crimes, and a person may be liable to pay damages to the person harmed and also be subject to criminal prosecution.

Responsibility and guilt The human and social significance of conviction for a crime is such that, in the Anglo-American system, special safeguards have been established to protect the innocent. Among these are two requirements that must be met if criminal responsibility is to be proven. First, the alleged offender must be charged with a specific act. He is to be tried for what he has done or failed to do, not for what he might have done or might do in the future. In other words, the defendant is held responsible for *something*, and that something must be susceptible of proof. Second, a person is criminally responsible only if he or she had what is called a "guilty mind" or "criminal intent," known in the law as *mens rea*.

Ideally, therefore, the specification of a crime includes both an act and a state of mind. Stealing is not merely the act of taking someone else's property; it also involves an intent to steal. Murder is more than homicide; it is homicide with "malice aforethought." It follows that the accused must have been capable of forming the intent. If a person is too young or was insane at the time of the alleged offense, then criminal responsibility cannot be established.

LAW AND MORALS

Many legal rules have little moral or symbolic significance. This variation is reflected in a traditional legal distinction between acts *mala prohibita* (wrong by prohibition) and acts *mala in se* (wrong in themselves).

Acts *mala in se* include, in addition to all felonies, all breaches of public order, injuries to person or property, outrages upon public decency or good morals, and breaches of official duty, when done willfully or corruptly. Acts *mala prohibita* include any matter forbidden or commanded by statute, but not otherwise wrong (Perkins, 1957: 57–58).

Many violations of motor vehicle codes, such as overtime parking or driving without an operator's license, would have no moral connotation if they were not prohibited by statute. True crimes are wrong not only because the statute says they are but also because the acts are deemed wrong on the basis of general moral standards.

The modern view is that acts *mala prohibita* are not really crimes and should be differently classified, perhaps as "public wrongs," "regulatory offenses," or simply "prohibited acts" (Perkins, 1957:701–702). They would thus avoid the stigma associated with criminal law, and this redefinition would help maintain the distinctiveness of the criminal law.

Between an extreme example of an act *malum prohibitum*, such as overtime parking, and a clear case of an act *malum in se*, such as murder, there are many gradations. The line between the two is blurred and moving. Littering in a public park, for example, might in an even more crowded world become *malum in se*.

Crimes without victims A significant portion of criminal law is concerned with conduct that consists primarily of affronts to the mores (see *CULTURE*, p. 60) rather than in clearly identifiable harms. Laws against sexual deviation, drinking, drugs, gambling, birth control, obscenity, and vagrancy are usually justified by reference to some harmful effect; but the alleged harm, however serious, is often hard to define, subject to debate, or only distantly connected to the offensive act. These are known as crimes without victims (Schur, 1965). Characteristically the "victim" is the person committing the act or someone willing to cooperate in the offending act, such as a prostitute.

The attempt to use law to coerce virtue raises difficult issues.

1. Moral pluralism and liberty The classic argument against legislating morals is found in John Stuart Mill's 1859 essay *On Liberty*:

The only purpose for which power can be rightfully exercised over any member of a civilised community, against his will, is to prevent harm to others. His own good, either physical or moral, is not sufficient warrant. He cannot rightfully be compelled to do or forbear because it will be better for him to do so, because it will make him happier, because, in the opinion of others, to do so would be wise, or even right. These are good reasons for remonstrating with him or reasoning with him, or persuading him, or entreating him, but not for compelling him, or visiting him with any evil in case he do otherwise (Mill, 1859/1910:73).

This argument slights the possibility that the integrity and cohesion of the social order may depend upon the continued assertion of a common morality (Devlin, 1959; cf. Hart, 1963). In effect, Mill said that the use of law to uphold the "common conscience," in Durkheim's terms, might have been necessary in archaic or primitive society but is not appropriate in a civilized community.

The reduction of liberty by the enforcement of morals may be a small problem when a single set of moral standards is widely shared in the community. But under conditions of cultural pluralism, when the law enters the area of morals it may clash with the beliefs and aspirations of substantial minorities. Honest and responsible citizens may be classified and treated as criminals, and criminal law may become an expression of the social and political dominance of some over others.

Sometimes laws against immoral conduct do not reflect a firm consensus based on traditional values. The history of Prohibition shows the leading role of narrowly based but powerful groups. Through sustained political action, "moral entrepreneurs" (Becker, 1963:147–163; Gusfield, 1963) can push through laws that do not necessarily have majority support. Even if there is consensus on the underlying value, there may not be agreement on the wisdom of embodying such values in a penal code.

2. Costs of criminalization The enforcement of morals has so many difficulties that there tends to be a negative effect on the integrity and reputation of the law.

Symbolic offenses tend to be vaguely defined, as in the case of vagrancy, obscenity, and outrage to public decency. This vagueness is a source of official uncertainty and leads to variable and arbitrary enforcement. The absence of a specific victim and the relatively private character of the forbidden activity create additional problems for the police. Without the help of complainants, the police feel they must exercise active surveillance over the community. Such practices as unlawful entrapment and illegal search and seizure' are a continuing temptation to police investigators who have no other means of knowing when a crime has been committed. Where evidence cannot be lawfully secured, police may employ harassment as an alternative to prosecution. Corruption may also result from reliance on informers and from continuing contacts between police and the underworld. The sheer difficulty of control requires enforcement to be selective and therefore discriminatory (Skolnick, 1966:204–229).

In branding nonconformers as criminals, the law tends to cast them apart from the legitimate community. The atmosphere of secrecy, suspicion, and deviousness that comes to surround such forbidden activities as homosexual relations, prostitution, and gambling may have its own degrading effect. Furthermore, what begins as a limited deviation may grow into a way of life, especially when the deviant comes to depend on criminal sources who supply the prohibited goods or services. In this sense, the legal sanction creates criminals. To the suppliers of contraband commodities, the legal prohibitions are a bonanza, creating opportunities for exploitation and gain they would not otherwise have (Packer, 1964:551–557).

Social definition of crime The problems that arise in the area of law and morals bring home the lesson that crime is a social product, not a natural phenomenon. It is society that decides what shall be considered a crime and therefore subject to police surveillance and control. When law is used to uphold morals, despite the high social costs of enforcement, an underlying policy decision may be obscured. It may be unconsciously assumed that the only problem of law enforcement is to win conformity to existing legal rules. There may be a question, however, whether all acts defined as criminal should continue to be so defined (Allen, 1964; President's Commission, 1967: Chap. 8).

THE PREVALENCE OF CRIME

It is important to distinguish crime statistics from the actual prevalence of criminal conduct. Crimes are committed by all segments of the community, and some that are very costly in wasted earnings or tax dollars receive very little official attention. Bribery and fraud are a way of life in many businesses and professions. These become public scandals from time to time, as in the case of bribes paid by multinational corporations or the misuse of Medicare funds by physicians. But the more routine forms of dishonesty, such as stealing by employees, insurance fraud, consumer fraud, and the like, are very frequent and seldom reported, although they may be dealt with privately by warnings and dismissals. The operations of organized crime account for billions of dollars in illegal goods and services, such as gambling, loan sharking, narcotics, and prostitution, as well as many crimes of violence.

White-collar crimes are "crimes committed by persons of respectability and high social status in the course of their occupations" (Sutherland and Cressey, 1974:40).

Police and community: accessible and remote

Table 13:1
Estimated rates[a] for crime index offenses, 1974,
and percentage change in rates 1960–1974, United States

Crime index offense	1974 rate per 100,000 population	Percent increase in rate per 100,000 population, 1960–1974
Murder	10	90
Forcible rape	26	175
Robbery	209	248
Aggravated assault	214	151
Burglary	1,429	183
Larceny-theft	2,473	141
Motor vehicle theft	461	152
Total	4,821	157

Source: 1974 Uniform Crime Reports, 1975:11.

[a] Rates are for specified crimes known to the police.

These have a special significance because, though technically condemned by the criminal law, they are widely tolerated and infrequently prosecuted. White-collar offenders do not fit the conventional image of the "common criminal," and the operators of the system are reluctant to treat them as such. Furthermore, many of the offenses, such as tax evasion and business fraud, are not considered really serious even though, it is sometimes argued, white-collar criminals "are by far the most dangerous to society of any type of criminal from the point of view of effects on private property and social institutions" (Sutherland and Cressey, 1974:41).

An alternative view suggests that some crimes are especially serious, or "core" crimes, because they threaten the elementary conditions of personal safety and community life:

Predatory crime does not merely victimize individuals, it impedes and, in the extreme case, even prevents the formation and maintenance of community. . . . Around one's home, the places where one shops, and the corridors through which one walks there is for each of us a public space

wherein our sense of security, self-esteem, and propriety is either reassured or jeopardized by the people and events we encounter (Wilson, 1975: 21, 24).

Thus crimes against the person—willful homicide, forcible rape, aggravated assault, robbery—and crimes against the household, especially burglary, are the core crimes that concern most people because they directly affect the peaceable conduct of everyday life. It does not follow, of course, that citizens should not be concerned about more remote offenses that affect the distribution of wealth and the quality of the society.

Crime index *Uniform Crime Reports* (UCR), issued annually by the Federal Bureau of Investigation (FBI), measures the trend and distribution of serious crimes in the United States. These include murder (the willful killing of another), forcible rape, robbery (larceny from the person by force or intimidation), aggravated assault (attacking a person for the purpose of inflicting severe bodily injury), burglary (unlawful entry of a structure to commit a felony or theft), larceny-theft (unlawful taking or stealing of property without the use of force, violence, or fraud), and motor vehicle theft. Table 13:1 presents crime estimates for 1974 in rates per 100,000 of population and the percentage changes in rates between 1960 and 1974. The increases reported are differences in rates and take into account the increase in population. In the 14-year period covered, there was a dramatic rise both in the absolute amount of such crime and in the crime rate.

Such official statistics are estimates covering only a fraction of even the limited kinds of crime included in the FBI index. Many such crimes go undetected, others are detected but not reported, and others are reported to the police but not officially recorded. Since unrecorded crimes do not appear in the statistics, the crime index is only a crude approximation of the true rate.

Some changes in reported crime rates may be the result of changed methods or improvements in reporting. When police records and reporting procedures are efficient, more crimes that come to the attention of the police get into the statistics. Such "statistical" as distinct from real changes are not taken into account in the UCR reports and indeed are hard to deal with in interpreting official data which involve numerous political jurisdictions. As police become indoctrinated in the importance of good record keeping, the completeness of records and therefore the measured crime rate will increase even if the actual rate remains stable.

Finally, changes in the age or sex composition of the population affect the crime rate. A population weighted in the older ages is expected to have a lower rate than a population with many young people, especially young men. Part of the increase in the U.S. crime rate in recent years is the result of just this kind of demographic change—a growth in the youthful population.

Attrition in the legal process The "career" of a crime suggests how difficult it is to estimate the incidence of criminality. What happens after a crime is committed is summarized in Figure 13:2, which is based on information reported in a national sample survey. These data come from reports of the people who were victims of criminal acts. Hence this kind of research is called a victimization study.

There are six stages in the figure, and at

Figure 13:2 Attrition in the legal process, 2,077 crimes reported

Source: After Ennis, 1967a

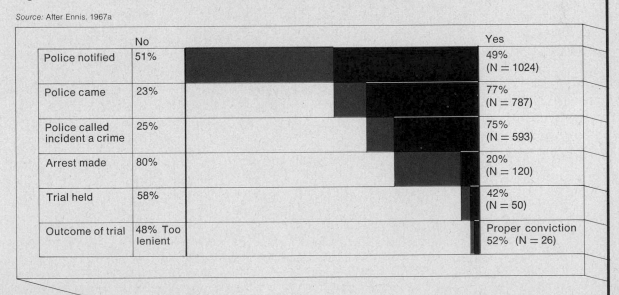

	No		Yes
Police notified	51%		49% (N = 1024)
Police came	23%		77% (N = 787)
Police called incident a crime	25%		75% (N = 593)
Arrest made	80%		20% (N = 120)
Trial held	58%		42% (N = 50)
Outcome of trial	48% Too lenient		Proper conviction 52% (N = 26)

each step events occur that affect the statistics.

1. Of 2,077 cases in which individuals were victims of a crime, only half (1,024) notified the police.

2. Once notified, the police came to the scene of the victimization or in some way acknowledged the event about three-fourths of the time.

3. Once they came, the police regarded the incident as a crime in three-quarters of the remaining cases.

4. Regarding the matter as a crime, the police made an arrest in 20 percent of the cases.

5. Once an arrest was made, there was a trial (including a guilty plea) in fewer than half the cases.

6. The outcome of the trial was thought to be a proper punishment in a little over half the surviving cases (Ennis, 1967a:48; Ennis, 1967b).

Official records are derived from the third stage in the attrition process, that is, crimes reported to the police and treated by them as crimes. In this survey the number was reduced from 1,024 to 593 between the stages of police notification and police definition of crimes. The smaller number, crimes actually reported to the police and officially recorded by them, is called "crimes known to the police." Such information, which is the basis of figures published in UCR is the best *official* index of crimes committed because it is the one "closest" to the crimes. The more remote an indicator is from the crime, the greater are the number of procedures that may distort the index. Therefore crimes known to the police are better indicators than arrest statistics, which are better than court statistics, which are better than prison statistics, for measuring the amount of crime.

The National Crime Panel survey To secure a serious-crime estimate that would not suffer from the limitations of official statistics, the National Crime Panel was established. Interviews were conducted twice during 1973 in national samples of 60,000 households and 15,000 businesses.

Victimization surveys, which include crimes not known to the police or not treated by them as crimes, show a much higher incidence of crime than do UCR reports. In other words, the victimization data are not affected by the attrition process.

An important aspect of personal crime is

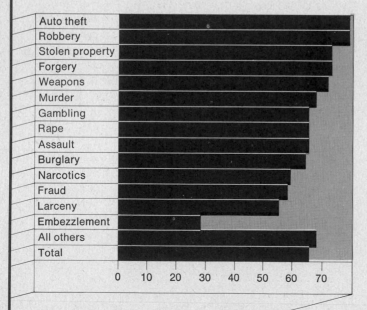

Figure 13:3
Percentage of repeaters
by type of crime
(persons arrested 1970–1974)

Source: 1974 Uniform Crime Reports, 1975:49.

the relation between the victim and the offender. The National Panel Survey for 1973 reports the percent of violent crimes involving strangers as follows: assault, 60; rape, 75; and robbery, 86. Although most of the crimes were committed by strangers, a large percentage of violent crimes are committed by persons known to the victim. (Law Enforcement Assistance Administration, 1975:3). In fact homicides, which are not included in the Panel Survey data, are more likely to be committed by people who know the victim rather than by strangers. Perhaps it should not be surprising that so many violent crimes are committed by persons known to the victim since the element of opportunity looms large in crimes against the person. Many crimes may not be reported to the police because the victim may wish to protect the criminal, may want to avoid embarrassment, may not want relations with the criminal to be further impaired, may prefer to seek redress without police involvement, or may fear reprisal. Such considerations are less likely to deter a victim to the same degree when the crime is committed by a stranger.

Recidivism The FBI's Uniform Crime Reporting Program includes a computerized criminal history file, which is used to provide evidence regarding "careers in crime." Of 207,748 individuals arrested during 1970–1974, 65 percent had been arrested twice or more before. Figure 13:3 shows the percentage of recidivism by type of crime. A special study was made of 62,236 offenders who were released during 1972. Of these, 67 percent were rearrested within three years (*1974 Uniform Crime Reports*, 1975:47).

Section four administrative justice

The model of a trial by judge and jury dominates the popular image of criminal justice. In fact, however, most cases do not come to trial. The police or the district attorney's office may decide not to press a charge, or the defendant may plead guilty.

In many communities between one-third and one-half of the cases begun by arrest are disposed of by some form of dismissal by police, prosecutor, or judge. When a decision is made to prosecute, it is estimated that in many courts as many as 90 percent of all convictions are obtained by guilty pleas (President's Commission, 1967:4).

The system is operated by *informal* magistrates who weigh evidence, interpret laws, and make most of the decisions. A policeman who decides to arrest a suspect, or not to do so, makes a complex judgment about the facts of a specific case, including what the person intended by the action and what might be the outcome of an arrest. The officer may decide that the apparent offender ought not to be punished because the law was not meant to apply in that case. For example, a statute forbidding card playing for money might not be enforced against "social" gambling if the police do not believe the legislature intended the law to apply to such cases. Often a law includes a broad definition of the offense in order to avoid loopholes; the police and prosecutors are expected to use discretion and enforce the law in the light of its "true" objectives (LaFave, 1965:89 ff.).

The exercise of discretion by law-enforcement officers, from the patrolman to the district attorney or sheriff, gives rise to an administrative system of criminal justice. The system is administrative because (1) the officials have tasks to perform and objectives to achieve—they are not passive dispensers of fairness—and (2) the officials belong to organizations that have internal problems and are subject to external pressures. Thus people who decide the fate of others do so not as fully independent judges but as officials who must keep organizational needs in mind.

A police officer who makes an arrest usually assumes that the person is guilty. The officer's assumption tends to be accepted by other officials in the system. Within an administrative setting, it is natural to conclude that mistakes are exceptional and that officials usually act with sufficient reason. This is called the presumption of administrative regularity. In the case of persons accused of crimes, this amounts to a de facto presumption of guilt. The advantages enjoyed by the accused from a legal presumption of innocence are reduced, and administrative officials, rather than the accused, are given the benefit of the doubt. The burden of proof tends to shift to the suspect; it becomes more difficult for him to maintain a posture of innocence; and the right to remain silent may appear obstructive.

PLEA BARGAINING

The dilemmas of administrative justice are sharply revealed in the practice of plea bargaining. The plea of guilty is negotiated by the prosecutor and defense attorney. The outcome is an agreement under which the accused will plead guilty in exchange for a reduced charge or a favorable sentence to be recommended by the prosecutor to the judge. Even when there have been no explicit negotiations, defendants relying on prevailing practices often act on the assumption that a guilty plea will be followed by a more lenient sentence.

From the standpoint of the courts, the plea of guilty is a matter of urgent economy. "There are simply not enough judges, prosecutors, or defense counsel to operate a system in which most defendants go to trial" (President's Commission, 1967a:10). In partial justification for giving a heavier sentence to the one of five defendants who refused to plead guilty, a federal judge wrote, in a 1960 opinion:

[If] in one year, 249 judges are to deal with 35,517 defendants, the district courts must encourage pleas of guilty. One way to encourage pleas of guilty is to establish or announce a policy that, in the ordinary case, leniency will not be granted to a defendant who stands trial (Skolnick, 1966:13).

However, the prevalence of plea bargaining cannot be entirely accounted for by the prospect of crowded court calendars and a "breakdown of the system." In fact, the high rate of guilty pleas is not recent, and bargaining by defendants and prosecutors has ancient roots (Wishingrad, 1974).

At least in the Anglo-American system, where prosecutors are given wide discretion regarding what charge to press or whether to press any charge at all, prosecutors cannot avoid the business of judging. This is especially true when crimes carry harsh penalties, and the prosecutor has to decide whether the defendant really deserves to be punished according to the strict letter of the law. Moreover, the prosecutor may not have the evidence to win a conviction. A combination of practical urgencies and a sense of individualized justice contribute to the inevitability of plea bargaining:

The idea that overwork forces the prosecutor to grant concessions to defendants in exchange for a bluffed out guilty plea all but ignores the prosecutor's concern for adjusting penalties to individual crimes and criminals in the interests of justice. It portrays the prosecutor both as a weakling and as an inhuman and unjust automaton who has been programmed to obtain the severest possible punishment for as many criminals as possible. Sadly enough, this damning but highly distorted portrait of the prosecutor is often painted by the prosecutors themselves (Rosett and Cressey, 1976:106).

This reminder is important, but not less important is the danger that unsupervised discretion will result in widespread abuses, including low-quality, "bargain basement" justice.

One such danger that has received attention is the possible effect on the role of the defense attorney (Blumberg, 1967; Sudnow, 1965). When most cases are subject to negotiation, and the issue is the size of the penalty rather than guilt or innocence, there is a tendency for defense lawyers to "cooperate" with the prosecutor by avoiding zealous or "obstructive" defense tactics. Prosecutors are more amenable when they are not forced to meet every possible challenge or the costs of every possible delay. A cooperative attitude on the part of the defense attorney is further encouraged when the client is not an isolated case but is part of a case load which the attorney must learn to manage efficiently.

Plea bargaining tends to win over the defense lawyer to the idea that the defendant is probably guilty of something. As a result, the defense may not take seriously the possibility of pressing for acquittal. In the *routine* case the pattern may well benefit most defendants. It is not known, however, to what extent attorneys become insensitive to the nonroutine case in which the interests of justice, and of the client, would be best served by standing fast on a plea of innocence.

There is always the danger that a defendant who would be found not guilty if he insisted on his right to trial will be induced to plead guilty. The defendant has an absolute right to put the prosecution to its proof, and if too much pressure is brought to discourage the exercise of this right, the integrity of the system, which the court trial is relied on to vindicate, will not be demonstrated. When the prosecution is not put to its proof and all the evidence is not brought out in open court, the public is not assured that illegalities in law enforcement are revealed and corrected or that the seriousness of the defendant's crimes are shown and adequate punishment imposed. Prosecutors who are overburdened or are insufficiently energetic may compromise cases that call for severe sanctions (President's Commission, 1967: 10).

Visibility Perhaps the major weakness of administrative justice is the relative *invisibility* of decisions. In principle, legal decisions affecting the rights of persons are formal and public and therefore subject to scrutiny, criticism, and control. When such decisions become part of administrative routines, such as patrolling an area, investigating complaints, or negotiating with defense counsel, they tend to be obscured, sometimes deliberately so. For example, a defendant may be asked specifically by the judge whether the guilty plea was made voluntarily and without inducements; yet there was inducement and even the judge may know it. Because of this hidden character, the process of plea bargaining has not been subject to formal review and assessment. Invisible decision making offers opportunity for bias, corruption, or simply random effects.

Yet administrative justice is inevitable, for no system of social control can operate without the exercise of judgment and discretion at all levels. The apparent answer is not to eliminate discretion—or the role of informal magistrate—but to make it more visible and more responsible. The presence of counsel at all stages can help increase both visibility and responsibility. In addition, such processes as plea bargaining can be made subject to greater control by formalizing the agreement to plead guilty, reducing it to writing, and thus making it subject to scrutiny. This requires explicit recognition that inducements to plead guilty have a proper and controllable place within the system of criminal justice. In 1971 the U.S. Supreme Court (*Santobello* v. *New York,* 404 U.S. 257) endorsed the legality of plea bargaining, and the Supreme Court of California, following suit, required that the terms of the plea-bargaining agreement be made part of the record. Such a development is not strange to legal history, which has often followed a pattern of formalizing hitherto informal procedures.

THE OFFICIAL PERSPECTIVE

The discussion of administrative justice suggests that in the legal order, as elsewhere, there is a persistent conflict between the needs of *systems* and the needs of *persons,* between institutional ideals and institutional realities. Legal agencies are going concerns, and they are prone to give the system the benefit of the doubt, assigning a high priority to its stability and survival. Viewed from the official perspective (or the system perspective), the goal of law is to uphold authority and order rather than to enhance rights and achieve full civic participation. In the official perspective, "one assesses the factors of freedom and security from the standpoint of the official processors of government" (Cahn, 1963:5). Almost invariably freedom comes off second best.

The sociological study of such legal agencies as the police or prisons is largely devoted to showing how administrative needs gain priority over other values, such as the right to protest or the humane treatment of prisoners. This approach should be compared with the discussion of oligarchy (Adaptation 18) and of the Methodist church (Adaptation 31). Both studies explore the official or system perspective in other contexts.

Section five social change and social policy

This section considers two fundamental issues that have, in recent years, raised serious questions about "law and order." The first has to do with the frustrations of social policy affecting the treatment of criminals, the second with the tension between freedom of speech and public order. Both issues reveal the changing values that underlie the changing law; both show how legal ideals depend on the sociological characteristics of prisons, police, and other agencies.

THE AIMS OF PUNISHMENT

Four objectives have played a part in forming social policy regarding punishment for crimes:

Condemnation As noted above social condemnation is a distinctive function of the criminal law. Criminal conduct is defined as morally blameworthy; it is not merely socially harmful or undesirable, for example, when farmers cause pollution by the excessive use of fertilizers. Because crime is blameworthy, there is a strong demand that punishment be (1) hurtful and (2) proportionate to the moral gravity of the offense.

The idea of condemnation is often phrased as a demand for retribution, expiation, or vengeance. The criminal has been wicked and should pay for his sin; the society as victim should take revenge. These ancient concepts are not essential to the policy of condemnation. Condemnation is a way of reaffirming the moral standards of the community; and it is a way of saying that the criminal deserves to suffer.

This association of punishment with condemnation has repelled many people because they see it as an unhappy reminder of an unenlightened past. As a result, the past century has seen a vigorous effort to minimize or even eliminate condemnation as a justification for punishment. That effort has never been wholly successful, perhaps because it is a challenge to the very idea of a criminal law.

Deterrence Many people, including legislators, are indifferent to the moral aspects of punishment. They see it rather as a practical device for inhibiting undesirable conduct. The assumption is that many people are potential criminals who weigh the costs of violating the law and are deterred by the threat of punishment.

If the commands of a legal system were not reinforced with the threat of punishment, many individuals would see no basis for believing that the legal system really meant what it said. . . . The imposition of punishment is a demonstration to society as a whole that the legal system is serious in its attempt to prohibit criminal behavior: punishment is the "convincer" (Zimring and Hawkins, 1973:87).

There is considerable variation in the effectiveness of deterrence, and little is securely known regarding what threatened punishment for what crimes will have what effect. However, since deterrence presumes rational calculation on the part of the potential offender, it is reasonable to conclude that *instrumental* crime—crime for gain or for a specific goal—is more susceptible to deterrence than *expressive* crime, such as a crime of passion or crime that reflects a personality need or quest for pleasure (Chambliss, 1967: 708).

Many criminologists believe that the severity of punishment is less important than its certainty and promptness. Harsh penalties are often counterproductive because juries, judges, and prosecutors are reluctant to impose them. To be deterred, the potential offender must give weight to the probability that the threat of punishment will in fact be carried out.

Isolation Most people who are in prison cannot commit crimes on the outside. Thus punishment is used to isolate or "incapacitate" a criminal. In the case of capital punishment, incapacitation is complete. On the other hand, imprisonment is not the only possible form of isolation. Other forms of close surveillance could be devised; and exile or "transportation" was for many years, in England and other countries, the preferred way of getting rid of people who were considered dangerous to the community. Indeed, the penitentiary is an American invention, dating only from the late eighteenth century.

As a means of crime prevention, isolation has a special justification. Isolation presumes that a person who has committed one crime will, if free to do so, commit another. Hence the justification for isolation is the presumed probability of recidivism.

As was noted above, rates of recidivism are indeed very high. These high rates reflect a selective factor, that is, the tendency of courts to sentence to prison mainly those who have a record of prior offenses. The high rates may also reflect the experience of being imprisoned.

More important than the recidivism rates of prisoners, however, is the large number of offenders who are not sent to prison as a result of the way the system of criminal justice works, and the possible concentration of potential offenders in relatively small segments of the population. One study showed that among 10,000 boys born in 1945, only 6 percent were chronic offenders, and these accounted for about two-thirds of the violent crimes committed by the entire cohort (Wolfgang, 1973:110–112). These and other studies have prompted the conclusion that

isolation as a means of reducing crime should be given much greater emphasis (Wilson, 1975: Chaps. 8, 10). However, it is not known how much expansion of prison facilities would be required to carry out such a policy and what the costs to the community would be.

Punishment as isolation shifts attention from the offense to the offender. If the objective is to remove a potentially dangerous person from the community, then the nature of the offense is less important than the character of the person. It becomes plausible to argue that individuals should be kept in prison until they are no longer a threat.

This conclusion is not necessary, however. One could argue that isolation is effective for crime prevention insofar as offenders are put away for definite periods in accordance with the criminal statutes. Even if they are let out again without being reformed, at least they will not contribute to the crime rate while they are off the streets. Nevertheless, when one says: "Wicked people exist. Nothing avails except to set them apart from innocent people" (Wilson, 1975: 209), the door is opened to a behavioral assessment of who is incorrigible, which is probably beyond the competence of social knowledge. An even cruder policy would be to lock people up on the basis of past offenses and throw away the key.

Rehabilitation During the past century the dominant aspiration of the system of criminal justice has been rehabilitation. In 1870 the National Prison Congress declared that "crime is a moral disease" for which "punishment is the remedy." It follows that "punishment is directed not to the crime but to the criminal" and "the supreme aim of prison discipline is the reformation of criminals, not the infliction of vindictive suffering" (quoted in Dershowitz, 1976:93).

This perspective gained wide support and in time became the dominant official viewpoint. Thus the 1972 edition of the Model Sentencing Act, sponsored by the National Council on Crime and Delinquency, says:

Persons convicted of crime shall be dealt with in

accordance with their potential for rehabilitation, considering their individual characteristics, circumstances and needs . . . Dangerous offenders shall be identified, segregated, and correctively treated in custody for as long terms as needed (quoted in von Hirsch, 1976:9).

Punishment as rehabilitation has reform for its object. It is decisively oriented to the offender rather than to the offense. Nevertheless, rehabilitation is a form of punishment so long as it involves coercive confinement and a coercive demand that the individual submit to treatment. Moreover, rehabilitation is not undertaken primarily for the benefit of the offender. It is offered as a rational mode of crime prevention.

The rehabilitative ideal has its origins in one of the great dilemmas of punishment: "Punishment must be severe enough to exert a restraining effect on others, but not so severe as to turn the person being punished into a more antisocial creature than he was before" (Packer, 1968:47–48). It is the fear that punishment will be counterproductive, in addition to more humanitarian objectives, that underlies the policy of rehabilitation.

Efforts at rehabilitation have involved a wide variety of techniques and programs: education and vocational training, counseling, individual and group psychotherapy, and efforts to transform the institutional environment—so-called milieu therapy—by creating a supportive atmosphere, reducing the distinction between custodial and treatment staff, and mobilizing peer groups for the transformation of values and perspectives.

Thus the rehabilitative ideal emphasizes individualized treatment; it is preventive rather than punitive in spirit; it invokes a medical model of crime and punishment; and it presumes that criminality is largely influenced by social and psychological deprivations.

The indeterminate sentence If rehabilitation aims to cure offenders, for how long should they be confined? The early proponents of rehabilitation did not shrink from the answer: as long as may be necessary to bring about the cure. Thus a corollary of rehabilitation is the indeterminate sentence. Indeterminate sentencing is widely used in the United States, and it takes many forms. The main point is that no definite time in custody is specified. Instead, the judge sentences the convicted offender to an indefinite term, the final decision to be made later on by a parole board or a similar agency.

A sentence is more or less indeterminate to the extent that the amount of time actually to be served is decided not by the judge at the time the sentence is imposed but rather by an administrative board while the sentence is being served (Dershowitz, 1976:101).

Most indeterminate sentence laws specify maximum and minimum terms.

The indeterminate sentence maximizes the discretion of the ultimate decision maker. Parole boards have sweeping powers to hold people in prison up to a maximum term, and they are largely free to use whatever criteria they wish in determining the date of release. Much may depend on the prisoner's willingness to conform to rules and accept treatment. Few parole boards have even stated their policies regarding the criteria for release (Heinz et al., 1976:4). The outcome is to leave the inmate dangling and encourage him to "play games" with the system by hypocritical participation in therapeutic programs.

Given wide discretion, parole boards respond to a variety of pressures:

For the sentence-fixer, the characteristics of the criminal must compete with the necessities of placating right-wing political pressure, displaying the necessary level of cooperation with law enforcement and prosecution, heeding the management interests of the correctional bureaucracy, keeping a finger on the pulse of seething unrest in inmate populations, trying to maintain some degree of consistency with colleagues of widely divergent views. . . . Along this route the normal defendant-inmate . . . is a lonely and almost forgotten actor. Possessing neither substantive legal nor political muscle, he is the pawn in an interest conflict that he can influence only by chance and which he seldom understands (Foote, 1972:32).

For these and other reasons, contemporary critics of the criminal justice system have become increasingly critical of the indeterminate sentence. There is a demand for more definite terms and for more limited discretion, whether exercised by judges or by parole boards.

The idea of "presumptive sentencing" is typical of recent proposals to reduce untrammeled discretion and yet retain some degree of flexibility. A presumptive sentence means that "a finding of guilty of committing a crime would predictably incur a particular sentence unless specific mitigating or aggravating factors are established" (Twentieth Century Fund Task Force, 1976:19–20).

Disenchantment and reconstruction The rehabilitative ideal has come to be thought of as a "noble lie" (Rothman, 1973:22). Others have referred to "the crime of treatment" (American Friends Service Committee, 1971: Chap. 6). This disenchantment is part of a more general skepticism about social programs. (See *EDUCATION*, p. 362.) A lowering of expectations has occurred because the programs presume more social knowledge than currently exists and because they are administered by institutions that are unlikely candidates for achieving high ideals or complex purposes.

The rehabilitative ideal suffers from three major defects. First, the treatment programs do not work, at least as means of reducing recidivism (Martinson, 1974). Second, the indeterminate sentence, a corollary of the treatment perspective, is increasingly perceived as unjust and ineffective. Third, it is fallacious to assume that psychological change can be coerced.

It has been suggested that the rehabilitative ideal can be redeemed or "liberated" if it is divorced from punishment. In other words, rehabilitative efforts should be continued but (1) "they must cease to be a purpose of the prison sanction" and (2) participation should be strictly voluntary and not coerced:

Rehabilitative programs must be expanded and improved but they must be related neither to the time the prisoner serves nor to the conditions of his incarceration. Prison training and treatment programs must be entirely facilitative, never imposed (Morris, 1974:xi).

A related approach perceives the policy of rehabilitation as humane custody, and the lowered expectations are expressed as follows:

In seeking to make criminal justice more redemptive and less punitive, we may have asked too much of institutions that can barely hold their own, let alone develop the competence to be curers of souls. . . . We may well conclude that the real worth of the "treatment perspective," in its various forms, has been to serve as a civilizing influence on correctional systems (Selznick, 1968).

CIVIL DISORDER AND FREEDOM OF EXPRESSION

A serious issue of legal policy arises when free public expression is weighed against the public interest in peace and safety. To balance these values the law must assess the dynamics of protest, the community structure, and the alternatives open to agencies of social control. Resolution of the dilemma hinges on understanding that social expectations about public order must be taken into account (Silver, 1967:1–24). For example, disputes between employers and employees were at one time considered serious threats to public order but later were accepted as normal conflicts of interest. In the nineteenth century and the early decades of the twentieth, many courts ruled that picketing by trade union members was inherently unpeaceful. An opinion of a federal circuit court in 1905 stated:

There is and can be no such thing as peaceful picketing, any more than there can be chaste vulgarity, or peaceful mobbing, or lawful lynching. When men want to converse or persuade they do not organize a picket line (quoted in Tanenhaus, 1953:188).

Laws banning picketing were in effect in some American jurisdictions until 1940, when the Supreme Court decided that picketing was a form of speech protected by the First Amendment (*Thornhill* v. *Alabama*, 210 U.S. 88, 1940). In this and later decisions the court enlarged the meaning of *speech* to include demonstrative acts of public expression. It thereby changed the standard of acceptable risks to public order.

Demonstrations and the law The communication of ideas by overt acts, even in a context of potential disorder, has been protected in Supreme Court decisions. In 1949 the court said that speech "may indeed best serve its high purpose when it induces a condition of unrest, creates dissatisfaction with conditions as they are, or even stirs people to anger" (*Harvard Law Review*, 1967:1774). In order for the larger community to discharge its civic responsibilities, it needs to be aware of the grievances of minorities. And overt demonstrations may be the only means available to groups that do not otherwise have ready access to the means of communication and to society at large.

The legitimacy of demonstrations is legally recognized, but only if other interests are safeguarded. The courts do not condone violence, intolerable burdens on traffic or the safety of the streets, or unjustified interference with private property. In the protection of these interests, modern legal doctrine is *contextual*, taking account of concrete circumstances. Thus, what a noisy demonstration is depends on the setting; words that may be incitement to riot for one audience may be acceptable before another. While violence is against the law, it does not follow that *any* act of violence justifies forcibly dispersing a crowd of demonstrators.

Similarly, obstruction of traffic cannot lawfully be used as an excuse for banning all demonstrations. Traffic regulation must be reasonable and take account of the alternatives available to the demonstrators. Demonstrators are entitled to seek access to large numbers of the public, preferably by making arrangements that do not excessively burden normal activities. The public can be asked to bear some inconvenience in the interests of free speech.

Caution The above discussion of the law of demonstrations reports the trend and some of the reasoning of judicial decisions, especially of the Supreme Court. But the Court's decisions may have only a limited effect on the day-to-day conduct of the police or of other officials who regulate demonstrations.

Crowd control versus crowd destruction The police have the duty of crowd control as distinguished from crowd destruction; they are not permitted to leap to the conclusion that the crowd is uncontrollable and that they are therefore free to act repressively. At most parades and public meetings, police are present to guide the path of the march or to ensure that a lawful assembly is not interrupted. At conventional parades, the police are little more than spectators; even when crowds are large and boisterous, the presence of a relatively few police suffices to maintain order. Rallies or demonstrations that express sharp divisions of opinion or unpopular causes and are marked by excitement and the threat of violence test the ability of the police to restrain themselves as well as unruly crowds.

Relatively few police in the United States are trained or qualified to deal with large public disturbances. Most of their work is carried on as individuals or in small work teams and deals with complaints involving one or two persons. The police are local officers scattered through numerous jurisdictions, each one self-contained, separately administered, and jealous of its autonomy.

When suddenly mobilized in large numbers to deal with potentially unruly crowds or with riotous conditions, the police, inexperienced and untrained for such work, may themselves be caught up in collective excitement. When police are worried by an unfamiliar task, fearful for their own safety, resentful of provocative acts, beset by rumors, and made anxious by extensive preparations for a disturbance, discipline may fail. Under such circumstances, police have used violence far in excess of what is necessary to control the crowd or to make an arrest. Innocent bystanders have been assaulted, and attacks have persisted long after the crowd has been dispersed.

Adaptation 33 recounts how faulty planning and administration, poor communications, and the breakdown of discipline may result in police violence and crowd destruction.

Adaptation 33 Stark: Police tactics and crowd destruction

On the evening of June 23, 1967, nine months before his withdrawal in 1968 from candidacy for a second term, President Lyndon Johnson attended a fund-raising dinner at the Century Plaza Hotel in Los Angeles. The antiwar movement was developing rapidly, and the Peace Action Council, which had operated for nearly a year as a loose confederation of local antiwar groups, planned what they hoped would be their first major peace march, a parade past the hotel while the president was speaking. Unable to block a parade permit, the police established stringent security measures but seriously inadequate provisions for crowd management and dispersion.

ASSEMBLY AND PREMARCH RALLY

The gathering place for the march was Cheviot Hills Park, about a mile from the hotel. The plan was to walk to the hotel and back again to the park. Alternative plans proposing dispersal areas beyond the hotel or a postmarch rally to draw people away from the hotel had been rejected by the police and the hotel. The march was to begin at 7:30 P.M. After 5:00 the crowd increased rapidly as people arrived from work. It was a good-natured and relaxed gathering, made up of the kind of people who were accustomed to proper, even cordial, interaction with the police. They were white, middle-class Americans. Many were business and professional men and women and housewives. There were numerous children and babies and a good number of students, some in hippie dress. But overall it was, as one observer de-

Source: Abridged and adapted from *Police Riots: Collective Violence and Law Enforcement* by Rodney Stark (Belmont, Calif.: Wadsworth, 1971), Chap. 1. Published in this form by permission of Rodney Stark.

scribed it, "one of the God-damnedest most respectable crowds you could imagine. I mean it was mainly Beverly Hills solid types, all those cute, earnest women and guys in $40 shoes."

The premarch rally began at 6:00, and at 6:30, while the speeches continued, white-helmeted policemen accompanied a civilian through the park. He handed out leaflets, copies of a restraining order obtained that morning which barred demonstrators from committing various acts—many of which it is unreasonable to suppose they would have done. They were barred from using stink bombs, smoke-making devices, "loosing any animal on the premises" of the hotel, and so on. They were also enjoined from congregating in front of the hotel or entering any private property within the hotel complex. Upon receipt of the leaflets some members of the crowd left, thinking the march itself had been banned. It had not.

The police barred all sound trucks from the parade, thus destroying the ability of parade leaders to communicate with, direct, or warn off the marchers. Some hand bullhorns were passed out among monitors, but these proved inaudible. Moreover, it was impossible to get word to the monitors about what directions they ought to give over their bullhorns. Still the crowd was jovial and confident. Most people felt they didn't really need monitors to walk in a short parade.

By 7:00 the 15,000 persons now in the park began to line up in preparation for the march. Immediately, the police cracked down, giving a hint of what was to come—"This is an illegal assembly. Your parade permit does not go into effect until 7:30." The march leaders got people to fall out of ranks and mill about until the time when standing abreast would be legal.

THE MARCH BEGINS

At 7:30 the first ranks moved out of the gate, where a pickup truck with sound equipment tried to join the parade. The truck was manned by several radicals who wanted to urge the crowd to engage in a massive sit-in once they reached the hotel. While the marchers flowed by, parade monitors formed a linked-arm circle around the truck in order to keep the truck out of the demonstration. The monitors took this action because sound trucks were illegal and their permit might be cancelled and because they did not want advocates of civil disobedience associated with the parade.

The police noted the incident and moved in. Told what was going on, a sergeant said, "All right we'll handle it." The sergeant motioned the truck out of the parade line, the driver signaled compliance and began to turn the truck slowly out of the march. Then an officer broke from the police lines and began to bash out the windows of the truck with his baton. Other police followed him and also began to beat on the truck. The police pulled people from the cab and from the back of the truck and beat them in front of the crowd. The police then beat and kicked others within reach around the truck, including several monitors. This incident, too, was a preview of what was to come.

IMPACTED CROWD

Meanwhile, at the hotel, 1,300 police officers with another 200 in reserve had been assembled to seal off the hotel from the marchers. However, they permitted several thousand spectators, both sympathetic and antagonistic to the march, to gather in front of the hotel, where for several hours they had merely requested the spectators to remain on the sidewalks. The injunction prohibiting congregating in front of the hotel was not announced or enforced at a time when it might have been possible for the spectators to leave.

And so on came the marchers. They had no internal communications. They had been denied a suitable dispersal area beyond the hotel. They were not marching past the hotel *to* somewhere, for they had been denied permission to hold a postmarch rally. As a march leader put it: "There was no focal point beyond the hotel to attract those in the march. . . . Therefore, the hotel itself became the focal point."

Furthermore, it turned out to be almost impossible for the marchers to pass the hotel. Passage was partly blocked by the crowd in front of the hotel. As the march approached, the police who had been keeping spectators on the sidewalks were withdrawn, and the crowd was permitted to spill into the street. The police positioned themselves at a critical bottleneck and blocked the only remaining space through which the march could have continued. As the march piled up in front of the hotel, the police continued to block the traffic lanes through which it could have passed. There was no way to proceed and no way to tell the marchers to halt. The police had created the very thing they said they most feared. They had stopped the march in front of the hotel and created a huge crowd.

The police felt something had to be done. They had no intention of permitting 15,000 people to stage a protest rally in front of a hotel in which the president was speaking. The reasonable course, however, would have been to open an adequate passage for the march and direct the marchers out of the area. Instead, at 8:25 a police captain took the microphone of the police sound van and announced that the assembly was illegal since, by stopping, the demonstrators had violated the terms of their parade permit. He then ordered the crowd to disperse, but he gave no instructions on how the marchers were to comply with this order. In fact the police had no plan by which the march could disperse. They confronted the march in an area where all routes, except to the rear, were blocked or so clogged as to allow only a trickle of traffic. They seem to have expected the parade to turn around on itself. Those in front could not. Marchers in the rear were not turned back but continued unsuspectingly to pour in, thus telescoping into a dense congregation in front of the hotel. Desperate to comply with police orders, some monitors instructed those near them in the crowd to march in circles and thus keep moving. It was an impasse: ahead, an unyielding line of police; to the west, another line; to the east, a steep embankment; to the rear, only a sea of unaware oncoming marchers.

The police asked the impossible, but they were determined. They used motorcycle wedges to force an open space between the crowd and police lines. But the density of the crowd forced those in front close to the police again.

POLICE VIOLENCE

When the police struck, they turned dazzling spotlights on the crowd and came in swinging. They beat everyone within reach while the crowd reeled back into tighter compression. Most were forced down the steep embankment (a 45-degree slope) into an underpass. But once down the slope, they were again boxed in. Baton-wielding lines of policemen beat them back up the steep slope, which was covered with slippery ice plant. The crowd formed human lifelines and passed infants, children, and the elderly up the slope.

Finally, the crowd was cleared from the hotel area. Women seeking lost children were turned away from the site. Police lines began to move into the neighborhood towards the park. Demonstrators were harassed wherever police found them. Some were chased into Beverly Hills. Others were diverted from parking areas where their vehicles were parked. Any group larger than five was considered an illegal gathering. This was interpreted to mean no more than five could ride in a single automobile and led to the stopping of many cars. Police violence was directed at anyone still seen to possess a picket sign. Innocent passersby were sometimes pulled from their cars and beaten or harassed.

Eyewitness accounts make it clear that a very large number of persons were beaten; 178 persons reported injuries to the American Civil Liberties Union. One can only conclude that the police used their clubs willfully and needlessly.

WHY DID IT HAPPEN?

Why was police planning so inadequate? Once the confrontation developed, why did the police behave so brutally?

Police plans were based on a faulty assumption about the kinds of people who opposed the war at that time and on a serious underestimation of the probable size of the crowd. The kind of people the people expected to turn out—kooks, radicals, hippies, and subversives—were those the police despised and those who, they thought, would pose a substantial threat to their own safety. Police planning relied on the fact that in Los Angeles earlier demonstrations against the war had never drawn

more than several thousand people. Even with the presence of the president, the police did not expect many more than 5,000 persons to turn out. Three times that many did.

Parade management always requires dispersal areas and adequate route supervision. The police vetoed available dispersal areas, and when the time came they denied the parade organizers the use of sound systems to direct the march. They seem to have felt that the march should not occur, and when they found they had no choice but to permit it, they essentially refused to condone it.

The police were unable to improvise adequate tactics on the spot. Later the chief of police said he gave the order to disperse the crowd when, looking down from a ninth-story hotel window, he saw a "bulge" in the crowd. Presumably from such a vantage point he might have worked out a dispersal route as well.

Finally, it is clear that the police were especially anxious because they were charged with the protection of the president of the United States. The deployment of 1,300 officers was designed to defend the hotel against assault, not to facilitate dispersal or order.

SUMMARY

1. The police were untrained for the task and inexperienced in handling large crowds.

2. Responsible officials tried to prevent the march and, when they failed to do so, strove to obstruct and frustrate it. This official attitude was known to the police rank and file.

3. Estimates of the size and character of the crowd were faulty, and intelligence work was incomplete. This also contributed to an anxious and punitive atmosphere.

4. The police were fearful for themselves and worried about their ability to protect the president.

5. Parade management by the police was directed at suppression rather than a smooth flow and ultimate dispersion into preplanned areas.

6. Lack of provision for communication among the marchers and between the police and the marchers made it impossible to evolve alternative plans in the emergency.

7. Police discipline collapsed.

References

Allen, Francis A.
1964 The Borderland of Criminal Justice. Chicago: University of Chicago Press.

American Friends Service Committee
1971 Struggle for Justice: A Report on Crime and Punishment in America. New York: Hill & Wang.

Becker, Howard S.
1963 Outsiders. New York: Free Press.

Blumberg, Abraham S.
1967 "The practice of law as a confidence game." Law and Society Review 1 (June):15–40.

Cahn, Edmond
1963 "Law in the consumer perspective." University of Pennsylvania Law Review 112 (November):1–21.

Carlin, Jerome E., Jan Howard, and Sheldon L. Messinger
1966 "Civil justice and the poor: issues for sociological research." Law and Society Review 1 (November):9–89.

Chambliss, William
1967 "Types of deviance and the effectiveness of legal sanctions." Wisconsin Law Review: 708–716.

Cohen, Jerome Alan
1966 "Chinese mediation on the eve of modernization." California Law Review 54 (August):1201–1226.

Cohn, Bernard S.
1959 "Some notes on law and change in north India." Economic Development and Cultural Change 8 (October):79–93.

Commission on Civil Rights
1961 Justice. Washington, D.C.:GPO.

Coons, John E.
1964 "Approaches to court-imposed compromise—the uses of doubt and reason." Northwestern Law Review 58:750–805.

Dershowitz, Allen M.
1976 "Background paper." Pp. 69–142 in Twentieth Century Fund Task Force on Criminal Sentencing, Fair and Certain Punishment. New York: McGraw-Hill.

Devlin, Patrick
1959 The Enforcement of Morals. London: Oxford University Press.

Ennis, Philip H.
1967a Criminal Victimization in the United States: A Report of a National Survey. Chicago: National Opinion Research Center. [Reproduced by the President's Commission on Law Enforcement and Administration of Justice.]
1967b "Crime, victims, and the police." Trans-action 4 (June): 36–44.

Foote, Caleb
1972 "The sentencing function." Pp. 17–32 in A Program for Prison Reform. Cambridge, Mass.: Roscoe Pound-American Trial Lawyers Foundation.

Galanter, Marc
1964 "Hindu law and the development of the modern Indian legal system." Unpublished. Prepared for the 1964 annual meeting of the American Political Science Association.

Gusfield, Joseph R.
1963 Symbolic Crusade. Urbana: University of Illinois Press.

Hart, H. L. A.
1963 Law, Liberty, and Morality. Stanford, Calif.: Stanford University Press.

Hart, Henry M., Jr.
1958 "The aims of the criminal law." Law and Contemporary Problems 23 (Summer):401–441.

Harvard Law Review
1967 "Regulation of demonstrations." Harvard Law Review 80 (June):1773–1788.

Heinz, Anne M. and associates
1976 "Sentencing by parole board: an evaluation." Journal of Criminal Law and Criminology 67 (March):1–31.

Kohlberg, Lawrence
1964 "Development of moral character and moral ideology." Pp. 383–431 in Martin L. Hoffman and Lois Wladis Hoffman (eds.), Review of Child Development Research. New York: Russell Sage.

LaFave, Wayne R.
1965 Arrest: The Decision to Take a Suspect into Custody. Boston: Little, Brown.

Law Enforcement Assistance Administration
1975 Criminal Victimization in the U.S.: A National Crime Panel Survey Report. Vol. 1. Washington, D.C.: GPO.

Lubman, Stanley
1967 "Mao and mediation: politics and dispute resolution in communist China." California Law Review 55 (November): 1284–1359.

Martinson, Robert
1974 "What works?—questions and answers about prison reform." Public Interest 35 (Spring):22–54.

Mill, John Stuart
1859/1910 Utilitarianism, Liberty, and Representative Government. London: Everyman's Library.

Morris, Norval
1974 The Future of Imprisonment. Chicago: University of Chicago Press.

Packer, Herbert L.
1964 "The crime tariff." American Scholar 33 (Autumn):551–557.
1968 The Limits of the Criminal Sanction. Stanford, Calif.: Stanford University Press.

Perkins Rollin M.
1957 Criminal Law. Mineola, N. Y.: Foundation Press.

Piaget, Jean
1965 The Moral Judgment of the Child. New York: Free Press. First published in 1932.

President's Commission on Law Enforcement and Administration of Justice
1967 Task Force Report: The Courts. Washington, D.C.: GPO.

Rosett, Arthur and Donald R. Cressey
1976 Justice by Consent: Plea Bargains in the American Courthouse. Philadelphia: Lippincott.

Rothman, David J.
1973 "Decarcerating prisoners and patients." Civil Liberties Review 1:8–30.

Schur, Edwin M.
1965 Crimes Without Victims. Englewood Cliffs, N. J.: Prentice-Hall.

Selznick, Philip
1968 "Preface" in Elliot Studt, Sheldon L. Messinger, and Thomas P. Wilson, C-Unit: Search for Community in Prison. New York: Russell Sage.

Silver, Allan
1967 "The demand for order in civil society: a review of some themes in the history of urban crime, police, and riot." Pp. 1–24 in David J. Bordua (ed.), The Police. New York: Wiley.

Skolnick, Jerome H.
1966 Justice Without Trial. New York: Wiley.

Sudnow, David
1965 "Normal crimes." Social Problems 12 (Winter):255–276.

Sutherland, Edwin H. and Donald R. Cressey
1974 Principles of Criminology. Ninth Edition. Philadelphia: Lippincott.

Tanenhaus, Joseph
1953 "Picketing as a tort: the development of the law of picketing from 1880 to 1940." University of Pittsburgh Law Review 14 (Winter):170–198.

ten Broek, Jacobus
1964, 1965 "California's dual system of family law: its origins, development, and present status." Stanford Law Review 16 (March):257–317; 16 (July):900–981; 17(April):614–682.

Twentieth Century Fund Task Force on Criminal Sentencing
1976 Fair and Certain Punishment. New York: McGraw-Hill.

Von Hirsch, Andrew
1976 Doing Justice. New York: Hill & Wang.

Wilson, James Q.
1975 Thinking About Crime. New York: Basic Books.

Wishingrad, Jay
1974 "The plea bargain in historical perspective." Buffalo Law Review 23:499–527.

Wolfgang, Marvin E.
1973 "Crime in a birth cohort." Pp. 109–115 in Sheldon L. Messinger (ed.), The Aldine Crime and Justice Annual. Chicago: Aldine.

Yale Law Journal
1970 "The new public interest lawyers." Yale Law Journal 79 (May):1069–1152, esp. 1103–1105, 1130.

Zimring, Franklin E. and Gordon J. Hawkins
1973 Deterrence: The Legal Threat in Crime Control. Chicago: University of Chicago Press.

Sources and readings

Introductions to law

Auerbach, Carl A., Lloyd K. Garrison, Willard Hurst, and Samuel Mermin (eds.)
1961 The Legal Process. New York: Chandler.

Berman, Harold J. and William R. Greiner (eds.)
1966 The Nature and Functions of Law. Mineola, N. Y.: Foundation Press.

Fuller, Lon L.
1968 Anatomy of the Law. New York: Praeger.

Summers, Robert S.
1972 Law: Its Nature, Functions, and Limits. Second edition. Englewood Cliffs, N.J.: Prentice-Hall.

Anthologies

Black, Donald and Maureen Mileski (eds.)
1973 The Social Organization of Law. New York: Seminar Press.

Schwartz, Richard D. and Jerome H. Skolnick (eds.)
1970 Society and the Legal Order. New York: Basic Books.

Simon, Rita James (ed.)
1968 The Sociology of Law. New York: Chandler.

Social analysis

Carlin, Jerome E.
1966 Lawyers' Ethics. New York: Russell Sage.
1962 Lawyers on Their Own. New Brunswick, N. J.: Rutgers University Press.

Friedman, Lawrence M.
1975 The Legal System: A Social Science Perspective. New York: Russell Sage.

Gluckman, Max
1968 Politics, Law and Ritual in Tribal Society. New York: New American Library.

Kalven, Harry, Jr. and Hans Zeisel
1966 The American Jury. Boston: Little, Brown.

Nonet, Philippe
1968 Administrative Justice: Advocacy and Change in a Government Agency. New York: Russell Sage.

Packer, Herbert L.
1968 The Limits of the Criminal Sanction. Stanford, Calif.: Stanford University Press.

Selznick, Philip
1969 Law, Society, and Industrial Justice. New York: Russell Sage.

Skolnick, Jerome H.
1966 Justice Without Trial. New York: Wiley.

ten Broek, Jacobus and editors of the California Law Review (eds.)
1966 The Law of the Poor. New York: Intext.

Weber, Max
1954 Law in Economy and Society. Edited by Max Rheinstein. Cambridge: Harvard University Press.

Criminology and criminal justice

American Friends Service Committee
1971 Struggle for Justice: A Report on Crime and Punishment in America. New York: Hill & Wang.

Chambliss, William J. and Robert B. Seidman
1971 Law, Order, and Power. Reading, Mass.: Addison-Wesley.

Cressey, Donald R.
1961 The Prison: Studies in Institutional Organization and Change. New York: Holt, Rinehart and Winston.

Newman, Donald J.
1975 Introduction to Criminal Justice. Philadelphia: Lippincott.

Radzinowicz, Leon and Marvin E. Wolfgang (eds.)
1971 Crime and Justice. Vol. 1: The Criminal in Society. Vol. 2: The Criminal in the Arms of the Law. Vol. 3: The Criminal in Confinement. New York: Basic Books.

Sutherland, Edwin H. and Donald R. Cressey
1974 Principles of Criminology. Ninth edition. Philadelphia: Lippincott.

Periodicals

Law and Contemporary Problems
Law and Society Review
Journal of Criminal Law, Criminology, and Police Science

Part Three
Master Trends

14 | Race and Ethnicity

Section one introduction

MASTER TRENDS

This is the first of four chapters dealing with master trends in the modern world: the many roles and functions of race and ethnic identity, the development of large cities as dominant forms of human habitation, technological and industrial change, and the transformation of political systems. The master trends of urbanization, technological development, and democratization—discussed in later chapters—interact strongly with the heritage of racial and ethnic oppression. The predicament of the big city in the United States is as much a problem of race as it is a problem of poverty or crowding or pollution. In South Africa, the migration of black Africans seeking jobs in expanding labor-hungry industries has created a black proletariat that has been segregated in large, racially homogeneous urban districts. The urbanization of blacks has both improved their job opportunities and increased their potential for political mobilization.

Throughout the world the technological, postindustrial society has created urgent problems of adaptation, especially for those millions, mostly minorities, whose unskilled labor is no longer in demand. And the extension of democratic participation in voting, in rights to education, and in employment is bound up with the demands of minorities to be granted full citizenship.

Race consciousness is a volatile and increasingly powerful force in the contemporary world. It has precipitated civil wars, created new nations, and generated a rising tide of expectations. Minorities are becoming more militant and more self-aware in societies at all stages of industrial and political development. This chapter views ethnicity as an engine of change, explores the historical roots and social dynamics of racial subordination, and assesses present tendencies toward integration, pluralism, or subordination.

THE SOCIAL DEFINITION OF MINORITIES

Minority group, the term most commonly used to identify a racial or ethnic population, is somewhat ambiguous. In the United States Indians, Africans, and European immigrants of various origins, although in some cases constituting large populations and in some localities preponderant, are called minorities. The term has even been extended to countries in which the minority is a clear numerical majority: South Africa, for instance, where the dominant European population is only about one-fourth the size of the black African "minority." *Minority* identifies a social condition, not necessarily a quantitative fact.

Sociologists often make a distinction between race and ethnicity. *Race* refers to differences between peoples based upon inherited characteristics, such as skin color; *ethnicity* refers to differences in socially acquired characteristics, such as language, religion, national origins, and culture. The importance of race, however, lies not in physical appearance or genetics, but in the social valuation placed upon it. It is not biological race that counts so much as the cultural interpretation of race. People have the ability to be color-blind, but they can also see racial differences where none exist.

The absence of distinct, inherited racial characteristics does not prevent one people from defining another as racially different. Throughout American history, waves of European immigrants were successively defined as racially inferior to earlier settlers and therefore were subjected to social isolation and oppression. As the descendants of immigrants became assimilated into the adopted society, they were redefined and accepted as part of the white stock—which is what they were to begin with.

In Canada, until recently the French and Anglo-Canadians were called races. In traditional Asia, outcaste groups are imagined to have origins different from the dominant population. The outcaste populations of Tibet, Korea, and Japan in popular speech are called races even though they have no distinguishing physical characteristics and are culturally similar to the dominant population in all respects except those connected with outcaste status. The popular belief is "that the outcastes are so different from oneself that they *must* be a different race" (Passin, 1955:40). Some of the beliefs about one of the Asian outcaste minorities, the Eta of Japan, are given in "Racism and Pseudorace." (See p. 444.) Similarities between these beliefs and those held about racial minorities in Western countries suggest a certain cross-cultural poverty of the racist imagination. The Japanese outcastes, who number only 2 percent of the population of the country are popularly assumed to be racially distinct, although the Eta are not genetically distinguishable from other Japanese (Price, 1966:6–33). The word *Eta* is an insult.

Prejudice and stereotypes Because prejudice is arbitrary and categorical, it is eroded by close interpersonal contacts and the press of reality. It tends to be perpetuated by simplifying assumptions called *stereotypes*. In stereotyping, a few characteristics are accepted as an adequate description of a minority, which may be composed of millions of people of all ages, educational backgrounds, and occupations. Although stereotypes can be favorable, highly favorable stereotypes are usually attributed to one's own group or a reference group, and most outgroup stereotypes are on balance negative. Even traits that have positive connotations are given a negative weight by a simple semantic shift: The Jew is shrewd, the Yankee provident; the Jew is stingy, the Calvinist frugal (cf. Merton, 1957:428–429). Categorical judgments are confidently presented as considered evaluations by persons who have little or no experience with the outgroup. But stereotyping is attenuated by critical attitudes imbued by education. Educated persons can be prejudiced, but it is somewhat harder for them to maintain the simplifying notions that justify prejudice (Simpson and Yinger, 1965:112–121).

THE VOCABULARY OF RACE

Every group has its vocabulary for outgroups, and the terminology is frequently demeaning

Racism and pseudorace: the Eta of Japan

A great deal of misunderstanding concerning the Eta exists in Toyoda.[1] . . . Most citizens prefer to avoid the subject of the Burakumin even in conversation. . . . Few city residents have ever been to the outcaste district, and most have never knowingly met an outcaste. Buraku dwellers do not affect the lives of the Toyoda people and do not constitute a recognized social problem. This lack of concern, however, in no way diminishes the attitudes of prejudice and hostility; rather, it propagates ignorance, obscurity, and even mystery. Four of the most general attitudes held by Toyoda informants toward the pariah caste are offered below.

Disgust is the most widely held and commonly verbalized attitude. Individuals who are unwilling even to discuss the outcastes distort their faces and exclaim, kitanai (dirty). These feelings are sometimes manifested more directly. For example, after one of the customers in a small wine shop noticed blood on the hands and shirt sleeves of a young outcaste, he shouted disparagingly at him and was joined by several others: "You are dirty, you animal killer! Look at the blood all over you! You are a filthy yaban [barbarian, savage]!"

Fear is another commonly found attitude of the Toyoda people. Outcastes are considered dangerous and capable of inflicting bodily harm. There are exaggerated stories of their physical prowess and fighting skill, and they are likened to the gangsters and hoodlums portrayed in American films. There is also the fear that surrounds the unknown. Burakumin are believed by some to be sinister characters with evil powers, and mothers sometimes frighten their children with gruesome tales of the Eta bogeyman. It is said, too, that the outcastes are afflicted with such contagious diseases as syphilis, gonorrhea, tuberculosis, and leprosy.

Because the Burakumin and their village are forbidden, the attitude of erotic curiosity prompts such questions as: Do the Eta look different? Are the women really beautiful? Are they rough, like gangsters? Do they actually speak a different language? What kind of food do they eat? Many wonder if Buraku girls are "better" than ordinary women; some young males have erotic desires for outcaste women; and restaurant hostesses often joke about an imputed enlargement or distortion of the genitals of the male Eta.

The spread of the final attitude, which might be termed objectivity, seems to be increasing steadily among the younger generation, but it has the fewest adherents in Toyoda. This attitude is not widespread because it depends primarily on observation. "Look at the Eta and their houses— they are dirty, they have dirty occupations, and they are diseased." "The Eta always marry each other, so their strain is weak. They are an exclusive, intimate group that rejects outsiders and any form of aid." "I feel sorry for the Eta because of their lowly position, but I will have nothing to do with them until they learn to live like other Japanese, that is, give up their occupations, marry outside their small community, clean up their villages, homes, and themselves, and drop their hostile clannish attitudes." Such beliefs are based less on legend than others but, as with Negro-white relations in

---

[1] *Toyoda* is a fictional name chosen to protect the privacy of persons in the real community. *Eta* signifies outcaste. *Buraku* refers to localities where the Eta live, *Burakumin* to the people of the Buraku—a designation commonly used in Japan for the outcaste group.

Source: John Donoghue, "An Eta Community in Japan: The Social Persistence of Outcaste Groups," *American Anthropologist* 59 (December 1957):1002–1004. Abridged by permission.

the United States, they operate as a self-fulfilling prophecy in maintaining the outcaste status.

The beliefs and myths of the Toyoda citizenry preserve majority group exclusiveness by associating the Burakumin with violations of some of the most fundamental and sacred Japanese values—those centering around purity, lineage, and health. The following are two of many popular legends heard in the city.

A young man met a beautiful girl in a restaurant. After a short courtship they were married, against the wishes of the boy's parents. They lived happily for a while, but when their children were born idiots with spotted complexions, it was discovered that the girl was a Burakumin.

This is probably the most widespread myth, as it is employed by parents to discourage children from affairs that might result in a love marriage. Even the most informed Japanese balk at the thought of marriage to an outcaste because of the popular notion of their weak strain from long intermarriage.

It was customary prior to the turn of the century for Burakumin to wash the bodies of deceased commoners in return for an offering of sake, but after the outcastes began to realize their emancipation, they frequently requested money for their services. Sometimes the demands were exorbitant. When the sum was refused, the Burakumin would threaten the family by vowing to drink the water used in bathing the body. The people were usually frightened into relenting to the Burakumin demands.

The legend illustrates the supposed barbaric quality of the Burakumin; not only were they mercenary, but they profaned the sacred, defiled the dead, and imbibed the impure and dirty.

and stereotyping. Minorities protest the public use of terms that stigmatize them or that carry ethnic connotations. Some Italian Americans insist that *Mafia* should not be used in the mass media because it associates a criminal organization with an ethnic population. The Anti-Defamation League of B'nai B'rith, as the name implies, works to reduce expressions of prejudice and discrimination against Jews and others.

Some minorities have now turned attention away from what they should not be called to what they should be called. A growing sense of identity and an effort to mobilize for self-betterment and political action have led to a choice of terms that communicate a sense of pride and activism. *Québécois* is one, *Chicano* another, *black* a third. *Québécois* signifies the regional base of French Canada and the aspirations of some French-Canadians for self-determination up to and including independence. *Chicano*, a word of obscure origin, is now a slogan for Mexican-Americans who have begun to react overtly against their subordinate status. The transition from *Negro* to *black* is a clear example of the instability of ethnic self-designation.

Negro into black In the late 1930s Robert E. Park observed:

Negroes . . . are more and more disposed to reject any terms or any racial distinctions that reflect and tend to preserve the memories of an earlier inferior status.

There is, finally, one small but significant change in the ritual of race relations that, it seems to me, needs to be specially noted. The great majority of Negroes now, after a good deal of discussion and differences of opinion, have adopted the term "Negro" as a racial designation in preference to another and more logical but less familiar expression like "Afro-American." Having adopted it, however, they spell it with a capital N (Park, 1937:xxiv).

Thirty years later *Negro* became unacceptable to many blacks. No doubt the acceptance of the word *black* was accelerated by the mass media, but the basic impulse behind the change was the growing self-awareness and assertiveness of blacks. *Black* is emphatic and simple. It is not contaminated with the connotations of subordinate status attached to *Negro* or its demeaning corruption, *nigger*. *Black* connotes an increased distance between the races, at least for a time, but it also declares an identity and pride in self.

Terminology is thus an indicator and an agent of social change. In half a century *Negro* changed from polite to general to unacceptable usage. An American sociologist commenting on the evolution of racial vocabulary has said, "I was born colored, I grew up Negro, I became black, and now I am Third World."

This chapter gives primary attention to minorities in the contemporary United States, but all sections draw comparisons with other countries and identify historical forces underlying present trends. It is hard to find a country untouched by ethnic problems, but some cases illuminate general issues and are of profound social significance. Canada, Switzerland, and South Africa for quite different reasons satisfy both of these conditions. Section Two gives attention to the role of slavery in the New World and discusses the other forces of conquest and dominance that bring minorities into being. Section Three deals with reactions to oppression and the growth of self-awareness and self-confidence among minorities. Section Four assesses the present condition of minorities under separatist and pluralist situations and measures the extent of socioeconomic subordination of several major groupings.

Section two conquest and domination

The constant factor in the making of modern minorities is the expansion of European society—through exploration, the conquest of distant lands, the subjugation of their inhabitants, and the establishment of Europeans as colonial rulers or as settlers displacing the original peoples. By European standards, North America, the Pacific islands, Australia, and Cape Colony in South Africa were thinly settled, and the populations were so inferior in military technology that resistance was hopeless.

The period of European exploration, conquest, and settlement set into motion the most sustained and pervasive contacts between different peoples that the world has ever seen. When it had run its course, there was hardly anyone left on the face of the earth who had not been affected in some way. Even isolated nomads in the Arctic and in remote deserts had encountered representatives of European civilization or the products of Western technology.

During the peak of empire building, all of the Western Hemisphere, Africa, Oceania, and much of Asia were carved into colonies or spheres of influence of European powers. Societies were brought into existence in which the dominance of one people over another was the foundation of the social order.

RAMPANT COLONIALISM

The style of European conquest, irrespective of national origin, was grounded in ignorance of other cultures, disdain for weaker peoples, and excessive application of force. Given the combination of avarice, religious zeal, and self-confidence, perhaps it could not have been otherwise.

As it was, the practices of the rulers were ethnocentric to a degree that is difficult to imagine in the modern world. The Europeans sometimes followed formal legal routines for the sake of keeping the record straight, but when they violated their own laws and mores, the violations were often condoned because the victims were not parties to the laws and were therefore not considered eligible for treatment due "civilized" men. Not being Christians, the natives could not take oaths; not being able to take oaths, they could not testify in courts. Consequently punishable offenses by whites never came to trial unless observed by another white who was willing to testify—a rare occurrence.

Although the home countries often had good intentions about the indigenous peoples, colonial administration at best was a difficult and often impossible task. The colonizers were distant in space and time from the restraints of home, and the explorers and settlers were chosen for their courage and self-reliance, not their forbearance and tolerance. When personal security hung in the balance, a handful of isolated men were likely to view the natives as expendable, and the natives soon learned not to be friendly.

The terms of submission There was variation from time to time and place to place, but the perceptions of the Indians of San Salvador by the conquistadores and the terms on which the Indians had to submit give a fair indication of what went on almost everywhere for a long time. But note that the brutality was not countenanced by a priest:

Columbus remarked of the Lucayans [the inhabitants of San Salvador]: "These people are very unskilled in arms . . . with fifty men they could all be subjected and made to do all that one wished." He and his compatriots tricked and cheated the Indians at every turn. Before entering a new area, Spanish generals customarily read a *Requerimiento* (requirement) to the inhabitants. This long-winded document recited the history of mankind from the Creation to the division of the non-Christian world by Pope Alexander VI and then called upon the Indians to recognize the sovereignty of the reigning Spanish monarch. ("If you do so . . . we shall receive you in all love and charity.") If this demand was rejected, "we shall powerfully enter into your country, and . . . shall take you, your wives, and your children, and shall make slaves of them. . . . The death and losses which shall accrue from this are your fault." This arrogant harangue was read *in Spanish* and often out of earshot of the Indians. When they responded by fighting, the Spaniards decimated them, drove them from

their lands, and held the broken survivors in contempt. As a priest among them said, the *conquistadores* behaved "like the most cruel Tygres, Wolves, and Lions, enrag'd with a sharp and tedious hunger" (Garraty, 1971:21).

Three centuries later the accents and locales were different, but one-sided "understandings" with more legal niceties led to the same consequences:

The British Government acquired territory throughout Africa by hundreds of treaties with African chiefs. Indeed, at one time the Foreign Office provided printed treaty forms for the use of officials and explorers. The Boers made a few such treaties; but whether British or Boer, all the treaties were in reality valueless. In the first place, the chief had no power to alienate land; in the second place, what he thought he was doing was to give the Europeans the usufruct [the right of use], not the possession, of it. In their ignorance of tribal custom, Europeans of all nations made what they thought were contracts by which the land became theirs, and to this day they all argue that their particular colony was acquired by genuine treaty. What really happened was that two totally different conceptions of land-ownership were in conflict, and neither side knew or recognized the conflict (Marquard, 1969: 12–13).

With the exception of South Africa, black Africa did not become a place of major settlement by Europeans. It was valued by the colonial empires for its products, which were sold in the world market, and for a long time its most important product was slaves. Much of Africa was already densely occupied, and European conquerors wanted to exploit the manpower rather than to displace it.

Although all conquered peoples were treated badly, the ones who mobilized credible military resistance were treated better. The New Zealand Maoris and some of the African and Amerindian peoples were formidable adversaries. In New Zealand, Canada, and the United States, treaties were made with the native peoples as "nations" that had legitimate governments and that cultivated their lands or used them in some other way that could be recognized by Europeans as true occupancy. However, compensation for confiscated land was rarely adequate, and conflicting ideas of what the contract entailed—that is, use versus possession—resulted in the same confusion as in Africa. In North America, treaties that invested control over a diminished part of tribal lands in the hands of the tribe "forever" were soon whittled away in subsequent treaties.

The experience of the Cherokee people, the great tribe of the Southern Appalachians, is a case in point. Between 1721 and 1783, ten treaties involving land cessions were made between Cherokee towns and Southern colonies or states. Between 1785 and 1835, 12 treaties were executed with the United States, and Cherokee holdings east of the Mississippi were almost extinguished (Royce, 1887:131, 378).

In some cases, and contrary to Indian custom, lands were ordered to be distributed to members of the tribes as personal holdings, but such property soon ended up in the possession of whites through purchase. The drama of conflict over land ownership is not yet concluded. More recently, land cases against the United States have been taken to the courts by Indian peoples. Grounds that inadequate compensation was paid, that force was applied, or that legal procedures were not followed have enabled the Indians to prevail and, generations after the despoliation, to receive some compensation.

THE PLANTATION

Three interacting factors were involved in the economic mobilization of undeveloped regions: ample land, scarce labor, and staple crops in demand on the world market. It did not matter much whether the land was in Asia, Africa, or the Americas nor whether the crops were sugar, tobacco, cotton, rubber, or something else; similar economic prob-

lems led to similar interracial situations. Settlers soon learned there was unoccupied acreage ready for the taking, and there was no reason for them to continue to work for wages. To make use of the "empty" land, the planters somehow had to control the movement of labor to keep their workers, and slavery was one institutional technique (Nieboer, 1900). Other methods used to solve the manpower shortage included induced immigration, convict labor, indenture, and the importation of contract laborers.

When the developers of the Hawaiian plantations, who were mostly Americans, found that Polynesians were an insufficient labor supply for the expanding agricultural economy, contract laborers were brought in from Asia. The largest groups were 45,000 Chinese in the last quarter of the nineteenth century, then 140,000 Japanese between 1890 and 1919, and then 125,000 Filipinos between 1909 and 1934. The recruited workers were unwilling to remain on the plantations and each grouping in turn left agricultural labor, creating a vacuum to be filled by newer immigrants (Lind, 1938; estimates by Norman Meller). The amalgam of peoples that make up contemporary Hawaii is thus in part a result of productive opportunities and a labor shortage. Forced labor is the ultimate solution to the problems of labor supply in the plantation economy.

In recent years there has been renewed scholarly attention to slavery in the New World (see, for example, Foner and Genovese, 1969:esp. bibliography, 262–268; Genovese, 1974). In large part the work has been stimulated by Tannenbaum's *Slave and Citizen* (1947), upon which Adaptation 34 is based. Subsequent research has somewhat blunted the contrasts posed by Tannenbaum regarding slavery in Anglo-America and Latin America. However, the slave trade and slavery are a stubborn heritage that cannot be erased from the study of race relations.

Adaptation 34 Tannenbaum: Slavery in the Americas

The slave trade from Africa to the New World continued for almost four centuries, until near the close of the nineteenth century. It involved the transportation of perhaps 20 million persons, untold millions of deaths and suffering, and the settlement and economic development of vast territories. In some measure all the nations of Europe participated, and each approached slavery and the slave trade with different historical experiences and different forms of institutional adaptation, particularly in law, religion, and economics.

Consequently there developed in the New World at least three identifiable slave systems, differing in the way the slave was regarded and treated. One system, practiced by the British, Americans, Dutch, and Danish, began with no effective slave tradition, no laws explicitly governing the status of slaves, and little religious concern about them. The Spanish and Portuguese system was based upon a continuing experience with slavery, a codified law regulating the status of the slave and relations between slave and master, and a religious appreciation of the spiritual personality of the slave. The French system lacked a slave tradition and law but shared the religious principles of the Spanish and Portuguese.

In all places the slave trade was extensive and profitable, and exceedingly cruel. The business developed special ways of handling the human cargo in which it dealt, and a kind of opaqueness to human suffering grew upon those engaged in it. Slavery itself became the dominant social institution where it was practiced. So inclusive was the influence of slavery that it might be better to speak not of a system of slavery but of the total pattern as a slave society. Wherever there was slavery, there was a slave society, not merely for the blacks but for the whites, not merely for the law but for the family, not merely for the labor system but for the total culture. Nothing escaped. The institution was the society in all of its manifestations. Nevertheless, there were differences in the degree of severity in the conduct of slavery. That of the northern nations was more severe, that of Spain and Portu-

Source: Slave and Citizen: The Negro in the Americas by Frank Tannenbaum (New York: Random House, 1947/1963). By permission of the publisher.

gal less so. The Dutch were probably the most severe, the Portuguese the least.

In the following discussion the British and American experience is compared with the Portuguese-Brazilian. In the former, the American South is the focus of attention. The British West Indies were an important part of the continental slave system as well as major slave users, and the islands were often a stopping-off "seasoning" place for slaves destined for the mainland.

SLAVERY IN BRAZIL

Although slavery had died out in the rest of Western Europe before the start of the modern slave trade from Africa, it had persisted in Portugal and Spain, and therefore Negro slaves were viewed in the same way as the Moors, Jews, and Spaniards who were slaves. The Mediterranean legal mores regarded slavery as the result of misfortune. The soul of the slave was thought to remain free. The master, who might have been a slave, had no greater moral status than the slave, who was protected by a body of law as a human being. Even

Human stowage in an eighteenth century slave trader out of Liverpool. These drawings were used in antislavery campaigns.

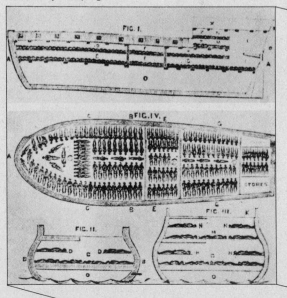

while in bondage, the slave had both a legal and moral personality.

Manumission Law, custom, and tradition were biased in favor of freedom and opened the gates to manumission. Tax gatherers did not oppose it, and the church ranked it among the works singularly agreeable to God. A hundred social devices narrowed the gap between bondage and liberty and encouraged the master to release the slaves and the slaves to achieve freedom by their own efforts. In Brazil, slaves could compel their masters to free them by reimbursing the original purchase price. And the right to have their price declared aided the Negroes in seeking a new master. The law further permitted the slaves to buy their own freedom in installments.

In effect, slavery under both law and custom had become a contractual arrangement between the slave owner and slave. There may have been no written contract, but the state behaved as if such a contract did exist and used its powers to enforce it. Slavery had thus from a very early date changed from being defined as caste because of innate inferiority or provision of holy script to a matter of the availability of money for redemption. By that fact it lost a great part of the degrading imputation that attached to slavery where it was looked upon as evidence of moral or biological inferiority. Slavery could be wiped out by a fixed purchase price, and therefore its taint was not indelible.

In addition to making freedom something obtainable for money, which the slave had the right to acquire, manumission was possible for other reasons. A Negro could be freed if unduly punished by his master. He was allowed to marry a free woman, and, as under the law the children followed the mother, a slave's children born of a free mother were also free. Slaves who participated in the armed forces were freed.

In the long run social arrangements and expectancies made a greater impact on manumission than did legal provisions. It was permissible for a slave child to be freed at baptism by an offer of a small sum. A female slave could seek a godfather for her baby, hoping that the moral obligation would lead to the child's freedom. It was both meritorious and pious to accept such a responsibility and to fulfill its implicit commitments.

The freeing of one's slaves was an honorific tradition. Favorite wet nurses were often freed. A parent having ten children could claim freedom. Slaves were manumitted on happy occasions in the family: a birth of a first son, the marriage of one of the master's children, the passing of a school examination by the young master, a family festival, a national holiday. Provision for manumission was also often written into the master's will. A cataloging of the occasions for manumission in Brazil might almost lead one to wonder at the persistence of slavery, but importations were large and continuous late into the nineteenth century.

Because, especially in cities, slaves were encouraged to hire themselves out and bring their masters a fixed part of their wages, they could accumulate their purchase price. Furthermore, the prevailing system of labor opened opportunities for escape from slavery in addition to legally provided manumission. Even in rural regions where cruelty, hardship, and inhumanity was probably most severe and where abuse was less subject to public scrutiny, slaves were allowed to sell products from their own plots and to save money for their freedom. The purchase of freedom was so accepted that many persons while still slaves bought the freedom of their wives and children. Among freed Negroes, cooperative societies were organized to pool resources and collect funds for freeing their brethren still in bondage.

Role of the church Without interfering with the institution of slavery where the domestic law accepted it, the church early condemned the slave trade and prohibited Catholics from taking part. Although the prohibition was not effective, it may have limited participation in the trade. Five popes between 1462 and 1839 condemned the slave trade, but the church did not interfere where slavery derived from established practices such as born slaves, slaves taken in war, those who had sold themselves, or those who had been condemned by a legitimate court.

The church's insistence that slaves and masters were equal in the sight of God was most important. Masters were obliged to protect the spiritual integrity of slaves, to teach them the Christian religion, to help them achieve the privileges of the sacraments, to guide them into a good life, and to protect them from mortal sin. The slave had a right to become a Christian. Baptism was considered an entrance into the Christian community, and the Catholic churches insisted that masters bring their slaves to church to learn the doctrine and participate in communion. Master and slaves attended church on Sundays, and the slaves gathered nightly before the master's house to receive his blessing. As Catholics, slaves were married in church, and the slave's family gained a moral and religious character. Married by the church, they could not be separated by the master.

Status of freed slaves Because slavery carried no taint, because it was a misfortune that had befallen a human being and was in itself sufficiently oppressive, the status of the freed slave carried little or no stigma resulting from prior slave status. Freed slaves and their descendants were incorporated into the community according to their skills and abilities, into the priesthood, the regular army, private and public employment, and even public office. Free Negroes had full rights before the law, and were allowed to hold property and take part in public life.

SLAVERY IN ANGLO-AMERICA

In the British colonies and the United States, both law and custom combined to equate the Negro with slave status. Because there was a great diversity of laws in the different jurisdictions and in any one place at different times, the following summary does not apply in all details to all places.

Legal status Because there was no legal tradition affecting slavery in Britain, when the first slaves were brought in contact with the English they did not know what to do with them. At first slaves were interpreted as indentured servants, but the analogy soon broke down. Indentured servants had a contract for a limited number of years, after which they would be free. The master assumed financial obligations. The relationship was recognized as temporary and dischargeable by a specified sum. The servant was a Christian and had rights to his wife and children, over whom the master had no legal control.

On the other hand, slaves had been bought from a third person. There was no time limit to their service. The master had no financial obligations to them. Slaves had no legal family and no rights in the law, and they acquired none by contract. The Protestant churches with their slow, hesitant, and doubtful approach to conversion increased the legal isolation of slaves. If they were neither free nor indentured servants, declaring them chattels solved the legal puzzle. But the powers of the master were then enormously increased, and the Negro slave was reduced to a beast of the field. The many thousands of instances of kindness, affection, and understanding between master and slave were personal and had no standing in the law. While the impact of the law could not completely wipe out the fact that the Negro slave was human, it raised a sufficient barrier to make most difficult the ultimate redefinition of the Negro as free. Negroes who could not prove that they were free were presumed to be runaway slaves and were advertised as such.

Religious disabilities In the British West Indies, slaves were denied the privileges of Christianity, and the Church of England did not recognize slaves as baptizable human beings. Although after 1700 there was no systematic opposition in the United States to teaching Christian doctrine to slaves, regulations forbidding assembly for worship before dawn or after dark, prohibition on Negro preachers, and opposition to Negro literacy impeded the development of religious life. The marriages of slaves were frequently not solemnized, and in any event, husband and wife, parents and children could be separated for satisfaction of the master's debts or simply as a business transaction.

Manumission In most British colonies, heavy taxes were imposed on manumission; financial payments were required of an owner who wanted to free his slaves by grant or will. South Carolina in 1740, as well as Georgia and Mississippi, provided that "all negroes, Indians (those now free excepted), mulattoes or mestizos, who are or shall hereafter be in the province, and all their issue and offspring, born or to be born, shall be and they are hereby declared to be and remain forever hereafter absolute slaves and shall follow the condition of the mother." There was no provision for self-redemption by purchase. Manumission thus was the only route to freedom, but in many slave-holding states and colonies a freed slave was obliged to leave the jurisdiction within a short time, never to return.

In several states manumission was valid only

with the consent of the legislature, and the master was often obliged to post a surety bond before manumission. In Tennessee (1801) manumission required a bond, court consent, and immediate departure. In Mississippi (1822) the master had to prove to the general assembly that the slave had performed a meritorious deed, whereupon a special act could be passed sanctioning the specific manumission.

Unlike in Brazil, there was no custom of freeing children at baptism and no godfather for the slave child, nor could the slave acquire money to purchase the freedom of his children. The slave had no redemption price and could not accumulate property to buy his freedom. Indeed he could acquire no property, for it would belong to his master. Manumission was an abandonment of the owner's authority, but it did not convey to the freed slave the civil and political rights of a freeborn person. In spite of being manumitted, the liberated Negro was not considered a free moral agent.

Emancipation In the United States and in the British West Indies, the abolition of slavery found both the Negro and white communities unprepared for freedom. The number of freed slaves was small and their role in the free community greatly re-

Humanity in bondage, nineteenth century: a South American slave mother.

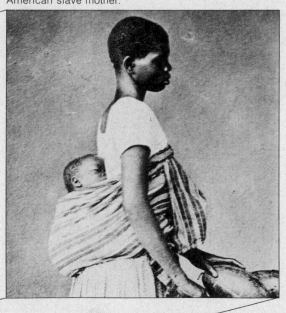

stricted; it was unable to absorb and direct the large body of slaves suddenly freed. On the other hand, in Brazil the centuries-long process of manumission and the hundreds of thousands of free blacks who occupied a wide range of positions in the social structure prepared the nation for abolition. By the time of emancipation Brazil had three times as many free Negroes as slaves. Even though it came later than in the United States, abolition came peacefully and as a manifestation of the national will.

CONCLUSION AND CAUTION

Nearly a generation has passed since Tannenbaum's essay was first published. Recent scholarship has thrown doubts on his more sweeping generalizations about the degree of protection given the slaves by law and the church in Latin America compared with British America.

Notwithstanding variations within every colony as a result of environment, economic conditions, social institutions, and the personality of owners, the Negro was everywhere a mobile and transferable possession whose labor and well-being were controlled by another man. Any comparison of slavery in North and South America should take account of the fact that Brazil alone had an area and variety comparable to all British America, and that the privileged artisans, porters, and domestic servants of colonial Brazilian cities can be compared only with their counterparts in New York and Philadelphia. Similarly, conditions in nineteenth-century Alabama and Mississippi must be held against those in the interior coffee-growing areas of south-central Brazil (Davis, 1966:243).

Although the question of the relative severity of slavery is an important and unresolved issue, the lasting significance of Tannenbaum's interpretation is not merely the suggestion that on the whole slaves in Brazil were better treated than slaves in British America; it is rather that the Spanish and Portuguese systems embraced practices and attitudes such as manumission and the acceptance of freed slaves that gave the two societies a different character, especially in the assimilation of Negroes in Brazil. The relative frequency of manumission and its institutional supports were crucial and as yet undisputed differences between Brazil and the United States. These differences not only affected the statuses of the former slaves but may have made a lasting impress on race relations in the two countries.

Section three accommodation and resistance

Slavery was the most important influence in the making of American minorities—more important than the conquest of the Indian tribes, the massive immigrations from Europe, and the lesser immigration from Asia. This is so because it created the largest of American minorities, established a fateful contradiction between political ideals and social realities, conditioned the movement of the frontier and the flow of Europeans to America, and built into American life a pattern of domination that is a continuing if declining theme. The slaves, freedmen, and contemporary blacks had to invent ways to cope with subordination, and their adaptations, past and present, influence the adjustment of other minorities in North America and around the world.

Before the days of organized, sophisticated, and militant resistance, some people with unique personal resources were able to make it on their own. Frederick Douglass (1960), a man of great intellectual and personal qualities, was one (Foner, 1950–1955). Sojourner Truth was another. (See p. 454.) But most people struggled simply to protect their families from the worst ravages of abuse and to live out their lives in a facsimile of peace.

In the 1940s Myrdal wrote that "from the actual power situation in America *the beliefs held by white people rather than those held by Negroes are of primary importance*" (1944:110). In the 1970s the statement is still true, but the beliefs of blacks are now given closer attention, and white beliefs have significantly changed. The changing patterns of protest during this century are summarized in Adaptation 35. The growing political competence and power of blacks and their diminished willingness to accept the collaboration of whites have been conspicuous elements of change.

Slavery was based upon absolute domination, but it did not separate the races. Although Negroes, free or slave, were excluded from restaurants and hotels except as servants, there was only rudimentary residential segregation under slavery. After the collapse of Reconstruction, when the federal troops were withdrawn from the South in 1877, the status of the freed slaves rapidly deteriorated. The accomplishments of the immediate postwar years were vitiated, and forms of social relations grew up that in some respects were as harsh and arbitrary as slavery itself.

LIVING WITH JIM CROW

Toward the end of the nineteenth century and with accelerating speed into the twentieth century, blacks were hemmed in, isolated, and controlled, first by informal rules and increasingly by local ordinances and state laws. Segregation and discrimination came to govern the conduct of blacks from the cradle to the grave, and they were utterly regulated, at least in their contacts with whites. Jim Crow was a new style of repression, not simply a modified form of the controls exercised under slavery (Doyle, 1937; Woodward, 1966).

The ordinances were so numerous and were enacted by so many legislative bodies that confusion and uncertainty were a part of everyday life. Black travelers were especially vulnerable because customs and laws varied so much from place to place. Even within the same city, rules were inconsistent and facilities differed. "For example, at the Union Station in Atlanta, Negroes may leave the waiting room provided for them and patronize the newsstand and lunch counter in the white waiting room. At the Terminal Station in the same city, they cannot enter the white waiting room for any purpose" (Johnson, 1943:46).

The Jim Crow laws put the authority of the state or city in the voice of the street-car conductor, the railway brakeman, the bus driver, the theater usher, and also into the voice of the hoodlum of the public parks and playgrounds. They gave free rein and the majesty of the law to mass aggressions that might otherwise have been curbed, blunted, or deflected.

Sojourner Truth: free woman

*Slavery is the ultimate institutional
assault on the personality, but some
slaves found the strength to surmount
the degradations of slavery and to
strive for freedom, both for themselves
and for others. The accounts of such
persons are rare in part because
illiteracy was an ingredient of the slave
condition, but the few documents that
survive reveal figures of heroic
dimensions. One such person was
Sojourner Truth, born in the 1790s in
Ulster County, New York, who had no
schooling and was illiterate.*

*For the first half of her life she was
known by her slave name, Isabella.
Separated from her parents before she
was ten, she was eventually bought by
a man named Dumont with whom she
remained for 18 years, "marrying" the
slave he designated. Dumont promised
to free her a year before slaves in New
York were due to be emancipated, but
when she asked for her papers he said
that he would keep her the additional
year because he had suffered losses
due to the birth of one of her children.
She stayed until the wool was spun to
repay the losses, but she then took her
youngest child and left. When Dumont
came after her, the family that had
taken her in bought her and her infant
and set them free.*

*Just out of bondage, she had resorted to the
law to free her son from an Alabama
plantation; later, as a domestic in New
York, she had been the first Negro to file
and win a suit for slander against
prominent whites. The latter case, involving
a much-talked-about religious scandal, had
occasioned two books—one grossly abusive
. . . the other championing her and
incidentally supplying us with such
material as the full employment record of
her first years in freedom (Pauli, 1962:11).*

Source: *Her Name Was Sojourner Truth* by
Hertha Pauli (New York: Avon Books, 1962) and
Feminism: The Essential Historical Writings,
edited by Miriam Schnier (New York: Random
House, 1972).

*Because religion was a dominant
influence on her, she spent the latter
half of her life traveling the country,
lecturing and preaching, hence the
name she took for herself: Sojourner
Truth. She addressed her audiences as
"children" because, she said, they were
all the children of God, and she was
old enough to be their mother anyhow.
Before the Civil War, her audiences
were mostly white, and she spoke often
for abolitionism, but after emancipation
she urged freed persons to grasp what
the war had won for them.*

*Abolitionism absorbed much of her
attention, but she was also a
campaigner for feminism, and she was
the only black woman to attend the
first national woman's rights
convention in 1850. In 1851 at a
women's convention in Akron, Ohio,
she gave a speech that is one of the
most eloquent entries in the feminist
literature, a portion of which follows:*

Well, children, where there is so much
racket there must be something out of
kilter. I think that 'twixt the Negroes of the
South and the women of the North, all
talking about rights, the white men will be
in a fix pretty soon. But what's all this here
talking about?

That man over there says that women
need to be helped into carriages, and lifted
over ditches, and to have the best place
everywhere. Nobody ever helps me into
carriages, or over mud-puddles, or gives me
any best place! And ain't I a woman? Look
at me! I have ploughed and planted, and
gathered into barns, and no man could
head me! And ain't I a woman? I could
work as much and eat as much as a man—
when I could get it and bear the lash as
well! And ain't I a woman? I have bourne
thirteen children, and seen the most all
sold off to slavery, and when I cried out
with my mother's grief, none but Jesus
heard me! And ain't I a woman? (Schnier,
1972:94–95).

*About 15 years later, when the major
issue was Negro suffrage, she said:*

I hear so much about colored men getting
their rights but, not a word about colored
women. . . . I want women to have their

rights, and while the water is stirring I'll step into the pool. Now that there's a stir about colored men's rights is the time for women to get theirs. . . . You never lose anything by asking everything. If you bait this suffrage hook with a woman, you'll surely catch a black man (Pauli, 1962:220–221).

After emancipation she concentrated her efforts on working for the welfare of freed persons and campaigned for government land in the West so they could become economically independent. She taught housekeeping skills to ex-slaves who had been field hands. When children were kidnapped from freedmen's camps to Maryland (while abolition was still being argued in the courts in that state), she persuaded frightened mothers to swear out warrants for the return of their children, as she herself had done many years before.

After the Civil War, public transportation in Washington, D.C., was legally desegregated, but few ex-slaves were willing to test their legal rights. Sojourner Truth took up the challenge and on her visits to the city seized every opportunity to ride. On one occasion her shoulder was dislocated when a conductor attempted to push her off a streetcar, but Sojourner Truth always insisted on her rights. Throughout her life this most modern of nineteenth-century women, slave or free, worked to change the system, and even in her old age she was a desegregation activist.

"Jim Crow" was a blackface minstrel character—a Negro impersonation created by T. D. Rice in 1832—that helped form the stereotype of a subservient, antic, childlike Negro male. Later Jim Crow came to refer to a pattern of racial domination.

The Jim Crow laws, unlike feudal laws, did not assign the subordinate group a fixed status in society. They were constantly pushing the Negro farther down (Woodward, 1966:107–108).

The multiplication of whites who could legally control the actions of blacks in specific situations encouraged white bullies to be openly aggressive in any situation. For them "nigger baiting" was a safe game, with the odds comfortably on their side. Daily life became increasingly insecure for blacks. They developed a style of etiquette that was a travesty of politeness. Obsequiousness, feigned ignorance, and strategies of apparent compliance thinly veiled their resentment. For example:

A Negro who lived in Atlanta, where Negroes board streetcars at the rear, went to Birmingham, where Negroes board streetcars at the front. Hence, on one occasion, when he stopped a streetcar, he got on at the wrong end. He said, however, that he apologized to the conductor by saying that he thought the car was going the other way (Doyle, 1937:235).

Public transportation has always been a focal point in the struggle against discrimination. It was a sphere in which minorities might be manipulated but also one in which they could and sometimes did strike back. Around the end of the nineteenth century, there was a flood of legislation segregating railways and later streetcars. It is a historical coincidence that in 1906 Montgomery was the first city in the United States to require separate streetcars for the two races, and in 1955–1956 it again attracted attention as the scene of the successful bus boycott that gave impetus to the movement led by Martin Luther King.

It must not be assumed that in the two generations after Reconstruction race relations were only aggressiveness on one side and subservience on the other, arrogance on one side and adaptive etiquette on the other. Most whites did not take part in abusing blacks, nor did they favor such acts, but not many had the courage or the will overtly to challenge the practices of the time. However, the new repressive rules were quickly rationalized by some whites as permanent and inevitable aspects of race relations. There were outbursts of personal defiance by blacks, occasional boycotts, and many individual acts of steadfast courage. Not the least of these were behaviors that are often misunderstood and stigmatized as "Uncle Tomism" but were in fact disguised defiance. As often as not, Uncle Tom behavior was a put-on, an ingenious social invention designed to reduce tension, escape abuse, and survive.

THE PASSING OF JIM CROW

Although remnants of Jim Crow still exist, rules upholding segregation are now more often violated than obeyed; and because they no longer have the support of law, they are usually violated with impunity. The causes of these changes are to be found in the

evolving protest movement, a complex phenomenon that is reviewed in detail in Adaptation 35. The first efforts to break down
segregation were relatively uncoordinated
and localized, but by the mid-1960s the civil
rights movement was national in scope, in
resources, and in objectives. The school
desegregation case was a truly national event,
and other events such as the Montgomery
bus boycott, the desegregation of the armed
forces (Fahy Committee, 1950; Moskos,
1966), the desegregation of professional
baseball, and the destereotyping of radio,
television, and film characters (Cripps, 1967)
proved that change was possible and helped
set the scene for further change.

Separatism The long-term trend has been
toward increased integration, but there have
been repeated countertrends, and the current mood is a mixed one, including a drift
toward separatism. Some black separatist
tendencies were responses to segregation
pressures from whites, and some were expressions of nationalism. Recent separatism
has been more militant than accommodative, and this has concerned both white and
black liberals whose common objective has
been to reduce the distance between the
races, to increase communication, and,
thereby, to maximize opportunities for
minorities—in short, to fulfill the American

promise. To strengthen their effectiveness
in the civil rights movement, liberals need
desegregation and increased interaction with
minorities. They are disillusioned to discover that they are expendable and that declining contact has accompanied visible
progress.

The major issues and problems of separatism were displayed in microcosm when
black studies and other ethnic programs
were established in many American universities. Controversy revolved around the degree of autonomy to be granted to the programs, the amount and character of student
participation in determining courses of study
and selecting staff, and, most important, the
degree of participation, if any, of nonminor-
ity students in these programs (Rustin et al.,
1969).

Under considerable pressure, some university administrations accepted the principle that black studies centers should be
exclusively black. When Antioch College
opted for an exclusively black program,
Kenneth B. Clark, a black educator and social psychologist, resigned from the board
of directors of the college. His action drama-
tizes the dilemmas introduced into the educational system when the values of race
pride and solidarity collide with the principle of integration.

457

*Adaptation 35
Meier and
Rudwick:
Patterns of
protest,
1900–1970*

Adaptation 35 Meier and Rudwick: Patterns of protest, 1900–1970

*The struggle of American blacks against oppres-
sion has been characterized by a number of
recurrent themes: accommodation, economic self-
sufficiency, black nationalism, legal reform, and
social protest. Thus far in the twentieth century,
protest has been the most lasting and powerful
force. The major components of the movement and
their competing strategies and tactics are discussed in the following survey of recent black
history in the United States.*

Source: Abridged and adapted by permission from "Introduction" by
August Meier and Elliott Rudwick in *Black Protest Thought in the Twentieth
Century*, Second edition, edited by August Meier, Elliott Rudwick, and
Francis L. Broderick. Copyright © 1965, 1971 by the Bobbs-Merrill Com-
pany, Inc.

THE STRATEGY OF ACCOMMODATION

As the nineteenth century drew to a close, the
position of blacks in American society was de-

W. E. B. Du Bois (1868–1963), American historian, sociologist, and activist. Either of his two early works, *The Suppression of the African Slave-Trade to the United States of America* (1896) or *The Philadelphia Negro* (1899), was sufficient to establish his place in the world of scholarship. In addition, at Atlanta University (1897–1910) he published a pioneering series of community studies using questionnaire and survey techniques. Du Bois participated in the foundation of the NAACP, in which he served as director of research and editor of the magazine *Crisis* from 1910 until 1934. Long a leader in the pan-African movement, he became a citizen of Ghana just before his death. (See Broderick, 1959; and Rudwick, 1960.)

clining steadily. Disfranchisement, lynchings, Jim Crow laws, and farm tenancy were their lot in the South. Throughout the country, labor unions excluded them from the skilled trades. After 1900 race riots became a commonplace in both North and South, with Negroes as victims of mob attacks upon the black minority. Under these conditions, protest and agitation waned, and a philosophy of accommodation gained the upper hand.

The most prominent representative of this trend was Booker T. Washington, principal of the Tuskegee Institute in Alabama. Between his famous Atlanta Exposition Address in 1895 and his death in 1915, Washington was the most prominent black man in America. Though he covertly spent thousands of dollars fighting disfranchisement and segregation laws, he publicly advocated a policy of conciliation and gradualism. Largely blaming black people themselves for their condition and describing the southern white man as "the Negro's best friend," he minimized the extent of racial prejudice and discrimination, accepted segregation and the separate-but-equal doctrine, depre-

cated political activity, favored vocational training and working with the hands at the expense of higher education and the professions, and recommended economic accumulation and the cultivation of Christian character as the best methods for advancing the status of blacks in America. Washington's ultimate aims were stated so vaguely and ambiguously that southern whites mistook his means for his ends. But his black supporters understood that through tact and indirection he hoped to secure the goodwill of white people and the ultimate recognition of the blacks' citizenship rights.

Despite Washington's prominence, black protest, though temporarily muted, did not completely disappear. The media of mass communication and the public at large, both black and white, regarded the Montgomery, Alabama, bus boycott of 1955–1956 as a radical innovation. But at the opening of the century Negroes had conducted boycotts of trolley car segregation in nearly 30 southern cities, in protest against Jim Crow arrangements then being introduced in state after state throughout the South. Curiously, these boycotts were ordinarily led by some of the most conservative members of the black community—businessmen and clerics who were often close friends of the accommodator, Booker T. Washington. Trolley car boycotts were a "conservative" protest movement in that they attempted to preserve the status quo against a radical change pushed by lower-class whites. As a tactic of withdrawal, the boycotts avoided rather than precipitated a confrontation with the racist whites.

BEYOND ACCOMMODATION

After the turn of the century, accommodation and separatism were challenged by a small band of militant black intellectuals. Led by W. E. B. Du Bois, at that time a professor at Atlanta University, they formed in 1905 the all-black Niagara Movement to oppose Washington's program, which they denounced as a failure. The Niagara group placed full responsibility for the race problem squarely on the whites. They denounced segregation, the separate-but-equal doctrine, and the disfranchisement laws. They maintained that economic progress was not possible in a democratic society without the protection afforded by the ballot and insisted that blacks could gain their rights only by agitation and complaint. These militant black integrationists spoke out against accommodation and black separatism at a time when these policies were endorsed by nearly all influential whites and the most powerful among the Negro leaders.

The NAACP Despite all of Booker T. Washington's efforts to crush them, the black radicals carried the message of protest and the demand for integration to prominent white progressives and socialists. Together, in 1909–1910, they formed the National Association for the Advancement of Colored People (NAACP), with the announced goal of fighting for black people's constitutional rights and the undeclared aim of curbing Booker T. Washington's power. Given the context of the times, it was the wealth, prominence, and influence of a small band of concerned whites that made it possible for the radical blacks to push their program with some degree of effectiveness. From the start, the NAACP branches were typically black both in members and leaders; but at the national

headquarters Du Bois, as editor of *The Crisis* and director of research, was the only black executive until James Weldon Johnson became the association's secretary in 1921.

It is very difficult today, with the NAACP under attack as gradualist and conservative, to understand that in 1910 contemporaries regarded its position on the race question as exceedingly radical. Through propaganda and publicity, through litigation in the courts and lobbying in the legislatures, the NAACP took the first legal steps in the lengthy struggle against disfranchisement and residential segregation.

The NAACP gained strength from the large numbers of southern Negroes who had migrated to northern cities and from a small but growing black bourgeoisie of professionals and business executives who served them. The NAACP did extraordinary service, giving legal defense to victims of race riots and unjust judicial proceedings. It obtained the release of the soldiers who had received life sentences on charges of rioting against intolerable conditions in Houston in 1917. It successfully defended black sharecroppers in Arkansas who in 1919 had banded together to gain fairer treatment, had become the objects of a massive armed hunt by whites to put them "in their place," and had then faced charges of insurrection when they resisted. A major effort of the NAACP during the 1920s was to secure passage of an antilynching bill. Though the law was not enacted, the NAACP rallied a great deal of public support, and the number of lynchings gradually declined in the nation.

The New Deal and rising expectations The election of Franklin Delano Roosevelt marked a turning point in American race relations. To be sure, the New Deal programs were not free of discrimination. Federal housing policies expanded urban ghettoes; the Agricultural Administration subsidized white landowners; and crop restrictions forced many black sharecroppers off the land. Nevertheless, black people shared in relief, jobs, and public housing, and black leaders, who felt the open sympathy of many highly placed New Dealers, held more prominent political positions than at any time since President Taft's administration. At the same time, the black vote had reached sizable proportions in many northern cities, creating an additional motivation for the

459

Adaptation 35
Meier and
Rudwick:
Patterns of
protest,
1900–1970

attention to black welfare among New Deal politicians. By 1936, blacks had deserted their traditional allegiance to the Republican party, the party of Abraham Lincoln. Finally, the emergence of the Congress of Industrial Organizations (CIO), which attempted to erase racial discrimination, gave some substance to the dream of an alliance of black and white workers for the first time since the decline of the Knights of Labor nearly a half century earlier.

In the favorable atmosphere of the 1930s, the NAACP broadened the scope of its legal work and continued its attack on the white primaries; ultimately (in 1944) the Supreme Court handed down a decision that ended Southern subterfuge on that issue. But the core of NAACP legal strategy in the 1930s was the long-range battle against segregation. For tactical reasons the chief emphasis was placed upon educational discrimination. The strategy adopted was to attack the obvious inequities—the lower salaries paid black teachers and the absence of graduate and professional schools for Negroes in Southern states—hoping that segregation would become so expensive and burdensome that it would fall of its own weight. Not until about 1950 did the association decide to attack directly the principle of segregation in the schools, on the grounds that segregated facilities were inherently unequal.

Nonviolent direct action In the early part of World War II two new movements anticipated later developments: the March on Washington Movement and the Congress of Racial Equality (CORE). In 1941 A. Philip Randolph, black socialist and president of the Brotherhood of Sleeping Car Porters, threatened a mass march on Washington unless President Roosevelt secured employment for blacks in the discriminatory defense industries. The president's Executive Order 8802 establishing a federal Fair Employment Practices Commission (FEPC) forestalled the demonstration. Even without enforcement powers, the FEPC set a precedent for treating fair employment practice as a civil right. The short-lived March on Washington Movement prefigured future trends as an explicitly all-black organization basing its strategy on mass action by the urban slum dwellers and concentrating on economic problems.

Randolph's approach was greatly influenced by the tactics of Gandhi's movement of nonviolent

resistance in India, as was his postwar campaign against Jim Crow in the armed services. But it was CORE that was chiefly responsible for projecting the use of nonviolent direct action as a civil rights strategy. CORE combined Gandhi's techniques with the sit-in, derived from the sit-down strikes of the 1930s. Until about 1959, CORE's main activity was attacking discrimination in places of public accommodation in the cities of the northern and border states. A cornerstone of its philosophy was that American racism could be destroyed only through an interracial movement.

In the wake of World War II, the campaign for black rights gained new strength. The political impact of the heavy black migration to northern and western cities now became evident. The growing black vote made civil rights a major issue in national elections, was a critical factor in the reelection of Truman in 1948 and the subsequent desegregation of the armed forces, and ultimately led to the establishment of a federal Civil Rights Commission in 1957. The NAACP and other organizations campaigned successfully in a number of northern and western states for laws guaranteeing fair employment practices, equal access to public accommodations, and nondiscriminatory housing. The NAACP, piling up victory after victory in the courts, successfully attacked racially restrictive covenants in housing, segregation in interstate transportation, and discrimination in publicly owned recreational facilities. *Brown* v. *Board of Education* in 1954 brought to a triumphant conclusion the legal campaign of the NAACP against educational segregation in public schools in the South. Meanwhile, the association's membership rolls filled with urban working-class blacks and, in the rural South, with relatively poor black farmers and even sharecroppers. Its program broadened, although not as extensively as its membership. It conducted drives to register voters, and it established housing and labor departments. Basically, the NAACP was expanding its work along the legal and legislative lines it had employed in earlier years.

CORE, by mid-century, was embarking upon demonstrations in the border states. Public accommodations were still its major target. CORE also began experimenting with direct action, including the boycott, to open up opportunities for industrial employment. And as early as 1947, CORE, in cooperation with a Christian pacifist organization, the Fellowship of Reconciliation, had conducted a Journey of Reconciliation—or what would later be called a Freedom Ride—in the upper South. Its purpose was to test compliance with the *Morgan* v. *Virginia* decision of the preceding year, in which the Supreme Court had declared segregation in interstate transportation unconstitutional.

BREAKTHROUGH IN ALABAMA

But what captured the imagination of the nation and of the black community in particular and what was chiefly responsible for the growing use of direct-action techniques was the Montgomery, Alabama, bus boycott of 1955–1956, which catapulted into national prominence the Reverend Martin Luther King, Jr., the man who most nearly achieved charismatic leadership in the civil rights movement in the 1960s. Like the founders of CORE, but unlike the great majority of civil rights activists, King professed a Gandhian belief in the principles of nonviolence. For King, who spoke of the creation of a "beloved community," love was more powerful than hate, and civil rights demonstrators who were beaten and jailed by hostile whites educated and transformed their oppressors through the redemptive character of their unmerited suffering. King won in Montgomery when a judicial ruling desegregated the buses. There were similar boycotts in Tallahasee, Florida, and in Birmingham, Alabama. These boycotts were widely heralded as indicating the emergence, especially in the South, of another "new Negro"—militant, no longer fearful of white hoodlums or police or jails, and ready to use his collective weight boldly. Seizing upon this new mood, King established the Southern Christian Leadership Conference (SCLC) in 1957, whose nonviolent program included both direct-action demonstrations and voter registration.

Martin Luther King's personal appeal did much to account for the popularity of direct action. But in fact blacks were ready for a new approach; the older techniques of legal and legislative action had revealed their limitations. Impressive as it was to cite the advances in the 15 years after the end of World War II—advances that included state laws and Supreme Court decisions—something was clearly wrong. Though the number of blacks registered to vote in the southern states

rose from about 200,000 to well over a million in the decade following the outlawing of the white primary in 1944, millions more were still disfranchised, especially in the Deep South. There, Supreme Court decisions desegregating transportation facilities were still largely ignored. After the 1954 decision against segregation in the public schools, the South countered with attempts by White Citizens' Councils to outlaw the NAACP, intimidation of civil rights leaders, "massive resistance" to Supreme Court decisions, and the forcible curtailment of black voter registration. Discrimination in employment and in housing abounded, even in northern states with model civil rights laws. Beginning in 1954, black unemployment grew constantly as a result of recessions and automation.

At the very time that legalism was thus proving itself a limited instrument, blacks were developing a new confidence in the future as they watched the rise of the new African nations, the success of King and others in nonviolent direct action in the South, the new laws and court decisions, the international situation, and the evident shift of white public opinion. In short, there had occurred what has appropriately been described as a revolution in expectations. Blacks no longer felt that they had to accept the humiliations of second-class citizenship, and consequently such humiliations, though fewer than they had been, seemed more intolerable than ever. Paradoxically, it was the NAACP's very success in the legislatures and the courts more than any other single factor that led to this revolution in expectations and the resultant dissatisfaction with the NAACP's program. An increasing black impatience and disillusionment accounted for the rising tempo of nonviolent direct action—including some by NAACP branches—in the late 1950s. It culminated in the student sit-ins of 1960 and the inauguration of what is popularly known as the Civil Rights Revolution, or Negro Revolt.

Toward radical militancy The black protest movement would never be the same again. The southern college student sit-ins began a chain of events that shook the power structure of the black community, made direct action temporarily preeminent as a civil rights technique, ended NAACP hegemony in the civil rights movement, accelerated social change in race relations, largely destroyed

461

Adaptation 35
Meier and
Rudwick:
Patterns of
protest,
1900–1970

the remaining barriers against the recognition of the blacks' constitutional rights, and ultimately turned the black protest organizations toward a deep concern with the economic and social problems of the masses. There was a steady radicalization of tactics and goals: from legalism to direct action and ultimately to black power; from participation by the middle and upper classes to mass action by all classes; from guaranteeing the protection of the black's constitutional rights to securing economic policies that would insure the welfare of the culturally deprived in a technologically changing society; from appeal to the white American's sense of fair play to demands based upon the power of the black ghetto.

First, direct action proved successful in a large-scale way in the South and won predominance over other tactics. The college student sit-in groups that suddenly flowered in the South formed the Student Nonviolent Coordinating Committee (SNCC) in April 1960, and many local ad hoc direct-action groups also appeared. Furthermore, the thrust from the youth stimulated the established organizations and created competitive rivalry among civil rights groups. And the competition in turn encouraged widespread use of direct action. Old techniques, some of them radical in their day, now seemed conservative and slow-moving; many youthful sit-in demonstrators regarded the NAACP as hopelessly outmoded and cripplingly dominated by the middle class, which lacked any concern for the welfare of the masses. New personalities challenged the entrenched leaders. The NAACP met the challenge by making direct action a major rather than a peripheral activity, and a number of its leaders in local branches become enthusiastic proponents of this tactic.

Voter registration—a conservative strategy of long standing—became, in the face of stubborn white resistance in Alabama, Mississippi, and Louisiana, a form of radical direct action. SNCC initiated the work of attempting to register voters in the rural counties of the deep South; CORE, some NAACP militants, and eventually SCLC followed.

As earlier goals, such as voting rights and desegregation of public accommodations, were gradually won, civil rights organizations became more concerned with the economic plight of the black masses who suffered from discrimination in employment opportunities and in the quality of education and housing. Blacks had always been relegated primarily to the low-paid, unskilled jobs. They consequently faced severe problems with the advance of automation.

All this led to a change in emphasis for the civil rights movement. Direct action, which since 1960 had been concentrated in the South, now reappeared in new forms in the North. There were school boycotts, rent strikes, and demonstrations against discriminatory employers and unions. With this change came another: More and more the masses of Negroes were participating in civil rights activity. The tactics of direct action had made it possible for ordinary citizens to participate in the fight for their freedom. Leaders, although they still came mostly from the middle and upper classes, increasingly articulated the needs and frustrations of the masses.

By 1965 direct action had passed its heyday. It had succeeded in desegregating public accommodations in the South and in obtaining thousands of jobs in retail stores and consumer-oriented industries in the North. It had played a central, even essential, role in the passage of the civil rights law of 1964 and the voting rights law of 1965.

Waning of nonviolence The competitive rivalry of the civil rights organizations, combined with the rising participation of the black masses, made the movement more militant, inclusive, and far-reaching in its demands and immediatist in its attitude. There was a tendency toward erosion of the principle of nonviolence. The growing participation of lower-class youth led to instances of spontaneous outbreaks of violence. And with the hardening resistance of the deep South and the difficulties inherent in attacking the deep-seated problems of employment, housing, and schools there was discussion among militants about retaliating in self-defense against the brutality of police and white hoodlums. A small minority was already advocating the deliberate use of violence. Thus hope kindled by progress and frustration created by obstacles joined to make blacks more militant, and one extreme of their militancy was represented by violence.

In the face of indubitable progress there were signs of increasing nationalist protest. This was the result of at least three forces: (1) a growing sense of confidence and self-respect based on the successes achieved; (2) disillusionment with the slow pace of change and the increasing brutality and white violence in the South, which gave blacks a greater sense of isolation at the very time that white support for the cause of civil rights was actually increasing; and (3) the rising participation of lower-class blacks, especially in some CORE chapters and in SNCC. Among lower-class people, nationalist sentiments have always been more deeply rooted than among the middle and upper classes; the alienation of the lower classes was actually heightened because of the rise in unemployment. The aspirations of these people had been raised, but in vain. They soon found that the civil rights movement had, in effect, passed by the lower classes. They were in fact worse off than before.

POWER AND SEPARATISM

It was among exactly such lower-class blacks that the most important nationalist movement of the early 1960s flourished. The Nation of Islam, or Black Muslims as they came to be called, was established around 1930 but did not grow rapidly until the recession of 1954. At its height the Nation of Islam was seriously weakened by a factional struggle between its top leader, Elijah Muhammad, and the minister of its Harlem temple, the dramatic spokesman Malcolm X. Early in 1964 Malcolm X left the movement and formed the Organization of Afro-American Unity. Malcolm X aimed at a less sectarian and more broadly based movement, but before he could get beyond setting forth the outlines of his program, he was assassinated. Yet for many, the very manner of his death combined with his fierce denunciation of white racism and his charismatic leadership elevated him to the level of the sacred and made him the single most influential symbol for the black nationalist impulses of the late 1960s.

Other nationalist tendencies also became prominent after 1960. The trials and successes of the movement gave blacks a new sense of dignity, self-esteem, and power. This led to a burgeoning interest in black history; as blacks gained pride and self-respect, they looked to the past in their search for an identity.

Black power At the very time that white support for the movement was rising, the most militant members felt increasingly isolated from the Ameri-

can scene. The radical left wing was growing disdainful of American society and the middle-class way of life and cynical about liberals and the leaders of organized labor. Any compromise, even if a temporary tactical device, had become anathema to them. They talked more and more of the necessity for revolutionary changes in the social structure, even of violence. They became increasingly skeptical of the value of white participation in the movement, and racially chauvinistic in their insistence that black power alone could compel concessions from the power structure of capitalists, politicians, and bureaucratic labor leaders.

Black power first articulated a mood rather than a program—disillusionment and alienation from white America, race pride, and self-respect or black consciousness. The precipitating occasion was James Meredith's march from Memphis to Jackson in the early summer of 1966, but the slogan expressed tendencies that had been present for a long time and had been gaining strength in the black community.

In politics, black power meant independent action: black control of the political power of the black ghettos and its conscious use to better the slum dwellers' conditions. It could take the form of organizing a black political party or controlling the political machinery within the ghetto without the guidance or support of white politicians. Where predominantly black areas lacked blacks in elective office, whether in the rural black belt of the South or in urban centers, black-power advocates sought the election of blacks by voter-registration campaigns and by working to redraw electoral districts. The basic belief was that only a well-organized and cohesive bloc of black voters could provide for the needs of the black masses. Even some black politicians allied to the major political parties adopted the phrase *black power* to describe their interest in the black vote. In economic terms, black power meant creating independent, self-sufficient black business enterprises, not only by encouraging black entrepreneurs but also by forming black cooperatives in the ghettos and in the predominantly black rural counties of the South. In the field of education, black power called for local community control of the public schools in the black ghettos. Throughout, the emphasis was on self-help, racial unity, and, among the most militant, retaliatory violence, the latter ranging from the legal right of self-defense to attempts to justify

463

Adaptation 35
Meier and
Rudwick:
Patterns of
protest,
1900–1970

looting and arson in ghetto riots, to guerrilla warfare and armed rebellion.

The paradox of black power Black nationalism, black separatism, and black revolutionary rhetoric have seized the headlines. But striking and important as the popularity of various forms of black nationalism have been since 1966 when black power became a slogan, it must nonetheless be emphasized that full participation in American society on an integrated basis is still the goal of the vast majority of black Americans. Though nationalist thinking enjoys considerable currency in middle-class black circles in the North as well as among ghetto youth, neither SCLC nor NAACP has adopted a nationalist program or ideology. The NAACP has counterattacked vigorously. Individuals like Kenneth Clark and Bayard Rustin, who were prominently associated with the earlier protest movement, have denounced the black separatists as segregationists and racists, undermining the very things the black protest movement had sought for so many years to bring about. Martin Luther King's last months were spent in developing a major project intended to demonstrate the continuing viability of the nonviolent direct-action strategy.

The popularity of the phrase *black power* and the vogue of separatist ideology in the late 1960s represent both a sense of power produced by the earlier successes of the movement and an escape into rhetoric caused by powerlessness to achieve continued rapid progress toward full equality. The slogan emerged when the black protest movement was slowing down, when it was finding increased resistance to its changed goals, when it discovered that nonviolent direct action was no more a

panacea than legal action had been, when CORE and SNCC were declining in activity, membership, and financial support. Impotent to make any fundamental changes in the lives of the masses, the advocates of black power substituted an ideology of separatism for one of integration. Ironically, this occurred at the very time that black people were closer to the goal of integration than ever before. Sixty years earlier the themes of racial unity and separatism had been part of an ideology of accommodation, and black radicals had demanded integration. The new black radical was now decrying integration as a white man's strategy of tokenism aimed at holding blacks in a subordinate position. Racial separatism had become part of a rhetoric of radicalism and militance, while the erstwhile radical program of integration was now denounced as conservative, and sometimes as downright racist.

It should be remembered that today, as traditionally, the main thrust of black protest has always been aimed at discrimination and segregation (the radicals of today distinguishing between voluntary separatism and enforced segregation); the central demand has always been for equal treatment with other citizens. The nationalist emphasis in militant black thought today is the latest expression of the ethnic ambivalence of blacks that is rooted in the contradictions of American society. Behind the revolutionary phrases of the black-power militants is usually a profound desire for an equal share and an equal status in American society. And the mainstream of black protest has always been firmly embedded in the basic values of American society. It aims not at their destruction but their fulfillment.

Section four plural societies

Observation of the complex, multiethnic colonies of Southeast Asia suggested the idea of plural societies:

Probably the first thing that strikes the visitor is the medley of peoples—European, Chinese, Indian, and native. It is in the strictest sense a medley, for they mix but do not combine. Each group holds by its own religion, its own culture and language, its own ideas and ways. As individuals they meet, but only in the market-place, in buying and selling. There is a plural society, with different sections of the community living side by side, but separately, within the same political unit. Even in the economic sphere, there is a division of labour along racial lines (Furnivall, 1948:304).

Key phrases emphasize that the societies are composed of different peoples who *mix but do not combine,* who live *side by side, but separately* (Cf. Smith, 1960; Kuper and Smith, 1969).

Plural societies are formed by historical

forces such as conquest, colonialism, and political independence. They may lose their plural character if the diverse populations share power and opportunity, find common interests, and reduce cultural differences.

By far the majority of all Mexicans share the dominant national cultural institutions and values. Only about 15 per cent of the population may be considered as Indians (based upon linguistic criteria) and, in terms of their basic institutions and values, a social and cultural segment distinct from the dominant culture. How large must such a segment be to qualify a society as pluralistic? If we look back into the Mexican past, however, there was a time when Mexico was more clearly qualified as a pluralistic society; at the end of the Eighteenth Century only 0.5 per cent of the Mexican population was European or Negro. Some 30.9 per cent were *mestizo*, and more than 60 per cent were Indians. It is safe, I am sure, to interpret these figures as representing different basic cultural institutions and values. It is inescapable that Mexico was once clearly a plural society and that it has become less so in the last 150 years (Wagley, 1960:779–780).

Thus societies may become less plural or they may split into smaller, more homogeneous units either by force or by consensus.

This section examines the situation in four countries:

1. Switzerland, a state in which language and religious differences are rather successfully accommodated, although with more stress than is sometimes supposed

2. Canada, with its significant cleavage on religious, linguistic, and territorial lines

3. South Africa, where sharp divisions among culturally or racially distinct populations are regulated by an extreme concentration of power

4. the United States, a complex multiracial, multicultural society.

PLURALISM IN SWITZERLAND

Switzerland is often cited as the ideal multicultural society; it successfully accommodates four different languages (German, Italian, French, and Romansh) and two major religions (Protestantism and Catholicism). German, French, and Italian are national and official languages (McRae, 1964).

Linguistically the country is about 75 percent German, 20 percent French, less than 4 percent Italian, and 1 percent Romansh. Romansh was recognized as a national language in 1938, but it has so few speakers (perhaps 50,000), that it was not made one of the official languages. Fourteen of the 22 cantons (political subdivisions) have German as the official language, three have French, and one Italian. Three cantons are officially bilingual in German and French, and one is trilingual in German, Italian, and Romansh. Despite the fact that Germans predominate, both in the number of cantons and in the percentage of the population, the ethnic interests and identities of the minorities are protected. In a strict majority-rule situation the minorities could be submerged, but this has not taken place because religious allegiances for the most part do not coincide with language and because the Swiss are more committed to national values than to ethnic values. Linguistic distinctions overlap and intersect with religion so that except for Italian speakers, who are 94 percent Roman Catholic, there are no solid linguistic-religious blocs (Mayer, 1968:715).

Living in peace and security for a long time, Switzerland is held up as a model country that has solved the tensions of cultural difference. It was not always so. Prior to the upwelling of political liberalism in the nineteenth century, Switzerland was repeatedly torn by religious wars. Furthermore, the conditions in other countries do not sufficiently resemble those in Switzerland to make Swiss pluralism a model to copy rather than merely to admire. The key to "the Swiss 'miracle' of unity in diversity rests upon a peculiar equilibrium of cross-cutting cultural divisions, which is historically unique and cannot be duplicated under different conditions" (Mayer, 1968:707).

Even under the most favorable circumstances, solidarity and tranquility are fragile.

Tension has occurred in the Jura region of Switzerland, where religion and language coincide and reinforce tendencies toward cleavage. Political conflicts have extended as far as movements to split off the French-speaking Catholic area into a separate canton (Mayer, 1968:720–741, esp. 734–741; *Economist*, June 29, 1974:35). Thus the hypothesis is supported that the Swiss miracle is in part an accident of crosscutting forces and not purely a result of political wisdom and toleration.

CANADA: DIVISION WITHOUT RACE[1]

Canada has been defined as "a collection of North American territories whose major problem is not the Black problem" (Rioux, 1971:123). Nevertheless, some Canadians refer to the French-British division as a racial problem, and until 1941 the Canadian census used the word *race* to distinguish the two European peoples. Unlike Switzerland, in Canada religious and language divisions coincide in the same territorial base. The French population of Canada has been stable at about 30 percent since federation in 1867, but the British have declined from 60 percent to about 40 percent. Indians and Eskimos make up only a little over 1 percent of the total and persons of diverse ethnic origins the remainder.

The French are highly concentrated in Quebec, where they sought and were granted many constitutional protections. French is an official language, and the people have special safeguards for their religious establishment and education. These guarantees tend to perpetuate their concentration in the Province of Quebec, which is more than 80 percent French and where more than three-fourths of French Canadians live. Geographic concentration combined with the constitutional recognition of their communal, religious, and cultural interests gives them a solid political base. They dominate

[1] Written in collaboration with Byron Sansom.

Quebec provincial politics and have occupied an important role at the national level. Three French Canadians have served as prime minister.

Basis of inequality Although they are not a suppressed political minority, the French are inferior to the British in socioeconomic status throughout Canada and especially in Quebec. The fact that they are subordinate even where they are in the majority has generated resentment and separatist movements (Hughes, 1943; Porter, 1968; Royal Commission, 1967–1970, esp. 1969:vols. 3A and 3B; Roseborough and Breton, 1968). Although the French (or Quebecers or Québécois, as they sometimes call themselves) have been inclined to blame this state of affairs on discrimination by British and American capitalists, who play a large part in the economic life of Quebec, other factors are also at work. Unlike the British and most other ethnic populations, the French were ill-prepared to take advantage of economic expansion, because the family, church, and parochial schools were not geared to an industrial economy (Porter, 1968).

As industrial and urban growth continue, the French have become increasingly urban and better qualified in technical skills. Industrialization may have heightened French awareness of their inferior status. The mass media, especially that owned by the French, have focused on their plight, not only in Quebec but throughout Canada. Whereas violence and open confrontation have been a part of Canada's ethnic history—for instance, the French resisted conscription during World War I and World War II—there has been a dramatic increase in protest activity since the late 1950s.

Ethnic stratification Scholars of Canadian stratification hold that the French have made small gains relative to other ethnic populations in the last several decades (Keyfitz, 1960; Porter, 1968). Such generalizations are based on analyses of Canadian census data, and these present problems of interpretation; for example, some occupational categories have been changed from census to census and some occupations are difficult to assign to specific categories. However, it is possible to estimate trends in occupational differentiation between the British and French by summarizing the census data into ten broad occupational categories. Table 14:1 gives the percentages of British and French male workers in these occupational categories for the census years 1931 and 1961 and the difference between the two percentages in each row. An Index of Dissimilarity is calculated from these differences. (See p. 468.)

The situations of both British and French improved, but the British remained clearly better off. The British are overrepresented in the higher and white-collar occupational categories (professional and technical; managers, officials, and proprietors; clerical; and sales) while the French are overrepresented in lower-ranking categories (farm laborers and foremen, and nonfarm laborers). There was a sharp decline in the percentage of French classified as farm laborers and foremen, and the growing technical orientation of French education paid dividends with an increase in the number of craftsmen and foremen. By 1961 they had achieved equality with the British in this category.

As might be expected from the occupational distributions, the French rank below the British in both income and education. In 1961 the mean annual income for the nonagricultural male labor force was $4,414; for men of British origin the figure was $4,852, and for those of French origin, $3,872. If the total is given an index value of 100, the British index is 110, the French index 88 (Royal Commission, 1969:vol. 3A, p. 16). A larger proportion of French have only elementary schooling, and a relatively large percentage of British have higher secondary or university schooling.

Cultural dualism British–French relations in Canada resemble the Mexican–Anglo problems of the southwestern United States in that two peoples are separated by language, religion, and culture. About 30 percent of Canadians reported French as their mother tongue in 1961, a figure that has remained nearly constant since 1931. But the percentage reporting English as a mother tongue increased from about 45 percent in 1931 to about 60 percent in 1961. Thus, there has been a decrease from about 25 to 10 percent for those reporting a mother tongue other than English or French. In other words, Canada has tended to become more bilingual than multilingual, and bilingual education is encouraged. In the Province of Quebec over 80 percent claim French as their mother tongue, about 15 percent English, and only about 5 percent some other language.

Canadian cultural dualism extends beyond language. In 1961 approximately 95 percent of the French in Canada professed Catholicism and about 80 percent of the British reported adherence to a Protestant faith. Closely related to religion is the organization of education into British and French schools, which reinforce differences in culture and historical identities.

In sum, Canada contains two distinct cultural groupings, to a large degree territorially and linguistically separate. The French have never embraced assimilation and acculturation, and French cultural nationalism has increasingly become translated into political separatism.

The politics of ethnicity Overt French protest has increased since the early 1960s. There were disruptions during Queen Elizabeth's visit in 1964, and some Quebec separatists used terror tactics in the 1960s. In 1970 political extremists resorted to kidnapping and assassinating Pierre Laporte, the Quebec minister of labor, who was garroted with the chain of his religious medal. This single demonstrative act was thus an attack on the political order, on a French-Canadian leader who was striving to achieve progress for the French within the political system, and upon the Catholic church.

Index of dissimilarity

The Index of Dissimilarity (ID) is frequently used to summarize the differences between two populations at the same time or the same population at two points in time. The occupational distributions in Table 14:1 offer a good example. The "difference" column shows the size of the percentage difference between British and French male workers in each category. Note that the difference is expressed in absolute terms. In calculating the ID, it does not matter which percentage is larger. When all of the differences in a column are added and divided by two, the result is called the Index of Dissimilarity: In other words, it is the sum of the differences between the x's (in this case the British) and the y's (the French), irrespective of which is larger, divided by two. It represents the percentage of one of the populations that would have to change occupational categories in order to achieve a condition of equality between the two populations.

When the ID is applied to the data reported in Table 14:1 for 1931 and 1961 and to data for the years 1941 and 1951 (not shown), an overall trend emerges. The differentiation between the British and French varied only slightly over an entire generation. In 1931, the ID was 12.9. By 1941, it had decreased to 12.0, perhaps as a result of French urbanization. However, between 1941 and 1951 the ID increased to 13.4. This increase is largely traceable to increased differentiation in occupations involved in war industries: professional and technical, nonagricultural managers, and operatives. Apparently the British were better placed in terms of both technical qualifications and residence to take advantage of the new openings that developed during World War II. Between 1951 and 1961 the ID decreased from 13.4 to 11.5 as a result of continuing French urbanization and the changing technical orientation of French education.

A decline in the ID from 12.9 in 1931 to 11.5 in 1961 does not suggest an impressive improvement in the relative position of the French during the 30-year span.

Table 14:1 Distribution of British and French males by occupational category, Canada, 1931 and 1961, in percentages

Occupational category	1931[a]			1961[b]		
	British	French	Difference	British	French	Difference
Professional, technical, and kindred workers	5.0	3.2	1.8	10.1	6.3	3.8
Farmers and farm managers	18.5	17.5	1.0	7.4	6.9	0.5
Managers, officials, and proprietors, except farm	8.0	5.6	2.4	12.6	7.9	4.7
Clerical and kindred workers	7.8	4.4	3.4	8.8	7.3	1.5
Sales workers	6.3	4.6	1.7	5.8	4.8	1.0
Craftsmen, foremen, and kindred workers	16.2	13.9	2.1	22.6	22.6	0.0
Operative and kindred workers	8.8	8.5	0.3	13.5	18.4	4.9
Service workers	3.8	3.7	0.1	5.6	6.2	0.6
Farm laborers and foremen	12.7	16.9	4.2	2.9	3.5	0.6
Laborers, except farm	13.1	21.8	8.7	8.2	13.2	5.0
Occupation not reported	0.1	0.1	0.0	2.6	3.0	0.4
Totals	100.3	100.2	25.7	100.1	100.1	23.0
Number in thousands	1,730	809	ID[c] = 12.9	2,071	1,303	ID = 11.5

Source: Compiled and computed from Census of Canada, 1931, Vol. 7, Table 49; and 1961, Vol. 3, Part 1, Table 21.

[a] Gainfully occupied males, ten years and over
[b] Males in the labor force, 15 years and over
[c] Index of Dissimilarity (see p. 468)

Some British and French favor minor reforms of political structure and practice, some a new constitution to replace the British North America Act (1867) with a more clear delineation of powers between the national and provincial governments. A more drastic constitutional change might grant Quebec special status as a province "not like the others." An even more radical approach proposes the formation of a confederation of two associated states—Quebec as one state and the rest of the provinces as another—united under a federal council with limited powers. The most radical position is separation.

The prospect of a major change has been given impetus by the Royal Commission of Canada on Bilingualism and Biculturalism (Royal Commission, 1967–1970). Established in 1963 by Parliament under Prime Minister Lester Pearson, the commission was to inquire into "the existing state of bilingualism and biculturalism in Canada and to recommend what steps should be taken to develop the Canadian Confederation on the basis of an equal partnership between the two founding races." The commission is both a symptom of crisis and a political adjustment. As directed, the commission report concentrates on the "equal partnership" approach and ignores the separatist option.

Canada is the scene of a test to resolve by

political means the strains of cultural cleavage, economic inequality, and historical tension. Two kinds of values are in conflict: (1) the ideal of a culturally homogeneous nation-state and (2) the ideal of a plural society sufficiently flexible to accommodate separate religious and linguistic identities that coincide with a geographic base.

SOUTH AFRICA: SEPARATE AND SUBORDINATE

Race affects the system of opportunity and power in many countries, but nowhere does it shape the social structure more completely than in South Africa. At a time when the world trend is to challenge segregation and subordination, South Africa has strengthened its controls over race relations. Thus the country is of particular interest and concern to students of race and is a focus of international controversy because of its policy of apartheid (officially "separate development") and because the dominant population is a numerical minority.

Color is the criterion of segregation and the principal determinant of stratification. In a total 1975 population of over 25 million, 4.2 million whites stand at the top of the social hierarchy. The whites are composed of English-speaking people, mostly urban and economically powerful, and the numerous Boers, descendants of early Dutch settlers, who are politically dominant.

The Dutch East India Company colonized the Cape of Good Hope in the seventeenth century, but British colonial power prevailed throughout South Africa in the nineteenth century. Even after their defeat in the Anglo-Boer War of 1899–1902, many Boers clung to national aspirations, and in 1948 they gained political power. They deprived black Africans and the Cape Coloured voters of political participation, wore down the opposition of other whites, and in 1961 declared the country a republic, removing it from the British Commonwealth. Thus the Boers changed from a subordinate minority with a unique cultural identity to a dominant minority in the Republic of South Africa. The names by which the Boers call themselves (Afrikaners) and their language (Afrikaans) express their self-definition as Africans and their homeland as Africa. Unlike colonists from England, France, or Portugal, they have no European home to which they might go. Afrikaners are becoming urbanized and increasingly involved in the country's industrial expansion, but their rural base is significant, and they remain inferior to English South Africans in both education and occupation.

Ranked below the whites are 2.4 million persons of mixed ancestry who are called Coloured or Cape Coloured from their geographic concentration; most of them speak Afrikaans. At a similar intermediate social ranking, there are more than 700,000 Asians, descendants of indentured laborers, mostly of Indian ancestry, who are concentrated in the eastern part of the country in Natal. At the bottom of the occupational scale, making up 71 percent of the population, are 18 million undereducated black Africans, referred to as Bantu from their principal linguistic family. These blacks belong to several linguistic subgroups and are to varying degrees urbanized and incorporated into the industrial economy.

Apartheid Racial separation and subordination have long been the way of life throughout South Africa, but both the scope and detail of government control have increased in recent years. Apartheid has been classified into three levels according to the amount of physical distance between the races (van den Berghe, 1966):

1. *Microsegregation*, the color bar, regulates the daily lives of nonwhites and limits their interaction with whites. In some respects this form of control resembles the Jim Crow practices of the U.S. South during the period of maximum domination. Nonwhites are assigned to segregated and inferior public and private facilities, and they live under numerous restrictions in their interactions with the other races. They are

Instrument of Apartheid: For identification and permission to travel and work in European areas, a non-European in South Africa is required to carry a passbook. Outside their own tribal areas, blacks whose passbooks are not in good order are subject to criminal penalties.

required to carry passbooks, and their geographic movements are rigidly controlled. Although nonwhites are the primary objects of apartheid regulations, whites must also obey segregation rules whether they want to or not (Marquard, 1969:Chap. 6). In the mid-1970s the government began to relax the extent and detail of controls. It is not clear how far this policy change will go and there is no sign that it will extend to the fundamental pattern of residential segregation.

2. *Residential segregation* has been greatly increased since the Afrikaner nationalists gained power in 1948. Racially mixed neighborhoods have been turned into homogeneous townships by massive shifting of racial groups. Nonwhite domestic servants are forbidden to live in the same houses with their white employers except under strict regulations. The policy is to make residential areas homogeneous, and nonwhites are mostly restricted to their own segregated sections except during working hours. New housing has marginally improved the physical situation for many blacks who formerly lived in shacks in deteriorated slums. As in urban renewal elsewhere, the residents suffer destroyed social networks and neighborhoods for the convenience of someone else. As the urban population grows to meet industrial demands, residential requirements also grow, and additional segregated townships are built—new and orderly, but bleak, cramped, fenced-in, and distant from the city center and places of work.

Densely settled and rigorously segregated, these areas concentrate both people and their discontents. The 1976 riots in the black townships drew international attention to the nature of South African residential segregation and dramatized for South African whites the despair harbored among the million Soweto residents and those who live in other townships.

3. *Territorial apartheid* looks toward a future in which the blacks will be settled in homogeneous territories called Bantustans, each inhabited by a separate linguistic grouping. This is the most controversial and confusing part of the complicated apartheid system. The policy would make South Africa into a multinational state within which each Bantu people would have its own "homeland" and eventually self-government. Critics have characterized the plan as substituting indirect rule for direct rule, but the black leaders are more assertive and demanding than the South African government bargained for (Lipton, 1972).

There are to be no separate "homelands"

for the different white ethnic groups, nor for the Cape Coloured and Indians. This does not mean they will be free of discrimination and segregation. Perhaps because the plight of the blacks is assumed to be more urgent, or because political leaders in the black African states champion their cause, the Bantu are a more conspicuous issue than the Coloureds and Asians.

Since the Bantustans cannot sustain themselves economically, the government is building industries within their borders and inducing businesses to set up industrial plants on their fringes. These expedients give work to some unemployed and underemployed Bantu. Although most of the locations are marginally suitable for industrial development, white entrepreneurs would benefit from tax and other concessions and from access to a supply of cheap labor. The earnings from the new industrial developments plus remittances from black workers in the white cities are supposed to make the black "homelands" economically viable.

Strains and dilemmas About 71 percent of the population are blacks, who have been allocated about 13 percent of the area of South Africa divided into seven or eight separate Bantustans. These are composed of numerous, scattered fragments rather than coherent geographic units, and the land reserved for blacks is incapable of supporting the present resident population. According to the plan, blacks not needed as workers in the white 87 percent of the country are to be "repatriated" to these "homelands," which they may never have seen. Even if born in white areas, they are defined as citizens of the Bantustans. Bantus remaining in the white areas to work are legally residents of the Bantustans and are treated as foreigners in white South Africa. But unlike foreigners they must obey the color bar and residential apartheid rules. Since most of their families live in the Bantustans, they are deprived of a normal family life.

The black population will more than double by the end of the century, but there is no plan to increase the size of the "homelands." In addition, various Bantu peoples have close linguistic and historical ties and have intermarried, but according to the plans, Bantustans cannot combine.

Despite their subordination, the Bantu play an indispensable role in the South African economy, and skilled and semiskilled black workers are essential to the success of industrial and mining enterprises. For these reasons or because of personal convictions, some whites oppose the more stringent forms of apartheid, and a minority of whites oppose it entirely. Apartheid costs the nonwhites most, but it also imposes direct costs on the conduct of business and government and heavy indirect costs in reduced economic efficiency. It cannot be said how far these costs are entering into official thinking. The relaxation already mentioned of some of the lesser forms of discrimination may signal the beginning of a trend.

South Africa is a beleaguered society. Within, there are growing pressures from increasingly militant nonwhite peoples and tensions between hard-line and more moderate whites. Political shifts in neighboring states reduce the security of the borders and expose the country to the increased possibility of guerilla action. Unrest in black townships and the shaky white Rhodesian regime compromise the South African government's efforts to achieve détente with its black African neighbors. Farther afield direct and indirect sanctions, ranging from sport to the UN, isolate the people and the leadership from international contacts. Whether such international pressures will encourage the moderation of South African racial policies is less than certain. It has been argued that to isolate the country further might have the opposite effect:

The country, separated as it is by thousands of miles from the remainder of the Western world, already suffers from an excess of isolation. Apartheid is to some extent the reflection of this isolation. The reactionary and racist tendencies within South African society positively thrive on it (Kennan, 1971:225).

Hard-line Afrikaaners are not likely to cave in before external pressure. Their determination and rigidity of outlook are deeply rooted in their own ethnic nationalism, and their police power rests on a modern military capacity. Even if apartheid must eventually collapse from its own internal defects, the question remains whether it can be replaced by policies of accommodation generated from within or only by revolutionary violence.

USA: AN ETHNIC KALEIDOSCOPE

A conspicuous feature of the United States is the diversity of ethnic origins and their modes of incorporation: native Americans by conquest and territorial displacement, blacks by slavery and immigration, Mexicans by conquest and immigration, Europeans by indentured and free immigration, Asians as contract labor and independent migrants. Each people has come upon a different scene, a different pattern of opportunities and difficulties with a different set of competitors. Furthermore, constant internal population movements change the patterns of interethnic contacts and alter the competitive situation. History can tell how a given ethnic grouping made its way, but it has little advice to offer other ethnic groups that encounter radically different circumstances. Poorly educated European immigrants and their children became successful in industry and business during a labor-hungry period of territorial and industrial expansion.

The children of Greek, Italian, Jewish and other European immigrants moved up the socioeconomic ladder farther and faster than was expected when their parents arrived in the urban slums of American cities. The second-generation children of those immigrants reached educational, occupational, and income rankings far beyond that of their parents, and in the case of Jews and Greeks, beyond that of native-born white Americans whose parents were born in the United States. Second-generation Italians also surpassed native-born whites of native paren-

tage in occupation and income and nearly equalled them in education (Broom, Martin, and Maynard, 1971). By all three measures, these new American populations have made a surprising achievement.

Today it is not sensible to expect blacks and Chicanos to succeed as Italian and Greek immigrants did, much less as well as the children of European immigrants. Machines have replaced manual labor, small enterprises can no longer compete with large rationalized business, and it takes a lot of education to go even a short way.

The opportunities of immigrants from Mexico have been especially limited by the subordinate status of Mexican-Americans already living in the southwestern states, who were a heritage of conquest.

When successive waves of Mexican migrants arrived in the post-1900 southwestern United States they found a large materially dispossessed minority with whom they had language, custom, kinship, and all manner of qualities in common, not least of which was that they both occupied the very bottom of the social structure. It does not make sense to view these large early waves of Mexicans as similar to immigrants from other lands to the U.S. because social-psychologically the post-1900 migrant from Mexico was not like the Irish immigrant whose identity-giving land was being left behind across a large ocean. Even the physical characteristics of these lands were continuous with that of land on the Mexican side. The immigrant to New York City was not like the migrant to San Antonio "returning" to land once part of his country, where he just as likely as not might have kin dating back to that era. When he arrived in San Antonio the powerful "Anglo" population could view him and define him precisely as they already defined his kin. The migrant himself upon arriving could simply take over the social-psychological repertoire of perspectives toward self and dominant others that his kin had already thoroughly established (Alvarez, 1971:21).

The nonwhite labor force The nonwhite labor force, more than 90 percent of which is black, differs markedly from the white labor force in the amount of unemployment and in occupational and educational character-

Table 14:2 Ratio of actual to expected[a] nonwhites
by occupational group, 1940–1976

Occupational group	1940	1950	1960	1970	1976[b]
White collar					
Professional and technical	.36	.40	.49	.64	.73
Managers and administrators (nonfarm)	.17	.22	.23	.33	.42
Clerical workers	} .12	{ .29	.46	.76	.87
Sales workers		{ .18	.23	.34	.35
Blue collar					
Craft and kindred workers	.27	.38	.49	.64	.67
Operatives and kindred workers	.57	.94	1.08	1.34	1.34
Nonfarm laborers	2.06	2.56	2.59	2.18	1.69
Service					
Private household workers	4.66	5.92	5.46	3.89	3.54
Other service workers	1.53	2.00	2.02	1.77	1.78
Farm					
Farmers and farm managers	1.31	1.22	.78	.45	.29
Farm laborers and supervisors	2.57	2.28	2.46	1.68	1.07

Source: For 1940–1960, Glenn, 1963:Table 1. Ratios for 1970 and 1976 are computed from basic data in Department of Labor, Bureau of Labor Statistics, *Monthly Labor Review* and *Employment and Earnings Report on the Labor Force.*

[a] The "expected" percentage of nonwhites in any occupational group is the same as the percentage of all workers in that group. For instance, in April 1976, 6.3 percent of all employed workers in the United States were sales workers and therefore one would "expect" 6.3 percent of employed nonwhites to be in that occupational group. In fact, only 2.2 percent of employed nonwhites were so employed. Thus the ratio of actual to expected is .35, that is, 2.2/6.3 = .35. If nonwhites were proportionately represented, the ratio would be 1.00; a ratio of more than 1.00 indicates overrepresentation and a ratio less than 1.00 indicates underrepresentation.
[b] Because of changes in the occupational classification and the form of questioning, data for 1976 are not strictly comparable with earlier years.

istics. Over the past 20 years, nonwhite unemployment has run double that of whites. In 1975 the average annual unemployment rate for nonwhites was 13.9 percent compared with 7.8 percent for whites (Monthly Labor Review, 99 April 1976:70). Furthermore, nonwhite unemployment is more harmful because it is likely to extend for longer periods. Nonwhites are concentrated in industries and occupations most vulnerable to changes in the economy, although the increasing numbers in government employment are cushioned against economic hardship.

Nonwhites are overrepresented in most of the poorly rewarded occupations and are underrepresented in the more highly rewarded ones. About one-fourth of nonwhites, compared with half of white workers, have white-collar jobs. One-third of

whites, but over two-fifths of blacks, have blue-collar jobs. Detailed analysis shows that the discrepancy between whites and nonwhites runs through the whole occupational structure. Table 14:2 reports changes in nonwhite representation in the occupational groups from 1940 to 1976. The table states how much the actual distribution of nonwhites in each occupation group differs from that "expected" if the nonwhites had their share. The nonwhite picture is clearly improving. In 1940 the nonwhite professional category reached only about one-third (.36) of the "expected" share, and by 1976 it had doubled to almost three-quarters (.73). Over the same period the ratios for farming occupations sharply declined, and nonwhites are no longer overrepresented in such occupations.

There is apparently a general upgrading

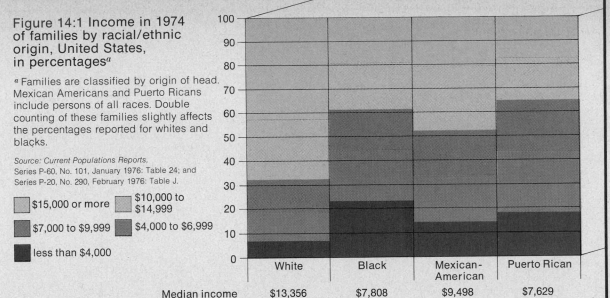

Figure 14:1 Income in 1974 of families by racial/ethnic origin, United States, in percentages[a]

[a] Families are classified by origin of head. Mexican Americans and Puerto Ricans include persons of all races. Double counting of these families slightly affects the percentages reported for whites and blacks.

Source: Current Populations Reports, Series P-60, No. 101, January 1976: Table 24; and Series P-20, No. 290, February 1976: Table J.

- $15,000 or more
- $10,000 to $14,999
- $7,000 to $9,999
- $4,000 to $6,999
- less than $4,000

	White	Black	Mexican-American	Puerto Rican
Median income	$13,356	$7,808	$9,498	$7,629

in both manual and white-collar work but relatively slow progress at the managerial level, in sales, and in top-level blue-collar work. The last can be explained by the low representation of blacks in craft labor unions, largely a consequence of discrimination, and the inferior seniority status of blacks. There are recent signs of improvement in nonwhite representation as managers, officials, and proprietors.

Within each of the 11 occupational groups listed in the table, nonwhites tend to be concentrated in the lower-paid occupations. For instance, most of the nonwhites in the professional and technical category are clergymen and teachers rather than doctors, lawyers, engineers, or other highly paid professionals (Broom and Glenn, 1967:111–113). The decline in farm labor and private household service is significant because it indicates a shift of nonwhites out of jobs where there is little or no prospect for advancement. Unfavorable though it is, the present occupational status of nonwhites is a considerable improvement over even the recent past.

A finer-grained analysis emphasizes the obstacles that stand in the way of equality: Blacks were found to be consistently at an occupational disadvantage compared to whites of the same educational levels, and the black–white gap became wider during the working career.

These findings provide evidence concerning the systematic way in which blacks are disadvantaged in the occupational system. They receive less education; while at school they have fewer opportunities to take on full-time or part-time employment; once they enter the labor market, they are less able to transform educational attainment into occupational attainment; the longer they work, the further behind whites they fall; and, finally, the higher the educational attainment of the black man, the worse off he is compared to whites with similar training.

These patterns add up to a massively discriminating occupational system, one which systematically provides less than equal treatment for blacks, even allowing for the poverty of their social backgrounds and their poorer schooling. This is one of the concrete meanings of institutional racism, a pattern of treatment whose outcomes may not be intended by any particular subsystem nor understood in terms of the prejudices of individuals, yet so pervasive that it can best be viewed as the output of the total society (Rossi and Ornstein, 1973:310).

Family income Inferior occupational distribution inevitably leads to relatively low in-

Table 14:3   Black legislators and other
officials holding office, 1962–1975

	1962	1966	1970	1975[a]
U.S. Senate, total	0	1	1	1
From the South	0	0	0	0
U.S. House of Representatives, total	4	6	13	17
From the South	—	—	2	5
State legislatures, total	52	148	198	281
In the South	6	37	70	124
Mayors, total U.S.	[b]	[b]	81	135
In the South	[b]	[b]	47	82
Other elected officials, total U.S.	[b]	[b]	1,567	3,069
In the South	[b]	[b]	763	1,702

Source: Potomac Institute, Democratic National Committee, *Ebony Magazine,* and Joint Center for Political Studies. Reported in *Current Population Reports,* Series 23, No. 38, July 1971:142; and No. 54, July 1975: 151.

[a] Figures are current as of May 1975.
[b] Figures not available.

comes. Figure 14:1 compares black, Chicano, Puerto Rican, and white family incomes. Although 42 percent of white families had incomes of $15,000 or more, none of the others reached half that percentage. Only 7 percent of white families fell below $4,000, but double the percentage of Chicano and triple the percentage of black families had incomes of less than $4,000. Of the three minorities, the Mexican-American profile is relatively advantageous and the black profile is the worst.

The continuing ethnic factor Black assertiveness has broken the quiet of the American ethnic scene, and other minorities have not been slow to follow. Two formerly silent or unheard groups, the Mexican-Americans and Indian Americans, have become both audible and politically visible, although their smaller numbers makes them less powerful than the blacks. Nevertheless, such political leaders as Cesar Chávez are beginning to gain recognition far beyond the confines of the ethnic community.

The substantial political strength of blacks is no longer in doubt. Table 14:3 reports a dramatic rise in the number of black office-

holders in the span of 13 years. Mexican-Americans number around 5 million, which is less than one-quarter the black total. Nevertheless, their regional concentration in the southwest facilitates political mobilization. By 1976 there were several national Mexican-American officeholders: one U.S. senator from New Mexico, one U.S. representative from California, and three from Texas.

The most rural of minorities — native American Indians — total considerably less than 1 million, and they are scattered in numerous small settlements. However, their growing urbanization is correlated with a sense of pan-Indian concern that crosses tribal identities (Wax, 1971:144–151).

Barring European immigration of unforeseen size, these minorities and probably the Puerto Ricans on the mainland will grow in both absolute and relative terms. Blacks, who now make up about 11 percent of the population, are projected to reach 14 percent by the end of the century (*Current Population Reports,* Series P-20, No. 203, July 6, 1970:1). The number of Mexican-Americans is likely to grow as a result of immigration as well as a relatively high rate

At the high tide of civil rights activism in the South. The 1965 Freedom March from Selma to Montgomery, Alabama. Center foreground is Dr. Martin Luther King, Jr.

of natural increase. A maximum 3 or 4 percent of the national total by the 2000 may be a fair guess. Although American Indians are increasing very rapidly (as are such other native peoples as the Canadian Indians, Pacific Islanders, New Zealand Maoris, and Australian aborigines), they will continue to be a small percentage of the total population.

References

Alvarez, Rodolfo
1971 "The unique psycho-historical experience of the Mexican-American people." Social Science Quarterly 52 (June):15–29.

Broom, Leonard and Norval D. Glenn
1967 Transformation of the Negro American. New York: Harper & Row.

Broom, Leonard, Cora A. Martin, and Betty Maynard
1971 "Status profiles of racial and ethnic populations." Social Science Quarterly 52 (September):379–388.

Cripps, Thomas R.
1967 "The death of Rastus: Negroes in American films since 1945." Phylon 28 (Fall):267–275.

Davis, David Brion
1966 The Problem of Slavery in Western Culture. Ithaca, N.Y.: Cornell University Press.

Douglass, Frederick
1960 Narrative of the Life of Frederick Douglass, An American Slave. Edited by Benjamin Quarles. Cambridge: Harvard University Press (Belknap Press).

Doyle, Bertram Wilbur
1937 The Etiquette of Race Relations in the South. Chicago: University of Chicago Press.

Fahy Committee (President's Committee on Equality of Treatment and Opportunity in the Armed Forces)
1950 Freedom to Serve! Equality of Treatment and Opportunity in the Armed Forces. Washington, D.C.: GPO.

Foner, Laura and Eugene D. Genovese (eds.)
1969 Slavery in the New World: A Reader in Comparative History. Englewood Cliffs, N.J.: Prentice-Hall.

Foner, Philip S.
1950–1955 The Life and Writings of Frederick Douglass. Four volumes. New York: International Publishers.

Furnivall, J. S.
1948 Colonial Policy and Practice. London: Cambridge University Press.

Garraty, John A.
1971 The American Nation: A History of the United States to 1877. Second edition. New York: Harper & Row and American Heritage.

Genovese, Eugene D.
1974 Roll, Jordan, Roll: The World the Slaves Made. New York: Pantheon Books.

Glenn, Norval D.
1963 "Some changes in the relative status of American non-whites, 1940–1960." Phylon 24 (Summer).

Hughes, Everett C.
1943 French Canada in Transition. Chicago: University of Chicago Press.

Johnson, Charles S.
1943 Patterns of Negro Segregation. Third edition. New York: Harper & Row.

Kennan, George F.
1971 "Hazardous courses in Southern Africa." Foreign Affairs 49 (January):218–236.

Keyfitz, Nathan
1960 "Some demographic aspects of French-English relations." In Mason Wade (ed.), Canadian Dualism. Toronto: University of Toronto Press.

Kuper, Leo and M. G. Smith (eds.)
1969 Pluralism in Africa. Berkeley and Los Angeles: University of California Press.

Lind, Andrew W.
1938 An Island Community. Chicago: University of Chicago Press.

Lipton, Merle
1972 "Independent Bantustans?" International Affairs 48 (January):1–19.

McRae, Kenneth D.
1964 Switzerland: Example of Cultural Coexistence. Toronto: Canadian Institute of International Affairs.

Marquard, Leo
1969 The Peoples and Policies of South Africa. Fourth edition. New York: Oxford University Press.

Mayer, Kurt B.
1968 "The Jura problem: ethnic conflict in Switzerland." Social Research 35 (Winter):707–741.

Merton, Robert K.
1957 "The self-fulfilling prophecy." Chap. 11 (pp. 421–436) in Social Theory and Social Structure. New York: Free Press. First published in the Antioch Review (Summer):1948.

Moskos, Charles C., Jr.
1966 "Racial integration in the armed forces." American Journal of Sociology 72 (September):132–148.

Myrdal, Gunnar with the assistance of Richard Sterner and Arnold Rose
1944 An American Dilemma: The Negro Problem and Modern Democracy. New York: Harper & Row.

Nieboer, H.
1900 Slavery as an Industrial System. The Hague: Martinus Nijoff.

Park, Robert E.
1937 "Introduction." Pp. xi–xxiv in Doyle.

Passin, Herbert
1955 "Untouchability in the Far East." Monumenta Nipponica 11 (October):27–47.

Pauli, Hertha
1962 Her Name Was Sojourner Truth. New York: Avon Books.

Porter, John
1968 The Vertical Mosaic. Toronto: University of Toronto Press.

Price, John
1966 "A history of the outcaste: untouchability in Japan." Pp. 6–30 in George De Vos and Hiroshi Wagatsuma (eds.), Japan's Invisible Race. Berkeley and Los Angeles: University of California Press.

Rioux, Marcel
1971 Quebec in Question. Translated by James Boake. Toronto: James Lewis & Samuel. First published in French in 1969.

Roseborough, Howard and Raymond Breton
1968 "Perceptions of the relative economic and political advantages of ethnic groups in Canada." Pp. 604–628 in Canadian Society: Sociological Perspectives, edited by Bernard R. Blishen, Frank E. Jones, Kaspar D. Naegele, and John Porter. Third edition. Toronto: Macmillan of Canada.

Royal Commission on Bilingualism and Biculturalism
1967–1970 Volumes 1–5.
1969 Volume 3A. The Work World: Part 1, Socio-economic Status. Part 2, The Federal Administration. Volume 3B. The Work World: Part 3, The Private Sector. Part 4, Conclusions. Ottawa: Queen's Printer for Canada.

Royce, C. C.
1887 The Cherokee Nation of Indians. Fifth Annual Report, Bureau of American Ethnology. Washington, D.C.: GPO.

Rossi, Peter H. and Michael D. Ornstein
1973 "The impact of labor market entry factors: illustrations from the Hopkins Social Accounts Project." Pp. 269–311 in Walter Müller and Karl Ulrich Mayer (eds.), Social Stratification and Career Mobility. The Hague: Mouton.

Rustin, Bayard, Martin Kilson, C. Vann Woodward, Kenneth B. Clark, Thomas Sowell, Roy Wilkins, Andrew F. Brimmer and Norman Hill
1969 Black Studies. New York: Philip Randolph Educational Fund.

Schnier, Miriam (ed.)
1972 Feminism: The Essential Historical Writings. New York, Random House.

Simpson, George Eaton and J. Milton Yinger
1965 Racial and Cultural Minorities: An Analysis of Prejudice and Discrimination. Third edition. New York: Harper & Row.

Smith, M. G.
1960 "Social and cultural pluralism." Annals of the New York Academy of Sciences 83 (January 20):763–777.

Tannenbaum, Frank
1947/1963 Slave and Citizen: The Negro in the Americas. New York: Random House.

Tomlinson, F. R.
1955 Report of the Commission for the Socio-Economic Development of the Bantu Areas Within the Union of South Africa. Pretoria: The Commission.

van den Berghe, Pierre L.
1966 "Racial segregation in South Africa: degrees and kinds." Cahiers d'Etudes Africaines 6 (No. 3):408–418.

Wagley, Charles
1960 "Discussion of Paper" by M. G. Smith (1960). Annals of the New York Academy of Sciences 83 (January 20):777–780.

Wax, Murray L.
1971 Indian Americans: Unity and Diversity. Englewood Cliffs, N.J.: Prentice-Hall.

Woodward, C. Vann
1966 The Strange Career of Jim Crow. Second revised edition. New York: Oxford University Press. A Galaxy Book.

Sources and readings

Bahr, Howard M., Bruce A. Chadwick, and Robert C. Day (eds.)
1972 Native Americans Today: Sociological Perspectives. New York: Harper & Row.

Bureau of the Census
1975 The Social and Economic Status of the Black Population in the United States, 1974. Current Population Reports, Series P-23, No. 54. (A summary of data on blacks, issued annually.) Washington, D.C.: GPO.
1975 Current Population Reports, Series P-20, No. 290. Washington, D.C.: GPO.
1976 Persons of Spanish Origin in the United States, March

Burma, John H.
1970 Mexican-Americans in the United States: A Reader. Cambridge, Mass.: Schenkman Publishing.

[Canadian] Royal Commission on Bilingualism and Biculturalism
1967–1970 Final Report. Five volumes. Ottawa: Queen's Printer for Canada.

Drake, St. Clair and Horace R. Cayton
1945/1969 Black Metropolis: A Study of Negro Life in a Northern City. New York: Harbinger Books.

Engerman, Stanley L. and Eugene D. Genovese (eds.)
1975 Race and Slavery in the Western Hemisphere. Princeton: Princeton University Press.

Fitzpatrick, Joseph P.
1971 Puerto Rican Americans: The Meaning of Migration to the Mainland. Englewood Cliffs, N.J.: Prentice-Hall.

Foner, Laura and Eugene D. Genovese (eds.)
1969 Slavery in the New World: A Reader in Comparative History. Englewood Cliffs, N.J.: Prentice-Hall.

Genovese, Eugene D.
1974 Roll, Jordan, Roll: The World the Slaves Made. New York: Pantheon Books.

Goldhagen, Erich (ed.)
1968 Ethnic Minorities in the Soviet Union. New York: Praeger.

Grebler, Leo, Joan W. Moore, and Ralph C. Guzman with Jeffrey L. Berlant, Thomas P. Carter, Walter Fogel, C. Wayne Gordon, Patrick H. McNamara, Frank G. Mittelbach, and Samuel J. Surace
1970 The Mexican-American People: The Nation's Second Largest Minority. New York: Free Press.

Kuper, Leo and M. G. Smith (eds.)
1969 Pluralism in Africa. Berkeley and Los Angeles: University of California Press.

Marquard, Leo
1969 The Peoples and Policies of South Africa. Fourth edition. New York: Oxford University Press.

Myrdal, Gunnar with the assistance of Richard Sterner and Arnold Rose
1944 An American Dilemma: The Negro Problem and Modern Democracy. New York: Harper & Row.

Park, Robert Ezra
1950 Race and Culture. New York: Free Press.

Shibutani, Tamotsu and Kian M. Kwan
1965 Ethnic Stratification: A Comparative Approach. New York: Macmillan.

Simpson, George Eaton and J. Milton Yinger
1972 Racial and Cultural Minorities: An Analysis of Prejudice and Discrimination. Fourth edition. New York: Harper & Row.

van den Berghe, Pierre L. (ed.)
1972 Intergroup Relations: Sociological Perspectives. New York: Basic Books.

Wagley, Charles and Marvin Harris
1958 Minorities in the New World: Six Case Studies. New York: Columbia University Press.

Wax, Murray L.
1971 Indian Americans: Unity and Diversity. Englewood Cliffs, N.J.: Prentice-Hall.

Woodward, C. Vann
1966 The Strange Career of Jim Crow. Second revised edition. New York: Oxford University Press. A Galaxy Book.

Periodicals

Ethnicity

Phylon

Race

Section one introduction

Like the domestication of animals, the beginnings of agriculture, and the mastery of metals, the emergence of the city is a definitive break with the past. Within the span of human existence urban settlement is a recent adaptation—perhaps only 4,000 years old. The ecological and social changes brought about by dense settlement are still evolving, and the consequences of the city for humanity and for the physical environment are only partially understood.

During the Neolithic Age, approximately 8,000 years ago, the first stable communities appeared. These were farming settlements of a few hundred people. As agriculture became more productive in the more favorable environments, some settlements grew substantially larger, but they were still made up of full-time farmers and were essentially rural dormitories rather than true cities. Even today in Africa and Asia there may be found settlements of several thousand persons that are overgrown villages rather than cities. Almost all of the inhabitants of those

places regularly till their fields. Clearly a large population and a food surplus are necessary conditions to produce urban life, but population size and a dependable food supply do not automatically make a city.

THE FIRST CITIES

Along the fertile river valleys of the Tigris and Euphrates, the Indus, the Nile, and the Yellow River, a fundamentally new social form appeared. Although many of the inhabitants of the first cities were still concerned with agricultural production, others had a wide range of occupational specialties not directly linked to the soil. The following are some of the modifications in the social order that were involved in the development of the first cities:

1. Increased occupational diversity and division of labor
2. Release of a few individuals from productive physical work to engage in symbolic work as priests and philosophers
3. Transformation of religious activities

related to fertility, rainfall, and the streams into the administration of the water supply (the irrigation system) and the management of lands and herds

4. Emergence of a political leadership

5. Increased differentiation of rewards for a wider range of tasks and responsibilities

6. Assignment of some manpower to protect the food supply and the city

7. Establishment of a market for the exchange of goods

Most of these features may be found in tentative forms in pre-urban settlements. It is the combination and dominance of a kind of social organization that characterizes the city: an ever-growing complexity and division of labor, increasing specialization, and the freeing of a few and then many workers from day-to-day subsistence tasks.

The emergence of the earliest cities in the fertile river valleys was followed by the growth of the Mediterranean city-states. The rugged terrain of Greece offered only a limited amount of land suitable for agriculture. This fact restricted city size and encouraged the impulse to settle distant places. By 600 or 500 B.C., a few Greek cities were establishing colonies throughout the Mediterranean, but such colonies remained largely dependent on the adjoining countryside for food and building materials. Colonialism, military conquest, and trade were powerful influences leading to occupational specialization in maritime and military crafts as well as the development of administrative skills. The physical nature of the city itself was shaped by the functions performed within it.

Cities, in the sense of civic communities, [were] signalized and symbolized by the wall that demarcated a primitive city's diminutive area from the vast surrounding countryside. . . . The Greek word for city—*polis*—originally meant citadel, and . . . the original polis at Athens became the "Acropolis," meaning "the summit citadel," when a populous open city crystallized round the foot of the rock (Toynbee, 1967:13B).

Periclean Athens Athens of the fifth century B.C. has been depicted as a mature and complex city-state with an elaborate division of labor; a pluralistic group structure linked to family, religion, class membership, and voluntary associations; a clearly defined parliamentary system; and public service based on citizen participation (Bowra, 1971; Breed and Seaman, 1971:631–645; Zimmern, 1961). This differentiated social order achieved unparalleled heights of creativity with a population of only a quarter of a million. The society was stratified into citizens (males who held the vote) and foreigners, women, and slaves (all of whom were denied the vote). At first stratification was tied to property, but this rule was eventually relaxed with the rise of a commercial class engaged in colonial trade.

Citizens made up less than one-fifth of the inhabitants of Attica (Athens and the surrounding area), and these men were able to carry out their obligations of universal public service because of the work of slaves, who made up about half the population. The slaves were not a mass of menial unskilled workers but included skilled artisans and men of learning who educated the sons of Athenian citizens. At least for sons of wealthy families, schooling continued until the age of 18, when all young men began two years of military training.

The degree of occupational specialization is suggested by Plutarch's list of laborers needed to construct the Parthenon:

. . . carpenter, moulder, bronze-smith, stonecutter, dyer, veneerer in gold and ivory, painter, embroiderer, embosser, to say nothing of the forwarders and furnishers of the material, such as factors, sailors and pilots by sea, and by land, wagon-makers, trainers of yoked beasts, and drivers. There were also rope-makers, weavers, cobblers, road-builders, and miners (quoted in Breed and Seaman, 1971:635).

Athens in the age of Pericles was a well integrated and socially differentiated city-state that contained a full range of social institutions and urban functions: skilled crafts, creative arts and advanced architecture, trade by land and sea, an organized military force, self-government, an intellectual elite, formal education, and religion linked to kinship—all of this with a population no larger than that of Akron, Ohio.

Diverse origins There are as many urban origins as there are independent cultural traditions with an urban way of life. Many of the qualities we think of as civilized have been attained by societies that failed to organize cities. Some Egyptologists believe that civilization advanced for almost 2,000 years under the Pharaohs before cities appeared in Egypt. The period was marked by the development of monumental public works, a formal state superstructure, written records, and the beginnings of exact science. In the New World scholars are still searching the jungles around Mayan temple centers in Guatemala and Yucatan for urban agglomerations of dwellings. For all its temple architecture and high art and the intellectual achievement represented by its hieroglyphic writing and accurate long-count calendar, classic Mayan civilization apparently was not based on the city. These facts do not detract from the fundamental importance of the urban revolution but underline its complex character. Every high civilization other than possibly the Mayan ultimately produced cities, and in most civilizations urbanization began early (Adams, 1960).

The population of ancient cities The Mediterranean seaports of the ancient world were centers of government, religion, and trade, and they grew and declined according to the fortunes of political and commercial empires. It is commonly agreed that Rome was the largest city of ancient times. The Roman census reported 900,000 in 69 B.C. Surely it was a city of the million class, but its maximum size, like that of other cities, is not known. In any case, the populations of early cities fluctuated widely.

The cities of the ancient world declined along with the empires they administered. By the middle of the fourth century A.D., Rome may have had a population of less than 200,000, and by the sixteenth century, as few as 50,000, but by then Rome, like other medieval cities, had begun to grow again in response to the stimulus of the market and the renewal of trade and travel (Pirenne, 1925).

THE PREVALENCE OF CITIES

Increased agricultural productivity to support a larger population, the displacement of surplus manpower from rural to urban areas, and the centralization of work in machine-powered factories—all these contribute to the expansion of cities. The explosive growth that has produced modern urbanized societies is a creature of industrialization and is hardly more than 100 years old. In 1800 a mere 2 percent of Europe's people lived in cities with populations of 100,000 or more (Davis, 1965:43). But with the Industrial Revolution, Western countries were rapidly transformed into urban societies.

Urban life is now the characteristic form of human settlement in Japan, Europe, Australasia, and North America. It is also the emergent form in most of the rest of the world, but the process is not uniform in pace or extent. In some regions, notably North America, temperate South America, western and northern Europe, Japan, Australia, and New Zealand, industrialization and urbanization have reduced the rural populations to a low level. Eastern and southern Europe have not moved so far in the direction of urbanization, and the regions of the developing world are characteristically less urban. Much of Africa and Asia remains predominantly rural.

Thailand, Burma, Nigeria, and India are among the least urbanized nations, with about 10 percent or less of their populations in metropolitan areas of over 100,000. The United Kingdom, Australia, Argentina, the

United States, Japan, and West Germany are among the most urbanized, with more than 50 percent of their populations in cities of 100,000 or over.

Within any region, the countries vary both in the percentage of the population that is rural and the pace of urbanization. For example, in eastern Asia, Taiwan declined from 48 percent to 36 percent rural between 1950 and 1970, while China declined from 89 to 76 percent. The percentage change was about the same, but Taiwan is classified as urban while mainland China is considered to be a rural country. Both Canada and the United States were about one-fourth rural in 1970. Japan changed from a predominantly rural to a highly urbanized (and industrialized) country in less than a single generation. Japan is exceptional, and a similar pace of urbanization should not be expected in the developing countries.

Three kinds of change make up the process of urbanization: (1) city growth, (2) a changed rural–urban population balance, and (3) change in styles and functions.

The increase in the number and size of larger cities, those in the over-100,000 class, is the most evident and worldwide change as urban areas fill up and spread into the countryside to form metropolises. (See Table 15:1.) In the 20 years ending in 1970, the number of cities with populations of at least 100,000 nearly doubled; they now total about 1,600. Those with at least 1 million persons more than tripled in the same period; they now number almost 200.

Massive migration from rural areas characteristically fuels rapid urban growth in advanced countries, in which case the rural population may be static or decline: In relative terms the country becomes more and more urban. Figure 15:1 shows that until the middle of the nineteenth century the United States was almost entirely a rural country. In 1840 the urban population was little more than 10 percent of the total; not until 1920 was the country urbanized in the sense that more than half of the population lived in cities. Currently three-fourths of Americans are urban dwellers. Despite the fact that the

Table 15:1　Number of large cities, by major world region, 1970

Region	City size 100,000–500,000	500,000–1,000,000	1,000,000 and over	Total
Africa	93	12	5	110
Asia	464	55	69	588
Europe	266	37	43	346
USSR	166	25	10	201
North America	141	27	28	196
Middle America and Caribbean	33	5	4	42
South America	64	15	13	92
Oceania[a]	9	4	2	15
Total	1,236	180	174	1,590

Source: Compiled from Davis, 1969:Table B, 83–111. Basic data are estimates. Cities are defined where possible to include the population of the urban area rather than merely the city proper.

[a] All large cities in Oceania are in Australia and New Zealand.

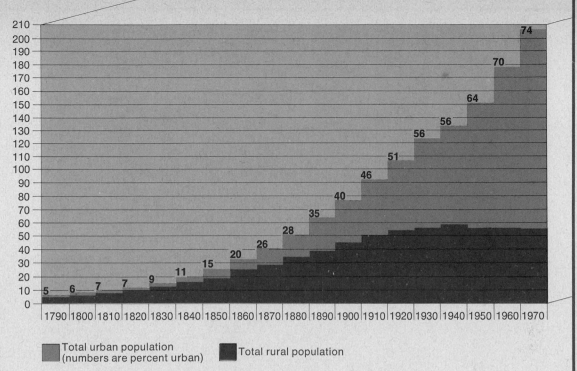

Total urban population
(numbers are percent urban)   Total rural population

Figure 15:1 Rural and urban population, United States, 1790–1970

Prior to 1950 some large and densely settled places were not defined as urban because they were not incorporated.
Figures for 1950 and later are reported under "new" criteria, which classify all the population
residing in urban fringe areas and in unincorporated places of 2,500 or
more as urban. This change moved almost 6 million persons from the
rural to the urban classification in 1950.

Source: Statistical Abstract of the United States, 1960:21; 1970:17.

United States is an urbanized country, the rural population continued to grow until around 1950. It has been nearly stable since then at about 54 million. However, cities can increase in size and number without changing a country or region from rural to urban. In eastern Africa in 1950 there were only four cities with more than 100,000 persons; in 1970 there were 14 cities with populations over 100,000 and two cities with populations over 500,000—a significant urban growth, but eastern Africa remained 90 percent rural.

Hand in hand with true urbanization in developed countries is the transformation of the productive functions of the nation and the labor force from primary to secondary and tertiary activities. (See *TECHNOLOGY AND CIVILIZATION,* p. 517.) As urban functions predominate, rural life and the forms of agricultural production also change: Farming becomes "agribusiness," dominated by and administered from urban centers. The life-styles of urbanism become more and more characteristic of the whole country, even in rural areas.

URBAN AND RURAL

Although there is agreement that some areas are rural and that others are urban, many localities are not obviously one or the other. How these localities and their populations are classified is important when trends in urbanization are traced or international comparisons are made.

The most commonly used distinctions are population density and size. The city is a locality in which a large number of people live and work in close proximity. The rural area, by contrast, has low population density or only a small number of people in a dense cluster. The minimum population size for a city is set at 2,500 by the U.S. Bureau of the Census, but a somewhat lower minimum would be more meaningful in the United States, since several demographic and economic variables, such as the sex ratio, change abruptly below 1,000 population (Duncan, 1957:35–45). Sociologists frequently add a third criterion—heterogeneity of the population in age, sex, and occupation—which excludes from the term city such settlements as peasant villages, mining camps, prisons, and many military installations.

The ecological city In addition to population density, size, and heterogeneity, urban sociologists also use other criteria to draw the line between city and noncity: (1) The *ecological*, or *natural*, city has a population density great enough so that most of the land is devoted to residential, commercial, and industrial use (including transportation); (2) it is separated from other cities by space (either land or water) devoted largely to agricultural or extractive use or not used at all; and (3) the space between cities is broad enough to make daily commuting across it impractical for most workers.

The ecological city includes the *legal* city (the city proper), its contiguous suburbs, and detached satellite settlements, which are socially and economically integrated with the central city. The U.S. census unit called the *urbanized area* is roughly equal to the ecological city. The larger ecological cities in the United States contain several legal cities. For instance, Greater Chicago includes the legal cities of Evanston, Glencoe, Skokie, Cicero, Harvey, and Park Forest, to name a few. The ecological city of New York includes Jersey City, Newark, Yonkers, and many other separately incorporated municipalities outside the limits of the legal city and even outside the state of New York. The populations of many urbanized areas now are more than double the populations of their central legal cities.

Since legal cities are often separated from one another by an invisible boundary—the middle of a street, a river, a bay, or a short span of open countryside—the ecological city is a more meaningful sociological unit. Because the use of data for the legal city rather than for the ecological city may be misleading, data for urbanized areas are usually employed in sociological research, as in Table 15:1.

After the 1960 and 1970 censuses, the press reported that most of the largest American cities had lost population, which implied that New York, Chicago, and Philadelphia are diminishing in importance. In fact, all of the largest ecological cities gained in population. The decline that was revealed occurred in *central* cities and was largely a consequence of decentralization of metropolitan areas.

Urbanization of the Third World Most of the major cities of Asia, Africa, and Latin America are located on the coast or on navigable rivers, indicating their origins in commercial and political colonialism. They serve as administrative centers for government and commerce, and *entrepôt* (transshipment) points for raw materials and the distribution of finished goods. Even the least industrialized of them administer the economies of surrounding districts and are focal points for the industrial activity in their respective countries.

However, many cities of the Third World lack the expanding industrial base that characterized the true urban revolution of developed nations. The push of rural population increase is at least as important as the attraction of opportunities in the city in creating pseudourbanization—urban growth without an adequate industrial development. These cities continue to perform the same roles they had in preindependence days—assembling raw materials for shipment to the factories of developed countries (McGee, 1967: Chap. 1). Despite political independence, Third World countries remain dependent upon socialist or capitalist industrialized powers.

Observers of rapidly growing cities in Latin America (Portes, 1971; Rodwin, 1965) and Southeast Asia (Evers, 1972; McGee, 1967) have commented on the force of sheer population pressure in altering the ecological patterns of old and new cities in new countries. Shantytowns, *barriadas*, *bidonvilles*—slums in any language—are the fastest-growing sectors of such cities. Middle and upper classes flee to new suburbs to place distance between themselves and their too-numerous and too-poor countrymen. In some cases the upper-class compounds are as isolated from the rest of the city as the foreign settlements used to be in colonial days. The native elites are isolated from the proletariat like colonial administrators from the "natives."

Even where there is forward planning for industrial development, surplus agricultural population floods the job market before plans can be implemented, as in the new industrial city of Ciudad Guyana in Venezuela. (See p. 502.) The stresses of such a rapid increase in the number of unemployed and underemployed persons may frustrate planning and retard the social and industrial development of the countries. Some of the most rapidly growing cities are located in developing countries, as shown in Figure 15:2. Vast rural reservoirs of population remain in Third World regions, and the social, economic, and political dislocations of massive and uncontrolled migrations to urban areas are only beginning. Developed countries never had to cope with such population pressure while they were undergoing urbanization.

Figure 15:2 World's fastest growing cities

The percentage figures indicate anticipated growth rates in the next decade.

Source: Development Forum, January–February 1976:8.

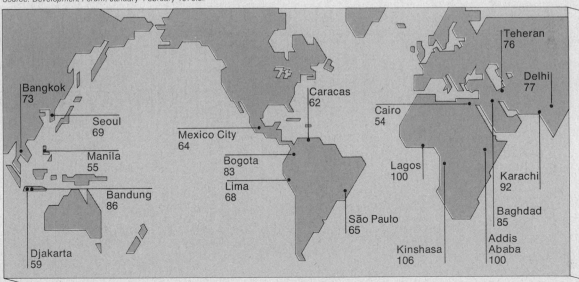

Section two the metropolis

On the northeastern seaboard of the United States, in Great Britain, in the Low Countries, in Western Germany, and in Japan, a new type of urban entity has grown up—the megalopolis. The megalopolis consists of two or more cities, once separated by broad bands of countryside but now joined by strips of urban or semiurban settlement. Within the connecting strips there is an intermingling of urban, suburban, and rural land uses and a new relationship of the urban and the rural. The residents of the "supercities" are more widely dispersed than the residents of traditional compact cities, and their activities are not organized around any one central core. However, they have a higher degree of interdependence than the residents of any other area of comparable extent.

Although the megalopolis has social and ecological unity, it lacks political unity. Unified planning and action are needed to handle transportation and resource conservation, which transcend the bounds of the politically separate cities, but most planning and social action within the supercities has been piecemeal. Institutional adaptation has lagged behind the needs of these new social entities.

ADMINISTRATIVE FRAGMENTATION

The numerous jurisdictions are jealous of their local authority and prerogatives, and

Exercise in futility? A traffic control center in Munich, West Germany

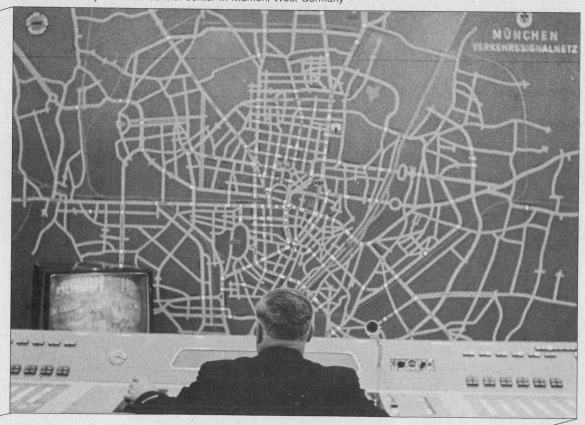

no "natural" agency has yet filled the gaps in management. The following comment, written during World War II, depicts Metropolitan London as a bombing target and as a problem in administration:

Centered on teeming Charing Cross, the London area is the most compact and circular conurbation in the world, and by the same token it is the most deadly target for aerial bombardment that man could ever have devised. . . . There are ten official Londons overlapping one another, like concentric circles around a bull's-eye, each one representing the metropolis in its various stages of governmental growth. These are the City of London, the County of London, Police London or Greater London, Port London, Drainage London, Water London, Electricity London, Transport London, Planning London, and Traffic London. Increasing in radius and in population from the London nucleus the whole southeastern corner of England is engulfed by the Metro London that began to emerge long before the present war (Lepawsky, 1941:828).

The analysis also enumerates the boundaries and functions of each London, which together make up the supercity.

The northeastern American megalopolis, called BosWash, with a population of over 36 million, is an extreme example of political fragmentation. This strip city extends from southern New Hampshire to the Virginia suburbs of Washington, D.C. One can travel from one end to the other of this supercity without leaving territory that is predominantly urban in its land use, its occupations, and the way of life of its people. Ten state governments, the District of Columbia, and hundreds of city, county, town, and village governments have jurisdiction over portions of this megalopolitan belt (Gottman, 1961).

Other megalopolises have declared their future shape: SanSan from San Francisco to San Diego, and JaMi along the Florida east coast from Jacksonville to Miami. No respecter of international boundaries, ChiPitts, the great industrial belt from Chicago to Pittsburgh, reaches across the Canadian border into southern Ontario.

CONCENTRATION AND DISPERSION

The beginnings of suburban expansion were recognized early (Weber, 1899), and a few commuter settlements had grown up along railroads near large cities some 50 years earlier. This movement involved few people, however, until the invention of the electric train and streetcar in the late nineteenth century made intermediate-range commuting both economical and convenient (Ogburn, 1946). Metropolitan areas then expanded outward along the train and streetcar tracks and took on a starlike configuration. Most people still lived within walking distance of the public transportation routes, which did not reach many of the outlying areas. The automobile eventually provided a more flexible means of transportation and led to a greater dispersal of people within the metropolitan area, but the full impact of the automobiles was delayed first by the Depression of the 1930s and then by World War II.

Migration from the central city to the outlying areas has had far-reaching social consequences. Suburbs are populated disproportionately by the young, married adults and their children, and the family tends to be child-centered. Single and unattached adults and married couples without children are rare. Children below the age of 13 and adults between the ages of 25 and 44 are overrepresented. The suburban sex ratio is well below 100. Fertility rates are higher than in the central city, but not as high as in rural areas.

On the average, residents of the suburbs are more affluent, better educated, and whiter than those in central cities. Fourfifths of suburban persons have a high school education or better; in central cities threefourths have that level of education. Median family income in the central cities runs about 80 percent of suburban incomes. Fifty-five percent of blacks live in central cities, but only 25 percent of whites live there (*Current Population Reports*, Series P-23, No. 37, June 24, 1971).

A larger proportion of suburban workers are in professional and business occupations. Many of the families are upwardly mobile and the move to the suburbs signifies their social mobility. Furthermore, high rates of geographic mobility characterize suburbia. Although most of the families are making payments on a home, the payments are regarded as rent, and equities are readily traded and sold. For those whose careers are most successful, each move may be to a more prestigious and expensive suburb and may symbolize a step in their upward mobility.

As in the rural neighborhood, primary relations in the suburbs are often based upon proximity of residence rather than upon commonality of interests. There is a return to neighboring and a trend away from the impersonality and anonymity of the central city. Participation in community organizations, including religious ones, is relatively high. Politically, suburbanites are more conservative than people in the central city. Morally, they are more conventional.

Each suburb tends to be homogeneous in the size and appearance of homes, in the income of residents, and in the patterns of consumption. Conspicuous consumption is avoided; getting ahead of the Joneses is apparently as strongly disapproved of as the failure to keep up with them. Even leisure activities are highly uniform.

Caution These generalizations do not apply to all suburbs and have sometimes been called the myths of suburbia. A study of a suburb populated by automobile workers questions that organizational participation is higher in the suburbs, that residential mobility is greater, that the suburbs are characterized by political conservatism and a renewed interest in religion, and that suburban culture is essentially middle class (Berger, 1960). The working-class suburb may itself be a deviant case, and generalizations based on suburban studies should be regarded as tentative.

A Canadian monograph is critical of generalizations based on studies of packaged suburbs, i.e., residential developments designed to provide a wide range of commercial facilities. Analysis of 15 different Toronto suburban areas finds much less "structure" in most suburbs than in the fully preplanned type and wide diversity according to such variables as socioeconomic status, ethnicity, density of settlement, the age of the settlement, past residential experience, and duration of residence in the suburb (Clark, 1966).

Density In urban nations, megalopolitan growth concentrates and redistributes population at the same time. Central cities become static or decline, but the metropolitan areas expand and their populations increase. Between 1960 and 1970 the U.S. population in urban areas grew from 125 to 149 million, an increase of 19 percent. The geographic area covered by the urban population expanded from about 40,000 to about 54,000 square miles, an increase of 35 percent. Hence the density of the growing urban population decreased—more people but in a larger area. It is estimated that two-thirds of the U.S. population lives on 1.5 percent of the land area, with an average urban density of 2,760 persons per square mile. The overall density of the United States is about 58 per square mile of land area, compared with 200 for China, 720 for Japan, and a worldwide density of 68.

In every decade since 1920, population has increased more rapidly outside than inside central cities. In fact, since 1960 central cities have been nearly static, but outside, metropolitan growth has averaged between 3 and 4 percent per year. The concentrating-dispersing forces of metropolitan growth are epitomized in the New York area. In 1970 Manhattan, with a population of 1.5 million, had a density of 70,000 per square mile, but that was a decline from 90,000 per square mile in 1950. The population of New York proper is now stable at under 8 million, but the suburbs of New York increased by 20 percent in the decade

Old rubbish into new land for high-rise apartments

beginning in 1960. The rule for defining an urbanized area is that it must have at least one city of 50,000 inhabitants and a surrounding area with a density of at least 1,000 per square mile. By that standard, the state of New Jersey with a density of 958 is almost entirely urbanized (*Bureau of the Census Release CB-72-100*, April 1972).

FULL LAND OR EMPTY LAND

With two-thirds of the U.S. population concentrated on less than 2 percent of the land area, it seems reasonable to assume that there is an ample reserve of land for the foreseeable future, but the kind of land and the way it is used are crucial. In a pure market economy, over a period of time competition determines land use on the criteria of cost and profit. Land is allocated to uses that yield the highest rents or earnings; there is competition between land uses as well as between land users. Land that is first utilized for grazing is taken over for cultivation, then for residential development, and finally for industrial or commercial use. Each change leads to more intensive use, with progressively higher financial yield per acre.

If there were a very large amount of desirable land, there might be little objection to letting free markets determine how any particular tract is used. However, productive land is in short supply, and the most fertile soils are often those on which it is cheapest to place real estate developments or factories. Building on slopes unsuitable for agricultural use costs more because of lower density and the need for expensive safeguards against erosion and slippage. According to some scholars, the added cost would counterbalance the cost of preserving the best arable land for agriculture.

In 1960 about 2.5 percent of all California land was in urban use, and in 1975 roughly 4 percent was urban. Although in absolute terms 4 percent may seem a small amount, "urban expansion occurs almost entirely on the very finest agricultural land" (Mrak, 1966:6). In fact, the increase from 2.5 percent to 4 percent is an increase of 60 percent in 15 years. The problem is complicated because the process of shifting land use changes the land. For practical purposes the urbanization process is irreversible, except over a long period of time and at large, perhaps prohibitive, costs. Some alterations are not reversible at any cost. Ecological study indicates that the planner should consider the cost of undoing the successively more intensive land use and should consider not doing in the first place what cannot be undone.

We know that today many cities have within their present boundaries enough vacant land to take care of growth for the next twenty years. We know that if we want to we can insist that housing and industry and other developments be located on lovely rolling hills instead of on desirable agricultural land. We know that we can run our highways along the edges of the fine land instead of through it.

Doing some of these things might cost us more money today than not doing them. But surely we will live to rue the day when we worried about the cost of housing developments and highways rather than retaining our finest agricultural areas for future production (Mrak, 1966:6).

THE ECOSYSTEM AND OPEN SPACE

The foregoing quotation is contrary to the precepts of urban land-use planning in that it calls for higher densities inside cities in order to preserve other lands for agricultural production. This collision of two enlightened attitudes points out that the interrelation of different social uses of land needs to be studied in a broader framework than heretofore. Large regions encompassing both rural and urban land uses are coming to be viewed as systems of patterned ecological relations in which changes in one part rebound upon the other parts of the ecosystem. However, the multitude of municipal, county, and state jurisdictions within any such region inhibit planning for the area as a whole. (On the concept of ecosystem, see pp. 535–537.)

The changed perspective toward open spaces was expressed first in efforts to preserve areas in their original natural condition for future generations. As cities grow larger and as more people can afford to travel, city dwellers seek respite from high-density environments. But the efficiency of automobile travel has changed the more

popular parks into rustic concentrations of urban density during the vacation season. Yosemite National Park is not immune to smog, crowding, and other characteristically urban problems. The broader view of the megalopolis and its ecosystem considers agricultural land not merely for its productive capacity but as part of the heritage of open space. Thus it has been proposed that such lands be taxed according to open-space values in order to encourage their owners to withhold them from industrial and high-density residential use. When agricultural and open lands are taxed according to their potential value as residential or commercial property, the owners are frequently forced to sell. In California, a system of agricultural preserves has been initiated which permits lower tax assessments for owners who contract to maintain the land in agricultural status for a term of years. Such plans are in their infancy, however.

Section three studying the city

THEORY OF URBANISM

Study of the city has been largely dominated by the contrast between rural and urban life. Common-sense observation suggests that living in the city is very different from living in the country or in a small town—more sophisticated but more superficial, more challenging but less protective, more exciting but more impersonal. The small town is assumed to be dominated by rural values and perspectives.

This interpretation of city life was summed up in an influential essay by Louis Wirth (1938), who expressed the point of view of the Chicago school of urban sociologists. It followed the tradition of Georg Simmel, whose "The Metropolis and Mental Life" (1903) made many of the same points. Wirth defined the city as "a relatively large, dense and permanent settlement of socially heterogeneous individuals" (1938:8), a definition that accords with commonly accepted views of urbanization, as discussed above in Sections One and Two. He argued that the size, density, and heterogeneity of cities call forth a whole series of individual and group adaptations that make up the distinctive features of "urbanism as a way of life."

Wirth saw the main effects of urbanism as (1) the transformation of social contacts, which become more impersonal, more transitory, more limited, and more superficial — in other words, secondary rather than primary contacts; (2) the emergence of an urban personality characterized by a fluid, multiple self-hood (see *SOCIALIZATION*, p. 103); (3) the dominance of formal social controls and special-purpose associations; and (4) the formation of relatively segregated groups with divergent life-styles. He described as perhaps the most general outcome of urbanism a weakening of social bonds, which accounts for the apparent prevalence of social disorganization in urban communities.

Psychic overload Wirth's theory is still considered unproven and open to question at a number of points (Morris, 1968; Fischer, 1972). Some aspects of his theory have since been modified to take account of new concepts and data. For example, the hypothesis first put forward by Simmel that city life produces "nervous stimulation" has been reformulated, using the concept of psychic overload:

This term, drawn from systems analysis, refers to the inability of a system to process inputs from the environment because there are too many inputs for the system to cope with, or because successive inputs come so fast that Input A cannot be processed when Input B is presented. When overload is present, adaptations occur. The system must set priorities and make choices. . . . City life, as we experience it, constitutes a continuous set of encounters with adaptations to overload (Milgram, 1970:1462).

Among the accommodations to overload are screening devices for limiting social contacts, for example, projecting a closed, unfriendly image by facial expression or by walking rapidly through the streets. (See

Adaptation 2.) More important, perhaps, is the emergence of new norms of noninvolvement:

Men are actually embarrassed to give up a seat on the subway for an old woman; they will mumble, "I was getting off anyway." . . . These norms develop because everyone realizes that in situations of high density people cannot implicate themselves in each other's affairs, for to do so would create conditions of continual distraction that would frustrate purposeful action (Milgram, 1970:1464).

The theory that norms of noninvolvement arise helps explain the perceived character of urban life without assuming that psychic overload occurs at every moment. The experience of overload is sufficiently frequent and stressful to make a psychic response of noninvolvement relevant and helpful, but the image of a constantly bombarded or harassed urban resident is exaggerated in fact and unnecessary to Wirth's theory.

The foregoing ideas serve to strengthen the theoretical underpinnings of the Wirth-Simmel argument, but factual reservations remain. Although it seems plausible, it is not known if the average city dweller actually experiences more nervous stimulation than the average small-town resident. A relevant fact is that "while the number of persons per acre increases with city size [up to a point], the average number of persons per room and per dwelling unit (where most of life is spent) actually decreases from rural to urban places" (Fischer, 1972:193). To account for the avoidance of social contacts, it may be unnecessary to assume a high degree of nervous stimulation. The more frequent encounters with strangers in the city, with ensuing strains and unknown outcomes, may be an adequate explanation in itself.

Perhaps the most important criticism of Wirth's model is that it does not apply very well to the preindustrial or premodern city (Morris, 1968:54). The ancient and medieval cities of the West and the Asian and African cities of more recent times have been large, densely populated, and heterogeneous. But traditional patterns of kinship, hierarchy, land use, occupational communities, and neighborhood settlement were dominant. These patterns limited the erosion of primary relations and forestalled the fragmentation of social experience.

The significance of this criticism is that the theory of urbanism is difficult to distinguish from a theory of modernization. Instead of identifying a distinctively urban phenomenon, Wirth's model may be drawing on some implications of the transition from *Gemeinschaft* to *Gesellschaft* or of the creation of a mass society. Since modernization occurs in cities and contributes to further urbanization, it is easy to see how the two processes intermingle.

On the other hand, many of the hypotheses suggested by Wirth are directly relevant to city life:

The clock and the traffic signal are symbolic of the basis of our social order in the urban world. Frequent close physical contact, coupled with great social distance, accentuates the reserve of unattached individuals toward one another and, unless compensated for by other opportunities for response, gives rise to loneliness (Wirth, 1938:16).

It may well be that the modern world, in and out of metropolitan centers, tends to produce a "lonely crowd" (Riesman et al., 1950). But the specific conditions of urban settlement tend to strengthen that tendency and, moreover, to give it a particular form and quality. The theory of urbanism is perhaps best understood as identifying a specific milieu within which the isolating and fragmenting processes of mass society are likely to occur.

Caution Wirth treated urbanism as a variable. In the real world, there is no such thing as a pure form of urbanism. The theory is a model, delineating what the urban world would look like in the absence of opposing forces:

The central problem of the sociologist of the city is to discover the forms of social action and organization that typically emerge in relatively permanent, compact settlements of large numbers of heterogeneous individuals. We must also infer that urbanism will assume its most characteristic and extreme form in the measure in which the conditions with which it is congruent are present. Thus the larger, the more densely populated, and the more heterogeneous a community, the more accentuated the characteristics associated with urbanism will be (Wirth, 1938:9).

The persistence of rural values and lifestyles within the city does not necessarily refute the theory. And the rise of suburbia may be considered, at least in part, a countervailing force. On the other hand, if too many facts have to be accounted for in other ways or treated as exceptions, the theory is likely to need revision in content or in scope (Gans, 1962:627).

SEGREGATION

The process of ecological succession as codified by plant and animal ecologists has a dramatic human parallel in the entry of a series of immigrant populations into the urban centers. The resulting segregation of visible ethnic and racial groupings in clearly defined social areas, often called ghettos (cf. Wirth, 1928; Drake and Cayton, 1945), has long been a major research focus, especially for the Chicago school of urban ecologists. The pattern is repeated in city after city and involves large numbers of racially distinct people and often physically decayed urban environments. Residential segregation imposes strains on the organization of cities, on the texture of urban life, on race relations, and on the culture and institutions of blacks and whites. The concentration of blacks and Puerto Ricans in central cities is the most recent and perhaps the most consequential of a long series of such segregated settlements.

Measuring segregation A study of the 207 largest American cities measured segregation by an index based on the distribution of whites and nonwhites according to their proportion within a given city. The index varies between zero and 100. An index score of 100 indicates complete segregation—no intermixture of whites and nonwhites in any block. An index of zero indicates proportional representation: for example, if 10 percent of the population of a city is nonwhite, 10 percent of the population of each block would be nonwhite (Taeuber and Taeuber, 1965).

In the 207 cities that had a population of 50,000 or more in 1960, the index values ranged from 60.4 to 98.1—in other words, from fairly high segregation to almost complete separation of whites and nonwhites. San Jose, Sacramento, Salt Lake City, San Francisco, and Bridgeport (Connecticut) had the lowest index values but were rather highly segregated by an absolute standard. Furthermore, all of these cities except Bridgeport contain a significant number of nonwhites who are not blacks; if the index had been computed for whites and blacks (instead of whites and nonwhites), the index scores would be significantly higher. This was not done because separate detailed data for blacks were not then readily available.

The most highly segregated cities were Fort Lauderdale, Orlando, Miami, West Palm Beach, and Jacksonville, all in Florida; Shreveport and Monroe in Louisiana; Inster, Michigan; and Winston-Salem, North Carolina. The mean segregation index was higher in the South (90.9) and North Central region (87.7) than in the Northeast (79.2) and the West (79.3), but there were very highly segregated cities in all regions. Degree of segregation did not vary consistently with size of city, number of nonwhites, or percentage of nonwhites.

The greater average segregation in the South than in other regions is a reversal of the historical condition. As recently as 1940, Southern cities were less segregated on the average than cities in the rest of the country, and at the beginning of the century there was only a moderate amount of segregation in some Southern cities. This does not suggest social equality. A relatively low rate of segregation coexisted with extreme

The vertical street: East Harlem. On street surveillance, see Adaptation 36.

socioeconomic subordination. Customarily black servants lived on the premises or behind the residences of well-to-do whites. The same living arrangements could be observed in a few upper-income neighborhoods in the North, but such residential patterns are disappearing.

Slums The word *slum* evokes an image of a densely settled, deteriorated ghetto area in the central city. Within limits this stereotype is valid, and the urban riots of the 1960s made many people who formerly knew only the word aware of the reality. A slum is an area that is no longer what it was and is waiting to be something else. A slum may be in the "transitional zone," in the terminology of the Chicago urban ecologists, but this is no guarantee that it will surmount its blighted condition. Only a part of the zone in transition will be taken into the expanding central district, and some slums have no future in the real estate market unless governments intervene.

Many slum inhabitants are new migrants from rural places or foreign lands. They are in the slum because they can find no other place in which to live, because they do not know their way around, because they cannot afford to live elsewhere, because segregation and prejudice exclude them from better environments, or because personal ties to kin or communal facilities hold them in the locality. Some slum dwellers are the "disreputable poor" who are going nowhere. (See *SOCIAL STRATIFICATION*, p. 174.)

Some slums are in outlying areas where squatters build their shacks out of refuse material on city dumps, marshlands, and other undesirable terrain.

During the Great Depression of the 1930's in the United States quasipermanent settlements of shacks and tents (called "Hoovervilles" in ironic tribute to the then President) grew up around the edge of cities and large towns in the agricultural regions of the far west. . . . Beyond the jurisdictions of both law enforcement and service agencies of the city, . . . they were also beyond the reach of building code, zoning, and sanitary ordinances (Howton, 1967:23).

Hoovervilles were transition areas for the unemployed who were waiting for economic recovery. The men were literate, had useful skills, and were ready to participate in the labor force, but they had to wait until the economy began to recover. When jobs opened up, most squatters moved to conventional living environments, but the years of deprivation took a heavy human toll.

Slums of the urban fringe are also found in vigorous postwar economies of Western Europe. Industrial expansion in France has stimulated the inflow of foreigners seeking to take advantage of job opportunities. About

700,000 of the 3 million immigrants are in the Paris area, where most of the Spanish and Italian workers are apparently able to find housing. The Portuguese and North Africans are less successful, and it is estimated that 100,000 homeless migrants have built *bidonvilles* (tin can cities) on the outskirts of Paris:

The North African bidonvilles are usually a mixture of cement and wood structures that lean against one another under corrugated iron roofs. Stones, bicycle tires and other objects are tossed on the roofs to hold down the sheets of iron. Narrow paths weave among the shanties.

The Portuguese bidonvilles are, on the average, better organized physically and socially. The Portuguese houses are usually larger, although, like the North Africans', have only two or three rooms. They are sometimes laid out in a row. One Portuguese bidonville even has an electricity line strung and television antennas sprouted from some of the shacks.

Electricity, however, is exceptional and most bidonvilles have no running water or heating except for coal and kerosene stoves. . . . Water is carried home in plastic tanks from a public pump, which may be as much as half a mile away (Jaffe, 1972).

Slums perform other functions in addition to housing unfortunate inhabitants out of the view of conventional society. It has been suggested that especially in developing countries, the *barriadas* (slums) function as an acculturative zone in transition where migrants from village society learn how the urban world works and how they can cope with it (Howton, 1967).

ECOLOGY AND THE URBAN ORDER

In half a century of intensive research, a number of theories of urban organization and research techniques have been devised to analyze the spatial pattern of cities. Two of the most influential are the approaches of social ecology and of social area analysis. Although more sophisticated techniques have subsequently been developed, both of the traditional approaches throw light on aspects of urban life.

The Chicago School of Urban Ecology

Studies of the ecological patterning of modern American industrial cities were originally developed by Park, Burgess, and their colleagues and students at the University of Chicago in the 1920s and 1930s (Burgess, ed., 1926; Park, Burgess, and McKenzie, eds., 1925).

A main concern of early human ecologists was to discover how human populations adapted to the natural environment and how social groups and institutions formed specific territorial arrangements, especially in cities. The major principles identified by Park and his colleagues were the ecological processes of competition, dominance, invasion, and succession, concepts borrowed from biological science.

In every life community there is always one or more dominant species. In a plant community this dominance is ordinarily the result of struggle among the different species for light. In a climate which supports a forest the dominant species will invariably be trees. On the prairie and steppes they will be grasses . . . the principle of dominance operates in the human as well as in the plant and animal communities. The so-called natural or functional areas of a metropolitan community—for example, the slum, the rooming-house area, the central shopping section and the banking center—each and all owe their existence directly to the factor of dominance, and indirectly to competition (Park, 1936:7–8).

For the Chicago ecologists, the central business district was the *dominant* area of industrial cities. In a growing city the central business district must expand, competing with the zone immediately outside it—the zone in transition, in Burgess's terminology. As a result of *competition* from the dominant center, land values in the transition zone are forced up, but the buildings and the neighborhood deteriorate. Old buildings are not repaired but are put to temporary uses, and new construction waits on *invasion* by the central business district.

Residents able to afford higher rents and the costs of commuting from outlying areas into the central business district begin to move to the periphery. When the change in land use from residential to business is complete, the process of ecological *succession* is halted—until competition and invasion begin again, perhaps because of the "need" to improve transportation networks and put freeways where office buildings once stood.

In the districts between business and industrial developments are slums, immigrant communities, rooming-house areas, "hobohemia," and bohemia. These areas tend to be separated by such barriers as transportation arteries, wedges of business and industry, parks, and topographical features that modify the concentric zonal pattern hypothesized by Burgess as the typical form of expansion for modern industrial cities. (See Figure 15:3.)

Chicago thus became a social laboratory for testing ideas about human ecology and the growth of the city. The ecological processes of competition, invasion, and succession were seen as sifting and sorting different social and cultural groups into natural areas within the urban community, creating a mosaic of segregated social worlds (Hunter, 1971).

Social area analysis A second approach to urban research was developed at the University of California, Los Angeles, in the 1940s. It was noteworthy for its attempt to view the residential segregation of social groups against the broad canvas of social change in modern industrial societies (Shevky and Williams, 1949).

Because the Bureau of the Census divides cities into census tracts, relatively homogeneous geographic units containing between 3,000 and 6,000 persons, the researcher had readily available data on small areas within the Los Angeles metropolis. Data on the tracts were interpreted in terms of three broad social processes or indicators: *social rank, urbanization,* and *segregation,* and tracts with similar scores were grouped together. These measures have also been called socioeconomic status, familism, and ethnicity. High urbanization signifies a low fertility ratio, many women at work, and

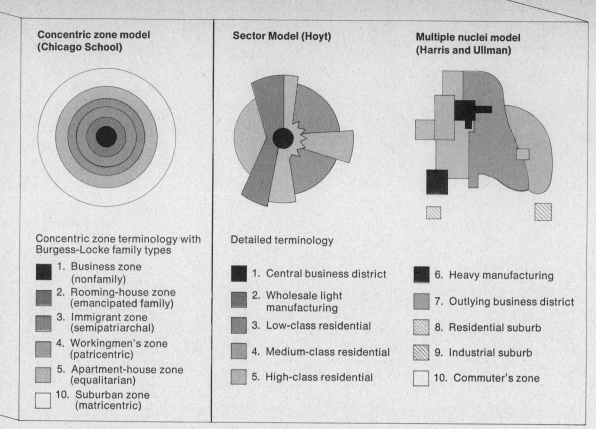

Concentric zone model (Chicago School)

Sector Model (Hoyt)

Multiple nuclei model (Harris and Ullman)

Concentric zone terminology with Burgess-Locke family types

1. Business zone (nonfamily)
2. Rooming-house zone (emancipated family)
3. Immigrant zone (semipatriarchal)
4. Workingmen's zone (patricentric)
5. Apartment-house zone (equalitarian)
10. Suburban zone (matricentric)

Detailed terminology

1. Central business district
2. Wholesale light manufacturing
3. Low-class residential
4. Medium-class residential
5. High-class residential

6. Heavy manufacturing
7. Outlying business district
8. Residential suburb
9. Industrial suburb
10. Commuter's zone

Figure 15:3 Three models of urban structure

Source: Concentric zone terminology after Burgess and Locke, 1953:101; detailed terminology after Harris and Ullman, 1945:12. By permission of the American Academy of Political and Social Science. Sector model after Hoyt, 1943.

few single-family dwellings, and it is therefore equivalent to low familism, that is, relatively weak commitment to family life. Conversely, high familism, which denotes a high fertility ratio, few women at work, and many single-family dwellings is equivalent to low urbanization.

As the growth of industry, towns, and mass communication brings more and more people into a condition of mutual dependence, there is an ever-increasing range and intensity of social relations among the members of industrial societies. This is called *societal scale* (Wilson and Wilson, 1945). Shevky and Bell (1955) identified three structural trends most characteristic of societies whose scale was increasing: (1) cieties whose scale was increasing: (1)

changes in the distribution of skills and occupations, (2) the separation of work and home as a result of the Industrial Revolution and the demographic transition to low mortality and low fertility, and (3) changes in the cultural composition of the population because of migration.

Both methods soon outgrew the metropolitan centers where they were first developed. The Chicago techniques have been widely applied, especially in the United States, and the social area approach more extensively in other countries.

Graphic models Methods of urban study that take land use as the point of departure lend themselves particularly well to graphic representation. Three familiar schemes are shown in Figure 15:3. The numbers of the zones have been coordinated to make the three diagrams easily comparable. The concentric model has six different zones, including Number 10, the suburban or commuter's zone. Different family types predominate in each concentric zone, and these are identified in the legend.

The sector model identifies five types of districts and the multiple nuclei model, nine types. The models do not list all the possibilities because the schemes emphasize different ideas about urban structure. Each could be broken down further: For example, service and shopping areas could be identified within the various residential districts. No diagram is given for the social area method, which presents another kind of graphic problem.

Each of the methods shown in the models contributes to understanding the social and physical aspects of large cities. Varying patterns occur in all large cities in urban industrial societies, but the graphic models call attention to different aspects of city life. Family characteristics usually show a distinct zonal pattern, supporting the Burgess concentric theory. Differences in social rank tend to be distributed along the lines of Hoyt's sector pattern (Salins, 1971:236), and the segregation of racial and ethnic groups is likely to display a multiple nuclei pattern.

Section four planning and renewal

Theories of the city come into sharp focus when social policies are debated. Almost everyone agrees that the tangled growth and evident decay of the modern city call for planning and reconstruction. But the assumptions of planning and the goals of reconstruction are subjects of continuing controversy. This section considers some of the issues at stake and how they relate to the sociology of urban life.

VARIETIES OF CITY PLANNING

The planning of cities is not new. Whenever a dominant political, economic, or religious elite has had a conception of what ends the city should serve, a kind of planning has emerged. Even the medieval cities of Europe were not haphazard growths (Mumford, 1938:51–58). They were given shape by the demands of fortification and defense and by the preeminence of major institutions, especially the church, the guildhall, and the marketplace. Medieval town-planning supported and symbolized the established social order.

Modern city planning has its origin in the reformer's dream. In the nineteenth century, many people recoiled from the congestion and squalor they saw about them, much of it due to the industrialization that greatly stimulated migration to the cities. In 1891 the chairman of the London City Council said:

There is no thought of pride associated in my mind with the idea of London. I am always haunted by the awfulness of London: by the great appalling fact of these millions cast down, as it would appear by hazard, on the banks of this noble stream, working each in their own groove and their own cell, without regard or knowledge of each other, without heeding each other, without having the slightest idea how the other lives. . . . Sixty years ago a great Englishman, Cobbett, called it a wen. If it was a wen then, what is it now? A tumour, an elephantiasis sucking into its gorged system half of the life and the blood and the bone of the rural districts (quoted in Howard, 1902:11).

Such sentiments as these helped create a movement for thoroughly planned communities.

The garden city and its critics A significant document of the city-planning movement is Ebenezer Howard's *Garden Cities of Tomorrow* (1902). Howard was an English reformer who saw the congestion of the cities and the depopulation of the rural areas as aspects of the same problem. The ideal, he thought, was a balanced environment, recombining city and countryside. New towns—founded on undeveloped land—would be so planned and so controlled as to retain the virtues of both urban and rural living. "Town and country *must be married* and out of this joyous union will spring a new hope, a new life, a new civilisation" (Howard, 1902:18).

In Howard's concept of the garden city, land was to be owned in common. As a result, one of the main causes of urban blight —the rise of land values as population density increases—would be avoided. The city could be planned without the rigidities that are introduced when privately owned land in some parts of the city becomes extremely valuable and without the pressure to increase densities and thereby push up the value of the land. This principle of common ownership, though vital in Howard's proposal, has had no practical influence on the development of comprehensive planning for large cities.

Another principle, more successfully transmitted, was the notion that every garden city should be protected by a permanent boundary of open land reserved for agricul-

ture and recreation. This greenbelt, in addition to offering opportunities for local agriculture, would give the city a definite limit and configuration. The greenbelt ideal has strongly influenced the perspectives of city planners, especially in the design of new towns. The creation of greenbelt towns was one of the programs of the New Deal administration during the 1930s (Stein, 1958: Chap. 8).

The garden city idea was part of a broader movement to harmonize and beautify the city. The emphasis was on more open space, new housing, new facilities, new city centers. In existing communities, a comprehensive survey would first be made, then a master plan would be developed for approval by political authorities. Planning for existing communities would be, of necessity, the main work of the new profession of city planning.

Jacobs (1961:17–25) argued that the idealists who proposed the garden city, the city beautiful, and related ideas were trying to solve the problems of urbanism by doing away with its distinctive characteristics.

Nostalgia and fantasy for an urban nation: Disney World, Florida

She felt the reformers were anticity, that they wanted to decentralize the metropolis and lower population densities, and that they hoped to substitute green for asphalt, quiet for noise, and a gentle ambiance for the crowd and turbulence of the big city.

In fact, a strong antiurban bias is apparent in many of the projects, as well as in the writings, of urban planners. For example, a discussion of new towns lists the following as "the basic evils and limitations of the old cities which New Towns and worthwhile redevelopment of existing urban areas must eliminate":

Dangers to health and life: The strained nerves, tensions, physical disabilities . . . resulting from "normal" urban life. . . .

Congestion: Life and movement is imprisoned by gridiron streets, forming an archaic pattern within which houses, factories, shops, and offices are crammed. . . .

Loneliness: Man is submerged in the colossal human swarm, his individuality overwhelmed, his personality negated, his essential dignity is lost in crowds without a sense of community.

Lack of nature: In the canyons of the city, nature is obliterated by the hard masonry. Man is lost in the stony urban desert. . . .

Waste of time, money, energy: In the city people are always going somewhere instead of doing things.

Ugliness: Monotony is produced by the endless repetition of similar rectangular blocks and the decaying wreckage of past disorder (Stein, 1958: 218).

These ills are to be remedied by such devices as the separation of pedestrian and automobile traffic, mainly through the use of superblocks; planned avenues of circulation; and defined neighborhoods of limited area, equipped with central meeting places. "Nature will dominate, and all cities will be green cities, with parks in the heart of each block and encircling belts of agriculture, natural playgrounds, and wilderness" (Stein, 1958:219).

This image of the city contrasts sharply with Jane Jacobs's view, presented in Adaptation 36, that city planning should build upon, rather than reject, the historic characteristics of urban living: high density, mixed activities, life in the streets.

Planning and preconceptions The movement for radical change and a new way of life has fallen far short of its goals. What began as a utopian social movement ended up as a practical profession whose members had to tailor their goals to what their clients would accept. And the staffs of local planning agencies have been, for the most part, civil engineers and architects, not urban sociologists. Nevertheless, the early reformers had a great influence on the spirit and style of city planning. This influence is most notable in the preference for open spaces, the emphasis on clearing slums and building new housing, the separation of urban activities into controlled zones, and the concept of a city plan as the product of professional expertise.

Contemporary criticism of city planning centers on its unspoken assumptions. Thus one line of argument stresses an unconscious middle-class bias:

The ends underlying the planners' physical approach reflected their Protestant middle-class view of city life. As a result, the master plan tried to eliminate as "blighting influences" many of the land uses and institutions of working-class, lower-class and ethnic groups. Most of the plans either made no provision for tenements, rooming houses, secondhand stores, and marginal industry, or located them in catchall zones of "nuisance uses," in which all land uses are permitted. Popular facilities that they considered culturally or morally undesirable were also excluded. The plans called for many parks and playgrounds but left out the movie house, the neighborhood tavern, and the local club-room; they proposed museums and churches but no hot-dog stands and night clubs; they planned for industrial parks, but not loft industry; for parking garages, but not automobile repair stations (Gans, 1968:62).

Planning involves the setting of standards and the assessment of need. But needs and standards are relative; much depends on a person's expectations and his prior experience. When housing is *extremely* bad, planners and residents are likely to be in close agreement. But above a certain minimum there is room for considerable difference of opinion. What is a slum to a planner may be a comfortable environment to the resident. Thus the effort to "renew" the Hyde Park–Kenwood area of Chicago, near the university, was resisted by black residents. For most of them, the movement into Hyde Park had been upward mobility. Their housing was better than they had before and better than they could find elsewhere in Chicago. People who had invested money and work in their homes resented having them defined as dilapidated. What seemed blighted areas to older residents were pleasant neighborhoods to new arrivals (Rossi and Dentler, 1961:185).

Conceptions of need have changed over the years:

The urban slum building of the 1890s was typically a dumbbell tenement with tiny windowless bedrooms in which up to twenty families shared a toilet. Today a dwelling unit is marked as substandard if it lacks a private bathroom for each family. . . . The present slum buildings of Harlem were the middle-class and even luxury apartments of prior generations. Structurally, they are solid masonry buildings with windows in every room, a major reason why rehabilitation rather than replacement has become an acceptable means of ministering to the housing needs of the poverty class. The average quality of the American housing inventory has been steadily rising but not as fast as our standards of what constitutes acceptable housing (Kahn, 1969:161).

Standards are elastic as well as relative. An urban working-class family, accustomed to sharing space, might prefer more room, but not at the sacrifice of other values, such as a better car, more food, or vacations.

It has been suggested that there are significant class differences in the way space is perceived and used (Fried and Gleicher, 1961:311–312). In the urban middle class, a sharp boundary is drawn between private

and public spaces. Privacy is a salient value, manifested in the siting of buildings, landscaping, arrangement of walks, and floor plans. Such public spaces as apartment hallways are paths to and from the private domain. They are not significant arenas of interaction, nor is there a sense of "territory."

The working-class style, in some places at least, is very different:

Social life has an almost uninterrupted flow between apartment and street: children are sent out into the street to play, women lean out the windows to watch and take part in street activity, women go "out on the street" to talk with friends, men and boys meet on the corners at night, and families sit on the steps and talk with their neighbors at night when the weather is warm (Fried and Gleicher, 1961:312).

The boundary between the dwelling and the environing social space is highly permeable.

The planners' symbolic world The preconceptions of planners are only partly the result of their social origins and life-styles; they stem also from the activity of planning itself. Planning creates a world of its own, a symbolic world of maps and models, zones and thoroughfares. This professional frame of reference fosters an image of the city that is often, and perhaps necessarily, remote from the urban reality as it is experienced by the inhabitants.

This point was brought out in a study of planning for Ciudad Guayana in Venezuela. In 1960 the Venezuelan government established a public corporation to develop the Guayana region and to plan the growth of the city. A team of planners and social scientists from the United States was brought in to help. Aware that there might be a significant gap between the planners' perceptions and those of the residents, interviews were conducted to discover how people perceived the urban environment. Most people, it was found, were parochial: They lacked a clear image of the city as a whole. On the other hand, the planners were short on understanding the texture of social space:

Whereas the planning team's habitual diagram of the city drew in the two major rivers, the Orinoco and the Caroni, followed by the location of the major settlements, most of the inhabitants concentrated on the urban environment, drawing little outside of it. . . . Their view was closely correlated with their use of the city, seldom extending beyond this experience, while, to the designers, many features of the city, such as the names and boundaries of barrios and many locally known buildings, were mostly unknown until our interviews were made. The inhabitants' world was a familiar territory unclear at the fringes of knowledge; the designer's world was thin in the center but bounded by the distinct outlines of rivers and urban development as sketched out on his maps (Appleyard, 1969:429–430).

Planning promotes a configurational bias, a tendency to stress the whole rather than the parts. This is understandable. After all, the prime mission of planning is to look beyond immediate decisions and activities, to consider larger patterns and long-run implications. Most planners would agree that there is a need for close integration of planning for the city as a whole and planning for the proximate settings of group life. To achieve that integration, however, planning must be in close touch with the realities of social space, that is, with actual expectations and uses.

Perhaps the deepest preconception of planning, a product of the planners' symbolic world, is the idea that physical arrangements decisively influence the quality of urban life. This preconception is shared by both orthodox city planners and their opponents (see Adaptation 36), so long as the main emphasis is on the arrangement of spaces and facilities.

Like the nineteenth-century reformers, the master planners assumed that people's lives are shaped by their physical surroundings and that the ideal city could be realized by the provision of an ideal physical environment. As architects and engineers, the planners believed that the city was a system of buildings and land uses which could be arranged and rearranged through planning, without taking account of the social, economic, and political structures and processes that determine people's behavior, including their use of land. This belief was supported by architectural ideology generally and also by plans for utopian and ideal cities which were constantly being proposed by architects and architecturally trained planners. It was reinforced by an oversimplified interpretation of the findings of urban ecologists, who seemed to correlate social pathology with the physical characteristics of residential areas (Gans, 1968:61).

In a sense, it is unfair to criticize planners for using the main tools of their trade. But when underlying assumptions are not fully understood or not tested, there is a danger that problems will be wrongly diagnosed and policies mistakenly formulated. Where the root cause of urban decay is poverty, discrimination, fear, and flight, new physical arrangements may help, but (1) their design must take account of actual life circumstances, for example, the specific needs of poor people for convenient health facilities and transportation to work; and (2) it must be understood that physical arrangements are not likely, of themselves, to alter the fundamental conditions of life.

Planning as process Partly in response to the criticisms and limitations discussed above but also as a result of changing responsibilities, theorists of planning have been trying to work out a new conception of the urban planner's role. Since World War II, planners have been actively involved in government programs, especially the design of new transportation systems and the rehabilitation of urban areas. These responsibilities have tied them closely to the decision-making process and have encouraged collaboration with economists, lawyers, systems analysts, and other specialists. As a result, there has been a growing tendency to abandon the earlier emphasis on long-range master planning. Instead of developing comprehensive plans, it is suggested, the main emphasis should be on *policy* or *program planning*:

I understand planning to be *a method for reach-ing decisions*, not a body of specific substantive goals. Applied within a fairly stable and widely shared value framework, planning is a rather spe-cial way of deciding which specific goals are to be pursued and which specific actions are to be taken. Seen in this way, it is directly antithetical to the more popular view among some practi-tioners, who are also called planners, in which planning is a social movement aimed at accom-plishing certain predetermined specific goals shared by members of the professional group or by other groups (Webber, 1963:320).

In policy planning, the planner participates in setting goals for urban change, but he does so in cooperation with other experts and in response to the needs and preferences of the community. The horizons of planning are broadened, but its aspirations are limited. There is an increased concern for social issues—such as the creation of jobs for de-prived populations—and physical planning becomes only a part of that larger effort. At the same time, planning as process is less dedicated to the achievement of an ideal human setting or even to the formulation of a long-range goal. Rather, the approach is in-cremental; it looks to the gradual improve-ment of existing conditions. Some would argue that this makes planning more real-istic, if only because the new programs "can be coordinated with the ongoing decision-making processes of city officials" (Gans, 1968:69).

Critics of the incremental approach point out that the policy planner is all too easily bound to the establishment and to the bu-reaucratic style of making decisions. It is difficult to be an independent analyst of existing goals and policies. Therefore some have suggested still another role: *advocacy planning*. The advocate planner is a technician speaking for special interests:

Advocate planners take this view that any plan is the embodiment of particular group interests, and therefore they see it as important that any group which has interests at stake in the planning proc-ess should have those interests articulated. In effect, they reject both the notion of a single "best" solution and the notion of a general wel-

fare which such a solution might serve. Planning in this view becomes pluralistic and partisan—in a word, overtly political (Peattie, 1968:81).

In practice, advocacy planning has been mainly associated with helping the under-privileged. The Cambridge, Massachusetts, group known as Urban Planning Aid de-fines its mission as the development of plan-ning strategies for low-income communities and "acting as planning advocate for these communities in order to make public plans reflect their needs" (Peattie, 1968:81). Of course, the same approach has long been used by more privileged interests, such as downtown business associations.

Although it seeks to disentangle planning from the status quo, advocacy planning re-mains, nevertheless, another form of plan-ning as process. As such, it suffers from the same limitation: The focus of planning is on special projects and programs, not on the city as a whole.

URBAN RENEWAL

The practical dilemmas of urban planning are sharply revealed in the U.S. govern-ment's programs for housing and urban re-newal (Greer, 1965; Abrams, 1964; 1965). Since 1954, local renewal agencies have sponsored a large number of projects, some of them very impressive. These include the reconstruction of parts of many downtown business areas and the creation of great com-plexes of apartments and offices, such as the Golden Gateway in San Francisco and Scol-lay Square in Boston. For the most part, how-ever, these renewal projects are not the end products of systematic planning but the re-sults of complicated interplays of eco-nomic and political forces. Although gov-ernment policies have encouraged local urban planning, far greater emphasis has actually been placed on stimulating private investment.

Urban renewal was first conceived as a potentially vast expansion of earlier efforts to provide more and better housing for the American people. In the 1930s the federal government had built some public housing for the poor and had begun a system of mortgage insurance to encourage expansion of the home-building industry. Mortgage insurance introduced the era of low down payment and proved to be an effective device for getting a large number of units built. The impact, however, was in the suburbs, not in the cities. A decisive fact was the availability of open land. A developer could readily buy a large tract, often farmland, and turn it into a suburban subdivision.

The new suburbs were white suburbs, and government perspectives and policies were largely responsible:

From 1935 to 1950, the federal government insisted upon discriminatory practices as a prerequisite to government housing aid. The Federal Housing Administration's official manuals cautioned against "infiltration of inharmonious racial and national groups," "a lower class of inhabitants," or "the presence of incompatible racial elements" in the new neighborhoods. . . . Zoning was advocated as a device for exclusion, and the use was urged of a racial covenant (prepared by FHA itself) with a space left blank for the prohibited races and religions, to be filled in by the builder as occasion required (Abrams, 1965:61).

In a sense, the government was engaged in planning by indirection. Without saying so explicitly, it was guaranteeing the exclusion of blacks and other minorities from the new government-sponsored housing.

The 1949 housing act offered a new departure, but it was fated to repeat the same pattern. Provision was made for breaking through the main barrier to urban redevelopment—the difficulty of assembling a sizable piece of land, several city blocks or more, at an acceptable cost. This was to be accomplished by bringing to bear the full power of government. A local renewal agency would be established, with the authority to condemn private lands, which would then be resold to private developers. In addition, the federal government would absorb a large part of the cost of the land.

The 1949 act limited the role of the federal government in two basic ways. First, the local renewal agency set up by the city would plan and supervise the projects. Second, it was contemplated that private enterprise would be the chosen vehicle of urban development. The private entrepreneur was not to be a mere government contractor. Rather, he would own, operate, and resell the facilities. Hence the fate of urban renewal was tied to the incentives that could be offered to private developers and builders.

Displacement of goals In 1954 Congress passed a new housing act. New incentives were offered to private enterprise, and the foundations were laid for a significant shift in the goals of urban renewal. Hitherto, the focus had been on slum clearance and housing, including public housing. But the first years of the program had shown that slum clearance was not necessarily profitable. It presumed a market for the new buildings or apartments, and in many cities that was not available. Fom the standpoint of the developer, it was far better to renew the city's "gray" areas than its slums. A gray area is a somewhat deteriorated district, otherwise well located—a good site for expensive housing:

The drive toward the better central sections and gray areas has been a perversion of the urban renewal purpose, and as more and more renewal projects fail, the better, not the worse, sites will be sought. Since a slum or blighted area is any section which the renewal agency designates as such, the site may be a slimy slum, a slim slum, or no slum at all. The existence of the slum is no longer the true reason for eminent domain, for displacement, for federal loans at low interest or for land subsidies. The main question is whether the section is good enough for a high-rental project (Abrams, 1965:116).

The 1954 act, sponsored by the Eisenhower administration, showed the way. Under its terms, an urban renewal project no longer needed to be justified as slum clearance. A site could be "blighted" and therefore only a potential slum in order to qualify for gov-

Money concentrates people. Houston rises abruptly from the coastal plain.

ernment support. With this authorization, the local agencies and the private developers moved more rapidly to initiate projects that were more in the nature of civic improvement than slum clearance.

Displacement of people

The most serious human aspect of urban renewal has been the eviction of thousands of residents. The local agency is required by law to help people relocate, and it must demonstrate that "decent, safe, and sanitary" housing is available. In fact, however, many people have suffered considerably as a result of the dislocation. They have had to pay higher rents, live in less satisfactory dwellings, and give up their accustomed ways of life.

If the tangible aspects of renewal are difficult to evaluate in the balance sheet of a cost-benefit analysis, how can one assess such intangibles as the cost of relocating an old woman whose only remaining satisfactions in life are taking care of the apartment in which she has lived for many years, going to the church around the corner and exchanging a few words with the neighborhood merchants? (Glazer, 1965:199).

Because a large percentage of the displaced families are nonwhite, it is sometimes charged that urban renewal amounts to black removal. Protests against displacement have led to political and legal action against renewal projects, some of which have been delayed for substantial periods. Legal assistance groups engaged in social advocacy (see *LAW*, p. 411) have made urban renewal a target.

Personal living space Research from opposite sides of the world and concerned with contrasting problems suggests that the way people see and use the "empty" space around their places of residence must be taken more fully into account by those who design communities and dwellings. More than personal satisfaction and well-being are involved, although these values should be enough to attract the attention of planners and architects. Even crime rates are related to building environments.

In New York City, it was found that high-rise housing projects had worse crime rates than other projects in the same area with similar densities and occupied by similar populations. The projects with lower crime rates were constructed in smaller units. It is thought that high-rise housing with blind corridors and empty staircases communicates a feeling of anonymity in the tenants. There is no "defensible space" for which they feel a sense of territory and responsibility. Short of knocking down the high-rise buildings, a redesign of the internal layouts reducing the number of families served by a corridor creates a feeling of ownership and belonging in the tenants and leads to a reduction in the crime rate. Small additional changes and the provision of common facilities, such as play equipment, fences, and improved lighting, also reduced the crime rate (Newman, 1972a; 1972b).

Although Australia is one of the most urban countries, a large majority of urban Australians live in dwellings with private open space. Such low-density forms of residence are criticized as being costly, inefficient, and aesthetically monotonous. But how do the residents use the space around their houses? And would public facilities do as well? A study in Adelaide, South Australia, gives a tentative answer to at least the first question (Halkett, 1976). Most of the gardens (yards) are not empty and wasted but are filled with the numerous activities of both children and adults who spend more than half their outdoor recreational time in private lots. Backyards are intensively used for a wide variety of activities, such as vegetable and flower gardening, house and car maintenance, reading, sunbathing, sleeping, playing games, hobbies, eating, and entertaining. It is not likely that a public area could provide the same wide variety of possible uses or engender the same sense of active involvement and pride of possession. Planners who urge denser settlement must therefore consider whether dense settlement may destroy the values of personal living space. "A suburban landscape which appears monotonous to a passing stranger may have unsuspected dynamic qualities that make it to its occupants anything but monotonous" (Halkett, 1974:4).

Adaptation 36 Jacobs: Principles of urban vitality

There is a wistful myth that if only we had enough money to spend—the figure is usually put at $100 billion—we could wipe out all our slums in ten years, anchor the wandering middle class and its wandering tax money, and perhaps even solve the traffic problem. But consider what we have built with the first several billions: low-income projects that become worse centers of delinquency, vandalism, and more general social hopelessness than the slums they were supposed to replace; middle-income housing projects that are marvels of dullness and regimentation, sealed against any buoyancy or vitality of city life; cultural centers unable to support a good bookstore; promenades that go from no place to nowhere and have no promenaders. This is not the rebuilding of cities. This is the sacking of cities.

Source: Abridged and adapted from *The Death and Life of Great American Cities* by Jane Jacobs (New York: Random House, 1961), pp. 4, 34–37, 143–221.

In understanding what makes for a viable, successful city, one overriding principle emerges. This is the need for an intricate and close-grained diversity. The components of this diversity can differ enormously, but they must supplement each other in certain definite ways. Four conditions are required for generating useful urban diversity; by deliberately inducing these conditions, planning can create urban vitality.

USES SPECIAL AND DIVERSE

Urban districts must have mixed uses. Besides residences, a city neighborhood needs stores, places of entertainment, office buildings, manufacturing plants, restaurants, banks, schools, libraries, haunts for browsers and lookers. One advantage of this mixture of uses is the safety it can provide for urban residents and visitors.

A well-used city street is apt to be a safe street. A deserted city street is apt to be unsafe. In mixed-use neighborhoods, people appear at different times, both night and day, and many of them are strangers. This encourages the people in buildings along the street to watch the sidewalks in sufficient numbers; nobody enjoys sitting on a stoop or at a window looking at an empty street. In cities, many people entertain themselves, off and on, by watching street activity. As they do so, they monitor and control each other as well as the transient stranger.

The basic requisite for such surveillance is a substantial quantity of stores and other public places. The activity generated by people on errands, or people seeking food or drink, is itself an attraction. That the sight of people attracts still other people is something city planners and architectural designers seem to find incomprehensible. They operate on the premise that city people seek the sight of emptiness, obvious order, and quiet. Nothing could be less true. The love of watching other people is constantly evident in cities everywhere.

This trait reaches something of an extreme on upper Broadway in New York, where the avenue is divided by a narrow central mall, right in the middle of traffic. The benches along this mall are filled with people, watching pedestrians, watching the traffic, watching each other. Eventually Broadway reaches Columbia University and Barnard College, one to the right, the other to the left. Here all is obvious order and quiet. No more stores, no more activity generated by the stores, almost no pedestrians—and no more watchers.

Typically, only cities can support a large number of small and special enterprises. The diversity of service stimulates still more diversity, both of services and of people.

As a rule, the larger a city, the larger the proportionate number of its small manufacturers. Big enterprises have greater self-sufficiency and do not need to be in cities. But small manufacturers must draw on many supplies and skills; they must serve a narrow market at the point where a market exists, and they must be sensitive to quick changes in that market.

The benefits that cities offer to smallness are just as marked in retail trade, cultural facilities, and entertainment. Towns and suburbs are natural homes for huge supermarkets and standard movie houses; there are simply not enough people to support further variety. Cities, however, are natural homes for supermarkets and standard movie houses *plus* delicatessens, Viennese bakeries, foreign groceries, art movies, and so on, all of which can be found coexisting, the standard with the special, the large with the small. Indeed, in lively and popular parts of cities, such as Greenwich Village in New York, the small much outnumber the large.

Recent city planning has resulted in the consolidation and segregation of the performing and other arts into islands of high culture known as cultural centers. This is a striking example of the current tendency to isolate the components of urban diversity from each other, depriving them of opportunities for mutual support in a complex system of interdependent uses.

Carnegie Hall, on West Fifty-seventh Street in New York, is a striking example of a cultural center that, being set in the midst of diversity, has helped to create still further diversity. The presence of Carnegie Hall on a lively mixed-use thoroughfare led to the presence of another use that depends on nighttime business—two motion-picture theaters. Because Carnegie Hall is a music center, it attracted to the neighborhood many small music, dance, and drama studios and recital rooms. All this is mixed with office buildings, as well as hotels and apartments having all kinds of tenants, but notably a great many musicians and teachers of music. The combination of daytime and nighttime use is especially stimulating to restaurants, and here there is a whole range, from a glamorous

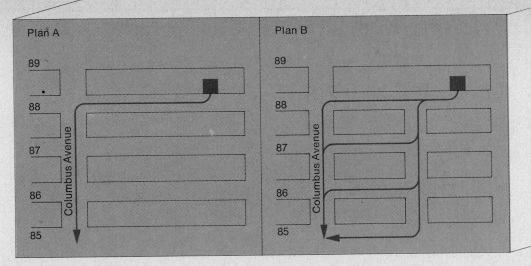

Figure 15:4 City street patterns

Source: *The Death and Life of Great American Cities* by Jane Jacobs (New York: Random House, 1961), pp. 179, 181.

Russian restaurant to an espresso café and a hamburger house. Dispersed among the restaurants are opportunities to buy rare coins and old books, health foods and thrice-worn Dior dresses.

The most ruinous plan that could be devised for this entire neighborhood would be to destroy Carnegie Hall and replace it with another office building. This was about to happen, as part of New York City's decision to segregate culture on a planner's island called Lincoln Center for the Performing Arts. Carnegie Hall was saved by a hair, although it is no longer the home of the New York Philharmonic, which has detached itself from the ordinary city and now performs in Lincoln Center. Cultural or civic centers are often tragic in their effects on cities. Multiple-use streets or districts should be treasured rather than destroyed by attempts to sort out and segregate their components.

STREETS SHORT AND NUMEROUS

Most blocks must be short; opportunities to turn corners must be frequent.

Figure 15:4 shows two patterns of streets and crossing: the long block (Plan A) and the short block (Plan B). Consider a person living on a long city block on the West Side of New York City, such as Eighty-eighth Street in Plan A. The arrow represents this person walking from his house over to and down Columbus Avenue, a main thoroughfare

from which he can get to other parts of the city. He may very well never enter the adjacent long blocks and would have every justification for doubting that these streets or their people have anything to do with him.

Suppose, now, that these long east–west blocks had an extra street cut across them as in Plan B— not a sterile "promenade" of the kind in which superblock projects abound, but a street containing buildings where things could start up and grow; places for buying, eating, seeing things, getting a drink. With the extra street, the Eighty-eighth Street resident would no longer need to walk the same monotonous path to a given point. He could choose alternative routes. The neighborhood would open up to him.

In Plan B, the supply of feasible spots for commerce would increase considerably. In Plan A (the actuality), Columbus Avenue is the only nearby place where tens of thousands of people from these oblong, backwater blocks meet and form a pool of use. In neighborhood A, there is so little street frontage on which commerce can live that it must all be consolidated, regardless of type, the scale of support it needs, or its distance from users. As a result, Columbus Avenue has its own kind of monotony—endless stores and a depressing predominance of commercial standardization.

Theoretically, almost all the short side streets of the East Side in the Sixties, Seventies, and Eighties are residential only. It is instructive to notice how frequently special shops like bookstores or dress-makers or restaurants have inserted themselves, usually, but not always, near the corners. The equivalent West Side does not support bookstores and never did, even though the West Side is full of intellectuals and always has been. Because of its long blocks, the West Side has never been physically capable of forming the intricate pools of fluid street use necessary to support urban diversity.

The myth that plentiful city streets are wasteful comes from the garden city theorists who decried the use of land for streets because they wanted that land consolidated into project prairies. Super-block projects are apt to have all the disabilities of long blocks, and this is true even when they are laced with promenades and malls. These prome-nades and malls are meaningless because there is seldom any active reason for people to use them. Even as alternatives for getting from here to yonder, these paths are meaningless because all their scenes are essentially the same.

BUILDINGS OLD AND NEW

The district must mingle buildings that vary in age and condition, including a good proportion of old ones.

Cities need old buildings so badly that it is prob-ably impossible for vigorous streets and districts to grow without them. If a city area has only new buildings, the enterprises that can exist there are automatically limited to those that can support the high costs of new construction. Well-financed supermarkets, chain restaurants, and banks are found in new construction. But neighborhood bars, foreign restaurants, and pawnshops go into older buildings, as do good bookstores and antique dealers. Well-subsidized opera and art museums often go into new buildings. But the informal feeders of the arts—studios, galleries, stores for musical instruments and art supplies—these go into old buildings. Old ideas can use new build-ings; new ideas must use old buildings.

The only harm of aged buildings is the harm that eventually comes of *nothing but* old age. But a city area is not a failure because all the buildings in it are old. On the contrary, the buildings are all old because the area is a failure. For some reason its enterprises or people are unable to support new construction. In a successful city district, some of the older buildings, year by year, are re-placed or rehabilitated. Over the years there is, therefore, a mixture of buildings of many ages and types. With the passage of time, the high building costs of one generation become the bargains of a subsequent generation.

Diversity, ruled out by the high costs of the large modern building complex, is apt to reappear, al-though in makeshift and shabby forms. Outside one vast housing complex in New York, whose standardized commerce is protected from un-authorized competition or augmentation within the project, there is an outcast huddle of stores, supported by the project residents. Clumped to-gether on a stretch of pocked asphalt left over from a gas station, they supply the project people with quick loans, musical instruments, cameras, Chi-nese food, odd-lot clothing. How many other needs remain unfilled? This question becomes academic when mingled building age is replaced by the economic rigor mortis of one-age construction, with its inherent inefficiency and consequent need for forms of "protectionism."

Neighborhoods built up all at once change little physically over the years. The physical change that does occur is for the worse. The neighborhood shows a strange inability to update itself, enliven itself, repair itself, or to be sought after, out of choice, by a new generation. It is dead.

DWELLINGS DENSE AND VARIOUS

The district must have a sufficiently dense con-centration of people and of dwellings.

Overcrowded slums are portrayed in planning literature as areas with a high density of dwellings. In fact they are, more and more typically, areas with a low density of dwellings. In Oakland, Cali-fornia, the worst and most extensive slum is an area of some 200 blocks of detached, one- and two-family houses. Cleveland's worst slum is a square mile of much the same thing. Detroit is largely composed of seemingly endless miles of low-density failure.

One reason why high city densities have a bad name is that high density and overcrowding are often confused. High dwelling density means a large number of dwellings per acre of land. Over-crowding means too many people in a dwelling for the number of rooms it contains. Garden city planners looked at slums which had *both* too many dwelling units on the land and too many people within individual dwellings and failed to make any distinction between overcrowded rooms and densely built-up land. Today we are much more apt to find overcrowding at low dwelling densities (when, for example, several poor families crowd into an old house built for single-family use) than at high densities (for example, tenements originally built for working-class families).

In order to increase the concentration of people in cities, high dwellings must be built. But how high should city dwellings go? If the object is a vital city life, the dwelling densities should go as high as necessary to stimulate the maximum potential diversity in a district. But if density becomes too high, it represses diversity instead of stimulating it.

Densities become excessive when they lead to standardized, monolithic construction. Packing the maximum number of dwelling units on a given acreage leaves little leeway for variety among buildings. All variations that reduce density are crowded out. Maximum efficiency, or anything approaching it, means standardization.

Popular high-density city areas have considerable variation among their buildings—sometimes immense variation. Greenwich Village in New York is such a place. It houses people at densities ranging from 125 to over 200 dwelling units per acre, without standardization of buildings. These averages represent everything from single-family houses to tenements to elevator apartments of many different ages and sizes.

The reason Greenwich Village has high dwelling density and great variety is that a high proportion of the land is covered with buildings. In most parts of the Village, buildings cover 60 to 80 percent of the land, leaving the other 40 to 20 percent as yards, courts, and the like.

Now, suppose only 15 to 25 percent of residential land is built upon, and the other 75 to 85 percent is left as open space. These are common figures for housing projects whose large expanses of open land are so hard to control in urban settings and produce so much dullness and trouble. Under these circumstances, high densities can be obtained only by building high-rise apartments. It is impossible to reconcile high density and variety unless ground coverages are increased and open space is decreased. In other words, high concentration of people cannot be combined with diversity if large expanses of green grass and open space are held out as an ideal for city life.

While high ground coverage is necessary for variety at high densities, it can become intolerable as it approaches 70 percent. High ground coverage can be compensated for in a number of ways. First, streets can be short and numerous; frequent streets are a form of open land. Second, public parks can be located in multiple-use areas where they will be really used. Finally, if nonresidential buildings are well mingled into dwelling areas, the net effect is to thin out the total number of dwellings and residents of a district. These strategies create open but used urban spaces, unlike the effort to relieve high densities by quantities of greensward which contributes little to an urban way of life.

CAUTIONS

The above discussion is controversial at many points, and the generalizations offered should be treated as hypotheses. A possible line of criticism is that the Jacobs model may be equating a working-class or ethnic life-style with urbanism. Other life-styles, equally relevant to the city, might require alternative physical arrangements. Moreover, much of what is attributed to spatial patterns may actually reflect a system of beliefs and sentiments. Whether a street watcher gets involved or maintains distance may indeed seriously affect public safety. But what a person feels and does will depend on his or her sense of relatedness to other people and the community.

References

Abrams, Charles
1964 Man's Struggle for Shelter in an Urbanizing World. Cambridge: Massachusetts Institute of Technology Press.
1965 The City Is the Frontier. New York: Harper & Row.

Adams, Robert M.
1960 "The origin of cities." Scientific American 203 (September):153–168.

Appleyard, Donald
1969 "City designers and the pluralistic city." Pp. 422–452 in Lloyd Rodwin and Associates, Planning Urban Growth and Development: The Experience of the Guyana Program of Venezuela. Cambridge: Massachusetts Institute of Technology Press.

Berger, Bennett
1960 The Working-Class Suburb. Berkeley and Los Angeles: University of California Press.

Bowra, Cecil M.
1971 Periclean Athens. London: Weidenfeld and Nicolson.

Breed, Warren and Sally M. Seaman
1971 "Indirect democracy and social process in Periclean Athens." Social Science Quarterly 52 (December):631–645.

Burgess, Ernest W. (ed.)
1926 The Urban Community. Chicago: University of Chicago Press.

Burgess, Ernest W. and Harvey J. Locke
1953 The Family. New York: American Book.

Clark, S. D.
1966 The Suburban Society. Toronto: University of Toronto Press.

Davis, Kingsley
1965 "The urbanization of the human population." Scientific American 213 (September):41–53.
1969 World Urbanization 1950–1970. Volume I: Basic Data for Cities, Countries, and Regions. Berkeley: Institute of International Studies, University of California.

Drake, St. Clair and Horace R. Cayton
1945/1969 Black Metropolis: A Study of Negro Life in a Northern City. New York: Harbinger Books.

Duncan, Otis Dudley
1957 "Community size and the rural-urban continuum." Pp. 35–45 in Paul K. Hatt and Albert J. Reiss, Jr. (eds.), Cities and Society. New York: Free Press.

Evers, Hans-Dieter
1972 "Urban involution: the social development of Southeast Asian towns." Unpublished paper read at the International Conference on Southeast Asian Studies, Kuala Lumpur, February 23–26.

Fischer, Claude S.
1972 "Urbanism as a way of life: a review and an agenda." Sociological Methods and Research 1 (November):187–242.

Fried, Marc and Peggy Gleicher
1961 "Some sources of residential satisfaction in an urban slum." Journal of the American Institute of Planners 27 (November):305–315.

Gans, Herbert J.
1962 "Urbanism and suburbanism as ways of life." Pp. 625–648 in Arnold Rose (ed.), Human Behavior and Social Processes. Boston: Houghton Mifflin.
1968 People and Plans. New York: Basic Books.

Glazer, Nathan
1965 "The renewal of cities." Scientific American 213 (September):195–204.

Gottman, Jean
1961 Megalopolis. New York: Twentieth Century.

Greer, Scott
1965 Urban Renewal and American Cities. Indianapolis: Bobbs-Merrill.

Halkett, Ian
1974 "Private gardens, private worlds." Community (December):3–5.
1976 An Analysis of Land Use in the Residential Garden. Ph.D. thesis, Australian National University, Canberra.

Harris, Chauncy D. and Edward L. Ullman
1945 "The nature of cities." Annals of the American Academy of Political and Social Science 242 (November):12.

Howard, Ebenezer
1902 Garden Cities of Tomorrow. London: Swan Sonnenschein.

Howton, F. William
1967 "Cities, slums, and acculturative process in the developing countries." Pp. 21–39 in Milton C. Albrecht (ed.), Studies in Sociology (Vol. III, No. 2, December). Buffalo: State University of New York.

Hoyt, Homer
1943 "The structure of American cities in the post-war era." American Journal of Sociology 48 (January):475–492.

Hunter, Albert
1971 "The ecology of Chicago: persistence and change, 1930–1960." American Journal of Sociology 17 (November):425–444.

Jacobs, Jane
1961 The Death and Life of Great American Cities. New York: Random House.

Jaffe, Mark S.
1972 "The shantytowns of Paris." International Herald Tribune (February 21):7.

Kahn, Alfred J.
1969 Studies in Social Policy and Planning. New York: Russell Sage.

Lepawsky, Albert
1941 "The London region: a metropolitan community in crisis." American Journal of Sociology 46 (May):826–834.

McGee, T. G.
1967 The Southeast Asian City: A Social Geography of the Primate Cities of Southeast Asia. London: Bell.

Milgram, Stanley
1970 "The experience of living cities: a psychological analysis." Science (March 13):1461–1468.

Morris, R. N.
1968 Urban Sociology. New York: Praeger.

Mrak, Emil M.
1966 "Food and land: the coming shortage." Cry California 1 (Summer).

Mumford, Lewis
1938 The Culture of Cities. New York: Harcourt Brace Jovanovich.

Newman, Oscar
1972a Defensible Space. New York: Macmillan.
1972b "Housing without fear." Time (November 27):69–70.

Ogburn, William F.
1946 "Inventions of local transportation and the patterns of cities." Social Forces 24 (May):373–379.

Park, Robert Ezra
1936 "Human ecology." American Journal of Sociology 42 (July):1–15.
1952 Human Communities: The City and Human Ecology. New York: Free Press.

Park, Robert E., Ernest W. Burgess, and Roderick D. McKenzie (eds.)
1925 The City. Chicago: University of Chicago Press.

Peattie, Lisa R.
1968 "Reflections on advocacy planning." Journal of the American Institute of Planners 34 (March):80–88.

Pirenne, Henri
1925 Medieval Cities: Their Origin and the Revival of Trade. Princeton, N. J.: Princeton University Press.

Portes, Alejandro
1971 "Urbanization and politics in Latin America." Social Science Quarterly 52 (December):697–720.

Riesman, David, in collaboration with Reuel Denney and Nathan Glazer
1950 The Lonely Crowd. New Haven, Conn.: Yale University Press.

Rodwin, Lloyd
1965 "Ciudad Guyana: a new city." Scientific American 213 (September):122–132.

Rossi, Peter H. and Robert A. Dentler
1961 The Politics of Urban Renewal. New York: Free Press.

Salins, Peter D.
1971 "Household location patterns in American metropolitan areas." Pp. 234–248 in Brian J. Berry (ed.), "Comparative factorial ecology." Economic Geography 47 (June supplement).

Shevky, Eshref and Wendell Bell
1955 Social Area Analysis: Theory, Illustrative Application, and Computational Procedures. Stanford, Calif.: Stanford University Press.

Shevky, Eshref and Marilyn Williams
1949 The Social Areas of Los Angeles: Analysis and Typology. Berkeley and Los Angeles: University of California Press.

Simmel, Georg
1903 "The metropolis and mental life." Pp. 409–424 in Kurt H. Wolff (ed.), The Sociology of Georg Simmel. New York: Free Press, 1950.

Stein, Clarence S.
1958 Toward New Towns for America. Liverpool.

Taeuber, Karl E. and Alma F. Taeuber
1965 Negroes in Cities: Residential Segregation and Neighborhood Change. Chicago: Aldine.

Toynbee, Arnold (ed.)
1967 Cities of Destiny. London: Thames and Hudson.

Webber, Melvin M.
1963 "The prospects for policies planning." Pp. 319–330 in Leonard J. Duhl (ed.), The Urban Condition. New York: Basic Books.

Weber, Adna F.
1899 The Growth of Cities in the Nineteenth Century. New York: Columbia University Press.

Wilson, Godfrey and Monica Wilson
1945 The Analysis of Social Change: Observations Based on Central Africa. Cambridge: Cambridge University Press.

Wirth, Louis
1928 The Ghetto. Chicago: University of Chicago Press.
1938 "Urbanism as a way of life." American Journal of Sociology 44 (July):1–24.

Zimmern, Alfred E.
1961 The Greek Commonwealth: Politics and Economics in Fifth Century Athens. Fifth edition. London: Oxford University Press.

Sources and readings

Breese, Gerald (ed.)
1969 City in Newly Developing Countries: Readings on Urbanism and Urbanization. Englewood Cliffs, N. J.: Prentice-Hall.

Bureau of the Census
1971 Social and Economic Characteristics of the Population in Metropolitan and Nonmetropolitan Areas: 1970 and 1960. Current Population Reports Special Studies. Washington, D.C.: GPO.

Comhaire, Jean and Werner J. Cahnman
1971 How Cities Grew: The Historical Sociology of Cities. Fourth edition. Madison, N. J.: Florham.

Fischer, Claude S.
1976 The Urban Experience. New York: Harcourt Brace Jovanovich.

Greer, Scott, Peter Orleans, Dennis C. McElrath, and David W. Minar (eds.)
1967 The New Urbanization. New York: St. Martin's Press.

Gutman, Robert (ed.)
1972 People and Buildings. New York: Basic Books.

Hawley, Amos H.
1971 Urban Society: An Ecological Approach. New York: Ronald Press.

Meadows, Paul and Ephraim H. Mizruchi
1969 Urbanism, Urbanization, and Change: Comparative Perspectives. Reading, Mass.: Addison-Wesley.

Morris, R. N.
1968 Urban Sociology. New York: Praeger.

Mumford, Lewis
1938 The Culture of Cities. New York: Harcourt Brace Jovanovich.
1961 The City in History. New York: Harcourt Brace Jovanovich.

Park, Robert E.
1952 Human Communities. New York: Free Press.

Scientific American 213 (September)
1965 Issue on cities.

Social Science Quarterly 52 (December)
1971 Urban Problems and Policies. Special issue.

Thomlinson, Ralph
1968 Urban Structure: The Social and Spatial Character of Cities. New York: Random House.

Toynbee, Arnold (ed.)
1967 Cities of Destiny. London: Thomas and Hudson.

16 | Technology and Civilization

Section one industry and society

Among the master trends of modern history is the rise of industrialism and, in our time, the beginnings of a transition to postindustrial society. These trends have created a social and economic order based on technological innovation and on large-scale, highly specialized systems of production. Industrialization began in Western Europe and has now become worldwide. People everywhere seem destined to know and experience, to enjoy or endure, the distinctive features of a technological society.

Section One reviews the broad sweep of change: early industrialization, including the experience of non-Western societies; basic shifts in the labor force as industrialism matures; and the idea of a postindustrial society. Section Two discusses the impact of mechanization on alienation and work satisfaction. Sections Three and Four consider the larger significance of technology for the place of humanity in nature, for the ecological crisis, and for culture.

SOCIAL RELATIONS AND CAPITALISM

Under feudalism, social life centered on the economically self-sufficient manorial estate controlled by a lord. An individual's occupation and status as free or serf were inherited. Unfree tenants or serfs were bound to the estate by tradition and law, and everyone, whether free or serf, was obligated to render services to the lord and pay taxes in goods or money.

The eventual breakdown of feudal rights and obligations released workers to go where early capitalist enterprises were located. Propertyless workers provided the free labor force required for industrial capitalism, and the entrepreneur was not responsible for his workers as the feudal lord had been. The entrepreneur could hire and fire according to the needs of his factory (Moore, 1951: 420–421, 425–427).

The great transformation In a famous passage of the *Communist Manifesto*, Marx and Engels wrote:

The bourgeoisie, wherever it has got the upper

hand, has put an end to all feudal, patriarchal, idyllic relations. It has pitilessly torn asunder the motley feudal ties that bound man to his "natural superiors," and has left remaining no other nexus between man and man than naked self-interest, than callous "cash-payment" (Marx and Engels, 1848/1959:9).

This theme has been echoed by most students of the rise of industrial capitalism. They have stressed the great break with the past that must occur if a traditional society, based on kinship and *Gemeinschaft*, is to take the road to economic rationality and the free market (Polanyi, 1944).

Capitalism brought with it a perspective of "possessive individualism" (MacPherson, 1962). The self-regulating market, in which each individual pursues personal economic advantage, was offered as the key to progress. But the price of that progress was a radical weakening of social institutions. Many of the traditional sources of meaning and belonging—locality, kinship, fixed status, religion—were undermined. And economic individualism became (and remains) an obstacle to regulation of private enterprise in the public interest, for example, to safeguard the environment or achieve social justice.

The spirit or ethos of capitalism is expressed in the virtues of individualism, hard work, thrift, self-discipline, accumulation, initiative, and rationality. These personal aspirations and disciplines were especially important during the formative years of capitalism. The historical origins of industriousness and economic rationality have been much debated. (Max Weber's theory that the Protestant Reformation contributed decisively to the rise of a capitalist spirit is discussed in *RELIGION*, Section Four.)

NON-WESTERN SOCIETIES

In the Western world industrialism arose from within, the product of many changes —in technology, commerce, politics, and social relations. By contrast, industrialization of the non-Western world came from the outside, at a later stage, and has often involved a greater social and cultural discontinuity.

In a peasant or village society, the coming of industrialism tends to break down what once was an integrated social system. When villagers take jobs in the city or even in a nearby factory or mine, the traditional fabric of social organization begins to unravel. The authority and unity of the family and community are undermined because the individual is less dependent on kinship ties. Economic change creates new roles, such as wage earner and storekeeper; money becomes visible and powerful; new forms of knowledge and skill in medicine and technology threaten the older community leaders. Traditional occupations lose their prestige.

As cheap goods, tools, and facilities become available, poverty and deprivation are no longer perceived as inevitable. Even small improvements in living conditions open horizons and raise expectations. Yet the slow pace of economic development and the effects of neocolonialism (see *POLITICS AND SOCIETY*, p. 559) may offer little chance of fulfilling those expectations.

In sum, the discontinuities between peasant society and industrialism are so great in many cases that economic development is slow and halting.

The dual society In some settings industrialization takes over completely. This is especially likely where an indigenous population is sparse and has a weakly developed technology. In Australia, for example, the small numbers of aborigines for the most part are peripheral to the industrial economy and influence it in no important way.

Another possibility is the emergence of a *dual society*, the coexistence of an industrial social system with a preindustrial one (Boeke, 1953). This occurs when industrialism is introduced into densely populated agrarian societies. The imported system may be mature capitalism, socialism, communism, or a blend of systems. Dual societies now exist in much of eastern and southern Asia, Africa, and Latin America. A chief characteristic of dual economies is the interrelation of traditional barter and a contemporary market based upon money.

In dual societies the divergent values of the industrial and preindustrial world affect each other in complicated and not always predictable ways. In an industrial society, there are many people who continue to accumulate wealth they may never spend, and even the ordinary worker may come to believe that he or she "cannot afford" to give up a well-paying job for one that is more congenial.

Preindustrial workers, however, do not want to accumulate wealth for its own sake. Employees often work hard to satisfy an immediate need but cannot be spurred to further effort once that need is satisfied. In industrial societies, higher pay usually holds down the rate of labor turnover. Preindustrial workers tend to leave the job when their requirements are satisfied, and higher pay may therefore increase labor turnover.

Family and economy in Japan Modern Japan is an example of continuities as well as breaks and shows that some traditional social forms may contribute to modern industrial organization. The persistence of a certain kind of familism is a key element in the organization of the modern Japanese firm and employee relations.

The most distinctive feature of the large Japanese firm is the system of lifetime employment.

Membership in the Japanese productive group is a permanent and irrevocable membership. Workers at all levels of the factory customarily work in but one company. They spend their entire career in that single firm which is entered immediately on completing their education. The firm will continue to provide the worker's income at whatever disadvantage to itself, and the worker will continue in the company's employ despite possible advantage in moving to another firm (Abegglen, 1958:128).

In addition, the mutual obligations of employer and employee are diffuse rather than specific (see *SOCIAL ORGANIZATION*, p. 38), and the company is highly paternalistic. It asserts authority over, and assumes responsibility for, many aspects of the employee's life. "Management is involved in such diverse and intimate matters as the worker's personal finances, the education of his children, religious activities, and the training of the worker's wife" (Abegglen, 1958:129; for cautions regarding this generalization, see Marsh and Mannari, 1971). One corollary is the wide range of compensations, which may include housing, food, and services; another is the adjustment of pay to personal circumstances, such as the size of the employee's family.

Wages and benefits are determined by seniority; a man or woman who has been with a company for 30 years makes, on the average, four times as much as a newly hired worker, though both may do the same job. Result: minimum unemployment and maximum morale year after year (*Time*, August 9, 1976:56).

This pattern of association has deep roots in culture and social structure. A study of Japanese society (Nakane, 1970) argues that *group consciousness* is a mainspring of Japanese life. Japanese are less concerned about social categories than about group membership. Thus if a person is asked what his occupation is, he is more likely to give the name of his company than to say that he is a carpenter or clerk or chauffeur. The fact of membership, of belonging to a functioning group or community, is more important than working at a similar trade or profession, having the same name, or sharing beliefs. The latter is consciousness of *kind*; the former is *group* consciousness.

Japanese group consciousness is strongly influenced by long-established attitudes toward family and kinship. In Japan the household has traditionally overshadowed the kinship system.

Thus the wife and daughter-in-law who have come from the outside have incomparably greater importance than one's own sisters and daughters, who have married and gone into other households. A brother, when he has built a separate house, is thought of as belonging to another unit or household; on the other hand, the son-in-law, who was once a complete outsider, takes the position of a household member and becomes more important than the brother living in another household. . . . Not only may outsiders with not the remotest kinship tie be invited to be heirs and successors but servants and clerks are usually incorporated as members of the household and treated as family members by the head of the household (Nakane, 1970:5).

The household model pervades Japanese social organization. Its perspectives have encouraged business paternalism and the identification of employees with the company. Among these perspectives is, first, a principle of exclusiveness. In Japanese society the ideal is a one-to-one relation: Paramount loyalty is to a single individual or to a single group. There is no room for overlapping group memberships, for serving two masters. Second is a principle of subordination. The household model, bringing together people who are heterogeneous in age, skill, status, and contribution, tends to create a vertical hierarchical order. The perceived moral rightness of the arrangement carries over into the modern world of employment. Japanese business firms have freely invoked

the symbolism of family to justify and reinforce these principles of exclusiveness and subordination.

WORLD LABOR FORCE

The transformation of modern society is clearly reflected in the changing composition of the labor force. Of the 4 billion people in the world, over 1.5 billion are economically active: 1 billion males and over 500 million females. It is estimated that in 1985, when the world's population will be nearly 5 billion, the labor force will have grown to about 2 billion. To employ so many people usefully will tax the administrative talents of many countries. The largest national working populations are China, over 300 million; India, 180 million; the USSR, 117 million; and the United States, 91 million (*Yearbook of Labor Statistics, 1974:*Chap. 1; *Statistical Abstract of the United States, 1975:*343).

The industrial sectors Productive economic activity is grouped into three major industrial divisions, or sectors: primary, secondary, and tertiary forms (Clark, 1957: Chap. 9). Primary industries include agri-

Families in the work force: In textile mills women and children have been and still are used as a source of cheap labor

culture, fishing, and forestry. Primary refers both to a stage of industrial development and to the fact that workers deal directly with raw materials. Mining is often classified as a primary industry, but because modern mining is essentially a machine operation and leaves few materials in an unprocessed condition, a case can be made for defining it as a secondary industry, and the latter definition is used here. Secondary industries, which include manufacturing and construction, convert raw materials into finished goods and complex products. Tertiary industries are professional and personal services, trade, transportation, communication, and commerce.

Industrialization The process of industrialization in what are now developed countries was accompanied by a redistribution of workers among the three industrial sectors.

The sequence of steps observed in many countries of the industrialized world has been generalized as a theoretical model of industrial development. In the early stages the labor force is preponderantly engaged in collecting raw materials and cultivating products for direct consumption as food, clothing, and shelter. With technological change and industrial expansion, agricultural productivity rises, releasing workers for construction and manufacturing, where their efforts yield higher earnings. The proportion of the labor force in agriculture decreases, and the proportion in manufacturing increases. Then with accelerating speed, workers enter service industries such as the distribution of products, the maintenance of trade and transport, education, health, public services, government, and administration. Because the industrial sectors are linked together, changes in one sector feed back upon the others. For example agricultural productivity is raised by advances in machine technology and by efficiencies in marketing and distribution.

Developing countries This model of indus-

trial change is reminiscent of the model of the demographic transition in that it describes a sequence of events that occurred in developed countries. However, the same pattern is less likely to take place in developing countries. In that respect, it also resembles the demographic transition model. (See *POPULATION,* p. 289.) Less developed countries with rapidly growing populations such as India and Indonesia will probably have the majority of their workers in primary industry for a long time. More than half of the world labor force are agricultural workers, and in Africa and Asia, three-fourths of the workers may be employed (or underemployed) in primary production. (See Figure 16:1.) The problem may be not so much to hasten such countries through the same steps of industrial development followed by advanced countries as to improve the efficiency of their primary production and enhance the quality of life for the population in rural settings. Thus the three dilemmas of modernization confront planners and politicians in a single package: the problem of uncontrolled population expansion, the problem of urban concentration, and the problem of industrial development.

Developed countries Although developed countries follow similar broad patterns of industrialization, they evolve unevenly and at different rates according to their resources, political policies, and organizational competence. Despite its high technological achievement, the USSR has lagged in agricultural productivity, and for an industrialized nation, a disproportionate part of its labor force—about one-quarter—is employed in agriculture. In contrast to the Soviet Union, the proportion of Japanese workers in primary production has rapidly declined. About 19 percent of the workers in this most industrialized Asian nation are employed in primary production. The comparable figure for the United States is about 4 percent and for Great Britain about 3 percent.

The secondary sector is predominant in such countries as Italy (41 percent), Belgium (41 percent), and West Germany (49 percent). The tertiary sector employs the largest proportion of workers in Sweden (46 percent), Japan (48 percent), Australia (59 percent), the United States (64 percent), and Canada (65 percent).

The U.S. labor force The evolution of the U.S. labor force is a good example of redistribution among the three sectors during the process of industrialization. In the early nineteenth century, the United States was an agricultural nation with three-fourths of its workers in primary production. But now, because of vastly increased agricultural productivity, only about 4 percent are in agriculture. In the 32 years following 1940, productivity of U.S. agriculture increased almost fivefold: In 1940 the average farmer raised enough to feed 10.7 persons; in 1972 he supplied enough farm products for 42 Americans and 10.4 persons abroad (*Statistical Abstract of the United States*, 1974: Table 1063). Labor is thus a declining component of farm costs, but expenditures for machinery and fertilizers have grown rapidly: Agriculture has become agribusiness.

The proportion of the U.S. work force employed in manufacturing and construction has remained constant at about one-third since the beginning of the twentieth century. Employment in services paralleled the growth of manufacturing until the beginning of the century when services rapidly outstripped manufacturing and construction. Service activities currently employ about 64 percent of the labor force, a larger percentage than in any other country except Canada. It is hard to predict how far the trend toward tertiary employment will extend. Some observers believe that the ceiling has nearly been reached, but the distribution of labor is dependent on technological change and political decisions that are barely foreshadowed in the contemporary economy. For example, changed attitudes toward resource

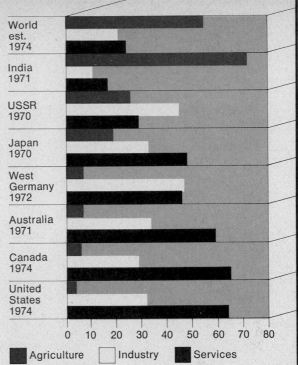

Figure 16:1 Distribution of the labor force by industrial sectors, world and selected countries (in percentages)

Source: Yearbook of Labour Statistics, 1974:Chap. 2A and country reports.

preservation and pollution control could have a profound effect on the work force, reducing investment in fertilizers and chemicals and increasing labor requirements.

The international labor market As the economies of nations become more intertwined, there is a flow of labor as well as capital and raw materials across national boundaries. The introduction of technically advanced industry to developing countries can be anything but a benefit when those countries have a surplus of unskilled and semiskilled labor and productive traditional industries that employ many workers. In a five-year period, textile companies in Indonesia created 86,000 new jobs in factories. At the same time 410,000 jobs were eliminated in traditional home craft production (Interna-

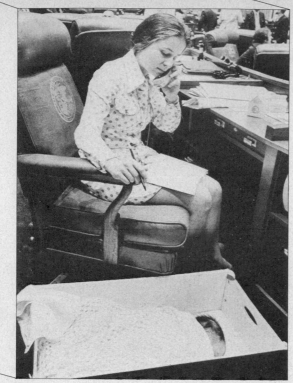

Accommodation at the workplace. An Illinois legislator keeps her daughter at her side.

tional Labor Organization bulletin). The total volume of goods produced may have been equally large, and the labor cost may have been reduced, but it is hardly what Indonesia needed. Nevertheless, getting factory jobs is better than what would have happened at an earlier period of economic imperialism. Then the factory jobs were created in the cities of the colonial power rather than in the developing country, for example, in Holland rather than in Indonesia.

In any case, countries with a growing surplus of underemployed workers realize that importing factories may have only a moderate impact on unemployment. Another remedy for surplus labor is for workers to go where jobs are, and throughout the period of industrialization migrants have sought out lands of expanding opportunity. (See *POPULATION*, p. 280.)

The industrial boom that followed the reconstruction of European industry after World War II created a severe labor shortage, which was met by the importation of hundreds of thousands of "guest workers" from less industrialized countries to more industrialized ones. At its peak—about 1972—there may have been 10 million foreigners working in northwestern Europe. The economic recession precipitated by the oil crisis turned the labor shortage into a labor surplus. When unemployment in West Germany reached 1 million, the country began to regard its 2.5 million guest workers with concern. But Germany is a Common Market (EEC) country, and workers from other EEC countries are in a privileged position.

Whatever the Germans do, they will not be able to send all of their guest workers home at a stroke. The 600,000 migrant workers from EEC countries —mainly Italy—cannot be touched, nor can a further 600,000 who have lived in Germany for more than five years or are married to Germans. The rest—mainly Turks, Jugoslavs and Spaniards—could, in theory, be gradually squeezed out as their one-year work permits come up for renewal. But many of them are doing jobs which few Germans would be prepared to do— although German-born dustmen are no longer the rarity they once were. Official estimates put the number of jobs where foreigners could be replaced by Germans at about 500,000. But the government knows full well that chucking its foreign workers out would make it very unpopular with the countries that have up to now been supplying this labour, and could backfire badly if the economy picks up again (*Economist*, January 18, 1975: 59–60).

POST-INDUSTRIAL SOCIETY

Changes in the labor force and in other basic indicators suggest that modern society should be perceived as moving to a post-industrial stage (Bell, 1967a, b; Touraine, 1971). This interpretation focuses attention on the transformations that have occurred since the Industrial Revolution of the nineteenth century. The most significant changes are the following:

1. The relative decline of industrial produc-

tion as the driving force of the economy and the representative activity of modern life When production was king, Henry Ford could turn out a basic Model T and the customer could have any color he wanted so long as it was black. White-collar workers made up a relatively small percentage of the labor force. The work ethic was largely unquestioned. With the shift to service occupations and to a consumer-oriented economy, production loses its primacy in both power and symbolism. Salesmanship and financial manipulation become the decisive qualifications for economic performance.

2. The enlarged social role of experts Although there is much room for debate regarding the relative power of business executives, government officials, and technical staffs, there is no doubt that the significance of the last group has greatly increased. (See Section Four.) Compared to the heyday of industrialism, the modern economy is heavily dependent on people with specialized knowledge. So, too, is modern government. One result is a marked expansion in the size and influence of academic institutions which train the specialists and serve as reservoirs of available talent.

The university . . . becomes the primary institution of the new society. Perhaps it is not too much to say that if the business firm was the key institution of the past hundred years, because of its role in organizing production for the mass creation of products, the university will become the central institution of the next hundred years because of its role as the new source of innovation and knowledge (Bell, 1967a:30).

This particular bit of prophecy should not be taken too literally. It is a way of stressing the growing importance of the "knowledge industry." In the not-so-distant future, the knowledge industry may find its home outside the university as we know it today — for example, in specialized research institutes.

Another consequence of the growth of expertise is the transformation of organizations, especially the development of post-bureaucratic forms. (See *ASSOCIATIONS*, p. 208.)

3. The expansion of participation The industrialism of the nineteenth and early twentieth centuries did not directly challenge the viability or distinctiveness of small-town and rural life. Although many people were drawn to the cities and to the centers of industrial production, those who remained could, for the most part, continue their accustomed ways. Society was more segmented, that is, divided into relatively distinct parts. But the modern economy demands and stimulates full participation. The technology of mass communications dominates marketing and creates a truly national society — more homogeneous, more closely interdependent, more vulnerable to breakdown. The postindustrial society, therefore, poses new problems of coordination and planning. It is a society that must be tended and "fine tuned." The market cannot be relied on to take care of itself.

4. The autonomy of technology Perhaps the most distinctive feature of postindustrial society is the preeminence of technology. Innovation is self-activating, no longer closely tied to the more urgent needs of production and consumption. An ever-expanding technology tends to create needs and to transform the human environment. Anxiety is growing that technological innovation is out of control.

These issues are discussed in Sections Three and Four.

Section two work and mechanization[1]

Sociotechnical systems It is useful to think of the settings within which people do their assigned work as "sociotechnical systems" (Emery and Trist, 1969). This idea emphasizes the close interdependence of technol-

[1] This discussion is based in part on materials prepared by Robert Blauner (see also Blauner, 1964). The relation between technical organization and human organization is discussed in Roethlisberger and Dickson, Chap. 24. (See Adaptation 12.) See also Perrow, 1967.

ogy and human relations. The sociotechnical system is a blending of the social and technical aspects of organization.

Technical system refers to the physical plant, the machinery, and the way mechanical processes are organized. The nature of the technology and the criterion of cost limit the alternative ways of getting the job done.

There is no technical system without a social system. The technical system determines important aspects of the group situation. For example, the technology may dictate how much detailed supervision is needed and what opportunities there are for informal contact among the workers. At the same time, the technical system depends upon the human factor—the skills, motivation, and discipline called for by the mechanical processes.

ALIENATION

In his early writings, Karl Marx advanced the theory of alienation, an influential hypothesis concerning the impact of technology on human relations in industry. In Marx's view, factory technology, the increasing division of labor, and capitalist property institutions brought about the estrangement of industrial workers from their work. Highly mechanized systems replaced craft methods of production in which artisans had been masters of their tools and materials. In the new factories intelligence and dexterity previously expressed in skilled crafts were "built into" the machines. Workers were left with routine and monotonous jobs. In the preindustrial period, both skilled craftsmen and peasants had considerable control over the rhythms and movements of work. But the machine system governed the pace of work and restricted the employee's free movements. This loss of freedom, this subordination to the machine, turned the worker into a mere instrument and made him feel *powerless.*

The increasing division of labor within the factory made jobs simpler, and each employee's area of responsibility diminished. In order to rationalize production, the work

was broken down into minutely subdivided tasks. The highly specialized operation might be very efficient, but it separated the worker from the total process. He did not need to understand how his work fit the whole. Responsibility, problem solving, and decision making were removed from the employees by the systematic division of labor and became the work of supervisors, engineers, and others on the technical staff. The fragmented relation of the individual to his work robbed him of a sense of purpose. This *loss of meaning* is another aspect of alienation.

Capitalism and alienation According to Marx, the property relations of capitalist society alienated the employee. The factory belongs to the entrepreneur, who has the legal and social power to hire labor, sell the products of the enterprise on the market, and take its profits for himself. The worker does not own what he produces. He has nothing to sell but his labor. Because the factory belongs to the capitalist, the worker is not likely to identify psychologically with its fortunes or its products. Because the profits do not benefit him personally, he is not motivated to work with all his energy and intelligence. Thus the property institutions of capitalism produce a third form of alienation—the employee's *sense of isolation* from the system of organized production and its goals.

Marx argued that capitalist economic institutions and modern factory technology deprive the employee of a truly human relationship to work. Loss of control means loss of freedom, initiative, and creativity. Specialization simplifies and degrades labor; it makes the goals of the enterprise so remote that a sense of meaningful participation in a work community cannot be attained. The worker does not identify with the productive organization but feels himself alienated from its purposes. When work does not permit responsibility, evoke a sense of purpose, or encourage larger identifications, the job is simply a way to make a living. Marx believed that unalienated productive work was a requirement for psychological well-being. Alienation reduces work to merely instrumental activity, which can only result in widespread suffering and degradation.

These ideas of the youthful Marx in the 1840s reflected a point of view widely held among intellectuals of the period. The rise of industrialism was viewed with misgivings, and intellectuals were concerned about the effects of the new order on the individual's organic relation to the community and work, and the identification of oneself as a creative and autonomous person. The concept of alienation, referring to estrangement from important sources of psychic and moral well-being, was "in the air." Specifically it was an important theme in the writings of G. W. F. Hegel (1770–1831), whose philosophy deeply influenced Marx's thought.

As Marx sharpened his attack on capitalism and predicted growing class conflict and political struggle, his emphasis shifted to the conflict of interest between workers and capitalists, and he did not pursue the theme of alienation. If he had done so, he might have come to realize that his critique was not uniquely relevant to capitalism. Rather, its most important elements apply to aspects of any industrial society, capitalist or socialist.

The theory of alienation in industry contains important insights regarding the effects of sociotechnical systems on human satisfaction. It illuminates some basic trends in modern work organization and accurately describes the situation of many employees. However, Marx greatly exaggerated the uniformity of modern industry. While the theory is suggestive, it underestimates the diversity of sociotechnical systems, some of which encourage a sense of responsibility and purpose.

INDUSTRIAL VARIATIONS

Empirical studies of modern work organization reveal that alienation occurs unevenly in the work force. These variations become evident when three industries with different technology—craft, assembly-line, and con-tinuous-process—are compared. The building, automobile, and industrial chemical industries are contemporary examples of each of these forms of technology. Each develops characteristic sociotechnical systems.

Craft technology The building industry is still largely based on craft technology. Its products are not standardized, and many traditional practices govern the way work is done. Historic craft specialities persist. The work force is predominantly skilled.

Craft workers are not dominated by the technical system. They control the pace at which they work, the quality of the product, and the quantity of output. They determine many of the techniques and methods involved in production and constantly meet to solve problems in the course of their work. Unlike other employees who often are under intense pressure, carpenters and masons are able to resist external control and maintain personal independence. This reflects the opportunities presented by the technology as well as the strength of the powerful craft trade unions.

Assembly-line technology Automobile production is based on the assembly line. As the incomplete motor vehicle moves along a conveyor belt, workers at every point on the line assemble one of the component parts. Three features of the assembly-line work organization are (1) extreme subdivision of jobs, (2) predetermination of work methods, and (3) the mechanically set speed of the conveyor belt. These features color the whole atmosphere of the assembly line.

The average assembler's job consists of only one or two operations. Little skill or training is required. The work is extremely repetitive, and little initiative is possible because engineers and time-study personnel have figured out in advance how each job is to be done. Assembly-line workers have virtually no control over their sociotechnical environment. The speed of the line brings about 50—in some plants many more—cars every hour and sets the pace of work and the quantity of output. The automobile worker

Table 16:1 Comparison of job satisfaction
and mental health by skill groups

| | Percentage reporting high scores | | |
	On job satisfaction index	On mental health index	Number of workers
Detroit factories			
Skilled and high semiskilled	72	48	(176)
Ordinary semiskilled	63	37	(128)
Repetitive semiskilled			
Not machine paced	41	29	(56)
Machine paced	28	13	(47)
Small-town factories			
High and ordinary semiskilled	72	56	(39)
Repetitive semiskilled	30	40	(40)
Detroit nonfactory			
High semiskilled	82	68	(28)
Ordinary semiskilled	60	49	(63)
White-collar employees	70	66	(68)

Source: Recomputed from Kornhauser, 1965:Table 5-1, p. 85. Interviews conducted during 1953–1954 with workers age 20–29 and 40–49.

cannot even leave his work station on the line without being relieved by another assembler.

Table 16:1 reports findings based on extensive interviews with about 650 workers in the Detroit area. Clear differences appear in both job satisfaction and mental well-being among workers at different skill levels and in different work settings. The lowest scores on mental well-being appeared among those working at repetitive, machine-paced tasks—that is, men on the assembly line.

Resistance to assembly-line work flared up dramatically in 1972 when a strike closed the highly automated General Motors plant in Lordstown, Ohio. Built in 1966, the Lordstown plant contains the world's fastest assembly line. When management attempted to bring the plant to maximum productivity —100 Vega compacts per hour—with elimination of some jobs and many other changes, the workers rebelled. The largely youthful work force refused to accept the increased pace and pressure.

Caution The assembly line is an extreme form of technology that is highly mechanized yet relies on a large number of human operators. The assembly line symbolizes the engineering mentality and has influenced other, less fully mechanized work settings. However, the numerical importance of assembly-line workers should not be exaggerated. Although no accurate census is available, it is estimated that less than 5 percent of American manual workers are on assembly lines (Blauner, 1964:91). A random sample of Detroit auto workers (Kornhauser, 1965) showed 11 percent in assembly-line work, although the total number of repetitive semiskilled workers (who include drill press operators, for example) was 25 percent of the sample.

Continuous-process technology In the technology of the modern oil and chemical industries, the product flows automatically through an extensive network of pipes and reactor units. Within each unit a particular process or reaction is carried out. Manual workers do not deal with the product directly, as they do in craft and assembly-line industries, but control the reactions of the invisible oils and chemicals by monitoring control boards, watching gauges and instruments, and adjusting valves. Only the maintenance crew, which repairs breakdowns in the automatic equipment, uses traditional manual skill.

Each team of operators is responsible for a particular chemical process and for the expensive equipment in its unit. Yet instead of feeling dominated by the towering technology, which in physical size and capital cost is many times greater than assembly-line technology, the operators feel they control the apparatus. Although production is regulated automatically, they control the pace at which they read instruments and patrol the plant. There is freedom of movement because automated work environments are relaxed and free of pressure. When operations are running smoothly, routine readings take up only a fraction of work time, and there is considerable "free" time.

Yet unpredictable breakdowns do occur, and then the energies of the workers are employed in locating the cause of the problem and restoring production to normal flow. The chemical operator's attitude toward breaks in production is in sharp contrast to that of the alienated automobile worker. The chemical worker feels in control when production is running smoothly; therefore he willingly works hard to eliminate the crisis. The assembly-line worker, on the other hand, feels powerless when the line is moving normally. He welcomes breakdowns and is likely to give a sigh of relief when the conveyer is stopped for repairs.

Many sociotechnical systems in modern industry cannot be classified as strictly craft, assembly-line, or continuous-process. Because of the great diversity in work environments, it is not possible to estimate the quality of human relations and the level of employee alienation throughout the whole industrial system.

RECONSTRUCTING THE WORK ENVIRONMENT

In 1972 a special report entitled *Work in America* was prepared at the request of the Secretary of Health, Education, and Welfare (HEW). The report reviewed various sources of discontent among American workers:

Many workers at all occupational levels feel locked-in, their mobility blocked, the opportunity to grow lacking in their jobs, challenge missing from their tasks. Young workers appear to be as committed to the institution of work as their elders have been, but many are rebelling against the anachronistic authoritarianism of the workplace (Senate Committee, 1973:xi).

In response to these and other findings, the HEW Task Force concluded that more effort should be devoted to the redesigning of jobs. Adaptation 37 is part of the report.

In Sweden a number of industrial enterprises have been experimenting with new ways of organizing work, including elimination of the assembly line. (See Herrick, 1971; Björk, 1975.)

Giant aircraft in a gigantic workplace: humanizing this environment is a challenge to the design of sociotechnical systems. McDonnell Douglas Corporation, Los Angeles, California

Adaptation 37 Task force report: The redesign of jobs

Most of the work redesign effort has confined itself to small work groups. Little of it has embraced the wider implications of the systems viewpoint and involved a plant or a corporation as a whole. The major exception to this trend is a General Foods manufacturing plant that was designed to incorporate features that would provide a high quality of working life, enlist unusual human involvement, and achieve high productivity. Management built this plant because the employees in an existing plant manifested many severe symptoms of alienation. Because of their indifference and inattention, the continuous-process type of technology used in the plant was susceptible to frequent shutdowns, product waste, and costly recycling. There were serious acts of sabotage and violence. Employees worked effectively for only a few hours a day and strongly resisted changes that would have resulted in a fuller utilization of manpower.

REDESIGN AT GENERAL FOODS

Management enlisted the advice and cooperation of workers and consultants from business schools, and together they designed a plant along the following lines:

Autonomous work groups Self-management work teams were formed and given collective responsibility for larger segments of the production process. The teams are composed of from eight to twelve members — large enough to cover a full set of tasks and small enough to allow effective face-to-face meetings for decision making and coordination. The teams decide who will do what tasks, and most members learn to do each other's jobs, both for the sake of variety and to be able to cover for sick or absent co-workers.

Integrated support functions Activities typically performed by maintenance, quality control, custodial, industrial engineering, and personnel units were built into the operating team's responsibilities. The teams accepted both first and final responsibility for performing quality tests and ensuring that they maintained quality standards.

Source: Abridged and adapted from Senate Committee on Labor and Public Welfare, *Work in America: Report of a Special Task Force to the Secretary of Health, Education, and Welfare* (Washington, D.C.: GPO, 1973), pp. 77–85.

Challenging job assignments An attempt was made to design every set of tasks in a way that would include functions requiring higher human abilities and responsibilities. The basic technology employed in the plant had been designed to eliminate dull or routine jobs insofar as possible. Still, some nonchallenging but basic tasks remained. The team member responsible for these operations is given other tasks that are mentally more demanding. The housekeeping activities were included in every assignment — despite the fact that they contributed nothing to enriching the work — in order to avoid having members of the plant community who did nothing but cleaning.

Job mobility and rewards for learning The aim was to make all sets of tasks equally challenging although each set would make unique skill demands. Consistent with this aim was a single job classification for all operators, with pay increases geared to mastering an increasing proportion of jobs, first within the team and then in the total plant. Thus, team members were rewarded for learning more and more aspects of the total manufacturing system. Because there were no limits to how many team members could qualify for higher pay brackets, employees were encouraged to teach each other.

Facilitative leadership In lieu of "supervisors" whose responsibilities are to plan, direct, and control the work of subordinates, a "team leader" position was created with the responsibility to facilitate team development and decision making. It is envisioned that in time the team leader position might not be required.

Managerial decision information for operators The design of the new plant called for providing operators with economic information and managerial decision rules. This enables production decisions ordinarily made at the second level of supervision to be made at the operator level.

Self-government for the plant community Management refrained from specifying in advance any plant rules; rather, it was committed to let the rules evolve from collective experience.

Congruent physical and social context Differential status symbols that characterize traditional work organizations were minimized in the new plant — for example, by a parking lot open to all

In this General Foods plant workers are organized into teams. The team members take turns at all of the work in their area, including equipment maintenance and cleanup.

regardless of position, a single office-plant entrance, and common decor throughout office, cafeteria, and locker room. The technology and architecture were designed to facilitate rather than discourage the congregating of team members during working hours. The assumption was that these ad hoc meetings often would be enjoyable human exchanges as well as opportunities to coordinate work and to learn about each other's jobs.

Using standard principles, industrial engineers had indicated that 110 workers would be needed to staff the plant. But when the team concept (rather than individual assignments) was applied and when support activities were integrated into team responsibilities, the result was a staffing level of fewer than 70 workers. While this 40 percent smaller work force is impressive, it is not the major economic benefit, because labor costs per unit are not a large percentage of the cost of goods sold in this particular business. The major economic benefit has come from such factors as improved yields, minimized waste, and avoidance of shutdowns. Significantly, these are productivity items that are related to technology but are especially sensitive to the work attitudes of operators.

What is particularly encouraging is the impact of this unique work setting on employees' extra-plant activities. For example, many workers have been unusually active in civic affairs—apparently significantly more so than is typical of the workers in other plants in the same corporation or in the same community. It has long been observed that workers in dull, isolated, or routine jobs seldom participate in community affairs, but this is the first instance where it has been shown that the redesign of work can have positive effects on community participation.

This General Foods plant is not a unique example, although the extent of the redesign is unusual. Several other cases illustrate the positive results of job redesign. Some clearly show the need for extensive planning before implementation should be attempted. For example, the first major experiment in Norway was carried out in the metalworking industry, a critical but unproductive sector of the Norwegian economy. A dilapidated wire-drawing plant was chosen for the experiment on the grounds that if improvements could be realized there, they could be achieved anywhere.

But productivity increased so much due to job redesign that the experiment was suspended: the unskilled workers in the experiment had begun to take home pay packets in excess of the most skilled workers in the firm, thus engendering bitterness.

REDESIGN OF BLUE- AND WHITE-COLLAR JOBS

At the Banker's Trust Company, many typists had repetitive jobs that entailed recording stock transfer data. Production was low, quality poor, and attitudes slack; absenteeism and turnover were high. The workers decided to try to redesign their own work tasks. Among other changes, they eliminated the work of a checker and of a special group that made corrections by assuming these responsibilities themselves. This change permits a $360,000 annual savings, and the social problems have been largely eliminated. Similar results have been reported at Traveler's Insurance with key-punch operators.

In a Corning Glass plant, women workers formerly assembled hot plates for laboratory use on an assembly line. Now each worker assembles a whole plate. Employees put their initials on each final product to allow identification with the work and to reference customer complaints. They also are given the opportunity to schedule their work as a group and to design work-flow improvements. Quality checks previously made by a separate group are conducted by the workers themselves. In six months following the change, rejects dropped from 23 percent to 1 percent, and absenteeism from 8 percent to 1 percent. During this same time, productivity increased. Also, the reputation of this division as an undesirable place to work was reversed. Other job-change projects have been conducted at Corning with more complex instruments.

Until 1967, Texas Instruments contracted for its cleaning and janitorial services. But the firm's engineers evaluated the plant as only "65 percent clean." Apparently, the contractor's ability to do the job well was reduced by a quarterly turnover rate of 100 percent.

Preceded by careful planning and training, the following actions were taken in a test involving 120 maintenance personnel:

• Cleaning service teams of 19 people were organized and were given a voice in the planning, problem solving, and goal setting for their own jobs.

• They were thoroughly trained in the job requirements and techniques and were provided with adequate equipment to do the job.

• They were held accountable for the overall job. The means of getting the job done were left to them. It was also the teams' responsibility to act independently to devise their own strategies, plans, and schedules to meet the objective.

• They were taught how to measure their own performance and were given the freedom to do so, both as individuals and as teams.

These were the outcomes:

• The cleanliness-level rating improved from 65 percent to 85 percent.

• Personnel required for cleaning dropped from 120 to 71.

• Quarterly turnover dropped from 100 percent to 9.8 percent.

• From the fourth quarter of 1967 until the fourth quarter of 1969, costs savings for the entire site averaged $103,000 per annum.

Participative management In the redesigned work settings mentioned above, one finds the workers participating in decisions on:

Their own production methods
The internal distribution of tasks
Questions of recruitment
Questions regarding internal leadership
What additional tasks to take on
When they will work

Not all of the work groups make all of these decisions, but the list provides the range within which the workers are participating in the management of the business or industry. Participative management does not mean participation through representatives, for, as experience has shown, that kind of participation may foster alienation through the inevitable gap between expected and actual responsiveness of the representatives.

Participative management means that, as the examples above illustrate, workers are enabled to control the aspects of work intimately affecting their lives. It permits the worker to achieve and maintain a sense of personal worth and importance, to grow, to be self-motivated, and to be recognized and approved for what he or she does. It gives the worker a meaningful voice in decisions in one place where the effects of his or her voice can be immediately experienced. In a broader sense, it resolves a contradiction in our nation— between democracy in society and authoritarianism in the work place.

Not all of a company's decisions, of course, are turned over to the workers when they participate in management. Upper-level managers continue to run the company, handle major financial transactions, and coordinate all the functions. Although they are no longer involved in planning the details of every operation in the company, they serve as expert consultants to the teams of workers. Some managerial jobs, however, do tend to be eliminated, such as some of the lower- and middle-management positions as well as intermediate supervisory positions without authority. But these jobs are frequently unsatisfying (supervisor jobs go begging in the auto industry) and unproductive. Without retraining opportunities for individuals in these jobs, however, they would either be put out of work or, with the threat of that possibility, oppose the redesign of work.

The concept of work design also needs to be applied to management, where participation can also usefully be increased. The work of managers needs to be redesigned not only because it is unlikely for authoritarian managers to support the humanization of work for lower-level workers, but also for their own physical and mental health.

Section three humanity, nature, and the ecosystem

The mechanization and dehumanization of work have preoccupied social analysts since the beginning of the Industrial Revolution. In that sense, the issues discussed in the preceding section are not new, although they remain urgent. Since the middle of the twentieth century, however, a deeper foreboding has entered the consciousness of technological society: the anxiety that great and irreversible changes threaten the complex structure of modern civilization and endanger the future of the human species.

This section considers (1) alienation from nature, (2) the technological foundations of the ecological crisis, and (3) some principles of conservation.

CONCEPTIONS OF HUMANITY AND NATURE

Human ecology is in part a subjective phenomenon. What people do to the environment depends on how they conceive it and what value they place upon it. In Western society, there is a long tradition that fosters an exploitative mentality, a conception of nature as wholly available to human needs and wants, untempered by any principle of restraint.

A human-centered universe Western culture has celebrated the unique human potential for individual freedom and reason. These philosophical perspectives have nurtured lofty ideals and remarkable achievements, but they have also helped create a view of humanity and nature prefigured in the biblical story of Genesis. God fashions man in his own image and appoints him lord of creation. "The earth is the Lord's, and the fullness thereof," but man is God's delegate. All things serve the purposes of him who shares in God's glory and His sovereignty.

Christianity built upon this Hebraic tradition and emphasized even more sharply the duality of humanity and nature. While rejecting the idea of a chosen *people*, Christianity accepted and reinforced the doctrine that humankind was the Lord's chosen *species*. The new religion encouraged spiritual humility and offered a model of self-sacrificing love. But there was no challenge to the unique worth or the rightful domination of the human animal.

St. Francis of Assisi has been called "the greatest radical in Christian history since Christ" because he urged the humility of the human species:

Francis tried to depose man from his monarchy over creation and set up a democracy of all God's creatures. With him the ant is no longer simply a homily for the lazy, flames a sign of the thrust of the soul toward union with God; they now are Brother Ant and Sister Fire, praising the Creator in their own ways as Brother Man does in his (White, 1969:350).

The Catholic church supported the expansion of a great Franciscan Order, but it rejected the heretical suggestion that all things created by God had something akin to a soul and were to be valued for their own sakes and not merely for their usefulness.

These perspectives of Western religion are neither universal nor inevitable. They contrast sharply with the religious ideas of much of the non-Western world, including preliterate societies. The great religions of Asia—Hinduism and Buddhism—tend to blur the boundary between humanity and the rest of nature (Morris, 1964:35). Doctrines of reincarnation and of cosmic consciousness have worked against the idea of human uniqueness and pride. Humanity finds nirvana—a perfect blessedness—in the renunciation of aspiration, in the extinction of selfhood, in unity with a universal spirit that encompasses all of nature.

In preliterate folk societies human beings belong to the natural order; they are both in it and of it; they are not set apart or placed above. "In this world view there can be no mysticism, because mysticism implies a prior separation of man and nature and an effort to overcome the separation" (Redfield, 1953:105). One manifestation of the primitive world view is animism, the belief that natural objects—plants, animals, even geological formations—are invested with a vital force or spirit no less real than that of human beings.

This conception of humanity-in-nature generates a principle of self-restraint:

Whether it be the spirit-inhabiting waterhole . . . of the Arapesh, or the rain-gods of the Zuni . . . these entities and dispositions are part of a man-including moral system. The universe is spun of duty and ethical judgment. . . . So we find everywhere in the uncivilized societies—and may therefore attribute the characteristic to the pre-civilized societies also—when man acts practically toward nature, his actions are limited by moral considerations (Redfield, 1953:106–107).

As depicted by Redfield and other like-minded anthropologists, primitive peoples do not feel free to work their will upon the natural surroundings.

It is easy to exaggerate the practical significance of a nature-affirming world view. Small communities with rudimentary technology are highly dependent on the environment as it is, including what it can offer in the form of game, fish, and other foods. Protecting the environment has a common-sense basis. In populous regions, however, the affirmation of nature has not necessarily saved the forests or protected the soil. Respect for nature may be offset by other values, such as the prizing of large families, with resulting overpopulation and pressure on the land. China and India are no strangers to the denuding of forests and the creation of deserts. Modern Japan is heavily polluted. Some environmental damage is very old:

Perhaps as far back as Neolithic time, the first ominous discordance [of man and nature] develops. The dry interiors of the Old World, from Cape Verde to Mongolia, are today a far more meager and more difficult human habitat than was true in early Neolithic. We know that their deterioration is much greater than can be accounted for by climatic change. . . . The inference, therefore, is that the discrepancy between vegetation and climate in the Old World is due to cultural influence. Specifically, ancient overgrazing by herding peoples is blamed for the bareness of much of the great interior of the Old World. The damage developed perhaps three or four thousand years ago (Sauer, 1938:766).

Until recent times, ecological destruction was a relatively slow, gradual, long-term consequence of human activity that appears, in the short term, innocent enough. Humanity's impact may be destructive regardless of how the world is conceived. Nevertheless, a conception of humanity in nature is a helpful reinforcement favoring the conservation of limited resources. Without such a perspective there is less chance of restraining the unbridled exploitation of nature.

The mentality of exploitation Alienation from nature—apartness and domination— breeds a mentality of exploitation. Nature is fully subordinate to humanity when it has no meaning except as a complex of natural resources. This broad perspective, when put into action, generates a number of more specific attitudes and commitments:

1. Nature is exploited according to felt human needs, but needs are constantly redefined and expanded as the capacity for exploitation grows. Once resources are easily available, especially if they are produced and marketed for profit, the luxuries of yesterday become the necessities of today.

2. The exploitation of natural resources becomes an end in itself. In that context, the very word *exploitation* loses its negative connotation. The full use of resources is seen as an aspect of progress, and it appears wasteful to neglect an unused potential. The concept of progress, called "development," is exalted; the concept of natural limitations is ignored.

3. Exploitation favors maximum productivity in the short run; the long run will take care of itself. The assumption is that nature

A memorial to species extinguished by man. More than 200 species of mammals, birds, and reptiles have become extinct within the last three or four centuries, mostly due to human intervention. About 800 species are listed as endangered by the International Union for Conservation of Nature and Natural Resources.

Aswan: assault on the Nile

Formally inaugurated in 1971 on Gamal Abdel Nasser's birthday, the Aswan High Dam of Egypt is the dead leader's monument. Bigger than any dam of its kind ever built, it is equipped to generate 10 billion kilowatts of power; it forms a lake nearly 2,000 miles square; it hobbles the mighty Nile River that spans half of Africa from the equator to the Mediterranean. The dam took 11 years to build and cost close to a billion dollars. The late President Nasser expected it to pay for itself in two years, double Egypt's national income and industrialize the poor agricultural state in ten years, and water an immense empty desert for his hungry, crowded people.

Egyptian government reports on its performance—it has been storing water since 1964 and producing power since 1967—are uniformly cheerful. Yet the dam has in fact greatly impoverished an already destitute nation, driven the fish from the eastern Mediterranean, exposed the whole Egyptian coast to erosion, endangered every bridge and barrier dam astride the Nile from Aswan to the sea, robbed Egyptian soil of the silt that had made it the most fertile on earth, threatened millions of acres with the blight of salinity, set off water-borne diseases, and squandered the very water it was meant to save.

THE NUTRIENT FLOOD

Five thousand years ago, the people of the Nile valley used to throw a beautiful virgin into the river every August to appease Hapi, god of the Nile, whose miraculous brown waters renewed their parched soil year after year. The Nile is the sole source of life in Egypt and its annual flood was one

Source: Abridged from Claire Sterling, "Aswan Dam Looses a Flood of Problems," *Life*, February 12, 1971. Reprinted by permission of International Famous Agency. Copyright © 1971 by Time, Inc.

of nature's exquisitely balanced wonders. Sometimes it brought too much water, engulfing villages, or else too little; and even in normal years about 30 billion tons flowed unused out to sea. But the water wasn't wasted. Every drop laden with rich sediment that emptied into the Mediterranean strengthened the aquatic food chain, nourishing marine life, and maintained the exact balance of salinity it needed; and every year the sediment added a little more to the delta land it had formed in the first place, sealed off underground seepage to sweet-water lakes, and shielded the sand dunes serving as dikes along the shore from the sea's powerful west-to-east currents.

Before reaching the sea, furthermore, the flood waters flushed away accumulating soil salts that would otherwise choke the life out of growing plants, dumping the salts at sea; and they left behind 130 million tons of that soil-building and enriching silt that has made the Nile valley the agricultural marvel it is. Now, because of the Aswan Dam, the Nile will never flood Egypt again. The swirling muddy water runs into Lake Nasser, behind the dam, and the priceless sediment sinks. Downstream from Aswan to the Mediterranean, 600 miles away, the water flows limpidly clear, and will forever.

After just six years, the aquatic food chain has been broken in the eastern Mediterranean along a continental shelf 12 miles wide and 600 miles long. The lack of Nile sediment has reduced plankton and organic carbons to a third of what they used to be, either killing off the sardines, scombroids, and crustaceans in the area or driving them away. The 18,000 tons of sardines, one-fifth of the annual fish catch, has disappeared. At the same time, salinity is rising as the Red Sea waters pour through the Suez Canal without the sweet Nile floodwaters to counteract them. Nobody knows what such environmental upheaval may eventually do to remaining plant and animal life in this corner of the Mediterranean.

THE SCOURING CURRENT

Erosion is eating at the delta coastline, exposed now to the full force of marine currents. Some parts of the coast are receding several yards a year. The silt-free water flows downstream much faster, carrying off not just fringes of coast but a quantity of the riverbed. This scouring process is undermining three old barrier dams and 550 bridges built since 1952. To slow the current and so prevent their collapse, the ministry of the High Dam plans to build ten new barrier dams between Aswan and the sea. The project, known as the Nile Cascade, will cost a quarter of a billion dollars—a quarter of what the High Dam itself cost.

Deprived of the Nile's life-giving sediment, many of Egypt's 6 million cultivated acres need artificial fertilizer already, as all of them will before long. Moreover, without the flood to wash salts away, soil salinity is already reaching ominous levels, not just in the heavily waterlogged delta but throughout middle and upper Egypt. Agronomists say that unless preventive measures are taken—at a minimum cost of over a billion dollars—millions of acres will be reduced to barren rubble in barely a decade.

THE FLOURISHING PARASITE

The one undisputed merit of the dam's stored water has been the conversion of 700,000 acres from flood to canal irrigation. This permits double-cropping that has added half again to the yearly production of these lands. Yet, because there are no floods, there are also no periods of dryness which, in the past, helped limit the population of bilharzia, a parasite carried by water snails. The bilharzia causes a debilitating intestinal and urinary disease in humans. Its carrier, the snail, loves the placid irrigation canals, where an infected human need only urinate or bathe to spread the wiggly tailed microscopic larvae and where a healthy human need only set foot to pick up the infection. One of every two Egyptians now has it; one of every ten deaths in the country is caused by it. In areas along new canals, the snails are quick to follow, and there the infection rate of bilharziasis has shot up from zero to 80 percent.

THE VANISHING WATER

These are terrible afflictions for a nation perennially threatened by famine as its people multiply, bursting the bonds of their narrow green valley only to be driven back by an implacable desert. Yet they might bear it all if the High Dam could give them the one thing they prize above every other: limitless water. It has not. For all the millions of dollars spent and to be spent, there is less water coming downstream from Aswan today than there was before, and there is not enough water behind the dam, and there may never be.

The planned capacity of Lake Nasser is 163 billion cubic meters, the minimum needed to cover the requirements of Egypt and the Sudan in a succession of lean flood years. It was to have reached that level in 1970, but it is not yet even half full. Limnologists studying the problem at the Lake Nasser Development Center in Aswan say it should be filling up around 1982. But Egypt's most authoritative limnologist, Professor Abdel Goher, thinks it may take 200 years.

More than 15 million cubic meters of water are probably escaping underground every year. The dam's planners assumed that fine clay from the incoming sediment would eventually seal any porous rock. But the sediment has been settling mostly in the lake's deep center along the old riverbed, and the Nubian sandstone lining the new lake's entire 300-mile western bank is capable of absorbing endless quantities of water.

Since Lake Nasser was to form in the hottest and driest place on earth, evaporation losses were bound to be staggering. Planners expected them to be an annual 10 billion cubic meters, but they failed to take into account the high wind velocity. The Egyptian Meteorological Institute has just completed a study showing that the rate is 15 billion cubic meters—half the total amount that used to be "wasted" by flowing unused to sea. The sad result of this seepage and evaporation is that Egypt is getting 10 billion cubic meters of water less every year than the celebrated Nilologist Dr. H. E. Herst has said it needs for irrigation, river transport, and the High Dam turbines.

THE REVENGE OF NATURE

Some might be tempted to blame the dam's Soviet builders for all these problems. But its West German designers were apparently unaware of possible miscalculations. So was the American secretary of state, John Foster Dulles, who offered to finance it and then changed his mind for political reasons.

In a plaque commemorating the dam's recent inauguration, Nasser's followers have written: "It was thanks to the Immortal Leader's struggle for freedom, socialism, and unity that the dam could be opened today." It is too late to wonder whether something more modest might have got them further in their eternal search for water, whether the Nile might have responded more generously if their leader had treated it with more of his ancestors' deference. He didn't and it didn't.

La Seine polluée

is infinitely bountiful, infinitely capable of recuperating from any negative effects of human intervention.

4. The environment is freely reconstructed and reconceived to fit human purposes. A river becomes a special-purpose resource for creating hydroelectric power. A forest is a tree farm. The bottom of a shallow bay is potential real estate. These perceptions justify unlimited use and control, including the creation of lakes, the rechanneling of rivers, and the opening of all lands to exploitation. Large engineering projects are perceived as heroic achievements rather than as alien and potentially dangerous intrusions. (See "Aswan: Assault on the Nile," p. 532.)

5. As peoples become independent of nature, they become more dependent on technology. Modern agriculture has created many high-yield hybrids as well as new varieties suitable for machine cultivation and harvesting (Kelly, 1967). But the new varieties depend on commercial fertilizers and mechanized farming. Although the "green revolution," based on high-yield grains, has greatly increased the food supply in nonindustrialized countries, new dependencies have also been created:

Typically the new grain varieties *must* have high fertilizer inputs in order to realize their potential. . . . Capital is required for fertilizer plants, fertilizer purchases, road construction, railroad construction, trucks, and so forth. Abundant water is also essential for most of the grains, requiring investment in tubewells, pumps, and irrigation ditches. Similarly pesticides and mechanized planting are necessary to get the most out of the new varieties (Ehrlich and Ehrlich, 1972: 121).

Technology is costly, and once an investment is made, there is a compulsion to expand its use to protect the investment. The result is an intensified commitment to the exploitation of resources.

THE ECOLOGICAL CRISIS

The mentality of exploitation, the rapid growth of technology, the spread of industrialization, and the burgeoning of world population have produced an ecological crisis. The crisis has two main components: pollution of the environment and exhaustion of resources. Pollution brings smog, dead lakes, undrinkable water, lethal radiation, dwindling fisheries, and the extinction of species. The depletion of mineral resources, including petroleum, is proceeding so rapidly that grave questions are raised regarding their future availability (Meadows et al., 1972:54–68). At the least, many minerals of special importance to modern technology will become increasingly expensive, a fact which has serious implications for the industrialization of Asia, Latin America, and Africa and therefore for the political future of humanity.

The ecological crisis presents problems that cut across many scientific disciplines. Ecology is in the highest degree an interdisciplinary subject. The contributions of sociology will include (1) identification of social factors, such as norms affecting fertility and living arrangements, that must be taken into account when predictions are made regarding future patterns of exploitation; (2) study of the possibilities and mechanics of social control to limit pollution and preserve the environment; and (3) analysis of perspectives that suggest revised social

goals and policies—for example, new meanings of conservation, new life-styles, and new conceptions of property and responsibility.

All who participate in the effort to overcome the crisis must share a basic understanding of ecosystems and of the forces that threaten them. The following paragraphs summarize some of the main elements of that understanding.

The idea of an ecosystem Ecology (from *oikos*, the Greek word for "house," and, by extension, "habitat") is the study of the adaptation of living things to the environment and the mutual relations that occur in the course of that adaptation. The environment includes other organisms as well as the inanimate physical setting. The basic data for ecology are spatial distributions. Ecology as a branch of the biological sciences developed during the nineteenth and twentieth centuries and was greatly stimulated by the writings of Charles Darwin (1809–1882) and by the German biologist Ernst Haeckel (1834–1919), who coined the term *ecology* in 1866.

Ecologists study ecosystems. An ecosystem is a specific pattern of interdependence and exchange involving organisms, their products, and the physical environment. A forest is an ecosystem. Closely observed, it is made up of many mutually dependent species, both plant and animal, whose survival and abundance are in part determined by the character of the soil, the contours of the land, and climatic conditions. Any reasonably bounded web of life can be studied as an ecosystem. Furthermore, the idea of an ecosystem may be applied to human society by studying, for example, the interdependence of population, activities, and resources (see *URBANIZATION*, p. 496).

From the standpoint of conservation, perhaps the most important contribution of this approach is that it increases sensitivity to the fragility of ecosystems. The concept of system suggests an equilibrium, but any given equilibrium may be very precarious.

Some ecosystems can absorb many shocks, easily reestablishing the basic state of the system. For example, the introduction of a new kind of fish might change the balance of species in a pond, but natural adjustments would tend to leave the system very much as it was, that is, a supportive habitat for broad types of plants, insects, and fish. The capacity of an ecosystem to make readjustments and maintain stability is largely dependent on the complexity of the system:

Complex communities, such as the deciduous forests that cover much of the eastern United States, persist year after year if man does not interfere with them. An oak-hickory forest is quite stable in comparison with an ultrasimplified community, such as a cornfield, which is a man-made stand of a single kind of grass. A cornfield has little natural stability and is subject to almost instant ruin if it is not constantly managed by man. Similarly, arctic and subarctic ecosystems, which are characterized by simplicity, tend to be less stable than complex tropical forest ecosystems (Ehrlich and Ehrlich, 1972:195).

Broadly speaking, the effect of technology is to simplify ecosystems, thereby making them highly dependent on specific resources, such as commercial fertilizers.

The displacement of nature Since about the end of World War II, pollution in the United States and the rest of the industrialized world has increased at a greatly accelerated pace, considerably faster than the population growth or the increase in gross national product. This dramatic increase can be traced to the introduction of new products (and the much more widespread use of old ones) that are peculiarly stressful to the environment (Commoner, 1971:Chap. 9). The reasons for that stress touch closely on alienation from nature.

According to Commoner, the new technology has one overriding characteristic: A natural organic product, or method of production, is displaced by one that is unnatural or synthetic. A good example is the replacement of soap by detergents. Another is the revolution in textiles, which substi-tutes synthetic fibers for cotton and wool. These new products are radically artificial. They are not fabricated from materials found in the received world of nature, as occurs when something is made of wood or copper. Rather, nature is reconstructed. The chemistry of plastics, detergents, and pesticides is based on the synthesis of new molecules. The widespread use of such artificial materials is an assault on the environment:

The structure of nylon and similar synthetic polymers is a human invention and does not occur in natural living things. Hence, unlike natural polymers, synthetic ones find no counterpart in the armamentarium of degradative enzymes in nature. Ecologically, synthetic polymers are literally indestructible. . . . Hence, every bit of synthetic fiber or polymer that has been produced on earth is either destroyed by burning—and thereby pollutes the air—or accumulates as rubbish (Commoner, 1971:162).

The ecological significance of chemical "progress" in fashioning new materials is discussed further in Adaptation 39.

A somewhat less radical displacement of nature is the growing reliance on artificial fertilizers. The use of such fertilizers in the United States has multiplied twelvefold in the past 25 years (Ehrlich and Ehrlich, 1972:229). The result is more yield per acre, with fewer acres and less labor needed for production. On the other hand, the ecological stress is severe. To produce the desired yields, excessive amounts of nitrates and phosphates (more than can be used by the crop) are applied to the soil. In contrast to organic nitrates found in humus, the excess inorganic nitrates do not remain in the soil. They are leached out and find their way to inland streams, rivers, and lakes:

The waters draining the farmlands of the Middle West are rich in nitrogen as a result of the heavy use of inorganic nitrogen fertilizers. Indeed, they have an estimated nitrogen content equivalent to the sewage of some 20,000,000 people—about twice the total human population of the Lake Erie basin. Thus, besides fertilizing their farms with nitrogen, the farmers are also fertilizing Lake Erie; their nitrogen contribution is of the same order of magnitude as that of the municipalities and the industrial polluters. The nitrogen balance of the lake has been seriously disturbed, and the abundance of inorganic nitrates encourages the growth of certain algae. . . . The bacterial decay of these masses of algae consumes oxygen, reducing the amount of oxygen available for fishes and other animals. Such blooms of algae and oxygen depletions are characteristic of lakes undergoing *eutrophication*, which may be loosely translated as "overfertilization" (Ehrlich and Ehrlich, 1972: 230).

Modern technology has made inorganic fertilizer cheap and plentiful. Under present conditions, organic farming, especially on a large scale, is much more expensive. The hidden cost of chemical farming, however, is pollution.

The use of feed lots for fattening cattle is another displacement of a more natural mode of food production, and it has increased greatly. Millions of cattle now spend less time on pasture and more time in feed lots. Consequently large quantities of organic waste are not returned to the soil (as they would be if the cattle were pastured) but are disposed of as sewage. Feeding grain to cattle rather than to people is inefficient and wasteful. When animals are fed grain, which people can eat, instead of grass, which they cannot, the advantage of converting inedible plants to edible protein is lost.

In the short run, chemical pesticides control unwanted insects better than their natural enemies do.

Unfortunately, many of the more effective natural enemies in agricultural crops appear to be more susceptible to the broad-spectrum synthetic organic insecticides and acaricides than are the pests against which materials are used (Huffaker, 1971:102).

The natural enemies are reduced in number not only by the effect of pesticides but also by the elimination, for a time, of their food supply. The frustrations of insect control are eloquent testimony to the significance of ecosystems.

Some displacements of nature may in time be remedied by the development of new technologies of recycling—for example, effective return of manure to the soil. But it is also probable that a new perspective will be required, one that rejects the historic Western belief that nature is infinitely manipulable.

RESTORING THE BALANCE

The ecological crisis has stirred considerable public reaction, including a certain amount of doomsday thinking, with prophecies of imminent catastrophe. In response, one group has proposed a global equilibrium model, based on an analysis of world resources and current rates of production and consumption. The model calls for radical social policies that would (1) stabilize world population by setting the birth rate equal to the death rate in 1975; (2) reduce both resource consumption and pollution per unit of industrial and agricultural output to one-fourth of its 1970 value; (3) shift social preferences from material goods to services, such as education and health; (4) divert capital to food production, to minimize the inequalities in world living standards; and (5) limit total average income per capita to about $1,800, which is "about half the present U.S. income, and three times the present average world income" (Meadows et al., 1972:165–166).

The effect would be a world in which the rate of growth of industrial output would be sharply checked, although stabilized at a level substantially higher than current production (three times the 1970 world average), and in which most people would have considerably more food and better services.

Such proposals, and the analyses on which they are based, must be examined with caution. First, the worth of the computer projections depends on the accuracy of the information supplied and on the validity of assumptions regarding continuing rates of growth, pollution, and resource consumption. Given the uncertainties of present knowledge and the rapidity of social change, substantial inaccuracies are inevitable. The models require continuing revision. Second, and perhaps more important, the authors of the proposal have little to say about how their social objectives are to be achieved, especially how the political issues are to be resolved. (For the second report to the Club of Rome, which gives more attention to political considerations, see Mesarovic and Pestel, 1974.)

Nevertheless, models of growth rates and their consequences and projections of possible future "steady states" are valuable guides to thought and planning. They are at least starting points for the formulation of goals and policies that can be responsive to the most important ecological constraints and to the gravest political concerns. Foremost among the latter is the imbalance between the world of the haves and the world of the have-nots.

Whatever one's attitude toward a coherent world plan, there is no avoiding a reappraisal of the premises of public policy. Among the most important issues are the following:

1. Limiting growth and development   It is clear that the ideal of unlimited economic growth is being seriously questioned. Although new scientific and technological breakthroughs are always theoretically possible, society can no longer rely on their occurrence to forestall ecological crises, including widespread famine.

The idea of limiting economic growth is a grisly joke to the millions of people who live at the borderline of subsistence. Therefore the affluent world must bear the burden, restraining its aspirations for ever-new levels of personal convenience and military security. It has been pointed out that compared to India, the population of the United States has a far greater detrimental impact on the land and makes a far greater claim, per capita, on world resources.

An Indian equivalent I define as the average number of Indian citizens required to have the same detrimental effect on the land's ability to support human life as would the average American. This value is difficult to determine, but let's take an

extremely conservative working figure of 25. . . . In Indian equivalents, therefore, the population of the United States is at least four billion. And the rate of growth is even more alarming. We are growing at one percent a year, a rate which would double our numbers in 70 years. India is growing at 2.5 percent. Using the Indian equivalent of 25, our population growth becomes 10 times as serious as that of India (Davis, 1970:14).

A policy of limiting economic growth would do nothing to reduce demands for greater equality, both among nations and within nations. Rather, it would unambiguously present to the haves the painful choice of reducing their consumption so as to increase the share of the world's goods available to the have-nots.

2. Building ecological criteria into government policies   It is easy to be "for ecology" in the abstract; it is much more difficult to establish effective incentives and controls. The constraints are both political and scientific. A democratic government is dependent on popular support, and ecology-oriented policies will be weak and superficial if the public is not willing to pay the costs of environmental protection. Hence public education remains vital. No less important is improved understanding of the social and economic factors that affect ecosystems:

Even with improved technology, large-scale recycling faces an uphill battle. Existing economic policies encourage the use of virgin rather than recycled materials, and these obstacles must be overcome before recycling can become environmentally and economically significant. Several federal programs . . . have undoubtedly lowered virgin material prices and induced greater consumption of these materials than would have occurred otherwise. Consequently, the reclamation of waste materials has been less profitable (First National City Bank, 1972:35–36).

The use of virgin materials is encouraged by federal tax policies offering such benefits to extractive industries as mineral depletion allowances. These policies reflect a historic commitment to maximizing the exploitation of natural resources. To make recycling effective, these special benefits would have to be diminished or removed.

3. Establishing new goals for technology
The taming of technology is not a negative enterprise. It is not antiscientific or anti-technological. On the contrary, technology itself must be enlisted in the cause of eco-logical restoration. Efficient recycling on a massive scale awaits new technologies of waste disposal, salvage, and composting; alternative energy sources, with low ecologi-cal impact, must be developed. Technology is also an indispensable adjunct of social control—for example, in devising tech-niques for measuring standards of perform-ance (Branscomb, 1971:976).

4. Building ecological considerations into daily life Any good citizen can insist that governments and businesses take environ-mental concerns into account in developing responsible policies for the utilization of scarce resources and controlling the dis-posal of wastes. Paradoxically, it is more difficult in democratic countries to persuade those same citizens to alter their daily lives with the same objectives in mind. People find it hard to limit their consumption of nonrenewable resources such as petroleum products even to the extent of obeying a speed limit which has been proved to save fuel and lives. The independent citizen thinks of his or her own self-indulgence as an inconsequential impact on the environ-ment—as in fact it is in statistical terms. Only the multiplication of numerous similar decisions imposes an insupportable burden on resources. An example of the cumulative effects of millions of decisions to own house-hold pets and to feed them commercially prepared products is outlined in Adaptation 38. It appears that ecology, which comes from the Greek word for house, may begin at home.

Adaptation 38 Fears: Pets, people, and the food supply

PETS V. PEOPLE

Pets are in competition with the human population for food as a consequence of the growth of the pet food industry and the increasing number of pets.

Before the Second World War, cats and dogs were usually fed cheap cuts of fish and meat which were relatively plentiful. Canning of pet meat was in its infancy; the few commercial prod-ucts contained mainly offal (parts of a butchered animal considered inedible by human beings) with some cereal. After the war the number of brands of tinned pet foods and the volume of sales grew rapidly. The sale of associated products, such as dog biscuits, increased similarly. Sales of pet foods in Britain rose from 20,000 tons in 1953 to 600,000 tons in 1974.

Many alterations in the composition of pet foods have occurred during the past 30 years, and today there is a wide diversity of products. Pet food tech-nology has become very sophisticated and has closely paralleled changes in the packaging of foodstuffs for human use. Today, very little of what goes into pet foods is unfit for human consump-tion. Large amounts of wheat, sugar, skimmed milk, soya, and other sources of vegetable protein are used, as well as the traditional meat items.

The vegetable ingredients of pet food could be, and are, used directly in human diets. Alterna-tively, any of the constituents of pet foods could be incorporated into the diets of farm animals and would then eventually be available for human con-sumption, albeit via a less efficient process. The inefficient use of valuable foodstuffs as feed for livestock has been much criticized. How much worse is the use of similar foods for pets?

In addition to their general effect on food sup-plies, the use by pet food manufacturers of various materials has been blamed for creating special-ized shortages. For example, there is a world scarcity of heparin for medical use (mainly as an anticoagulant) partly because its natural source,

Source: Abridged and adapted from Robie Fears, "Pet foods and human nutrition," *New Scientist* (March 18, 1976):606–608. Published in this form by permission of Robie Fears and *New Scientist*.

hog intestine, is turned into pet foods. Another shortage was emphasized by the recent campaign to stop pet food manufacturers from using whale meat in their products, as they were endangering the population of certain species of whale. The subsequent response by the pet food companies showed they were susceptible to public pressure.

PET POPULATIONS

In the United States, the dog population increased from 15 million in 1935 to around 40 million in 1974; the birthrate of cats and dogs is now estimated at 3,000 per hour compared with 450 human babies. (The annual pet food bill is six times that spent on baby food.) Reliable estimates suggest that there are about 6 million dogs and 5 million cats in Britain and that the dog population is expanding by 4.4 percent per annum; 26 percent of all homes owned one or more dogs and 16 percent owned a cat. In the United States, 46 percent of homes owned a dog.

Delegates at the World Food Conference in Rome in November 1974 agreed to provide the poorer countries with 10 million tons of cereal yearly for three years, as the forward planning strategy for food aid. This figure is probably a minimum estimate of the needs of the developing countries, which may have a cereal deficit of 85 million tons by 1985. At present the richer countries distribute about £600 million ($1.25 billion) worth of food annually as aid. In comparison, dogs and cats in Britain alone consume each year a minimum of 1.5 million tons of assorted foodstuffs, worth approximately half as much as the value of food distributed by the rich countries to the poor ones. As a substantial proportion of pet food is still of animal origin, this 1.5 million tons could be translated into a very much larger volume of cereals. It is not possible to achieve a quick transfer of resources devoted to pet foods into aid for the developing nations. Nonetheless, a comparison between pet foods and food aid does focus attention on our priorities and shows how major problems might be solved by a redirection of effort.

STRATEGIES OF CONSERVATION

In the long term, it is difficult to predict what will happen to the pet population. China, for example, has banned the keeping of dogs as pets because of their need for food. In the West, it has been suggested that eventually pets will be confined to zoos (although this same prediction has also been made for farm animals). In the short term, it is unlikely that pet keeping will be dramatically curtailed. Any widespread antagonism to cats and dogs in the foreseeable future will be caused not by a revulsion at their consumption of limited food supplies but rather in response to other problems, particularly health problems, associated with their behavior.

If it is considered desirable to relieve some of the pressure made by the heterogeneous pet population on the total supply of foodstuffs, however, the following points might be considered.

First, the dogs' requirements for food could be reduced simply by keeping smaller dogs; a Scottish terrier eats about a quarter as much as an Alsatian. A higher license fee for larger dogs is one suggestion considered by the Working Party on Dogs constituted by Parliament.

Second, the number of unwanted strays could be reduced. Although strays may consume relatively little conventional pet food, they constitute a large and totally unnecessary population. Ultimately, a reduction in the number of unwanted animals can only be brought about by more efficient contraceptive mechanisms for pets and by a greater sense of responsibility from owners.

Third, to reduce the wastage of valuable resources as pet foods involves replacing constituents of most value in human diets (for example, soya) with items that would be less readily eaten by people. It is difficult, however, to imagine a potential constituent of pet foods which has not already been recommended for human use. Deep-sea fish, oil-seed residues, and leaf protein may all be underutilized at the moment, but they have great potential for human diets. It would be distressing if oil-seed residues from countries such as India and Nigeria were used in Britain for feeding to pets in addition to their present use as feeds for farm animals. It is bad enough to waste home-produced commodities in pet foods; it is surely worse to import foodstuffs from developing countries for this purpose.

Certain pet food manufacturers consider that their future lies in exploiting single-cell and vegetable proteins, but this would be a retrograde step, as single-cell proteins have an enormous future in human diets. It is possible that an "artificial" provider of energy such as 1,3-butanediol (which is efficiently utilized by animals such as pigs, chicks and rats when fed at 15 percent in the diet) may find a place in pet foods. And, being derived from petroleum, it does not require land for production, in the conventional sense. The Celanese Corporation has filed a petition with the U.S. Food and Drug Administration for the use of 1,3-butanediol in intermediate-moisture pet food.

Additional fiber may also have a useful place in pet diets, especially in view of the recently reported benefits to human nutrition. An increase in fiber content, besides reducing the proportion of valuable foodstuffs, would help to prevent the obesity which is so common in dogs.

WHO GETS THE PROTEIN?

In general, the composition of pet diets should follow the criteria applied to diets for livestock, where it is now generally recognized that attention should be given to using foodstuffs that are not directly useful to man. Unfortunately, unlike livestock, common pets are carnivorous and do not have four stomachs and so cannot be fed the foodstuffs such as bagasse (sugar cane or sugar beet residue) and citrus pulps which have been recommended for farm animals. Probably the biggest problem is providing pets with sufficient protein. Dogs seem to require more protein than people—about 12 percent of energy provided as good-quality protein. This is commonly translated into about 20 percent mixed protein (soya/fish meal).

In terms of food consumption the population of the world is not 4 billion but 19 billion "population equivalents"—the extra being the animals associated with man. Recent figures show that consumers in the richer countries account, on the average, for 997 kg (2,193 lb) of grain per head per year. Some 63 kg (139 lb) are eaten directly and 934 kg (2,055 lb) indirectly as animal products. People in poorer countries consume 181 kg (398 lb), almost all directly as cereal—an intake approximately equivalent to that of a medium-sized dog in Britain. The latter is enjoying food of better nutritional value.

Adaptation 39 Commoner: Principles of ecology

Ecology has not yet developed the cohesive, simplifying generalizations exemplified by the laws of physics. Nevertheless, a number of generalizations are already evident from what we know about ecosystems; these can be organized as an informal set of laws of ecology.

EVERYTHING IS CONNECTED TO EVERYTHING ELSE

The single fact that an ecosystem consists of multiple interconnected parts that act on one another has some surprising consequences. Our ability to picture the behavior of such systems has been helped considerably by the science of cybernetics. . . .

Cybernetics derives from the Greek word for helmsman; it is concerned with cycles of events that steer, or govern, the behavior of a system. The helmsman is part of a system—the ship—that also includes the compass and the rudder. If the ship veers off the chosen compass course, the change shows up in the movement of the compass needle. Observed and interpreted by the helmsman, this event determines a subsequent one: the helmsman turns the rudder, which swings the ship back to its original course. When this happens the compass needle returns to its original, on-course position and the cycle is complete. If the helmsman turns the rudder too far in response to a small deflection of the compass needle, the excess swing of the ship shows up in the compass—which signals the helmsman to correct his overreaction by an opposite movement. Thus the operation of the cycle stabilizes the course of the ship.

Ecological systems exhibit similar cycles, although these are often obscured by the effects of

Source: Adapted from *The Closing Circle* by Barry Commoner. Copyright © 1971 by Barry Commoner. Reprinted by permission of Alfred A. Knopf, Inc.

Fattening cattle: Edible plants into edible protein

daily or seasonal variations in weather and other environmental agents. The most famous examples of such ecological oscillations are the periodic fluctuations in the size of fur-bearing animal populations. For example, from trapping records in Canada it is known that the populations of rabbits and lynx follow ten-year fluctuations. When there are many rabbits the lynx prosper; the rising population of lynx increasingly ravages the rabbit population, reducing it; as the latter become scarce, there is insufficient food to support the now numerous lynx; as the lynx begin to die off, the rabbits are less fiercely hunted and increase in number. And so on. These oscillations are built into the operation of the simple cycle in which the lynx population is positively related to the number of rabbits and the rabbit population is negatively related to the number of lynx.

In such an oscillating system there is always the danger that the whole system will collapse when an oscillation swings so wide of the balance point that the system can no longer compensate for it. Suppose, for example, that in one particular swing of the rabbit-lynx cycle, the lynx manage to eat all the rabbits (or, for that matter, all but one). Now the rabbit population can no longer reproduce. As usual, the lynx begin to starve as the rabbits are

consumed; but this time the drop in the lynx population is not followed by an increase in rabbits. The lynx then die off. The entire rabbit-lynx system collapses.

This is similar to the ecological collapse which accompanies the eutrophication of a lake. If the nutrient level of lake water becomes so high as to stimulate the rapid growth of algae, the dense algal population cannot be long sustained because of the intrinsic limitations of photosynthetic efficiency. As the thickness of the algal layer in the water increases, the light required for photosynthesis that can reach the lower parts of the algal layer is sharply diminished, so that any strong overgrowth of algae very quickly dies back, releasing organic debris. The organic matter level may then become so great that its decay totally depletes the oxygen content of the water. The bacteria of decay then die off, for they must have oxygen to survive. The entire aquatic cycle collapses. . . .

All this results from a simple fact about ecosystems—everything is connected to everything else: the system is stabilized by its dynamic self-compensating properties; these same properties, if overstressed, can lead to a dramatic collapse; the complexity of the ecological network and its intrinsic rate of turnover determine how great a stress it can sustain, and for how long, without collapsing; the ecological network is an amplifier, so that a small perturbation in one place may have large, distant, long-delayed effects.

EVERYTHING MUST GO SOMEWHERE

This is a somewhat informal restatement of a basic law of physics—that matter is indestructible. Applied to ecology, the law means that in nature there is no such thing as waste. In every natural system, what is excreted by one organism as "waste" is taken up by another as food. Animals release carbon dioxide as a respiratory waste; this is an essential nutrient for green plants. Plants excrete oxygen, which is used by animals. Animal organic wastes nourish the bacteria of decay. The wastes of the bacteria—inorganic materials such as nitrate, phosphate, and carbon dioxide—become algal nutrients.

A persistent effort to answer the question "Where does it go?" can yield a surprising amount of valuable information about an ecosystem. Consider, for example, the fate of a household item which contains mercury, a substance with serious environmental effects. A dry-cell battery containing mercury is purchased, used to the point of exhaustion, and then thrown out. But where does it really go? First it is placed in a container of rubbish; this is collected and taken to an incinerator. Here the mercury is heated; this produces mercury vapor, which is emitted by the incinerator stack, and mercury vapor is toxic. Mercury vapor is carried by the wind, eventually brought to earth in rain or snow. Entering a mountain lake, let us say, the mercury condenses and sinks to the bottom. Here it is acted on by bacteria which convert it to methyl mercury. This is soluble and taken up by fish; since it is not metabolized, the mercury accumulates in the organs and flesh of the fish. The fish is caught and eaten by a man and the mercury becomes deposited in his organs, where it might be harmful.

Tracing such an ecological path is an excellent way to counteract the prevalent notion that something regarded as useless simply "goes away" when it is discarded. Nothing goes away; it is simply transferred from place to place, converted from one molecular form to another, acting on the life processes of any organism in which, for a time,

it is lodged. One of the chief reasons for the present environmental crisis is that great quantities of material have been extracted from the earth, converted into new forms, and discharged into the environment without taking into account that everything has to go somewhere. The result, too often, is the accumulation of harmful amounts of material in places where, in nature, they do not belong.

NATURE KNOWS BEST

This principle is likely to encounter considerable resistance, for it appears to contradict a strongly held idea about the unique competence of human beings. One of the most pervasive features of modern technology is the notion that it is intended to improve on nature—to provide food, clothing, shelter, and means of communication and expression that are superior to those available to man in nature. Stated baldly, the third law of ecology holds that any major man-made change in a natural system is likely to be detrimental to that system. . . . I had found it useful to explain this principle by means of an analogy. Suppose you were to open the back of your watch, close your eyes, and poke a pencil into the exposed works. The almost certain result would be damage to the watch. Nevertheless, this result is not *absolutely* certain. There is some finite possibility that the watch was out of adjustment and that the random thrust of the pencil happened to make the precise change needed to improve it. However, this outcome is exceedingly improbable. The question at issue is: why? The answer is self-evident: there is a very considerable amount of what technologists now call "research and development" (or, more familiarly, "R&D") behind the watch. This means that over the years numerous watchmakers, each taught by a predecessor, have tried out a huge variety of detailed arrangements of watch works, and have discarded those that are not compatible with the overall operation of the system and retained the better features. In effect, the watch mechanism, as it now exists, represents a very restricted selection, from among an enormous variety of possible arrangements of component parts of a singular organization at the watch works. Any random change made in the watch is likely to fall into the very large class of inconsistent, or harmful, arrangements which have been tried out in past watch-making experience and discarded. One might say, as a law of watches, that "the watch-maker knows best."

There is a close analogy in biological systems. It is possible to induce a certain range of random, inherited changes in a living thing by treating it with an agent, such as X-irradiation, that increases the frequency of mutations. Generally, exposure to X-rays increases the frequency of all mutations which have been observed, albeit very infrequently, in nature and can therefore be regarded as *possible* changes. What is significant, for our purpose, is the universal observation that when mutation frequency is enhanced by X-rays or other means, nearly all the mutations are harmful and the great majority so damaging as to kill the organisms before they are fully formed.

In other words, like the watch, a living organism that is forced to sustain a random change in its organization is almost certain to be damaged rather than improved. And in both cases, the explanation is the same—a great deal of "R&D." In effect there are some 2 to 3 billion years of "R&D" behind every living thing. In that time, a staggering number of new individual living things have been produced, affording in each case the opportunity to try out the suitability of some random genetic change. If the change damages the viability of the organism, it is likely to kill it before the change can be passed on to future generations. In this way, living things accumulate a complex organization of compatible parts; those possible arrangements that are not compatible with the whole are screened out over the long course of evolution. Thus, the structure of a present living thing or the organization of a current natural ecosystem is likely to be "best" in the sense that it has been so heavily screened for disadvantageous components that any new one is very likely to be worse than the present ones.

This principle is particularly relevant to the field of organic chemistry. Living things are composed of many thousands of different organic compounds, and it is sometimes imagined that at least some of these might be improved upon if they were replaced by a man-made variant of the natural substance. The third law of ecology suggests that the artificial introduction of an organic compound that does not occur in nature, but is man-made and is nevertheless active in a living system, is very likely to be harmful.

The varieties of chemical substances actually found in living things are vastly more restricted than the *possible* varieties. . . . Obviously, there are a fantastically large number of protein types *not* made by living cells. It is likely that many of these possible protein types were once formed in particular living things, found to be harmful, and rejected through the death of the experimental organism. . . .

One of the striking facts about the chemistry of living systems is that for every organic substance produced by a living organism, there exists, somewhere in nature, an enzyme capable of breaking that substance down. In effect, no organic substance is synthesized unless there is provision for it degradation; recycling is thus enforced. When a new organic substance is synthesized with a molecular structure that departs significantly from the types occurring in nature, it is probable that no degradative enzyme exists, and the material tends to accumulate.

All artificial organic compounds that are active biologically ought to be treated as we treat drugs, or rather as we should treat them—prudently, cautiously. Such prudence is impossible when billions of pounds of the substance are produced and broadly disseminated into the ecosystem where they can reach and affect numerous organisms not under our observation. Yet this is precisely what has been done with detergents, insecticides, and herbicides. The often catastrophic results lend considerable force to the view that nature knows best.

THERE IS NO SUCH THING AS A FREE LUNCH

This "law" derives from a story that economists like to tell about an oil-rich potentate who decided that his new wealth needed the guidance of economic science. Accordingly, he ordered his advisers, on pain of death, to produce a set of volumes containing all the wisdom of economics. When the tomes arrived, the potentate was impatient and again issued an order—to reduce all the knowledge of economics to a single volume. The story goes on in this vein, until the advisers are required, if they are to survive, to reduce the totality of economic science to a single sentence. Their response is the "free lunch" law.

In ecology, as in economics, the law is intended to warn that every gain is won at some cost. In a way, this ecological law embodies the previous three laws. Because the global ecosystem is a connected whole, in which nothing can be gained or lost and which is not subject to overall improvement, anything extracted from it by human effort must be replaced. Payment of this price cannot be avoided; it can only be delayed. The present environmental crisis is a warning that we have delayed nearly too long.

Section four technology and culture

The central place of technology is reflected in the themes and values of modern culture, including major ideas of social theory. Implicit in a number of nineteenth- and twentieth-century theories of society is a postulate of *technological determinism.* In such theories the growth of culture is seen as closely dependent on the capacity of man to control his environment. Specific ways of dealing with nature determine social organization, which in turn decisively affects values, forms of government, and even religion and the arts.

MARX AND HISTORICAL MATERIALISM

The most influential social theory taking technological evolution as its starting point is found in the writings of Marx. (See *SOCIAL STRATIFICATION*, p. 186.) Marx, with his collaborator Friedrich Engels, developed the doctrine of historical materialism, which holds that changes in technology invariably produce changes in the way work is organized, including the distribution of authority and power within the work unit. Taken together, the technology ("forces of production") and the organization of work ("relations of production") form the *material substructure* of the society. This substructure defines the nature of the society, for all other institutions are "superstructure," ultimately serving and dependent upon the material base. The following is a sample of Marx's argument:

[2] This section was written by Philippe Nonet in collaboration with the authors.

These social relations between the producers, and the conditions under which they exchange their activities and share in the total act of production, will naturally vary according to the character of the means of production. With the discovery of a new instrument of warfare, the fire-arm, the whole internal organization of the army was necessarily altered, the relations within which individuals compose an army and can act as an army were transformed, and the relation of different armies to one another was likewise changed.

The social relations within which individuals produce, the social relations of production, are altered, transformed, with the change and development of the material means of production, of the forces of production. The relations of production in their totality constitute what is called the social relations, society, and, moreover, a society at a definite stage of development, a society with a unique and distinctive character. Ancient society, feudal society, bourgeois (or capitalist) society, are such totalities of relations of production, each of which denotes a particular stage of development in the history of mankind (Marx, 1849/1956:146–147).

In the Marxist scheme, technology generates economic institutions but then drops out as the immediate determining force. The economic system, not the technology as such, produces vested interests and the class struggle.

Furthermore, the pace of technological progress depends in part upon the nature of the economic system. Marx thought modern capitalism had a unique capacity to accelerate the development of technology. In capitalism, he argued, producers are compelled to initiate technological change in order to increase productivity and survive competition.

Marx saw the disturbing effects and the human costs of technological advance. Nevertheless, he welcomed it and looked with optimism on its promise for humanity. The historic role of capitalism, as Marx saw it, was to develop the technological resources that would overcome oppressive scarcity and create a truly free society. At the same time, this great productive apparatus would require a higher degree of organization and planning than capitalism could provide. Hence, owing to technology, capitalism would eventually make the advent of socialism not only possible but inevitable. And socialism, too, would depend upon advanced technology.

VEBLEN: THE REGIME OF WORKMANSHIP

Like Marx, the American economist and social critic Thorstein Veblen (1857–1929) believed culture and social organization were determined by technology, or what he called the "state of the industrial arts." Veblen's celebration of technical progress was even more emphatic than Marx's. He saw in technology the source of important values — encouraging a rational, matter-of-fact approach; satisfying an "instinct for workmanship," that is, a propensity to find pleasure and pride in a job well done; promoting a concern for reducing waste; and achieving a more productive use of resources. In his view, such concerns and talents grow naturally among workers in technical occupations (Veblen, 1914). With technological progress, he argued, technicians would become increasingly indispensable and would acquire the power to reorganize the production and distribution of goods in accordance with their own standards of efficiency and rationality. Veblen imagined an ideal society, where a "Soviet of Technicians" would establish a "regime of workmanship" and achieve the dream of a rational and just economy (Veblen, 1921).

However, Veblen thought modern capitalism would be a major source of resistance to technological progress, not the powerful stimulant Marx had envisioned. He saw a fundamental conflict between workmanship and the pecuniary values of salesmanship, between technology and ownership, between the technician's concern for the quality and rationality of production and the businessman's quest for profit.

Veblen hoped that in the long run, technicians would become aware of the dependence of industry on their skills and would undertake "a conscientious withdrawal of efficiency," that is, a strike "to incapacitate the industrial system for such time as may be required to enforce their argument" (Veblen, 1921:166–167). In this way the Production Engineers would overturn the Guardians of the Vested Interests and acquire the power to realize the potentials of modern technology and industry.

The optimism of Marx and Veblen, characteristic of most nineteenth-century evolutionary theorists, is not shared by more recent writers. The contemporary mood is pessimistic, permeated by anxiety for the negative effects of technology on human values.

THE TECHNOCRATIC AGE

The term *technocracy* evokes the picture of a society in which technology pervades and dominates all spheres of life, efficiency prevails over self-expression and personal values, and the growing authority of technical experts undermines democratic ideals. The vision of a technocratic age has haunted the contemporary imagination, in social thought as well as in literature (Mumford, 1970; Ellul, 1964; Huxley, 1946; Young, 1958).

These writings should be understood as pointing to risks associated with technological progress rather than to an inevitable trend. Technical advances create opportunities as well as dangers. They can serve humane as well as destructive ends. As productive capacities are increased, many values are brought within closer reach; human efforts may be shifted from burdensome tasks to new goals.

Culture lag Technological progress is risky because new devices are put to work before there is the capacity or the will to control destructive side effects. Sociologists have long observed that changes do not occur in a coordinated way even in closely related parts of culture and social organization. Although the different parts of society—for example, industry and education—are interdependent, changes go on at different rates. Industry may develop a need for skilled personnel that the educational system is unable to supply without retraining of teachers. Pressure is brought on the school system to make adaptive changes in its training methods, but while this adaptation is going on, a period of maladjustment occurs. This period of delay has been called *culture lag* (Ogburn, 1922:200–214).

Ogburn emphasized that changes in "material" culture—the realm of technology—often outdistance changes in other components of social life. In time, ways of adjustment, which Ogburn called the *adaptive* culture, are developed. Some elements, such as the social organization of work, adapt to new technologies fairly easily and completely. The mores, on the other hand, resist longer and adapt only partly.

Caution In discussions of culture lag, it is often assumed that technology is the first to change. That is often true but need not be so. For example, public attitudes and government policy, especially in wartime, may stimulate drastic increases in the rate of technological change. Furthermore, the fastest possible adjustment to technology is not necessarily the best. A delayed adaptation may be based on fuller experience and a better assessment of what is required for effective adaptation. Under modern conditions, it cannot be taken for granted that technology must call the tune.

The tyranny of means In technocracy, the relation of means to ends is inverted: Ends no longer fully govern the choice of means; instead, the capacities and requirements of technology tend to determine what ends will be pursued.

The controversy over commercial supersonic aircraft (SST) offers a striking example of the inversion of means and ends (*Congressional Digest*, 1970). Key arguments for the project were: (1) supersonic transportation is technologically feasible; (2) the research required to design the aircraft would preserve the lead of the United States in aerospace technology; and (3) government support for the project would help maintain the aerospace industry, with its technical competence and productive capacity. The economic feasibility of the project and the effects of supersonic booms remained unquestioned for several years after work had begun. When opposition arose, it had to cope with the resistance of a variety of government offices and private groups which had acquired a vested interest in the program. The fact that the SST *could* be built came close to deciding that it *should* be built.

One sign of the technocratic spirit is a preoccupation with efficiency. The imperatives of short-run returns undermine competing values. When there is strong pressure for results, attention is focused on activities and objectives that can be readily measured or assessed. Subtle values and broad social purposes tend to be set aside because they make decisions more complex, more uncertain, and more difficult to justify. Furthermore, comprehensive values are less likely to enlist group support than are narrower ends that promise definite payoffs for specific interests.

A drive toward efficiency undermines values in three main ways: (1) *intangible* ends, such as those bearing on the quality of life, lose out when they are balanced against pursuits that can yield measurable results; (2) *long-term* ends which require complex planning, such as conservation, are readily displaced by more practical short-run goals; (3) values that entail *multiple* ends—for example, the combination of teaching and research in higher education—are simplified

The electronic dossier

Most Americans do not realize the vast size and scope of today's credit-reporting industry. For example, the Associated Credit Bureaus of America have over 2,200 members serving 400,000 creditors in 36,000 communities. These credit bureaus maintain files on more than 110 million individuals.

The Retail Credit Company investigates individuals who apply for insurance or employment. Their files include dossiers on 45 million individuals and contain information on drinking, marital discord, adultery, as well as a person's general reputation, habits, and morals. A typical investigation takes 30 minutes, with much of the information coming from neighbors.

One of the fastest-growing credit-reporting firms is the Credit Data Corporation of California, which has 20 million files on computer tape. During recent hearings, the firm's president testified they were adding 50,000 files a week and estimated that within five years information on every American who has applied for credit could be in their computer data bank.

Perhaps the most serious problem in the credit reporting industry is the storage and communication of inaccurate or misleading information. Errors can crop up in a variety of ways:

*1. Confusion with other persons
Recently, a New York assemblyman was denied credit for no apparent reason. Only after repeated calls to the credit bureau did he learn that the credit bureau had confused him with*

Source: Abridged and adapted from a statement of Senator William Proxmire, upon introducing the Fair Credit Reporting Bill. U.S., Senate, Committee on Banking and Currency, *Hearings Before the Subcommittee on Financial Institutions*, 91st Cong., January 31, 1969, pp. 427–436.

someone else. A person less persistent might still have a falsely blemished record, particularly if he did not happen to be an assemblyman.

2. Biased information A record of slow payment or nonpayment in a person's credit file does not necessarily mean he is a poor risk. Perhaps he had a legitimate dispute with a merchant and withheld payment until the merchant lived up to the terms of the contract. While merchants have a wide variety of collection weapons, about the only bargaining power consumers have is the threat to hold up payments. Unfortunately, the consumer's side of the story does not find its way as easily into the files of the credit bureau as does the merchant's version.

3. Malicious gossip and hearsay Potentially damaging personal information is most prevalent in the files of credit-reporting agencies that specialize in investigating people who apply for insurance or employment. The information is often obtained from neighbors or co-workers who are offered the opportunity to indulge in anonymous character assassination. A Pennsylvania woman was turned down for major medical insurance. After repeated interviews with company officials and the Pennsylvania insurance commissioner, the woman's husband finally learned the reason. A credit report indicated she was an alcoholic. In actual fact, the woman had never consumed more than a dozen drinks in 20 years of married life.

4. Computer errors With the growing trend toward computerization, the incidence of computer errors is on the increase. A California credit-reporting agency mistakenly labeled a whole file drawer of good credit risks as bad credit risks. An aerospace engineer has written: "I am especially concerned by the possibilities of error afforded by computer systems, which spew forth incorrect data and half-truths due to the dogmatic nature of computer programming and the limitations of human operations."

Garbage in, garbage out. This UNIVAC computer stores and retrieves vast quantities of information at high speed; but the quality of the information depends on human intelligence and human control.

and reduced to a single objective.

The vulnerability of values in the technocratic age is illustrated by the threats to privacy that have accompanied the growing technology of information and surveillance. With the development of electronic means of communication, new surveillance devices, especially the telephone tap, have made possible easy and almost undetectable invasion into the most private aspects of individual life (Miller, 1971; Westin, 1967; Senate Judiciary Committee, 1971).

The privacy of conversations, including telephone calls, is protected under the Fourth Amendment of the U.S. Constitution. Except in cases involving threats to national security, evidence obtained through a wiretap may not be admitted in a criminal trial unless a court gives the government a search warrant authorizing the tapping (*Berger* v. *New York*, 388 U.S. 41, 1967). But this principle conflicts with a long-standing rule allowing the introduction of evidence obtained by informers. The evidence secured by an informer or undercover agent is treated in law as equivalent to the testimony of any witness; the special relation between the informer and the government may affect the credibility of his testimony, but not its admissibility. People must bear the risk that parties to conversations may reveal what they heard. In a recent case, an informer carrying a concealed radio transmitter engaged the accused in a conversation, which was overheard through the transmitter by government agents acting without a warrant. A deeply divided Supreme Court held the evidence admissible. In a strong dissent, Justice Harlan argued:

Authority is hardly required to support the proposition that words would be measured a good deal more carefully and communication inhibited if one expected his conversations were being transmitted and transcribed. Were third party bugging a prevalent practice, it might well smother that spontaneity—reflected in frivolous, impetuous, sacrilegious, and defiant discourse—that liberates daily life. Much offhand exchange is easily forgotten and one may count on the ob-

Woman with Loaves by Pablo Picasso (1905). Modern mass-produced bread—soft and spongy, thin of crust—is a distant relative of Picasso's loaves.

scurity of his remarks, protected by the very fact of a limited audience, and the likelihood the listener will either overlook or forget what is said, as well as the listener's inability to reformulate a conversation without having to contend with a documented record. All these values are sacrificed by a rule of law that permits official monitoring of private discourse limited only by the need to locate a willing assistant (*United States* v. *White*, 401 U.S. 745, 787–788, 1971).

Computers create similar risks of intrusion and abuse of power simply by making large amounts of information available quickly and at very low cost. (See "The Electronic Dossier," p. 548.)

The regime of experts In technocratic society, experts steadily widen their influence in business and government, while political

leaders, private entrepreneurs, and the public lose confidence in their own ability to make independent judgments. This is not to say that experts have actually displaced the political or business leaders. Most students of postindustrial society argue that ultimate power resides where it was. "It is not the technocrat who ultimately holds power, but the politician" (Bell, 1967a:34). But the style of decision making and much of the content is increasingly subject to the influence of technicians.

However, the regime of experts entails risks for democratic values: (1) It undermines the legitimacy of public participation and criticism and (2) it diminishes the authority of elected officials. Citizens and politicians are laymen who find themselves compelled to defer to those who "know better." This problem underlies tendencies toward the formation of self-perpetuating oligarchies in large-scale organizations. (See Adaptation 18; on the role of experts in government, see Lipset, 1950; Wilensky, 1967.)

VOICES OF RESISTANCE

Modern man is at best uneasy in the technocratic age. There is a sensed loss of community and of moral purpose; for many, the new world is opaque and threatening. In some quarters modern technology is explicitly rejected in favor of a more natural style of life; elsewhere alienation is expressed more indirectly, in feelings of impotence and disarray and in a symbolism of despair.

Literature of the absurd While much of modern design and architecture celebrates technology, other currents in art and literature picture the technocratic world as inhuman and absurd. Charlie Chaplin's movie *Modern Times*; Franz Kafka's novels *The Castle* and *The Trial*; George Orwell's negative utopia in *1984*; and the theater of the absurd, including Samuel Beckett's *Waiting for Godot*, are some of the best-known examples of this trend. Some of the key themes in these works are: (1) the social and personal disorganization that follows the imposition of a technocratic order; (2) the basic irrationality of purportedly efficient but unresponsive systems; and (3) the powerlessness of man before the technological apparatus that supposedly achieves his mastery over nature. The despair expressed in the art and literature of the absurd reflects in part a pessimism that grew out of the experience of totalitarianism in the 1930s and 1940s and its use of technology for repression and war. The despair also reflects a fatalistic belief in the inevitability of technological change and the irreversibility of its destructive effects.

Return to nature Another tendency, which has its main support among middle-class youth, is more hopeful about reversing the drift of history. In this view, salvation is to be found in a return to the natural environ-

ment. There people can respond freely, according to their basic needs and talents, without subordinating themselves to the imperatives of technology (Roszak, 1969; Reich, 1971). The freedom and innocence of a state of nature is to be found outside the city, on subsistence farms. In the arts, a revival of interest in handicrafts and in folk music reveals similar aspirations.

It is doubtful that a truly consistent stand against technology can be viable in modern society, except as a marginal counterculture. The counterculture can be an effective source of criticism and a center for the affirmation and renewal of humane values. But in the long run, a return to nature can succeed only with appropriate technological support; it cannot succeed if it offers low levels of subsistence, long hours of labor, inadequate medical care, and minimal education.

References

Abegglen, James G.
1958 The Japanese Factory: Aspects of Its Social Organization. New York: Free Press.

Bell, Daniel
1967a "Notes on the post-industrial society (I)." Public Interest (Winter):24–35.
1967b "Notes on the post-industrial society (II)." Public Interest (Spring):102–118.

Björk, Lars E.
1975 "An experiment in work satisfaction." Scientific American 232 (March):17–23.

Blauner, Robert
1964 Alienation and Freedom: The Factory Worker and His Industry. Chicago: University of Chicago Press.

Boeke, J. H.
1953 Economics and Economic Policy of Dual Societies. New York: Institute of Pacific Relations.

Branscomb, Lewis M.
1971 "Taming Technology." Science 171 (March 12):972–977.

Clark, Colin
1957 The Conditions of Economic Progress. Third edition. London: Macmillan.

Commoner, Barry
1971 The Closing Circle: Nature, Man and Technology. New York: Knopf.

Congressional Digest
1970 "Congress and the supersonic transport." Vol. 49, no. 12 (December):289–310.

Davis, Wayne H.
1970 "Overpopulated America." New Republic (January 10): 13–15.

Ehrlich, Paul and Anne H. Ehrlich
1972 Population, Resources, Environment: Issues in Human Ecology. Second edition. San Francisco: Freeman.

Ellul, Jacques
1964 The Technological Society. Translated by John Wilkinson. New York: Knopf.

Emery, F. E. and E. L. Trist
1969 "The causal texture of organizational environments." Pp. 241–260 in F. E. Emery (ed.), Systems Thinking. Baltimore: Penguin.

First National City Bank
1972 Environmental Quality and New York City. New York.

Herrick, Neal Q.
1971 "Activities to enrich work in other developed countries." Paper delivered at the 138th meeting of American Association for the Advancement of Science, December 127, Philadelphia.

Huffaker, C. B.
1971 "The ecology of pesticide interference with insect populations." Pp. 92–104 in J. E. Swift (ed.), Agricultural Chemicals—Harmony or Discord for Food, People, Environment. Berkeley: Division of Agricultural Sciences, University of California.

Huxley, Aldous
1946 Brave New World. New York and London: Harper & Row.

Kelly, Clarence F.
1967 "Mechanical harvesting." Scientific American 217 (August):50–59.

Kornhauser, Arthur
1965 Mental Health of the Industrial Worker. New York: Wiley.

Lipset, S. M.
1950 Agrarian Socialism. Berkeley: University of California Press.

McDermott, John
1967 "Crisis manager." New York Review of Books 9 (September 14):8.

MacPherson, C. B.
1962 The Political Theory of Possessive Individualism. Oxford: Oxford University Press.

Marsh, Robert M. and Hiroshi Mannari
1971 "Lifetime commitment in Japan: roles, norms, and values." American Journal of Sociology 76 (March):795–812.

Marx, Karl
1849/1956 T. B. Bottomore and Maximilien Rubel (eds.), Karl Marx: Selected Writings in Sociology and Social Philosophy. New York: McGraw-Hill.

Marx, Karl and Friedrich Engels
1848/1959 Lewis S. Feuer (ed.), Basic Writings on Politics and Philosophy. Garden City, N. Y.: Doubleday.

Meadows, Donella H., Dennis L. Meadows, Jorgen Randers, and William W. Behrens III
1972 The Limits of Growth. New York: Universe Books.

Mesarovic, Mihajlo and Edouard Pestel
1974 Mankind at the Turning Point: The Second Report to the Club of Rome. London: Hutchinson.

Miller, Arthur R.
1971 The Assault on Privacy: Computers, Data Banks, and Dossiers. Ann Arbor: University of Michigan Press.

Moore, Wilbert E.
1951 Industrial Relations and the Social Order. New York: Macmillan.

Morris, Ivan
1964 The World of the Shining Prince: Court Life in Ancient Japan. New York: Knopf.

Mumford, Lewis
1970 The Myth of the Machine. New York: Harcourt Brace Jovanovich.

Nakane, Chie
1970 Japanese Society. Berkeley: University of California Press.

Ogburn, William F.
1922 Social Change. New York: Viking Press.

Perrow, Charles
1967 "A framework for the comparative analysis of organizations." American Sociological Review 32 (April):194–208.

Polanyi, Karl
1944 The Great Transformation. New York: Holt, Rinehart and Winston.

Redfield, Robert
1953 The Primitive World and Its Transformation. Ithaca, N. Y.: Cornell University Press.

Reich, Charles
1971 The Greening of America. New York: Random House.

Roszak, Theodore
1969 The Making of a Counter Culture. Garden City, N. Y.: Doubleday.

Sauer, Carl
1938 "Theme of plant and animal destruction in economic history." Journal of Farm Economics 20:765–775.

Senate Committee on Labor and Public Welfare
1973 Work in America: Report of a Special Task Force to the Secretary of Health, Education, and Welfare. Washington, D.C.: GPO.

Senate Judiciary Committee
1971 Federal Data Banks, Computers, and the Bill of Rights. Hearings Before Subcommittee on Constitutional Rights, 92nd Cong., 1st sess., February 23–March 17.

Touraine, Alain
1971 The Post-Industrial Society. New York: Random House.

Veblen, Thorstein
1914 The Instinct of Workmanship. New York: Viking Press.
1921 The Engineers and the Price System. New York: Viking Press.

Westin, Alan F.
1967 Privacy and Freedom. New York: Atheneum.

White, Lynn, Jr.
1969 "The historical roots of our ecologic crisis." Pp. 341–351 in Paul Shepard and Daniel McKinley (eds.), The Subversive Science. Boston: Houghton Mifflin.

Wilensky, Harold L.
1967 Organizational Intelligence. New York: Basic Books.

Young, Michael
1958 Rise of the Meritocracy. London: Thames and Hadson.

Sources and readings

Bell, Daniel
1973 The Coming of Post-Industrial Society. New York: Basic Books.

Bendix, Reinhard
1956 Work and Authority in Industry. New York: Wiley.

Blau, Peter M. and Otis Dudley Duncan
1967 The American Occupational Structure. New York: Wiley.

Blumberg, Paul
1968 Industrial Democracy. London: Constable.

Burns, Tom (ed.)
1969 Industrial Man. Baltimore: Penguin Books.

Ehrlich, Paul and Anne H. Ehrlich
1976 Population, Resources, Environment: Issues in Human Ecology. Third edition. San Francisco: Freeman.

Ellul, Jacques
1964 The Technological Society. New York: Knopf.

Ferkiss, Victor
1969 Technological Man: The Myth and the Reality. New York: Braziller.

Kranzberg, Melvin and Carroll W. Pursell, Jr. (eds.)
1967 Technology in Western Civilization. New York: Oxford University Press. 2 vols.

Miller, Delbert C. and William H. Form
1964 Industrial Sociology. New York: Harper & Row.

Miller, G. Tyler, Jr.
1975 Living in the Environment: Concepts, Problems and Alternatives. Belmont, Calif.: Wadsworth.

Moore, Wilbert E.
1965 The Impact of Industry. Englewood Cliffs, N. J.: Prentice-Hall.

Mumford, Lewis
1934 Technics and Civilization. New York: Harcourt Brace Jovanóvich.
1967 The Myth of the Machine. New York: Harcourt Brace Jovanovich.

Nef, John U.
1964 The Conquest of the Material World. Chicago: University of Chicago Press.

Silberman, Charles
1966 The Myth of Automation. New York: Harper & Row.

Periodicals

Economic Development and Cultural Change
Human Organization
Journal of Human Resources
Manpower
Technology and Culture

17 | Politics and Society

Section one the creation of nations

The transition to modern society has been marked by an ever-increasing interdependence of politics and society. Two dimensions of this master trend are especially important: the enlargement of political *control* and the expansion of *participation*. These themes and variations upon them recur throughout this chapter.

Recent history has seen a great expansion in the size, scope, and significance of political institutions. Politics has become inextricably mixed with the major social changes discussed in the preceding chapters. The repression and resurgence of ethnic groups, the crises of urbanization, the use and mastery of technology—these and other worldwide problems have made modern governments activist and omnipresent. There was a time when government could be largely restricted to setting minimum rules for social conduct, levying taxes, and waging war. But today even conservative leaders, who would like to limit the role of govern-

ment, find themselves driven to unprecedented measures of social intervention. Like it or not, big government is here to stay; it cannot escape responsibility for the health of the economy, the decay of the cities, or racial conflict. Nor can it ignore the rising aspirations of hitherto subordinate and silent millions.

NATIONALISM

Of all the social forces in the modern world, none is more important than nationalism. The nation is in many ways the decisive unit of social organization. It can summon profound loyalties; it can organize great economic and military efforts; it can give to millions of people a consciousness of kind, a sense of common fate, and a collective identity.

For many centuries kinship, social class, and local community were the centers of loyalty. In Europe, nationhood emerged only gradually as new institutions (1) defined and defended national boundaries, (2) broke down local barriers to trade and communication, (3) became politically integrated under an effective central government, and (4) created a system of education with an official language which transmitted a sense of common heritage.

Many conditions had to exist before these changes could be accomplished. Germany and Italy did not become fully organized nations until the nineteenth century, although centuries earlier the Florentine, Machiavelli (see *SOCIAL STRATIFICATION*, Section Five), wrote an eloquent plea for the unification of Italy. In France and England vigorous monarchies contributed to the formation of nations, even though the royal houses had to change their own perspectives and self-images. The ruler had to "make up his mind whether he was the first of the nobles or the first of the magistrates and administrators" (Guerard, 1959:xi). As kings and queens came to think of themselves as chief administrators, they built up a corps of tax collectors, judges, police, and other officials throughout the country, completely dependent on the central government. This helped lay the basis of the modern nation-state.

The emergence of nations is a phenomenon of *widening loyalty and consciousness*. If national identity is to be achieved, loyalty must extend beyond the immediate bonds of locality and kinship. The individual embraces a more general and abstract idea—the concept of being French, Indian, Tanzanian, or Swiss. Extending or generalizing the sense of civic identity is one of the most profound aspects of nation building.

National consciousness broadens loyalties and gives them focus and depth. New aspirations are created, especially the demand for national autonomy. The nationalist patriot wants his own government to symbolize and protect the identity of his country. In this sense, nationality also *limits* perspectives.

The combination of these broadening and limiting effects of nationalism generates a potent political energy. Nationalism creates power by making more people available for

Jawaharlal Nehru (1889–1964) was the political heir of Mohandas Gandhi (1869–1948). Gandhi led the movement for Indian independence and developed the tactic of Satyagraha, a form of collective action, often involving civil disobedience, based on militant, self-sacrificing nonviolence. In his time Gandhi was the greatest charismatic figure of the non-Western world. A religious as well as a political leader, he became known as Mahatma, "great soul."

Nehru was born into a prosperous, upper-caste family. He was educated in England and joined Gandhi's movement about 1919. He spent ten years in jail, off and on, and was released for the last time in 1945, shortly before he became Prime Minister of India.

participation in its larger community. At the same time, this potential energy is given impetus and direction by the tendency of nationalism to draw upon and enhance patriotic pride and fervor.

Today the nation-state plays an ambiguous role. On one hand it is a threat to world stability. On the other hand, its capacity to mobilize people and change old ways of life makes the nation the major agency of modernization. All over the world economic development and nationalism are closely associated.

COLONIALISM AS NATION BUILDING

For four centuries (1500–1900) European powers penetrated the preindustrial areas of Asia, Africa, and the Americas. Spain, Portugal, Holland, France, Belgium, England,

Italy, and Germany—all took part in the great commercial and political adventure called *colonialism.* (See *RACE AND ETHNICITY*, Section Two.) They sought resources, markets, settlements, pride, power, and religious conversions. As they exploited, traded, settled, aggrandized, subjugated, educated, and converted, they brought with them the culture of the Western world, which they transmitted with obscure intent and uneven success to at least the top layers of the societies with which they dealt.

Where the Europeans came to stay and were not merely casual visitors, traders, or pirates, they faced the problem of establishing order. In doing so they themselves unconsciously laid the foundations for the emergence of new nations. They did this in three ways:

1. By defining national boundaries In many areas the colonial governments simply drew lines on a map and gave a name to the new "country." Indonesia and the Philippines are good examples:

The scattered lands inhabited by the peoples of Malay stock, including therein the Philippines, the entire Indonesian archipelago, and such parts of the Malay Peninsula as were primarily Malay were not laid out by nature or originally so settled by man as to make any one political partition of them more self-evident than another. The existing frontiers are, as far as both geography and ethnology are concerned, essentially arbitrary and reflect the limits of the colonial spheres carved out in the conflict of imperialisms (Emerson, 1960:124).

The new national boundaries were set partly for administrative reasons, so that the responsibilities of the colonial governor for a given territory could be fixed. Boundaries were also needed to establish claims and work out accommodations with rival European powers.

2. By creating a more integrated social organization The colonial administrator typically established centralized control over his domain. He had to pacify the territory, collect taxes, and protect his fellow countrymen as they exploited and developed the resources of the colony. To achieve these ends, transportation and communication were improved, a national currency was established, and at least a rudimentary educational system was created. The result was easier and safer movement within the colonial boundaries, both for government agents and for the native peoples. Patterns of mutual dependency sprang up. It was easier to do business with people inside the colonial boundaries, and this tended to establish new and enduring social bonds.

3. By stimulating national consciousness The colonial government, it is said, created the conditions of its own destruction. By its very existence as a central administration for a defined region, the colonial government brought a new focus of loyalty and pride to people who would eventually demand freedom in the name of patriotism and national honor.

Perhaps most important, the colonial government itself became the target of opposition and rebellion. Anticolonial sentiment stimulated national consciousness, even among settlers from the home country. Among non-Europeans, those who struggled for independence did not seek a return to the situation as it was before the Europeans came. Rather, they sought independence for that nation which was the creature of the colonial power. For example, after the Indonesians gained their freedom following World War II, they laid claim to the entire territory of the old Netherlands East Indies, which includes Irian (West New Guinea), although the people of New Guinea are unlike the Indonesians in both race and culture.

Colonial nationalism has been strongest where the colonial government was most constructive. Where it invested in economic development, educated the people, brought them into government administration, and created or allowed such free institutions as political parties and trade unions, nationalism grew rapidly. The British were relatively benign colonial rulers. By the same token they did much to make rebellion a practical possibility.

Direct and indirect rule The policies and practices of the colonial powers in dealing with a diversity of problems followed no single pattern. However, there were two main types of colonial rule, and these had different effects on national development.

Under *direct rule* the colonial power set up its own administration and tried to regulate in detail the economic and social life of the colony. For example, the British in Burma replaced the old monarchy with a governor-general

. . . whose staff gradually increased until the Secretariat came to house all types of departments and ministries expected of a modern government. Burma proper was divided into eight divisions, each consisting of three or four districts. In a ruthlessly logical fashion two or three subdivisions were created in each district, two to four townships in each subdivision. The townships were each divided into nearly fifty village tracts that became the prime units of local government (Pye, 1962:82).

This is an extreme example of the effort to bypass existing social organization and superimpose a centrally controlled administrative hierarchy.

In exercising direct rule, the colonialists used the principles and methods they knew. They introduced Western concepts of law and administration, as the British did in creating a civil service and a Western-style judiciary in India. Direct rule limited and sometimes destroyed indigenous institutions, but it allowed the recruitment of educated native persons to serve in the government bureaus.

Under *indirect rule* colonial authority was exercised through local leaders — kings, tribal chiefs, and village elders. This was the policy of the Dutch in Indonesia and of the British in some African territories. This system tended to minimize the Western impact and support local institutions and customs.

The choice of direct or indirect rule was usually pragmatic, depending on the traditions and strength of the colonial power. If it had only a weak outpost in the colony, intermittently reinforced or supplied from a home base thousands of miles away, it was obviously prudent to come to an agreement with the local leaders who would, for a price, control their own populations. Indirect rule required fewer paid officials and was cheaper.

Economic policy influenced the choice of direct or indirect rule. Where the colonialists sought only a kind of tribute of cocoa, rubber, or some other product, this could be done through the use of local chieftains. On the other hand, if the colonized population was seen as a market for goods manufactured abroad or if local manufacturing was developed, direct rule was more effective.

What are the effects of direct and indirect rule on nation building? Paradoxically, direct rule, though apparently more oppressive, lent itself more readily to the evolution of a united nation. Direct rule tends to create a cohesive political community *before* independence. When independence is achieved, the new rulers have something to work with. At least part of the job of centralization and training has already been done.

Indirect rule often helped make social change more acceptable to a tradition-bound people. Working through existing institutions has the effect of moderating the pace of change and associating it with a familiar and accepted local authority. On the whole, however, indirect rule kept the society weak, fragmented, and unprepared to enter the modern world. Usually indirect rule did not foster the development of an educated class. The central government, dependent on the cooperation of village leaders, remained weak.

The strength of traditional authorities sustained by indirect rule creates difficulties after independence. When the colonial power leaves, the local leaders are reluctant to give up their power, and they lack a strong commitment to the new state. Hence they represent a force for separatism along regional or ethnic lines.

Caution The distinction between direct and indirect rule is not hard and fast. There are few pure cases of one or the other. The colonial powers did what they thought would work. Even under a policy of indirect rule, they were not necessarily sensitive to local needs or institutions. In some cases, they reorganized communities in the interests of efficiency. "If the traditional structure was too large . . . it was simply broken up. If the traditional units were too small, a number were amalgamated" (Young, 1965:131).

Tribalism The architects of the new nations of Asia and Africa must take account of preexisting social organization. In their quest for modernization they lead populations still largely bound by tradition. Many millions of their people are untouched by the Western world. To them the immemorial ties of personal relatedness, ritual, and traditional authority are the true sources of security and satisfaction. For thousands of villages, isolation is still a paramount fact of life.

In the Congo, the village of Lupupa has its own way of describing the world:

The earth is conceptualized as a round, flat platter; if one approaches the edge (although the distance is too great to conceive of this as a real possibility) and is not careful, he will tumble off and into a limitless sea beyond which is only the unknown. In the exact center of this platter is Lupupa and, by extension, the Congo, while somewhere around the rim are placed America, Belgium, and Portugal. These three countries, it is evident, figure in the world scene because they are the only ones known — America, because there had been American visitors there, Portugal because of the presence in Tshofa [a nearby village] of a Portuguese trader, and Belgium for obvious reasons. . . .

The most sophisticated person in the village knew that this picture of the world was untrue, and told us so. He had learned the truth in school, he said, and the world, far from being a flat platter, was in reality a flat triangle, with Lupupa in the center, and Belgium, Portugal, and America at the various angles of the figure (Merriam, 1961: 176).

Among these people, nationhood has little meaning. Moreover, for villagers the idea of a nation is very new, whereas local legends may trace the tribe back to the beginning of the world. It is reasonable to expect some reluctance to trade their old identity for a new one.

The tribe is a kin-based, tradition-centered unit of social organization composed of people who share a sense of personal relatedness rooted in a real or imagined common descent. Tribal society of the African Gold Coast "was an amalgamation of family units into larger and larger kinship groupings in which totemic genealogy provided a major social guide" (Apter, 1955:80). Tribes may occupy a particular territory, but territory is less important for tribal organization than for the modern nation-state. It has been estimated that there are as many as 6,000 tribes in Africa (Murdock, 1959:425–456).

Although many tribes are very old, tribalism is a more recent phenomenon:

In much of Africa tribal consciousness was almost unknown in traditional rural life. Tribalism was a product of modernization and the western impact on a traditional society. In southern Nigeria, for instance, Yoruba consciousness only developed in the nineteenth century and the term, Yoruba, was first used by Anglican missionaries. . . . Similarly, even in the 1950s, an Ibo leader, B. O. N. Eluwa, could travel through Iboland attempting to convince the tribesmen that they were Ibos. But the villagers, he said, "couldn't even imagine all Ibos." The efforts of Eluwa and other Ibo leaders, however, successfully created a sense of Iboness. Loyalty to tribe is in many respects a *response* to modernization, a product of the very forces of change which colonial rule brought to Africa (Huntington, 1968:38).

In the context of village life, the tribe is likely to be narrowly conceived and, in any case, has a weak hold on awareness and loyalty. The larger tribal identities were in part created by lumping together groups for administrative purposes even when no strong bond of kinship was recognized. In addition, tribalism was encouraged by local leaders as a way of mobilizing political support, especially in the cities.

Traditionally, the tribal bond was an extension of family loyalties. A person belonged to the tribe through family membership, and the authority of the tribe over the individual was channeled through the kinship group. This pattern was effective in rural areas where the family was an economic unit and organized virtually the total life of the individual. As the tribesman moves to the city, however, family authority and identity weaken. The tribe comes to have a more direct influence on the person. In a subtle way, this may serve as a transition to a sense of national citizenship, because loyalty is shifted to a larger unit, even if the immediate effect is to obstruct national unity.

NATIONHOOD AND MODERNIZATION

The emerging independent nations of Asia and Africa encounter many problems not faced by earlier new nations. Earlier ones developed at the same time as industrialization. Today's new nations must live with the fact that much of the world is rich, powerful, and highly advanced in industry and technology, and they enter a world scene charged with political and ideological conflict. For these and many other reasons, the present strains of nation building are more acute.

Neocolonialism A special constraint on the former colonies is their continued dependence on the *métropole*, the country that ruled before independence. The economic dependency is often so great that it is perceived as another form of subjugation—neocolonialism.

Like so many other political expressions, neocolonialism is a pejorative term applied indiscriminately or shunned absolutely according to ideological preferences. There is little agreement about its meaning even among those who habitually use it, and it covers almost any kind of contact between the highly industrialised and the economically backward countries, ranging from politically uncontaminated trade to outright military intervention. As far as the latter is concerned, there is not much point in calling it neocolonialism, as it constitutes the oldest and the most common instrument of subjugation. So it

seems advisable to restrict the meaning of "neocolonialism" to the exercise of power based on economic and technical superiority without assuming formal sovereignty and without a recourse to arms. As the possession of power, however, seldom fails to bring some profit, we could emphasise the economic end-result and define "neo-colonialism" as "the exercise of political influence in a legally foreign territory on the basis of economic power and with the aim of enhancing or maintaining profits" (Andreski, 1968:177).

After independence, many of the old economic patterns continue. Some may be mutually beneficial in the short run: The *métropole* gets raw materials, a market for its finished goods, and all the profits it can extract; the former colony gets a certain amount of capital investment, therefore jobs, and productive capacity, and a percentage of the profits in the form of taxes. But the new nation retains its dependent economic status. The more powerful partner sets the terms of the relationship. For instance, foreign capital may be available in a sector of the economy that promises little or no local employment, as in the extraction of petroleum. The investment may only make worse the former colony's dependence on a single commodity that is very vulnerable on the world market, such as coffee or sugar. Even foreign aid has its costs because of restrictive conditions. "The hard truth is that the underdeveloped countries have to pay for all the 'aid' they receive" (Dos Santos, 1970:233).

Caution It should not be supposed that new nations have ever found an easy road to stability or to democracy. The history of nation building in premodern Europe was to a large extent a record of disunity and struggle. Strong ethnic divisions or significant local attachments were obstacles to national unity. Weak leadership, internal warfare, unstable boundaries, and political repression were everyday facts of life. In these respects, the new nations of the contemporary world are no more backward than were the then-emerging nations of the West.

The revolution of rising expectations For

many centuries the lives of millions of people in tradition-centered societies remained unchanged. A poor existence and short life were fatalistically accepted. But one of the sources of change in the modern world is the breakdown of these traditional perspectives, the increasing demand for better health, more comfort, and all else that technology can provide. The change has been so drastic that a new term has been coined — *the revolution of rising expectations*.

These new expectations are partly due to lessening isolation. As communication increases, bringing news of high living standards to remote places, people become aware of alternatives to poverty. The newly awakening peoples feel that they too are entitled to the benefits of advanced technology.

Aspirations are also raised by the dynamics of nationalism. The governments of the new nations attempt to bind together their formerly heterogeneous peoples by building up internal trade, improving transportation and communication, expanding educational facilities, establishing government-sponsored health clinics, damming rivers for electric power, and creating military establishments. Indirectly, these activities introduce new values and perspectives.

The struggle for independence from the colonial power brought with it hopes for a better life. In the course of the struggle, nationalist propaganda offered visions of a rosy future once the foreigners were ejected. The very fact of a changed status helped produce the sense of an expanding world.

The revolution of rising expectations should be viewed in the light of an important generalization: *Poverty or hardship as such does not produce rebellion or other collective action; rather, action is stimulated by a new awareness of alternative possibilities.* As Leon Trotsky, a leader of the Russian Revolution of 1917, said, "In reality the mere existence of privations is not enough to cause an insurrection; if it were, the masses would always be in revolt."

Democracy and the modernizing elite In the new nations there is continuing tension between democracy and authoritarianism. The dominant trend is toward increased popular participation in political life — voting, membership in mass parties, attendance at political rallies and demonstrations. Political awareness is part of the larger process by which national consciousness and loyalty are created. Voting for nation-centered parties and for national officers helps build a national civic identity. In addition the new leaders seek popular support against the more traditionalist or separatist chiefs or other political opponents.

The emphasis on public participation in political life does not necessarily mean that a great deal of political freedom is allowed. Indeed, there may be less freedom of political action and participation than was permitted by the previous, more traditionalist elite:

Because the populist regime depends on the systematic cultivation of formerly isolated and ignored groups, it must rely on exhortation and propaganda to a greater extent than does the pre-populist regime. . . . In such a society, where mass opinion is stirred, the expression of any opinion becomes all the more significant because it is no longer confined to the homogeneous and articulate thin layer at the top. The populist regime suppresses freedom at the top because freedom may now penetrate the lower levels and have serious consequences (Berger, 1962:423).

A characteristic political form in many of the new nations is the one-party regime. A broad mass organization absorbs and supplants contending factions. In some cases, the single mass party is mainly an instrument of control. However, such parties are attractive to modernizing leaders who want a political form that will (1) contribute to emerging national consciousness and head off movements that might grow up around ethnic or regional interests, (2) establish a commitment to some basic policies — for example, a broadly socialist perspective, (3) increase the chances for disciplined action to advance modernization, and (4) provide a transition to more complete democracy. Mexico and

Tanzania are examples of one-party democracies. (On Tanzania, see Cliffe, 1967.)

The modernizing elite is mainly committed to economic development and increased national strength. It is less concerned with political forms and may use the term *democracy* as a slogan and a call to action rather than as a description of a specific way of making decisions. Such labels as *tutelary democracy* or *guided democracy* describe regimes that encourage some forms of mass participation but maintain effective control at the top.

Section two social revolution

THE MEANING OF SOCIAL REVOLUTION

Broadly understood, a social revolution is any profound transformation of society or of some aspect of society. Thus an industrial revolution points to extensive changes in values and in social organization. A managerial revolution alters the social composition of the industrial and governmental elites in modern society (Burnham, 1941). In this context, the word *revolution* does not suggest the method of change. It is assumed that many forces, acting in a variety of ways, have a profound and cumulative effect upon the social order.

A more restricted concept of social revolution focuses upon a definite set of events. In this meaning social revolution is a form of collective action with the following features:

1. The action aims to overthrow a government and to oust the social groups that support it from positions of power.

2. Popular support is mobilized through such direct action as mass demonstrations, rioting, refusal of soldiers to obey their commanders, and seizure of factories or of large agricultural holdings. These acts challenge existing authority and set passive elements of the population into motion.

3. Demands are general rather than limited, extending to basic changes in the political and social order.

There is a high probability that violence will be used in a revolution of this sort, either in the course of mass action or by soldiers recruited to the revolutionary cause. However, force is not essential to a social revolution. Little or no violence may occur if the government is weak and chooses to capitulate in the face of a well-organized and widely supported revolutionary group. Revolutionaries may use force *after* they come into power, in suppressing opposition to the new regime, even though they used little force in actually taking over the government.

The social revolution as a form of collective action is distinguished from the coup d'état, in which a group outside the government takes over power, though with limited goals and without stirring a general social upheaval. Thus in 1962 the military leaders in Peru formed a junta and ousted the existing government in order to nullify the results of the presidential election. This coup had none of the features of a social revolution. On the other hand, a coup d'état can be *part* of a social revolution. A case in point is the Bolshevik coup in November 1917, which ousted the Provisional Government formed when the czar was overthrown the preceding

A scene from the October Revolution, Moscow, 1917: Russian soldiers demonstrating under the banner of communism

March.[1] In this case the coup was a phase of the broader drama called the Russian Revolution.

Although they may involve mass action, social revolutions do not necessarily favor the extension of political democracy. The German Nazi regime of 1933–1945 was created by a social revolution, but it was contemptuous of democracy and extinguished democratic institutions. Nor were the Bolsheviks (later called communists) favorable to democracy. In each case, a self-appointed vanguard asserted the right to speak for the people and rule in their name, without, however, submitting itself to the test of free elections. The Nazi and communist revolutions are examples of a great historical paradox: the use of mass action and the summoning of popular support for dictatorial movements and governments.

THE REVOLUTIONARY SITUATION

The conditions that make a society ripe for revolution are complex and varied, and no simple formula can be stated. Nevertheless, several conclusions can be drawn from the evidence of history.

1. Aspiration is as important as deprivation in stimulating revolution. The significance of rising expectations has already been indicated. (See Section Two.) Commenting on the French Revolution, Tocqueville said:

Thus it was precisely in those parts of France where there had been most improvement that popular discontent ran highest. This may seem illogical—but history is full of such paradoxes. For it is not always when things are going from bad to worse that revolutions break out. On the contrary, it oftener happens that when a people which has put up with an oppressive rule over a long period without protest suddenly finds the government relaxing its pressure, it takes up arms against it. Thus the social order overthrown by a revolution is almost always better than the one immediately preceding it, and experience teaches that, generally speaking, the most perilous moment for a bad government is one when it seeks to mend its ways. . . . Patiently endured so long as it seemed beyond redress, a grievance comes to appear intolerable once the possibility of removing it crosses men's minds. For the mere fact that certain abuses have been remedied draws attention to the others and they now appear more galling (Tocqueville, 1856/1955:176–177).

The lowest, most oppressed strata of the population do not take the lead. Social revolutions are likely to be organized and led by groups that are fairly well-off economically. For example, the Jacobin clubs of the French Revolution, which were important centers of agitation and organization, were of distinctly middle-class composition. (See Table 17:1.) The members "represent the abler, more ambitious, and successful of the inhabitants of a given town. It is as if our present-day Rotarians were revolutionists" (Brinton, 1957:102).

The respectable and relatively well-situated revolutionists revolt because they feel that the existing order does not give them the social status and the freedom of action to which they are entitled. For many, this represents a quest for full recognition and complete economic opportunity rather than a desperate effort to escape intolerable conditions.

Deprivation, however, does play a part because the revolutionary situation is often marked by severe hardships brought on by food shortages, a sharp decline in the value of money, new and burdensome taxes, or a demand for unpopular military service. Desperation at the lower levels of society may produce sporadic outbreaks that highlight the weakness and incompetence of the government, encouraging the better-off elements to take action. At the same time, those most deprived become available for mass action in support of the revolutionary leaders. For all groups, it is *relative* deprivation that sharp-

---

[1] These are New Style dates, according to the Gregorian calendar. Before the revolution, Russia used the Old Style (Julian) calendar. Under that system, the czar was overthrown in February 1917, and the Bolsheviks seized power in October. The terms *February Revolution* and *October Revolution* are sometimes used in referring to the Russian events of 1917. These dates are equivalent to March and November under the New Style, which conforms to Western usage.

ens resentment and stirs revolt (Davies, 1962:5–19).

2. Social revolutions occur when the ruling elite is weak and divided. In the revolutionary situation a state of disorganization spreads throughout the whole society. The revolution is a crisis of confidence, and the wealthy and the powerful lose self-confidence or cease to care. Members of the ruling elite are affected by new ideas and by criticism of the existing order. Just before the French and Russian revolutions, many of the nobility were highly critical of the regimes and doubtful that the old way of life could continue for long. Beset by internal criticism and self-doubt, the government hesitates to take strong countermeasures. Yet it is incapable of instituting the reforms that might stave off the revolution. Or such action may come too late.

Consequently, there is a breakdown of solidarity within the governing class. Some of its members openly espouse revolution and even undertake to lead it. These upper-class rebels may be conservative in their backgrounds and social views, but they feel that the crisis can be met only by overthrowing the government.

3. The crisis puts at issue the type of government represented by the existing regime. Limited rebellions may demand only that particular men in power be turned out. Thus kings sometimes have been forced to abdicate, to be replaced by another member of the royal family thought to be more competent, less corrupt, or simply more willing to follow the policies proposed by the rebels. In a social revolution, however, the attack goes beyond particular officeholders. A change in the form of government is demanded. The interests of those who derive their privileges from the existing form of government and its institutions are threatened.

Thus the revolution reveals weakness and incompetence at the top, widespread loss of confidence in the existing political order, and the availability of alternative groups in the society whose aspirations and self-confidence are high. Clearly, revolutionary

Table 17:1
Social composition of the Jacobin clubs during the French revolution, in percentages

	Moderate period 1789–1792	Violent period 1793–1795
Middle class	66	57
Working class	26	32
Peasant	8	11
Total	100	100
Members	4,037 in 12 clubs	8,062 in 42 clubs

Source: Brinton, 1957:101.

change is not a simple thrust from below. It is preceded by a corrosion that affects the entire social system.

THE NATURAL HISTORY OF REVOLUTIONS

The overthrow of the old regime is not an end but a beginning. What is most significant in social revolutions occurs *after* the initial event. How far social change will be pushed and upon what principles the society will be organized depend on the character of the revolutionary leadership.

In the classic cases of France and Russia, power was at first transferred from the monarchy to a group of moderates who represented the official parliamentary bodies and who sought a limited change in the nature of the government and society. But these men had inherited an ineffective government organization and a host of political and social problems. Moreover, they were unprepared to assume the leadership of an aroused and excited public, because their moderate views inclined them toward compromise and gradual change rather than toward direct action and drastic measures. At the same time, they were committed to a new atmosphere of political freedom, and this made them hesitate to curb those who held more radical views. The radicals believed that the changes accompanying the overthrow of the old government were not enough. They insisted that the political revolution should become a social revolution.

Dual power The weakness of the moderates is acutely revealed in the existence of dual power. In the early stages of the Russian Revolution, rival governments appeared. One was the official government, controlled by the moderates; the other was an unofficial government.

Lenin, the leader of the Russian Bolsheviks, described the situation in this way:

What has made our revolution so strikingly unique, is that it has established dual power.... By the side of the Provisional Government, the government of the *bourgeoisie*, there has developed *another*, as yet weak, embryonic, but undoubtedly real and growing government—the Soviets of Workers' and Soldiers' Deputies.... This power is of the type of the Paris Commune of 1871. The fundamental characteristics of this kind of power are: (1) Its origin is not in a law previously considered and passed by Parliament, but in the direct initiative of the masses from below, everywhere. . . . (2) Instead of the police and the army, institutions separated from the people and opposed to the people, there is the direct arming of the whole people; orderly government is thus insured by the armed workers and peasants themselves, by the armed people itself; (3) officials, bureaucrats are also either displaced by the direct rule of the people, or at any rate, placed under special control (Lenin, 1929:115).

Lenin wrote this statement in April, 1917, about a month after the overthrow of the czar and six months before he himself was to assume power.

Russia of 1917 is the clearest case of dual power. On one side was the Provisional Government; on the other were the Soviets (councils) within which the Bolsheviks and other radical groups were active. The same phenomenon, though not always so plainly evident, has occurred in other revolutions. In the English revolution of the 1640s, the radicals controlled the New Model Army, which represented a dual power rivaling the moderate-controlled Parliament. In the

French Revolution of 1789–1795, a network of radical Jacobin societies provided the organizational basis of dual power.

The essential sociological feature of dual power is the withdrawal of loyalty by groups capable of establishing an alternative government. Such groups take varied forms. Sometimes they have a geographical basis, as in the American South just prior to the Civil War; at other times, a sector of the official government—often the army—may become a "government within a government"; or new organizational forms may appear, based upon preexisting political parties, churches, trade unions, or other associations. In the 1930s a dual-power situation was created by the German Nazis, who built a network of organizations, including their own military units, that challenged the existing civil authority.

A pattern of dual power also existed in Palestine during the period of rising Zionist influence prior to the establishment of the state of Israel in 1948. Although the British governed Palestine under a League of Nations mandate, a number of Jewish organizations, notably the labor federation (Histadrut) and a military organization (Haganah), constituted a separate system of community institutions. A similar situation has prevailed in Northern Ireland since the late 1960s when the Irish Republican Army, paramilitary Protestant forces, and the government all began to struggle for control.

The phenomenon of dual power suggests two conclusions regarding the dynamics of social revolution:

The dramatic days of insurrection, when the old government is deposed, may only confirm and complete, with a minimum of violence, a transfer of power that has already occurred. If the unofficial rival government has established its own machinery and won over the loyalty of units of the army or police, the revolution will already have taken place. In such cases, the final showdown will bring no surprises.

Social revolutionists do not so much seize power as destroy and re-create it (Pettee,

1938:4–5). The old institutions, already weakened, are helped to die. New ones, typically more vigorous and ruthless, are established. These new groups do not simply replace the old. They are more dynamic and bring additional resources into political life. Therefore, the total quantity of effective political power is increased in the course of the revolution.

Victory of the extremists

The great social revolutions witnessed a deepening conflict between the moderates and the radicals. In part, these conflicts took place *within* the rival or shadow governments. The extremists pressed their views inside the Soviets, the Jacobin societies, military staffs, or other bases of dual power. When they became dominant there, they were ready for a final test of strength with the legal government of moderates that had replaced the old regime.

Although characteristically the extremists are only a small part of the total population, they come to power in two basic ways. First, by intimidating opponents, both physically and psychologically, they neutralize large parts of the population. As the crisis deepens, more and more people withdraw from political participation. Political life tends to be polarized, with high activity at the extremes but passivity among large numbers. Fear and confusion put many on the sidelines. The political arena is abandoned to those who are most ruthless and determined.

Second, because of their discipline and political passion, the extremist minorities are able to take advantage of popular manifestations of resentment or desperation. They place themselves at the head of the "masses," that is, of the most active and excited elements. This greatly increases their power, at least temporarily.

Once in power, the radicals establish a revolutionary dictatorship. Firmness and terror are the order of the day. Step by step, all opposition is suppressed. New and drastic measures are introduced, and the social revolution is imposed from above. The government itself is now the main source of social change and the chief mobilizer of the people. Especially in the revolutionary dictatorships of communism and fascism, there is an emphasis on demonstrations of mass support, with huge parades and meetings addressed by the revolutionary leaders. Instead of holding elections, the leaders offer these direct activities as evidence of popular approval.

Thermidor

The leaders of the French Revolution underlined their break with the past by instituting a new calendar. For the warmest season of the year they chose the name Thermidor ("gift of heat"). On 9th Thermidor of the year II (July 27, 1794), the revolutionary leader Robespierre was deposed. He was executed the next day. There followed a period of reaction against the militancy of the revolution, and the way was paved for Napoleon Bonaparte. This transition, to some extent duplicated in other social revolutions, has since been called the Thermidorean Reaction.

As a phase in the natural history of revolution, the Thermidorean Reaction has the following significance:

1. The centralized power created by the revolution is taken over and stabilized by a "strong man"—Cromwell in England, Bonaparte in France, Stalin in Russia.

2. Revolutionary fervor is reduced, and accommodations are made with more moderate groups and older traditions. The revolutionary extremists are suppressed; peace is made with older institutions, such as the church; historic nationalist aspirations are reasserted.

3. The reaction is not complete. There is no return to the prerevolutionary situation. Although many of the ideals of the revolutionaries are shucked off, the chief social changes brought about by the revolution are maintained and consolidated. Thus under Stalin, socialism became identified with state ownership of industry and state initiative in economic development, but the revolutionary ideals of workers' control and the classless society were abandoned.

The outcome A great social revolution is not the work of a handful of conspirators or fanatics. Disciplined minorities play a decisive role, but the upheavals occur because there are real problems that the old order seems incapable of solving. Some of these problems are immediate and relatively temporary, such as might be brought on by defeat in war or an economic crisis. They are not likely to lead to a social revolution unless important sectors of the society are ready to accept fundamental changes in the positions of great institutions or social classes.

The Russian Revolution was begun by idealists who included in their number both moderates and extremists. "They dreamed of power with the object of abolishing power; of ruling over people to wean them from the habit of being ruled" (Koestler, 1946:59). But the regime they created soon humiliated and destroyed the generation of militant idealists. Within a few years, a dictatorship had suppressed all opposition and set itself to build up its own and the coun-

try's power. Indeed, the chief accomplishment of the revolution was the modernization of Russia (Strachey, 1960:7–8).

Caution The above discussion identifies patterns that are discernible in at least some revolutions. However, it is not possible to generalize for all revolutions. There is no single pattern of revolutionary history, no inevitable set of stages.

Nationalism and social revolution In a number of cases, including the Nazi regime in Germany, national feeling provided much of the political energy for staging the revolution and supporting its victorious leadership (Kautsky, 1962). The French Revolution, too, had its nationalist aspects, especially in the defense of the revolution against foreign armies representing governments hostile to the overthrow of the aristocracy. Adaptation 40 is a case study showing how national aspirations can be combined with revolutionary action.

Adaptation 40 Johnson: Peasant nationalism and communist power

Following the outbreak of the Sino-Japanese war in 1937, the Chinese communist party (CCP) enlarged the territory under its control by establishing guerrilla bases in rural areas behind the Japanese lines. By the time of Japan's surrender in 1945, one-fifth of the population of China lived in the guerrilla bases and followed the CCP, but the communist government of China was not formally proclaimed until October 1949.

The communists' success during the war was in marked contrast to the decade preceding the war, when they first tried to organize the peasantry. Al-

though the CCP was in effective control of various small enclaves in the Chinese countryside from 1927 on, its efforts during that period to set up rural "soviets" were far less successful than during the blackest period of the Sino-Japanese war.

Many interpretations of the communist rise to power in China have been advanced since the revolution of 1949. Some analysts emphasize the economic distress of the Chinese peasantry and the attraction of communist proposals, such as land reform. Others contend that the appeals of communism are irrelevant because communist parties are self-serving conspiracies indifferent to the attitudes of the populations under their control. Still others argue that the Chinese communist success was due to military superiority alone, and they discount the social and political environment

Source: Abridged and adapted from *Peasant Nationalism and Communist Power* by Chalmers A. Johnson, with the permission of the publishers, Stanford University Press. © 1962 by the Board of Trustees of the Leland Stanford Junior University.

of wartime China as of secondary importance in producing a communist victory.

The view advanced here is that the communist rise to power should be understood as a species of nationalist movement originating in resistance to the Japanese occupation of China during World War II. The Chinese masses—the peasants—were unified and brought to political consciousness in the course of the drastic restructuring of Chinese life that accompanied the Japanese conquest of north and east China. This wartime awakening became the basis for a new order in China following Japan's collapse: After the war the resistance leaders were confirmed by their followers in positions of legitimate national authority.

The following account is based in part on a study of documents in the archives of the Japanese army and other Japanese agencies, made available after World War II.

PREWAR CHINA

Before World War II, Nationalist China, controlled by the Kuomintang party (KMT) and its leader, Chiang Kai-shek, was violently anti-Japanese. This early nationalism was an expression of Westernized, or cosmopolitan, educated Chinese. But for all the political activity and ferment among the prewar elites, their movement was a head without a body. Nationalism was a powerful sentiment among leadership groups, but the social milieu in which they acted was not nationalistic. The Chi-

567

Adaptation 40
Johnson:
Peasant
nationalism and
communist
power

Chairman Mao Tse-tung, leader of the Chinese Communist Party, on campaign against Chiang Kai-shek, north Shensi, 1947

nese peasantry had no stake in the Chinese literary culture. (China's total population in 1949, estimated at 557 million, was about 90 percent villagers.) The earlier humiliations of China at the hands of the European powers were largely meaningless to the agricultural masses. The prewar peasant was absorbed in local matters, had only the dimmest sense of "China," and was politically quiescent.

Until 1927, the CCP had shared with the KMT the leadership of the early anti-imperialist, anti-Japanese movement among the intellectual and urban classes. However, with the establishment of Chiang Kai-shek's regime in 1927, the KMT purged the CCP, and the communists withdrew to Kiangsi province in south China. From 1929 to 1934 the communists consolidated and enlarged their position in Kiangsi, but in 1934 KMT armies drove out the communists, forcing the Long March to Yenan in north central China, where the communists gained effective control of a number of guerrilla bases.

EFFECTS OF THE JAPANESE INVASION

The most important consequence of Japan's invasion in 1937 and subsequent occupation of China was its impact upon the peasant masses. The invasion heightened the peasants' interest in and awareness of national defense, citizenship, treason, legitimacy of government, and the long-range betterment of the Chinese state. In short, the war mobilized the peasantry, creating the conditions under which mass nationalism could emerge.

Because of the isolation of the peasantry from Chinese nationalist elites, Japanese intelligence had expected little or no resistance on the part of the peasants. However, the devastation and exploitation that accompanied the Japanese invasion produced a radical change in the political attitudes of the northern Chinese; north China became the center of guerrilla resistance during the war.

A number of factors contributed to the awakening and mobilization of the peasantry:

A visible, ruthless enemy The hostile activity of easily identifiable foreign soldiers against Chinese soldiers and civilians had a decisive political effect. Although the peasantry, on the eve of the war, was no more opposed to the Japanese than to other authorities, it became anti-Japanese because of the conduct of Japanese troops. Anti-Japanese feelings, stimulated by the invasion itself, were exacerbated by the "mop-ups" which were aimed directly at the peasantry.

Because the Japanese could not distinguish a guerrilla from a villager, they took ruthless action against the entire rural population. In Hopei, the Japanese implemented a "three-all" policy — "kill all, burn all, destroy all." The essence of the policy was to surround a given area, kill everyone in it, and make the area uninhabitable. For example, in May 1942, Japanese forces surrounded the village of Peihuan in central Hopei, pumped poison gas into the tunnels that were used as shelters by the peasants, and killed 800 Chinese. The effect of such actions was to arouse even the most parochial of village dwellers. The peasants became receptive to a new political appeal — the defense of the fatherland.

Flight of local officials As the armies of the Chinese central government retreated, most local officials went with them, and a political vacuum was created. The villagers responded by establishing self-defense forces and, in some cases, guerrilla units. Hundreds of local anti-Japanese governments were set up behind Japanese lines. The feeling of belonging and of having a stake in government was entirely novel to the Chinese masses; it brought an exhilarating sense of self-determination.

The Japanese puppet government In 1940, the Japanese established a puppet government, whose purpose was to create popular support for the invaders. Because of inept administration, continuing Japanese exploitation, and heavy-handed military activities, the facade of Chinese sovereignty surrounding the Japanese-sponsored government never won the support of the Chinese peasantry.

These developments broke the hold of parochialism on the Chinese peasant. The war destroyed the rural social order and sensitized the Chinese peasant to new associations, identities, and purposes. The new environment was the most favorable the communists had encountered since the party's founding in 1921.

ROLE OF THE COMMUNIST PARTY

The source of the communist party's authority in China today dates from the wartime period when it led the mobilized masses of previously noncommunist areas in their struggles with the Japanese army. Propaganda, organization, and military action were the means by which the communists took advantage of the opportunity created by the Japanese invasion, the crumbling of existing authority, and the response of the peasantry.

Propaganda The propaganda effort launched by the CCP was remarkably free of communist ideology. The communists did not repeat their political failure of the prewar period; they eschewed old slogans of class warfare and radical redistribution of property and concentrated solely on national salvation. An example of the wartime propaganda is a CCP leaflet found by the Japanese army:

Exterminate the Traitor, Peace Preservation Committees! Japan has invaded our Shansi, killed large numbers of our people, burned thousands of our houses, raped our women in countless numbers, robbed us of our food and wealth, trampled on the graves of our ancestors, forced our wives and children to flee, destroyed our famous places, . . . and made the joy of peace impossible. . . . Everybody! Rise up and join a guerrilla self-defense unit! Exterminate the Peace Maintenance Committee which sells out the nation! Defend our anti-Japanese patriotic people's government! Assist the all-out resistance of Commander Yen! Act in unison with Army and people to overthrow Japanese imperialism!

Organization A second source of communist strength was the organizational expertise of the communist army. Communist-controlled troops included regulars, guerrillas, and militia. The regulars were uniformed, mobile divisions, field forces with the best equipment and officers. They were transferred from one area to another in response to military developments. The guerrillas were full-time military units but remained in the area where they were mobilized and were not usually in uniform. Often guerrilla units were set up prior to the arrival of regular communist forces and were subsequently incorporated into the communist army. The militia was made up of farmers, both men and women, who engaged in local military activities as needed. They also collected intelligence, controlled movements between villages (by means of

an elaborate passport system), and mined roads.

As guerrillas and militia, the peasants encountered the enemy and identified with the resistance. The regular forces, however, provided the organizing leadership. Training and propaganda activities were the special duties of political departments attached to all regular communist military units.

Political specialists or cadres used regional dialects to communicate with the majority of the people. A communist army guide entitled "Problems of Working with Youth in Peasant Villages" emphasized the necessity of obtaining information on the political, economic, and cultural life of the village, as well as on pro-Japanese sentiment. The manual also instructed political workers to dress and talk like peasants and to respect local superstitions.

The manual also said, "the broad peasant class is the chief object of mass movement work, but the peasantry has two distinctive characteristics: (a) a conservative or nativistic viewpoint, and (b) limited organization with no clear perception of the future." To meet this difficulty, the manual advised that initial efforts be directed at handicraft workers, middle-school students, small-businessmen, and "self-respecting" bureaucrats and landlords who sense the existence of a "national crisis." The support of such people would facilitate work with the peasants.

Mass-movement associations The end product of a successful campaign was the creation of mass organizations. The most common were National Salvation Associations, separately organized for peasants, women, young people, workers, teachers, merchants, and cultural workers. These large, hierarchically structured organizations had little internal democracy; their chief function was to educate their members politically and train them in reading and other skills. From these associations, auxiliary resistance units such as self-defense corps, stretcher units, and transportation corps were recruited.

Although they were not intended to exercise political power, the mass associations contributed to the guerrilla government by electing representatives. The aim was to afford the population a sense of direct participation in the resistance movement and thereby to ensure continued popular support

569

Adaptation 40
Johnson:
Peasant
nationalism and
communist
power

for the communist army. The mass associations' true contribution to Chinese political life was not democracy but, as the communists themselves stated, mass mobilization.

Guerrilla warfare A third factor accounting for the success of the CCP was the effective military action of the communist army against the Japanese. When the communist armies engaged the enemy, they inflicted serious damage. The usual Japanese report, however, was "No enemy force encountered"—a consequence of the communist armies' strict adherence to the principle of guerrilla warfare: Fight only at times of your own choosing. The success of such tactics depended on support from the rural population, for guerrilla warfare is not so much a military technique as a political condition. In guerrilla warfare, the conflict is between a professional army, possessing the advantages of superior training and equipment, and an irregular force, less well trained, less well equipped, but actively supported by the population. The people free the guerrillas from dependence on supply lines, provide them with nearly perfect intelligence concerning enemy movements, and hide fugitives.

CONCLUSION

Between 1937 and 1945 north China witnessed a confrontation between two expanding political domains: the Chinese communists and the Japanese. Having squeezed out the Kuomintang as a third participant early in the war, they fought between themselves—winner take all. When the Japanese were defeated, the Chinese commu-nists took all of north China (except for some major cities that the KMT managed to reoccupy for a few years). North China thus became the chief stronghold from which the communists waged their successful civil war against the KMT during 1947–1949.

In China, communist power rests basically upon indigenous national aspirations. The reality underlying that power is a quickened national awareness and an unprecedented mobilization of the people. The transformation took place under the banner of communism, but its roots lie deeper than attachment to communist political ideas and leadership. The nationalist foundation of communist rule must inevitably lend a distinctive character to the evolution of communism in China.

Caution *The preceding discussion does not settle the question whether, in the long run, the Chinese communists would have gained victory even without the Japanese invasion. According to one observer,*

in view of the underlying social discontent and endemic civil war there is every reason to suppose that even if the Red Army had been defeated, Communists would have continued to exist and to have retained potential for sudden expansion in favorable circumstances that were bound to occur. The Japanese invasion certainly helped and speeded the process, but it seems to have been contingent rather than necessary to the rise of Communist power (Bernal, 1970:47).

These issues are the subject of debate among students of Chinese communism (see, for example, Ch'ên, 1965).

Section three totalitarian society

In the nineteenth century, social change was perceived as social progress; the future of society seemed clear and hopeful. Industrialism and democracy would advance together. Traditional society based on fixed status, privilege, and ignorance would be swept aside. A new and permanent era of rationality and enlightenment would gradually extend its sway. This optimistic view of a progressive society assumed that the darkest pages of human history, measured by brutality, tyranny, and political hatred, belonged to the past.

In the twentieth century, there is a more pessimistic note. Industrial society and the technology on which it is based have conferred many benefits. But they have also produced some unexpected and drastic responses. One of the most important of these responses is the emergence of twentieth-century totalitarianism. Mussolini's Italy, Hitler's Germany, Stalin's Russia, and Mao's China are the main examples. Thus totalitarian regimes have been sponsored by ideologies of both left and right.

Totalitarianism represents a fusion of state and society, an entire social system in which politics profoundly affects the whole range of human activities and associations. The totalitarian social system differs markedly from older authoritarian dictatorships. In the latter, power is concentrated in the hands of a ruling few, but many spheres of life, such as religion and the family, are more or less free from state control. Autocratic rulers of the past were often cruel, despotic, and ready to sacrifice others to their own power and glory, but they lived in societies poorly adapted to the exercise of centralized power. It is one thing to have the trappings and the doctrine of autocracy; it is another to have the means to put it into practice. Modern technology and social organization provide the most advanced tools of political dictatorship. It draws upon sophisticated methods of mass indoctrination and the manipulation of individuals and groups.

TOTAL POWER

In totalitarianism the government accepts no limitation on the amount or kind of coercion it may use to achieve its ends. It can execute people, exile them, place them in prison or in labor camps—all without effective restraint. Totalitarian power is also unlimited in scope. It is all-embracing. The government asserts the right to control and regiment every phase of life.

Total power is not easily achieved or maintained. Every totalitarian regime supplements conventional powers of government by new devices and strategies for subjecting people to detailed surveillance and control. The most important controls are the following:

1. The official political party Although there are no significant contests in the totalitarian state, much effort is devoted to maintaining a party organization. The regimes are sometimes called *party states* because of the important role played by the

single political party in strengthening the top leaders. The totalitarian party consists of a relatively small percentage of the population but includes the most dedicated supporters of the system.

The party is a training ground for future leaders and administrators; it is an army of volunteers who stimulate and reinforce support for the government; its members greatly enhance the capacity of the government to observe the population and report subversive activities. Within the party, there are sometimes conflicts and debate among top leaders, but the membership itself does not participate in the determination of policy or the selection of leaders. The party is a dependable instrument of total power controlled from the top.

2. Official ideology The totalitarian government is a propagandist and agitator that demands total conformity to an orthodox set of political beliefs. The government gains prestige as the spokesman for a new set of moral beliefs. The ideology provides material for the political indoctrination of the people, who thus learn whom to hate, what to cheer, and why they must sacrifice; loyalty is tested and "dangerous thoughts" detected and combated. Under totalitarianism the official ideology stands unchallenged. No competing doctrines may be openly promulgated. Furthermore, the official ideology is not restricted to politics, religion, or economics; it is a total ideology, guiding all phases of conduct and belief. The common thread is subordination of the individual to the will of the state.

3. Monopoly of public communication The government takes over the entire system of public communication: newspapers, radio, television, cinema, and publication of books, magazines, and even academic journals. This monopoly has several uses for totalitarian rule. Most important, the prohibition of independent media of communication stifles the organization of opposition groups, since they cannot maintain themselves without some means of communication. In addition, the government can filter out any news that might create unfavorable attitudes or undertake campaigns of "public education" to create a favorable climate of opinion.

4. Control of organized group life When the totalitarian regime comes to power, it either breaks up or takes over most independent social groups, including trade unions, business associations, youth groups, churches, schools, and political parties. It even places loyalty to the state above loyalty to family and friends. It attempts to curtail the autonomy of primary groups, especially in the early stages of totalitarian rule when the values transmitted by the family may not conform with those of the state.

But totalitarianism is not the absence of social organization. On the contrary, associations of all kinds are created and supported by the totalitarian state. Government-controlled youth leagues, hiking clubs, trade unions, and other "people's" organizations have multiplied under both fascism and communism, but such social groups are not independent. They are instituted and controlled from above to mobilize people for courses of action desired by the ruling elite and to prevent the development of independent groups and opinion.

5. A managed economy The totalitarian state assumes control over the main sectors of the economy, especially the big corporations and banks. Total power is not possible when the government must defer to the independent decisions of businessmen or when the free play of the competitive market is allowed to decide who produces what and how much and at what price. Under communism all major enterprises are owned and run by the government. Hitler permitted private ownership to remain, but the government controlled business management.

6. Arbitrary police power Because totalitarian regimes depend on the extensive use of arbitrary police power, they are often referred to as *police states*. The police become weapons in the struggle for total power, and special police agencies, partly secret, act as arms of the government in maintaining political surveillance of the population and in ferreting out potential opponents. Moreover, the police are not restrained by legal requirements of speedy trial or fair treatment.

In its quest for total power, the totalitarian state combines the threat of violence with organization and mass persuasion. The ultimate achievement of total power would rest on complete and willing acceptance of the system and its existing leaders by the population. However, no totalitarian government is willing to test its hold on public opinion by removing the threat of imprisonment or worse or by permitting the open debate of public issues.

Since the death of Stalin in 1953, there has been considerable relaxation of totalitarian control in the Soviet Union:

Purges of the elite within the Communist Party and political terror directed against the population at large were for a long time defined by many observers as distinctive and irremovable features of Soviet totalitarianism. Political controls of essentially nonpolitical activities and restrictions on freedom of movement and expression continue to characterize Soviet society. But the formerly ubiquitous forced labor camps have apparently largely been closed down, the purging of the ranks of the Party greatly reduced, and even the treatment of defeated "enemies" at the highest levels of the Party transformed from inevitable shooting to probable demotion and "internal exile" (Inkeles and Geiger, 1961:249).

In communist countries trade unions are controlled by the state, and the right to strike is not recognized. In the Soviet Union under Stalin (1922–1953), trade unions were agencies for promoting labor discipline and production and for administering welfare services. In 1958, as part of the post-Stalin trend toward easing totalitarian control, union powers were expanded, and unions were made more effective in protecting workers' rights. While wages are not subject to collective bargaining, the local unions have become more active as critics of management and as participants in redressing worker grievances. The central organization of Soviet trade unions is described as follows:

573

Section four
social
foundations of
freedom and
democracy

At the top the union central committees and the Central Council of Trade Unions, led by trusted communists; function as agents of the Communist Party and the state, more like sections in a governmental department of labor than as independent trade union centers. The national union bodies are not independent organizations expressing the will of their members. Their rights were given them by the party, not derived from the power of the working class. At any time, their work is oriented to the current instructions from the party. But they also have the duty and right to speak in the name of workers before governmental bodies. . . . Top union leaders, as communists, have strong reasons for seeking gains in living and working conditions that affect morale and confidence in the system. The CCTU functions as a watchdog over the unions, to see that they work along approved lines; but also to a degree it acts as a watchdog for the workers, seeking better protection of their interests (Brown, 1966: 319–320).

The relaxation of totalitarian control in the Soviet Union has been accompanied by an increased concern for consumer needs, some restraints on police power, and possibly a greater degree of professional and academic freedom. However, the government retains the decisive instruments of total power. The government's continued stability and self-confidence may reduce the harshness with which these powers are used; if this goes on for a long time the totalitarian character of the system may change.

TOTALITARIANISM AND INDUSTRIAL SOCIETY

Although as a political system the totalitarian state is alien to constitutional democracy, there are some similarities that should not be overlooked.

1. The modern totalitarian state is a vehicle of rapid industrialization. Its power rests on advanced technology. Its values include a prizing of scientific and engineering progress. Indeed, in accordance with Marxist doctrine, the communists accept material progress as the main criterion of social worth. Insofar as advanced industrial organization defines the character of a society, communism has points in common with other industrialized systems.

2. Totalitarian society, like the rest of the modern world, is a participant society. The totalitarian rulers ask more of their people than simple obedience. Through a large variety of government-controlled organizations and programs, the people are called upon to participate actively in public life— to volunteer for special duties, to show enthusiasm for their leaders, to read the government newspapers, to join in public criticism of lesser officials, to vote for the official slate of candidates. The more totalitarian the society, the greater is the emphasis on mobilization, on driving the population toward greater effort to serve the state.

The emphasis on participation plus the glorification of "the people" in totalitarian ideology lends a pseudodemocratic cast to life in the totalitarian world. The very term *democracy* becomes identified with participation and popular consent, even if it does not involve the free choice of leaders, freedom of speech, or freedom of association. In the democratic age, the symbols of democracy, and some of its forms, are associated with even the harshest dictatorial regimes. Mass dictatorship is a parody of the democratic ideal.

Section four social foundations of freedom and democracy

The often anguished politics of the modern world direct renewed attention to salient issues that have troubled statesmen and scholars for 2,000 years: the problem of freedom, that is, the protection of the individual from oppression, and the quality of self-government, that is, the degree to which civic participation is widespread, rational, and effective.

This section deals with these issues by considering (1) the legitimacy of authority, (2) pluralism as a foundation of freedom, and (3) political participation.

POWER AND LEGITIMACY

Legitimacy is power justified by reference to accepted values. When power is legitimate, it is called *authority*. By means of legitimation, consent to the exercise of power is gained, and governing is freed from primary reliance on naked force. The quest for legitimacy is universal, but the principles of legitimacy vary: Each culture justifies authority in accordance with its major values.

Some rule, and others obey, in part on the basis of shared beliefs in the desirability of the arrangement. However, though legitimacy justifies a system of power, it does not follow that principles of legitimacy are "mere quackeries designed to trick the masses into obedience" (Mosca, 1939:71). Rather, such principles answer real needs felt by rulers and ruled alike.

Legitimate power tends to be restrained power. Principles of legitimacy state what power-holders cannot do as well as what they are justified in doing. For example, if a principle of legitimacy calls for popular elections, then the governing group cannot appoint its own successors but must hold elections to justify its continued power. In the case of monarchy, established principles of legitimacy governing accession to the throne, such as the right of birth or election by a council of barons, checked the power struggles of feudal lords. The principles of legitimacy support the broader notion of a restraining law that stands above the rulers, to which they are responsible and by virtue of which they govern.

"Even the tyrant must sleep," wrote Thomas Hobbes, and dictators as well as democrats strive for legitimacy. The authoritarian ruler may recognize only a very blunt and crude principle of legitimacy—for example, "I rule because my father ruled." The principle is crude because it does not permit questioning of specific decisions; once the grant of authority is made, it is unlimited. In a constitutional democracy, a complex system of legal and political principles restrains official conduct. However, even a crude legitimation is the first indispensable step toward a system that permits the questions:

By what right do you govern? How do you justify your decisions?

The contribution legitimacy makes to freedom depends on the specific principles invoked. When Hitler justified his regime by claiming to represent the historic spirit of the German *Volk*, or when appeal is made to tradition as the basis of authority, it is difficult to make the principle an effective basis for criticizing and restraining the exercise of power. When legitimacy rests on specifically delegated power or on a particular competence, the possibilities of critical assessment are enhanced. (On authority and legitimacy, see Weber, 1947:324–362; Friedrich, 1958. On legitimacy "in depth," see Selznick, 1969:30.)

PLURALISM

Political freedom can be realized only in group membership. Single individuals are too weak to face governmental encroachments on their freedom. But they can protect themselves by joining with others. The collective power of organized groups also enables individuals to resist arbitrary interference with their liberty in other spheres of life. The freedom of workers is enhanced because unions can prevent management from treating them arbitrarily.

The existence of diverse social groups contributes to political freedom. Professional associations, trade unions, business organizations, churches, and political parties, for instance, generate social power that can protect individuals, standing between them and hostile forces.

The theory that pluralism is an indispensable condition of freedom can be understood by comparing three patterns of social organization:

Concentrated power When power is in a few hands the freedom of individuals and of other groups is endangered. There is so much strength on one side that opposition can be isolated and quickly destroyed. This situation is encountered where one group dominates a community.

When a single group or combination of

groups achieves a virtual monopoly of power, it no longer has to take account of the interests of other groups. There are no effective checks on its power. Even if it is motivated by high ideals, any group with a monopoly on power endangers the freedom of others.

Fragmented power Another danger to freedom occurs when power is so widely dispersed among competing groups that no group or combination is strong enough to organize the community and establish effective social control. A frontier society, in which each man is his own police force, is a case in point. Moreover, where power is fragmented, the community is vulnerable to any strong group that may arise. The conquest of England in 1066 by a small force from Normandy was made easier because of the fragmented character of social organization. Power was dispersed among many local lords, bishops, and kin groups.

Countervailing power Freedom is best protected when there are a number of groups powerful enough to check each other and strong enough to maintain social order and organize the main activities of the society. Such a pattern of social organization is called *pluralist.*

[The pluralist society is] characterized by the presence of large, well integrated groups representing significant divisions of interests and values. The various groups are limited in their power by the fact that the interests of other groups must be taken into account. The power of the state is limited by the power of organized public opinion and large special interest groups; the pressure exercised by business interests is counterbalanced by the forces of organized labor; both management and labor must take into account the interests of an integrated consumers' movement and other public agencies; no one religious group possesses a monopoly of spiritual values, and the various religious groups learn to accommodate themselves to one another; religious thought is denied absolute sovereignty over ideas by the presence of independent secular thought maintained by a free press, free universities, free literary movements, learned societies and organized scientific research. In the sphere of production, a pluralist society might allow for the operation of more than one form of economic organization: not only corporations and single entrepreneurships, but worker owned cooperatives and state organized collectives as well (De Gré, 1946:535).

Functions of pluralism Social pluralism limits the power of groups by providing a system of social checks and balances (see Dahl and Lindblom, 1953:303–306):

1. It encourages competition among groups and rivalry among leaders and therefore inhibits monopolies of power.

2. It limits leadership control by increasing the chances that members belong to several organizations. Each group tempers its attack on others to keep from losing the cooperation of those members who belong to the other organizations.

3. Participation in a pluralist society encourages such skills of democratic politics as the use of bargaining and negotiation.

4. Pluralism increases the availability of sources of information independent of government, church, or any single organization. This permits people to consider criticisms of, and alternatives to, existing policies and leaders.

If pluralism is to be a workable pattern of social organization, there must be a shared belief in its validity. This consensus need not run deep, however; it may depend merely on the shared beliefs of "influentials" rather than on solid support and full understanding by the entire public (McClosky, 1964:373).

The significance of pluralism for both freedom and democracy was underlined by Tocqueville when he said: "If men are to remain civilized, or to become so, the art of associating together must grow and improve in the same ratio in which the equality of conditions is increased." (See Adaptation 41.)

Critique of pluralism The pluralist theory outlined above has some important limitations:

1. The theory is more relevant to freedom than to democracy. The principle of countervailing power points to an indispensable precondition for the protection of individual and group liberties, but it does not require a large amount of public participation. The pluralist model is fulfilled if autonomous groups exist, each limiting the power of the others.

2. Individual freedom is not necessarily fully protected by pluralism. Although the individual stands to benefit when large organizations compete and bid for his support, a world of large organizations leaves many people defenseless against powerful leaders. (See *ASSOCIATIONS*, Section Four.) Moreover, people, such as nonunionized employees, who do not belong to effective organizations that can protect or promote their individual interests, may be left out in the cold.

3. Pluralism is compatible with the so-called elitist theory of democracy (Thompson, 1970:22–26). That point of view is expressed in the following definition of democracy: "The democratic method is that institutional arrangement for arriving at political decisions in which individuals acquire the power to decide by means of a competitive struggle for the people's vote" (Schumpeter, 1950:269). Thus understood, democracy is the opportunity to choose among competing leaders. The public is essentially passive and does not have an important role in making decisions or formulating policy. The participatory aspect of democracy is minimized (Pateman, 1970: Chap. 1).

4. Countervailing power tends to create "veto groups" (Riesman et al., 1950:239) that are able to block concerted action by the majority. Thus pluralism may lead to social stalemate. In the United States, this condition appears in the relative ineffectiveness of both the Congress and the state legislatures, which accounts in part for the disposition of courts to assume enlarged responsibilities, as in the cases of school segregation and legislative reapportionment.

These criticisms do not refute the basic truth in pluralist theory, but they do indicate its limitations. Although pluralism ac-counts for a vital aspect of democratic society, it does not offer a complete model. Pluralism speaks to the minimum conditions necessary for freedom and democracy; it does not assure that higher aspirations—for civic competence and civic participation—will be served.

Caution The *doctrine* of political pluralism should be distinguished from pluralism in the descriptive sense. Whether or not a society is pluralist in its social organization is a matter of fact. The term pluralism is also customarily used in discussing ethnic or cultural diversity. An ethnically plural population may or may not participate in a pluralist political order. (See *RACE AND ETHNICITY*, Section Four.)

PARTICIPATION

A larger view of democracy suggests that everyone should be interested in government and act effectively. The ideal, however, is often far removed from the political reality. Moreover, participation is a very general term. There are many different kinds of participation and many variations in its extent and quality. It is not obvious which pattern best serves the democratic ideal.

Rates and kinds In recent decades the political scene in the United States has been marked by a sharp increase in the number of marches, sit-ins, and other forms of demonstrative political activity. The increase is reflected in the trend of responses to a statement, put to successive national samples between 1952 and 1968: "Voting is the only way people like me can have any say about how the government runs things" (Converse, 1972:328). In 1956, 1960, and 1964, roughly 25 percent said that voting is *not* the only form of political influence open to most people. In 1968 this percentage rose to over 40 percent, suggesting widespread recognition of the role of demonstrations in changing society. The increase was most marked among the better-educated. Studies have shown that the better-educated are more ready to accept the legitimacy of dramatic and unconventional forms of political participation as well as the legitimacy of the demands put forward, and, in addition, they are better equipped to apprehend the link between demonstrations and subsequent changes in government policy. It should also be noted, however, that by the early 1970s many activists had turned away from demonstrations as a preferred form of political activity in favor of participation in the electoral process.

Compared with some other nations, voter turnout in the United States is low. During the 1920s only about half the electorate voted in presidential elections. Currently a presidential election brings out over 60 per-

cent of potential voters, but the turnout in off-year congressional elections is considerably lower—in 1974, about 39 percent. In Italy voter participation runs close to 90 percent, and in Denmark, West Germany, and Great Britain it falls in the 80–85 percent range (McClosky, 1968:255).

In Australia, which has been a leader in voting reform and where the secret ballot was first introduced (hence the "Australian" ballot), all persons eligible for the vote are registered, unlike in the United States, where the registration laws are obstacles to electoral participation. Voting in Australian general elections is compulsory, and failure to vote without good excuse is punishable by a fine. Thus the turnout in Australia is nearly complete—by U.S. standards, spec-

577

Section four
social
foundations of
freedom and
democracy

Political participation in a new country: The Prime Minister of Gambia, seated, receives a message from a village leader during an election campaign.

Table 17:2 Voting participation, United States,
November 1974, in percentages

	Highest participation		Lowest participation	
Age	45–64 years	57	18–20 years	21
Sex	Male	46	Female	43
Race	White	46	Black	34
Education, whites	College (5 years or more)	67	Elementary (0–4 years)	21
Education, blacks	College (5 years or more)	59	Elementary (0–4 years)	25
Family income (annual)	$25,000 and over	61	Under $5,000	32
Employment status	Employed	47	Unemployed	28
Marital status	Married, spouse present	50	Married, spouse absent	24

Source: *Current Population Reports,* Series P-20, No. 293, April 1976:Tables 4, 5, 6, and 8 (sample survey).

tacularly high. This does not mean that all Australians vote thoughtfully as the lawmakers intended. Some voters deliberately spoil their ballots so they will not be counted as a sort of protest vote. A small percentage automatically give their preferences to candidates whose names are listed first. In Australian parlance, this is known as the "donkey vote."

In assessing rates of voting, one should distinguish between the circumstances that tend to discourage voting and those that tend to raise it artificially. Table 17:2 makes clear some of the factors that depress voter participation in the United States: low education, low income, second-class citizenship. However, high voter turnout does not necessarily mean that political involvement is high, that alienation is low, and that voters are well informed. The contrary may be true if voting is not really voluntary:

Voting turnout in national elections in traditional rural villages in Turkey has been higher than that in larger cities, including the national capital, despite the fact that villagers have extremely little education and virtually no contact with the mainstream of national political communications. . . . Frey believes that most voting occurs to comply with the wishes of the headman of the village, or some other influential person with

whom the voter may be linked in the traditional village social structure. He concludes that the villagers are "more voted than voting" (Converse, 1972:287).

In totalitarian and one-party states, there is usually strong pressure by the government to maximize voter turnout. At various times in U.S. history, turnout rates have been artificially inflated by bribing people to go to the polls and "vote right"; by multiple voting, made possible when registration procedures are absent or ineffective; and by the custom of voice vote or some other form of nonsecret ballot. There was a decline in voter turnout in the United States around the turn of the century which was apparently attributable to the introduction of the secret ballot and better controlled voter registration (Converse, 1972:276 ff.).

Recent efforts to increase the registration and voting of disprivileged minorities are having an effect on voting behavior.

There is some indication that the proportion voting in the South increased in 1970 over 1966, running counter to the trend in the rest of the country. Southern Negroes as a group appear to have moved in the direction of greater involvement in the political process than was the case in the previous Congressional election. A clear instance of this is found among Southern Negroes living in

579

Section four
social
foundations of
freedom and
democracy

the Central cities of large metropolitan areas . . . who voted at a rate which was about 15 percentage points above their 1966 level (*Current Population Reports*, Series P-20, No. 228, December 1971:5).

Quality of participation Much debate has centered on whether the American voter is rational (Key, 1966). In part the debate is stimulated by the disposition of social science to emphasize the nonrational springs of action—that is, to look beyond what people say to what they do and to the circumstances that affect their decisions. But social science findings are not incompatible with rationality. For example, a finding that some people "vote their pocketbooks" is consistent with both rationality and an awareness of social circumstances.

A voter may be rational in one respect but not in all. At least three kinds of rationality may be distinguished: (1) rationality as knowledge and competence, (2) rationality as action in furtherance of perceived self-interest, and (3) rationality as intellectual consistency and adherence to principle.

The complexities of modern politics make great demands on the understanding of the electorate. Candidates must be judged not only by the party they represent but also by the particular wing within the party. A multitude of complex issues, from foreign policy to tax programs, need to be assessed for their long-run as well as short-run effects.

Voters are very different in their political skill. The educational and job experiences that produce such skills are not uniform throughout the population. Social position has much to do with the ability to write letters, use the telephone easily, read the newspapers, and speak at meetings. Both poise and knowledge affect political competence. The conditions of lower-class life probably do not train people in techniques of cooperation and leadership that are taken for granted among middle- and upper-class people.

Whether or not people have the skills, many do not feel competent to deal with po-

litical affairs. A sense of impotence keeps them out of politics. The higher the education, the more likely the individual will feel political participation does (or can) have an impact. (See Table 17:3.) "Among the poorly educated, lower-income manual workers the sense of involvement in public, and particularly international, affairs tends to be extremely limited and passive" (Almond, 1950:130; see also Campbell et al., 1960). Even among higher-status groups, there are those who feel at the mercy of forces beyond their control.

The great differences in feeling or affect that people bring to politics result in part from the wide variety of motives behind political interest. Traditionally, Americans have been exhorted to participate in politics in order to defend their private interests and to fulfill their duties as citizens. Self-interest is indeed a potent political incentive. The farmer, for example, must attend to politics in an era of government-supported prices, crop quotas, and subsidies. But many citizens do not see a direct relation between their private interests and politics. Even

Table 17:3
Education and the sense of political efficacy

Education	Percentage scoring high on sense of political efficacy	Number
Eighth grade or less	0	18
Some high school	14	596
High school graduate	28	1,347
Some college	45	388
College graduate	58	353
Total		2,702

Source: See Table 17:4.

To measure differences in the sense of political efficacy, a national sample was asked such questions as: Would you say that people like you have quite a lot to say about what the government does, or that you don't have much say at all? Scores were based on positive responses to four questions, scores of three or four being classified as "high."

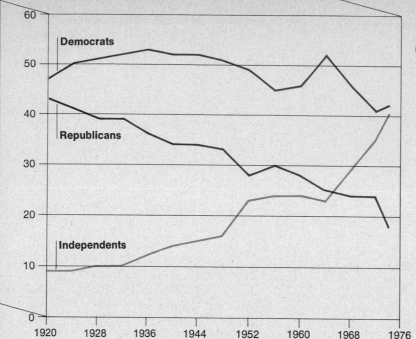

Figure 17:1
Party identification, 1920–1974
(in percentages)
Source: Nie et al., 1976: Fig. 5.1.

when their personal interests are clearly related to government action, they may feel incapable of having an effect on action or may feel that expressions of concern are pointless.

Party adherence and the independent vote
Figure 17:1 shows the changes in party identification over half a century. In 1920 the numbers of Republicans and Democrats were nearly in balance, and independents made up only one-tenth of the electorate. By 1974 the ranks of Republicans had declined to a minority of less than one-fifth. Democratic adherents had also declined to about two-fifths of the electorate, and they were equaled by the number of independents, who increased markedly after 1964. There is evidence that over the years, and especially since 1964, new voters contributed signifi-

Table 17:4   Strength of party identification and concern over election outcome, in percentages

	Strong party identification	Weak party identification	Independents
Care very much or care pretty much	82	58	55
Don't care very much or don't care at all	18	42	45
Total	100	100	100
Number of cases	(429)	(525)	(383)

Source: Survey Research Center 1968 American National Election Study (SRC 45523), University of Michigan, Inter-University Consortium for Political Research.

cantly to the increasing number of independents (Nie et al., 1976:63ff.).

Among the more important conclusions of modern research on voting is an assessment of the independent voter's role in the political process.

The ideal of the Independent citizen, attentive to politics, concerned with the course of government, who weighs the rival appeals of a campaign and reaches a judgment that is unswayed by partisan prejudice, has had such a vigorous history in the tradition of political reform—and has such a hold on civic education today—that one could easily suppose that the habitual partisan has the more limited interest and concern with politics. [However], far from being attentive, interested, and informed, Independents tend as a group to be somewhat less involved in politics. They have somewhat poorer knowledge of the issues, their image of the candidates is fainter, their interest in the campaign is less, their concern over the outcome is relatively slight, and their choice between competing candidates, although it is indeed made later in the campaign, seems much less to spring from discoverable evaluations of the elements of national politics (Campbell et al., 1960:143).

Table 17:4 shows that 82 percent of people who strongly identified with a political party cared "very much or pretty much" about the outcome of an election. The corresponding percentage for independents was 55 percent. Many persons without party affiliation or with weak party identity "care," although not so large a proportion as strongly affiliated citizens.

The view of the independent voter as uninterested and uninvolved has been challenged in a study of "switchers" in presidential elections. The research shows that many independents choose candidates in the light of the positions they hold on important issues (Key, 1966). Probably there are two kinds of independents: those who care little about political outcomes and have no urge to affiliate with a party and those who wish to be free of party ties so as to form their own political opinions.

Adaptation 41 Tocqueville: The democratic age

In 1831, the French government commissioned Gustave de Beaumont and Alexis de Tocqueville to study the prison system and prison reform in the United States. Far more important than their specialized report On the Penitentiary System of the United States, *however, was Tocqueville's analysis of the entire political system of the new country, published as* Democracy in America. *Part One appeared in 1835 and Part Two in 1840. Only 26 years old when he went to America, Tocqueville became a celebrated author and political thinker almost overnight. Edward Everett, in a commentary published in* North American Review *(1836), wrote: "We regard his work . . . as by far the most philosophical, ingenious, and instructive, which has been produced on the subject of America" (Mayer and Lerner, 1966:xi).*

Tocqueville saw the United States as a social laboratory. Here was a new country in which democratic institutions were being rapidly developed and given free rein. Here, if anywhere, the full significance of democracy might be studied. His aim was to draw some lessons from this experience for the guidance of his own countrymen. In pursuing this task, Tocqueville adopted a distinctly sociological perspective. He asked: What social conditions sustain the democratic political order? What are the consequences of democracy for manners and customs, for nonpolitical institutions, for the quality of life?

The following passages from Tocqueville show some of his major concerns. The passages have

Source: Abridged and adapted from *Democracy in America* by Alexis de Tocqueville, trans. Henry Reeve, ed. Francis Bowen (Cambridge: Sever and Francis, 1862). For easy reference to other editions, general locations of quoted passages are shown.

not been edited for this adaptation but are taken directly from the translation.

It is not, then, merely to satisfy a legitimate curiosity that I have examined America; my wish has been to find there instruction by which we may ourselves profit. Whoever should imagine that I have intended to write a panegyric would be strangely mistaken, and on reading this book, he will perceive that such was not my design: nor has it been my object to advocate any form of government in particular, for I am of opinion that absolute excellence is rarely to be found in any system of laws. I have not even pretended to judge whether the social revolution, which I believe to be irresistible, is advantageous or prejudicial to mankind. I have acknowledged this revolution as a fact already accomplished, or on the eve of its accomplishment; and I have selected the nation, from amongst those which have undergone it, in which its development has been the most peaceful and the most complete, in order to discern its natural consequences, and to find out, if possible, the means of rendering it profitable to mankind. I confess that, in America, I saw more than America; I sought there the image of democracy itself, with its inclinations, its character, its prejudices, and its passions, to learn what we have to fear or to hope from its progress [I. Introduction].

DESPOTISM AND DEMOCRACY

No sovereign ever lived in former ages so absolute or so powerful as to undertake to administer by his own agency, and without the assistance of intermediate powers, all the parts of a great empire: none ever attempted to subject all his subjects indiscriminately to strict uniformity of regulation, and personally to tutor and direct every member of the community.

When the Roman Emperors were at the height of their power, the different nations of the empire still preserved manners and customs of great diversity; although they were subject to the same monarch, most of the provinces were separately administered; they abounded in powerful and active municipalities; and although the whole government of the empire was centred in the hands of the Emperor alone, and he always remained, in case of need, the supreme arbiter in all matters, yet the details of social life and private occupa-

tions lay for the most part beyond his control. The Emperors possessed, it is true, an immense and unchecked power, which allowed them to gratify all their whimsical tastes, and to employ for that purpose the whole strength of the state. They frequently abused that power arbitrarily to deprive their subjects of property or of life: their tyranny was extremely onerous to the few, but it did not reach the many; it was fixed to some few main objects, and neglected the rest; it was violent, but its range was limited [II. Bk. 4, Chap. 6].

The notion of secondary powers, placed between the sovereign and his subjects, occurred naturally to the imagination of aristocratic nations, because those communities contained individuals or families raised above the common level, and apparently destined to command by their birth, their education, and their wealth. This same notion is naturally wanting in the minds of men in democratic ages, for converse reasons; it can only be introduced artificially, it can only be kept there with difficulty; whereas they conceive, as it were without thinking upon the subject, the notion of a single and central power, which governs the whole community by its direct influence. Moreover, in politics as well as in philosophy and in religion, the intellect of democratic nations is peculiarly open to simple and general notions. Complicated systems are repugnant to it, and its favorite conception is that of a great nation composed of citizens all formed upon one pattern, and all governed by a single power [II. Bk. 4, Chap. 2].

I believe that it is easier to establish an absolute and despotic government amongst a people in which the conditions of society are equal, than amongst any other; and I think that, if such a government were once established amongst such a people, it would not only oppress men, but would eventually strip each of them of several of the highest qualities of humanity. Despotism, therefore, appears to me peculiarly to be dreaded in democratic times.

On the other hand, I am persuaded that all who shall attempt, in the ages upon which we are entering, to base freedom upon aristocratic privilege, will fail; that all who shall attempt to draw and to retain authority within a single class, will fail. At the present day, no ruler is skillful or strong enough to found a despotism by reestablishing permanent distinctions of rank amongst his subjects: no legislator is wise or powerful enough to preserve free institutions, if he does not take equality for his first principle and his watchword. All of our contemporaries who would establish or secure the independence and the dignity of their fellow-men, must show themselves the friends of equality; and the only worthy means of showing themselves as such is to be so: upon this depends the success of their holy enterprise. Thus, the question is not how to reconstruct aristocratic society, but how to make liberty proceed out of that democratic state of society in which God has placed us [II. Bk. 4, Chap. 7].

FREEDOM AND ASSOCIATION

Aristocratic countries abound in wealthy and influential persons who are competent to provide for themselves, and who cannot be easily or secretly oppressed: such persons restrain a government within general habits of moderation and reserve. I am well aware that democratic countries contain no such persons naturally; but something analogous to them may be created by artificial means. I firmly believe that an aristocracy cannot again be founded in the world; but I think that private citizens, by combining together, may constitute bodies of great wealth, influence, and strength, corresponding to the persons of an aristocracy. By this means, many of the greatest political advantages of aristocracy would be obtained, without its injustice or its dangers. An association for political, commercial, or manufacturing purposes, or even for those of science and literature, is a powerful and enlightened member of the community, which cannot be disposed of at pleasure, or oppressed without remonstrance; and which, by defending its own rights against the encroachments of the government, saves the common liberties of the country [II. Bk. 4, Chap. 7].

There are no countries in which associations are more needed, to prevent the despotism of faction or the arbitrary power of a prince, than those which are democratically constituted. In aristocratic nations, the body of the nobles and the wealthy are in themselves natural associations, which check the abuses of power. In countries where such associations do not exist, if private individuals cannot create an artificial and temporary substitute for them, I can see no permanent protection against the most galling tyranny; and a great people may be oppressed with impunity by a small faction, or by a single individual.

Alexis de Tocqueville was born in Verneuil, west of Paris, in 1805 and died at Cannes in 1859. He studied law and, as a young man, began a career in the judiciary. In succeeding years he developed a broad interest in the structure of French society, especially in the problems created by the interplay of a continuing aristocratic tradition and the rising tide of democracy. His book on democracy in America has been called "perhaps the greatest work ever written on one country by the citizen of another."

The most natural privilege of man, next to the right of acting for himself, is that of combining his exertions with those of his fellow-creatures, and of acting in common with them. The right of association therefore appears to me almost as inalienable in its nature as the right of personal liberty [I. Chap. 12].

Amongst the laws which rule human societies, there is one which seems to be more precise and clear than all others. If men are to remain civilized, or to become so, the art of associating together must grow and improve in the same ratio in which the equality of conditions is increased [II. Bk. 2, Chap. 5].

TYRANNY OF THE MAJORITY

In my opinion, the main evil of the present democratic institutions of the United States does not arise, as is often asserted in Europe, from their weakness, but from their irresistible strength. I am not so much alarmed at the excessive liberty which reigns in that country, as at the inadequate securities which one finds there against tyranny.

I do not say that there is a frequent use of tyranny in America at the present day; but I maintain that there is no sure barrier against it, and that the causes which mitigate the government there are to be found in the circumstances and the manners of the country, more than in its laws.

It is in the examination of the exercise of thought in the United States, that we clearly perceive how far the power of the majority surpasses all the powers with which we are acquainted in Europe. The authority of a king is physical, and controls the actions of men without subduing their will. But the majority possesses a power which is physical and moral at the same time, which acts upon the will as much as upon the actions, and represses not only all contest, but all controversy [I. Chap. 15].

When the ranks of society are unequal, and men unlike each other in condition, there are some individuals wielding the power of superior intelligence, learning, and enlightenment, whilst the multitude are sunk in ignorance and prejudice. Men living at these aristocratic periods are therefore naturally induced to shape their opinions by the standard of a superior person, or superior class of persons, whilst they are averse to recognize the infallibility of the mass of the people.

The contrary takes place in ages of equality. The nearer the people are drawn to the common level of an equal and similar condition, the less prone does each man become to place implicit faith in a certain man or a certain class of men. But his readiness to believe the multitude increases, and opinion is more than ever mistress of the world. Not only is common opinion the only guide which private judgment retains amongst a democratic people, but amongst such a people it possesses a power infinitely beyond what it has

elsewhere. At periods of equality, men have no faith in one another, by reason of their common resemblance; but this very resemblance gives them almost unbounded confidence in the judgment of the public; for it would not seem probable, as they are all endowed with equal means of judging, but that the greater truth should go with the greater number.

The fact that the political laws of the Americans are such that the majority rules the community with sovereign sway, materially increases the power which that majority naturally exercises over the mind. For nothing is more customary in man than to recognize superior wisdom in the person of his oppressor. The intellectual dominion of the greater number would probably be less absolute amongst a democratic people governed by a king, than in the sphere of a pure democracy, but it will always be extremely absolute; and by whatever political laws men are governed in the ages of equality, it may be foreseen that faith in public opinion will become a species of religion there, and the majority its ministering prophet.

If the absolute power of a majority were to be substituted, by democratic nations, for all the different powers which checked or retarded overmuch the energy of individual minds, the evil would only have changed character. Men would not have found the means of independent life; they would simply have discovered (no easy task) a new physiognomy of servitude. There is,—and I cannot repeat it too often,—there is here matter for profound reflection to those who look on freedom of thought as a holy thing, and who hate not only the despot, but despotism. For myself, when I feel the hand of power lie heavy on my brow, I care but little to know who oppresses me; and I am not the more disposed to pass beneath the yoke because it is held out to me by the arms of a million men [II. Bk. 1, Chap. 2].

DEMOCRACY AND ANOMIE

In certain remote corners of the Old World, you may still sometimes tumble upon a small district which seems to have been forgotten amidst the general tumult, and to have remained stationary whilst everything around it was in motion. The inhabitants are, for the most part, extremely ignorant and poor; they take no part in the business of the country, and are frequently oppressed by the government; yet their countenances are generally placid, and their spirits light.

In America, I saw the freest and most enlightened men placed in the happiest circumstances which the world affords: it seemed to me as if a cloud habitually hung upon their brow, and I thought them serious, and almost sad, even in their pleasures.

The chief reason of this contrast is, that the former do not think of the ills they endure, while the latter are forever brooding over advantages they do not possess. It is strange to see with what feverish ardor the Americans pursue their own welfare; and to watch the vague dread that constantly torments them, lest they should not have chosen the shortest path which may lead to it.

Their taste for physical gratifications must be regarded as the original source of that secret inquietude which the actions of the Americans betray, and of that inconstancy of which they daily afford fresh examples.

If, in addition to the taste for physical well-being, a social condition be super-added, in which neither laws nor customs retain any person in his place, there is a great additional stimulant to this restlessness of temper. Men will then be seen continually to change their track, for fear of missing the shortest cut to happiness.

Amongst democratic nations, men easily attain a certain equality of condition; but they can never attain as much as they desire. It perpetually retires from before them, yet without hiding itself from their sight, and in retiring draws them on. At every moment they think they are about to grasp it; it escapes at every moment from their hold. They are near enough to see its charms, but too far off to enjoy them; and before they have fully tasted its delights, they die.

In democratic times, enjoyments are more intense than in the ages of aristocracy, and the number of those who partake in them is vastly larger; but, on the other hand, it must be admitted that man's hopes and desires are oftener blasted, the soul is more stricken and perturbed, and care itself more keen [II. Bk. 2, Chap. 13].

When every one is constantly striving to change his position; when an immense field for competition is thrown open to all; when wealth is amassed or dissipated in the shortest possible space of time amidst the turmoil of democracy,—visions of sudden and easy fortunes, of great possession easily won and lost, of chance under all its forms, haunt the mind. The instability of society itself fosters the natural instability of man's desires [II. Bk. 2, Chap. 17].

THE WORTH OF DEMOCRACY

In the present age, when the destinies of Christendom seem to be in suspense, some hasten to assail democracy as a hostile power, whilst it is yet growing; and others already adore this new deity which is springing forth from chaos. But both parties are imperfectly acquainted with the object of their hatred or their worship; they strike in the dark, and distribute their blows at random.

We must first understand what is wanted of society and its government. Do you wish to give a certain elevation to the human mind, and teach it to regard the things of this world with generous feelings, to inspire men with a scorn of mere temporal advantages, to form and nourish strong convictions, and keep alive the spirit of honorable devotedness? Is it your object to refine the habits, embellish the manners, and cultivate the arts, to promote the love of poetry, beauty, and glory? Would you constitute a people fitted to act powerfully upon all other nations, and prepared for those high enterprises which, whatever be their results, will leave a name forever famous in history? If you believe such to be the principal object of society, avoid the government of the democracy, for it would not lead you with certainty to the goal.

But if you hold it expedient to divert the moral and intellectual activity of man to the production of comfort, and the promotion of general well-being; if a clear understanding be more profitable to man than genius; if your object be not to stimulate the virtues of heroism, but the habits of peace; if you had rather witness vices than crimes, and are content to meet with fewer noble deeds, provided offences be diminished in the same proportion; if, instead of living in the midst of a brilliant society, you are contented to have prosperity around you; if, in short, you are of opinion that the principal object of a government is not to confer the greatest possible power and glory upon the body of the nation, but to ensure the greatest enjoyment, and to avoid the most misery, to each of the individuals who compose it,—if such be your desire, then equalize the conditions of men, and establish democratic institutions.

But if the time be past at which such a choice was possible, and if some power superior to that of man already hurries us, without consulting our wishes, towards one or the other of these two governments, let us endeavor to make the best of that which is allotted to us, and, by finding out both its good and its evil tendencies, be able to foster the former and repress the latter to the utmost [I. Chap. 14].

CONCLUSION

Tocqueville's argument may be summarized thus:

1. In the democratic age, equality becomes a paramount value. This equalizing tendency breaks down the power and self-confidence of traditional elites. Whatever their defects, these elites did exercise some restraint on kings and other sovereigns. Democracy tends to create a strong centralized government before which all citizens are equal. Tocqueville thought this equality might become an equality of weakness. As a result, he saw a latent despotism in democratic society.

2. To make the citizens stronger, Tocqueville emphasized the importance of the autonomous association in the democratic community. He would have seconded the slogan of his contemporary, the French anarchist Proudhon, who said, "Multiply your associations and be free."

3. Tyranny can be cultural and psychological as well as political. Democracy, which gives all opinions equal worth and honors the views of the majority, may usher in an age of conformity. This danger he referred to as the "tyranny of the majority."

4. Democracy and equality tend to stimulate ambition, loosen social bonds, and lessen respect for established forms of conduct. Thus democracy tends to be anomic and runs the risk that dissatisfaction will produce irrational political responses. Tocqueville did not use the term anomie, which was given currency by Durkheim. (See Adaptation 3.) In addition to the idea of anomie there are many similarities in the perspectives of Durkheim and Tocqueville.

COMMENT

Tocqueville's analysis should be understood as a diagnosis of some of the inherent weaknesses of democracy. In this sense, it is similar to the study by Michels. (See Adaptation 18.) Tocqueville wrote mainly as a friend of democracy. Although he drew on his aristocratic background and inclinations, he also expressed his faith in self-government.

References

Almond, Gabriel
1950 The American People and Foreign Policy. New York: Harcourt Brace Jovanovich.

Andreski, Stanislav
1968 The African Predicament. London: Michael Joseph.

Apter, David E.
1955 The Gold Coast in Transition. Princeton, N. J.: Princeton University Press.

Berger, Morroe
1962 The Arab World Today. New York: Doubleday.

Bernal, Martin
1970 "Was Chinese communism inevitable?" New York Review of Books 15 (December 3):43–47.

Brinton, Crane
1957 The Anatomy of Revolution. New York: Random House (Vintage Books).

Brown, Emily Clark
1966 Soviet Trade Unions and Labour Relations. Cambridge: Harvard University Press.

Burnham, James
1941 The Managerial Revolution. New York: Day.

Campbell, Angus, W. E. Miller, and D. E. Stokes
1960 The American Voter. New York: Wiley.

Ch'ên, Jerome
1965 Mao and the Chinese Revolution. London: Oxford University Press.

Cliffe, Lionel
1967 One Party Democracy: The 1965 Tanzania General Elections. Nairobi, Kenya: East African Publishing House.

Converse, Philip E.
1972 "Changes in the American electorate." Pp. 263–337 in Angus Campbell and Philip E. Converse (eds.), The Human Meaning of Social Change. New York: Rusell Sage.

Dahl, Robert A. and Charles E. Lindblom
1953 Politics, Economics and Welfare. New York: Harper & Row.

Davies, James C.
1962 "Toward a theory of revolution." American Sociological Review 27 (February):5–19.

De Gré, Gerard
1946 "Freedom and social structure." American Sociological Review 11 (October):529–536.

Dos Santos, Theotino
1970 "The structure of dependence." Papers and proceedings of the 82nd annual meeting. American Economic Review 60 (May):231–236.

Emerson, Rupert
1960 From Empire to Nation. Cambridge: Hårvard University Press.

Friedrich, Carl J. (ed.)
1958 Authority. Cambridge: Harvard University Press.

Guerard, Albert
1959 France: A Modern History. Ann Arbor: University of Michigan Press.

Huntington, Samuel P.
1968 Political Order in Changing Societies. New Haven, Conn.: Yale University Press.

Inkeles, Alex and Kent Geiger
1961 Soviet Society, a Book of Readings. Boston: Houghton Mifflin.

Kautsky, John H. (ed.)
1962 Political Change in Underdeveloped Countries: Nationalism and Communism. New York: Wiley.

Key, V. O., Jr.
1966 The Responsible Electorate. Cambridge: Harvard University Press.

Koestler, Arthur
1946 Darkness at Noon. New York: Modern Library.

Lenin, V. I.
1929 The Revolution of 1917. Vol. 20. New York: International Publishers.

McClosky, Herbert
1964 "Consensus and ideology in American politics." American Political Science Review 63 (June):361–382.
1968 "Political participation." Pp. 252–265 in International Encyclopedia of the Social Sciences. Vol. 12. New York: Macmillan.

Merriam, Alan P.
1961 Congo: Background of Conflict. Evanston, Ill.: Northwestern University Press.

Murdock, George P.
1959 Africa. New York: McGraw-Hill.

Nie, Norman H., Sidney Verba, and John R. Petrocik
1976 The Changing American Voter. Cambridge: Harvard University Press.

Pateman, Carole
1970 Participation and Democratic Theory. Cambridge: Cambridge University Press.

Pettee, George S.
1938 The Process of Revolution. New York: Harper & Row.

Pye, Lucian
1962 Politics, Personality and Nation Building: Burma's Search for Identity. New Haven, Conn.: Yale University Press.

Riesman, David, in collaboration with Reuel Denney and Nathan Glazer
1950 The Lonely Crowd. New Haven, Conn.: Yale University Press.

Schumpeter, Joseph A.
1950 Capitalism, Socialism, and Democracy. New York: Harper & Row.

Selznick, Philip
1969 Law, Society, and Industrial Justice. New York: Russell Sage.

Strachey, John
1960 "The strangled cry." Encounter (November):7–8.

Thompson, Dennis F.
1970 The Democratic Citizen. Cambridge: Cambridge University Press.

Tocqueville, Alexis de
1856/1955 The Old Regime and the French Revolution. Translated by Stuart Gilbert. New York: Doubleday.

Weber, Max
1947 The Theory of Social and Economic Organization. Translated by A. M. Henderson and Talcott Parsons. New York: Oxford University Press.

Young, Crawford
1965 Politics in the Congo. Princeton, N. J.: Princeton University Press.

Sources and readings

Bendix, Reinhard (ed.)
1968 State and Society. Boston: Little, Brown.

Campbell, Angus, Philip E. Converse, Warren E. Miller, and Donald E. Stokes
1966 Elections and the Political Order. New York: Wiley.

Chasin, Barbara and Gerald Chasin
1974 Power and Ideology: A Marxist Approach to Political Sociology. Cambridge, Mass.: Schenkman.

Coser, Lewis A. (ed.)
1966 Political Sociology: Selected Essays. New York: Harper Torchbooks.

Eckstein, Harry and David E. Apter
1963 Comparative Politics: A Reader. New York: Free Press.

Eisenstadt, S. N.
1971 Political Sociology: A Reader. New York: Basic Books.

Eisenstadt, S. N. and Stein Rokkan (eds.)
1973 and 1974 Building States and Nations. 2 vols. Beverly Hills, Calif.: Sage.

Hagopian, Mark N.
1974 The Phenomenon of Revolution. New York: Dodd, Mead.

Kirkpatrick, Jeane J.
1975 Political Women. New York: Basic Books.

Kornhauser, William
1959 The Politics of Mass Society. New York: Free Press.

Lipset, S. M.
1960 Political Man. New York: Doubleday.

McConnell, Grant
1966 Private Power and American Democracy. New York: Knopf.

MacIver, R. M.
1947 The Web of Government. New York: Macmillan.

Moore, Barrington, Jr.
1966 Social Origins of Dictatorship and Democracy. Boston: Beacon Press.

Tocqueville, Alexis de
1966 Democracy in America. Edited by J. P. Mayer and M. Lerner. New York: Harper & Row.

Verba, Sidney and Norma H. Nie
1972 Participation in America: Political Democracy and Social Equality. New York: Harper & Row.

Periodicals

American Political Science Review
Foreign Affairs
International Affairs
Journal of Politics
Political Science Quarterly

Credits

Name Index

Subject Index